More praise for *Song for the Blue Ocean*

"I hereby nominate Carl Safina to be the person in charge of telling us what's really going on in the world. . . . He is an ecologist with the soul of a poet. . . . The book is a page-turner. . . . Prescient and powerful . . . Safina has done what I could only dream about: he has written a plaintive, sensitive, caring, intelligent, indignant paean to his beloved waters and their threatened habitats."

—Richard Ellis, *Los Angeles Times Book Review*

"Engrossing and illuminating . . . Passionate and enthralling narrative . . . What elevates his book above the usual environmental tract and makes it so compelling and involving is that he is genuinely besotted by fish, and his enthusiasm is infectious."

—Thurston Clarke, *The New York Times Book Review*

"A haunting melody. A howl. A lament. And at times, a dirge. *Song for the Blue Ocean* is all of these, and much more. What Rachel Carson's *Silent Spring* did to spur public outrage over pesticides, we can only hope Carl Safina's magnificent, profoundly disturbing book will do to halt overfishing and the catastrophic depletion of marine species."

—Barbara Lloyd McMichael, *The Seattle Post-Intelligencer*

"Environmental writing sometimes shuns the human side of things. Safina's focus on real people—men and women afraid for their livelihood—is one of the unexpected strengths of a book rich in science and natural observation."

—*Civilization*

"Everywhere he goes, Safina finds testimony to the enchantments of the living sea and the pleasure it brings to those who sense its grace. . . . Invaluable . . . [*Song for the Blue Ocean*'s] poetic and powerful reenchantment of nature makes it great."

—James William Gibson, *The Washington Post*

"Carl Safina's moving portrait of our remarkable and endangered water planet is a message of warning and of hope: If we act now, there is time left to leave our children a living planet. As a new century dawns, *Song for the Blue Ocean* will help inspire progress toward that most critical end."

—Kathryn Fuller, director, World Wildlife Fund

"Safina's thought-provoking narrative describes species, sketches local history, and introduces the key players to tell their sides of the story. His moral is clear: marine scientists can no longer stand aside and merely monitor what's happening to the seas. Their special knowledge and professional passivity (which they call 'objectivity') make them as accountable and liable for the damage being done as the most aggressive gilnetters, longliners, purse-seiners or cyanide fishermen. . . . A must-read for anyone concerned about the future of marine fisheries."

—George Reiger, conservation editor,
Field and Stream and *Salt Water Sportsman* magazines

"Sad, serious, wondrous, wise, provocative, funny, full of adventure, but above all, *Song for the Blue Ocean* is inspirational. You will never think about fish—or the ocean—the same way again after Carl Safina works his magical way with you in this action-packed saga. Carl Safina is to the sea what Aldo Leopold was to the land—an articulate visionary."

—Sylvia Earle, chief scientist emeritus,
National Oceanic and Atmospheric Association

"Carl Safina's firsthand account of the plight of our oceans is both authoritative and impassioned, revealing the human side, and costs, of our use of the sea. This is the most readable and compelling book on ocean conservation to date."

—Julia Packard, executive director, Monterey Aquarium

Song for the Blue Ocean

Song for the Blue Ocean

*Encounters Along the World's Coasts
and Beneath the Seas*

Carl Safina

A Holt Paperback

John Macrae Books/Henry Holt and Company

New York

Holt Paperbacks
Henry Holt and Company, LLC
Publishers since 1866
175 Fifth Avenue
New York, New York 10010
www.henryholt.com

"Move" is from *Green Age* by Alicia Suskin
Ostriker, © 1989. Reprinted by permission of
the University of Pittsburgh Press.

The excerpt from the *Annual Review of Ecology
and Systemics* is reprinted with permission from
the *Annual Review of Ecology and Systemics,*
Volume 9 © 1978 by Annual Reviews, Inc.

Library of Congress Cataloging-in-Publication Data
Safina, Carl, 1955–
Song for the blue ocean : encounters along the world's coasts
and beneath the seas / Carl Safina.
p.   cm.
"A John Macrae book."
Includes bibliographical references and index.
ISBN-13: 978-0-8050-6122-2
ISBN-10: 0-8050-6122-3
1. Fishery conservation.   2. Marine ecology.   3. Marine
resources conservation.   I. Title.
SH327.7.S34   1998   97-12663
333.95'616—dc21   CIP

Originally published in hardcover in 1998 by
John Macrae/Henry Holt and Company

First Holt Paperbacks Edition 1999

Designed by Paula R. Szafranski

Cartography by Jon C. Luoma

Printed in the United States of America

15   14

For Rose and Mercédès

Move

Whether it's a turtle who drags herself
Slowly to the sandlot, where she digs
The sandy nest she was born to dig

And lay leathery eggs in, or whether it's salmon
Rocketing upstream
Toward pools that call, *Bring your eggs here*

And nowhere else in the world, whether it is turtle-green
Ugliness and awkwardness, or the seething
Grace and gild of silky salmon, we

Are envious, our wishes speak out right here.
Thirsty for a destiny like theirs,
an absolute right choice

To end all choices. Is it memory,
We ask, is it a smell
They remember,

Or just what is it—some kind of blueprint
That makes them move, hot grain by grain,
Cold cascade above icy cascade,

Slipping through
Water's fingers
A hundred miles

Inland from the easy, shiny sea?
And we also—in the company
Of our tribe

Or perhaps alone, like the turtle
On her wrinkled feet with the tapping nails—
We also are going to travel, we say let's be

Oblivious to all, save
That we travel, and we say
When we reach the place we'll know

We are in the right spot, somehow, like a breath
Entering a singer's chest, that shapes itself
For the song that is to follow

—ALICIA OSTRIKER

Who knows what admirable virtue of fishes may be below low-water-mark, bearing up against a hard destiny, not admired by that fellow creature who alone can appreciate it! Who hears the fishes when they cry? It will not be forgotten by some memory that we were contemporaries.

—HENRY DAVID THOREAU

Contents

Preface

When I was a boy, on warm spring evenings in the rich light before sunset my father would often take me down to the pebbly shore of Long Island Sound to hunt striped bass. At the shore, with the sparkling water, the coursing terns, the iridescence of a freshly caught fish, the world seemed unspeakably beautiful and—I remember this vividly—so real. It seemed so real. Compared to the other families in our neighborhood—the ones with absentee businessmen fathers and kids with television dependency—I thought that my father and I, with our secret fishing spot, were very, very lucky. When one is growing up with a sense of place, the world seems secure and filled with promise.

The arrival of bulldozers on our shoreline was an unfathomable catastrophe. In a youngster's worldview, the country map is small. Loss of my beach amounted to expatriation. And no one is so long-remembering as a refugee.

In graduate school, I arranged to do field work on the ecological relationships between seabirds and fishes. This would allow me to spend many hours out in the coastal ocean habitats that had opened my heart on my boyhood shores. At least now I was far from the bulldozers. My research began to develop into a reputable body of work, and to be published by well-regarded scientific journals. By all outer measures I was beginning a promising career as a research ecologist.

But something else was happening during the course of my studies. Magnificent creatures that I was just getting to know in the ocean, like giant tuna, sea turtles, marlin, and sharks, were growing scarcer each year. The oceans were being depopulated; the creatures were not just being used—they were being used up. Watching them disappear, I felt helpless. It was almost as though the bulldozers had found me again, and were at work in the ocean.

Sixty million buffalo once roamed the rolling green prairies of North America. They supported human cultures for thousands of years. But after a few decades of exploitation by industrial-age people, they were reduced to relics, symbols of profligate waste and dull self-interest. From my own vantage point—

my research and fishing activities—it seemed that a last buffalo hunt was occurring on the rolling blue prairies of the oceans. The sea, as I watched, was being figuratively and literally strained. Overfishing was draining the ocean's vitality, compounding the bulldozers' work in the coastal wetland nurseries. Though overfishing threatens the very people who engage in it, this simple connection seemed as lost on many fishers as overhunting had been on the buffalo hunters.

To plumb the extent of the changes I saw among the oceans' creatures in my home waters, I undertook a journey of discovery beyond the blue horizon. I went to search out the oceans' messages, and to bring those messages ashore. I traveled in a variety of roles: scientist, observer, advocate, guide, tourist, fisherman. The following pages record my journey. I will be your guide and interpreter. But ultimately you must judge what the oceans' creatures and its peoples have to say, and what it means to you.

Montauk, N.Y.
1997

Acknowledgments

This *Song* is sung by a chorus, and I have given many people space to tell their own stories because I thought they were far more interesting than was I. Many other unsung people helped work the stage and theater. Among these, I extend my utmost thanks to Jan Beyea for basic logistical help and advanced moral and professional support, and to Joanna Burger for career-long enthusiasm, mentoring, and friendship. Gary Soucie's frank criticism and sharp insights improved this book immensely. Valerie Harms offered important encouragement and incisive aid at several pivotal points, and Jean Naggar, Jack Macrae, Rachel Klauber-Speiden, and James Lincoln Collier helped the manuscript see the light of day.

A Pew Scholars Award in Conservation and the Environment provided crucial funding for time and travel, without which this book would simply not have been possible, and it would be difficult to overstate my debt to J. Peterson Myers and the selection committee for the big nod. For other major, essential funding, and truly wonderful supportiveness, I am forever indebted to Sarah Clark-Stuart, Angel Cunningham, Wolcott Henry, Scott McVay, Julie Packard, Rich Reagan, Josh Reichert, Jeanne Sedgwick, Mark Valentine, Tom Wathen, and Ted Williams. We all owe a debt of gratitude to the David and Lucile Packard Foundation and the Pew Charitable Trusts for their major commitment to help ensure a future that includes abundant life in the world's oceans.

Rutgers University and the National Audubon Society provided exemplary assistance with financial logistics, and I thank Jim Cunningham, Carole McNamara, Teri Moresco, and other National Audubon staff members for facilitating the leave of absence during which this book was written.

Joanne Cardinali, John and Nancy DeBellas, Dave Witting, Richard Wagner, Joe Cavallaro, Pete DeSimone, Bob Leonti, Peter Martin, and Michael Sutton did everything from reading draft chapters to helping land big fish, but mostly they afforded the finest kind of friendship and priceless memories of times and tides over many years, experiences that inspired much of my subsequent thought and work and inspire me still.

The philosopher Albert Camus once wrote, "A man's work is nothing but this slow trek to rediscover . . . those two or three great and simple images in whose presence his heart first opened." My father, Carlo Safina; cousin Lou Safina; and uncles Tony Aragona and Sal Aragona helped instill and nurture my earliest enthusiasms for the sea.

Michael Gochfeld, Ed Ricciuti, Cecily Kihn, Marcy Cohen, Dylan Ford, Steve Coll, Becky Shuford, George Reiger, Ada Graham, Frank Graham, and Brock Evans lent early encouragement and read manuscript sections. Marlene Cole, Ken Able, and David Nemerson helped with transcribing, accommodations for writing, and essential moral support. Ed Miller, Chris Miller, Joan Kaiser, and Joel Piereth at Westlake Marina in Montauk, Long Island, made me feel welcome and comfortable during extended bouts of writing and revising.

During this endeavor I have benefited greatly from the sparkling support, camaraderie, and thoughtfulness of Don C. O'Brien Jr., Ken Hinman, Lisa Speer, Dave Wilmot, Dorie Bolze, Maggie Mooney-Seus, Suzanne Iudicello, Jerry Leape, Sonja Fordham, Greg Stone, Scott Burns, Mike Testa, Sonny Gruber, Jack Musick, Bob Hueter, Jane Lubchenco, Sylvia Earle, John C. Ogden, and Vikki Spruill. The award-winning Living Oceans Program team of Marilyn England, Merry Camhi, Pat Paladines, and Mercédès Lee made me look good at work and covered expertly for me during long absences in the field and abroad.

This is a work of nonfiction. In certain instances, however, names or minor details have been altered to protect individuals, and some quotes and situations have been edited for clarity. In my travels and during development of this book a large number of extraordinary people were willing to take time, bear with me, and open my eyes to many remarkable places, ideas, and efforts. In many ways, this is their book. At the risk of accidentally omitting some important individuals, I must acknowledge Ed and Susan Wickersham and their sons Jeff and Tim, Zeke Grader, Bill Kier, Larry Landis, Felix Smith, Jason Peltier, John Roberts, Chuck Morones, Eldon Lundberg, Stacey Cepello, Sue Sutton, John Sutton, Sue Knox, Chris Leininger, Jim Tate, Zach Wiley, Roz Vostinak, Beth Hunning, Stuart Knox, Rod Kaiser, Pete Lawson, Bill Pearcy, Ted Strong, Andy Kerr, Glen Spain, Peter Moyle, Brian Vincent, Hans Radtke, Fran Recht, Jane Nicolai, Randy Fisher, Larry Six, Lighthawk ("the environmental air force"), Donella Meadows, Rod Fujita, Steve Johnson, Dick Good, Paul Engelmeyer, Bill Baake, Mike Reed, Jim Lichatowich, Rich McDonald, Willow Burch, Don Riswick, Randy and Brenda Wall, Les and Fran Clark, the Reverend Irene Martin, Jim Bergeron, Bob Eaton, Tom Getty, Ivan Larsen, Steve Fick, Sydney Schneidman, Dan Daley, Jerry Bouck, Ed Chaney, Antoine Minthorn, Jerry Abrams, Charlie Horton, Rich Ruais, Steve Weiner, Tim Voorheis, Roger Hillhouse, Frank Cyganowski, Frank Mather, Barbara Block, Bob Eakes, Richard Roe, Leonard Ingrande, Allen Peterson, Dave Linney, Joe McBride, Billy Campbell, Leon

Perkins, Tim Tower, Sonny McIntire, Gil Radonski, Alex Adler, Chris Weld, Don Barry, Roger McManus, Charlie Johnson, Lisa King, Theo Isamu, Minoro Ueki, Noah Idechong, Francis Toribiong, Rob Lester, Bob Johannes, Lyle Squire, Yvonne Sadovy, Tom Graham, Larry Sharron, Devon Ludwig, Vaughan Pratt, Perfecto Pascua, Jeremy Jackson, Bernard Nietschmann, Armstrong Wiggins, Héctor Guzmán, Ross Robertson, George Burgess, Jim "Sea Ethic" Bohnsack, Estelle Ruppert, and all the people mentioned herein. I thank them all, and I hope that this book helps make their views and efforts better appreciated and better understood.

Song for the Blue Ocean

BOOK ONE

Northeast

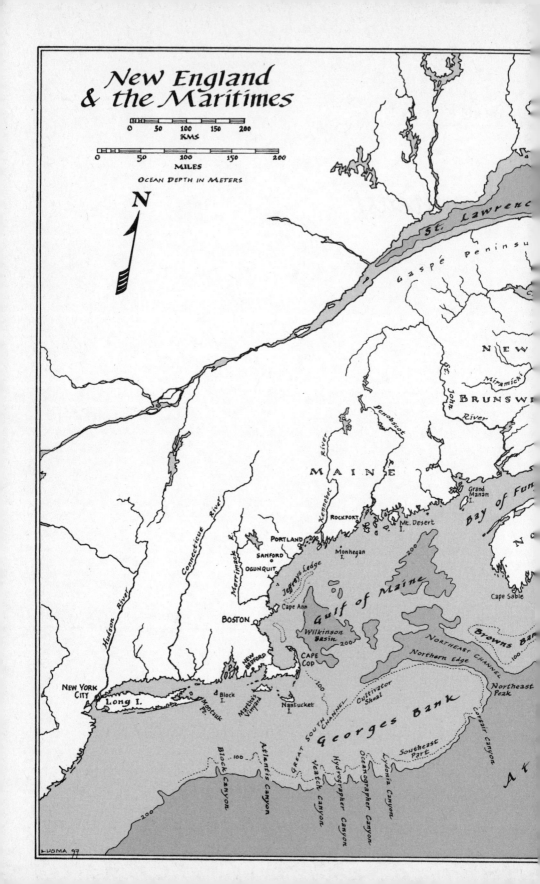

New England & the Maritimes

0   50   100   150   200
KMS

0   50   100   150   200
MILES

OCEAN DEPTH IN METERS

N

St. Lawrence

Gaspé Peninsu

N E W

Miramichi

B R U N S W I

River

St. John

River

M A I N E

Penobscot

River

Kennebec

River

Grand Manan I.

Bay of Fun

N

ROCKPORT

Monhegan I.

Mt. Desert I.

PORTLAND

SANFORD

OGUNQUIT

Jeffreys Ledge

200

Gulf of Maine

Cape Sable

Cape Ann

BOSTON

Wilkinson Basin

200

Browns Ban

NORTHEAST CHANNEL

100

NEW BEDFORD

CAPE COD

Northern Edge

Northeast Peak

NEW YORK CITY

Long I.

Block I.

Montauk

Martha's Vineyard

Nantucket I.

100

GREAT SOUTH CHANNEL

Cultivator Shoal

Georges Bank

Corsair Canyon

Southeast Part

100

Block Canyon

200

Atlantis Canyon

Veatch Canyon

Hydrographer Canyon

Oceanographer Canyon

Lydonia Canyon

200

LUOMA 97

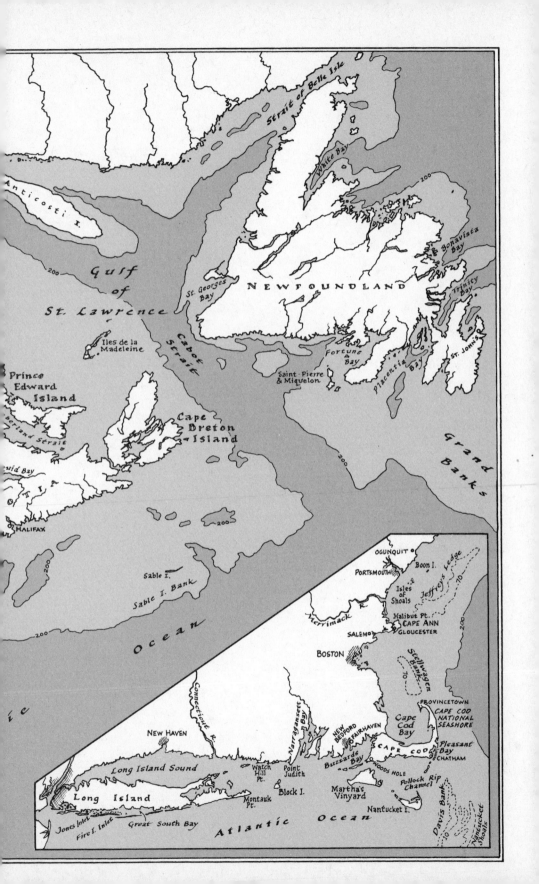

A few inches from where I stood, human history ended. The bronze age, the industrial revolution, the space age—gone. One hundred years ago, one thousand years ago, one million years ago, ten million years ago, much of the world looked like this. Sixty million years ago, the creature I was now watching, the shark slowly circling me, looked like this. Already perfected. In the beginning, all was void, and darkness was upon the waters. Ancient before Creation itself: the eternal sea.

A slick plain like molten glass stretched away to the far horizons, where it seemed to meld upward without boundary into the deep blue sky of outer space. Just arcing out of night, the new sun sent an apricot-colored wash into the moist dawn like watercolor touched to wet paper. Thirty miles at sea, adrift in an open eighteen-foot boat, the world seemed freshly created and miraculous, laden with possibility. Even nowadays, the ocean at first light has that kind of power. The shark angled away, so unhurriedly that I could hardly mark the moment when its shape, so startling when it had first appeared, finally vanished.

For two hours, my drifting boat rode a soft swell, the sea heaving and subsiding as though breathing, and I rising and falling gently as though resting my head on my lover's chest. During that time the only thing I noticed was that the sun had purged the atmosphere of excess moisture, had sharpened the outline between sea and sky. The sky now seemed a circular curtain around the rim of not planet Earth but planet Ocean.

What caught my eye was a faint chevron bulging ever so slightly from that molten, glassy sea, fifty yards from where I sat adrift. As I rose to my feet to study it, the chevron grew to a distinct wake. A wake without a boat. The wake ran along the surface for a few seconds, accelerated, and exploded like a revelation.

A giant bluefin tuna, among the largest and most magnificent of animals, hung suspended for a long, riveting moment, emblazoned and backlit like a saber-finned warrior from another world, until its six hundred pounds of muscle crashed into the ocean like a boulder falling from the sky. The jagged tear it left in the sea was marked by an emerald patch of fine bubbles rising slowly to the surface until the spot healed, slowly turned blue again, and became indistinguishable.

Wind and sea remained kind to me and my small craft for the duration of the morning, and I found my way back over the horizon, through the inlet, and home, without incident. Ashore, the vision of that giant tuna never dissipated.

That morning I saw something. Not new—after years of fishing, it was certainly not the first tuna I had seen—but I saw something differently. I saw this fish not as a struggling opponent at the end of a line, not as potential dollars at the fish house, not as a prop against which my "sport" was framed, not as the prospective evening meal, but as a wild animal, perfect master of its element, no less spectacular than a grizzly bear or an eagle. No less spectacular, but perhaps even more venerable. "In a world older and more complete than ours," Henry Beston wrote in *The Outermost House,* "they move finished and complete."

The bluefin tuna is clearly complete. Some say it is nearly finished. Scientists calculate that the bluefin population off the eastern seaboard of the United States and Canada has declined sharply since the 1970s, plummeting nearly 90 percent. They say reproduction is now very low. But commercial fishermen in New England—*good* fishermen and good people—say this is hogwash, that the fish are abundant, increasing in numbers. This debate is more than academic, because an adult bluefin may be worth more money to the person who can kill one than any other animal on the planet, elephants and rhinos included.

Probing for the truth to this debate requires following the bluefin, and the bluefin's trail leads us in many directions. It leads across and through oceans. It leads into a dense human jungle filled with shadowy figures, vinelike tangles of crisscrossing agendas, and thickets of politics. In this odd jungle, on the trail of a giant fish, our attention is continually diverted by side paths, made by other creatures, crossing the main trail again and again, leading intriguingly into the dark underbrush where we cannot follow. In this watery jungle, the bluefin's path may cross the swordfish's, the cod's, even the scallop's, and we may pause long enough to examine their tracks before we press onward. But most of all, the bluefin's trail leads through the looking glass of the ocean's surface, revealing that while the ocean may look the same as it has for millennia, it has changed, and changed greatly.

The Gulf of Maine

"I think there may be something to show you here," Charlie Horton is saying through my headphones. Horton likes the color of this water. After flying over miles of oceanic desert, skimming wave upon wave unrelieved, this blue oasis is coming alive for us, finally.

Two sleek finback whales are plowing furrows in the surface below us, at an uncommonly swift pace. Charlie banks his airplane for a better look. As he's visually locked onto them, I glance down between the struts and am startled to see a school of very, very big fish. "Right here! Right here!"

Horton banks hard and the plane wheels in a tight, gut-jumping circle. "Yup, tuna!" he says. "Good ones! Some five-hundred-pounders in that bunch." About a hundred giant bluefin tuna are traveling peacefully just under the surface. The animals I am looking at are so large, I expect them to behave like dolphins; that they are not coming to the surface to breathe air feels somehow uncomfortable. I have to remind myself—it seems so odd—that these large creatures are truly fish.

Close your eyes. Think fish. Do you envision half a ton of laminated muscle rocketing through the sea as fast as you drive your automobile? Do you envision a peaceful warrior capable of killing you unintentionally with a whack of its tail? These giant tuna strain the concept of fish. "Fish," anyhow, is a matter of dry taxonomy, the discipline that tells more of your origins than of who you are now. "Fish" is a label, like your surname that relates you to both your disgraceful uncle and your extraordinary cousin, yet says nothing of you. Name is not destiny. Your relationship to those around you—your ecology, if you will—defines you in the moment.

The giant tuna rise in unison, their backs breaking wakes like a flotilla of small boats. As they continue cruising, one of them splashes and sprints forward a few yards, like a thoroughbred jittery before a race, its behavior hinting strongly of enormous power in repose. What sense of the world, what *feeling,* moves this animal? Is it impatient? Is it thinking?

Questions large and small come forward. The airplane turns a slow arc.

Below, in plain sight, swim giant creatures from another dimension, confined below the surface no less than we are confined above it. They feel not the breeze but the tides; they have never pressed a solid surface; they breathe by moving forward and can never rest. How may we know them?

Charlie watches the bluefins a moment and jots a note about their number and location. Charlie Horton is a professional fish spotter, finding bluefin tuna and swordfish from the air, then guiding a commercial fishing boat to them. Today, though, Charlie isn't working with a boat. He has only me to worry about. I have formally requested that the National Marine Fisheries Service and the U.S. Fish and Wildlife Service begin a process that could end commercial fishing for bluefin tuna. But I've arranged to come fishing (as Charlie refers to flying) with him and with others in New England, because many fishermen insist that bluefin numbers are increasing and that the petition should be withdrawn. I want to see if I can get their sense of things, and try to understand their lives and livelihoods a little.

We continue onward, hurtling over the shimmer, searching, scanning. White bursts—these too may be giant bluefins—draw our attention. Rather than tuna, several hundred white-sided dolphins come into focus, undulating crisply through the sea surface below. They glide up to snatch breath without breaking stride, then run along submerged, until coming easily again for the next inspiration of air. All this they do in one fluent movement, seemingly having as little need to think about breathing as we. Their fluid maneuvers are excruciatingly beautiful, a living embroidery of motion through the ocean's wrinkled cloth. Having never watched dolphins from the air before, I am surprised that the animals are not evenly spaced. Certain individuals consort more closely together than others. I wonder if these are parents with their grown offspring, families, relatives, perhaps friends. Behind and following the dolphins, crisscrossing and coursing just above the waves, flies a loose flock of shearwaters, oceanic wanderers who touch land only when nesting. A blue shark appears, lazily wagging its way along just beneath the surface.

All the animals gathered in this one area have my riveted attention, but Charlie sheers away, and we continue along at 107 knots.

For the next thirty miles, we see little but ocean and sky. Charlie scans intently and tirelessly, as many square miles of sea surface pass beneath us. The shimmer mesmerizes me. After what seems a long while, Charlie says, "Look west."

A couple of miles away, the activity of half a dozen whales whitens a small area in the rolling blue universe. Another isolated oasis. A hundred and twenty miles an hour is fast, and we cover the distance to the whales in a blink. Now at least a dozen finbacks and humpbacks trouble the surface below, over an area perhaps four miles in diameter. One humpback breaches and crashes back, sending up an astonishing geyser of spray and foam. Remarks Charlie, "When you see whales like this, you could see tuna anywhere around here."

Up ahead, an enormous finback is doing some heavy breathing at the surface, sending up columns of steamy vapor each time it exhales. Signaling a deep dive with its arching back, the whale sounds straightaway like an arrow, out of sight. Directly below, two humpbacks, a mother and calf, erupt suddenly through the surface, blowing hard. Another mother and calf soon follow, up from infinity. We watch the whales moving along beneath the surface between breaths, their long and slender pectoral fins waving like the graceful arms of dancers. The whales roll forward in unison, lifting their massive tail flukes toward the sky, then flowing seamlessly into a sounding dive, digging straight down into very clear water for a few wonderfully extended seconds, before finally dissolving into that deep eternal indigo.

Charlie goes into a search pattern. His judgment that this is a place worth scrutinizing pays off. We spot a school of a dozen giant bluefins and turn hard to circle them. Their movements appear stiff, as though their massive musculature is packed into too tight a skin. Autumn is upon us, and after summering on rich feeding grounds, the bluefins are nearing their fattest. The big fish swim tautly. Their tails—sickle shaped, capable of flexion but stiff, fibrous like fiberglass—wag ever so slightly. I am looking down at a pod of zeppelins reshaped for speed. Were Atlas to put down the world for a moment and pick up a giant bluefin, it would balance in his fingers like a dart, with its greatest mass gathered up front, to carry the momentum and deliver the impact. Widest just behind the head, the animals I am watching taper rapidly toward their propelling tails. When a giant bluefin tuna decides to move, it does not so much swim through the water as split it like a wedge.

Charlie asks whether his abrupt maneuvering is making me queasy. His questioning brings me back inside my body, and I realize that the engine noise, the vibration, and the frequent sharp banking and rapid changes in altitude are getting to my stomach a little bit.

We head off to the southeast, crossing miles of featureless water over many long minutes, scanning, always scanning. Each time we go searching, my stomach recovers. Each time we find life and begin to bank hard and wheel, queasiness returns.

Off in the eastern distance, a hundred or so shearwaters and gulls are sitting on the water in scattered groups, like salt and pepper on a blue plate. We investigate. A dead whale, well decomposed, hangs vertically, producing a slick that runs for miles. Charlie banks tightly and swoops in. My poor stomach gives another tug. I dig into my sweatshirt for a package of little crackers and unthinkingly toss a handful toward my mouth; they bounce off of my headset's featherweight mouthpiece and scatter on the cabin floor.

Several large, well-gorged blue sharks—"blue dogs" as Charlie calls them—lounge with languid leisure in the fetid slick. They exemplify carnivorous contentment. Most assuredly, this is blue shark heaven. When blue dogs die, they must hope to go to the big, reeking whale carcass in the sky. Charlie only glances at the sharks, but he watches the birds' behavior carefully. These birds prey on the same fish and squid as do the tuna, and birds' behavior can betray tuna hunting near the surface. Charlie tells me that once, while watching shearwaters swimming underwater, feeding on small herring, he saw one of them get hit by a blue shark during a dive. "When the shearwater come to the surface, one wing was not working. He began going in circles. The shark appeared, chasing that bird round and round like you wouldn't believe. Finally wore the shearwater out and nailed him." Blue shark heaven can be shearwater hell. We leave the scene.

A plump humpback, grand and beautiful, pops out at about two o'clock, to the south, idly doing barrel rolls in the water. Charlie notices an enormous streak of subtle color deep under the whale and explains, "That streak is a big school of sand eels that the whale's been feeding on." Tuna eat sand eels too, so we check this area carefully.

Charlie circles tightly, and centrifugal forces make themselves felt in my abdomen. Two "little" twenty-five-foot-long minke whales ("minke" rhymes with "kinky") surface nearby. With their white-tipped flippers, the minkes look like they're playing Ping-Pong. They abruptly disappear. Minkes were of no interest to whale hunters until the much larger whales were reduced to near extinction. Now actively hunted by Norwegians and the Japanese, who disingenuously say they hunt them "for scientific purposes," their meat is consumed in Japan. The hunts are used as a pretext for killing other, highly endangered, protected whales, whose meat is then labeled "minke"—as DNA tests of whale meat from Japanese markets have proved. These minkes, though, remain safe from whale hunters at present.

A basking shark, gray and huge, comes into focus as though entering from the Dreamtime. Estimated length: thirty feet. It slices a slit with its immense dorsal fin. Like the great whales, this gentle giant subsists on tiny animals, straining them from the water with the cave that is its mouth. The placid monster swims unhurriedly at the surface, a life within temporal and spatial dimensions we can only begin to guess at.

Several small pods of giant tuna appear near the surface not far from the basking shark. Inexplicably and impressively, some of the giants come through the surface and crash. Horton, who has seen this a thousand times, cheers. These massive tuna *are* magnificent animals.

We have covered a lot of territory this morning, and seen remarkable things. Accustomed to plodding along the sea surface in a boat, I find the airplane's great speed, which allows us to cover so vast an area and find so many pockets of life at such a breathtaking pace, literally a new experience of space and time. A fish spotter can cover, apparently, the entire Gulf of Maine in a day, keeping close tabs on where, in the moving waters, the life is concentrated.

Having come all the way across the Gulf to an area east of Provincetown, Massachusetts, Horton is heading us down to Chatham, at the elbow of Cape

Cod, for lunch. He asks what I want to eat, so he can radio our order ahead. All I can think of is crackers to settle my stomach. Horton turns the aircraft to the southwest, and the outline of Cape Cod appears vaguely in the hazy distance. "That last bunch of tuna was really nice; six- or seven-hundred-pounders. *Jeez* they were beautiful," he says as he reaches for the funnel and "relief tube" that drains to the outside of the aircraft. "I can fly forever when the sky and sea are this gorgeous. In the air, looking for fish—I love this. Every time I come up here, I thank the Lord."

Amen.

Earlier this morning, when I was a poorer man than I am now, I drove to the Sanford, Maine, airport and met Charlie Horton for the first time. Horton relies on finding bluefin tuna for a significant part of his income, but according to the Atlantic tuna commission, the bluefin's breeding population has dropped nearly 90 percent in just fifteen years, and many scientists expect continued decline. The National Audubon Society has recently petitioned the government to list the bluefin under the Convention on International Trade in Endangered Species, usually called CITES (pronounced SIGH-tees). This would effectively suspend commercial fishing for bluefin. I wrote the petition. I did so after American and Japanese representatives to the tuna commission told me that, despite the precipitous decline reported to them by their own scientists, they had no intention of reducing bluefin catch quotas.

The commission's formal name is the International Commission for the Conservation of Atlantic Tunas. It is usually referred to by its acronym, ICCAT (pronounced EYE-cat). ICCAT comprises roughly twenty member Atlantic-rim countries, plus Japan, which is both a major fisher of Atlantic tunas and the major importer and consumer of bluefins. Founded in the late 1960s, the commission assumed authority for "tunas and tuna-like species," including marlins and swordfish. The commission's charter mandates that it manage for "maximum sustainable yield," meaning, essentially, the most fish that can be taken from a healthy population without causing it to slide into long-term decline.

But according to the commission's own scientific reports, most species the commission has authority for have, in fact, declined sharply since the 1970s. Species now at their lowest levels in history include: bluefin tuna, blue marlin, white marlin, eastern Atlantic yellowfin tuna, albacore tuna, bigeye tuna, and swordfish. Though the commission claims to be "managing" the fisheries, the only catch quotas it has are for the bluefin and for swordfish. But those quotas have always been much higher than the commission's scientists recommended—and much higher than the populations could withstand. The commission has in effect presided over the depletion of many of the Atlantic's big fishes. This illustrious résumé suggests that the acronym ICCAT might as well stand for International Conspiracy to Catch All the Tunas.

I wrote the bluefin petition with the hope that one international treaty organization—CITES—could force another international treaty organization—ICCAT—to act responsibly. Ideally, threat of action under CITES—which could categorize the fish as endangered—will pressure the tuna commission into reducing catches enough to let the bluefin population rebuild. In the long term, many more people would benefit from a rebuilt bluefin population—as, of course, would the fish themselves. The downside is that until the population rebuilds, people who fish for a living—good, decent, hardworking people—could be financially hurt by lowered catch quotas. But the same people will be hurt anyway if the tuna commission refuses to reduce catches and the bluefin declines even further. It is a situation that could have been avoided had the tuna commission lived up to its responsibilities and its name all these years.

But that is only my opinion. And it is based largely on the assumption that the scientific information developed by the tuna commission is accurate. Millions of dollars ride on that question. A CITES listing for bluefin tuna would suspend exports of the fish between the east coast of North America and Japan, the major market. Animals listed on CITES's Appendix I, such as the African elephant, are considered to be in danger of extinction, and they or their parts may not be brought across national boundaries. This is the mechanism that banned international trade in ivory. If the bluefin were to be listed and the fish barred from export, the price would crumble. At U.S. prices, fishing for days or weeks to catch one rare giant bluefin tuna, as is done now, would no longer be profitable, and the fishery would become commercially extinct.

But with the Japanese market, the bluefin is worth fantastic money. Fishers can be paid, depending on the quality and condition of the individual fish, more than $50 per pound for a fish that can weigh hundreds of pounds (the largest bluefin tuna on record weighed nearly 1,500 pounds). Although the mighty bluefin tuna is capable of trans-Atlantic migrations, probably more bluefins from the east coast of North America cross the Pacific, because the next step in the transaction is a one-way air-freight ticket to Tokyo. Here wholesalers auction the fish to retailers. One bluefin tuna recently sold for $83,500, nearly $117 per pound. The 715-pound giant was to be reduced to 2,400 servings of sushi, which, because of the exceptional quality of this individual fish, would be served to elite businessmen and government officials for $75 per serving, bringing in, altogether, an estimated $180,000. One fish.

Besides high prices, the bluefin commands an awed, almost mystical respect and devotion among those who know the animal most intimately. One says, "If you talk to enough fishermen, you may sense how much we really love the bluefin and how much they mean to us. I think it's the way the Indians felt about the buffalo." But people love the bluefin in different ways. Fishers, conservationists, governments, and international treaty organizations continually embroil themselves in bitter international struggles over control and salvation of the fishery.

Perhaps only wolves, African elephants, and the great whales inspire the same intense controversy and anger over their exploitation and "management." While various factions struggle to control the fishing and the money it generates, fishermen around the world hunt the bluefin with everything from harpoons to airplanes to satellites.

But none of this struggle was apparent in the gracious way Charlie Horton greeted me when we met on the runway this morning, before leading me to his bright yellow single-engine Super Cub.

Horton, zipping up his leather jacket, began the flight as he always does, preparing for the worst. "If we have to ditch, I won't have time to explain things. You reach in here and pull out the raft and two survival suits to keep us from freezing to death. If we don't have time to get the suits, that's fine. You pull this handle, and you *should* have a four-man raft in all its glory. Hang onto that raft, because if you let·go, it's going to take off in the breeze and you'll never catch it. To be safe, we have to anticipate trouble." That anticipation has already saved Charlie's life once.

We got clearance to take off and climbed into the Maine morning. A thin ribbon of green water edged the shore; then the bottom dropped away, leaving the blue ocean shimmering, a constantly changing patchwork quilt of breeze patterns and slicks.

We climbed to two thousand feet. A mile from shore, the surface was sprinkled with thousands of lobster buoys, a broad band of colorful dots stretching along the coast to the ends of vision. Looking down, it was difficult to imagine how the lobstermen can tell whose buoys are whose, but it was easy to understand why the huge lobsters one sees mounted on restaurant walls are mostly from long ago.

While I pondered lobsters, Charlie checked a nautical chart showing the sea-floor topography of the Gulf of Maine. Looking at the ocean, he does not see the surface so much as envision the bottom. On Charlie's map, all drawn detail is underwater. Except for the names of a few coastal towns, the land lies blank and incidental, an empty border to the sea, most useful for jotting notes. Charlie studied the map and determined a route across the Gulf that would take us over several major sea-floor features that—while remaining hidden beneath hundreds of feet of water—affect what one sees on the surface. The ridges, hills, canyons, and slopes on the bottom of the sea affect the movement of masses of water. These water masses, differing in temperature, nutrients, and oxygen, form a moving mosaic of habitats that determine the distribution of fish.

"Hundred and seven miles, hundred eighty degrees. Take us, depending on what we find and how much we dally on the way, maybe three hours going down to Chatham," he announced.

We headed south under a clear sky, over the ocean's blue expanse. Before long, the land set behind us and dropped out of sight, and we were without any apparent point of reference.

"Let me show you how I can tell where we are," Charlie offered. His map is superimposed with gridded "loran"—short for Long-Range Navigation—lines, and his plane is equipped with a device that receives signals broadcast from government sending stations and, by triangulating, electronically calculates and displays its exact location. Virtually all planes and fishing boats have loran units or satellite positioning systems on board, allowing them to find and return to pinpoint locations on a trackless ocean with push-button ease.

"I can punch in the position of every group of fish I see," Charlie explained, sliding the map over to me and interpreting notations made on a separate piece of paper. "This is from the last time I was out. I had a school of thirty-five small tuna at this point. Then over here, I saw one lone fish, a pretty good-size one." To return to where he saw something last evening or last summer, Charlie punches a button, and the loran unit gives the heading, reads off the distance to go, draws a steering diagram, and displays ground speed and time till arrival.

Fishermen are the last major hunter-gatherers in modern culture, pursuing wildlife on an industrial scale with all the tools of the space age brought to bear. But if finding fish from the air seems a high-tech approach—and it is—the irony is that the boats Charlie works with catch the huge fish by throwing spears. Space age or not, all hunters, be they bushmen or boatmen, must be able to find and capture quarry in what remains of the concealing wilderness. Despite the tremendous advantage of the plane for revealing the fish's position, the person wielding the hand-thrown harpoon must possess considerable skill if the operation is to be profitable. Approaching a wild, wary fish worth thousands of dollars, while a circling pilot, several crew members, and their families are depending on you for the rent, requires the "stick man" to summon a level of concentration and alert, unthinking attention that can best be appreciated only by those who do it.

Once a tuna is hit by the harpoon, the technology again advances to the electronic age. The harpoon is rigged with a hot wire that electrocutes the fish. In the old days, the fish would run out a harpoon rope attached to a big buoy and a flag. Pulling the rope and buoy would tire the fish until it could be retrieved. Occasionally, an exceptionally powerful fish would continue to run until the flag was lost from sight. One old-timer explained, "Some fish, Christ, they can just keep going and going and going. One time we stuck a fish and his buoy flag just disappeared. One week later, it come sailing back into the bay again. The fish was still alive on it." Nowadays, Charlie explained, the zapped fish is dead within seconds. "That hummer will go about fifty feet and roll over, belly up, just like that. You haul them right aboard."

On his best day last month, Charlie saw twelve schools of tuna within five miles of each other. The boat working with him harpooned seven fish. "Those giants were pretty tame, because we were way out beyond where most boats go," Charlie said. "They're not usually so easy to approach. Bluefin tuna are becoming more educated. A few years ago, you could fly an airplane over the top of these fish, and it didn't bother them at all. This year, particularly, I notice that if you're at anything less than four or five hundred feet, they'll go right down. They hear the engine or see a shadow and they know it means trouble. And as the season gets along and the fish get more harassed, they're more wary. They learn. So we've got a very unusual fish here. Most fish don't seem to have the memory that the bluefin has. It never ceases to amaze me how smart they are. If the swordfish was as smart as the bluefin, he wouldn't be an endangered species, which, in my opinion, he is. He's in trouble. With the tuna, I think we're in good shape, I really do. I think there are a lot of bluefins around and I hope it stays that way. I only wish the swordfish were doing as well as the bluefin tuna."

Before he started fishing with this airplane in 1984, Charlie worked on a boat that did a lot of swordfish harpooning south of Martha's Vineyard and Nantucket. He used to see six or eight a day and get three or four, on average. On the best days, the top guys could harpoon thirty or forty swordfish. "And then all of a sudden we didn't see them from the boat anymore, so I got the airplane. But it dropped right off." In 1985, the last year that boat fished, the crew caught three swordfish the whole season. "After that," Charlie said, "as far as I know, nobody even saw a swordfish south of Martha's Vineyard." So he started swordfishing with Canadian boats on Georges Bank. "Three years ago we got a hundred and thirty swordfish for one boat. Last year we got thirty. This year, fifteen. They're doing the same thing out there on Georges now, in my opinion, that we saw south of Martha's Vineyard. Drying it right up."

Charlie believes the swordfish's biggest problem is caused by long-lining. A longline is a line some twenty to eighty miles long, with over a thousand baited hooks. Swordfish do not begin breeding until they weigh over a hundred pounds, and the ones harpooners saw at the surface were generally quite big. But longlines catch large numbers of small swordfish. Complained Charlie, "They get swordfish *two feet long!* They throw the little pups overboard dead. It's a terrible shame to kill a twenty-pound fish that could have grown to six hundred."

If airplanes, radios, sea-floor charts, loran, and video sonar are not enough to reveal the fish, pilots and boat captains can subscribe (via onboard fax, if that is their preference) to daily satellite-generated maps of sea-surface temperature patterns, so they can maintain a big-picture view of water movements in the habitat mosaic. The owner of several tuna-netting boats, his diamond ring glinting in the sunlight, once told me this story: "This summer, I saw on the satellite charts that a big finger of warm water had broken off from the Gulf Stream and was coming inshore. It was just the right temperature for yellowfin tuna, so we rushed one of our boats there. He loaded up with five hundred tons of yellowfin in six days, unloaded, went back, and loaded up four hundred tons in the next six days. Got eleven hundred tons total for the sea-

son; most yellowfin tuna we ever got." This is not the same as poachers finding bears by tuning in to their radio collars, perhaps, but the analogy suggests
itself. It's not that technology is bad, but without good management guided
by long-term thinking and mindful of natural limits, technology can get mis-
used. The unpleasant reality of this—the collapse of overfished animals and
the destruction of fishing economies—has been presented to us many times,
laid at our feet like a dead bird brought by the cat, and we have been too over-
wrought each time by the tragedy and the sight to examine it and ask where
all these dead birds are coming from, and with what effect. In the U.S. alone,
the Department of Commerce estimates that fisheries depletions cost billions
of dollars annually, and hundreds of thousands of lost jobs.

After a thoughtful pause, Charlie said, "You know, I've thought about the
Audubon Society trying to restrict bluefin tuna exports to Japan, and I said,
'What the heck are these guys getting into this for?' They're supposed to be bird
guys, right? But, the truth is, the fish guys have done a lousy job. I mean, a really
lousy job. So I'll support anybody that'll save these resources. I don't want to see
these damn fish disappear so that when young fellas come along there's nothing
for them. It's possible we could wipe the fish out, just like it's possible to wipe
out any species."

The shoreline of the outer Cape is coming into crisp view, with its undulating
white line of breakers. The beige bluffs, amber beach-grass meadows, green
patches of forest, emerald salt marshes, and meandering channels sprawl in
resplendent repose, their concerted colors a visual ode to joy. We fly along the
national seashore at Truro, past Wellfleet, and over a lobsterman hauling his
traps. Though it's Sunday, the beach is almost devoid of people. It is September,
and those who neither fish nor have an eye for migrant birds have retreated back
indoors, leaving the most beautiful month to a few lucky people. At Pleasant
Bay—an understated name—white boats, tugging at their moorings like ponies,
punctuate blue channels.

We land smoothly on grass alongside the Chatham runway. One just-landed
plane is being towed off the airstrip, having run out of fuel before it reached the
end of the pavement. The pilot is laughing.

In the snack bar, several fish-spotting pilots compare impressions: "I saw a lot
of blue sharks today, not too many porpoises."

"Listen, I don't know where your boat is, but I tell you, it'd be worth it to get
them over to the BB buoy. Sand eels are thick there. That's where you're gonna
find the tuna."

"All week we've seen fish where my boat is today, except the weather hasn't
been calm enough to get to them. Now that the weather is finally good, there's
a big seine netter down there waiting to move in on them the moment they
show."

. . .

After lunch, we taxi into the sunshine and head southeast. A line of billowy clouds on the far horizon accents the blue clarity of the sky. The ocean looks bluer still, almost cobalt.

Mile after mile of rolling blue prairie flows below us, stretching to the ends of the earth, revealing nothing.

Clear, blue offshore waters are oceanic deserts, with pockets of dense life separated by great expanses of relative emptiness. In terrestrial deserts, the amount of life is limited by lack of water, while in oceanic deserts life is limited by lack of nutrients. Camel-like, many open-ocean creatures are in effect desert-adapted animals, able to cross vast tracts of barren habitat until they find the oases containing the food they need.

Thirty miles offshore, we spot a tuna seiner and a couple of planes. Perhaps they've found an oasis. Climbing until comfortably out of their way, we head toward them. Approaching, we realize there's a crowd—four or five planes, a seiner, several harpoon boats, and several rod-and-reel boats pulling fake squids across the surface in hopes of luring a bite. Boats hunting tuna will travel far, running for hours and crossing miles of relatively lifeless sea, to get to where fish are. This area is filled with shearwaters, too. Enormous drifting mats of rockweed indicate that here is a great whirling eddy. Such eddies concentrate oceanic life, making it vulnerable.

The tuna seiner *Ruth and Pat* has just slid its net skiff astern. Working together, the skiff and seiner are making a big circle around a small group of giant tuna, surrounding them with the net. The water below us is about 40 fathoms—240 feet deep. The seiner's net cannot reach that depth, so they have to hope they can purse the bottom of the net closed before the fish dive out. The net is so large that when the circle is completed and a curtain of netting surrounds and undermines the school, the giant fish will suspect nothing until much of the net is winched back aboard the boat.

Above the seiner, a couple of planes are making tight circles. Charlie tells me that the pilot spotting for the *Ruth and Pat* "is a gentleman and a real conservationist. He's cried about what's happened to the swordfish." The radio suddenly crackles as two of the pilots below us begin arguing heatedly about just whose fish these are. The more heated of the two claims he saw the fish first and that before his boat could arrive the other pilot alerted the *Ruth and Pat,* which was closer and got to the fish first. Like a tern joining a feeding flock, another plane arrives. At twenty-five hundred feet, I am happy to be well above this tense, dense pack. We notice another school of giant bluefins running under the surface. About ten boats are streaming in now from all directions, from several miles around. The fish have been found out.

A glance back at the tuna seiner reveals that something has gone wrong. They have somehow lost one end of the net, and they send two small launches to make tight circles in the open spot, trying to prevent the tuna from approaching the breach. Now the wind is causing more problems, blowing the boat into the net circle, so that the shape of the net is starting to resemble a kidney. They regain control, and as the netting is hauled aboard and the circle becomes smaller, a dozen giant tuna, trapped and frantic, their metallic flanks reflecting the sun like signaling mirrors, are frothing what is left of the ocean being drained away from them.

In *The Silent World,* Jacques Cousteau described being in a net in the Mediterranean with sixty giant bluefin tuna as it was drawn up for the kill. He wrote:

> The noble fish, weighing up to four hundred pounds apiece, swam around and around. . . . We pondered how it would feel to be trapped with the other animals and have to live their tragedy. Dumas and I were the only ones in the creeping, constricting prison who knew the outcome, and we were destined to escape. Perhaps we were over-sentimental but we were ashamed of the knowledge. I had an impulse to take my belt knife and cut a hole for a mass break to freedom.
>
> The death chamber was reduced to a third of its size. The atmosphere grew excited, frantic. The herd swam restlessly faster, but still in formation. Their eyes passed us with almost human expressions of fright.
>
> . . . Never have I beheld a sight like the death cell in the last moments. The fish were out of control. . . . With the seeming momentum of locomotives, the tuna drove at me, head-on, obliquely, crosswise. It was out of the question for me to dodge them. Frightened out of sense of time, I . . . surfaced amidst the thrashing bodies. There was not a mark on my body. Even while running amok the giant fish had avoided me by inches, merely massaging me with backwash when they sped past.

The New England tuna netters' annual season starts in late August, and in two months each of five seining vessels, crewed by about six or eight fishermen, will catch a million dollars worth of bluefins, their annual free allocation of a public resource, courtesy of the U.S. government. Two men jointly own three of the five seiners, earning a tidy sum each autumn. While thousands of other fishermen struggle to earn a living from this depleted resource, these five boats, providing only 3 percent of the employment in the fishery, are disproportionately allocated roughly 25 percent of the quota—and their fatly paid lobbyists work like sled dogs to ensure that they hang onto it.

We sheer away from the crowd. The sea surface begins rippling in places as the tide, running over submarine ledges, forms textures and rips on the water.

After traveling several miles, we cross a drift line of seaweed and flotsam—quite long—marking the border of two large water masses. On one side of the line the sea is a plankton-rich, opaque green, of coastal origin. On the other side, clear blue: water from far offshore. This is a special place of meeting. Like a forest edge against a meadow, the two water masses are two ocean habitats.

In the sea no less than on land, the confronting frontier between habitats holds dual potential, attracting the denizens from both sides. Temperatures on each side of such lines are often several degrees apart, forming a partial barrier and leading edge for the travels of swimming animals. Such zones of convergence become charged with synergy. Fronts like this one, where nutrients from continents (their presence betrayed by the dense plankton they are nourishing) become newly available to creatures in clear ocean-desert waters, often gather dense concentrations of life, at all levels of the food web. In the ocean, the fluid mosaic of habitats exists on an immense spatial scale, and right now we're looking directly at the encounter of two big pieces in that mosaic. But tomorrow, this boundary may be miles away or, if there is a churning storm, it may be history.

Over the greener water, Charlie says, "This looks a little too cloudy for bluefins." We cross to blue water. Near the separation zone, a humpback whale surfaces abruptly with a sharply explosive spout of steamy exhalation, then gushes a swimming pool's worth of water out of its pleated throat and swallows its enormous mouthful. Several hundred seabirds, mostly shearwaters, flock excitedly around it, foraging for injured and disoriented fish spilling from the whale's jaws. A second humpback surfaces, mimicking the first, then a third appears, rolls over majestically, and dives in a backflip.

Deep under the drift line of flotsam that marks the water-mass boundary is an enormous dark streak: more sand eels. The tiny animals sand eels feed on—and in turn *their* food—are also concentrated along these habitat edges. Several dozen white-sided dolphins come leaping and streaming into view.

We begin a circling search. A giant ocean sunfish lies basking on its side like a five-hundred-pound dinner plate. Sunfish have no commercial value at present, so they go on living placidly, eating their jellyfish, giving little grief and getting little trouble in return. I have met ocean sunfish from a small boat and found them surprisingly curious as they circled closely, fixing me with their man-in-the-moon faces, seeming to make direct eye contact.

"Blackfish!" says Charlie suddenly, with almost tense excitement, upon spotting two pods of pilot whales (called blackfish in New England). "I never tire of seeing these," he says with absorbed affection. Charlie swoops and abruptly changes altitude, moving the plane up and down like a magnifying glass as he tries to get the best perspective. Having emptied my second and last bag of crackers a while ago—most of which again bounced off my mouthpiece and are scattered at my feet—I'm starting to feel queasy once more and I start burping, which past experience tells me is a bad sign.

It does not matter. This is an excellent vantage for studying these animals. As the pods approach each other head-on, all the individuals in each group close ranks, bunching quite tightly. Are they nervous? Shy? As the two groups meet and begin to commingle, their spacing again relaxes. Perhaps a moment of apprehension at meeting new individuals has passed.

Painting a rusty stain under the sea nearby is an enormous streak of "red feed," shrimplike invertebrates related to Antarctic krill. Three finback whales are churning hungrily through the russet clouds. Big reddish streaks, many half a mile long, drift everywhere we look now. The leviathans come in through the extravagant provender, pumping their great flukes. With their immense mouths agape and remarkable throats distended, the whales propel themselves into the prodigious profusion of food, running the length of it, rolling on their sides and turning upside down, flashing their white chevrons. Reaching the edge of the swarms, they turn on their tails, swimming back though the teeming hordes, lazily gulping great populations of little animals. A basking shark abets this mass annihilation of inglorious invertebrates like a quiet accomplice, a great, gray, ghosting appetite, neither to be hurried nor denied.

Charlie remarks, "*Boy,* there are some whales in here!"

This place is *alive!* In every direction now, creatures far larger than dinosaurs cavort and carry on, blowing voluminous clouds of breath and breaking the sea's surface in rings of foam. The scene is ages old. Pleistocene Park. Everything here is giant. The mammals are giant; the fishes, giant; the scale of creatures enlarged to match the oceanic scale itself. The vast sea seems boundless and expansive. From our commanding view the ocean stretches off like a tight azure drum around the rim of the world, and here against the center of this drum pounds the rhythm of the living. I feel utterly captivated, connected and rhapsodic; I feel that somehow a sweepingly enlightening, profound realization awaits just beyond consciousness—like a forgotten dream sensed upon waking—if I can take this scene in for a few more moments, just long enough to let myself open fully and encompass it.

"All right, let's get out of here," Charlie says. "We'll see more giant tuna as we go north, I'm sure."

We head back toward Maine, pushed by a tailwind. Charlie, constantly attentive to the sea surface, takes a sip out of his water jug and continues scanning. For thirty-five miles we see only water and sky. The brimming intimacy of the whales' oasis melts away with distance, and the ocean again assumes the vaguely threatening dispassion of a vast saltwater desert.

In a surprisingly short time we are back where we found the dead whale this morning. Still here. It is late afternoon, the time of day, Charlie says, when tuna are usually traveling to the west, heading into the sun. So many mysteries. Charlie suddenly points out a dozen giant bluefins, each well over five hundred pounds, swimming in parabolic formation—a graceful arc—just under the surface. The fish are advancing as if strung together, with the two outermost fish taking the rest of the school through the water as though pulling the ends of a net.

Most fishes' schools show synchronous movements, but not social structure or cooperation. The giant bluefins' parabola formations are the next dimension in schooling, the most advanced social grouping among fishes. "The most striking feature of tuna schools is the degree of organization," wrote Brian Partridge and his colleagues from the University of Miami, who studied bluefin groups in New England waters. "Giant bluefin exhibit the most rigidly defined school structure which has yet been observed in any fish."

Not every bluefin school looks the same, though, because the rules determining the schools' structure and form—the position and spacing of the individuals—are based on the number of fish present. The animals at each end of the parabola must be able to see each other in order to maintain the formation. If there are too many fish in the school and too much distance from one end of the parabola to the other, the outer animals cannot maintain visual contact, and the school must be organized differently. So bluefin parabolas are usually formed by groups containing fewer than fifteen individuals.

Bluefins' parabolas serve two functions. One, they provide significant energy savings from easier swimming. With their pectoral fins outstretched, the bluefins take advantage of the lift generated by their neighbors (similar to geese flying in formation); they can also gain increased thrust without increasing effort by "pushing off" of the compaction of water against each other. Second, and more importantly, the parabola formation functions as a dragnet, allowing the bluefins to corral and envelop prey schools they encounter as they travel. As this linear formation advances, the bluefins at each end are the school's leaders, the middle ones the followers in a sense, but each animal is on the front line. The bluefins in their parabolas, say the scientists, practice "cooperative hunting of the sort usually associated with cetaceans [whales and dolphins] or group-living carnivores such as lions or wolves."

The label "fish" says as much about their lives as a toe tag in a morgue. Taxonomy be damned. Watching them, I imagine the giant bluefins watching *one another* closely as they travel, monitoring each other's pace, their great bodies glowing softly in the water like polished tin, producing soft halos around themselves, their enormous eyes swiveling as they search. I imagine looking now ahead for prey, then glancing across at the lead fish, looking over at your neighbor, checking your schoolmates' flanks for signs of an excited flush of color indicating someone has spotted prey in the distance, beyond your field of vision.

According to the loran, these bluefins are only a quarter mile from where we first saw tuna this morning; they may be some of the same fish. Shearwaters rushing toward white explosions nearby call our attention to about thirty medium-sized tuna, between one and two hundred pounds, chasing frantic prey fish at the surface. The prey spray into the air, looking oddly like flocks of sparrows rising and disappearing. By the time we make another circling pass, more than seventy-five tuna have surfaced and are rushing prey, a drama of great beauty and confusion. Charlie makes note, then proceeds, commenting almost wistfully several times about how beautiful those giants in parabola formation looked. He turns for home. One of the most memorable days of my life is drawing to a close.

We hit the runway at five-thirty. Charlie says, with exceptional graciousness, "Any time you want to come out with me, you can. I can use a pair of eyes like yours to help me spot." When I had offered to buy Charlie Horton lunch, he'd said, "I'll get lunch. You can get dinner." Arriving here, it turns out he had no intention of staying for dinner. He was headed up toward Rockport for the night, and he took off after refueling.

Ogunquit

Life in Ogunquit, Maine, may not be red in tooth and claw, but it certainly is red in claw. Lobster icons accost from every direction, including the tops of flag-poles. Lobster T-shirts clutter shop windows, watercolor paintings of lobsters await buyers on the sidewalk, and restaurant signs sport huge red lobsters. One might not suppose that a significant tourism industry could rest upon the graven image of a huge marine invertebrate that, basically a seagoing bug, is unlikely table fare. But here it is.

The day spreads a dense overcast with a raw, moist wind that shudders fitfully through the trees and scuds the ocean white, inspiring fear of winter and of growing old. Undaunted senior tourists, having already grown old and appear-ing fearless, go from bed to breakfast, traveling the sidewalks in force, in and out of the countless boutiques and galleries, buying up the lobster shirts for their grandchildren. I find my way along the street to Barnacle Billy's restaurant.

Steve Weiner seems more like a country lawyer or businessman than a fisher-man. Direct and earnest without being aggressive, he has a successful salesman's grasp of the subtleties of human politics on a one-to-one level. The main thing—the *one* thing—he wants me to come away with, he tells me, is the realization that the guys up here are very sincere in their belief that the bluefin tuna are recovering from the devastation of the 1960s and early '70s and that the resource, as he refers to the animals, is doing well. He buys lunch and refuses to let me pay for our drinks.

Steve is bright, and I do not doubt his sincerity. He is an officer of the East Coast Tuna Association, an unlikely amalgam of various commercial bluefin tuna fishers, including such oft-feuding types as purse seiners, rod and reelers, and harpooners, all of whom get in one another's way on the fishing grounds. They have laid aside their differences (at least in public, at least usually) to unite polit-ically against a variety of threatening people who would reduce the number of fish they are allowed to catch, such as the National Marine Fisheries Service, sportfishing groups, conservation organizations, and scientists of the American Fisheries Society.

I am here to get Steve's take on all this, to hear what other fishermen around here have to say, and to get a feel for how Steve's crew works the water. Steve has a reputation as one of the best bluefin harpooners around, and he says that the weather forecast for tomorrow looks good.

In the morning I rise at six and walk down to Barnacle Billy's to see if Steve and his crew will search for fish today. Harpooners are fussy. They need ideal weather, both to cause the giant fish to rise and stay up, and to facilitate seeing and pursuing them near the surface. A flag suggests a wind of only about ten miles per hour. The ocean looks calm.

Tim Voorheis, a small, ruddy-faced, strawberry-haired spotter pilot in his early forties who works solely with Steve, shows up a moment later carrying a cup of coffee. Steve and Tim judge this a good day to go fishing. Their mate, Kevin, a stocky, chain-smoking guy in his midthirties with curly reddish hair and an upturned nose, says the Weather Service predicts a big storm for tomorrow. "S'posed to blow forty." This being the day *before* the storm, he says, it's a very good day to hunt. "The tuna sense the storm coming, and rise to the surface." Why they would do that, I don't know; more mysteries. Steve's brother, Brooks, comes over and says, "This is gonna be the day—day before the storm."

Steve's boat, the *Elizabeth Ames,* is a graceful Down East–style lobster boat, but rigged strictly for bluefin harpooning. A huge tank, into which giant tuna are immediately immersed in iced seawater after capture, occupies much of the deck. This chilling preserves the quality of their flesh and hence their appeal to the Japanese palate—and wallet. The price paid varies according to the fat content of the fish (something the fishers can't control but that generally increases as the season progresses on the feeding grounds) and the freshness of the surprisingly delicate flesh, which can show, only a few hours after death, a change in color that will cost money.

Buyers will take a core sample or sliver out of the fish and scrutinize it in the palm of their hand for color, freshness, and fattiness—the more fat the better—before offering a price. Tainting, leanness, bruises, unsightly gaff tears, or any other external damage can even render a fish "nonexportable," knocking the price down 90 percent and sending the fish to an ignoble fate in an American sushi bar or, worse, a fish market, which will sell it as steaks to be cooked.

The *Elizabeth Ames* has a high crow's nest for spotting and a long "pulpit" extending from her bow, from which the harpooneer practices his craft. Everything aboard is orderly, a well-kept boat reflecting a well-organized crew. Steve also owns another boat, run by another crew. From their home port farther north, the *Elizabeth Ames* has been down in Ogunquit for several days to be closer to a group of fish. Steve, Brooks, and Kevin, with Tim in the air, make up the usual crew on this boat. Brooks earns about half his living from fishing and the rest of it from selling chemicals, a business in which Steve has also enjoyed considerable success. Brooks says that in the off-season most guys fill in with carpentry and odd jobs.

I follow Tim out to the airport. At seven-twenty, the sun is climbing and a big moon still shines broadly in the pale morning sky. Tim's proud plane is a gleaming Piper Cub, vintage 1946. Had he told me the plane was a year old, I would have believed him. "It's important to me that the plane looks good and functions perfectly and reliably," he says. "I wouldn't go up in the air in most planes." Tim puts his lunch into the plane, in a metal *Bonanza* school lunch box featuring Pa, Little Joe, and Hoss. I stuff myself with crackers in a preemptive, on-the-ground strike against air sickness. We wait for some ground fog to burn off. Tim started fishing more than twenty years ago with Steve and Brooks. He started flying in 1977. For a couple of years he tried to convince Steve that he needed a spotting plane, and the crew finally agreed that to stay competitive, they should have one. He's been spotting full-time during the tuna season for the last five years.

We taxi into the sun and lift off, rising to behold a maze of ridges suspended in distant fog. We head directly east over creeks meandering through bright green marsh grass. Tim begins scanning before we've even crossed the shoreline. We shoot over the barrier beach, out into the nearby ocean, over the lobster buoy zone, and a couple of miles farther offshore before heading south toward an area where, the VHF radio reports, the rod-and-reel fleet has already hooked a few tuna this morning. Someone on the radio reports seeing some 150-pounders about forty miles east of us. Steve, west of us in the boat, has seen some medium-sized bluefins in the two-hundred-pound class—still not adults—busting up the surface. Brooks tells us over the radio that their sonar is detecting dense herring schools near the bottom.

We're at eleven hundred feet, heading into the sun past picturesque little Boone Island rock with its lighthouse. Tim says that as kids they never had to go beyond this area, seven miles from shore, to look for tuna.

We head south toward the Isles of Shoals. A breeze blows up, making white-caps. Beginning a little east of the Isles, the rod-and-reel fleet stretches out densely to the south about as far as we can see, several hundred boats, each throwing at least a hundred pounds of fish—chum—overboard during the course of a day, each hoping to fool a giant fish into eating a spiked offering. The chumming fleet's quota for the season is nearly filled. The harpooners can't wait for all these chummers to get off the water, so they can have more of the place, and the fish, to themselves. The purse seiner *White Dove* comes into view to the south, having already netted fifteen giants this morning.

One of the pilots broadcasts the news, which I'd gotten over the phone yesterday, that congressional pressure has prompted the National Marine Fisheries Service to recommend against listing bluefin as endangered under the CITES treaty. In other words, they have turned down my proposal. Tim, relieved, tells me that if I take the time to understand his fishery I'll come to realize that there are far more fish out here than the scientific reports estimate.

We pass the Merrimack River. A long, well-defined drift line of pollen has come out on the tide with the river water, making a big semicircular streak outside the river. It reaches about three miles into the ocean, then bends back to the shore. Tim makes a few tight circles around what look like small streaks of flotsam. He says these are striped bass. As the sun glints they disappear, then they look like streaks of flotsam again. The light keeps changing and the image keeps vanishing in the glare and the wind streaks. I say, "Are you sure those are really fish?" He nods vigorously. Finally, I can clearly see two of the streaks swimming off.

By ten o'clock, Tim and I have not seen a tuna. Tim is unhappy with the way the weather is shaping up and says the fish very rarely stay near the surface when the wind breezes up from the northwest like this. He tunes to the government weather channel for the updated forecast. I'm starting to feel chilly and button up my quilted shirt. Tim takes us to a place about twenty-five miles offshore, where we spot a humpback calf alone at the surface. We swing over for a look and can see a light patch beneath it in the murky green water. Apparently, its mother. Admiring the calf, Tim says he can't comprehend how anybody could kill a whale.

We head back to Boone Island. Tim belches into the headphones and says, "The tide's nearing slack, a better time to see fish." The wind drops out again. The water goes slick. Another pilot radios to say he just saw thirty or forty giants come up suddenly, run along just beneath the surface for a few minutes, and then go down. "Now some of the fish may be starting to show themselves," Tim says.

It's becoming clear that this is a game of changing surface conditions and of waiting for the fish to make themselves vulnerable. Wait we do. Tim searches indefatigably. Lack of sleep is catching up with me, and with the droning of the engine and the monotonous glitter of the sea below, I can't help dozing, though I'm ashamed to do so.

Tim turns landward for some fuel and a leg stretch. We come in with a crosswind and the plane bounces jauntily as our wheels bite the runway. At noon, after refueling and a candy bar, we're ready to leave again. Tim turns the key and nothing happens. He says, "That's interesting." He hops out and checks a couple of things, turns the prop a little by hand, gets back in, and turns the key again. Nothing. He goes back out and looks around. Flips a couple of switches. Says he's gonna try it one more time. Says, "If nothing happens this time—." He turns the key again. The engine starts, and off we go. Into the wild blue yonder.

The ocean's surface has slicked to a glassy calm. "This is better tuna weather," Tim says enthusiastically. "If it stays flat like this, they may show."

A breeze comes up again, flecking the surface with whitecaps and exasperating Tim. "Damn wind is just hangin' on," he says. "I hate days when it does this." Tim complains that the weather has been killing them. The red pennant we saw flying at the airport already warns of the bad weather predicted for tomorrow.

We're coming over a place called Jeffreys Ledge, about forty miles from the coast. The bottom here—the ledge—comes up from 120 to 30 fathoms (720 to 180 feet). At such high spots, currents force deep, nutrient-rich water up over the bottom contour, bringing some of it close to the surface, where ample light penetrates. Here, those nutrients become newly available to single-celled planktonic plants that need both the nutrients *and* the surface light, together, to photosynthesize food. The resulting "bloom" of rapidly reproducing plankton forms a rich grazing ground for minute animals and larval fish. These attract small fish, which are hunted by bigger fish. In short, the entire food chain sets up shop, eventually drawing in the ultimate predators—and here we are. Shearwaters and gulls, scattered in small groups, sit resting. A line of drifted vegetation catches our attention, and we notice a school of several hundred smallish fish along it. Tim puts the shadow of the plane directly across the school. "Bluefish. If they were tuna they would have spooked."

He calls Steve to check in. "If the tuna were gonna show, you'd think they woulda shown by now."

Tim decides to give me my first flying lesson. "Put your feet on these two pedals. These are the rudders. Press on the right rudder a little bit, and give the stick some pressure." I have trouble coordinating the rudder and stick, and I am unclear about how much pressure it takes before the aircraft responds. We begin climbing upward. I realize that I need a little forward pressure on the stick most of the time.

"O.K., now how do I control the airspeed?" I ask. Tim shows me what to do. "Now what altitude do you want me to maintain—eleven hundred feet?" I realize that I am, for the moment, flying the plane. My eyes become glued to the altimeter, but since there is a short lag between the actual altitude and the altimeter's reading, I keep going up and down, up and down, trying to get right on eleven hundred feet. While I'm biting hard on the tip of my tongue, I suddenly notice Tim laughing to himself.

"What would you do if I had a heart attack?" he asks.

"I'd have a heart attack too, of course." I tell Tim, "O.K., I'm gonna be turning now, so just keep an eye on what I'm doing because I'm not too sure. . . ." I turn the plane, tentatively at first, and am pleased at the sensation of acquiring the feel of an entirely new skill.

Tim stops laughing long enough to say kindly, "Not too bad! Kinda smooth!" The flying is straight, flat, and uncomplicated, and I relax enough to try to take a swig of soda. I succeed only in hitting my mouthpiece with the bottle. I seem to have a learning disability about this. Satisfied to think that at least I have more talent for learning how to fly than for feeding myself, I return control of the plane to Tim.

A group of about a hundred dolphins comes into view; this would make a good picture. As we circle over them, I snap some photos through the window. With my attention fixed on the grace and patterning of the animals moving below, I try to slide the window open for a better shot. But instead of pushing the window tab I hit the throttle lever mounted alongside the sill, making the engine suddenly race. The plane surges forward with a great roar, startling Tim, who doesn't understand what is happening. I understand exactly what is happening, and immediately pull the throttle back.

Tim says I've given him that heart attack.

The surface of the ocean, which has been changing constantly throughout the day, again goes calm. Tim announces that we now have ideal conditions. A voice on the radio says, "There's not enough wind to blow the stink off a dog, but we've all been at this long enough to know that the right weather doesn't always mean they're gonna show like they're supposed to." I've already been at this long enough to know he's right.

Tim says, "We should see something soon."

Ahead, I see something, odd-looking and vaguely shark-shaped, drifting intriguingly below the surface. Tim says it's a discarded piece of fishing net.

A mile beyond that, several hundred gulls, forming a fluttering cloud, are following hard behind a working dragger. As the net is hauled up, some of the gulls snatch fish being forced from the mesh by water pressure. Others are grabbing discarded fish being shoveled from the deck because they are too small or too damaged to be marketable. The wasted fish are a good deal for the gulls, even if relying heavily on handouts weakens their character. But the fish, the fishermen, and the rest of us pay a price for such waste. Waste is not the only issue here, nor is the problem merely local. Using everything netted would not fix the biological effects of catching billions of very young fish, seabirds, rare porpoises, and other animals throughout the world's seas. Each year, fishing boats draw up an estimated twenty-seven million metric tons of marine life that, dying or dead, are thrown overboard—*a quarter of the whole global catch.* Such unwanted creatures are collectively known as by-catch or by-kill. Shrimp trawlers—the largest source of adult mortality for endangered sea turtles—generate the most by-kill: For each pound of shrimp kept, two to eight pounds of sea creatures are killed and dumped. In the western Pacific, the region with the highest by-kill, an inconceivable—but measurable—nine million metric tons of marine life are killed and discarded annually.

At five in the afternoon, we throw in the towel and head back. I take out my remaining crackers and, having successfully found my mouth, absentmindedly munch through half a box during the homeward flight. After we land, Tim invites me to have dinner with him again at Barnacle Billy's, where he eats every night. I can't imagine a good reason not to, except that I'm getting sick of the place. On the other hand, they have good clam chowder and Tim and the others are great company.

It's dark by the time I get to the restaurant, and I park in an unlit lot a couple of blocks away. Closing the car door, I look up at the full September moon and imagine being out on my beloved home waters off Montauk, hunting striped bass under this magnificent night sky of early autumn. Struck by a sudden unexpected twinge of homesickness, I walk swiftly down the street to the light and noise of Barnacle Billy's.

Today's weather, as predicted, is garbage from the fishermen's point of view, so Steve Weiner has arranged for a group of fishermen to gather at the Super 8 Motel at noon to see Tim's aerial photos of tuna.

Rich Ruais, a tense man in his early forties with a meet-the-Beatles haircut and a thin, flat mouth, accompanies the fishermen. Ruais is a paid, full-time lobbyist for the East Coast Tuna Association. He also worked on the staff of the New England Fishery Management Council during the 1980s, when the council allowed the free fall of New England populations of cod, haddock, flounder, and other important species, sending them to their lowest levels in history and creating widespread unemployment.

Also joining us is Roger Hillhouse, a man in his early sixties with a casual, self-assured demeanor, piercing blue eyes, and more logged hours looking at tuna from an airplane than anyone else in the world. Roger has been finding fish from the air for thirty-six years, first in the Pacific and then on the East Coast.

Roger thinks this year the tuna are spending more time hunting, staying deep and out of sight, because they are having difficulty finding enough food. Part of the reason: bluefish, a swift, efficient fish known for its voracity. "They drive all the food fish out. Bluefish are miserable things."

Though my own scientific field research on bluefish in the mid-1980s indicated that, as Roger says, prey flees—or is eaten—in the path of bluefish schools, Roger's attempt to blame bluefish for troubles with tuna perplexes me, because bluefish had been coexisting with tuna for a long time when Roger first looked down upon vast, virgin schools of bluefin tuna off the Atlantic seaboard as though looking at money in the bank.

Roger's career encompasses the whole history of the East Coast bluefin fishery; he's seen it all. Roger co-owns three of the five bluefin seine-net boats, and he came into the fishery with the first boats in 1962. "The California sardine fishery I had been flying in was shot from overfishing—and now, thirty years later, they still haven't recovered—so we came here looking for small tuna fish for the canneries. We found school after school, and we loaded up."

Following their success, Roger says, roughly twenty other boats came in. "They began to wipe out all the medium-size fish. Then, fifteen years of netting the small fish robbed the whole young size class out of the population. There was nothing growing up. Boats were catching four-hundred- and five-hundred-ton boatloads of little eight-, ten-pound bluefin tuna off New Jersey. The captains were paid fifty dollars a ton, regardless of size.

"I saw the California sardines collapse and I know what can happen. I promised myself years ago I'd never knowingly participate in the destruction of another fishery. That's why I support bluefin conservation."

Though the Atlantic tuna commission estimates that the number of breeding bluefin has declined by nearly 90 percent, these fishermen tell me the scientists grossly underestimate the numbers. They say they have aerial photos to prove it. Tim pulls out his slides, and the lights go out. An impressive school of bluefin tuna appears on the wall. "You can count one thousand fish on the surface, I think, on this one. I could see schools of medium-sized fish like this for fifteen miles around me. And they probably stretched all the way to Canada. That was the only day of the season that all those fish came up. Otherwise you would never know, in God's world, that there were that many fish there. These are a very mystical fish, and that's probably why all of us in this room are chasing them. It isn't the money. It's the mystique of these fish."

Tim hits the button and another picture appears on the wall. "You can count six hundred right on the surface here." Another slide. "Here you can see three hundred right on top." Click. "This is a bigger school. You just start counting and it's incredible."

Steve Weiner says, "Let me just tell you that the most fish we've seen in our lives was on a day when we caught one fish. And we're pretty decent at harpooning. That's because it was just flat-ass calm. The fish could see us. We couldn't get *near* those fish. And you see, if you look at catch rates, it would seem to you that there weren't very many fish there that day. But really there was an ungodly amount of fish there. We would have loaded that boat if we'd had a five-mile-an-hour wind to mask our approach. If other people cared as much about their fisheries as the commercial tuna fishermen do—as we do—about ours, we'd have very healthy fisheries worldwide. The bluefin regulations are working and the fish are coming back."

As frustrated as the fishermen are that the scientific information does not fit their impressions, their impressions alone do not entirely disprove the official estimates. Even if there are now only forty thousand adult bluefins (down from perhaps ten times as many), as the scientists estimate, it may still be possible to see several thousand fish in the course of transiting the region by air on one of those days when many schools inexplicably surface. And other fishermen, primarily old-timers and those south of Cape Cod, paint a very different picture of bluefin abundance.

The New England fishermen's main complaint is that no one will take their anecdotal information into account. But taken as a whole, for *all* the fishermen I've talked to up and down the coast, the anecdotal information does not contradict the scientific estimates. A pattern emerges from the anecdotes: Fisher-men north of Cape Cod see and catch consistent numbers of bluefins—though not as many as in the old days—while in many places south of the Cape the fish-ing is a shadow of what it was in the past. On Long Island, a large, stationary fish trap just off the beach used to catch giant bluefin regularly. "In the sixties we'd sometimes have half a dozen giant tuna in the trap when we'd go check it in the morning," the former trap tender told me, "but we didn't catch any in the last twenty years we operated." Tuna tournaments were once held in Rhode Island, where the best fishing spots were within two or three miles of shore. Charter-boat skipper Al Anderson says, "We haven't seen bluefin tuna in those areas in nearly two decades." Montauk marina proprietor Ed Miller says, "What's surprising about the bluefin tuna fishing is how fast the big fish have declined around here. The first time I went giant-tuna fishing I caught three giants that day. I was so close to Rhode Island I was watching people swimming on the beach. You didn't have to go offshore in those days. I don't know if it's overfishing or natural, or some combination, but it sure has gone downhill fast." Pictures from the 1930s show more than a dozen giant tuna hanging at one dock after a day of sportfishing off New Jersey, where nowadays perhaps only a dozen giant bluefins will be landed in that state in an entire season. A commercial-trawler captain from Long Island told me, "When I started tuna fishing in the early eighties it was pretty easy to catch giant tuna locally. Now, you have to take your boat up to New England." People from Long Island who *have* taken their boats to New England say the fish from the south have simply moved up to those waters, not dwindled. This may be correct, but it may also be wishful thinking.

Tim clicks the remote and a dead whale surrounded by sharks appears on the wall. "These are the biggest blue sharks that I've ever seen; that's a sixty-foot whale. Some of those sharks were around fourteen feet long. There were literally hundreds of sharks feeding on that carcass."

One of the other fishermen, who had been at the scene in a boat, says, "Those sharks were coming right up and sniffing the boat and opening their mouths. It scared my friend and me. My friend got some good pictures of the sharks and of the whale. He said his wife would be grossed out when she saw the whale pic-tures, because, with the whale all bloated up like that, it's very obvious you're looking at a male whale."

"What killed that whale?" I ask.

"He met up with a gill net. Had netting on his upper jaw. We saved a whale out there last year, a humpback that had tangled in offshore lobster gear. He was completely traumatized and heading for the beach, with thick line wrapped on him and dragging big orange plastic buoys. I saw him on my way out and we got Gary Grenier to cut him free. He put a knife on a long pole and cut that stuff off. And when he did, the whale just laid there, as if, 'Thank you.' It was a neat thing to see."

Obviously, the men in this room care about the living things around them, and one of the men pipes up, "The guys that we fish with around here love the bluefin. Truly. More than they love their wives."

"A lot more."

"Many of them aren't married because of these fish. They *were* married and they aren't married now because of the bluefin."

"I read in the newspapers that we're fishing because they're worth a lot of money. It's not the case. Money is the excuse we give our wives to rationalize why we're out there."

"We love these fish. We'd be the first guys to stop fishing if we thought they were in trouble. We spend more hours on the water—. Listen, I'm telling you this is a healthy, recovering fishery. You read about 'commercial fishermen destroying it,' and, granted, it's happened in a lot of other fisheries. The bluefin tuna fishery is healthy. It's made up of guys who are responsible, and we have a future in this fishery. When I see this stuff they print, I lose my faith in government, I lose my faith in science, I lose my faith in the *New York Times,* I lose my faith in everything. I mean—really!"

Tim says, "To me, the giant bluefin tuna is a symbol of all that is great in the world, every living creature. To me it's the most magnificent creature on earth, maybe even more so than man himself."

Dave Linney says, "There's another half to this. My daughter goes to college on tuna fish money. It's very important to me."

Talk turns to the Gulf of Mexico, where the giant bluefins that survive the summer in New England go in wintertime to spawn. No one has seen bluefins spawning, but Roger believes they come in small groups and gather at water-mass fronts along concentrated drift lines of floating seaweed and other flotsam that hold prey. He thinks they don't begin breeding until a group has reached a few dozen. This makes sense; lots of fish breed in groups, because with external fertilization, commingling eggs and sperm in seawater, group-spawning helps ensure fertilization of more of the drifting eggs. "So," Roger says, "I've always contended that longline fishing inhibits these tuna from getting together into these larger groups, and interferes with spawning activity. Nineteen seventy-three, before the Japanese really went into the Gulf with longlines, produced the most successful spawning that we ever recorded, by numbers of young fish we later netted. That was our last big year for young fish. The Japanese came in '74, caught five thousand tons of breeders, and this went on for a number of years and then they left. But they were immediately replaced with local long-liners. Something is interfering with these fish. My contention is that long-liners picking them in the Gulf are disrupting spawning, keeping them from getting together in large schools. We're not seeing any big, major year classes, like '73. We are not seeing the babies—we are not seeing the spawning."

I wonder how Roger could assume that the netting of so many young fish that he was involved in for over a decade would have no eventual effect on the number growing up to become adults and, consequently, the numbers of young fish spawned in the last few years. But if I have any doubt that these fishermen blame Gulf long-liners for damaging their fishing, Steve erases it by saying, "I told Rich today, I said, 'Rich, it's not for me to find ways for those guys in the Gulf to fish responsibly. If they want to fish—if there's a way that the long-liners can exist as a legitimate fishery, then they better come up with it pretty quick.' "

Steve continues, "The amount of fish they're cutting off dead because they can't legally keep them is scary. The Gulf of Mexico is important, but also outside the Gulf; long-liners up north in the summertime—. I mean, if I had my way, the damn longlines—."

Roger reminds us again that long-liners destroyed the swordfish.

Steve says, "I see long-lining as our biggest problem." Steve also tells me he's just heard that Honduran long-liners landed several hundred tons of bluefin last year. He says that the bluefin traffic through Mexico and through other countries that are not members of the Atlantic tuna commission—and so not bound by any catch controls—is a big concern and a big problem for them. These are the same migratory fish that spend the summer off New England. He also believes that Japanese catches in the Gulf Stream far offshore in winter are hurting this same population.

Now, for the first time, I am hearing the bluefin fishermen say there are problems in the fishery. Until now, I have heard only that the bluefin is abundant, healthy, and increasing in numbers. This causes me to wonder whether, perhaps, some of the fishermen really do believe that the bluefin faces problems and, in the temptation to point fingers, are allowing their guard to slip a little.

Regardless of the answer to that question, there is little doubt that the situation in the Gulf of Mexico has been problematic. In 1981, Japanese long-liners were asked to leave U.S. waters in the Gulf because management agencies and U.S. fishers had been outraged by high Japanese catches of bluefin tuna and billfish.

But by 1987 the size of the U.S. longline fleet already far exceeded anything the Japanese had sent to the Gulf. Louisiana's tuna landings (mostly yellowfin tuna) exploded in the 1980s, from thirty-five thousand pounds in 1984 to over twelve *million* pounds in 1988, a 3,400 percent increase.

The composition of the Gulf fishing fleet changed markedly during the mid-1980s, as many longtime captains bailed out of the fishery. Members of the Gulf's relatively young Asian-American community, already involved in shrimp fishing, took advantage of the cheap tuna-fishing equipment on the market. These Asian-Americans (mostly immigrant Vietnamese) innovated unorthodox techniques, particularly the use of live bait instead of frozen. Live bait was much more effective, but keeping it alive required drilling large numbers of holes in the boats' hulls to flood bait tanks with continually changing seawater. The remaining older captains were unwilling to punch holes in their hulls because of the safety factor and suffered a competitive disadvantage. This inflamed racial tensions.

Further intensifying the competition, bluefin tuna were available for shorter and shorter periods, perhaps because the bluefin population was declining. Yet escalating Japanese prices kept many boats targeting bluefins. Tensions flared as competition rose and operations became marginal.

As profits declined, vessels began pirating one another's gear. With boats setting longline gear stretching twenty miles or more and fishing thousands of hooks, another vessel could work the first ten miles of gear, stealing buoys, radar reflectors, and fish, while the owner of the gear was still setting the line. Observers witnessed several armed confrontations, noting, "No shots were exchanged but most of the Asian-American boats were heavily armed with illegal automatic weapons, many of them relics of the Vietnam War." By the late '80s, competitive tensions and piracies were so cutthroat that on two occasions when observers were aboard Asian-American long-liners that became disabled, other Asian-American long-liners within sight of them would not abandon their gear to go to their aid, ignoring radio distress calls. On both occasions, other boats came long distances to rescue the ailing vessels.

After the National Marine Fisheries Service cut funding for observers aboard Gulf long-liners in 1987, Louisiana State University's Coastal Fisheries Institute, seeking to fill the void, tried to initiate their own observer program in 1988–89. But the university report noted, "The observers had a difficult time securing trips during the bluefin season as so much illegal activity was going on that the captains didn't want witnesses. A common practice was for a boat to keep all of the bluefin it caught (they were only allowed to keep 2 per trip) and pass on those it couldn't legally land to other boats in exchange for a percentage of the sale price." Since prices for giant tuna were running from twenty-one to thirty-six dollars per pound in the New Orleans area, "this proved to be quite profitable."

Filled quotas and the season's official closure didn't stop some vessels from landing giant bluefins. A Japanese dealer continued buying, keeping one step ahead of the law by moving to different parts of the Louisiana coast as National Marine Fisheries Service agents tried to catch up with him. Vessels selling bluefin to him would partially unload their catches at each of five docks to avoid remaining at one dock too long. The buyer was constantly moving among these docks and must have come within a hair's breadth of getting nailed on a couple of occasions, because several giant tuna carcasses were found floating in nearby bayous. The buyer eventually left with a wad of green, having given federal fisheries enforcement officers the slip.

The Atlantic tuna commission had recommended years earlier that no fishing be directed at giant bluefin in their Gulf of Mexico spawning grounds. But the Fisheries Service never acted to close certain areas during bluefin spawning, or to require fishing gear that could catch yellowfin tuna but would break free under the surge of a giant bluefin. The service's only further gesture was to limit the number of bluefins that a boat could land per trip and to require boats bringing back bluefins to also land twenty-five hundred pounds of other fish. In other words, the fishery for giant bluefin tuna worth thirty dollars per pound was supposed to become a "by-catch only" fishery—officially closed, but with a "tolerance" of one giant bluefin per day per vessel. This may have looked good on paper to somebody, but it only resulted in continued targeting of bluefin *plus* additional fishing for things like sharks, yellowfin, and whatever was available, to make up the legally required "target" catch. Rumor had it that even giant sunfish were kept—and then thrown into Dumpsters—to make the quota for "target" species, to justify the bluefin they had "incidentally" caught at the beginning of the trip.

Long-liners fishing for tuna also catch marlin and sailfish, which cannot be sold if caught in Atlantic, Caribbean, or Gulf waters (an intended conservation regulation). But most of the billfish hooked on longlines die during the hours they struggle before the longline is hauled. These (and the occasional drowned mammal or endangered turtle) are slipped back into the sea—their magnificent corpses a boon for crabs. A few live marlin and sailfish, hooked just before haulback, are occasionally brought alongside alive. Many captains simply cut the unmarketable fish free because a large, panicked, thrashing fish with a big pointed bill on its snout poses more trouble than a seventy-five-cent hook is worth. But for some captains, seventy-five cents is seventy-five cents, and the worthless fish ruin hard-gotten live baits. On these boats, the fish is immobilized and the hook retrieved. The university's observers explained, "Immobilized fish were recorded as 'dead' since it was unlikely that fish beaten over the head with baseball bats would survive." It seems catching marlin in the Gulf of Mexico has changed since Hemingway's old man Santiago, his palms bloodied from struggling with a great fish for days, apologized to the marlin for harming it. Apparently, for some captains, long-lining means never having to say you're sorry.

The afternoon is wearing on, and Roger Hillhouse suggests that we reconvene later at a local restaurant. At the restaurant, the hour, the setting, and the smell of food—and a few drinks—allow the conversation to unwind and drift. The men forget the issues and the controversy for a while and trade stories culled from a lifetime of adventures among wild animals in nature.

Roger begins telling stories from his West Coast days. "I used to fly a lot at night. I could identify twenty-three species at night by the shape of the school's glow, but the first night I flew, I mistakenly set a guy on a school of squid. Squid grab onto the net, and when they do, water won't pass through it. That guy had two or three hundred ton of squid pulling on his net, and the boat started leaning over like this; it almost tipped over! I knew what a school of squid looked like after that!"

In his early years, Roger spent a lot of time searching out dolphins—most fishermen call them porpoises—swimming above yellowfin tuna. Why Pacific yellowfins and dolphins swim together remains uncertain (mutual admiration has been suggested), though it almost certainly involves food. But one does not need to understand a relationship to exploit it. Setting nets around dolphins to catch yellowfin tuna became Roger's living. Because dolphins were often drowned in this way, public outcry eventually led American tuna canners to buy only tuna caught in ways that are "dolphin safe." It's interesting that many people who are aghast at the thought of harming a dolphin, of snuffing so bright a life, will glibly down a sandwich made from the wild creature with whom the dolphin swims, without pausing to reflect on where and how it may have lived, or with how many dolphins it might have exchanged glances.

Roger has plenty of dolphin stories from those Pacific days. "After we got into yellowfin tuna fishing, I was flying off Mexico once and I found two adult killer whales swimming in a circle. Inside the circle was one porpoise and a baby killer whale. The baby was chasing the porpoise around. Every time the porpoise would try to escape the circle, the adults would block it off and turn it back. I watched for over thirty minutes; I couldn't believe that they actually train their young."

Roger continues, "Once, we found a school of porpoise that we wanted to set the net around, and started working these porpoises in the usual manner. But every time we'd start to set, they'd do something abnormal. Pretty soon I looked behind them. About two or three miles back were about twenty killer whales." Eyebrows go up around the table. "Oh yeah—those porpoises *knew.* The killer whales never changed pace. Just kept coming. These porpoises went this way and that way and back and forth. Every time they'd make a zigzag, the killers would be getting a little closer. And when those killer whales got within half a mile"— Roger pauses for effect, and several of us lean forward a little—"they suddenly sped up and *charged!* They swept right into that school of porpoises and tuna, and they *attacked.* One would grab a porpoise and swim a short distance with it hanging out of its mouth, trailing blood. Then he'd let that half go and grab another one, or a tuna. They just kept chomping 'em up. Never did I *ever* see so much blood in the water."

Soon, inevitably, a shark story comes out of the bag, and one of the men relates an incident from his adolescence. "It was tuna season and we was out looking. My father was down in Casco Bay helping to seine herring, and my mother and I went out tuna fishing in his boat. It was a very quiet and calm day. I saw this wake plowing right along and I says, 'There's one to the right a little bit.' So I get on the harpoon stand out over the water, up close enough to see him. I saw it wasn't a tuna fish. It was a great white shark. It turned and swung right at the boat, just five feet alongside, looking the boat all over, and then went back out and kept going. My mother stuck her head out of the wheelhouse and said, 'Why don't you try to see if you can hit him?' I thought, 'See if I can hit him?' Well, I didn't want to hit him with the harpoon point, because he'd just turn and break the pole and I'd lose it. So I took the dart off, and I'm holding just the harpoon pole with no point on it. I throw it as far as I can, and I miss him. Well, he turns *right* around and comes back, full throttle. His snout comes out of the water, his mouth opens, and he hits the bow of the boat: *Wham!* Like that. Hard. I hadn't even hit him! Imagine if I'd hit him! Well, I says to my mother, I says, 'Don't prick with him any more.' But she was laughing like hell! And she starts to turn around and go for him again. He hears us coming, and he turns around and starts for *us* again. I had just the pole in my hand, no point. When he went under the stand I jabbed it right down and hit the top of his head. When I did *that,* he came right up out of the water, and I'm only about five feet off the water on the harpoon stand. His mouth is open so big I could drop a bushel basket right into it. He's right below my feet and I'm looking down at this huge angry mouth, full of teeth ready to bite my legs off. Oh, *boy!* My mother thought it was a rip! I didn't think it was so damned funny. But she was just laughing like hell."

One of the men says, "Speaking of things that fish like to eat, so to speak, in the old days we saw plenty of food fish like herring and mackerel and squid. On the surface everywhere. And boy, you don't see much of it anymore."

"No, there ain't much herring around compared to years ago."

Another adds, "The whiting are nearly gone, too. That was a favorite—probably one of the favorite things that tuna fish liked around this area—the whiting."

"Yup. Boy, there used to be whiting everywhere. That's gone. If tuna had to live on whiting, they'd be some skinny, I'll tell you."

We linger at the restaurant until about ten-thirty. Brooks Weiner drives me home in the rain. He says, "We all really appreciate your coming. You're the first guy to really come and see and talk with us. Even if you come to the same conclusion that the fish are in bad shape at the end of this, we respect you for having come to check it out. You know the old saying: 'Believe half of what you see and none of what you hear.' At least you've made an attempt to see for yourself."

I go inside feeling not flattered but humbled, because had I been Brooks, I am not sure I would have had the class to say such things.

Rain falls all through the night. I wake in the morning to dense fog and drizzle. It's cool, and I can see my breath. Autumn.

By eight-thirty, the fog opens up. The flag is limp, but I see a front approaching. The ocean's flat pewter expanse broods under an unsettled, lead-throated sky. One lone sailboat on the dark sea summons from somewhere a luminous shine, its sails glowing like a polished pearl upon gray velvet.

Morning fog and the impending front have the bluefin hunters waiting out the weather ashore. Dave Linney, whom I'd met yesterday, owns a nursery and spends his summers harpooning tuna. He is a powerfully built man with big, weather-beaten hands, green eyes, and a raccoon tan line on his face from wearing glacier glasses while scanning the glare for bluefins. His boat, *Peregrine,* is named after my favorite bird. Linney looks as though he was born wearing a flannel shirt. One would never suspect that he has an MBA and worked at Citibank in Manhattan for six years. Born in Indiana, Linney is the son of a banker who summered in Maine. As a member of the town zoning board, he helped to develop some of the best town wetlands protection regulations in this state.

Dave invites Leon Perkins, an old-timer whose experience with bluefin spanned half a century, to join us. I ask Perkins if there are any contrasts between the old days and now.

"In the old days, before spotter planes," Perkins begins, "an area wouldn't get fished for a while. And the fish would go there and after a few days they'd be tame as logs. Then someone would find them and get nine, ten fish. The next day everybody'd steam over and there'd be a wicked kill and then the fish'd go right down again. With the advent of the Jap high prices, everybody's got planes now and the fish don't have a chance. Spotter planes are the worst thing that ever happened to tuna fishing, conservationwise. Of course, I was here when the first purse seiners came, with *their* planes. That was the beginning of the end of abundant tuna. You can't have big tuna if you catch all the small ones, and those guys were targeting the small ones for the first decade or so."

Dave remarks that many people still bemoan what the seiners did to the fish in the sixties. "And," he says, "when you see a seiner take three hundred giant tuna in one set, you think, 'Wow, that could be my whole decade—maybe twenty years—of fish-catching right there.' It can make you a little bit resentful about it."

Perkins says that when he started in 1936, a person went tuna fishing for fun. If you made your expenses, you did well. Since around 1975, the bluefin fishery has evolved into a cash-producing fishery, an important part of a person's annual earnings; though he says, "Nobody in their right mind could count on tuna being their sole source of income."

He adds, "In the early years, we sold tuna for their livers. I assume they used them for vitamins or oil. There'd be about seven or eight pounds of liver in a fish in the early part of the season; maybe fifteen pounds in the fall when the fish was fat. The liver was worth more than the whole fish itself, and I've sold many a giant tuna for seven pounds of liver. I can remember when fifteen cents a pound seemed good. When the price went to a dollar, it seemed unbelievable." Two men he knows recently sent two tuna, caught the same day, to Japan on consignment. They got $53 per pound for one and over $40 for the other, and made $35,000 for the two fish.

I am also curious about Perkins's impressions about other kinds of fish. "The problem is," he says, "when one fish declines, tremendous pressure gets shifted onto some other. People who have got to make boat payments go in on some new fish and then, *whammo! That* goes. Compared to the others, the tuna fishery looks like the most healthy one around right now."

I ask, "Do you think there are as many tuna around now as in the old days, Mr. Perkins?"

"I don't know. See, I don't know anything about this deep-water, offshore fishing they're doing now, because, Christ, most of the time we only went five or six miles. There were a lot of fish around in the old days. You'd see fish all day long, but in the late afternoon, they'd really be thick. The most we got in a season was one hundred and thirty-two, but most every year it was over a hundred."

I ask Linney how that compares to today. "The best harpooners," Dave replies, "get about thirty-five per season. Average guys get between fifteen and twenty, and a lot of guys get less than ten." Dave says that although nobody may want to admit this up front, there are certainly fewer giants now than there used to be. But he quickly adds that he thinks there are many more small and medium fish in the last few years than a decade or so ago.

Tim Tower has just walked over. Tim runs a boat that takes paying anglers out to catch cod, pollock, and other species for recreation and food. In the early 1970s, Tim fished for giant tuna with a hand line—no rod, no reel, just a line—a method still in common use. Tim adds, "I probably caught thirty fish a year; not too many."

Dave snorts. "To you thirty fish a year is not too many? Don't make me sick!"

"Well, you know, it was 1972, '73, and '74—"

Perkins says, "Speaking of hand-lining, remember Suzanne Graves? A fish took a line, she ran up and grabbed it, and it dragged her right to the stern on her knees. Burned her hands all to hell. Third-degree burns. She went to the hospital. But we got the fish. The next week she was back out there, with both her arms bandaged up like a praying mantis."

Dave tells me that Tim wrote a thesis on tuna. "Yeah," Tim says, "my bachelor's thesis from Alfred University. I don't know where my copy is. Probably all outdated now. Tuna have changed a lot since then. I wrote about their behavior. When they're hunting, they will zig and zag and try and herd a school of small fish into a center, sort of like a bunch of coyotes chasing a fawn deer. When they get them where they want them, they'll keep the fish herded in the center, in between them, in a big tight ball—"

"By the way," Perkins interjects, changing the subject, "I'll tell all of you a story. I'm watching that Marty Stoufferheimer, or what the hell ever his name is, there on *Wild America* last night, and he says harbor seals can't sleep in the water. But I can attest they can. Your father and I were down outside Portland Lightship one hot day. Dead calm and, Jeez, it was just broiling down like the Sahara Desert. And we saw this damned seal laying there. And of course, your father, he was always putting me up to something. He says, 'How close do you suppose we can get to that seal?' So we edged up to that danged seal and Harry took the harpoon and just touched him with the end of the pole, and I got the worst bath that I ever got in my life when that son of a gun woke up! And I'll tell you one thing, Marty Stoufferheimer, or what the hell ever his name is, when he says they can't sleep in the water, he doesn't know what he's talking about."

• • •

The evening holds a distinct chill. Though the equinox is still a few days away, there is no hint of summer left. At 10:55 P.M. someone comes to my door and does not knock but slips a note into the louvers and leaves. I open the door and read: "Dear Dr. Safina— Tomorrow will be too windy. However, Sunday and Monday are supposed to be beautiful. Have a pleasant night. Sincerely, Lori at the front desk."

Windy or not, a day this beautiful has to be lived. The day is bright and clear, the sky blue, and the dry air feels light. A northerly wind stirs a primal urge to move. The geese feel it, and so do I. Perhaps it is a last internal vestige from a time, long ago, when we migrated with the seasons across open plains, following the animals we pursued for food. Perhaps that is why the sight of migrating geese arrests our attention, why we feel the pull. We want to go, to travel in fresh or moody weather, taking in each newly revealed vista.

I buy a ticket and hop aboard Tim Tower's *Bunny Clark* along with a couple of dozen hopefuls who would like to connect with a thumping fish or two for dinner. Tim has earned a reputation as a superlative captain, and, astonishingly, twenty-eight fish caught from his boat have made it into the record books of the International Game Fish Association. He encourages release of the fish on his boat, and he has had his own tags made up with his name and address on them. Tim has tagged and released huge cod of over sixty pounds—a size most serious cod fishers don't see in a lifetime. Many of the fish tagged on his boat have been recovered elsewhere.

Punching the tickets as he welcomes passengers aboard, Tim keeps up a humorous banter, saying, "It's important to hold onto this ticket, because if you leave the vessel during the cruise, it will allow you to come back on."

I ask how the fishing has been, and the humor and twinkle drain from his face. "I catch more big fish than anybody in Maine," he says, "and it's getting tougher for me. In 1983 we got almost a thousand trophy-sized fish. This year we've only caught about sixty. Price of cod went up last week and a lot of gill-netters and draggers out of New Bedford and Gloucester started working this area, and we can already see the difference. We used to catch a pile of redfish. No more. It's true of every species now."

Tower pulls the *Bunny Clark* from the dock and out of the tiny cove that is Ogunquit's harbor, into the ocean. Tim fingers the loran's keypad, and the information that will get him to our first spot appears on the display screen. "The haddock is probably the biggest example. We talk about haddock in numbers now instead of tons. This boat's caught seventy-four haddock this year. And it's the biggest year I've had for haddock in three years. Last year we caught twenty-three. In the past, you couldn't count them. We had literally tons of haddock. I used to row a skiff out sometimes and fill it full of haddock. I could catch more haddock in one day in that skiff than this boat has caught in two hundred and sixty-two trips this year. When I was a kid I had two halibut spots. You couldn't catch a halibut now if you tried."

Stewardship of these fish and management of the fisheries is the official responsibility of the New England Fishery Management Council, one of eight regional fishery management councils created in 1976 when the United States Congress enacted the Fishery Conservation and Management Act. The act was prompted by the devastating effect that fleets of enormous fishing and process-ing ships from distant nations were having on fish populations and dependent fisheries along U.S. shores. The act had two goals: to Americanize fisheries in U.S. coastal waters and to conserve the fish. The former goal, achieved with Yan-kee efficiency, extended U.S. control from twelve out to two hundred miles and phased out foreign fishing. To accomplish the latter goal, the act established the regional councils and appointed those most knowledgeable about the fisheries—people who fish—to be responsible for regulating fishing activities. As writer Ted Williams noted seventeen years later, "The act was a grand experiment in human nature, rooted in the conviction that if you lead people toward righ-teousness without looking back to see if they're following, their innate goodness will rise and envelop them, and they will march resolutely past temptation, ascending with you straight and true to celestial heights neither they nor anyone else ever dreamed they could attain." Well, as Lily Tomlin says, "No matter how cynical you get, it's not cynical enough."

The council system's uniquely idealized form of representative self-government did not work as intended, because people with financial stakes in the outcomes of their own self-regulation do not always act ideally. Putting billions of dollars' worth of fish in front of the industry and asking them to police themselves was not terribly realistic.

American fleets soon surpassed the catching abilities of the recently departed foreigners, with the help of misguided boat-building subsidies that shoved U.S. fishing power far beyond the fishes' abilities to reproduce. The councils made hardly a move to restore, conserve, or even regulate. Throughout the 1980s, the councils repeatedly avoided an ounce of prevention, deferring economic discom-fort. By the early 1990s, these forgone ounces of prevention threatened to cost a ton of cure. Many fish populations, especially in New England, were in tatters. Ironically, inaction intended to avoid economic discomfort was now costing New England $350 million annually and more than fourteen thousand jobs. (Though New England is the most notorious case, the same principle operates nationally: The federal government estimates that fish depletion costs the United States $8 billion annually, and three hundred thousand jobs.) This is only the human side of the disaster.

On Georges Bank, previously regarded as among the richest fishing grounds on the planet, the formerly dominant cod (once reverently referred to as King

Cod in fishing communities), pollock, and haddock were replaced by dogfish and skates (often called "trash fish" by fishers) that surged into their vacated niches. Overfishing had stood the Bank's natural ecology on its head. Some people speculated that King Cod and his royal court—now refugees in their own kingdom—might suffer a fierce competitive disadvantage in trying to regain the throne from species that were once the court jesters, even if the fishing boats were forced to stay home. (But within a decade even the once-scorned dogfish would be overfished, allaying fears that it could still pose a threat to cod and raising new fears that it, too, was in trouble.)

Year after year, the New England Fishery Management Council never got its act together, despite continual controversy and withering hand-wringing. Some council members began blaming seals and even porpoises for the scarcity of groundfish. ("Groundfish" is a collective name for cod, haddock, hake, pollock, flounders, and a variety of other species that are found near the bottom—hugging "the ground." The term might as well refer to the way these animals have been treated—ground down to nubs.) In 1991, the Conservation Law Foundation sued for failure to rebuild the groundfish populations, then at an all-time low. "The lawsuit is a blunt instrument," CLF's director, Doug Foy, admitted, "but nothing else was working."

The lawsuit forced the process along but did not fix the problem. In 1994, the National Marine Fisheries Service's Dr. Vaughan Anthony, who chaired a new scientific assessment of the cod population, said, "This is a terrible situation, bordering on disaster. . . . We couldn't find anything good to say about this species, or I'd say it now." A Fisheries Service report also used the word "disaster" to describe the yellowtail flounder situation and with the highly unusual use of an exclamation point in a scientific document, concluded, "The stock has collapsed!" Only eight fish out of a hundred were surviving from one year to the next. The breeding population had declined 94 percent in three years, leaving reproduction "the poorest on record." The last very successful yellowtail flounder spawning had been in 1987. But 60 percent of the catch from that year group were too small to sell when they were caught, and they were discarded dead. Allen Peterson, the Fisheries Service's regional director, declared, "The patient is hemorrhaging. We've got to stop the bleeding before we can treat the wound."

The Fisheries Service stepped in over the management council and closed large portions of the famed Georges Bank, New England's major fishing ground.

King Cod and his court have a long, long way to go before they regain the motherland and are once again vital and robust populations. But even if that ever happens, the fishing communities of New England may yet become the biggest long-term losers in the whole scenario, because by overfishing they have undercut their own economic power. As fishing businesses go under, the dockside space is being bought up for condos, waterfront restaurants, marinas, and the like. To the extent that the fishing industry puts itself out of business now—and this process is well under way—there will be that much less harbor space available for a fishing industry to re-expand in the future even if the fish do come back and the ecosystem recovers.

But New England's fishing communities are relatively lucky compared to their neighbors. Just to the north, in Newfoundland, the cod crisis reached nightmare proportions. Here, crass or unenlightened self-interest by fishers can't be blamed, because the fisheries management system is not democratic. Here, the government agencies with the authority were not greedy, just negligent. Who is at fault? The people who are *paid for* (the words "responsible for" cannot be made to fit here) running Canada's Department of Fisheries and Oceans. Who pays? As always, the human victims of bad management are the fishers; the bureaucrats' paychecks remain unaltered. Recognizing far too late a mistake of catastrophic dimensions, in 1993 the Canadian government did the unthinkable and closed—shut down—the cod fishery, throwing twenty-five thousand fishing people, who live in communities with virtually no other employment, onto the government dole (adding taxpayers to the list of victims). Thus, Newfoundland cod—like New England haddock and halibut—was now commercially extinct. The international debacle in this region is the worst fishery management failure in the world (this could change; there are challengers in the making).

Around the year 1500, explorer John Cabot had described the Grand Banks as so "swarming with fish [that they] could be taken not only with a net but in baskets let down with a stone." Within seventy-five years, the fish were supporting a boom. One colonist noted that the cod "draweth many nations thither and is become the most famous fishing of the world." Now it is famous for another reason. Where was once a natural system of unimaginable richness, spurring the colonization and prosperity of northeastern North America, there is now a $2 billion welfare burden and 60 percent unemployment. To people whose families have lived in the region for centuries, it is an apocalyptic transformation.

Aboard the *Bunny Clark* today, Tim Tower does not need to read about the 1500s, nor does he need his university diploma, to know what has been lost. "We used to catch big sea pollock, twenty to forty pounds, along the shore. You never see that anymore; never see that," he says, shaking his head and looking at his shoes. Sad and angry at the same time, he sees the basis of his livelihood being chipped away and taken apart, fish by fish.

And rock by rock. "These trawlers' net-dragging gear is destroying the rocky bottom structure and the growth on it that the fish need as habitat," Tim says. "Give you an example: There used to be a great pollock spot out on the back side of Jeffreys Ledge. There was a hell of a school of pollock there. One other person knew about it, and he knew a dragger captain who was having hard times, and he took some pity on him, and he gave him the loran numbers. The next morning, the dragger was working that peak. The first tow, he got eighty thousand pounds of pollock. We never caught a significant amount of pollock on that spot ever again. And I'll tell you something; after that dragger left, the entire bottom habitat was changed. What used to be a sharp, jagged peak on the sonar was a round, flattened hump. In the northeast corner there used to be a real sharp edge, and all these little anemones and stuff used to grow on there. Now, it's nothing like it used to be. You can still catch a pollock there occasionally, but—" Tower ends his sentence with a dejected wave of his hands.

Not far away, four large draggers are plowing along in parallel, separated by only about a quarter mile. "That's what we call gang trawling," Tim says. I ask if it's as coordinated as it looks. Answering obliquely, but getting straight to the point, he says, "They're just trying to catch everything."

In July 1991, Massachusetts congressman Gerry Studds had declared, "We cannot stand by and watch cod and flounder and haddock—the bread-and-butter species of Georges Bank—become the nautical equivalents of the dodo bird and the passenger pigeon." The comparison is a chilling one. At one time, passenger pigeons numbered in the billions. Breeding colonies extending "for twenty-eight miles, averaging three or four miles wide" were reported as late as the 1870s. In the late 1800s, millions of passenger pigeons were caught commercially in nets for human consumption each year. By 1889, the American scientific journal the *Auk* carried an article by ornithologist William Brewster, who had searched for remaining concentrations of passenger pigeons. Though he believed the greatly depleted bird was not on the verge of extinction, Brewster warned that the passenger pigeon was overexploited and inadequately protected. "The theory is that the birds are so infinitely numerous that their ranks are not seriously thinned by catching a few million breeding birds in a summer. . . . The netters, many of whom strike me as intelligent and honest men, seem really to believe this. As they have local influence, and the powerful backing of dealers in the cities, it is not likely that any really effectual laws can be passed until the last of our Passenger Pigeons are preparing to follow the Great Auk and American Bison." (The great auk, a flightless seabird, was driven extinct in 1844 after being overhunted for, among other things, cod bait.)

The passenger pigeon, though in decline, was indeed not on the verge of extinction in 1889. So nothing much was done. But the pigeon (like many fishes) apparently needed the social stimulation of large groups in order to breed, and when the population declined to a certain threshold, it suddenly collapsed. Twenty-five years later, the last passenger pigeon on Earth died in a zoo.

The statements about the passenger pigeon's supposed invulnerability are remarkably similar to what people once said about the great whales, and to what we frequently hear today about many species of fish. This is understandable. It is hard to accept that the wild animals you depend on are dwindling, and harder still to accept it if your activities might have contributed to the problem. That is human nature, regardless of what kind of animals are involved. But the passenger pigeon's sad story, and the human capacity for denial, should be kept in mind. Those who do not learn from history, as we are seeing, are indeed doomed to repeat it.

For Tim's fares today—the people on whom Tim Tower relies for a living now, the people who have paid Tim to find fish—fishing is tough. We move to several spots but catch very little. Most fares catch nothing at all. It's the first time this year that Tim's paying customers catch not a single cod. The mood is somber as we motor back toward port.

At the dock, Tim earnestly thanks everyone for coming and asks them to give a round of applause to his mate. I applaud heartily, wishing I could put a few tons of cod in the water for Tim's next trip.

Is it really possible that the bluefin tuna, the world's most valuable fish, could be exempt from all these problems and the kind of thinking that has demolished the vitality of the region's other great fisheries? Tomorrow I am heading south to Massachusetts. Those I've met here tell me I'm welcome back anytime. I will miss them.

Cape Cod Bay

"I'm not an anticonservationist," Gerry Abrams is saying. "Certainly, I rely on natural resources to earn a living, I always have. And I'm certainly not an anti-environmentalist, because I personally believe that many, many of the resources that have been good to me over the years financially, businesswise, have problems related to habitat loss as much or more than to overfishing. But I don't buy the argument that man is the thing that is expendable in the quest to correct what-ever is wrong. Particularly with fish like tuna that swim across national bound-aries, given the state of our economy, if we're going to err, we ought to err on the side of employment."

"But what happens when resources get depleted?" I ask. "You must worry about that, because you've seen it and it affects your business, right?"

"Absolutely, O.K.? But what I'm saying is, if we need to err, we ought to err on the side of employment. We can't have Americans doing all the sacrificing for conservation and other countries not cooperating. We can't afford to give out that kind of foreign aid."

"What about the idea of the United States leading an international effort to get other countries to cooperate in reducing catch quotas for bluefin tuna until the fish recover?"

"Wait a minute! Just a minute. That's bullshit and I'm going to tell you why it's bullshit. You're talking about reductions? We never talked about increases and you're talking about reductions! For what? We never thought the bluefin was in bad shape to begin with! Don't risk your reputation on this yet. Wait and see what happens. Don't be in a rush to accept the hysteria. You don't know shit about bluefin tuna, and reading a report doesn't make you an expert."

I had just met Gerry Abrams. At four-thirty A.M., when I stepped outside in the dark, Gerry was waiting for me in his Lincoln. "Hello, Mr. Abrams," I said, extending my hand.

"Mr. Abrams was my father," he said in a thick New England accent. "My name's Gerry." It was a charming introduction and the nicest thing I ever heard Gerry say. Gerry is an ambitious fish dealer, and founder and "president emeritus," as he says, of the East Coast Tuna Association. Solemnly dedicated to making a dollar—and he has made many—he is one of several people who claim credit for first arranging to ship fresh bluefin tuna from New England to Japan for the sushi connection. Gerry is a man of middle age and round features. His round head is balding. His round eyes are made rounder by bifocals. Dressed in a blue windbreaker and khaki pants, Gerry is impeccably groomed, with a close-cropped mustache, manicured hands, and polished nails.

At five-thirty we leave the Gloucester–Cape Ann Marina on Gerry Abrams's thirty-one-foot, state-of-the-art sportfishing boat, the *Lady Jane*. His boat is equipped with autopilot, loran, video sonar, cellular phone, radios. We negotiate the river in darkness, with Gerry at the wheel. As we break the river mouth, the blush of first light begins to tint the horizon. Gerry pushes the throttles forward, the boat rises up onto plane as it gains its cruising speed, and we head northeast.

Dawn begins pushing back the covers of night and the sun rolls out of bed. The ocean is slick calm, the sky overcast except over the eastern horizon, where the clouds end abruptly with a jagged line like a torn piece of paper. I am looking back at the cloaked, receding coastline when Gerry taps me on the shoulder, calling my attention to a stunning, late-September sunrise.

This is the height of the bluefin tuna season in New England. In early autumn, the giant bluefins' wariness slips a little as they begin feeding heavily to fatten for their fall migration. Autumnal gluttony, necessary for surviving the strain and privation of self-powered, long-distance travel to wintering grounds, is part of the persona of migratory animals, be they the songbirds ashore or the fish off the beach. The desperate need to feed and fatten is the reason that fish of all kinds appear out of nowhere in the fall. On the inshore edge of the bluefin tuna's summer range, for example, swift fleets of bonitos, hordes of bluefish, and schools of striped bass, all of which spent the summer subtly, now surge and strike along the beaches. Their savage hunger constantly shadows the imponderably large schools of anchovies, herring, mackerel and other prey that represent the natural productivity of summer. As sheltered estuaries and coves begin to feel the lash and chill of northerly storms, millions of these small fishes, unable to remain in their shallow sanctuaries because insuperable cold will soon be upon them, move out into the dangerous Atlantic gauntlet.

Of the many fish that move in autumn, the bluefin tuna's migratory travels are farther ranging and more complicated than most. Scientists say the tuna's routes to winter breeding areas are "not well documented." Perhaps someday they will be, though with research money becoming scarcer, that will be difficult. For now, once they leave the summer feeding grounds, the blue giants are swallowed into Atlantic vastness until they arrive in the Gulf of Mexico to breed.

Because giant tuna in the act of spawning have never been seen by scientists, what little we know about their lovemaking is based on the distribution of bluefin larvae. Though they are among the largest animals in the world, bluefins begin life as tiny larvae, as do most fish and amphibians. This is different from sharks and the other vertebrates—mammals, birds, reptiles. Prior to the early 1970s, when bluefin larvae were first found in the Gulf, no one was sure where the giant fish spawned. Though scientists have searched along the eastern seaboard, few bluefin larvae have ever been found anywhere off North America except in the Gulf of Mexico and the Straits of Florida.

When bluefin eggs hatch, the larvae become part of the drifting plankton, traveling at the mercy of currents and suffering extraordinary mortality. There is nothing really quite like plankton in the land or air environments. But in the ocean, plankton is fundamentally important. Living near the surface of the sea, the plankton community is composed of single-celled plants—phytoplankton—and minute animals—zooplankton. The microscopic plants are the pastures of the sea, and they produce something like 70 percent of the oxygen we breathe. The animals, a bizarre and minute zoo of predatory invertebrates and menacingly armed fish and crustacean larvae, spend all their time consuming the plants or murdering each other. A more dangerous neighborhood can scarcely be imagined. Identifying planktonic larvae, which bear no resemblance to their parents and often look very much like larvae of other species, is difficult, exceedingly tedious work. A bluefin larvae five millimeters long (not even a quarter of an inch) is a toothy, spike-headed animal with huge eyes and a minute, eel-like body. There is no hint that its cells carry in their DNA the blueprint for one of the world's most highly developed and most sought after large creatures. So what scientists know about the spawning of bluefin they know circumstantially, from the distribution of larvae. All that's really known about the adults' breeding behavior is that giant bluefins disappear from New England in late autumn and appear in the Gulf of Mexico in winter in breeding condition. Except for some that do not make it that far, like the one Gerry hopes to catch today.

Gerry's mate, Austin Dorr, slices up two hundred pounds of herring on the way out. These slices—our chum—will be doled overboard to attract giant tuna and diminish their wariness. Austin is sixty-two years old. He's got a ruddy complexion, a couple of broken teeth in front. He moves and speaks with the sort of kindly, earnest, confident-but-modest Jimmy Stewart manner that was more characteristic of Americans back when the United States thought of itself more as America the Beautiful. As if to emphasize that he was lucky enough to grow up in a Will Rogers era I can scarcely fathom, Austin reflects, "I've never had a bad day."

The tuna fleet appears on radar before we can see it. Gerry speaks of the importance of all these boats to the economy. Gerry says you can't get a room in

Gloucester right now because so many people have come here at the height of the season trying to catch a giant tuna. He says that all the fishers are buying bait every morning, buying fuel, visiting the coffee shops, gassing up their cars, and populating the restaurants. If the fish were in trouble, he says, we wouldn't fish. But he declares most emphatically there are plenty of giant bluefin. "And we are restricted by a quota while the Europeans fish unrestricted. All these fish we protect on our side of the ocean swim to the east. We're helping build the fishery in the Mediterranean." This is a theme that Gerry repeatedly returns to, but it is not clear how much of this is accurate and how much is finger-pointing. Some bluefins from the American coast cross the Atlantic to Europe, in variable proportions, each year, riding the Gulf Stream. And some easterners also cross to the west. Information from tagging and other studies suggests that the rate at which bluefins cross the ocean from west to east is somewhere around two percent. Gerry believes this information is wrong, politically motivated, and that the Atlantic hosts one large, freely mixing population. But while people like Gerry Abrams argue about the rate at which bluefins migrate back and forth across the Atlantic, everyone agrees that many Atlantic bluefins cross the Pacific, in jet planes bound for Tokyo.

Nonetheless, bluefin tuna, among the most migratory of animals, range widely throughout the world's oceans. Populations inhabit both sides of the Atlantic and the Pacific. In the western Atlantic they range from Nova Scotia to the tropics. They have coursed these waters since before the bordering lands were named. But the first time anything human gazed upon an ocean, no bluefin had set a fin against the sea, because bluefin tuna did not yet exist; the bluefin is a young species, only about one to two million years old, having evolved *after* the earliest hominids. Nowadays, over the course of a year, their Gulf-to-Gulf transits have them breeding in the winter-warm Gulf of Mexico, then chilling out during summer in the Gulf of Maine; patrolling oceanic ridges in dim, cool waters, keeping mackerel and herring edgy. But some of them range even farther, traveling south of the equator or riding the Gulf Stream to waters off Europe, from which they may or may not return west eventually. Younger bluefins generally don't move as far. They spend the winter distantly offshore of the U.S. Atlantic coast, in the relatively warm waters of the Gulf Stream. Adolescents are often intercepted in the Gulf Stream by Japanese long-liners hunting the more oceanic bigeye tuna on the high seas of the North Atlantic.

For most of human history, animal migrations utterly mystified people. Animals simply appeared in certain seasons, then vanished. The little we know about the movements of animals like tuna chips away at great mysteries. The reason that animals of different ages sometimes migrate to different places in different seasons is that what they need to grow and survive changes throughout life. Adults must travel to certain breeding grounds to reach conditions best for survival of their young. Those still too young to breed will move as little as is necessary to stay within waters of tolerable temperatures and to track their food supply.

Imagine, then, their movements. Imagine the giants in winter, finding their mates and exerting their passions in the warm and sunny Gulf of Mexico, chasing the flying fish like thunder in the tropics. Imagine their surviving children of several years ago swimming hidden in the Gulf Stream far to the north and east. While winter gales rage overhead and whip the sea surface into foaming mountains embedded in fog before driven snow, the young bluefins course the warm vein of the Gulf Stream, trailing the scent of their prey schools, bathed by the very same water that bathed their spawning parents weeks earlier at the Gulf Stream's source.

Facts hint at further mysteries. Over thousands of unmarked miles the bluefins come and go, flooding into these New England waters during summer like high tide, expelled for the winter like an exhaled breath. Somehow, all these animals know where to go: into the Gulf Stream or down to the breeding grounds. What instincts rule their motivations and desires? After seven winters in the Gulf Stream, what impulse, what *sensation,* first turns their head south to seek their spawning ground? They move of their own volition, and we have no knowledge of their urges.

Why some bluefins from the western Atlantic catch the Gulf Stream for a long ride across the ocean to mingle among the eastern Atlantic population, no one knows. That population once ranged all the way from Norway to northern Africa. The Norwegian fishery, which took more than eight thousand metric tons in 1962, went into extinction in the mid-1980s. Interestingly, some bluefins tagged off the east coast of North America in the 1960s were recaptured off Norway, suggesting that their disappearance from Norwegian waters might possibly reflect, at least partly, a population decline in the western Atlantic. The eastern bluefin population, reduced to a fifth of its former size, bears a large, virtually unregulated commercial fishery. Catches in the eastern Atlantic and the Mediterranean (where they also spawn) exceed twenty thousand tons per year— in some years twice that. Several countries fishing on this population neither belong to the Atlantic tuna commission nor heed the commission's recommendations to refrain from netting masses of young bluefins in their first year of life. Zeroing in on the vast, easily caught schools of young fish is exactly the tactic that led to the rapid mining and long-term depletion of the population off eastern North America. History repeats. Heavy pressure is also exerted on the big fish, for the export sushi market.

Bluefins live in the North Pacific, too, breeding around Japan and the Philippines in spring and early summer. Juveniles are carried northward by the Kuroshio, or Japan Current. Some spend their first winter near Japan, while others continue on a spectacular six-thousand-mile arc across the wide Pacific and may stay off California and Mexico for more than a year. The costs—in energy and time—of such an enormous migration preclude crossing the ocean in each direction within a single year. Fishermen regularly encounter large, mature bluefins enormous distances from the fish's spawning grounds during breeding season, meaning that not all adults breed each year. The Pacific migrants' trip back west may take two years. In the intervening period, the fish are lost from human observation. No one knows whether a bluefin may cross the Pacific repeatedly during its lifetime; nor whether some visit the central Pacific without continuing farther east; nor, in those that have gone east to the coast of California and Mexico, how they find their way back. Nor why, exactly, they are built and inclined to make these long treks. In pondering these simple questions, we stand on the ragged edge of scientific knowledge as on some wilderness coast, the answers yet beyond us.

The Atlantic and North Pacific bluefins are one species, northern bluefin *Thunnus thynnus.* A second species, the southern bluefin tuna, *Thunnus maccoyii,* migrates through the temperate Southern Hemisphere between thirty and fifty degrees south latitude. Spawning only in the Indian Ocean south of Java, southern bluefin undertake prodigious, complex migrations far from their natal source, around the southern Indian Ocean gyral, sometimes ranging past the Cape of Good Hope into the South Atlantic. This tuna's far-ranging hegiras may take two to three years to complete, perhaps the most time-consuming migrations of any creatures on the planet.

These migrations involve navigational abilities that stand quite outside human faculties. We study sensory deprivation in humans by suspending volunteers in water, yet these animals are fully oriented in the trackless oceans by senses we either lack or use in entirely different ways. Tuna and some other migratory fishes have magnetite crystals in their brains, a built-in compass. To our five-sense mosaic of the world, a tuna's magnetic perception is extrasensory; we cannot imagine the sensation of it.

The southern bluefin's history of exploitation follows a familiar pattern, traceable to a familiar source: Japanese demand for wild fish. In 1971, some twelve hundred Japanese long-liners worked the waters off Australia. The population was mined down. Catches peaked at more than twenty thousand tons in 1982; then the fishing began to fail. Fishery officials reduced the number of boats. But remaining vessels compensated for declining catches by increasing the length of fishing voyages and the amount of fishing gear set. Each vessel, in one extended trip lasting over a year, might bait and set over a million hooks (each year, long-liners set well over 100 million hooks in the Southern Ocean)—making the ocean a treacherous place indeed, and not just for tuna. By-kill of albatrosses, other seabirds, and leatherback turtles has been severe.

In 1991, scientists expressed alarm about "a severe decline in the southern bluefin population" to "a dangerously low level," estimating that the population dropped more than 90 percent since 1960. Australian and New Zealand scientists believed existing fishing restrictions were not adequate to prevent further decline. The Japanese, whose quota had been cut 75 percent during the 1980s, now pushed for a catch *increase.* But by 1997, Australia felt compelled to reduce Japanese catches in its waters again because the tuna population remained hazardously low. Whether the fishery managers will act differently in this instance than they have almost everywhere else, and restrict fishing activities enough, for long enough, to allow this species' recovery, remains to be seen.

Meanwhile, human appetites around the world drive an effort to scour the oceans in search of tunas. Fisheries expert Dr. James Joseph, head of the Inter-American Tropical Tuna Commission, says, "Over the next fifty years, the world's population is expected to double [and] . . . rational management of the world's tuna . . . in an even more crowded and competitive world will not be easy." By the late 1980s, about four tons of tunas were yanked from the oceans each minute. In 2000 it will be twice that. The bright yellowfin and the surface-loving little skipjack tuna bear the brunt of this—about 75 percent, by weight, of the kill. Bigeye tuna, a sushi favorite, and albacore, beloved by American moms preparing sandwiches, absorb 20 percent or so. Commanding the most extravagant prices, served to the wealthiest diners, and making up only 5 percent of the world tuna catch are the beleaguered bluefins.

But Gerry is telling me that any talk of bluefin scarcity is sandbagging by "elite recreationalists." He says that the scientific assessments have always been distortions of the truth and that scientists have always been the tools and puppets of the elite recreationalists, unwilling to hear anything about the *real* number of fish.

It is difficult at first for me to understand what Gerry means, exactly, by "elite recreationalist," because many recreational fishermen sell their tuna to Gerry. I slowly gather that an elite recreationalist is a recreational angler who believes that excessive fishing is hurting fish populations.

As we approach our intended spot, about a hundred boats, all anchored and chumming for tuna, appear out of the haze. Some are commercial boats. Many are "recreational" boats—that is to say, their crews are weekenders and vacationers who rely on nonfishing salaries for a living. But at current prices, all bluefins caught here are sold, making everyone a commercial fisher in one sense. Gerry says that this is only one little spot out of many and that there are so many boats fishing because there are so many fish. If the haze clears, we should see the other fleets.

We set the anchor on a ridge in three hundred feet of water, fourteen miles offshore. The surface end of the anchor line is attached to a buoy so we can drop the boat away from the anchor at any moment to chase a hooked fish, which might otherwise empty the big reel of hundreds of yards of line in a few moments or tangle in other boats' anchor lines and break off. The sonar shows dense schools of small fish—young mackerel—in the upper fifty feet.

Austin readies three fishing rods. This is some of the heaviest-duty rod-and-reel equipment made. The line is 130-pound test (it takes 130 pounds of pull to break it), and the hooks are the size of a man's index finger. Austin puts a hook through a piece of herring, then puts a piece of polystyrene foam in the hooked bait to offset the sinking rate of the steel and allow the bait to appear to be drifting more naturally. He sends the bait 120 feet down, attaches a balloon to the line as a float, and sails the balloon a few yards behind the boat. Two other baits are similarly deployed, one at ninety feet and the other at seventy-five.

Once a giant bluefin is hooked, tiring it requires applying such great pressure that the angler must be strapped into a specially designed chair in order to fight (the word "play" is inappropriate) the fish. Gerry allows that if we hook a fish, I'll be "in the chair." Putting some reservations aside (the philosopher in me is ill at ease, but the fisherman in me is excited at the prospect—and right now we are fishing), I sit while Austin makes the necessary adjustments on the foot rests and bucket harness. The harness, in which the angler sits, attaches to the reel with heavy brass clips. Austin describes to me how, if a fish is hooked, I am to get into the chair and pick up the clip on each side of the harness. He will put the rod into the socket on the chair and I will immediately attach these two clips to the reel. The reels are adjusted to let line slip off at forty pounds of pull. If the line does not slip—if the reel jams, for instance—a hooked giant tuna will easily exert enough thrust to break it—if something else does not break first. Austin shows me how, when the rod is yanked, I will be pulled off my seat as the bucket harness, attached to the rod, catapults me forward. What prevents me from being pitched overboard attached to the fish is that the harness is strapped to the chair, so I become part of the boat, essentially—as long as everything holds. Bolts on fighting chairs have broken and people have been pulled overboard, attached fatally to both chair and fish.

The bluefin's immense strength and stamina are not mere by-products of its size. Some sharks get big, but the strength of a five-hundred-pound shark does not compare to that of a five-hundred-pound bluefin. Marlin get big—and they are strong—but their endurance does not match a bluefin's. When a bluefin tuna pulls a person out of a chair and threatens to break clips, straps, and bolts, that person is experiencing the combined, coordinated functioning of millions of muscle cells that are among the most powerful and specialized in any creature.

What allows a tuna to generate such dangerously explosive thrust, merely by wagging its tail, is a package of natural adaptations that exquisitely integrate specialized muscles, specialized circulation, and specialized external design. Making the bluefin so unbelievably tough is a body thoroughly designed to penetrate cold, food-rich waters and rule as the top predator there; its muscles function more effectively in cold water than those of any other fish. Of more than thirty thousand fish species plying the world's waters, the bluefin is among the few that have developed the ultimate weapon of vertebrates: heat.

Internal heat generation confers tremendous survival advantages upon an animal, allowing prolonged alert activity despite large changes in surrounding temperatures. Whereas chilling retards an animal's behavior by slowing the rate of chemical reactions in its body, heat conveys superior ability to see clearly, react, chase prey, or avoid predators. Mammals and birds all pay the costs of being warm-blooded—finding and metabolically burning additional food—to gain these advantages.

But a seemingly insurmountable problem confronts fish: The properties of water make it physically impossible for an animal with gills to raise its body temperature metabolically. Fish do not have the option, not even theoretically, of increasing their temperature by simply increasing metabolism.

Here are the difficulties: As fish breathe, their gills transfer oxygen from the surrounding water into the bloodstream. The blood delivers its oxygen throughout the body to the cells of muscles and organs. In the cells, the oxygen is used—is metabolized—to perform work. The work produces heat, which warms the blood slightly as it is being pumped back to the gills. But as blood passes continually through the gills, it is chilled (its heat is carried off) by the surrounding water.

Here are the particulars: Water contains very little oxygen—less than 3 percent of the oxygen that air contains. Any animal working to extract such meager oxygen must move an enormous amount of water over the gills' surface. But heat diffuses out of the gills ten times faster than oxygen diffuses into the blood. So, by the time the blood has acquired the oxygen it must take back to the muscles, it is as cold as the surrounding water. Increasing metabolism, which would produce more heat, would consume more oxygen, which would require faster blood flow, which would increase heat loss at the gills. Regardless of whether a fish is resting, chasing prey, or fleeing at top speed, it will always remain a cold fish. Bottom line: An animal with gills cannot raise its body temperature through metabolism because the properties of water make it impossible.

Achieving the impossible requires finding extraordinary solutions, and tunas, billfishes, and certain sharks have done just that. Their marvelous methods for warming are so complex that scientists' understanding of them has taken a century and a half to unfold and is still incomplete.

Key to these fishes' solution to their heat-loss dilemma are complex systems of intermingled veins and arteries. These vascular webs were named *rete mirabile,* or "wonderful network," by the French anatomist Georges Cuvier, who in the 1830s first described—but did not understand—them. Today we know that a *rete* is a heat-exchange system that actually uses the blood's heat-losing property to *heat* the blood. This may sound impossible, but it works.

In the *rete*'s vascular network, arteries and veins branch again and again and again, forming an intermingling mass of fine, parallel arterioles and veinules. When warmed venous blood coming from the muscles enters this vascular network, its heat dissipates across vascular walls into adjacent, cooler, arterial blood coming in the opposite direction from the gills. By the time this arterial blood passes entirely through the *rete* and enters the muscles, it is already warm. This countercurrent heat exchange is astonishingly efficient: 97 percent of the heat leaving the muscles is recaptured by incoming arterial blood. (The *rete*'s arteries and veins do not branch so finely as to form capillaries, across which oxygen would also begin to diffuse.) By thus ingeniously and precisely separating heat from the blood exiting the muscles, and sending this heat back into the muscles before it would be lost through the gills, the big fishes have performed evolutionary judo on the laws of physics.

In tunas, and also in the lamnid sharks (great white, mako, porbeagle, and salmon sharks), this countercurrent heat exchanger surrounds the red muscles that power the fish's sustained swimming. This red muscle is the major source of metabolic heat that is recaptured and recirculated by the heat exchanger, allowing the warmed cells to work at their utmost efficiency and maximum power output. In most fishes, the red muscles used for sustained swimming are located along the fishes' sides, where they can lose heat to the adjacent water through the skin. In tunas and the warm-blooded sharks, evolution has moved this muscle inward, away from the skin, toward a more central location within the fishes' bodies. (The dark red circle in a steak cut from the body of a tuna or mako shark is a cross-section of the animal's red muscle bordered by the "wonderful network" that conserves warmth in the living wild fish.) The overwhelming swimming power generated by tunas is closely linked with the evolutionary movement of the red muscle deeper within the body. The red muscle and *rete* arrangement of the bluefin tuna and the mako shark, two animals far removed in evolution, have been independently shaped by natural selection to resemble each other closely—one indication that this system indeed conveys tremendous survival advantage.

In addition to warming their muscles, the tunas and the lamnid sharks also have heat exchangers warming their eyes and brains (aiding vision and response) and their viscera (which greatly speeds digestion by stoking the fire in their bellies).

The body temperatures of most warm-blooded fishes remain warmer than the surrounding water but vary somewhat as water temperatures fluctuate. The superlative bluefin goes an additional step. Bluefins keep their body temperature relatively stable despite wide fluctuations in water temperature. A bluefin ranging from Canada to the Bahamas during its annual migrations, in water temperatures spanning 45 to 86 degrees Fahrenheit (7° to 30°C), maintains its body heat around 80 to 90 degrees (between 28° and 33°C). While it is breeding in the Gulf of Mexico, the bluefin's core temperature may be only a few degrees warmer than the surrounding water. Yet a few months later, while the same giant bluefin is hunting herring off Nova Scotia, its temperature may be fully 36 degrees Fahrenheit (20°C) warmer than the chill, midforties waters it is coursing.

Thus the bluefin tuna—one of the most highly evolved of all fishes—can regulate its body temperature as well or better than any other fish in the world. Researchers are unsure how they do so, but it appears that they can engage the heat exchanger when they need to conserve muscle-generated heat in cold water and disengage it, shunting blood around it, when they need to dissipate heat in warm water. This ability to thermoregulate, coupled with their enormous, heat-conserving size, has allowed the bluefin to become the widest-ranging of the tunas, penetrating from the tropics into sub-Arctic latitudes. The bluefin's warmed body enables it to venture actively into cold waters where the fishes that it eats are most abundant—and to hotly pursue and catch prey.

Austin begins throwing herring chunks uptide. We will throw chunks and wait all day or until a fish bites. This is all-or-nothing fishing. It can go from deadly boring to out of control in a heartbeat. After waiting hours, days, weeks without a strike, in the next moment something may happen that you will remember the rest of your life—if the fish does not pull you overboard. We wait, toss pieces of herring, and eat sandwiches. Gerry makes some calls on his cellular phone, evading radio eavesdroppers.

Without my prompting, with the tone of a mentor and the enviable conviction that he is doing something genuine and real, Austin explains every move he makes around the bait and the fishing gear. He says, "Chumming is an art. There are some great chummers out here; I mean *great* chummers!" He takes pleasure in describing to a newcomer what goes on in the fleet. "Sometimes a boat gets a hot streak, then it might go cold. I used to fish with a woman who caught nine tuna in eleven days. This boat next to us over here was catching tuna every day last week."

Gerry says some boats will catch consistently, though many boats do not catch any. Only about 5 percent of these boats get a fish during the year, and of those, most get only one. A few, though, get far more. "While others get none or one, some will get twenty fish for the season. One guy has caught forty-two giant tuna on a rod and reel here this year, including ten in one week. No one can figure out what he's doing so right while some boats around him have caught nothing all season."

Gerry adds, "The few boats that catch consistently are better than we are. They know something we don't know." One boat that was on a really hot streak was visited by scuba divers from other boats, trying to figure out what they were doing differently, and their cabin was broken into several times by people looking for clues.

Newly arriving boats crowd in on us. A small boat named *Decapod* seems lost, looking for a spot to anchor among all the boats. I count 113 boats in the fleet we are fishing in. We can now see the next fleet to the north, too. And there are more fleets beyond. Gerry says there are boats chumming all the way to Monhegan Island, some ninety miles up the coast. I can't help thinking that if there are a hundred boats in this spot alone and a hundred in every other spot around Cape Cod Bay that holds tuna, it seems unimaginable that a tuna could pass the season without encountering numerous opportunities to swallow a fish with a hook in it. Indeed, it seems inconceivable that a tuna could survive the season unless it had learned—by observation—what not to touch.

A boat attempts anchoring too near and is chased away in no uncertain terms by Austin. It is important to be reasonably clear of neighbors. You may hook a fish that entangles a nearby boat's anchor line and breaks free. Or they may hook a fish that crosses your own anchor. A fishing line attached to a rapidly running hooked tuna can easily cut through anchor rope, leaving a boat—perhaps your boat—unable to fish for the rest of the day and with expensive lost equipment to replace: an anchor, twenty feet of chain, a thousand or more feet of rope.

A hooked tuna can turn into a bandsaw engine not just because of the power of its smoldering inner muscles but because those muscles propel an exquisitely designed exterior. Water is eight hundred times denser than air, and its friction and drag challenge a predator that must not only match but overtake, out-maneuver, and *catch* prey that is smaller and therefore inherently more agile. All other things being equal, a small animal can make tighter turns than a larger pursuer. This is why all other things can't be equal. To survive, the predator must devote considerable metabolic energy and structural adaptation to gaining advantage in the chase. Turn off the engine of a flying plane and you will begin to glide. Stop pedaling a bicycle and you will coast for an easy distance. But shift a speeding boat into neutral and it will plow heavily into the water at nearly a dead stop. Boats do not need brakes, though a boat encounters water's drag on only its bottom. But a fish is entirely embedded in water. For a big fish to achieve speeds in the neighborhood of fifty miles (ninety kilometers) per hour—twice as fast as many modern outboard boats generally cruise—it must develop tremendous thrusting power and it must deploy this thrust with exceptional efficiency.

The bluefin tuna's highly advanced red muscle cells generate that extraordinary force. Tunas' high-performance gills are crammed with more surface area—and their blood packed with more oxygen-carrying hemoglobin—than all other fishes. Cells produce power when a protein called myoglobin delivers oxygen (from the blood) to cell structures called mitochondria (in biology class, they called these the "power plants" of the cells). Mitochondria use the oxygen to make ATP, a chemical that acts as the cell's refined fuel. These fishes' red muscle cells have some of the highest mitochondria densities and myoglobin volumes in the animal kingdom. The red muscle of a tuna contains ten times as much myoglobin as the red muscle of a bird or mammal. An angler startled and bowed by the almost frightening thrust of a running tuna is experiencing the combined, coordinated energy unleashed by these supremely forceful cells.

Tunas possess a remarkable array of external characteristics designed both to transmit their great muscle power and to eliminate drag. During a sprint—to pursue squid or to avoid a warm-bodied mako shark, for instance—tunas can retract their largest fins into grooves and slots, eliminating the fins' drag. (Speed is one of their most striking characteristics; the name tuna derives from the Greek "to rush.") Among the big high-performance fishes, tunas alone possess a row of small rudderlike fins, called finlets, running along the top and bottom rear third of their bodies, where the body tapers sharply. As the fish moves forward, their finlets produce little vortices, breaking up the laminar flow of water that would otherwise create significant drag behind them as they rush forward. Tunas, billfishes (swordfish, sailfish, spear fishes, and marlins), and the warm-blooded sharks all have horizontal keels near their tails; these stabilize the fish, enhance its turning ability, and minimize water resistance as the fish lashes its caudal fin from side to side. Their stiff, sickle-shaped tails create tightly whirling eddies of water, in whose curl the fish is actually propelled, as if it is surfing on its own wake; the fish, in essence, creates its own tailwind to shove it forward. So the shape and motion of their tail subverts water's dragging density for the tunas' own high-paced purposes. Again these remarkable animals turn challenging, seemingly disadvantageous aspects of their environment to their advantage. Engineers from the Massachusetts Institute of Technology are now designing underwater vehicles based on the shape and propulsion method of the tuna, as a way to achieve previously undreamed-of efficiency. Taken together, the bluefin's integrated internal and external systems allow it to summon its explosive attack capability, its jolting power.

Gerry says, "It's a good thing most of these guys can't catch these giant tuna. These fish are too big and dangerous. Accidents can happen." Among Gerry's close acquaintances is a captain who lost a man once when the boat hooked a giant bluefin. The captain, at the throttle, put the boat into forward as the man was still struggling to clip into the chair's harness. The man lost his footing and was pitched overboard. Horrified, the captain shifted into reverse. In the confusion, the man in the water was struck by the propellers. His body was found in a trawler's net several days later. The captain, Gerry says, "has never been the same since."

With more than a hundred boats in view, we continually scan the fleet for any sign of action. About a half hour after we start chumming, a distant boat hooks a fish and begins maneuvering through the crowd, with captain and mate yelling directions to each other, trying to get around other boats' anchor lines. Gerry kisses three pennies and whimsically throws them overboard for good luck. He makes another phone call. Even though it's Sunday, and he's out on his boat, he's conducting business at a rapid clip. His next call is to a nearby spotter pilot, a friend of his.

At eight-thirty, an adjacent boat hooks a giant fish on a heavy hand line—just a tub of coiled line and a pair of heavy gloves—and leaves its anchor buoy. Our video sonar suddenly prints a big fish at 118 feet, represented by a large red dot on the screen. Austin works the bait. The fish on the video vanishes, perhaps having eaten our free lunch and wisely avoiding the oldest trick in the book. "The one y' see ain't the one y' get," he says. The adjacent boat loses the fish; the hook has pulled free. About five minutes later there's another boat working a hooked fish at the periphery of the fleet. Not long after that, a boat called the *Sneak Away* out of Cohasset, Massachusetts, hooks up two hundred yards from us.

Gerry complains he doesn't like this kind of fishing. He'd rather be alone, away from the fleet, trolling around. The phone rings. Gerry says pugnaciously to whomever he is speaking, "They just want the fish for themselves. We're not going to let their greed get us." The sonar marks another fish at 160 feet. Is it eyeing our bait? Does the sight of the lines frighten it?

Small mackerel suddenly appear behind the boat, taking little shards of herring. Gerry rigs a light rod with four bare hooks and a small sinker at the end. He drops it down a few feet and starts jigging up and down. The mackerel jump onto the bright gold, bare hooks as though created to do so. He catches them two, three, four at a time, kills them, and tosses them overboard to add to the chum. We mark another tuna at 161 feet. A boat named *Marlin* motors slowly by, dragging a freshly caught giant bluefin by its immense tail. The startling sight of the tail, which is much wider than the shoulders of the man standing next to it, arrests my attention. Austin remarks, "That's a little fish." Another red smudge appears on our screen at 130 feet. Surely this fish has looked at our deepest bait.

Forty-five minutes pass with no further action among our hundred neighbors, then a boat called *Semana* hooks up. Amid confused yelling and frantic maneuvering, their crew chases after the fish and struggles to remain clear of other boats. *Semana* has trouble around an anchor, clears it, eventually gets the fish up close, harpoons it, and gaffs it amid much excitement and shouting.

Gerry says, "I don't know why they do all that screaming."

An adjacent hand-lining boat suddenly hooks a fish, as another hand-liner drags a large tuna through the fleet back to its anchor buoy.

At nine-forty the *Renegade* hooks up and fights furiously as it maneuvers hastily past our stern. The reel is whining loudly, the powerful giant swiftly ripping yard after yard after yard of line off the reel despite the heavy drag. Fighting a bluefin requires—uniquely—that anglers apply psychology, but to do so the people must maintain control of the struggle. *This* fish is out of control. If the bluefin can make a long first run, it will begin to understand how to remain away from the boat, and it will pick a distance, usually the distance at which the boat becomes visible, and refuse to come closer. It will run, you will break your back to regain some line, and during that time the fish will be growing stronger again. When it reaches that point it has chosen, it will fight a standoff, exerting just enough pressure to stay put. You will sweat to put half a turn on the reel's handle, then strain your whole body to lever the fish up enough to take another quarter turn. And in a few cycles like this, all the while with the rod bent brutally and the line quivering, you will gain a few feet. The fish will tear off one yard of line. Then it may feel strong enough for another sprint and decide to go, and you will ache to watch yards of line melt away amidst a spray of fine droplets, as the side plates of the humming reel grow hot.

In the early days, when reels were more prone to seizing because their drag systems lacked modern materials like Teflon, people thought it necessary to let the fish run long on its first, fresh, burning dash, so it would begin to tire without jamming or breaking the tackle. After that first run (if there was any line left on the reel—and frequently there was not), the pressure was increased. But the fish would fight on for hours. Even after World War II, with nylon line of modern strength, a giant bluefin tuna, if allowed a long first run, would frequently fight four, five, even ten hours or more. Now the idea is to put on heavy pressure initially, to make the fish think that trying to run far is hopeless. Fish fought this way are usually brought to the boat in under an hour, and often considerably sooner. But a particularly "hot" fish can still be uncontrollable during a long first run and then decide to wage a war of attrition. And from all continuing appearances of the scrambling crew and the screaming reel, the *Renegade* is attached to a hot fish that, right now, is still out of control.

Somewhere in the blue, this panicked animal's muscle cells are madly combusting all available oxygen, their mitochondria detonating maximum, full-throttle power. With fins retracted into slots and stiff, slicing tail propelling it deeper and away against the drag of the reel and line, the giant works crazily to break the connection. Under such heavy exertion, the fish may by now be shunting blood around its thermal exchangers to avoid overheating, dumping excess warmth at the gills. The bluefin is buying time, increasing the chances that something will go wrong on board the boat, that something will seize or pop or crack or burn or scrape, causing the line to part. This huge fish is fatiguing the man, far behind, who is breaking a sweat and already gulping air through his mouth. But it is also going into oxygen debt, exhausting itself.

The adjacent *Sara K* hooks up, as does the *White Whale*. The three boats line up in a row, struggling to control their giants. *Renegade* and *Sara K* fight side by side, perilously close to each other.

The rest of the sizable fleet seems quiet and without action.

White Whale's fish comes up thrashing, furiously throwing cascades of spray. A harpoon is poised and lowered several times. The men cannot quite force the animal within range for the final thrust. Ultimately, the giant bluefin, which has taken them in a wide circle, brings *White Whale* too close to its own anchor buoy. Now the fish is getting them into trouble. A man in the stern jabs the harpoon frantically several times, but the fish remains just out of reach—just, barely, too deep. The line wraps up in the buoy and tangles, giving the fish its chance. *White Whale* has run out of time. The exhausted bluefin, seeming dazed, hesitates. Diesels roar, enveloping the crew in a large plume of black smoke as the boat backs down hard, heavily slopping water over the transom. In a do-or-die effort, the harpoon is thrust and, this time, hits the animal and takes hold. The doomed bluefin's gigantic head suddenly shoots through the surface, a head big enough to silhouette a man's torso, with an eye like a horse's.

Gerry says, "If this fishery is stopped, who's going to buy these reels, this line, this fuel, this bait? Do you know how many boxes of herring are sold each morning? All this commerce is for the bluefin. Who's going to buy six-thousand-dollar fighting chairs? If it wasn't for the bluefin, these people wouldn't be out here doing this and supporting all this commerce and all this economy." Sweetening the scene for Gerry, too, is that many of these very same bluefins will be sold through him, and he will ship them to Japan.

The *Renegade* is still working hard near us. "Reel! Reel!" the captain screams. The exhausted man in the fighting chair puffs, "I can't reel anymore." This bluefin is clearly beating him up, wearing him down. And now the man is reacting too slowly, taking too long, making mistakes. The giant tuna breaks the surface and then sounds, making a short run, angling under the hull, taking the line toward the propellers. The boat roars forward to clear the line. Again they labor the fish up. Again it breaks the sea a short distance astern, and they back the boat rapidly toward it. Suddenly the bluefin's movements are short and desperate. Another man on deck throws a harpoon, striking the great fish. It lies arrested in shock, completely spent. A woman sinks a gaff hook into it and ropes its tail.

Gerry idly catches more mackerel, bops them, and throws them overboard. "The tuna don't bite as well now as they did in the old days. There are too many boats in the last ten years and too much noise overhead."

The fleet falls quiescent, and Austin says the bite may be over. An hour passes.

At ten-forty a reel on the *Martha Jean* begins screaming. And it keeps screaming for many long seconds under a heavily strained rod while the crew scrambles to drop off of their anchor buoy, get the other lines in, and commence the chase.

Another red smear appears on our video sonar, at 125 feet. Nothing touches our hooked baits. For all the action around us, the vast majority of boats have, like us, not had a touch. Says Gerry, "Even for those who know how to fish, it's a chance game. DeNoia over there in the *White Stallion* is an excellent fisherman, but he hasn't caught a fish yet this season despite lots of time put in. The *Marlin* is a good fisherman, an old-timer. He's gotten only one this year, the one he got this morning." Gerry says, "It's our turn next."

I ask mischievously, "If we catch a fish, are we going to tag and release it?"

Not one to joke about money, Gerry says severely, "There's not a tag in this whole fleet." Gerry tells me that the difference between a marine biologist and God is that God doesn't think he's a marine biologist. He says there are basically as many fish as ever. The fish may be getting hook-shy, that's why it's not like the old days. But there are plenty of fish. It's just that there's so much pressure on them they're getting smart about lines, learning to avoid them. "You can only kick a dog so many times before it doesn't like your shoe."

Austin says, "We used to see them more right behind the boat and stick them right behind the boat with the harpoon. We don't see that anymore because the fish are getting smart. They're down there, but they're getting smart."

Gerry, suddenly and inexplicably roused to anger, says, "The National Marine Fisheries Service is perpetrating a deliberate lie that bluefin have become scarce. They refuse to believe anything fishermen tell them. It's a Big Lie." Gerry gets in my face and says with a look both earnest and menacing, "I'm going to tell you something that I'd tell my son. You're a young guy. Don't stake your reputation on believing the bluefin is in trouble. The bluefin is not a legitimate conservation issue, because the resource is not threatened. Abundance is tremendous." Shouting now, he says, "It's up to people like myself to stand up to the government and change things, because if we don't, this country won't be the same for our children as we and our forefathers knew it."

The things Gerry feels compelled to stand up to include efforts by fishery scientists and conservation groups to convince the International Commission for the Conservation of Atlantic Tunas to lower bluefin catch quotas. But nothing in the commission's annals should give Gerry cause for worry. The commission's managers have a long history, a tradition—a culture—of ignoring their own scientists' advice. Ignoring their scientists is perhaps the one area in which they excel. In 1981 the commission's scientists concluded that the western Atlantic's bluefin tuna population was depleted and that catches "should be reduced to as near zero as feasible." The commission's managers responded by setting an annual catch quota of 1,160 metric tons, ostensibly for "scientific monitoring." The fishing industry howled, and in 1983, this "scientific" quota was summarily raised to 2,660 metric tons. (A decade later, the U.S. National Marine Fisheries Service commented on the wisdom of this by noting that if the commission had simply not raised the catch quota in 1983, the adult population would by 1993 have grown to three and a half times what it then was, while steadily increasing rather than declining.) Throughout the 1980s, the annual "scientific" quota remained unchanged while the commission's own data showed the breeding population declining each year. No one on the commission asked, "If this is for science, how many fish carcasses are required to reliably monitor population trends?" No one asked because the quota was not really intended for scientific objectives. It was intended for commercial objectives. But because the scientists had recommended a catch near zero, the commissioners tried to perform cosmetic surgery by calling the commercial quota "scientific monitoring."

I have this on good authority. By 1990, the commission's scientific committee estimated that the breeding population had declined roughly 90 percent since 1975. Worse, they reported that the "scientific monitoring quota," at the level it was set, "will cause the decline of the adults to continue." At a meeting of the U.S.'s ICCAT commissioners and their "advisers" from the fishing industry, I raised my hand. Should we not ask, I queried, how many fish we need to kill in order to monitor the trends in the population, and should we not then limit the scientific monitoring quota to that level, until the population can recover? The commission's U.S. advisory committee chairman responded from the podium, "It isn't actually a scientific quota, and we never really believed it was."

Other organizations began weighing in with new statements. The U.S. National Marine Fisheries Service scientists wrote, "The objective of stemming the decline in adult population size will not be achieved under the management program now in effect. In order to stem further decline in the adult spawning stock . . . it is necessary to reduce the allowable take 50% or more." North America's largest professional organization of fisheries scientists, the American Fisheries Society, stated, "The present management regime will not allow the stock to recover, poses an unacceptable risk of there not being enough adult fish to spawn new generations of tuna, and is counter to the long-term interest of both fishery producers and consumers. . . . Although the threat to the biological integrity of the stock is of most concern, the economic losses incurred to date are staggering and cannot be recovered." The society's president warned, "Failure to implement strong conservation measures would be a serious mistake which could cause concerned countries to find solutions through CITES and the Endangered Species Act."

Gerry Abrams's East Coast Tuna Association began to aggressively fight this "Big Lie" perpetrated by these "elite recreational fishermen" and their "government agency puppets" by hiring a full-time lobbyist and hiring as political consultant a lobbying firm partnered by a former White House political director and by the man who would become chairman of the Republican National Committee during the next presidential campaign. Meanwhile, the East Coast Tuna Association and the National Fisheries Institute—a seafood industry lobbying firm whose vice president also happened to be one of the U.S. commissioners to ICCAT—persuaded Congress to pass a law prohibiting the U.S. National Marine Fisheries Service from setting lower bluefin quotas than the ones the tuna commissioners agreed to at ICCAT's annual meeting. Effectively, the fishing industry and commissioners from other countries such as Japan were now setting fishing quotas within U.S. waters. The National Marine Fisheries Service had to go along with it whether they liked it or not—and they did not.

These maneuvers were designed to keep fishery management isolated from fishery science. Gerry Abrams was indeed doing an admirably effective job of standing up to the government.

Meanwhile, the disparity between the scientists' advice and the managers' actions drew the attention of conservation organizations. These groups also discovered that, among the other problems, the bluefin fishery was so poorly monitored that U.S. catches actually *exceeded* the quota by 25 percent. This part was the Fisheries Service's own fault, and they were sluggish in moving to correct it. So in the spring of 1991, several members of the conservation community met with the U.S.'s chief government-appointed representative to the Atlantic tuna commission, Carmen Blondin, and asked him to remind the Fisheries Service in writing that it was important that the U.S. remain within its quota, as we are legally obliged to do. While saying he agreed "wholeheartedly" that this was important, he would not commit those sentiments to paper. It was as though legal obligations and wholeheartedness took a back seat to fears of ruffling the fishing industry and its political allies—who controlled government appointments.

In an attempt to make the Atlantic tuna commission responsive to its scientists, mindful of its legal obligations, and accountable for its actions, the National Audubon Society had formally requested that the U.S. Fish and Wildlife Service propose listing the western Atlantic bluefin tuna population in CITES's so-called Appendix I. If the Fish and Wildlife Service agreed to propose the listing, the 120-plus CITES signatory countries would vote on the tuna proposal when they next met, in Kyoto, Japan. If the fish was listed, export to Japan of East Coast bluefin tuna would be suspended, taking the financial incentive out of the fishery. My hope was that dangling this sword over the tuna commission's head would force them to clean up their act and to reduce catch quotas prior to the CITES meeting, thus putting the bluefin on the road to recovery while making a CITES listing unnecessary.

Abrams's East Coast Tuna Association's lobbyists persuaded five influential members of Congress to pressure the Fish and Wildlife Service to kill the CITES idea. They did.

All things considered, the tuna association has been wildly successful. But Gerry, not one to let down his guard, is disturbed and angered by the new and meddlesome presence of conservation organizations. He sees the National Marine Fisheries Service, already the puppet of elite recreational fishermen, as likely to try to enlist even more allies in its attempt to destroy the American bluefin tuna fishery.

Three P.M. No fish have been hooked in several hours. No marks on the sonar. Where did they go? Why? The day has grown gray and nasty. We bring in the lines and run home. On the way back Gerry and Austin sing song after song, including such old favorites as "You Are My Sunshine" and "God Bless America."

Two hours later, we are on the concrete dock at Gerry's waterfront packing house in a light drizzle, watching one of his men decapitating a giant bluefin with an electric saw. The *Marlin* arrives with the fish we saw them towing earlier. *Marlin* is up visiting from Long Island, where the giant bluefin season is a thing of the past. A woman in her midfifties, who fought the fish, tells me she's been fishing for tuna since the 1960s and this is her 111th giant bluefin over five hundred pounds. I am impressed.

Two more Long Island boats arrive. One is buying bait for tomorrow and one has caught a fish. Its flanks gleam luminously and the deep blue color of its back sets off its steely, silver-gray sides and the bright yellow of its finlets. Its body looks polished and lacquered.

Gerry says, "You see a fish like this and you think, 'What a magnificent fish!' But the thing you have to remember is, it's just a fish. It's like those little mackerel I was catching and throwing into the chum today, only bigger. It's just a fish, just a big mackerel."

Rain is falling into blood puddles on the concrete bulkhead. Gerry's employees are working hard, unloading the bluefins Gerry is buying, and dragging plastic totes of herring and whiting that Gerry is selling for bait. The entire packing house is handling nothing but bluefin business.

"I don't do it for the money," Gerry says. "I do it for one purpose: to try to ensure that your children and my children and everybody's children and grandchildren have the same opportunities in this country that I have enjoyed and that I appreciate."

Gerry drives me back to the hotel and tells me that in Bimini this year there were more bluefins than ever before. After spawning in spring, the adult bluefins head up through the Straits of Florida as they migrate toward their summer foraging range off New England and southern Canada. The tuna must swim through a narrow bottleneck off Bimini, which earned the name Tuna Alley around the time Ernest Hemingway fished for giants there. The water is so clear ("gin clear," they call it), the sand so white, and the fish so easily seen, that Bimini may be the best single place to try to actually get a sense of abundance by directly observing wild adult bluefins as they pass through.

Anxious to follow up on Gerry's good news regarding Tuna Alley, I find Alex Adler, a professional fisherman who catches bluefin commercially in Cape Cod Bay during this time of year and runs a charter sportfishing boat out of Islamorada, in the Florida Keys, the rest of the year. Alex has been running a boat chasing giants in Tuna Alley off Bimini each spring since 1980.

"There is no comparison," he says flatly, "in the size of tuna schools between the early eighties and now."

"So you *are* seeing more bluefins now than before?" I ask for clarification.

"No! The opposite! There's no comparison between how *many* we saw *then* and how *few* we see *now*. Before 1984, especially, the schools of giant bluefins were a lot bigger. Where we now see five to twelve fish in pods, in the past the schools were frequently sixty to eighty fish, and I'd often see schools of two hundred to four hundred fish. At times, there were groups of tuna spread over an area a mile long and half a mile wide; not a solid school that size, mind you, but many groups of fish all throughout an area that big, hundreds and hundreds of giant tuna."

Adler tells me that what has hurt tuna more than anything, in his opinion, is long-lining and catches of juvenile fish. He claims that swordfish long-liners fishing between January and March off Bimini and Walker Cay in the Bahamas and in the Abaco Trench catch and discard many bluefins they are not allowed to keep. "I've had long-liners tell me that, once in a while, they have to cut off anywhere from thirty to seventy-five dead bluefins in one evening's set," he says. "This is not every night, but once in a while they get into a concentration like that." As for catching young fish, which is commonly done, particularly south of Cape Cod, he explains philosophically, "You can't have college students if you don't let anybody get through high school." He believes the fish should be protected until after they've reached adulthood and have had a chance to spawn.

I ask how his seasons in Cape Cod have been and he says last year he caught six fish. He adds, "It's great to have a shot at catching a fish worth ten grand, but they're worth so much money now, these guys will take the last buffalo. You know what I mean? It's a sad deal. Deep down, I know the bluefin is in danger. The fishery isn't what it was; we used to hand feed them up behind the boat here in the bay a lot. They're being caught in many different ways, and it's all adding up."

Curious about the runs at Bimini in the old days, decades ago, I drive down to Woods Hole on Cape Cod to talk to Frank Mather. Now a white-haired octogenarian, Mather has more of an institutional memory about the old times than probably anyone. Born in 1911, he earned a degree in naval architecture and marine engineering from MIT.

"I worked in that field until after the war, then I kind of got bored with it. We always used to come to Woods Hole for the fishing, and I was aware of these crazy scientists doing mysterious work here. I got tired of commuting here to go fishing, so I tried to get a job here."

Mather took a job at the Woods Hole Oceanographic Institution as a research technician in 1945, measuring waves. Five years later, he was doing pioneering research on tuna. Bluefin became his obsession. Mather designed a method of tagging the fish and became the first researcher to learn that some bluefins cross the ocean on their migrations. It was some of Mather's work, describing the abundant, untapped tuna schools, that interested the California seine netters in making their first exploratory trips to the East Coast for bluefin.

But by the late 1960s, Mather's research indicated that the bluefin was in trouble. At that time, so many small fish had been caught that several entire age groups were virtually missing from the population. Mather feared, prophetically, that as the adults grew old and died there would be few younger fish to replace them.

Though his frame has grown old, Mather's legendary energy still enables him to pack more into life than most of us. When I met him in Woods Hole, he had just come back from Costa Rica, where he had caught several hundred-pound-plus sailfish on a fly rod. A researcher who formerly worked for Mather told me, "He'd work circles around us. And after he retired, he'd hire college kids to run his boat and fish recreationally with him. He fished so hard these kids couldn't keep up with him. He'd exhaust them and they'd quit. Of all the people I ever worked for, I respect Frank Mather the most."

Mather clears the fly rods off his living room couch. The walls are hung with aged black-and-white photos of people fishing for tuna from old-style boats; there are several of giant tuna hanging at the dock beside a younger man. His voice is a bit shaky, but Mather's blue eyes twinkle mischievously as he talks.

"When I started my research, we were studying age and growth, and we were doing a lot of taxonomy, just trying to identify the species of tuna that lived off the East Coast. Nobody even knew which species of tuna were which in the western Atlantic when we started. The taxonomy was all screwed up.

"It was unbelievable how many fish there were back then. Not just tuna. We used to count sharks and we'd get to a hundred before lunch and we'd quit counting. Now, most days you don't see a shark. Nineteen forty-eight was a boom year for tuna. We'd leave the dock at ten in the morning. We just trolled one rod with old linen line. We were very amateurish. One week we averaged ten hundred-pound tuna a day. In other words, we were practically sinking the boat. We'd see so many fish at the surface, you had your choice of which of the schools to go to.

"In '63, we had an incredible run of four-year-olds: about sixty-five-pound fish. They just stayed on top, and from the boat you could look down and see more of them. Pilots said that the whole east side of the Cape, all the way from Provincetown to Nauset, about forty miles, was just white with these schools.

"When the seiners started, that was the kind of school they were catching— young fish. They'd make a set and get a hundred tons of ten-pound fish, about twenty thousand young bluefins. And they were getting sets like that all the time. They were catching almost everything they saw. An aerial spotter said in '67 that he only saw two schools that year that didn't get caught. They'd be able to catch almost every fish in the school, except if the net broke or if sharks ripped it. A lot of fish were wasted because if a boat netted a hundred-ton school and only had room left on board for ten tons they would just drop the rest, which were already dead. Roger Hillhouse, the spotter pilot who's still part owner in three seiners, wrote a letter saying they were devastating the tuna just like the buffaloes and the passenger pigeons. His colleagues beat him down enough that he kind of kept quiet after that. He's the only commercial guy I knew who had a farsighted attitude. This was in the early seventies, about the same time I was saying the fish were headed for trouble and other people were saying I was full of nonsense. Now they say the breeders are down ninety percent since 1970, but the young fish were already creamed in 1970."

Intent on following up on the schools of fish that swam past Bimini, I ask Mather if he had ever witnessed the migration of tuna through the Straits of Florida. "I was there once," he replies. "As we were running, the captain, who was up on the bridge, called out, 'Tuna!' and we looked. There were just *armies* of tuna. I don't even remember seeing any gaps between the schools, but there must have been. Clear water, absolutely white bottom. Each fish stood out like a horse turd in a glass of milk. It was all so exciting. There was just an absolutely unbelievable number of fish."

It's blowing about forty knots and the trees are shaking violently as I head south to Rhode Island. Rain is pounding so hard on my windshield that, though my wipers are tapping double-time, I'm having difficulty seeing anything at all. I search the car radio for something I can stand to listen to, and after two passes through the entire dial amid a wall of noise, I pause on a Beatles tune with an aptly oceanic sentiment: *I'd like to be / Under the sea / In an octopus's garden / In the shade.* The Fab Four, who, lest we forget, were the first to posit that we all live in a yellow submarine, sound fresh enough to lift even this dreary day a bit. Once they finish, I turn the radio off and listen to the drumming rain and the slapping wipers, which have an appeal of their own.

My magical fishery tour has now brought me into the venerable fishing port of New Bedford, a dingy city of potholed streets, evangelical video-ministry storefronts, alcohol-abuse recovery centers, potential clients of said centers, and a general air of gloom. Nothing seems to say New Bedford; every sign says Whaling City. It's a claim to fame, if a dubious one. This town has a long history, but it seems to have senesced rather than matured. Maybe it's just the weather. I skirt the downtown and cross the bridge to Fairhaven. Black clouds are screaming across the harbor. The rain bounces hard and heavy off the windshield, and I slow down again. I'm already an hour late.

Frank Cyganowski, at age seventy another elder statesman of the fishery, is a tall, slender man whose blue eyes are framed by bushy eyebrows, his white hair combed straight back. He and his wife, Ruby—whose big, dark eyes suggest she must once have been a knockout—occupy a modest little suburban house, with a tiny yard and neighbors hard by.

Cyganowski feels he retired from tuna seining prematurely. "I should still be out there fishing. I didn't retire with very much money, and if I'd stayed in I could be a wealthy man nowadays." He needs the money, he says, because he's supporting his divorced daughter and her children.

Born and raised just a few miles from where he now lives, Frank is crusty, cantankerous, but friendly. Boats and fishing have been his life, but one of the few signs of Frank's long fishing history is a tiny, mounted bluefin tuna in the living room. Frank was one of the original seine netters and was a partner of Roger Hillhouse's.

Frank takes me to a local bar and grill for lunch and, the pace of his speech measured, deliberate—a bit wistful—tells me his story. "I've seen so many fisheries disappear," Frank says, looking down at his crossed hands. "When I lived on Narragansett Bay, you could fill your skiff with blue crabs." He looks up at me. "Bay scallops? Anywhere you wanted to go you could catch 'em with a dip net. Oysters? There was a big oyster industry. In fact, one of my jobs was running an oyster boat. The oyster beds got buried in the '38 hurricane. They never came back. All the oystermen went out of business. Why didn't they come back? Sewage. Chlorine. If chlorine will kill a germ, then sure as hell it will also kill a tiny fish egg or scallop larvae.

"Herring? My *God!* In the old days, you went out herring fishing at night. You had to go when there was no moon, otherwise the water wouldn't fire." The ocean is full of planktonic organisms that create their own light—similar to a firefly's—if disturbed, as by swimming fish. Their "fire" is much easier to see on dark nights. Frank continues, "It was a sight to behold. Any direction you'd look, the ocean just teemed with life. You'd see fish swimming away and once in a while big streaks behind from predators chasing them. Sometimes you'd see a school of herring or mackerel so big you'd think you were running into shallow water. It was like a million-watt bulb lit up all over the ocean. And they were *everywhere!* To catch herring was a matter of picking a school.

"Mackerel? Roger Hillhouse used to see such mackerel schools from the air he'd radio our boat and say, 'There's a school of mackerel here as big as Buzzards Bay.'

"Then the Russian fleet came in. And the Poles, the Bulgarians, the East Germans, the West Germans—. They caught three hundred and forty thousand tons of mackerel here in one season—that figures to over half a billion fish! Pretty soon the mackerel gave out. They also wiped out the hake, the herring, the whiting—. Hell, by the time Congress put the two-hundred-mile limit into effect in '76, everything was *gone!* The whiting still haven't come back; swordfish and tunas used to gorge themselves on whiting. The red hake, there's damn few of *them* around, even.

"And they never came back, because after they put in the two-hundred-mile limit, all the banks started begging people to invest in American fishing vessels. And then Americans just continued where the Russians and other foreign fleets left off. That's what happened."

The waitress comes by for our orders.

"Hell, the fish that were around here before the Russians came would have sustained the United States' fleet forevermore. The only thing the Russians weren't taking were bluefin tuna. I started fishing for tuna in 1962. Four boats started fishing bluefin. Next thing you know, there were boats coming here from every direction. The bluefin couldn't stand that kind of pressure. While we were catching the small fish, giants were being caught by traps along the shore. There were traps all the way up to Maine. The traps caught mackerel, or whatever, but when the tuna showed up, they'd catch a lot of giant bluefin. Trap men hated the bluefin because they'd wreck their traps and were only worth nickel-a-pound for pet food. The traps disappeared when the mackerel disappeared and the herring died out.

"We used to wait for the tuna to show at Delaware Bay near Cape May. We didn't know that, starting about the first of June, the fish were coming in past Cape Hatteras, North Carolina. We found out about it once when we were in Cape May. We sold an engine to a guy from North Carolina, and he says, 'How come you guys don't fish off Oregon Inlet?' I says, 'Why, any fish down there?' He says, 'My God, tuna fish like crazy, every spring.' So I told Roger what the guy told me.

"So Roger set out to fly to Oregon Inlet, North Carolina. But he never got that far. He got to Virginia. He came back and dropped a note in a bottle to us, because there were some Canadian seiners around and he didn't want them eaves-dropping over the radio. Roger's note said: 'See you down there in the morning. Wait till dark to move.' We didn't get to Roger's spot till two in the afternoon. Tuna? My *God!* I mean, coming right along the beach—school after school after school.

"First set we made was fifty tons of forty- to sixty-pound fish. By nightfall we were loaded. We had a hundred and ten tons. So we steamed back up to Cape Henry and went up the Chesapeake Bay all the way up to Cambridge, Maryland, where Bumblebee had a plant. We unloaded, then we steamed back there and got loaded again in nothing flat.

"But the stuff you're hearing now about bluefin being scarce, it's all propaganda, all a ruse. True, the West Coast boats that came over here in '63 and '64 did quite a job on fish of a hundred to five hundred pounds, which there was a great abundance of. There were five big, thousand-ton seiners. They used to unload their catches in New Brunswick, Canada. They caught yellowfin in the Pacific, and they'd come up here with only two or three hundred ton of yellowfin tuna, and they'd fish all this area. They'd fill their boat up with bluefin and go to Canada. They always referred to bluefin as yellowfin in their reports. They killed thousands and thousands of tons. But they didn't wipe 'em *all* out."

Frank says, "I should still be out there. When I was a young man I spent a few years as captain of a motor yacht for a millionaire on Long Island, until he died at age eighty-six. Hell, I'm only seventy. He used to enjoy harpooning swordfish for sport. The year before he died, at age eighty-five, he harpooned fifteen swordfish. In the 1960s we'd see a lot of swordfish. Can't find a swordfish out here now. The long-liners catch 'em. *That's* the thing that ought to be stopped—the long-liners. Jesus Christ, they're bringing in tiny swordfish carcasses of twenty pounds, thirty pounds. It's a damn crime."

Lunch arrives. Chicken for me, roast beef for Frank; and I am glad I did not order the grilled swordfish. The waitress smiles and places our food before us. "Looks good," I say.

"Yep," says Frank Cyganowski. "Finest kind."

A dense, long silence follows while we eat, as Frank reminisces to himself and I daydream about what it would have been like to grow up when one could see wild swordfish every day in the same areas I've traveled regularly for fifteen years without hope of seeing one. Nowadays, forty or more miles of line, thousands of hooks, and a trip eighty miles or more (often many more) from shore are required to catch what one man in the 1960s could catch with a harpoon in an afternoon, in plain sight of land.

The place has gotten crowded and loud, and eerily and bizarrely, from the din of the bar, a snatch of conversation seems to float out of the noise, as happens sometimes. A man says, very slowly and declaratively, and not to us, "They—will—come—*back!* I hope." Frank doesn't seem to have heard him, but I'm hoping it's an omen.

By all accounts, the swordfish was a remarkable animal to encounter. And by any measure, the swordfish is a superbly attuned predator. The broad sword of the fish, the flat blade extending half a body-length from its snout, can be used in defense. But it is also a hunting weapon designed for defeating the defensive grouping of prey fishes. Usually, the denser the prey school, the safer are the individuals in it, because predators have great difficulty singling out, separating, and running down a meal. But swordfish have turned this defensive grouping against their prey, because their sword allows them to charge, slashing, into a dense school of fish, then leisurely turn and pick up the dead and injured.

In the 1970s and early 1980s, Dr. Francis Carey, a Woods Hole Oceanographic Institution scientist, brilliantly provided a startling first—and perhaps last—scientific glimpse into the behavior of wild swordfish. He radio-tracked a dozen swordfish off New England, New York, Florida, and Baja California. He installed temperature sensors adjacent to the brain, attached a depth gauge to the dorsal fin, and affixed a radio transmitter so the fish could be followed. Few such studies have been attempted because the technologies, expense, and logistics required for oceanic research on wild big fish are so daunting. Further, as Dr. Carey noted, "The experiments require extraordinary luck for catching the fish in good condition." And, the work was hazardous. One crew member nearly lost an eye to the slashing bill of a swordfish they were working with on deck.

During daylight hours, Carey's radio-tagged swordfish often made abrupt and very deep dives below the thermocline (an invisible boundary where temperature changes sharply) into cold, dim waters. One swordfish descended to astonishing daytime depths of up to 600 meters (nearly 2,000 feet). During such dives, the swordfish left surface waters as warm as 75 degrees Fahrenheit (24°C) to enter water as cold as 43 degrees Fahrenheit (6°C). To endure this kind of rapid heat shock in water, the animal must possess adaptations for coping with sharp changes of temperature and withstanding prolonged cold while actively hunting.

Foremost among its adaptations for diving through the thermocline, the swordfish can keep its brain temperature above the temperature of the seawater, maintaining elevations of more than 27 degrees Fahrenheit (15°C). Brain temperatures of Carey's tracked swordfish changed only half as much as the water temperature, then stabilized at relatively high temperatures, even during dives where surrounding water temperatures fluctuated significantly. (One striking exception was a swordfish whose brain cooled very rapidly while it suddenly began drifting deeper and deeper. The scientists speculated that it was killed by a shark. If it was, the shark was probably a mako, a warm-bodied animal that is the only fish known to prey on adult swordfish.) The billfishes have approached the challenge of cold water more conservatively than tunas and warm sharks. The adaptations of swordfish and their kin allow enhanced performance as top predators without the higher costs of heating their entire bodies: Only the brain and eyes are warmed significantly. Rapid changes in brain temperature can disrupt behavior or even be lethal. Warming the eyes improves the visual response to prey or predator. Warming both brain and eyes gives these animals a terrific advantage: the ability to break through ocean-temperature barriers while maintaining a clear image of prey pursued in cold, often deep and dark, water—prey whose own brains are chilled.

The eyes and brain of billfishes are warmed by a muscular furnace unlike anything else in the animal kingdom. Discovered in the 1980s, this unique system is most highly developed in the swordfish. Tunas and the warm sharks *conserve* heat incidentally generated by their muscles. But the billfishes, rather than merely conserving muscular heat, have gone an additional step, evolving an organ specialized to *produce* heat for their brain and eyes.

A unique muscle at the base of their brain is specialized to produce *only* heat, and no movement. Dr. Barbara Block, who has studied these organs, discovered that they are highly developed. Their cells have extraordinary capacity to oxidize, or burn, fuel. This capacity is the cells' power potential. Remember what's involved here: The protein myoglobin delivers oxygen to cell structures called mitochondria, which use the oxygen to make ATP, a chemical that acts as the cell's refined fuel. The faster this happens, the higher the cell's power output. Cells in the swordfish's heater muscle have very high amounts of myoglobin and contain the highest densities of mitochondria of any known cells in the animal kingdom. This amplified capacity for power allows the heater to keep the eyes and brain of a swordfish warm for hours in frigid water.

Normal muscle cells do work—move—when energy from ATP is used to pump calcium back and forth across a specialized membrane and stimulate contractions in certain proteins. In swordfish heater cells, the energy from ATP is superabundant, so the cells have very high horsepower and should be capable of a lot of work. But in these heater cells, the proteins that would be stimulated into movement are missing. So the elevated energy released by quickly using up ATP and rapidly pumping calcium is producing *only* great heat, and no moving work. The process is one of designed futility; the heater's cells have uncoupled energy generation from force production. By analogy, if a normal muscle cell is like the engine and drivetrain assembly of a car, releasing energy and producing motion, the swordfishes' heater-muscle cells are like an auto engine with the drivetrain disconnected. This is the swordfish's furnace of muscle, a muscle with its engine revving.

In the kingdom of the brine, the warm-eyed fish is king. All blood coming into the head via the carotid artery is passed through the furnace. Most of this warmed blood then flows across the back of each retina, warming the eyes for visual acuity. To prevent the heat from being lost when this blood moves on to the gills, a countercurrent heat exchanger at the base of the heater organ recaptures the heat and keeps it in the animal's head. And a layer of fat cells both insulates and fuels this furnace. In addition, through evolution swordfish have lost a bone beneath the brain (the basisphenoid), and the absence of this bone barrier facilitates heat transfer between the heater organ and the brain itself. Specialized nerves controlling voluntary action exist in the heat-producing muscle, implying the animals control heat voluntarily, like they control swimming. A swordfish can turn down its cranial heater in warm water, and then crank up its furnace to produce more warmth while swimming in the cold depths. In water of 57 degrees Fahrenheit (14°C), they can maintain a cranial temperature of 84 degrees (29°C). To achieve such great temperature differentials, the swordfish's heat-producing organ has to be extremely efficient. And indeed, among the billfishes, the swordfish has taken the heater farthest. A swordfish's head warmer is twice as large as that of a comparably sized blue marlin, enabling the swordfish to penetrate higher latitudes and deeper waters than any other billfish. Blue marlin can dive down to 200 meters (about 650 feet; not nearly as deep as a swordfish), and their heater keeps their eyes and brain warm for less time in cold, deep water. White marlin, the smallest marlin, must spend most of their time near the warm surface.

In addition to the furnace, the swordfish has adaptations to conserve body warmth (though not as advanced as tunas'). Dr. Carey discovered that when they come to the surface after a deep dive, swordfish can warm ten times faster than they had cooled. One swordfish tracked in cold water for eight hours leapt repeatedly when it returned to the warm surface. It might have been trying to increase its blood flow, increasing the speed at which its cooled blood could be warmed by the warm surface water flowing over its gills.

But this could not entirely explain how rapidly its body warmed. How can the animal alter the rate at which it gains or loses heat? When the swordfish is in cold water, one of its main arteries can be closed to shunt more blood through its heat exchanger, conserving heat in its swimming muscles, and slowing cooling. When the animal comes up from cold depths to the warm surface, this artery can be opened to shunt cooled blood around the heat exchanger, now greatly speeding the rate blood is *warming* across the gills as its temperature rises to match that of the warm surface water. This is what brings swordfish, sharks, and tunas to bask at the surface during the day (where they are visible and vulnerable to planes and harpoons). They are coming to warm up from the cold.

Around New England's Georges Bank, Carey's swordfish moved off the bank at night, out over much deeper water, hunting at or above the thermocline and often coming near the surface under cover of darkness. During these movements, the swordfish sometimes crossed between different habitats, going from pastel green, algae-rich water on the bank to clear, blue, oceanic water at night, like a lion moving from the daytime shade of riverside thickets into open plains under the cloak of darkness. Several of the tracked animals commuted to the same spot on the bank every day, usually descending in early morning with large schools of prey fishes (visible on the tracking vessel's sonar). Prey often descend to deep, dark depths during the day to avoid many predators that either need light to see or air to breathe. But the swordfish can follow prey into the dim depths, tracking and hunting with the aid of its enormous—and warm—eyes.

The eyes of a swordfish are so large they can mesmerize. In *Men's Lives,* Peter Matthiessen describes his first attempt to harpoon a swordfish, back when they were common off Long Island. "I was wound tight with expectation as I ran forward to the pulpit, freed the long harpoon lashed across its rails, and stared ahead at the two curved blades [the dorsal and tail fins] tracing a thin slit on the water. The beautiful fish was . . . a swift and graceful distillation of blue-silver sea. Its round eye, a few inches beneath the shining surface, appeared huge. I was still staring when the night-blue fish shivered and shot away, leaving only the deep sun rays in the sea." The seasoned fisherman who was Matthiessen's companion chastised, "I put you right on that fish, but . . . you just stared at him, and you know why? You seen the eye. . . . My old man taught me never to look at the eye. . . . That fish rolled his eye out and he fixed you, and you ain't the first. Nobody believes how big that eye is, and by the time they get over the surprise, the bow is past him and that fish is gone."

By the 1980s, Dr. Carey and his students, having just begun to understand the swordfish as a wonderful, complex animal, were forced to terminate their studies as the great gladiators of the sea grew scarce. "Swordfish have become ever harder to catch," Carey wrote.

How fast things can change. Only a couple of decades earlier, one B. K. Gilbert accompanied a multiday swordfishing trip on Georges Bank to research a report on the harpoon fishery for the Fisheries Research Board of Canada. At that time, boats would routinely strike, or "iron," a swordfish, throw over a keg at the end of the harpoon line, then send a man in a dory out to retrieve and subdue the creature, while the main vessel continued looking for fish. The report includes an excerpt from Gilbert's daily log, describing a "typical day":

> Shortly after 9 AM (before engine was started for day), a swordfish was sighted off the bow. Gave chase and ironed it fair. . . . Ironed second swordfish at 9:10 AM. . . . Ironed third swordfish at 9:26 AM. Hauled second swordfish at 9:45 AM. . . . Ironed fourth swordfish at 10:21 AM. Striker missed the next one. Ironed fifth and sixth at 10:45 AM. We lost No. 6 when line fouled on the propeller. Seventh and eighth ironed at 11:40 and 11:45 AM, respectively. Twenty-two boats now visible. At noon, we passed an ironed swordfish which was leaping at the surface. . . . Ironed fish at 1:00 PM, 1:45 PM, 1:50 PM. . . . Ironed another swordfish at 2:10 PM. It dove about 5 seconds after being hit. Another, ironed at 2:20 PM, dove almost immediately. At 2:25 PM dory alongside without his fish. . . . Ironed swordfish at 3:45 PM. Some porpoises off the bow. . . . The weather was excellent, clear and calm all day. Most of the fish were not finning but were sighted underwater and fairly close to the boat. Had they been finning, a far greater number of fish would have been seen and presumably more

caught. . . . [T]here must be a large body of swordfish in the area. . . .
2 at 5:20 and 2 at 6:30 PM. Fishing over for the day. Total catch 16
swordfish.

This log entry was penned in 1959, and by the time people born in that year
would celebrate their twenty-fifth birthday, this description of a "typical day"
would whisper like something from the irretrievable past. That simple, almost
inconceivable log entry—a written passage in more than one sense—serves not
merely as elegy and eulogy for the days when swordfish were a strong neighboring presence. It describes our own lost youth, the world many of us inherited.
That was our birthright, and our children's, a world away from the one we are
passing on. The much-diminished swordfish lives still. Let's not be comforted by
its mere existence, but rather insist upon remembering the shape the world is
supposed to have: round and whole. And may that vision of abundance someday
gather power enough to levitate the dead.

Shores of Three Continents

A steady twenty-five-knot wind has the flags in Montauk, Long Island, standing well out from their masts. I don't need to glimpse the water to know it's been blowing long enough to build a challenging groundswell. It will be lumpy on the ocean if we're lucky. More likely, we'll be blown out.

Joe McBride is angry. As president of the Montauk Captains and Boatmen's Association, he has repeatedly asked the Fisheries Service to reduce the number of young bluefin tuna each boat is allowed to kill each day, so their annual quota—and his association's fishing season—will last until the fish migrate for the winter. The service has never acted on his requests. Now, the quota is filled, and they are shutting the season down at its height. Today will be the last day.

Dawn pokes a timid finger into an angry red autumn morning. Sailor, take warning. McBride and mate Billy Campbell are already at work on McBride's *My Mate,* readying the boat in the gloam. Joe has short, slightly receding Frank Sinatra gray hair and a paternal countenance. McBride is fifty-eight and has seven grandchildren. For thirty years, he was an assistant principal and dean in the New York City school system. He'd built up his charter business on weekends and during summers for twenty years before retiring three years ago.

"I'm very fortunate," he says. "I never made a million dollars, but I'm able to do what I want to do." He taps his pipe on a piling, continuing, "In the city, I'd work for six hours and twenty minutes a day, yell at a few teachers and a few kids, and go home. Now I'm 'retired' and I work fifteen, sixteen hours a day, but I enjoy it. I meet interesting people, and some of the fish you can catch here are fantastic."

McBride's boat, a forty-one-foot Hatteras, has two new Cummins diesels. "I needed the new engines to give me the ability to go where I need to, because we have to go farther and farther offshore to catch the same fish. Where we used to go ten or fifteen miles, now we go thirty, forty, fifty miles, for the same fish. And, there are fewer of them." In his search to please his customers, his new "very economical" diesels burn approximately seventy-five gallons of fuel a day.

At five-fifty A.M., McBride's four customers for the day arrive, toting three six-packs of beer and several bags of chips. They've paid $750 and driven two hundred miles for a day of fishing, and they appear to be looking forward to it. The leader of today's group is a golf pro at a country club, where the party became acquainted.

A hundred and twenty pounds of butterfish and other creatures—the day's bait—comes over on a wheelbarrow. We wrestle aboard a garbage pail full of ice. In dim light, other boats begin pulling away from their slips. I open a bag of potato chips and a cola. Breakfast of champions.

Joe gets on the radio and calls a couple of boats, trying to interest several captains in joining him on a two A.M. departure later in the week for a car trip to Washington. Joe exhorts his colleagues to come along, saying he wants to "shake up the National Marine Fisheries Service" and show them that the charter fishing industry is not to be slighted. But not all the captains are enthusiastic. Defending their business interests in Washington means canceling a day's chartering and a day's pay.

My Mate's engines suddenly grumble to life, vibrating the deck and filling my nostrils and eyes with acrid diesel exhaust. We motor slowly out of the harbor along with several other charter boats, then throttle up as we round the jetties and turn east along Gin Beach. Montauk Point lighthouse is visible five miles ahead, its beacon piercing a morning flush with storm. Once around the point we will turn south and get a sense of whether the sea conditions are navigable for the forty-mile run to where the migrating fish have been camped during the last few days.

In the dawn's early light we round the point and get our first look at the ocean. The sea—dark, angry, and confused—is all gray foam and rollers. Captain McBride reaches for the throttle. "Look at this—forced to slow down already." He instructs Billy to give the fares a choice. Billy explains to them that we can either scrap the trip now or continue and see what we get hit with. The fares don't look too seaworthy, but they are talking a tough game. We go for it.

For the time being, anyway.

Just south of Montauk Point, and stretching south for about five miles, lie Montauk Shoals. At a depth of only fifty to seventy-five feet, the shoals kick up under strong tides and rough seas. And this morning they put up a nasty account of themselves. Several of the charter boats throw in the fish rag and turn back. Captain Joe hesitates, then veers sharply off course, trying to get off the shoals and into deep water more quickly, where we may not have to take such a beating. Joe squints through the spray-hazed glass surrounding the bridge. Several boats, including two of the best charter boats in Montauk, are still pounding along with us. They're all on the radio discussing their options. Joe releases the microphone key and says to me, "If *these* two boats turn back, I'm turning back."

McBride pushes onward. *My Mate* undulates through the lumpy sea, throwing walls of spray. Joe suddenly yells, "Hang on!" and I try to find a way to jam my feet against something solid. He steers the boat into a big, foaming comber, slightly too late to cut into it head-on. The boat shudders heavily, hesitates, and starts to yaw slightly before digging back in. McBride mutters something about his vessel suffering. More boats turn back, but not the two that Joe has decided to measure his mettle against. We're down from eighteen knots to seven. A veritable crawl, especially considering there are still more than thirty miles of this between us and our destination. That's as the gull flies; but in addition to going slowly, we are deliberately forty degrees off course, tacking as much as possible to get off the shoals. McBride is working the wheel and throttles constantly, weaving and veering around individual waves and holes.

As an uncommonly big roller curls threateningly, a drifting lobster buoy, trailing a long floating rope capable of disabling the boat if it tangles the propellers, prevents us from turning where we need to. "Hang on!" Joe yells again. Unable to position the boat properly, we take the full force of the big wall of water, broadside. The boat pounds heavily and is enveloped in spray.

The fares are in the cabin, out of sight. The loran tells us we're now about ten miles off Montauk Point. We plow on into deeper water, the heavy groundswells becoming less prone to curling into breaking waves. Just as it seems we're getting used to the seas, Joe yells again: "Hang on!" A tremendous crash from below sends Billy scrambling down to see what has happened. It's nothing major. Several heavy big-game rods and reels have fallen from their cabin-ceiling holders. The fares are startled, but fortunately, no one was struck.

In a few minutes, with the water further deepening, we settle into a routine pounding and occasionally turn into some of the larger, steeper groundswells.

Conversation again becomes possible. McBride relights his pipe, then—with both hands back on the steering wheel—says through clenched teeth. "Years ago, if you were shark fishing in September, as many of us did, you'd often see giant tuna swimming through your chum. I remember one day somebody saying, 'Jeez, a whole school of sharks.' And I looked down and there was a school of giants. This kind of thing happened frequently. If you were fishing for giants, your chances of catching one were very reasonable, whereas now, there have been only about twelve or fifteen giants caught in the Montauk area this entire year. In the past, there were always plenty, there were always some southeast of Block Island, some in the Butterfish Hole, places like that. Now they're pretty much only up in the Cape. They were always up there, but we used to have them here, too.

"When I started, people fished for tuna for enjoyment, not money. Gradually, it became a dollar fish and the pressure went up." He puffs on his pipe, mingling the scent of pipe tobacco with salt mist and diesel fumes. "I have nothing against a guy making a legitimate dollar, as long as it doesn't destroy the species. But now people are even selling these young fish we are going after today, to local restaurants where they're not worth very much. I'm not going to let people kill small fish for fifty cents a pound. Most of the captains, including myself, request that the fares take home no more than they're going to eat."

Billy appears again at the top of the bridge ladder and asks to check out my binoculars. Billy knows his seabirds. Shouting back and forth over the engine noise between the bridge, where I'm sitting, and the cockpit, where he's standing with legs apart, trying to steady the binoculars, we together identify greater, Cory's, and sooty shearwaters. In the winter, the off-season for charter boats, Billy used to work on long-liners fishing for tilefish, and he admired the different birds that survived at sea at that harsh time of year. While he's straining for a better look at one distant flying bird that is going flap-flap-glide, flap-flap-glide and might be the season's first fulmar, he adds, "But some long-liners shoot shearwaters because they'll eat the bait off the hooks as the longline is being let out." He puts the binoculars down, and with one hand gripping the ladder and the other indicating the rolling sea, continues, "When it's rough like this, the boat will plow downhill in a following sea as you're setting the longline, and as the gear gets strung out real hard, thirty baits can come popping up at the same time. The shearwaters will dart in for those baits, so they shoot them. I hate seeing that, because I love birds. I especially love the gannets. They're so graceful when they dive. But sometimes you get eight or ten a day killed on your gear. They hit the baits as they're going out, get hooked, and get pulled down." This bird by-kill is not just local, either. Long-liners in various parts of the world kill enough albatrosses to endanger several species of the great ocean-roaming birds with extinction. Australia recently declared the magnificent wandering albatross endangered, and officially designated long-lining a "key threatening process." Once, seafarers believed killing an albatross would bring the worst of luck. Some fishers have developed ways of keeping birds away from their baits, such as trailing long streamers that frighten them. But nowadays, in most places, little is done to discourage seabirds from taking baits—except killing them.

Coming up to the bridge and getting back to tuna, Billy tells me, "When I was a teenager, there were a lot of giant tuna around Long Island. Some boats caught eight, nine giants in a day. Used to go with a friend of mine. Used to see swordfish, marlin. The place was *alive* out there. Y'know? Anybody who thinks the ocean is as alive now as it was then is crazy. Anybody who says that, wasn't there years ago. Y'know?"

Joe adds, "We used to make half-day trips for white marlin, there were so many so close. That all ended when long-lining jumped up. Don't get me started on long-liners."

Billy continues, "When I started commercial fishing, we used to get so many tilefish, that as we were hauling the gear the blue sharks would gather behind the boat, and we'd watch them eatin' tilefish right off the line—bing! bing!" Billy's eyes gleam with a childlike excitement, and he begins to speak in present tense. "And we're going fast as we can, pullin' 'em in. I get on the leader and try to get it out of the shark's mouth. For a fifteen-year-old kid this is like, 'Wow! They *pay* me for this?' I loved it. It was fun then. Now—." The gleam vanishes and Billy is suddenly past forty again, working for a day's pay. "It's so businesslike now. Now a lot of the fares want to know how much the fish are worth, and 'What's my cut?' Y'know? When I was a kid nobody ever asked 'What's my cut.' It was just 'How're they bitin'?'

"Same thing like with sharks. When I was twenty years old I was running a night bluefishing boat, and I kept hearing about this guy 'the Monster Man,' who went sportfishing for sharks. To me it was a joke. I had to move the boat three or four times a night to get *away* from sharks. They'd swarm around, eating the bluefish off the lines. Now, blue shark fishing is still good early and late in the season, but during the middle of the summer it drops off to nothing. We used to catch a lot of duskies. *Big* duskies. Dusky and brown sharks were our summer fishery. We *always* got lots of brown sharks." Dusky and brown, or sandbar, sharks have declined by 80 to 90 percent since the 1970s. "Porbeagle sharks were gone because of overfishing even before my time."

Joe adds, "There are also far fewer mako sharks, because they're good to eat. But what really hurt sharks was when the value of fins went up in the late 1980s." Prices rose sharply when several fish dealers established export channels to the Orient (especially Hong Kong and Taiwan), where shark fins are prized for soup, and where vast quantities of fins from around the world are sent. The U.S. government encouraged commercial shark fishing, to fill the gap left by swordfish depletion.

Joe continues, "It was only the fins that were really worth money, and suddenly some commercial fishermen were just cutting the fins off and letting the sharks drift away to die. We caught a shark that must have gotten away while they were slicing its fins off, because it still had its tail. It had a long-liner's hook in its mouth." In very few years, many species of sharks declined significantly, because their biology—late maturation and low reproduction—makes them highly vulnerable to overfishing.

For hundreds of millions of years sharks gave more grief than they got. But by the 1980s the party was over for the quintessential predators, and sharks were being killed by the tens of millions worldwide each year. In 1993, the U.S. Fisheries Service belatedly implemented a shark-management plan with catch quotas for the East Coast of the United States. Sharks were by then so overfished and the fishery so overcrowded with boats that the first six-month quota was caught in twenty-eight days—even though the quota was set twice as high as the sharks' reproductive rate, because of political compromises forced by shark finners. (After four years of ensuing rancor and continued declines, pressure from conservationists and shark scientists finally halved this quota in 1997.)

McBride takes a meditative draw on his pipe, then admits, "*We* used to waste sharks, too. Guys would bring in ten sharks a day, for pictures or what-have-you, and a lot of them just got dumped. But then with Jack Casey's tag-and-release program through the Fisheries Service, we got educated, and stopped it. Now, we tag and release most of them. This year we've gone through about four hundred tags. That's four hundred sharks that we've caught and made a living from, that are still alive, still breeding. We're able to re-utilize the fish and not kill as many. And tagging is interesting. I tagged a sandbar shark here off Montauk that was recovered seven years later off Venezuela. I also tagged a blue shark that was recovered off Portugal. Before tagging, we never understood how far these animals went."

For the last fifteen minutes, Joe's been watching our sea-surface temperature gauge, which, after remaining inert for nearly thirty miles, has been edging up steadily by a tenth of a degree at a time. The total temperature gain has been three degrees, and for the last few minutes it seems to have reached a plateau at 67 degrees Fahrenheit. We have crossed a habitat boundary, an edge of two water masses, that has been relatively stationary here for a few days.

McBride finishes our conversation by adding, "With all the changes we've seen, nowadays we spend a lot of time trying to educate people not to take all they can catch. Gradually, conserving works economically to the benefit of our industry. It's just not a good policy to encourage people to kill fish that they don't need."

Captain Joe, for all his talkativeness up to this point, is more intent on hunting now, scrutinizing the sonar closely. He glances again at the loran, then at some scribbled numbers from yesterday. He throttles down, and the engines' roar quiets to a diesely growl. We're about forty miles offshore. The water here is an extraordinarily clear deep blue, unlike anything ever seen inshore.

Billy has spent a lot of the last half hour cutting bait fish into pieces for chum. In addition to the butterfish and squid, there's an assortment of unmarketably small fish Billy got from a trawler. Billy points out to me that prominent among this by-catch that makes up today's chum are very young haddock, a species now commercially extinct in the northeast, a species Tim Tower in Ogunquit had complained were now so rare. Once, this was among the most common fishes in the region, a valuable mainstay of the commercial fleet. Billy slices up the young haddock, shaking his head as he does.

The bluefins that have been in this area are babies, about three years old and forty pounds. The limit on bluefin tuna this size is four per person per day. Joe has been trying unsuccessfully for several years to get the federal government to cut this to two per person.

Joe announces to the fares, "The fishing is likely to be good here today, and in the excitement it's easy to take a lot of fish, but please don't take more fish than you can use, because we need to conserve. If we get them good, we can keep catching and just release them. But please don't kill more than you can use."

One of the group, a fellow named Paul, tells McBride that he owns a restaurant and that he can use all the fish we can catch.

While Captain Joe and Billy ready the lines, the fares, who weathered the rough ride in remarkably good form, are still sitting in the cabin, eating sandwiches and swigging soft drinks. From inside the cabin the golf pro, a fortyish man named Harry, calls, "Here, fishy-fishy. I'm prepared to do battle with monsters of the sea."

Joe encourages them to come out of the cabin and onto the deck.

Billy explains to them that they will rotate the task of continually tossing pieces of fish overboard. Two lines, baited with similar chunks of fish, are tossed in among the fish bits. To hide them from the tuna, small, dark-colored hooks are buried deep in the baits. Even at this young age, bluefin tuna are keen-eyed and wary. "Bluefins are *smart*," Billy says to me. "Smarter than yellowfins."

Several herring gulls, black-backed gulls, and greater shearwaters come to our seagoing soup kitchen, competing for pieces of our chum. Joe and Billy feed the bait in among the chunks, letting it out sixty feet or so, then repeating the process. Having the bait drifting back is more deceptive to the wary tuna, which sometimes eat every free-drifting piece of chum yet avoid every piece of bait dangling on a line. Even when speedily shooting through the offerings and appearing quite ravenous, the tunas display impressive discriminatory abilities.

Before our third line can be put out, one bait is hit by a fish but quickly rejected. The strike snaps the fares to attention. The person who is designated as the chummer, momentarily distracted from his task, is quickly instructed by Joe, "Never, ever, stop chumming. No matter what."

Nothing further happens for a while, and Joe, announcing that we'll make a short move, starts the engines. This is not a day for patience. McBride knows that the fish have been moving around in bunches, and he wants to find them. Studying his video sonar while cruising at reduced speed, Joe suddenly slows to a stop and says, "O.K., we're marking them very good between forty and sixty feet. Wow, marking like an SOB!"

In a hurry, chum and lines go over. Nothing touches the baits. The fish are clearly here, but they are not biting. Perhaps they can be finessed. On the latter hypothesis, the last few feet of line is changed to a lighter, less visible leader. As Billy and I are letting out the lines, he suddenly locks his reel and lifts the rod tip smartly. A fish is hooked.

The golf pro—prepared to do battle with monsters of the sea—takes the rod. Joe gets a second fish hooked up almost immediately. The golf pro works hard. These young fish are remarkably strong. They tear line off the reel in long runs against the drag. Joe and Billy work fast and smoothly. The fish arc left and right, the tight line ripping and hissing through the surface. "Move to keep the fish in front of you," instructs Billy. The anglers slip and struggle around the cockpit, and rods are hastily passed over and under each other to keep crossed lines from tangling during the pandemonium.

"You thought this was going to be like goldfish!" one of the spectating fares remarks enigmatically through a crammed mouthful of potato chips. After a tough five minutes, the first fish nears the surface and a gaff hook meets it. It is deftly swung aboard.

The man with the chips says, "It's *beautiful!* What is it? Look, the fins move! Wow, this fin goes into a slot!"

Billy says, "It's a bluefin tuna. They're very hydrodynamic, that's why their fins are like that."

"Keep chumming," Joe says laconically.

Fish two is decked. Billy compliments the anglers on their skill. To bleed the fish and thereby maximize the quality of their meat, Billy deftly pokes a knife into a precise spot on each side of each fish. Pressurized blood spurts in red jets from their heat-exchange systems. The fishes' stiff tails are drumming the deck in panic, splattering blood everywhere. Billy grabs them one at a time and swings them into the fish box. The fish hit the ice shivering in an attempt to put on the blinding burst of speed they are capable of. But their tails can gain no purchase. There is nowhere to go. Millions of years of evolution toward perfection in temperate oceans have left them utterly unprepared for a tiny sea of ice. Bits of shaved ice shower over the deck before the lid can be slammed on the fish box, sealing the young bluefins in their dark, frigid coffin.

The golf pro is now chumming, daintily minimizing direct contact with the fish chunks. A school of little tunny, a small and (fortunately for them) unpalatable species of tuna, invade the chum line like a ricocheting hail of darting silver bullets.

Joe instructs the golf pro to chum more heavily. He wants to make sure some chunks are getting past those little tunnies. Fish are now streaking through the chunks. We miss two strikes. A heavy but unseen fish creates a large swirl behind the boat. We catch a skipjack, one of the smallest species of tuna in the world—usually under ten pounds—and generally canned (as are yellowfins) as "chunk light tuna." Ten minutes later, we release a little tunny.

For the next twenty minutes there are no more hits, though fish occasionally shoot through, grabbing pieces of chum. McBride gets on the radio. The *Sunbeam,* a large boat from Waterford, Connecticut, reports that they've "got 'em good" and invites us to join them. We move two miles to join the big boat, a hundred-footer with two dozen anglers on board. We get right in behind the anchored *Sunbeam,* whose impressive chum line contains an equally impressive number of tuna.

A fish hits the first line out, but we miss the strike. Almost immediately after that, Billy hooks one. Billy hands his rod off to Brian, a rotund, fiftyish house builder who is wearing a white business shirt and office shoes. The fish runs off many yards of line, then darts down deep and goes under the boat, forcing Brian, at Bill's instruction, to bend over the side and thrust the rod into the water to avoid tangling the line in the propellers. Brian, who has never been fishing before, struggles awkwardly for a few minutes and breaks a sweat. In the heaving roll, and with his office shoes slipping in the blood on deck, Brian fights heavily for a few more minutes and becomes exhausted. He hands the rod off to me. The fish, also tiring, seems under control and can be brought to the boat. Billy gaffs the bluefin, a forty-five-pounder. Despite its power, still quite a baby.

Brian gasps, "That fish wore me right the hell out! Did you guys get a picture of me?"

Joe instructs the golf pro to keep chumming.

Another strike refocuses everyone's attention, but the fish feels the line and rejects the bait before it can be stung. Another rod bends over. Al, a thirty-something window cleaner who also has never fished before, can't handle the fish. Against the strongly struggling tuna, and with poor footing, he simply cannot winch any line back onto the reel. The fish suddenly surges for its life and breaks the line.

Five minutes later, another fish bites and is hooked. It makes a very fast run away from the boat but becomes the fourth one to go into the ice box. McBride instructs me to cut more fish into chunks. I open the deck hatch and bring out one of two remaining forty-pound boxes of bait fish. Captain McBride climbs to the bridge and tunes in the radio's weather channel. The marine weather forecast is calling for a harder blow. But the wind is actually moderating and the hazy ocean is flattening to a slick roll. For now, anyway.

Near noon, the *Sunbeam,* away from which we have drifted, calls to report a hot bite going on. Within two minutes, we miss a strike. Then another hits, which Joe hooks before handing the rod to Al. Joe yells, "Chunks! Keep the chunks coming!"

The tuna describes a big circle. Billy says to Al, "O.K., now dip down, move around the corner. Dip. Keep reeling. O.K., come left."

Joe again yells, "Chunks!"

The fish comes up and zips away, then turns back. It surfaces and circles, its tail beating a rapid, noisy flurry of foam. The gaff swings out, and a moment later the tuna lays trembling and gasping in spasms on the deck.

At noon, after five quiet minutes, we move back to the anchored *Sunbeam.* They are throwing enough chum to hold the fish. Joe calls for more chunks: "Keep chumming, even if the boat is sinking."

After a quiet twenty minutes, a common bonito, another small member of the tuna tribe, comes over the side and is invited to join us for dinner. Joe says, "These are excellent eating." A short while later we move back to the mother lode—or perhaps more correctly, the nursery lode. This one spot seems full of tuna, but we had to cross forty miles of ocean to find this particular place, at a time of year when, in seasons past, the fishing was fast and furious only ten or fifteen miles from the Point. And other noted areas to our west along the south shore of Long Island—which held good numbers of young tuna in years past—are reporting an absence of them, as they have for the last few years. In those places, fishing like this is history, "the good old days." (It will turn out that fishing like this will pretty much become history here, too, within a few years as poor spawning success during the 1990s and increased competition for the fish conspire to produce scarcity.)

The customers have now acclimated enough to life on deck that they are letting out the baits themselves. Paul, the restaurateur, hooks a bluefin. A sleek sixty-five-pounder, it runs strongly and takes him around the transom but is overcome in about five minutes. The customers admire it as it lays quietly gasping.

Joe yells, "Chunks!"

Before this fish is iced, another is hooked. Brian takes it. When his fish is added to the others on the ice, the box is full. The top fish is slamming its tail against the lid every few seconds, like a man pounding with his fist. Joe tells me that a large tuna sank a boat last year. The fish, which was put into a box built into the boat's hull, broke through the box's wall with its tail. "Boat sank like a rock."

Paul hooks up. Then Joe hooks another and hands the rod to Al. The fish Paul has been wrestling with nears the boat and is gaffed and swung aboard. Paul says, "Beautiful! Wow!" The fish carries someone else's hook and a broken line. Paul spreads his fingers to loosen his hand and forearm muscles. "This gets to you after a while."

There's another bonito, then a shark bites off a hook.

"That was a good drift," says Billy.

The deck is slick with clotted blood, and before it can be washed off, Brian slips and falls heavily but says he's O.K. Paul's fish is shuddering and drumming on the deck. The bars and spots on its side flush and then fade as it dies.

Skipjacks are behind the boat now by the dozen, their neon-blue markings flashing as they shoot by. At a quarter past one, I take the last few chunks on deck and throw them overboard. There is another big box of bait in the hold, but Joe climbs to the bridge and starts the engines. As the engines warm, a larger fish hits a bait Al was letting out. He grapples with it, grunting with exertion. It's a seventy-pounder. The instant it hits the deck, Joe puts the boat in gear and heads for home. Billy pulls the plug on the fish box and gallons of bloody water shoot out. Our wake reddens.

I climb to the bridge. Joe tells me, "I know we've got another box of bait, but I didn't want to kill any more fish today. These guys wouldn't go for releasing the fish, so I stopped when they got two bluefins apiece. That's plenty."

Joe's still hopping mad about the impending season closure, which means canceled bookings and returned deposits that have already been spent. He says he doesn't want to kill more fish, he just wants to have the season last. If the Fisheries Service would just halve the daily limit, the season could last twice as long, for the same number of fish.

Joe McBride sits, suited and attentive, with a bunch of sullen chartermen who have made the nine-hour drive from the port of Montauk to Washington, D.C. The U.S. commissioners to the Atlantic tuna commission meet twice a year with their official advisory committee. A diverse array of government officials, fishing-industry lobbyists, lawyers, scientists, fishermen, and conservation advocates occupy the small auditorium, garbed in everything from pin-striped business suits to T-shirts and baseball caps.

The advisory committee's role is to present ideas and information to the commissioners, to help them develop the policies and goals that the U.S. will bring to the table when delegates from some twenty countries convene in Madrid, Spain, for the annual ICCAT meeting.

In practice, the advisers form less a committee than an unruly mob of conflicting interests, deep resentments, and bitter personal hostilities. Several members of the advisory committee have brought lawsuits against each other and against the National Marine Fisheries Service, charging violations of fishing restrictions, negligent monitoring of quotas, and failure to file legally required impact assessments of bluefin fishery regulations. Three U.S. commissioners preside, themselves at cross-purposes. By law, one commissioner must represent recreational users of the resource; one, commercial users; and one, the U.S. government. (No slot exists for someone to represent conservation and public interests.)

The auditorium is carpeted and muted. Tension, thick as mist, adheres to everything in the room. It soon becomes plain that the users are warring among themselves. The constituents and advisers do not so much inform as bully the commissioners with angry and inflammatory hortatory speeches, across-the-room accusations, and occasional outbursts of foul language. The level of decorum approximates that inside a sausage factory. In addition, the government commissioner maintains a deep personal grudge against the director of the National Marine Fisheries Service, whose advice he ignores. First-timers here, as am I today, are immediately struck by the way the tone and the contentiousness impede communication and progress.

Scientists from the National Marine Fisheries Service present their latest information on the various billfishes and tuna species for which the tuna commission has assumed authority. The graphs for blue marlin, white marlin, swordfish, and bluefin tuna all look similarly bleak. In each graph, fishing mortality is headed up and fish are headed down. Fisheries Service staff members give a lengthy presentation on swordfish. Adults have declined sharply in the last two decades. The graph shows a forty-degree slope downward. Fishing pressure on large fish is higher than previously thought, and the adult population, in a veritable free fall, is down about 80 percent since the 1970s. Young swordfish, ages two to four, are suffering high fishing mortality. In fact, more than 80 percent of the female swordfish caught are juveniles too young to spawn, killed before they can breed. Worst, the North Atlantic is now so infested with longlines, and fishing pressure is so crushingly intense, that survival of young through adulthood is down to about 3 percent what it once was. At that rate, the Fisheries Service fears commercial extinction of this swordfish population within ten years.

Dr. Eric Prince reports on U.S. attempts to initiate research work with Caribbean countries. He shows a slide of a Venezuelan long-liner, its deck loaded with swordfish. The U.S. has been unable to initiate work with Trinidad, though it's a major landing port for Taiwanese long-liners. The Japanese have given Grenada and St. Vincent some longline boats designed to catch yellowfin tuna, and Prince says Japanese advisers are on the islands instructing fishermen on how to handle the catch so it can be exported to Japan for sashimi.

The bluefin tuna presentation, upon which millions of dollars of competing interests are focusing a laser glare, is made by Dr. Gerry Scott. Scott, addressing those who would kill the messenger, is visibly and understandably nervous. In this lion's den the pressure in the air is so intense that my own palms are getting clammy as I just sit in the audience. Maybe it's just the lights, but Scott is sweating so profusely from his hands and face that sweat drips onto his overhead transparencies as he stands at the machine to explain them. Scott shows projections for the next five years, concluding, "The population of adult bluefins is very likely to continue to decline through the period of our projections unless catches are reduced by about half." I involuntarily wince upon hearing this, though I had read the summary earlier and was not surprised by the presentation. What I am cringing at is the thought of being him, having to deliver those words to this assembly.

A round of volleys from differing perspectives follows. Ken Hinman, director of the National Coalition for Marine Conservation, stands and delivers: "It is vividly clear that the ICCAT program is not working toward rebuilding the population within our lifetimes. The science demands a fifty percent reduction in fishing mortality, at a minimum."

Mike Sutton of the World Wildlife Fund rises next. A newcomer to the tuna debate, Sutton is a biologist, lawyer, and highly skilled conservation advocate. His diverse background in fish research, law enforcement, and international fisheries issues, including whaling, poses him as a triple threat in this room. Sutton says that both fish and fishermen suffer the results of shortsighted management. Long-term thinking is most favorable to both the bluefin and to the fishermen, he says, because fishing activity will be able to expand if the bluefin population is allowed to rebuild. Half the people in the room seem at least to accept the statement. The rest glower.

Gerry Abrams, flanked by his own crowd of constituents, plays the artful dodger. Gerry's preferred habitat is the dark forest of scientific uncertainty, and he weaves skillfully among its shadows. "Last year, when the Audubon Society proposed that our exports of bluefin to Japan be suspended, they were relying on a 1990 ICCAT assessment that was based on some data that needs to be changed, but the updated assessment that we have just been given was done without applying the corrections that were agreed to by NMFS—"

"That's not true," interrupts Dr. Brad Brown of the National Marine Fisheries Service. "The corrections suggested by your consultant were made."

Abrams sidesteps and pirouettes: "I'm not going to have a scientific argument over it because, first of all, I'm not a scientist, and, second of all, the science is not the most reliable science in the world. I would simply point out, again, that if we're going to err, we ought to err on the side of employment."

Dick Stone of the National Marine Fisheries Service addresses the commissioners, saying, "If you go back to the 1981–82 language, it says we're to 'ensure stabilization or increase.' That's the exact language. If you want a recommendation, since ICCAT operates under a 'maximum sustainable yield' policy, I think we could ask our scientists where we would need to rebuild to in order to produce the maximum sustainable yield."

Dr. Brown picks up the ball, saying that for the western Atlantic, the total weight of all breeding bluefins in the population would need to be about thirty thousand tons to produce the maximum sustainable yield. This compares with the current estimate of less than six thousand tons, under which the depleted population is declining.

When recognized in his turn, Captain Joe McBride rises with the bearing of an Indian chief and speechifies on behalf of his surrounding tribe of charter-boat skippers. "I'm representing today approximately thirty charter-boat captains from Long Island who were confronted a week ago with a serious problem. Our fishery for the small fish was closed a month earlier than last year because our quota has been reached. That might be a very necessary conservation measure. You gentlemen are the people we rely on for our information, and we are willing to support your science. We support better conservation. Five years ago, we respectfully requested that you halve the daily limits. If you had done that for us, there would never have been the need for this closure that is costing us significant amounts of money. For five years, we have been willing to take as much as a seventy-five percent reduction in daily mortality so that we can maintain our businesses for the duration of the season. My question is: Why have we gotten no positive response from the Fisheries Service? We will no longer tolerate having our business cut off in the month of October, when the season is at its height, by the whim and fancy of bureaucrats in Washington. This is wrong; it's not good management, it's not even good politics. Thank you for your consideration."

The officials explain that this meeting is about international policy matters, not domestic allocations and regulations. No action can be taken here to reduce the daily limit. That must wait for a more appropriate forum and a future rule making. No one responds directly to the points Captain McBride has expressed. Having said his piece, he and his disgruntled constituents file out for the long ride home, feeling—correctly—that nothing much was accomplished for their time and their canceled fishing day.

Steve Weiner, the harpoon boat owner who helped me get to know the fishermen of Ogunquit, now president of the East Coast Tuna Association, says to the remaining group, "We've got to solve this issue of catching the younger fish, or all else is for naught. That's the future of this fishery. But we're wasting a lot of time by not focusing on it. We've got to lay off these small fish. Of the forty fish I caught this year, ten were mediums—juveniles. I'm willing to give up catching any juvenile fish, anything under three hundred pounds."

One Jim McHue, an aged sport angler and veteran of many identically factious meetings in years past, rejoins, "We can cut back on the small fish, but not as an excuse to do nothing about the giants, the breeders. You can't look at the hole and ignore the donut. Let's work from the big picture here."

Sensing that we might be nearing a constructive discussion and perhaps a substantive proposal, a tuna industry representative steers the conversation away from the issues and back to the topic of scientific uncertainty: "Our science is not definitive. We don't know the real degree of error."

"I've listened to attacks on the science, but I haven't seen any alternate science presented," replies Mike Montgomery, the commissioner representing recreational fishing interests. "I'm prepared to support our scientists. It's better to err on the side of the stock, though I know employment is tough."

Abrams, ever ready to fend attacks on—and seize an opportunity to reiterate—his main point, rejoins angrily. "The President himself!" he booms, then pauses, as if to gather behind his words the solemnity of the U.S. presidency and the momentum of the popular vote. "The President *himself* has said: 'If I'm going to err, I'm going to err on the side of employment.' We've been hearing the same assessment of bluefin for a decade and it's incorrect! NMFS said in 1981 that 'it's too late to save the bluefin.'"

Breaking in angrily again, the Fisheries Service's Dr. Brown shoots back: "You've said that before, and I'd like to see that in writing. I've been through the papers and I have never found that."

Chief commissioner Carmen Blondin, letting his feud with the Fisheries Service begin to show, cuts Brown off. Gerry Abrams continues with the air of a man who is dusting himself off after being unpleasantly and impudently accosted. Dramatically pausing for a moment and lowering his volume to an emphatic hush, he concludes, "The best way to improve our database is to continue fishing under the current quota."

All of this leads subtly to a catch-22, hardwired into the commission's process, that makes these advisory meetings like the heater muscle in the head of a swordfish—generating intense heat but no motion. After venting all this rancor and hostility, the committee can go no further, can decide nothing. Nor are the commissioners required to decide upon a position, despite the formal presentation from the scientists. This is because the final scientific report will not be put together until two weeks hence, when the scientific committee meets in Spain just before ICCAT's managers meet. And the commissioners say they cannot decide any policy until the final report is unveiled, because it might contain changes.

The advisory committee chairman, a tuna industry rep, says, "There's no doubt about the decline that occurred in the past. That reality is embedded in cement. From what we've heard here, it seems clear we need to do something. But the final assessment may show some changes."

"Yes," says chief commissioner Blondin, nodding gravely, "we need to see what the final report says."

And there it sits.

Blondin confidentially tells several of the attendees, including me, that he's glad the discussion about listing bluefin tuna under CITES is hanging over Japan's head, because it will make it easier for him to get Japan to agree to quota reductions. He tells us that internally he's smiling, but he can't let anyone know that. He asks his ad hoc confidants not to hang him and to consider the various diplomatic problems he has to deal with.

No one takes these remarks too seriously, because, in the final analysis, actions will speak for themselves. Blondin, by his earlier refusal to state in writing that staying within our quota is important, exemplified how cynically the managers have winked off their legal responsibilities under the ICCAT treaty, and the scientists' warnings. A cynical atmosphere breeds cynics. By operating at this level of cynicism and countercynicism, each person involved is debased and diminished. Myself among them.

A wind-driven November rain slashes the darkened window as I settle into my seat for the overnight trans-Atlantic red-eye. I am hoping to gain insight into the dynamics that have left the tuna commission so inert and ineffectual.

One hundred and thirty attendees from twenty countries converge at the Hotel Pintor, a rather dingy establishment in downtown Madrid, for the annual Atlantic tuna commission meeting. Most countries send three or four people. The U.S. delegation, all thirty-five members of it, comprises commissioners, government fishery scientists, fishery managers, congressional staff, State Department employees, a factious and unruly assortment of commercial and sportfishing industry reps, and environmentalists.

The commission's scientific committee has reported in their final document that catches must be reduced by half. Usually, the U.S. commissioners read the final report and "decide" their position ad lib (for over a decade they've opted for the same: no reduction in the quota despite the continuing decline in the population). This time, things are different.

Prior to coming here, the U.S. commissioners were instructed to seek a 50 percent reduction in catch quotas, to bring management into line with the scientific advice. This is the first catch reduction proposed by an ICCAT member country in a decade. It did not happen all by itself. Conservation advocates spent much of the fall working against bitter tuna-industry lobbying. Maneuvering escalated to the White House when tuna exporters hired heavily connected lobbyists to obtain congressional and presidential pressure on the Fisheries Service to seek *increased* catch quotas. Conservationists countered with their own White House contacts and prevailed, and the policy to seek a 50 percent catch quota reduction, based on the advice of the scientists, emerged.

Before the weeklong meeting even begins, Carmen Blondin briefs the U.S. delegation, explaining that the U.S. position is politically unrealistic and unachievable. "Impossible," he says.

With an attitude like that, it will be.

In the hotel ballroom that has been converted for the meeting, the commissioners take their seats around a long central table, with little flags and plaques identifying their countries at their places. English, French, and Spanish are simultaneously translated through headsets for everyone in the room.

Efficiency is not a prominent characteristic of the commission. An hour and a half of opening speeches, most of which reiterate that there will not be enough time to do all that needs to be done at the meeting, is followed by a half-hour coffee break, which is followed by lengthy individual introductions of each attendee from some twenty countries, except—thank goodness—the U.S. During all this, I peruse the long-awaited scientific report, which shows a decline for the fifteenth consecutive year in the number of breeding bluefins in the west Atlantic; the total decline is estimated at roughly 90 percent.

After the close of the first day of meetings, Blondin again tells us that the 50 percent cut is not politically feasible. One liberally drinking delegate says to me, "What happened to our position for a fifty percent reduction in the quota? We just gave up on it? Just like that? I've been coming here since 1983, and nothing—*ever*—happens. Nothing. Nothing. Nothing!" Commissioner Mike Montgomery complains to me that he's being kept in the dark by Blondin and by the commissioner representing the commercial fishing industry.

I am invited to dinner with several of the U.S. delegates and their wives (90 percent of the official attendees are men). Gerry Abrams cranks up his repertoire of off-color and off-taste jokes. Soon he's improvising his brand of ethnic humor. When my steak and fried potatoes arrive, Gerry turns to me and says, "Those potatoes look as greasy as Italians." Conversation trails off around the table. Heads turn to Gerry. Glances turn to me. With my eyebrows raised, I stare into my food for a long moment, then decide to pass up the bait like a bluefin on Gerry's sonar screen, and let the remark hover in the air around Gerry like a bad stink, until it dissipates on its own.

When it does, Gerry and Commissioner Montgomery, who is a wealthy California lawyer, muse together about how great it will be to "have Cuba back" in a few years. Abrams says he can't wait to fly his plane there. "To gamble in one of my casinos?" inquires Montgomery. Gerry tells Montgomery that he spent two hundred thousand dollars last year lobbying on the bluefin issue. Listening to the two of them brings to mind a characterization I once read of "men so rich they handle their wallets the way they handle their testicles when they soap themselves."

I arrive back at the hotel late, with a headache and in need of sleep. Sounds of lovemaking from the next room drown out street traffic. My neighbor, a member of the U.S. delegation who had come to Madrid alone and who will leave alone in a few days, is not alone tonight.

Negotiations on quota reductions become deadlocked the next day. The Canadians say catch reductions are out of the question. With their cod fishery in trouble, they can't afford to ask their fishermen for another cut.

Canada's strongest personality at the meeting is Jim Beckett, a stern-looking man with wild eyebrows and some equally wild notions. Beckett tells me that bluefin population levels in the 1960s, when the first intensive commercial fishing began and scientists made the first abundance estimates, may have been unusually high. He also tells me that cod populations in the sixties may have been unusually high. Though the data shows—"appears to show"—the populations in decline between the 1960s and now, he speculates that the abundance—"the apparent abundance"—of the sixties was, perhaps, *abnormal*. Perhaps he's never read the early explorers' and settlers' descriptions of catching cod and other fish with baskets and pans, or talked to any old-timers. Denial seems Beckett's forte. Denying the problem puts him in the strongest position psychologically to argue against reducing the tuna catch, which Beckett is here to do. Whether this is the wisest position is another question.

The Canadians say the U.S. position on bluefin tuna is disingenuous and hypocritical. "You want reductions?" they ask. "Then stay within your quota." Blondin's earlier refusal to state that it is important for the U.S. to remain within its quota has rightfully come back to haunt.

That night after dinner, Sport Fishing Institute president Gil Radonski—a longtime proponent of reducing bluefin tuna catch quotas—and his wife, along with several commercial-fishing-industry representatives, are robbed at knifepoint on the street outside Plaza Mayor. Hearing of this, Gerry Abrams responds, "Goddam Gypsies! We hired them to get Radonski, but they obviously botched the job." Gerry alone laughs.

At midweek, I ask U.S. senior fishery manager Dick Schaefer, "If your boss asks you what we've accomplished, what will you tell him?"

"Nothing," Schaefer responds. "We've accomplished nothing so far."

To which an eavesdropping delegate adds, "Just like every year."

The Japanese, too, are resisting talk of quota reductions. Japan's spokesman puts maximum spin on the scientific report in his hortatory remarks. But many of his statements clash with the scientific information available to each of us in the new report.

In a thick accent, he announces, "This year we are pleased to see the stock has been showing a stable trend."

Actually, the scientific report shows the breeding population down more than 20 percent from last year's low.

"Current catch limits should result in increases in the population within five years."

The scientific report projects that unless quotas are halved, the population will likely continue declining.

"We see no reason for further catch reductions. Seeking a change in the quota does not seem responsible."

The scientific report is silent on what would be responsible. Responsibility, it appears, is beyond the realm of science.

The Japanese go on to suggest that artificial "seeding" (stocking) can increase the number of tuna in the oceans. Significant progress has been made, they say, by Japanese researchers raising bluefins in captivity. "We are willing to offer our knowledge," he says.

But according to one of their delegates, in their twenty years of research they have yet to obtain a single ripened egg from their captive bluefin tuna. Instead, they raise young wild-caught fish to marketable size.

Sweden's scientist, Lennart Nyman arrives. Sweden has formally proposed that the western Atlantic bluefin be listed under CITES. When the U.S. government announced it would not pursue listing the bluefin under CITES, the National Audubon Society and World Wildlife Fund had already initiated discussions with Sweden, whose own once-productive bluefin fishery had vanished in the last two decades. Sweden saw merit in the proposal. They had no idea what lay ahead.

Dr. Nyman, a tall, slender, distinguished-looking man with a neatly groomed beard, has come to make an official statement on behalf of Sweden. Nyman is a sharp and knowledgeable person with a glib sense of humor, and his business card reflects his combination personality: both serious and jocular. It shows two affiliations, "National Swedish Board of Fisheries" and "International Society of Arctic Char Fanatics." (Arctic char, a relative of the brook trout, is a lovely fish of the far north.) Nyman seems much amused with the commission proceedings and appears to view the assembled delegates as a parliament of buffoons. But he tells me that the Japanese head of delegation, Mr. Shima, a hoary-haired old warrior with a severe limp who also represents Japan's whale hunting interests at other conferences, had been enraged about Sweden's proposal, and in an un-Japanese loss of cool, berated the Swedes, calling them "stupid." Nyman says, "But all you need to do is look at ICCAT's own graphs; they say everything."

Japan states publicly that Sweden's endorsement of listing the bluefin tuna under CITES is irresponsible, inappropriate, and counterproductive. "The decline in breeding-age bluefin has been expected, and is part of the management regime."

I cannot make sense of this, so I ask a Japanese delegate to clarify. He explains that the catch quotas were set to allow continued catches high enough to reduce the surviving adults, with the idea that management will protect the young fish coming up the ranks into adulthood. This perspective rests—indeed, relies totally—on the assumption that the number of young fish is unrelated to the number of adults. He further explains that catching most of the adults will not reduce numbers of young fish because each adult lays millions of eggs and survival rates of eggs and larvae are dictated by variable rates of natural mortality.

But it seems to me that if each adult lays several million eggs and survival rates vary, then the more adults, the more young. That's just basic logic. Saying that the bluefin's chances of successfully reproducing the next generation cannot be threatened even if the breeding population is reduced by more than 90 percent, because each fish lays so many eggs, seems like saying you can't destroy an oak forest by clear-cutting it, because each tree makes so many acorns.

These guys, I am thinking, must know that they are blowing smoke. Because it seems improbable that there is no documented relationship between the numbers of adults and young, I check a couple of widely available documents that I have brought with me, to see what scientists really know about it. The scientific report of the 1991 World Meeting on Bluefin Tunas states, "Larvae survey results have shown a decline in larval population and thus probable spawning stock." Indeed, larval densities in the Gulf of Mexico spawning areas have dropped 75 to 90 percent since the 1970s. I found the most direct evidence in the new ICCAT report that was distributed to everyone at the meeting. When I took the estimated number of breeders in each year and graphed it against the estimated number of one-year-olds the following year, the result was a clear correlation. Not a straight line, mind you, because of things like natural variability in mortality, but the correlation was, in scientific terms, "statistically significant." Large adult populations generally spawned the strongest year classes of young fish, and the smallest breeding groups produced the worst breeding failures.

The smallest breeding populations are those of the last few years. These are the depleted groups that the Japanese, U.S., and Canadian fishery managers say (with one hand on their wallets and the other on a rabbit's foot) will produce a strong class of youngsters—eventually. While the managers work under fishing-industry pressure to keep quotas high, the carcasses of the last 10 percent or so of the western Atlantic's parent bluefins are migrating across the Pacific in cargo planes bound for Tokyo, generating many millions of dollars while going from sea to sushi.

So it seems to me that there are two problems with the Japanese argument that even if we catch most of the adults there will be plenty of young to replace them. One, it is wrong, according to information in the scientific reports in everyone's folder. Two, it is a high-risk gambit, especially since there has not been a strong year class of young fish since the 1970s, and only a couple of mediocre spawnings among many poor years in the 1980s and '90s.

Bluefin spawning is not the only issue in which the Madrid delegates are dodging the facts like skillful matadors. When Spain complains bitterly to France because French fishers are drift-netting for albacore tuna in defiance of the United Nations' ban, France asks whether the recent scarcity of albacore around Spain might not be due to climate changes affecting the fish's migratory routes. Clumsy try, and no one bites.

The meeting breaks. Time for a new adventure in dining. I order fried baby eels in cheese sauce. I've eaten my share of smoked eels, and I've eaten some pretty strange things in my travels, including bee larvae, but this soft mound of baby eels makes me gag. While I'm nearly retching on my supper, the U.S., Canada, and Japan enter closed, after-hours sessions to discuss the western Atlantic blue-fin. Canada is unwilling to accept even a phased-in reduction and wants further restrictions on U.S. catches of small fish. But the Japanese, who themselves catch almost entirely immature fish, balk at such suggestions, except for the very small-est ones they neither catch nor consume. The Japanese seem more concerned about the fish reaching Tokyo than reaching sexual maturity. The talks mire.

In the morning, in the full session, the delegates begin lengthily reading aloud from statistical reports that we already have before us. When the meeting grinds into budget sessions, I spend the afternoon in the hotel lobby, chatting with bored attendees.

Daily, the commissioners from most countries are doing their best to ignore and show their disdain for the Swedes. The Swedes complain repeatedly to the secretariat that although they have been invited here, they are not being allowed to address the conference. After they have waited all week, it is looking like Swe-den won't get a chance to speak. Finally, in the closing minutes of the last full session, they barely get onto the agenda to read their statement. Nyman bluntly observes that the western Atlantic breeding population appears headed for extinction. He points out that the population may hit some low threshold beyond which it could suddenly collapse, as happened with Icelandic herring. Nyman reminds the delegates that Sweden's sport and commercial bluefin tuna fisheries are already gone. He emphasizes that a reduction in mortality is urgently needed, especially for the western Atlantic population.

No comments follow from the floor, because the commission delegates have voted not to appear to legitimize Sweden's proposal by discussing it.

Canada, the U.S., and Japan are again meeting in all-day closed sessions to dis-cuss reductions. At seven-thirty P.M., Blondin emerges to brief us. The Canadi-ans are barely budging. Canada scoffs at Sweden's CITES proposal, believing it has no chance of passage. The Canadians will accept no more than a 20 percent reduction phased in over two years. But, Blondin says, "The Japanese would buy into a more rapid destruction of recovery, I mean, more rapid *production,* excuse me, of recovery."

Why the movement? Japan has had bad experiences with CITES. CITES listed all the whales and sea turtles, leaving Japan looking bad for deciding to continue importing these animals and their products from outlaw countries not party to CITES. After taking a public-relations beating, Japan relented and decided to comply with CITES, because their image as the world's leading wildlife scofflaw was so costly in global opinion. A CITES listing on bluefin tuna would seem a symbolic catastrophe to the Japanese, who appear paranoiacally convinced that this proposal is not aimed at conservation but, rather, they tell me, is a well-planned strategy "to destroy our food culture" and "put fisheries into chaos."

As if they are not in chaos already.

. . .

Andrea Gaski of the World Wildlife Fund and I join Dr. Nyman for dinner. Nyman lampoons commission diplo-speak throughout the evening. "The observer from Sweden would like some butter. Are there any comments from the floor?"

"I would like to have more time to assess fully the allocation of butter resources to a noncontracting nation having observer status, although I praise the distinguished observer for his interesting choice of wine."

"We should study the butter proposal further, and reconvene this panel next year," adds Andrea.

Thursday night's negotiations between the U.S., Canada, and Japan go till two A.M. In the morning the meeting table is littered with beer, soda, and water bottles, and ashtrays are piled high. Blondin says they have no agreements. Japan is willing to buy into a 50 percent temporary, phased reduction, because of the political expediency of doing so to avert a CITES listing. The U.S. and Japan now have the option of bringing a vote to the floor. Canada would almost certainly be defeated in a vote because an alliance of the U.S. and Japan on any quota cut would be convincing to most, if not all, of the other countries. To the surprise of many, the U.S. position seems suddenly within reach.

But Blondin says that he is committed to consensus and will not risk "embarrassing" the Canadians with a vote. To those of us who have grown cynical in an atmosphere of cynicism, this represents an intentionally sidestepped opportunity for the U.S. delegation to achieve its officially instructed goal.

The negotiators go back behind closed doors. I mill around the lobby. A fisherman representing swordfish long-liners from the United States tells me that bad times are causing people to leave the fishery. More than half of the boats have quit swordfishing in the last few years because of vanishing returns. Unlike many of the bluefin tuna fishermen, he tells me that the science reflects what he sees on the water. He says Sweden's CITES proposal is a stick of dynamite—dangerous, but potentially able to do considerable good if it gets the tuna commission moving without destroying it and hurting fishers. Not everyone sees the constructive strategic value in the CITES proposal. Spain has initiated action to keep Sweden out of the European Community unless Sweden changes its position on CITES.

At ten A.M., we get the word. There will be a four-year, phased quota reduction of 25 percent. There will be no sale allowed of fish less than thirty kilograms (about sixty-six pounds). After four years, the quota will automatically revert back to the current level, unless they decide otherwise when the time comes. Doing some quick arithmetic, I calculate that, because it will take four years for the quota to drop 25 percent, the actual reduction in the kill for the entire period will be only about 17 percent. According to the scientists' projections in ICCAT's report, this will not stop the population's decline.

At a final delegation meeting, Blondin says we've made progress in protecting the resources on which we all depend. Diplomatically, there is little doubt that the meeting and the compromise were successes. But according to the scientific analysis, reducing the catch quota by only 25 percent over four years will force the breeding population lower. Gerry addresses the delegation, saying again that if we must err, we must err on the side of employment, then repeats for the delegation his joke, in case some of us hadn't heard earlier, that the Gypsies botched his setup to kill Radonski. Gerry, alone, has the last laugh.

But not all the comedy acts have taken their turn on the stages of the world. Four months later, in March 1992, CITES's 120-plus member nations and a host of nongovernmental organizations and observers convene in Kyoto, Japan, for their two-week biannual conference. They have come to debate which forms of life will be afforded protection under the Convention on International Trade in Endangered Species.

In opening ceremonies at the resplendent conference facilities in the evening, a Mr. Nakamura, head of the Japan Environmental Agency, observes "CITES seeks harmonization between conservation and utilization of wildlife. If wildlife cannot exist there will be poor quality for human life. A better world for wildlife means a better world for human life." The mayor of Kyoto points out, "Love of nature is at the core of Japanese culture."

"DOWN WITH SWEDEN!" "BLUEFIN IS NOT TOY FOR ENVIRONMENTALISTS!" In the morning, we are greeted by an indignant picket line of Japanese seafood representatives.

Only 1 percent of Japan's total imports of all tuna species, and roughly 15 to 20 percent of its worldwide bluefin tuna imports, would be affected if the proposal is adopted. But Japanese delegates, as they had four months earlier in Spain, repeatedly tell members of the conservation community, "This is the same sort of thing you did to us on whales, sea turtles, and drift nets, and we will not let this happen with bluefin tuna. If you succeed here, you will go on to the next species and the next until you destroy our food culture."

The faces here because of the bluefin proposal are familiar; and they are also the same ones that attend the International Whaling Commission meetings. An amazingly small handful of individuals handle an amazingly large proportion of the world's fishing negotiations—and they are not what I would call conservationists.

Most countries here have sent between one and five delegates. Japan's CITES delegation is augmented by heavy reinforcements: forty-nine persons in all. For several days, Japan and Canada work feverishly to force Sweden to withdraw the proposal prior to a vote. In closed meetings, the Japanese pound the table and make economic threats.

Swedish delegation head Dr. Sven Johanssen says wearily, "Imagine the worst kind of pressure that can be applied by one country to another and you have an idea of what the Japanese and Canadians are doing to us. I'm sorry to say it's out of our hands now. The ambassadors are arguing it out back in Stockholm. We will have to do as instructed." Constantly shadowed by a mosquito-like cloud of reporters, endlessly harangued by members of Japan's large delegation, the Swedes grow more worn and worried-looking every day.

The U.S. officially opposes the proposal, but the personal biases of the individuals on the U.S. delegation—particularly National Marine Fisheries Service and Fish and Wildlife Service staffers—keep their opposition efforts halfhearted, even while official U.S. rhetoric hangs tough. Still, though, they offer no support to the Swedes.

Not all of Japan's personnel are deployed against the Swedes. There are well over one hundred countries represented here, so the Japanese delegates split up. Delegates from the Pacific tropical island nation of Vanuatu and from the Dominican Republic tell me the Japanese have warned that if they support the Swedish proposal, they can expect Japan to cut their economic aid. A delegate from Zimbabwe says, "I am sickened by the manipulations on the bluefin tuna." One member of the Philippine delegation says they were instructed to vote against the bluefin proposal—the Japanese had already met with their fishing minister back home—but would vote for listing the bluefin, against instructions, if special arrangements can be made for a secret ballot on this species.

The conservation groups are split on whether to try to invoke CITES provisions allowing secret ballots. Some of the groups are against the idea, on principle, because open ballots make countries more accountable. Others realize that, on the bluefin issue, secret ballots are the only way to get a true and honest vote because Japan is intimidating so many delegates.

A peculiar bluefin tuna "briefing book" appears at ICCAT's booth, containing a six-page statement by "The Federation of Japan Tuna Fisheries Cooperatives, in agreement with the International Commission for the Conservation of Atlantic Tunas [ICCAT], the Inter-American Tropical Tuna Commission, the National Fisheries Institute of the United States [the seafood industry lobbying firm employing one of the U.S.'s tuna commissioners], the U.S. East Coast Tuna Association [Gerry Abrams's bluefin exporters], the International Coalition of Fisheries Associations" and others. This does nothing to dispel impressions that ICCAT has conflicts of interest and works neither independently nor objectively.

ICCAT's booth also displays a variety of graphs, all with lines going up. Puzzled because so many species of tunas and billfishes are declining, I take a close look at the axis labels. These are graphs of weight plotted against age! The commission has hung graphs showing that as fish get older, they weigh more! This is the only way ICCAT can force its data into graphs showing lines going upward. They are keeping their embarrassing, down-trending graphs of fish populations safely out of sight, hidden like dirty magazines.

Fierce conflict over the bluefin proposal is reflected in the attentions of reporters from around the world; only the fight over elephants and ivory receives more press attention. In an informal early poll on bluefin positions, sixteen countries will definitely vote no; two are probably no; sixteen probably yes; eight definitely yes; three undecided. The rest: unaccounted for.

Bluefin tuna will come up for a vote this afternoon, right after consideration of the rare brown hyena. The bluefin is being taken out of turn, two days early, not during consideration of fishes but inserted between mammals and birds. Rumor has it that the Swedes have requested this because they desperately need relief.

For lunch, several of us go into Kyoto for sushi. The racial homogeneity of Japan's streets is in stark contrast to the international conference. In the sushi bar the only bluefin we see is on television. The CITES debate has made big news here.

Reentering the conference hall following lunch, the Swedes are absolutely mobbed by reporters, cameras, and lights.

At 2:24 P.M., right after delegates close debate on the brown hyena (its name is placed into Appendix II; exports will be monitored), Sweden is asked to make its statement on tuna. Dr. Sven Johanssen addresses the hundreds of people in the conference hall: "Our objective is the restoration of bluefin populations to sustainable levels." He recounts the decline of bluefins off Sweden during the 1960s and notes that the Scandinavian coast bluefin fishery has suffered a drop in catches from eight thousand tons annually to zero. (One of the delegates had shown me photos of tremendous catches taken from Swedish waters in years past.) Turning his remarks to the western Atlantic, he tells the assembly that unless a 50 percent reduction in bluefin catches takes place, "complete collapse" can be expected in a few years. He points out that the decline in the western Atlantic is continuous, not fluctuating as it would be if natural conditions were responsible rather than overfishing.

"Sweden will consider constructive alternatives to the proposal if they meet the following conditions," he continues. "One, ICCAT must pursue catch reductions. Two, ICCAT must improve data collection and research. Three, all nations fishing for bluefin tuna must cooperate with ICCAT. Four, ICCAT must keep CITES fully informed on their progress. If a commitment to these points is made, Sweden is prepared to withdraw its proposal."

The chair gives Canada the floor. Jim Beckett, of Canada's Department of Fisheries and Oceans, disingenuously says that bluefin population trends in the 1980s were the result of catches in the 1970s rather than continued overfishing, and that the ICCAT program is now bearing fruit. Other species, he says, have been fished harder and are still O.K. (None of this is true, and this characteristic denial of reality will within months finally destroy Newfoundland's cod fishery, proving Beckett and his colleagues profoundly wrong.) Canada, he says, accepts Sweden's modest conditions.

Representing Japan, a Mr. Imamura, counselor of the Fisheries Agency, explains that his country shares the view of Canada, and accepts the conditions made by Sweden.

Morocco, an ICCAT member, says that Sweden's suggestions and conditions fit within the framework of ICCAT to restore and sustain the bluefin fishery.

For the United States, Fisheries Service director Dr. Bill Fox says the U.S. shares Sweden's deep concern, especially for the western Atlantic population. "We thank and commend Sweden for offering the means to resolve this contentious problem." The United States, he says, accepts Sweden's conditions.

Sweden says, with palpable relief, "Hearing the preceding comments, we will withdraw our proposal."

The chairman says, "Thank you. This concludes the debate on this item."

Not so fast. Immediately, a hand shoots up from among the delegates. Roger McManus, president of the Center for Marine Conservation, who is here representing the World Conservation Union, has something to say. So do the delegates from a number of countries. So do twenty or so environmental group representatives.

The chairman glances at McManus and immediately looks down, announcing, "The next species on our agenda will be . . ."

And that is the end of the bluefin proposal.

It turns out that to squelch debate, Canada and Japan had insisted that no floor statements be permitted from anyone besides the fishing countries. Sweden, under severe duress, had acquiesced. With those countries agreed, the CITES Bureau determined ahead of time to bar any other remarks. This was highly irregular; statements were allowed on every other proposal throughout the conference, including those withdrawn for various reasons.

McManus, furious that the U.S. delegation allowed this, lambasts U.S. Fisheries director Fox outside the conference hall, saying, "It's a slap in the face of all of us who had something important to say." Delegates from Nigeria and Botswana are also upset, saying the countries involved in stifling the debate brought dishonor on the CITES treaty and on themselves.

A press conference to handle clamoring reporters' questions about the bluefin tuna issue is hastily convened in an adjacent room. The Swedish head of delegation, Dr. Johanssen, looks terrible. A reporter from Japan's public television station asks him whether he thought this issue turned too political for the biological considerations to be objectively weighed.

Johanssen, brightening a bit at what must seem the first semisupportive question a reporter has asked since he arrived in Japan, answers, "Yes, you are quite right. We came here expecting to debate the biological merits of our proposal, but rapidly realized there were other factors that would decide the issue."

The reporter asks if the fishing countries, by accepting Sweden's conditions, have committed to cut the catches in half.

A Japanese representative says, "Rather than talking about a fifty percent cut, I think we can say we can cooperate. The situation is more complicated than a fifty percent cut, but we believe our goals will be achieved."

Afterward, the conservation groups lick their wounds. "Politics dominated over biology," says Mike Sutton.

"We lost," says McManus.

Don Barry, Sutton's boss at the World Wildlife Fund, observes philosophically, "Only once every decade does a species issue gather so much momentum so fast. Win, lose, or draw, the nature of the debate on bluefin tuna and on marine fishes has been changed completely, and will never again be the same." Then he adds, "Still, though, CITES conferences were better in the good old days during the seventies, when the debates were focused on biology, and there was a lot less politics."

"And a lot more sex," someone adds.

An American woman who works as consultant to the Japanese fishing industry in Washington, D.C., comes by. She squeezes my arm and says with a wink, "I want to thank all the conservation groups for making this a lucrative year."

Tokyo isn't noted as a place to go to unwind, but following the CITES conference I've arranged to meet Jack Moyer and spend a few days with him and his wife, Lorna. Jack, age sixty-seven, is a lanky marine biologist who settled in Japan after the Second World War and established a marine research station on Miyake Jima in the Izu Islands, which he has run for the last forty years. He is now deeply involved in environmental education for children, and he writes on marine conservation issues for a large Japanese scuba magazine. Lorna, from the Philippines, is forty years his junior. About their age disparity, she says, "My father beat me and I was raised by my grandparents, so I like old people." Lorna has magnificently survived a horrific childhood. She grew up amid thieves and murderers. Her friends lived at a garbage dump. Added to her formative experiences was the harassment of corrupt police. She once spent a couple of nights in a Philippine jail, in a cell with no bed and no toilet, just a concrete floor, for peddling dried fish without a vendor's license. To taunt her, the police ate her confiscated wares outside her cell.

Now, life is better. Jack is touchingly kind to Lorna. When Lorna begins to say, "Jack has taught me—," Jack breaks in and says, "I don't want to teach you anything. I just want to explain to you how I feel so that you can better know who I am." He says to me, "In a mixed-culture marriage such as ours, I feel you can't tell your partner what values are right. You have to let your caring foster interest, and then let your relationship and values grow together."

Lorna met Jack in the Philippines while Jack was investigating the smuggling of endangered sea turtles and she was volunteering community service work (despite all the abuse Lorna has endured, she is a caring and gentle woman of grace). They decided to marry a few weeks later. Her entire family was against the marriage, except her grandmother. Lorna says, "Even I had misgivings that he might really be planning to take me to Japan to sell me for prostitution."

Prostitution holds an oddly prominent place in their consciousness, but it holds an oddly prominent place in Tokyo, too. On public phone booths and utility poles all over the city, one sees color-photo stickers advertising provocative girls. Lorna says it is unpleasant, in fact hazardous, for any Southeast Asian woman to be alone on the streets in Japan after six P.M. Assuming that any non-Japanese Asian woman is a harlot, men on the street often offer her money or make lewd comments. Jack adds that although 99½ percent of the men are good guys (not a high enough proportion to inspire confidence in a crowded city of so many millions), it is dangerous for Lorna on the street at night because she could be taken and drugged; once her abductors got her addicted, they would force her into prostitution by controlling her with drug withdrawal and dependency. Lorna adds that soon after she came to Japan she lost her way in the city and was nearly tricked into involuntary whoredom by a man offering to help her find her way—if she gave him her passport. Jack explains that the reason he and Lorna are always well-dressed is that, due to their age difference and her being from the Philippines, people on the street assume she is a prostitute unless they look well-off. From the stares I see them get on the sidewalks, it does not seem that clothes solve the problem entirely. Jack acknowledges that, not being Japanese, he and Lorna have a tough time fitting in Japan, despite Jack's long residency.

Jack's life in Japan has otherwise centered on coral reefs, and many new species of reef fish were discovered at his field station. He tells me sadly that 80 percent of the coral reefs surrounding Miyake Jima have now been destroyed by development on the island.

We search out a sushi bar for lunch, and inquire about bluefin tuna. Jack translates. "The chef says, 'No bluefin tuna. . . . I used to have bluefin. . . . Those days are long gone. . . . Long ago, you could get bluefin *toro,* the really good belly cut, from the average shop. Now, too expensive. Now, only for rich people and politicians—with expense accounts.' The best tuna he can afford now is bigeye."

Bigeye it is, then. Today, we will treat ourselves. We enjoy some very fresh bigeye tuna *toro,* Pacific yellowtail (*hamachi*), and *iko* (squid); we have sushi and sashimi—raw slivers of fish with and without rice and a seaweed wrap, respectively. The sushi chef chats with us and says that he has never been on a boat, never seen a living tuna.

Early the next morning, I meet Jack in the dark. We are going to the fish market. At five A.M. we park and walk a few blocks, falling in step with a crowd of rubber-booted pedestrians from surrounding blocks, all headed toward Tsukiji market. Trucks, motorized carts, bikes, and hand dollies all converge on an enormous complex of hangarlike buildings making up the world's largest fish bazaar. An open pickup rattles by, piled with tuna.

The market is already going full force, already several hours into its normal workday. There is great noise and confusion; the place is mobbed with people and crowded with the open stalls and booths of hundreds of vendors. This market is so immense and jammed that I cannot see to the end of it.

We see mackerel, bonito, herring, eels, tilefish, cuttlefish, jacks of many kinds, shrimp colorful and shrimp drab, and clams of all sorts. We see sea robins, skipjacks, loaches, cutlassfish, trumpet fish, halfbeaks, flounders, yellowtail. Large and small, dead or alive. Mahimahi, or dolphin fish, is perhaps the most beautiful fish in the world, but its colors vanish so rapidly upon death that the fish must be seen alive to be seen at all; here they lie stacked and pallid. And—aha!—here swims the infamous, seemingly inoffensive fugu, an almost comical-looking puffer, parts of which are so deadly to eat that the fish is used for ritual suicide. Fugu may be prepared for the rest of us only by specially licensed chefs who've served years of apprenticeship. Adventures in dining end here.

As we stroll, we encounter a continually mounting array of various squid species from around the world—some the size of my little finger and some the size of my nightmares. There are whole squid, cleaned squid, squid in their own ink, fresh squid, cooked squid. One squid species, the thickness of my thigh, with hooks like snake's teeth ringing every suction disk on every arm, is the most menacing-looking creature I have ever gazed upon.

New kinds of crustaceans, mollusks, and fishes, including many, many creatures I am unfamiliar with, are revealed every few steps. There are odd-looking squillas (mantis shrimp), and a kind of clam with a siphon as big as my forearm. Jack, who knows much about the biology of fishes that are utterly new to me, points to one and says, "This species, *Sebastes inermis,* is a simultaneous hermaphrodite." That is to say, it is both male and female at the same time (some other fishes are sequential hermaphrodites; they change sex). Jack is surprised to see a particular type of flying fish, which, he says, had been fished out. He asks the merchant in Japanese, who replies that, yes, this is the first time in years that they have been available. Jack points to a fish in the genus *Callionymus* and says, "I have a fish in this genus named after me."

From Maine have arrived sea urchins and lobsters. Some of the vendors have huge tanks set up with live fish, and suddenly I am face-to-face with a tank of tautog and summer flounder, here—as am I—from New York. My reaction surprises me. I *know* these fish. I have met them while snorkeling back home on Long Island and have watched them struggle with the conflict of being wary and curious at the same time. I have caught, and, yes, killed and eaten them. And enjoyed it. But here, on the other side of the world in this unfamiliar place, we meet as old friends. Silly, but I am overtaken with a feeling of poignant connection, as though I am visiting comrades taken prisoner of war. I cannot help putting my hand to the glass. The fish, disoriented, crowded, reduced to meat that is still breathing—belaboredly—do not react at all. They are neither curious nor frightened. Their shock, a tender mercy, has them numbed.

A hand truck quickly going by strikes me, shoving me aside. My fault for not paying attention. Carts and dollies are zooming along every which way, pushed or pulled by very busy men to whom time is definitely money. To a newcomer, there is unspeakable confusion and bustle. But although we are frequently in the way, no one is yelling at us, and I am thankful for the Japanese skilled politeness and civility in crowds. People—wholesalers, retailers, housewives—bump and jostle.

One section holds the giants. Bluefin tuna, blue marlin, yellowfin tuna, swordfish, striped marlin, bigeye tuna. Potential bidders are inspecting the fish, which are individually identified, and making notes on cards. They check each fish over carefully, as though buying an automobile (many of which would cost far less). They check the wedge of tail section that is exposed for them, noting its color and fat marbling. They poke with the aid of flashlights into the tunas' body cavities. One man tells us that Mediterranean bluefins are taken too close to the spawning grounds, and because spawning takes so much energy they are not fat enough to yield prime meat. He says they are best six months after spawning, as far from the breeding season as possible. Jack tells me, "These guys speak with great authority, but they all have different opinions. Nevertheless, how they *think* is how they buy." Another pile of tuna, these clearly second-rate, are frozen and mounded like small logs. These fish have been kept at −60 degrees centigrade (−76°F), and they are hard as stone. A bucket-fronted truck rams the pile of tuna ice-logs and carries off a load.

We bump into Israel's CITES delegation. Fancy meeting! They say it was a pity that Sweden was left hanging out to dry like that, that several countries should have cosponsored the proposal to take some of the pressure off the Swedes and ensure a debate on the biological merits. Yes, we agree, a pity.

Marketeers are continually whizzing past in motorized carts. Adding to the sense of confusion and noise are the sounds of hawkers, cash registers, phones, and the whack and thump of fish being slaughtered and butchered all around. Under bright lights, still-quivering fish are rapidly sliced apart and turned into meat.

There are crabs. Crabs in water. Crabs in sawdust. Familiar blue crabs from the temperate Atlantic. Land crabs from tropical South Pacific islands. Big crabs, little crabs.

Eels. In tanks. In mesh bags. On ice. Black. Silver. With stripes. Without.

Octopuses large and tiny. Live, fresh, or pickled. Dark, pale, or scarlet.

Eggs. From salmon, from urchins, from herring, from many, many others.

Mackerel of all kinds, halibut, prawns, seaweeds, sea squirts, spiny lobsters, fried larval fish, live larval fish. Anchovies and goosefish.

Down one lane and up another. We do this for four hours, and I never gain a sense of the perimeter of this market. In Madrid, I had visited the world's second-largest fish market—no comparison. This blows Madrid away. One buyer tells us he services thirty-six big retail markets, selling two hundred tons of fish per day. And he is just one guy we spoke with at random. Jack says as we find an exit, "I've been here about five times, and I've never been where we were today." Outside wait hundreds and hundreds of trucks. And this scene repeats every day. Every single day, drawing fish from all the world's oceans.

Fast-forward nine months. At its next annual meeting in Madrid, the tuna commission attempted to avoid scrutiny. It refused to allow the World Wildlife Fund's observer into the meeting and banned WWF's statement requesting that the commission adopt a bluefin recovery plan. This left World Wildlife's Mike Sutton with unlimited free time to schmooze delegates over coffee in the lobby outside the meeting room and to distribute and explain the banned statement.

Gerry Abrams frequently repeated his mantra that we must err on the side of jobs. But by now, the conservation groups had their own mantra: Halve the catch quota and institute a management plan to rebuild the population. If that were done, the fishery could support many *more* jobs.

Obviously feeling pressured by the events of the last year and a half, the commission directed its scientists to evaluate rebuilding options for Atlantic bluefin populations. Was ICCAT awakening from its long hibernation, or was stalling being elevated to an art form?

During the ensuing year, with Republicans out and Democrats into the White House, Gerry Abrams's East Coast Tuna Association dropped their Republican lobbyists like spoiled tuna and hired former senator Paul Tsongas, who had vied unsuccessfully for the Democratic presidential nomination. Tsongas and his law firm helped open doors for the fishermen, allowing them to garner the support they would need to reverse the U.S. policy for quota cuts. Several members of Congress began pressuring the Department of Commerce to abandon their scientifically derived position that the bluefin catch quotas must be halved.

ICCAT's next revised scientific assessment of the bluefin's status was the bleakest ever, reporting that any earlier cause for guarded optimism had crumbled into firm predictions of continued decline. The new assessment noted that it would now take many years for the population to recover "even at zero catch." For the first time, the commission grudgingly acknowledged that the number of young fish "does depend on" the spawning population's size. The current low population of breeders, the report admitted, is not likely to produce a strong class of young fish.

This time no amount of politics could dispel the pall of the scientific report and the possibility that CITES would act to list the species at its next conference.

The tuna commission's managers budged significantly, agreeing to a 50 percent reduction in catch quotas, phased in over two years. Even though their scientists gave this only about even odds of stabilizing the population at a low level, it was a big step.

Responding to the announcement on behalf of Canadian fishermen—and the 60 percent of Newfoundlanders newly unemployed by the cod closures—Ron Bulmer, the president of the Fisheries Council of Canada, said, "The cod crisis has taught us a valuable lesson that others are going to have to learn: that we must err on the side of conservation."

south of Block

A few months *before* the tuna commission agreed to cut the western Atlantic bluefin catch quota in half, I had taken World Wildlife Fund vice president Mike Sutton out on the ocean to catch, tag, and release a few large blue sharks. As dawn brightened a mild new summer day we headed southeast from Montauk toward an underwater ridge south of Block Island. In recent days, interesting reports had been trickling in from an area about fifteen miles beyond our destination—sightings of uncommon numbers of young bluefins. We were still running when I first caught a glimpse of what looked like it might be a large flock of shearwaters, barely visible in the hazy early morning air a couple of miles south of us. I turned the wheel ninety degrees off course and we went to investigate.

Our plans for the day immediately changed as we witnessed a scene unlike any I had seen before, or have since. The tuna had moved west, and we had run into them. I wrote an unusually detailed entry in my boat log:

> An incredible day with bluefin tuna schools over an area stretching at least five miles. The tuna stayed up all day, blitzing baby butterfish and traveling in huge green-frothing schools that often covered about an acre each, frequently moving at 7 knots. The sound was a rolling roar, like thundering herds on blue prairies. The butterfish glittered like sparse raindrops ahead of the busting schools, jumping in random directions rather than coordinated sprays. In the water the little butterfish seemed disoriented and dispirited, awaiting the onslaughts with nowhere to run, until the thundering herds were amongst them, the rushing tuna completely overwhelming their schooling defense by ripping through them *en masse* on a broad front. Feeding activity peaked around 5 pm. Also saw 2 white marlin—it's been a while! Lots of sea horses noticed among floating weeds.

Most of those fish were young four-year-olds from the last moderately strong spawning of bluefin tuna in the western Atlantic, in 1989. This age-group represented a small spike of abundance, hope, and opportunity, preceded and followed by years of generally dismal reproduction in the Gulf of Mexico spawning grounds. They were now about seventy pounds on average, and we saw *thousands* of them. This was the generation most at stake. We had helped convince the federal government a year earlier to ban the sale of such young fish, and we felt hopeful that this vigorous group of juveniles might be shepherded into adulthood and allowed to spawn new generations. Protection of this year class might make the difference in rebuilding the bluefin population, so it seemed particularly promising that mounting pressure on the tuna commission might finally prompt them to cut the catch quota in half.

When the tuna commission met and indeed agreed to halve the western Atlantic bluefin quota, they left themselves a year before fully implementing the cut. In that time the tuna industry's flag bearers and lobbyists scrambled like mad dogs, leaning heavily on congressional representatives, bureaucrats, and a variety of scientists.

The scientists found a data error that, when corrected, indicated that the population was down "only" about 85 percent instead of 90 percent or so. Using this skimpy pretext, the East Coast tuna industry was able to turn the politics around again. They shifted their strategy, drawing attention away from their own overfishing by pointing fingers at people overfishing in the Mediterranean. Tagging studies in the 1980s indicated that only about 1 to 2 percent of American bluefins go to Europe every year, but the industry argument was: "Since some of the fish cross the ocean, people in the Mediterranean are catching our fish and *they* are the problem—and we demand an increase in our quota." While the logic was not exactly watertight, politically this tack was a winning ploy: No politician or bureaucrat could possibly lose out by criticizing foreigners while working to please their own constituents.

Even though the industry's own paid scientific consultants showed that rebuilding the bluefin population to levels of the mid-1970s within twenty years would require cutting the West Atlantic quota by about *80* percent, all conservation efforts crumbled in the path of immediate money politics. First, the tuna commission rescinded the 50 percent catch reduction before it was ever implemented. Then, they abandoned a commitment to adopt a recovery plan.

By now a new government commissioner, Will Martin, was in charge, and though he spoke silver-tongued to conservationists—using all the right buzzwords about "sustainability" and "precaution"—he was careful not to anger or disappoint the tuna industry. With an emboldened tuna lobby pressing closer, nipping his heels and snarling for more, Martin threw precaution to the wind. Someone said he developed Stockholm (a.k.a. Patty Hearst) syndrome—adopting the personality of one's captors—but that would be taking credit away from decisions that were his. After helping rescind the quota cut, he led the charge for two quota *increases* in 1994 and 1996, the first of which he enigmatically called a "conservation measure"; the other increase he referred to oddly and oxymoronically as "keeping the status quo." (He said he expected that this latter 154-ton increase would soon be offset by regulations requiring all fish discarded dead at sea to be counted against the quota, so there would be essentially no net mortality increase. He was the only one who believed this might happen in the forseeable future. And in fact it didn't.) In a Department of Commerce press release, Mr. Martin said, "The modest quota increase for western bluefin tuna sends an appropriate signal that when conservation works, the concessions of our fishermen can be rewarded by increases in harvests."

Concessions? Much of this struck me as utterly disingenuous and intentionally misleading. I was not the only one who saw it this way. Dr. Paul Boyle of the New York Aquarium for Wildlife Conservation faxed me the press release and wrote in the margin: "How has it 'worked'? Seems like the usual self-congratulation for grossly inadequate outcomes! An increase in the W. Atlantic strikes me as completely inappropriate."

Just how inappropriate? The commission's own scientists had written clearly that the new quota Mr. Martin was pushing for would entail a 10 percent chance of driving the population to extinction within a decade. But his mind was set.

In sum, the cuts and subsequent increases in the quota amounted to a round-trip that by the late 1990s put the catch almost back up to where it had been in the late 1980s. The only thing that really changed was that the fish, bumping along at a low population level, were now reproducing worse than ever. Scientists searching for bluefin larvae in the Gulf of Mexico have been unable to find any recently, suggesting that the spawning population may be reaching the point of collapse.

Yet all was not *absolutely* riddled with cynicism, not *totally* bleak. With swordfish in a nosedive and the long-liners in a panic of their own making, the commission cut the North Atlantic swordfish quota by a third for 1997, effective through to 1999. If that commitment is honored and extended, it should help to at least stabilize the swordfish's populations. Lord knows, those broadbills need a break, though prompting a recovery would require further cuts.

But like many agencies entrusted with stewarding natural resources, the Atlantic tuna commission has always confused process with progress and progress with success. Procedure is still the commission's chief product. There are still no management plans, no recovery timetables, no recovery goals, and not one population of tuna, swordfish, or marlin managed to produce the "maximum sustainable yield," as the commission's own charter requires. Virtually all these species are overexploited.

The population of bluefin in the Mediterranean Sea continues to bear a fishing free-for-all, with catches twice the sustainable level. A commission recommendation to freeze catch levels was ignored, followed by the highest take of bluefin ever. It is only a matter of time before the need for restraint becomes universally apparent—if not by foresight then by hindsight.

As for bluefin off the east coast of North America, with the fish from the last mediocre spawnings of the late 1980s nearing maturity in the late 1990s, fishers thought they saw a recovery in the slight bulge that was entering the adult population. But I suspect that when the snake passes this egg, it will probably be skinnier than ever, because so few young are coming up the ranks behind them. I hope, as I often do, that I am wrong.

Kenyan conservation scientist David Western, who had tried to have Kenya initiate a global CITES proposal for the bluefin but "had to withdraw under political pressure from Japan and other countries that have a deep vested interest," remarked, "It is one of those species for which politics overrides any concern. . . . The tuna is still an issue. It will continue to become a bigger issue."

I suspect it will, because in my opinion the bluefin tuna remains the most purposely mismanaged large animal in the world.

On Long Island, I went to salve my disappointment with sushi. The head chef recommended some longline-caught bigeye tuna that he'd just gotten from Ecuador. The thought of drowned albatrosses bothered me, but I nodded anyway even while I wondered how much longer I could justify doing so. It *was* delicious, but that was never the question. I told the chef I'd read that bluefin was overfished; did he think that was true?

In slightly broken English he responded, "Overfished, yes. Bluefin, we can't afford. But, yes, overfished." Then he added, "Did you eat sushi last week?"

"No, *I* can't afford to eat sushi every week." I grinned.

"Last week, no tuna!" he exclaimed. "Last week, almost no sushi restaurants in whole New York area have tuna. For first time, no tuna any kind in market. Overfished. I think: In ten years, maybe no more tuna for sushi."

I took a sip of my warm *sake* and wondered at the meaning of having met someone more worried about tuna than I.

Spring is a time of renewal, and needing a jump-start on feeling renewed, I accepted an invitation by marine scientist Barbara Block to join her crew in Cape Hatteras for a few days in early 1997 to implant new high-tech electronic tags into large bluefin tuna.

Dr. Block, a protégé of Frank Carey (the man who'd developed acoustical tags for tracking swordfish), has learned more about tunas and marlins in the wild—their evolution, physiology, and behavior—than anyone. Though still in her mid-thirties, Block has earned a reputation as a brilliant, world-class biologist. In quality, quantity, and diversity, her work already far surpasses most scientists' entire career output. She'd assembled in Cape Hatteras a retinue of graduate students, post-doctoral fellows, biologists, and wildlife veterinarians, mostly from her Stanford University lab in Monterey, California. Block was again pushing the envelope on new technologies, having just helped develop two kinds of computerized "tags" that actually store data on an animal's movements, allowing scientists, for the first time, to understand the travel patterns of wild fish in the ocean over long periods.

Spring was indeed in the air as I drove south along the Outer Banks. Though March had barely begun to shudder off the grip of winter, the afternoon was shirtsleeve warm, and northward-migrating birds were streaming up the beach even as the gulls and gannets of winter continued working still-chilly waters. Along the Atlantic coast, early spring does not follow winter so much as overtake it.

Barbara Block had come to Hatteras to execute a research program designed specifically to take scientific advantage of a unique situation. Sportfishermen had discovered a concentration of bluefin tuna in the Gulf Stream nearby. This allowed scientific access to these animals that was unparalleled anywhere else in the world, for two reasons: One, the fish were ravenously hungry and aggressive and astonishingly easy to catch; two, the commercial season for large bluefin was still closed for the winter and the fish could not be killed or sold, so many sportfishing boats were willing to cooperate in a tag-and-release program.

I found the house Dr. Block and her team had converted to a research station, and, after a dinner of fresh striped bass caught from the surf by several of the scientists, Barbara showed me the new computerized instruments she and her colleagues had developed for this project. The first, called an archival tag, is implanted into the fish (it is a little larger than your index finger) and it logs the fish's position, depth, body temperature, and surrounding water temperature for as long as several years. Block explained, "The tag wakes up every two minutes to take the data, and stores the information in an electronic memory." A short light-sensing wire stalk protruding from the instrument senses the interval between dawn and dusk, allowing the unit's microprocessor components to calculate latitude and longitude using time of daylight and an internal clock. Another, even more remarkable new instrument stores all the same information, but at a pre-set interval that can range from days to several years the tag unit electronically detaches itself, comes to the sea surface, and begins transmitting its stored information to an orbiting satellite—which then sends the data to Block's laboratory! These "pop-up tags" had proven themselves in pool tests with captive yellowfin tuna, but Barbara had put the first ones into wild bluefins only a week or so before I arrived. She'd programmed these to come off within a few days, and to the amazement of no one who knows Barbara Block, they were working well.

With this technology, we will be able to learn, for the first time, a lot about what these animals really do: how they use their habitat, how they behave—how they *function*. We will be able to understand them more on their own terms, as though we could pull back the sea's covers and just *watch*. Perhaps the more we understand these animals' complexities, the more they will surprise and delight us, and the more we will appreciate them.

For the first time in years, I had a hard time sleeping due solely to excitement. Anticipation of seeing what I consider the most excitingly innovative—and some of the most important—wildlife research in North America kept me hoping the alarm would soon signal time to rise.

Wind howled all night, but dawn came calm, and we prepared for a day at sea. Block and several assistants switched on the computers that seemed to dominate the house, and via the Internet they downloaded the most recent satellite maps of sea surface temperatures, showing the position of the Gulf Stream's edge.

In a thirty-five-foot New England–styled boat named *Bullfrog,* we threaded our way through a menacing-looking Hatteras Inlet and headed offshore. We didn't need the maps to tell us where the Gulf Stream was. Twenty miles from the inlet, rough and white-capped seventy-five degree water was steaming eerily into the cool air as though we'd sailed into a great cauldron. Using sonar, we searched along the Stream's temperature edge for an hour, two hours. Three hours. The game plan was to find a school, chum them up, and then either catch fish or have hooked fish transferred to us from other boats for tagging. When a boat called to report they were hooked to a fish, we—and three dozen or so other boats in the fleet—raced over like a flock of terns converging. Arriving boats began throwing whole herring, and the school of big fish came up crashing through the surface as chum disappeared in deep boils and explosions of foam, and boats began hooking up around us amid screaming birds and shouted instructions.

We heaved a tennis ball attached to the end of our line into the boat with the first hooked fish. They unsnapped their leader from their line and snapped it onto ours, thus transferring their hooked fish to the end of our line.

I was in the chair and readied on the rod, and when the line shot tight the big fish snapped me to my feet in the harness, a single safety cord holding me into the boat. The rod arced under a fresh surge downward and to my shock I felt my knees begin to buckle. For a few worried moments it seemed the fish would actually collapse my stance the way a winning arm wrestler's relentless pressure crushes his opponent. Then the line began slipping from the reel, I regained my footing, and over a few minutes I worked the already tired fish up.

Captain Bob Eakes opened the transom door and grabbed the straining leader. By way of a splattering of language best described as colorful, he shouted for the mate to turn the *Bullfrog* down-sea. With several people pulling, a following wave helped shove the three-hundred-pound animal onto the deck.

Waiting as the fish slid through the door and onto a padded mat were Block and several assistants—all in boots and waterproof overalls—one of whom immediately started a stopwatch. Biologist Chuck Farwell instantly shoved a hose into the gasping giant's mouth to irrigate the gills with oxygen-rich seawater. "Beautiful fish; *nice* fish," he breathed as he covered the beast's shifting eye with a dark wet cloth to calm it. Its laquered back was deep blue, its flanks edged with a lighter, luminous electric blue that bordered a burnishing bronze, finally grading to the metallic silver-gray of its belly.

The deck was tense and quiet as the team quickly moved into kneeling positions around the animal and got to work. Farwell swiftly removed the hook and handed one end of a measuring tape to Block, then called out the fish's length to a man with a clipboard. Thirty-one-year-old Dr. Heidi Dewar, scalpel ready, bent to work. Seas had grown increasingly sloppy, and some water sloshed across the deck, causing the fish to slide a little. Surgeon Dewar waited a moment. Then she pushed the scalpel through the giant tuna's leathery hide, making a slight incision and shaving a tiny sliver of muscle for later genetic analysis. She handed the muscle sample to Block, who placed it in a waiting vial, labeled it, and passed it up to a waiting assistant. Block inserted the internal tag. While Dewar sutured the small wound, Block darted two external tags into the animal's back, marking this fish as the bearer of an internal archival tag, worth a cool thousand dollars to the finder—value added to the world's most valuable fish.

We swiveled the mat and slid the fish head-first back into the sea, and it took off like a shot and vanished. In another boat, Dr. Eric Prince of the National Marine Fisheries Service and wildlife veterinarian Tom Williams of the Monterey Bay Aquarium were also putting Dr. Block's state-of-the-art instruments into husky tuna.

The invasiveness of all the handling and surgery was a little disconcerting, but a far stretch better than bleeding and icing the bluefins for a trip to Tokyo would have been. In Cape Cod Bay, when I'd facetiously asked Gerry Abrams if he planned to tag any fish we might catch, he'd answered, "There's not a tag in this whole fleet." Here, there were *only* tags. All the fish being caught on the sport boats were being released, and captains said they felt "honored" to be able to pass fish off to scientists for the high-tech research.

These bluefins were not the five-hundred-pound-plus monsters commonly caught in New England. They averaged two hundred to three hundred and fifty pounds. Many were the eight- to ten-year-old fish from the last moderately productive spawning years in the late 1980s—some from the same age class I'd seen demolishing butterfish off Block Island a few years earlier. They were now just maturing, and in a year or so—if they survived—would probably venture to the Gulf of Mexico to join the remaining older fish for their first breeding.

Three out of the initial fourteen fish our boats handled carried hooks from previous encounters. One fish had two older hooks, plus ours, suggesting that pressure was high. Some local captains wanted to be able to kill one fish per day, and already, fishermen from New England were pressing for a winter opening so they could bring their commercial boats down here to export fish.

All in all, I saw the abundance of these young adult fish here less as deliverance than as a fragile and inspiring opportunity. Used as an excuse for increased exploitation, their potential would be squandered. Shepherded into the future, they could perhaps salvage a last best chance to spawn strong new generations and avoid having the bluefin go the way of the buffalo—a relict reminder of a time of plenty.

Bullfrog's engine roared as we raced toward our last fish transfer of the waning day. In late afternoon the big tuna became very active, and watching them crashing herring thrown behind our boat was so astonishing it kept distracting me from scientific duties on deck. Each handful of fish that hit the surface instantly drew a gleaming, seven-foot-long, wide-bodied rocket from the deep. Often two or three big bluefins raced competitively for the same fish, their fins slicing the surface like drawn sabers of charging horsemen, with the winner sending up geysers and drawing cheers and then blasting the herring like there was no tomorrow. But we were here to help ensure that there *was* a tomorrow, and seeing all these fish shot us through with great hope and exuberance. These speeding torpedoes were no buffalo, no mere remnants. These were the rushing vitality and power of the sea incarnate. These, we hoped, were the future.

BOOK TWO

Northwest

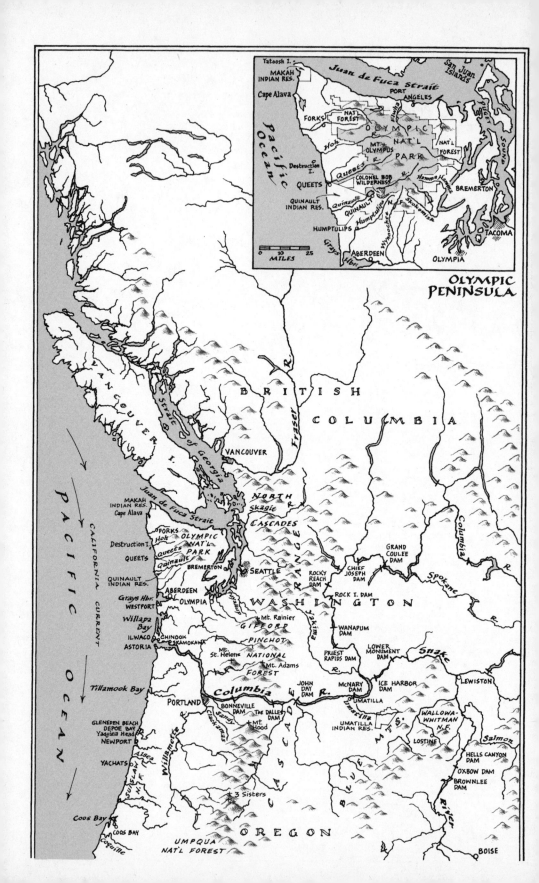

OLYMPIC
PENINSULA

Inset map labels:

Tatoosh I.
MAKAH
INDIAN RES.
Cape Alava
FORKS
Hoh
Destruction I.
QUEETS
QUINAULT
INDIAN RES.
HUMPTULIPS
ABERDEEN

Juan de Fuca Strait
San Juan Islands
PORT ANGELES
NAT'L FOREST
OLYMPIC NAT'L PARK
MT. OLYMPUS
NAT'L FOREST
COLONEL BOB WILDERNESS
Queets R.
Quinault
Quinault
Hamma Hamma R.
BREMERTON
Wynoochee R.
Humptulips R.
N.F. Skokomish
Grays Hbr.
OLYMPIA
TACOMA

Pacific Ocean

0   10   25
MILES

Main map labels:

PACIFIC OCEAN

CALIFORNIA CURRENT

VANCOUVER I.

Strait of Georgia

VANCOUVER

BRITISH COLUMBIA

Fraser R.

NORTH CASCADES

Skagie R.

Juan de Fuca Strait

MAKAH
INDIAN RES.
Cape Alava
FORKS
Hoh
Destruction I.
QUEETS
Queets
Quinault
QUINAULT
INDIAN RES.
ABERDEEN
Grays Hbr.
WESTPORT

OLYMPIC NAT'L PARK

BREMERTON

SEATTLE

OLYMPIA

ROCKY REACH DAM

CHIEF JOSEPH DAM

GRAND COULEE DAM

Columbia R.

Spokane R.

ROCK I. DAM

WASHINGTON

CASCADE RANGE

Willapa Bay

ILWACO
ASTORIA

CHINOOK
SKAMOKAWA

Mt. Rainier

GIFFORD PINCHOT

Mt. St. Helens

NATIONAL

Mt. Adams

FOREST

Yakima R.

WANAPUM DAM

PRIEST RAPIDS DAM

LOWER MONUMENT DAM

Snake R.

ICE HARBOR DAM

LEWISTON

Tillamook Bay

PORTLAND

Columbia R.

Clackamas

Sandy

BONNEVILLE DAM

THE DALLES DAM

JOHN DAY DAM

Mt. Hood

McNARY DAM

Umatilla

UMATILLA INDIAN RES.

Umatilla R.

BLUE MTS.

WALLOWA-WHITMAN N.F.

LOSTINE

Salmon R.

GLENEDEN BEACH
DEPOE BAY
Yaquina Head
NEWPORT

Alsea R.

Willamette

Siuslaw R.

YACHATS

CASCADE RANGE

3 Sisters

HELLS CANYON DAM

OXBOW DAM

BROWNLEE DAM

Coos Bay
COOS BAY
Coquille

UMPQUA NAT'L FOREST

OREGON

BOISE

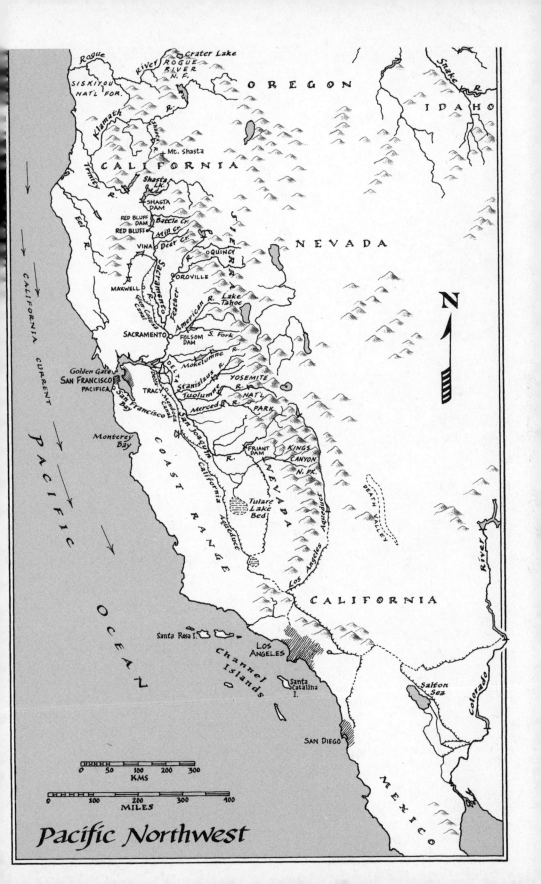

Rogue River
Crater Lake
ROGUE RIVER N. F.
SISKIYOU NAT'L FOR.
Klamath R.
Shasta R.
Trinity R.
+ Mt. Shasta
Shasta Lk.
SHASTA DAM
RED BLUFF DAM
RED BLUFF
Battle Cr.
Mill Cr.
VINA Deer Cr.
○ QUINCY
OROVILLE
MAXWELL
Sacramento R.
Feather R.
Glenn Colusa Canal
American R.
Lake Tahoe
SACRAMENTO
FOLSOM DAM
S. Fork
Mokelumne R.
Golden Gate
SAN FRANCISCO
PACIFICA
San Francisco Bay
DELTA
Delta Mendota Canal
TRACY
Stanislaus R.
YOSEMITE
Tuolumne R.
NAT'L
Merced R.
PARK
San Joaquin R.
Monterey Bay
FRIANT DAM R.
KINGS CANYON N. PK.
COAST RANGE
California Aqueduct
Tulare Lake Bed
SIERRA NEVADA
DEATH VALLEY
Los Angeles Aqueduct
Santa Rosa I.
Channel Islands
LOS ANGELES
Santa Catalina I.
Salton Sea
SAN DIEGO
Colorado River

O R E G O N
I D A H O
Snake R.
C A L I F O R N I A
N E V A D A
C A L I F O R N I A
M E X I C O

PACIFIC OCEAN
CALIFORNIA CURRENT

N

0   50   100   200   300
KMS

0   100   200   300   400
MILES

Pacific Northwest

In a quiet stream high in the mountains' dark forest, a single salmon, scratched and dazed and already spotted with a rotting white fungus, is finning weakly in the slow current. Hers has been a life of almost magic and miraculous luck. She has done all a salmon can do. And here, spawned out, spent, fulfilled, that life will end. A time to die. She drifts slowly downstream until she hits a gravel bar. And for the first time since she hatched and wriggled from the gravel of this very stream, she stops swimming, forever.

From the ocean—from a fish's-eye view—the place of spawning must seem like the gates of heaven itself, since the prospect of getting there entails a pilgrimage up toward the mountaintops and into the enshrouding clouds. And if the holy among humans are inspired to ascend similar high places to come closer to God and receive visions or commandments for the ages, it is perhaps as remarkable and holy that the salmon commit so fully and so fatally to their hegira of sex and sublimation, death and rebirth, unwitting though they probably are.

I wonder if a vision of her life is passing before her as she lies here with that one unblinking eye staring up at the enormous trees overhead and the sunlit sky beyond them. I suppose not. I can only suppose that she has no recollection of the urges that have driven her, no recall that as a youngster she left this stream to travel under the ocean's broad roof to the deep heart of the sea and back. And I suppose she cannot now remember fighting her way against the river's torrent and leaping up sunlit falls and choosing a strong mate. Does she even know that she has laid her eggs, fulfilled her part in shaping the future? Can she remotely realize that each day she lived, comrades fell to natural catastrophes and cunning predators and diseases and accidents and nets and hooks and the structured works of humanity? As she lies dying here, can she possibly understand that she has survived?

Everything that could ever go right for a salmon has gone right for her. But for most salmon here along this coast, the reverse applies.

. . .

Once, salmon were merely the world's most complicated fishes, spending part of their life as freshwater fish, part as saltwater fish, and yet another part again as freshwater animals bent single-mindedly upon self-destruction through reproduction—immortality through suicide. These different stages demand extreme physical changes and navigational abilities as advanced as any living being's and more advanced, by far, than most. Ranging as they could from the Continental Divide to the center of the ocean and back within one relatively short, humble, heroic life, the salmon's story was exceptional by any measure.

That life and story has become increasingly complex. Nowadays, one cannot see the salmon's world without adding to the tale the plot complications of logging, agriculture, hydropower, dams, politics, pesticides, foreign markets, private property rights, public property fights, recreational, commercial, and subsistence fishing, and artificial reproduction. And one cannot see *those* subplots without confronting the heights and depths of the human spirit, no less than a salmon can confront life without ranging between the purest of springwaters and the bottomless depths of the deepest sea.

Shuttling as they do like silver threads between upland and ocean, abyss and summit, salmon tightly stitch the interlock between continent, torrent, and tide, binding together everything humans do to land or water. And we do much.

The Great Northwest of the United States and Pacific Canada have become the world's extinction epicenter for ocean fishes. Nowhere else in the world are ancient lines of marine fishes vanishing with such haste. Pacific salmon have disappeared from about 40 percent of their breeding range in Washington, Oregon, Idaho, and California. In this region, salmon are either extinct, endangered, or threatened in two-thirds of the area they occupied ten decades ago. Extinction is an unusual form of death, because while most death adds a spoke to the wheel of life, extinction carries a peculiar finality—an end of lineages, a preclusion of futures. As the poet Gary Snyder put it, "Death is one thing, an end to *birth* is something else."

Hope paces impatiently. Salmon are still abundant in Alaska, and lessons learned in the Northwest—if we learn them—could be applied there; there is still time. The Pacific Northwest, then, offers much we could study. The Northwest is perhaps the best place in the world, for example, to study finger-pointing elevated to art. So rarefied and pervasive is this trait that even the best and the brightest seem to do it unconsciously, by subtle alterations of emphasis, the way you shift unthinkingly in your chair if you need to displace pressure. It is also a place to study an extreme range of views and policies, from people who tried to exterminate salmon with poison to people who worship the fish.

Either way, whether salmon represent your demons or salvation, they loom large here. Think of the Northwest, and salmon soon come to mind. Only a few wild animals symbolize the heart and soul of a region. Tigers in India, lions and elephants in Africa, kangaroos in Australia. In North America, the buffalo of the Great Plains and the salmon of the Pacific Northwest supported economies, cultures and human self-identities. And though white settlers destroyed the buffalo in greed and in genocide against the natives, they embraced the salmon. The immigrants, like the native peoples, saw in salmon something deep, powerful, moving, and valuable—even if they approached the fish with less awe, less reverence, and, consequently, less success than the natives had for millennia. Certain other animals still *symbolize* their regions. But salmon are unique because their symbolic power *and* their economic value have survived together to the threshold of the twenty-first century. And this holds the best hope for salmon and the people who need them.

Yaquina Head

While the insomniac ocean fitfully tosses its head on the wild Oregon coast, the adjacent forest sleeps in deep shadow. Night's cocoon is slowly opening into morning's glory. No wind troubles the sky. And I am driving as fast as I can because I'm about to be late.

Dick Good and his yellow Labrador retriever Lucy are up and about by the time I arrive at Newport harbor. A couple of sea lions on the dock lie bellowing to the cool dawn.

At five-thirty, we cast off the dock lines. The forty-five-foot boat pulls from its slip as familiarly as a dog begins its morning walk. Inside the *Pamala Jean*'s wheelhouse, it's warm and cozy. Tangled wires and dangling trolling lures hanging near the many electronics—radios, sonars, radar, loran map-plotter—create a confused clutter. Survival suits, designed to keep a person insulated for hours in cold water if the boat sinks, are stored under the galley table.

"How many people experience joy and excitement on their way to work each day?" Dick asks rhetorically as we motor through the harbor. Many years of earning a living as a commercial salmon troller have brought Dick Good a level of skill and knowledge—not to mention the freedom that eludes most of us—that is enviable by almost any standard.

But Dick is going bankrupt. After staying tied to the dock almost a week because of bad weather, Dick caught *one* salmon yesterday. His way of earning a living is going down the tubes. It is a slow and agonizing death, and even a glimpse of it conveys a sense of the terrible misfortunes that can befall good and hardworking people. A day on the docks here is like a walk through a hospital ward where all the doors are open, exposing the suffering patients.

Good has lived in Olympia, Washington, all his life. He caught his first fish at age seven, forty years ago. Despite the hard knocks, Dick looks a decade younger than he is. Perhaps it is not the problems one confronts but the level of optimism and generosity with which one confronts them that earns us our faces by the time we turn forty. Dick is certainly the most optimistic and generous fisherman I've ever met. But while a lifetime of optimistic fishing may have taken years off his looks, at the rate problems are piling up it may yet take years off his life.

When he was in his early twenties, Dick was a cabinetmaker by trade. Twenty years ago a retiring troller gave Dick his license, thinking he was bestowing a great favor. In the 1970s, Washington had twenty-three hundred active commercial salmon-trolling licenses. Now there are six hundred. This year the salmon fisheries were shut down entirely along much of the coast. Below San Francisco, fishing for chinook salmon is open for a few months, and some fish are being caught. This year there is no recreational salmon fishing out in federal waters between the Canadian border and San Francisco—the first time this has ever happened. Recreational fishing is open in state waters within a few miles of the beach in Oregon, but there are no fish there this year, so everyone has stopped trying. There is no commercial salmon fishing at all in Washington this year—another first.

Most salmon fishers on the coast have called it quits. A few from Washington have, like Dick, scattered to the north and south. About a third of the boats now in Newport are here from Washington, creating some resentment among the locals. Refugees from the great salmon famine, they are holding on by their fingernails.

Dick is wearing shoes with soles worn to wafers and a gray wool sweater. He has dull strawberry blond hair and a strawberry blond steel-wool beard. His light blue eyes, set among wrinkles, peer hopefully from under the filthiest cap on the Pacific coast. The cap, which in its youth was blue, bears the name and emblem of the Washington Trollers Association, and its disrepair seems to reflect the tenor of life here.

Dick is married, with no kids. His wife boards horses. "She understands my need to fish, and I understand her need for horses. Neither one of us has made what you would call a smart career move in life."

I say, "You must both be romantics."

"We're both selfish. We want to do what we want to do. This is such a wonderful life, if you can make enough money to get by. There was always a lot of independence. On a whim, we might go from California to Alaska. I know a guy who came to the dock in the spring to take his boat for a quick preseason shakedown. He didn't come back to port until October, and when he came back his truck was so covered with parking tickets it looked like a Christmas tree."

Dick tells me that a previous owner of his boat named it after a girl in his high school class. "She hung around the older guys. Now—small world—she shows horses with my wife. So when someone asks where I am, my wife says something like, 'He's on *Pamala Jean,* painting her bottom.' We have great fun with the double intenders."

Dick used to be home a lot. Now he's away more, living on the boat. "If I go to Alaska, I'll be away two to three months. My wife and I are real good friends, so I don't like being away from her."

As Dick steers *Pamala Jean* slowly through the harbor, I comment that it looks like a very nice boat.

"Oh," he beams with pride, "this is a *real* nice boat. Getting old, though. This fleet is turning into a bunch of antiques. Look around here," he says, serving up the harbor with a waving hand. "A lot of boats in this fleet were built in the forties and fifties. Some, as long ago as the teens. Nobody's building new trollers. Why would they?"

Lucy whines and Dick absentmindedly massages her behind her ears with his thumb and forefinger.

As we slide slowly under the Newport harbor bridge and between the long rock jetties, Dick verbally paces the narrow confines of his options. "If I'm going to stay in fishing, I'll have to find someone willing to sell me an Alaska permit. There's still a very viable salmon fleet working in Alaska. That's the only place left to speak of. There's no such thing as a full-time troller here anymore. You either need crabbing or something else, or a job on shore." To go crabbing, he would need to find someone willing to sell their permit. To get into groundfishing, he would need to obtain yet another permit.

"The only thing really open to me is albacore. But this boat is marginal unless the albacore are inside of a couple of hundred miles from shore." Seeing my surprise, he says, "Yeah, well, it's usually an offshore shot." Most serious albacore boats are sixty to seventy feet long, and albacore fishing involves trips of five to ten days, trolling all the daylight hours. Last year the big scores were made fifteen hundred miles offshore in the extreme Pacific. "There's nowhere to hide out there. If it gets real windy, you just put your hat on backwards and hang on. I'm not going beyond two hundred miles. It's a nice boat, *but*—. You've gotta be sensible."

I'm trying to imagine being "only" two hundred miles offshore in this boat, and working alone for a week. Salmon season here is only open a couple more weeks. After that, he'll run for the albacore—where he can't hide. Dick's easily foreseeable life will end in October, when the tails of the albacore turn south ahead of the advancing North Pacific autumn. "After that, I don't know. The next few years are real up in the air right now. I just don't know."

Salmon fishing employed about eight thousand people full-time on the West Coast until recently, second only to wood products. If you include the ripple of processors and other employment, the rolls swell to sixty thousand workers, comparable to wood. As recently as the late 1980s (when catches were already much lower than historically), recreational fishing generated over $900 million annually, and the commercial catch generated over $200 million. Dock value of the Northwest's commercial salmon catch dropped 93 percent from 1980 to 1994.

Meanwhile, the world salmon market is—ironically—glutted, largely with captive-raised and Alaskan wild fish. Distant sources keep prices depressed for local fishers even as regional catches hit all-time lows.

Pacific salmon are hunted in rivers and on the high and open seas by Canadian, American, Korean, Russian, and Japanese fishers, and recent annual catches hover near a million tons. Fishing is often intense, and in many areas, only about 20 percent of adult fish returning to spawn get past the hooks and nets, into the rivers. While fishing is an important source of mortality, habitat loss, dams, agriculture, logging, and all the unnatural ills kill more fish—especially young ones—and depress the ability of the world to support salmon.

For salmon as for many other things, including logs from here in the Northwest, the major market is Japan. The Japanese eat more salmon than anyone, a third of the world's catch. They eat them raw. Pickled. Fried. Smoked. Pasted. Salted. Baked. Souped. They eat their livers. Their sperm. Their heads. A large percentage of the Alaskan catch—most of it—makes a stop at Tsukiji.

Salmon farming is also increasing—rapidly—accounting for about half the salmon eaten by humans. But the Japanese prefer the taste and texture and appearance of wild fish, which they consider incomparably superior to farmed. Upon that assessment, the Japanese and I find common ground.

There is a sandbar at the end of the jetties. The boats ahead disappear in the swelling combers. The seas are about six feet, with a few much larger. Our round-bottomed boat starts rolling. Dick says, "I think this is going to be a stabilizer day." By hand, he heaves overboard the two sixty-pound planing plates—what he calls flopper-stoppers—on chains. "They slow me up, but they make the ride more comfortable." Their effect is marked and immediate.

On the radio, two other boats carry on a cryptic conversation. Someone says, "Are you going where you said you were?"

The other answers, "I'm going where I was yesterday. I heard that after I left, the bait moved in, with some birds." Bait means prey fish, attractive to both seabirds and salmon.

Dick says, "That guy you hear—Louie—is over seventy years old. Been fishing on that boat since the 1950s. Hell of a fisherman. *Tough* fisherman. Stays out longer than anyone. But he's beginning to make mistakes now. Last night, he anchored off a place he thought was Yaquina Head, but it was really the next headland south. He used to be very quiet on the radio, listening, lurking, taking it all in, then making his moves. Now, he rambles." Dick knows where Louie was yesterday, and the news about the bait catches his interest. That's where we'll head today.

After a pause during which he is intent on setting his course, he says oddly, "I have only a couple of tons of ice downstairs. Normally, I can hold up to fifteen tons of fish. With so little ice on board, I don't think I could hold more than eight or ten tons of fish."

If people like Dick Good have had the ability to live their dreams, it now seems more like sleepwalking. One imagines gently shaking his shoulder, saying, "Dick . . . Dick, wake up. . . . Dick . . . you caught only *one* salmon yesterday."

It is as though idealism has turned on the people running these remnant boats. They were once romantics but are now just plain unreasonable. It's not that Dick isn't painfully aware of what is going on. "I don't want the salmon to become a museum piece," he says. "I don't think that's necessary. They're incredibly tough fish, and we have enough left to get them back if we get the streams back in shape."

It's a biologically astute synopsis. But the political will to do this has never existed. Looking intently ahead through the spray-soaked windshield, he continues, "The dams on the Columbia did more damage to salmon than all the fishermen that ever lived. Plus logging, population growth, runoff from cities degrading streams. A salmon that's caught in the ocean obviously does not get upstream to spawn. But what use is going up a river if the habitat is no good?"

"This here," he says, taking both hands from the wheel momentarily to indicate the world around us, "was the coho coast. Then the hatcheries ignored the biology, and had the opposite effect from what they wanted. Hatcheries helped bring complete collapse to the coho salmon in Oregon. Putting out too many fish. Putting the wrong fish in the wrong streams. Now we've got the drought, and the warm ocean water. Going into that, the salmon were already stretched as far as they could go. They had nothing to spare for coping with bad weather or bad ocean temperatures." He's referring to the unusual atmospheric conditions and warmer-than-normal sea temperatures that have affected this coast and much of the eastern Pacific in recent years.

A bird that might be a puffin flies by in the distance, along with a line of murres.

"It's a big ocean. Maybe we've trained the fish to stay offshore. I don't know."

Over the radio, Dick exchanges morning greetings with the person who gave him Lucy. Clipping the radio microphone back into its holder, he says that in Newport right now there are about fifty to sixty salmon boats. Ten years ago, at this same time of year, there were three hundred. Just here in one harbor. The average age of the people fishing in this fleet is now over forty-five. "Only the hard-core are left," he says. "There are no young people coming in."

Two sooty shearwaters fly by. Newport's lights were the last visible feature of the harbor, until they vanished in a woolly fog. We are in twenty-eight fathoms, eight miles southwest from the harbor entrance, four miles offshore; quite close by Dick's standards. "For me, this is the beach."

Dick lets the outriggers down. They squeak rustily, as if sore. The 'riggers are forty-five feet long, wooden, set at a sixty-degree angle when they are deployed. From the outriggers are suspended cables attached to downriggers—hydraulically retrieved lead balls weighing forty-five to sixty pounds each—and from the cables stream the fishing lines. Dick fishes six cables, with four lures positioned thirty feet apart, vertically, on each cable, the legal limit of twenty-four. He alternates "hoochies"—plastic skirts resembling squid—and spoons, with metal flashers ahead of the hoochies to get the attention of salmon. There are bells on the end of the outriggers, to announce strikes. Dick says, "I like to troll at two point three to two point eight knots. Some guys have a knack for knowing whether to go faster or slower. I just blunder along and do whatever feels right."

Putting the lines out takes fifteen minutes. At six forty-five, we are trolling. "I can't stack more than four lures per cable, because I'm required to try to stay down below the coho. They say coho are endangered, but I'm skeptical of government findings. If the Department of Fish and Game said the sun rises in the east, I wouldn't believe them. There have been times when they said there were no salmon, but they were there. Right now—I don't know. The way it's looking, there're not a lot of fish. It's too early to tell. I'd hate to think they're right this time.

"Coho used to be our bread and butter. Now, we've had to learn how to catch chinooks. I like chinook fishing. There's more of a hunt to it. You're just looking for a few premium fish. It's not mass production."

If he likes fishing that is not mass production, then he must love this fishing. Referring to yesterday, I ask him how you make money catching one fish.

"You flat don't. But I didn't lose *too* much yesterday, because we were fishing close, and I only burned about twenty gallons of fuel. I saw I wasn't going to make a lot of money, so I rationalized quitting early to come in and change the oil. Today isn't shaping up too swift, either, as far as I hear on the radio; only one fish has been caught so far." He adjusts his cap and says, "I need about ten fish per day to make some money. The price is two to two-and-a-half dollars per pound. In 1989, we were getting three-and-a-half to four dollars a pound. The price is shot because Norway and the Chileans dump extremely low-priced farmed fish onto the market."

I ask if anyone is making a profit. He says, "No one here is. A lot of these boats will go to Alaska in July."

I ask, "Then why is anyone fishing here now if everyone is losing money?"

"We're gambling. It always seems like there's the potential for some money. I'm trying to scrape together three thousand dollars for a life raft we're soon required to have. I've got two thousand dollars so far. I thought I could get by this year with no major expense, and go into the season with a couple of thousand dollars. Then the autopilot broke. That was eighteen hundred bucks. Then there's a thousand dollars I need for dockage. I guess you could say a guy has to be pretty stupid to stay in this fishery where we're trying to make just enough money to keep fishing so we can continue to lose money. But it's such a way of life. It's not a job that you can exchange for another one." Dick opens a nonalcoholic beer, takes a thoughtful suck, and adds, "If I hadn't quit drinking eighteen years ago, I wouldn't have been able to afford keeping this boat. And if I still had to make mortgage payments on the boat, I don't see how I could do it."

The top of a nearby boat disappears in the trough of a large swell. Six additional boats are coming into our area. The sea is a dark aquamarine, soupy with phytoplankton—good salmon water.

Someone on the radio says, "Just one fish can perk up a guy's day. But so far we're unperky."

Dick says, "Well, we heard the feed was supposed to be here, but so far I haven't seen any on the sounder." He scans with binoculars. There are about ten boats in sight. Only a few birds—shearwaters—are working this area. We're certainly not on a mother lode. Dick, ever observant for anything that could tip the odds, calls another boat: "Did you make that turn because you got a fish?"

"Yeah. But it was kind of a puny thing."

The boats look pretty as the sea begins to glisten. Dick seems to like the fact that I am admiring them. "I think they're the prettiest boats made," he says. "Even some of these mud-ugly boats. When they get out on the ocean with their outriggers spread, they look beautiful."

I try to imagine an accountant saying, "I think we have the prettiest cubicles." This is small-scale commercial fishing at its best. Except for the lack of fish.

The diesel hum is soporific. Louie, the old-timer, reports over the radio that he has a couple but complains about slow going.

Someone says, "I think we're setting a new record. I didn't think you could tow gear for so long without catching a fish." Dick knows every voice on the radio, and he tells me that was Dennis. "He's hard-core." Apparently, one of the greatest compliments that can be paid by a colleague in this elimination derby is to be called hard-core.

Dick checks the lures. "We need a fish real bad. I haven't had a zero in my log book for years. I'm not in the habit of fishing for nothing."

On the radio, someone says, "I just lost a very good fish that popped a new sixty-pound-test leader."

These are commercial fishing boats, yet the fishing is so poor each boat is reporting each strike and even fish lost!

Dick says to me, "When the fishing was good, the radios were quiet because everyone was busy."

Dick puts on a green wooden lure his father made and checks its motion close to the boat. It swims with a seductive wiggle. Satisfied that this lure is in working condition and could catch a salmon, he hopefully lowers the wiggling trickster out of sight.

I notice that Dick has a cold. He says, "I broke into a sweat last night, and I'm coughing now. I'm losing money fishing, but with all the bad weather last week, I certainly can't afford to take another day off."

Except that every day he fishes he loses money a little bit faster.

At eight-thirty, we have some cereal and milk for breakfast. He gets a call on his cellular phone from his wife, which brightens him. "The fishing's great!" he tells her. "It's the catching that's the problem."

Another boat calls to report catching two big ones. That's Jim. Jim's from Alaska, "from a little town where they had so little to do that they switched spouses every winter." Still in a sharing mood, Jim generously gives his loran numbers over the air. Dick checks his coordinates, turns the wheel for the spot where the two big ones were, and says to me, "With so few fishermen left, there is less secrecy about where the fish are. We all know we need all the help we can give."

We troll the spot for a while, then Dick makes a turn. A few minutes later Dick mutters to himself, "I don't know why I turned. I should have worked that spot better, because that's where Jim caught his." He turns to me and says, "I'm getting desperate."

At nine o'clock, one of the outrigger bells starts jingling.

"Hey! There's one!" shouts Dick happily.

The jingling stops. He squints both hopefully and worriedly at the bell. "God," he says, invoking the deity in a somber tone, "I hope it didn't get off."

He hits the switch that sets the line hauler in motion. "It's not looking real good."

But the fish is there.

It's a chinook salmon. Smallish; about eight pounds. A little under two and a half feet long. A three-year-old.

He hand-over-hands the leader, smoothly grabs the flasher with one hand, and deftly gaffs the fish with the other. He quickly clubs the salmon to prevent it from thrashing. Dick says, "This may look unceremonious, but I don't want the fish slamming around and losing scales. This fish is pampered for the market."

I interpret his self-consciousness over the clubbing as a sign of his respect for the fish and a reminder of a common irony: the bond between love and destruction. The gleaming fish goes still in a spreading pool of blood.

This animal is bullet-shaped, sleek, strong-looking. Its back is purplish black. The sides, bright silver. In the transition zone between the purple-black and silver, each scale is lavender or purple, in a different luminously iridescent shade, and framed in black. These scales together make a miniature gallery of abstract paintings, like an exhibit of similar lacquered works by the same artist, gathered and brilliantly displayed side by side so that the slight variations among them set up a subtle shimmer that draws the eye. With a magnifying glass, one could enter this gallery and stroll at leisure. The array of scale alongside scale, panel alongside panel, each differing ever so slightly, is so subtle and exceptional that if one could enlarge this presentation to fill a wall it would light up a whole room. Depending on the angle of my head and the light, the iridescent colors change from purple to gold to green. The salmon's eye is a pale jade, with a blue-black pupil. The head, a gunmetal blue-gray. Its small teeth, sharp. Its pearl-white belly shines with a light lavender cast, and its dorsal and tail fins bear troutlike speckles.

Dick immediately guts the fish, a female. He throws her beating heart to Lucy, who gobbles it. Tiny crabs fill the salmon's stomach. (Recently a biologist told me that at one time the Pacific sardine migrated up the coast in extraordinary numbers, and predators like hake, sea lions, and salmon followed them—a big floating, moving food web. In the summer, the sardines were fattening, their oil content increasing rapidly from fourteen barrels of oil per ton of sardines to fifty barrels per ton. Salmon that were getting ready to come upstream—and some of them went nine hundred miles upriver on the Columbia without feeding—had an extremely rich source of food. I remember the biologist saying, "Of course, the sardine collapsed due to overfishing, but the predators continue to make the migrations. Now, salmon have to eat crab larvae of far less nutritive value.")

After the salmon is buried in ice, Dick redeploys and readjusts the boat's trolling speed. We now have one salmon in a hold that can take ten tons of fish. Dick calls a friend to tell him of the fish we've just caught.

The water temperature, measured at leisure, is 53½ degrees on the Fahrenheit scale. A dozen boats are in view, several within a mile of us. The overcast turns the ocean a blue-green-gray color that has no name.

An hour passes, which Dick fills by gabbing on the radio. At ten o'clock, a twin of the first fish offers the supreme sacrifice. Dick says, "It's no trophy, but we'll take it to town and trade it for money." The fish is worth about sixteen dollars. "Hey," he says sarcastically, "I've already paid for the dozen herring I brought for bait."

Five minutes later, we catch a baby of about sixteen inches. With care, and deftly, Dick slips it off the hook and back into the sea without touching it. "Grow up," he admonishes.

We turn to go back over the area. The sonar shows lots of baitfish here.

Seeing how terrible the fishing is, and how much the remaining fishermen are struggling, I begin to wonder who is catching whom and whether the fish will ultimately be the victors in this awful war of attrition.

The sky begins to brighten, the sun sending through the clouds shafts of light so glorious that men have long thought gods dwelled in such a heaven. The sun pops out, and clear-cuts on the distant hills become visible.

Ever the optimist—as everyone left in this game must be, to a fault—Dick indefatigably continues to check all his lines. One has a broken leader. Dick repairs it, then pauses to take a pill for his heart arrhythmia.

By lunchtime, we tally each salmon that the commercial fishing fleet here has taken: Jim has two. Don has one. Dennis, up ahead, has two.

A voice on the radio asks, "Are you still fishing, or did you have enough sense to go in?"

"Still fishing," Dick says.

"Me too. But I don't know why."

"I know what you mean. You just hate to keep grinding up and down all day long. Maybe tomorrow will be a better day. Better days are coming. I hope." Then to me he says, picking up on our conversation, "I think it will be worthwhile for us to have been here this year. I hope to be able to buy my life raft. And all of us are contributing to the local economy. In port, we're paying for our dockage and buying food and fuel. So I think it will be worthwhile for us to have been here."

It's the first time I've ever heard someone justify his business on the grounds that the money he is losing is helping others.

Dick checks all the gear again. "God! I don't know how we can scratch through so much water without getting *something!*" Then he gives himself an attitude adjustment by adding, "But you can't be discouraged and be a troller. There'll be better days."

"Whoopee!" calls another boat. "I am very deserving of this fish."

The echo sounder shows heavy schools of prey fish, and Dick leaves the pilot house to become his own deckhand again, checking the lines. "We used to have deckhands, but there's not enough money left to hire anybody." Dick admits he's been lazy about checking the hooks for weeds. "I usually check the lines more often, because that's the right way to do it." One after the other, the lures come up. One after the other, they come clean and fishless. One after the other, the lures are lowered back out of sight. By the time everything is checked, he says with a dazed disillusionment bordering on mild shock, "Jeez, I'm getting awfully tired of looking at bare hooks."

In 1985, Dick Good caught nine hundred coho salmon in four days. A friend had seventeen hundred. "That was the last good coho year," Dick says, adding oddly, "I really hope they're wrong about coastal coho. If they're right, they should close it."

Picking up again on an earlier thread in the conversation that Dick has apparently been ruminating over, he says, "I think what I said about no one making a profit was wrong. I think Louie's made a few bucks."

The term "death spiral" is one you hear from time to time on this coast. Glen Spain of the Pacific Coast Federation of Fishermen's Associations used it when he was telling me that there haven't been any full-time salmon fishers since 1988, "when we went into this death spiral of poor stream habitat, poor ocean conditions, degraded estuaries. The five thousand boats that fished for salmon in the Northwest in the 1980s," he said, "generated one and a quarter billion dollars in annual economic impact. For every job on a boat you have up to eight jobs on the prefishing and postfishing ends." He told me that there is no more valuable fish out here pound for pound than adult chinook. In terms of economic spin-offs, one adult fish may generate five hundred dollars in personal impact. "But if you look at the ten-year average, we have ninety-seven percent loss in this fishery if measured with either landings or money."

At one P.M., the bell on the starboard outrigger starts tinkling. Dick immediately begins shouting, "Hey, hey! We've got one!"

This fish is a fine, fat chinook of about fourteen pounds. It has a damaged jaw and gill cover, long healed over, from a near-fatal encounter with the hooks of men sometime in its opaque past. Dick says, "Somebody did me a favor, or maybe I once let this one go."

A radio voice interrupts our celebrating, saying, "I don't know, Dick. Looks pretty bleak. I'm sharpening knives and trying to find stuff to do. I wanted to stay around here, but I'm not going to make any money this way."

Dick says to me, "He's at a spot thirty miles offshore, and he hasn't caught a fish yet today." Dick replies into the microphone that at this rate it would be better to sit in port and pay just the dock fee and not the fuel.

The other fisherman has just arrived at the same conclusion. "I just don't look forward to doing this another day. I'm not going to do this tomorrow."

The salmon famine claims another. For him, this way of life has just ended. This man is discouraged, but as Dick says, you can't be discouraged and be a troller.

A woman named Marlise comes on the radio: "I've got my rose-colored glasses on today. We're living in hopes and memories. I wish I'd never caught a fish here. Then we wouldn't be doing this."

Another fisherman on the radio says in a tight, humorless voice, "I've got bills coming up and I'm running out of time."

Another boat reports two more fish.

Dick says to me, "I can think of a lot of reasons to stay at this until nightfall. If we saw fish. If we were catching fish. If I thought we were going to catch fish. If the wind wasn't blowing. If I felt better."

At four-fifteen, we quit. "We brought up a lot of empty hooks there today. I don't know where I'm going to be tomorrow." He begins to haul the gear. On the last line, he finds a shining fifteen-pounder. "That's a thirty-dollar fish."

"Beautiful fish," I agree.

"Yeah, they're great animals."

A small, dark, solitary porpoise appears, like a luck charm. We'll need more porpoises, because our twenty-four hooks have put four salmon on two tons of ice in a hold built for fifteen tons of fish.

"This is better than yesterday, when I only caught one." Dick is an optimist among optimists. I am beginning to think that even hope can turn self-destructive when it is abused. If cheerful sanguinity can be thought of as something to guard you from bad things—a sort of psychological immune system—then Dick may be suffering the equivalent of an autoimmune breakdown, where the system can no longer discriminate what it should be protecting and what it should be deflecting.

Since midday, the seas have been building. Most of the boats are complaining about the weather and about getting beaten up as they head toward port. A few of the swells are now twelve feet high, and I don't feel so swell myself.

We get into Newport at six. I ask Dick if I can buy one of the fish from him. To my surprise, he tells me it is illegal for him to sell to me; he can sell only to licensed dealers. In an act of incomprehensible generosity, he gives me one of the salmon. I feel faced with a dilemma. Sometimes, it is as charitable to accept a gift as to give one. I take the fish and walk to my car. Returning to the boat, I tell Dick I want to make sure I haven't left my jacket or anything in the cabin, and stuff a twenty-dollar bill under a dishrag on the galley table.

Because the fishers are from out of state, none of them has an automobile here. Five of us walk to a diner: Marlise Pederson and her husband and fishing partner, Jack, have joined us, along with a guy named Murray. Marlise is a rotund woman, wearing salmon earrings. Her rose-colored glasses are off now. She says to me as we walk down the street ahead of the men, "The main question—the one I keep asking myself—is: Are we defunct? Are we done? It's a pretty important question for us." In a hush, she says, "We caught *one* fish today." She asks rhetorically, "Can we even have an economy without our resources—the fish, the logs from forests, et cetera? Can we all just work for the government?"

She comes from a long line of fishermen. Her grandfather and his brother fished in Norway, as did her father and all her uncles. She herself has been a fisher of salmon—exclusively salmon—for twenty years, though she took a bachelor's degree in economics from the University of Washington. "That was a long, *long* time ago," she says, looking both wistful and forlorn. Choices made. Paths chosen. Perhaps she has chosen a dead end and has taken twenty years to come to it.

In the restaurant, the fishermen are amazed to see that one Dungeness crab costs nearly seventeen dollars. "I'm not accustomed to paying for crabs," Dick says.

Murray has heard a tantalizing rumor that someone caught eighteen fish yesterday at a spot thirty-five miles offshore.

We all order seafood. They speak of Alaska. Murray says it used to be nice when you could go home after a trip. They agree that the closure in Washington was warranted, but they also agree—and this is the droning mantra of this community—that even if there really is too much fishing, unless something is done for the spawning habitat in rivers, the salmon problem won't be solved by simply ending fishing. They speak of how short various fishing seasons are because of the number of boats competing for limited quotas. Black cod season is ten days. In Alaska, halibut season was down to twenty-four *hours!* "For that, you need an animal crew that's not afraid of any kind of weather."

Jack says no thanks.

The last time Murray was in Newport was six years ago. "What a contrast," he says. "There were plenty of fish then. Plenty of boats in the harbor. Everyone had money." Now, they are all operating on hope, and diversifying in the meanwhile. Marlise has begun working in a tax office. Jack does some carpentry. Murray does some fiberglassing on boats—not exactly diversifying *out* of the fishery.

Jack picks an advertising flyer from a rack outside the diner and idly thumbs through it as we walk back to the boats, skimming ads. One in particular arrests his attention. It is from a lawyers' office, and he reads part of it aloud: "Divorce seventy-five dollars. Bankruptcy, ninety-five dollars." Jack says, "Let's see: How many more days will it take for us to catch enough salmon to afford bankruptcy?"

The next morning, I see Marlise and Jack on the dock. They have chosen not to go fishing today, and they seem slightly dazed by the gravity and implications of having made such a decision.

Driving out through Newport, I pass a florist shop bearing the sign, "If all else fails, send flowers."

Yachats

Where I am standing, the Pacific Ocean meets the rushing Alsea River with a gleaming, reckless, torn line of white surf tripping across the river's shallow bar. To understand a salmon's situation you must begin where the fish itself begins: in the rivers. Salmonlike, you must leave the ocean and head upstream. The Alsea, terminating on Oregon's central shoreline, is one of hundreds of rivers sliding through the Northwest's coastal forests before colliding with the sea. They include some of the continent's largest—Sacramento, Klamath, Rogue, Columbia, Skagit, Fraser—draining an area ten times the size of New England.

The rugged, folded land that cradles and nurses these rivers is dominated by three great and youthful mountain chains: the Coast Ranges, facing the ocean from California to the Olympics of Washington; the Cascades, farther inland, their snaking crest more distantly paralleling the coastline; and the Rockies. These mountains slit the streaming sky and rend the weather. The moist sea breezes sweeping up their westernmost flanks get cooled in the high chill, producing rain, as much as one hundred inches a year of it, making true rain forests near the coast. And every cloud that falls to earth west of the Continental Divide sends water that washes the backs of salmon on its way to the sea.

Everywhere, from the seeps to the deeps, wherever water slips over ground, those fish are moving. And within and throughout this region, those fish are on people's minds, are why people come here. Here is a recreational vehicle park called King Silver—its huge sign a salmon wearing a jeweled crown, its "camping" spaces occupied by the trailers and motor homes of on-the-road retirees. Another sign announces the Chinook Salmon RV Park. The Yachats Crab and Chowder House and the Flounder Inn Tavern both feature beers named after salmon: Coho Pacific light, Steelhead extra pale ale, and others. The people here pay homage to salmon.

What we call "the Northwest" is a big and diverse place: rivers, rain forests, mountains, fjords, arid inland prairies, and the edge of the ocean, and I am beginning to feel that, more than anything, these fish are what make it all one unified region. What Timothy Egan wrote rings true: "The Pacific Northwest is simply this: wherever the salmon can get to."

A family is strolling the lonely, windy beach as the sky darkens again and rain comes on strong. Gulls, hunkered against the dismal weather, are loafing on the sandy strand as though they've been doing this all their lives and have gotten really good at it. A deep, dark trough separates beach—wide now, at low tide—from outer bar, where the rollers pile up high and emerald, swell, and break. For the whole sweep of vision over the rough, gray, whitecap-salted ocean, only one boat confronts the eye.

To the south, a high, fog-shrouded forest plunges steeply and spectacularly to a wild, deserted beach. One might imagine that this is how the world appeared when God first saw it and pronounced it Good—planet Earth fresh-baked and straight from the oven, before we started carving at it.

In reality though, the Northwest has looked very different. Twelve thousand years ago or so, after the last slow-dance with glaciers, the air here first carried the voices of mammoth hunters across open steppes. Over protracted time they developed fishing skills and a fishing culture. At some of the earliest archaeological sites along the Columbia River, those from nearly ten thousand years ago, salmon bones are absent. A thousand years later, there they are, and sites active about eight thousand years ago contain abundant remains of salmon. The people had learned the value of these fish.

The native tribes of the Northwest became the richest people in North America. They had wandered into a region replete with teeming salmon and shellfishes; copious fresh water; limitless rot-resistant wood for houses, boats, and weapons; abundant mammals upon which to use those weapons in the forests and sea; plentiful mushrooms, roots, berries, and other food plants; and a climate so mild that most birds that elsewhere are migratory saw no reason to move in winter. Nowhere else on the continent could people live off the land this easily, and they found it unnecessary to either farm or follow game herds as the continent's other native peoples did. And so they lived in the luxury of large permanent settlements, so plentifully endowed, so well supplied, so generously lardered, that they filled their abundant leisure time with a culture so rich that scarcely a spoon or fish hook was fashioned into less than an ornamented work of art.

Living as they did amid the world's richest salmon factories, the people built their culture around fishes. All houses faced the water. For travel offshore, dugout canoes up to sixty feet in length were sent against the seas. For inland hunting or berrying or gathering trips, smaller, fleeter canoes traveled upon natural highways of flowing freshwater. Creatures of the waters became family crests or spirit helpers, carved into everything from totem poles to food bowls, woven into baskets, painted on possessions, tattooed upon one's very flesh, and everywhere incorporated into the patterns of life.

"There are few people more expert in the art of fishing," wrote John Jewett, who lived among the Moachat Nootka (on what is now Vancouver Island) for two years after being taken captive in 1803. Of salmon, Jewett remarked, "Such is the immense quantity of these fish, and they are taken with such facility, that I have known upwards of twenty-five hundred brought into Maquinna's house at once." Not that catching them was necessarily easy. "I used frequently to go out with Maquinna . . . in a canoe, to strike the salmon . . . but could never succeed, it requiring a degree of adroitness that I did not possess." Another impressed traveler in a different part of the coast wrote, "Where Boston eyes would detect nothing, Indian sees a ripple and divines a fish."

The natives developed many methods of taking salmon, including trolling with hook and line, spearing, netting, and trapping. Various traps included a "particularly cunning" crib set at the foot of a waterfall, into which salmon fell back after an unsuccessful attempt at leaping the fall. "I have seen more than seven hundred salmon caught in the space of fifteen minutes," penned Jewett.

Many other fish were also abundant. Beyond the kelp beds—sometimes far beyond, on the open ocean—cod, halibut (ranging up to two hundred pounds), sablefish, and others stalked the sea floor and were taken with baited hooks suspended from buoys artfully carved to resemble bobbing seabirds or otters. Herring, smelt, and the vitamin-rich eulachon, or candlefish, teemed in schools so large and dense they could be struck from the ocean's surface with rakes at rates of six hundred an hour. "It is astonishing to see how many are caught by those dexterous at this kind of fishing, as they seldom fail, when shoals are numerous, of taking as many as ten or twelve at a stroke, and in a very short time fill their canoe with them," wrote Jewett. In shallow coves, herring laid immense quantities of delectable eggs on kelp or on branches suspended from floats for this purpose.

Gigantic sturgeon lurked in deep river bottoms. In 1864 Sir Arthur Birch wrote: "It is great fun to watch them spearing Sturgeon which here run to the enormous size of 500 & 600 lbs. These Indians drift down with the stream perhaps 30 canoes abreast with their long poles with spear attached kept within about a foot of the bottom of the River. When they feel a fish lying they raise the spear and thrust it at the fish seldom missing. . . . & you see sometimes 2 or 3 canoes being carried off at the same time down river at a pace by these huge fish."

Not every sea creature required an artfully refined technique for its capture. Easy to get were various types of clams, mussels, oysters, cockles, octopus, and other inhabitants of the intertidal zones. Anyone who could wade could help gather these.

The sea provided not only a living but an origin. One day, Raven coaxed the first people to come out of a clamshell and, born of the seashore, they went off to populate the lands. The Northwest became perhaps the most densely populated nonagricultural region of the world. Twenty-eight persons per square mile—eight times the population density of the interior, and roughly the density of present-day Kansas and Arizona—lived on the coast that would become British Columbia. In 1824 Sir George Simpson of the Hudson's Bay Company wrote, "The native population on the banks of the Columbia River is much greater than in any other part of North America that I have visited. . . . The shores are actually lined with Indian Lodges at the Fishing Season." They caught something like eighteen million pounds of salmon each year before white faces arrived, far more than have been caught in any of the last fifty years.

These riches supported several distinct cultures, but all held the fish in mystical reverence, propitiated with sacred rites and ceremonies. The Indians did not practice conservation as we know it—essentially restraint. They had no need for restraint. But they understood that their dependence on the fish was so great that anything upsetting the relationship between humans and salmon would be catastrophe. They reasoned that scarcity might be caused by disrespect (we have confirmed their suspicions), and they sought to maintain good relations between the Indian people and the salmon people. The Coast Salish, Tlingit, and Kwakiutl peoples—though unrelated to one another—all believed that chinook, sockeye, pink, chum, and coho salmon were not really fish at all, but five tribes of people living in a great magic village under the sea at the end of the horizon. Every summer these undersea tribes sent their young men and women, disguised as fish, to meet the Indian people and to provide for them. Nothing was regarded as mere food. Nor was food regarded as something secured wholly through wit and skill. The people regarded fish and other animals as having voluntarily and compassionately placed themselves in the person's grasp. Arrival of the first spring salmon was a momentous event. If this scout was not afforded the proper deference, the salmon people might be offended and decide to stay away. Accordingly, First Salmon ceremonies were held. Prayers to the first salmon caught included such supplications as, "Do not feel wrong about what I have done to you, friend Swimmer, for that is the reason why you came . . . that I may eat you. . . . Now protect us . . . call after your father and your mother and uncles and aunts and elder brothers and sisters."

It is not too difficult to see why the natives worshiped these fish. Imagine an animal that is born in mountains, travels backward on river currents hundreds of miles to the sea, disappears in the deep ocean for years, and then reappears hundreds of times larger and fights its way into the clouds while fasting, to spawn upon its deathbed.

The attributes of salmon are many and varied. In his book *The Good Rain,* Timothy Egan says, "An outsider has trouble understanding this infatuation with salmon. They're just fish. . . . But then you go to a waterfall deep in British Columbia's high country and see leaping sockeyes. . . . Now you think of them as athletes. You check the elevation, nearly 3,500 feet above sea level . . . and they become alpinists. . . . And then you slow-cook one in foil over a fire . . . and they are delicacies."

. . .

We know much more than we understand about salmon. For all the *perceived* values of salmon, the vast interior reaches of the animals are cloaked with mystery. Who are these beings, and why do the things they do with their lives have the magic to inspire all peoples who have known them?

Salmon. The name means "leaping one"—from the Latin *salire,* to leap. And what leapers they be! A salmon can put four body lengths between its tail and the water. "It would be inconceivable, if not actually witnessed, how they can force themselves up, and after a leap of ten to twelve feet retain strength enough to stem the force of the water above," wrote Captain Charles Wilkes in 1841. But the sight of fleets of athletic creatures defying the forces of gravity and the rush of falling water is only the most visible image of a life that is extraordinary on any scale.

Pacific salmon include the chinook, sockeye, coho, chum, pink, and—confined to Asia—masu. (There is nothing odd about the eyes of the sockeye; the Indians called them *sukkai,* and the transcription has suffered.) In the same genus are the steelhead and coastal cutthroat trout, which are seagoing races of inland trout species. The steelhead is usually classed as a salmon because it is highly oceanic. The cutthroat tends to stay local, and most people do not consider it a salmon. (The Atlantic salmon, *Salmo salar,* the leaping leaper, is in a different genus and not closely related.)

Modern Pacific salmon evolved from a common ancestor about eight million years ago, after continental drift opened the North Pacific to the upwelling of deep, nutrient-rich Arctic waters toward the surface, triggering a great abundance of small animals that could be preyed upon. Salmon began venturing into this cool environment, with much success. The cooling also set the stage for successive ice ages. Isolated by glaciations and consequent several-hundred-foot sea-level changes, salmon populations continued to evolve independently to better fit local conditions, and when they were rejoined during thaws between ice ages some had changed so much as to become virtually incapable of interbreeding— they had become different species.

The natural geographic range of Pacific salmon extends generally from central California up and around the Pacific Rim and down the Asian coast to Japan. They also run Arctic rivers fronting nearly two thousand miles of this world's most frozen ocean, from Russia's Lena River east across Alaska's north coast to Canada's Mackenzie River. Inland, in North America, they span the area from the coast to the Continental Divide, and they seasonally invade a vast area of Alaska's interior.

Even this expansive view shortchanges them, ranging as they do not just into rivers and around the rim of the North Pacific but across the great ocean as well, wherever the water is cold enough.

. . .

But the distribution of species is nothing compared to the feats called forth from individual fish. A chinook salmon returning from the sea can dig into the very heart of North America, boring a thousand miles up the Columbia River system into the Rockies, or nearly *twice* this distance up the Yukon River—across Alaska and into Canada. And a fish just entering freshwater, with many hundreds of miles yet challenging it, may already have traveled two thousand miles just to reach the river mouth.

Fishes that spawn in freshwater but live the greater part of their lives in the sea are called anadromous. The streams provide more security for eggs, but food is limited there, so young fish go to feed in virtually limitless ocean pastures, where they can grow large. Larger fish lay more eggs and produce more young. In the biological arms race that is life on the Earth, success in reproduction is the only measure of success in living. Going to sea allowed these formerly freshwater-confined fishes to increase their habitat area many thousandfold, increasing their market share on life. These are the major evolutionary advantages of anadromy. But the benefit of spawning in streams has turned into an Achilles' heel—the need to breed in freshwater near humankind.

Virtually all salmon die after spawning, even those that breed in low reaches near the sea. The Pacific salmon's nuptial death sentence is made more mysterious by many individuals among Atlantic salmon, steelhead, and cutthroats who do survive, reenter the sea, and eventually return to spawn more than once. If it can be done, why don't they all do it? Whatever the reason, it remains hidden.

Salmon lay only two to five thousand eggs, while some marine fishes lay millions. But compared to the tiny eggs that most marine fishes abandon to near-certain death, salmon eggs are enormous and carefully deposited, endowed with prodigious nutrient reserves from their parents' estate. Consequently, salmon hatch as robust babies with big yolk sacs that enable them to grow for weeks within the gravel's relative safety, before emerging and committing themselves to the challenges of stream life. These advantages are relative, not absolute. Relative to ours, their chances are appalling: one in three thousand. Still, that is an incredible advantage over odds approaching one in tens of millions for a bluefin tuna.

After emergence, salmon spend varying lengths of time in freshwater before moving toward the ocean. Some spend only a few days, some a year or more, depending on species and location. Where the growing season is short, staying longer in freshwater enables youngsters to enter the sea at a larger size, which reduces their risk of being eaten by oceanic predators.

All the foregoing complexity is in fact oversimplification. Salmon break every rule they make, and exceptions to generalizations are so many as to strain human capacity to hold them in the mind. Some salmon do not even spawn in truly fresh water; certain populations of pinks and chums spawn in brackish tidal areas near river mouths. Sockeyes have twenty-two different patterns of time in freshwater versus time in salt, ranging from fish that migrate to sea before they reach their first birthday and return to breed and die in two years to those that spend four years in freshwater and three winters in the ocean. Chinook have at least fourteen different patterns; coho, twelve; chum and cutthroat, six; and steelhead, four.

Diversity is their evolved response to the unpredictability of rivers. Maturing at different ages and in different years lessens the risk that any given generation will be eradicated by a catastrophic environmental disaster such as an egg-killing drought or deluge, a stream-blocking landslide, a volcanic explosion, or extreme water temperature in a particular year or place. High odds of dying young have produced dozens of ways of trying to beat those odds.

When the time comes for the young fishes to make their saltwater debut, they undergo a dramatic transformation in body shape, coloration, and physiology—a kind of radical prepuberty—to prepare them for the ocean's hazards. This makeover is called "smoltification," and posttransformation juveniles are called smolts. The young salmon now finds itself living within a narrowed, fusiform body designed for long-range travel. That new body possesses the typical camouflage of fishes that roam the high and open seas—dark blue-green back, silvery sides, and pearly belly—instead of the earth tones and spots that helped it remain inconspicuous against riverbed pebbles.

Perhaps most complicated are the *unseen* changes that transmogrify the youngsters from freshwater to saltwater animals. Migratory tendencies and direction-finding capabilities develop. A body designed for freshwater (pumping water out the kidneys to prevent flooding, and taking up ions through gills to maintain electrolyte balance) reforms itself for saltwater (*removing* sodium and chloride ions at the gills, while *conserving* water at the kidneys). More than a dozen hormones manage these changes. Timing is critical: Juvenile salmon transferred prematurely to saltwater suffer stunted growth and thyroid dysfunction and often die.

Helped along by rivers flowing high with spring snowmelt, ocean-bound smolts move out of the rivers facing into the stream, traveling backward on the current. The journey takes anywhere from a few days to several months. Seaward migration is timed to coincide with peak abundance of such foods as copepods, larval shrimp, amphipods, isopods, larvaceans, mysids, arrowworms, pteropods, and the larvae of fishes, crabs, and mollusks.

In late spring young salmon begin leaving estuaries, facing full saltwater and the pulse of oceanic existence, confronting a formidable new array of temperatures, turbidities, tides, currents, food densities, and predators. Not surprisingly, this time is often marked by a calamitous spike of mortality—often amounting to 50 percent right off the bat. Most losses go to predators—everything from deadly isopods to larger salmon to sharks and other fishes, gulls, loons, dolphins, seals, and sea lions. Young salmon cohorts may sustain *daily* mortality rates of 2 to 8 percent in their first forty days in the sea.

Those still alive when each day dawns are growing rapidly (the best defense against predators), gaining between 3 and 8 percent of their body weight daily in the first few months, sometimes quadrupling in size during the first ocean summer. After the first few months at sea, mortality gradually drops by an order of magnitude. Still, with predators ranging from halibut to humpback whales, overall mortality for salmon while in the ocean is very high by our standards; 50 percent would be phenomenally good, and for many cohorts natural mortality reaches 95 percent before it is time to head home. Add fishing, and only 1 to 4 percent of the smolts that had entered the ocean typically make it back to their natal rivers.

The ocean may seem a "black box" into which young salmon disappear and from which large, vibrant, surviving adults burst forth, but some things are known about salmon sea life. While some populations remain near shore, many others make spectacular migrations rivaling those of any bird. Migrations are adaptations toward abundance, evolved to optimize feeding, survival, and reproductive success by tracking favorable conditions across space and through time. In the fall, millions of young salmon abandon North America and disperse into oceanic space. Most migrate northward over the continental shelf, swimming two body lengths per second for up to seventeen hours each day, averaging about ten to fifteen miles daily. In its first few months at sea a young salmon may thus travel seventeen hundred miles from its natal river. Reaching the Gulf of Alaska by late fall, they depart the continental margins, turning south toward the cool, subarctic, central reaches of the great ocean. This is the general pattern. Steelhead are the most boldly oceanic, forgoing the coastal trek and striking out directly from the continent toward the heart of the great blue universe.

Asian salmon migrating east mingle with those from the Americas in the Bering Sea and Gulf of Alaska, resulting in a great, interdigitating, racially integrated salmonic nation stretching all the way from North America to waters off Japan, Kamchatka, and the Asian mainland. The southern border of this nation of fishes is the Subarctic Boundary (about forty degrees north latitude; from about San Francisco to northern Japan). North of this front are the cool, low-salinity, highly productive Arctic-influenced waters, with their abundance of large and nutritious prey. South of the boundary is the warm, high-salinity ocean-desert domain, a different country, where the monarchy is composed of the tunas and billfishes.

The tunas' and billfishes' remarkably hydrodynamic, sickle-tailed, specialized body forms and warm-blooded physiologies contrast startlingly with the "generalized" design of salmon. Yet salmon have risen to the position of dominant open-water fish across much of the ocean. The generalizations of a salmon's body represent an optimized shape for the many differing tasks it is called on to perform, from traveling the wide and trackless ocean, to surmounting rushing flows and waterfalls challenging their upstream swim, to digging a nest with a broad tail. For these diverse needs, their body serves well. Remarkably well. Of all the cold-blooded fishes, salmon are unsurpassed in their physical capabilities.

The first live salmon I ever saw were waiting for the rising tide to let them over the bar at the mouth of the Klamath River in California. I was not expecting them, and I received the rare and sparkling joy of fresh discovery. It was the summer I graduated from college, and Greyhound buses and my thumb had gotten me from New York to the West Coast, where, like Balboa, I first gazed upon the great Pacific. Small fleets of impatient big chinooks and a few steelheads ventured hurriedly across the wide, shallow bar, while a much larger group of fish, waiting on the seaward edge where the surf was breaking, strove to avoid sleek seals that had gathered to assault them while the water was low. Not all the salmon succeeded in evasion, and seals occasionally surfaced with a struggling fish in their jaws. Backed by giant redwoods and standing thigh-deep in the last of the ebbing tide, I watched astonished as pods of excited fish dashed past my knees. I was armed with a fishing rod, as I always was in those days whenever water was in view, but this was unlike anything I had ever seen before—these fish seemingly more driven, wilder, more primeval. The last thing on these fishes' minds was food, anyway, so I cradled the rod and let the scene etch itself deep behind my eyes, and I fell under the salmon's spell. When some time had passed, a hefty chinook of about twenty-five pounds came floating downstream, bled nearly to death after tearing itself from a gill net set illegally up the river. I loosed a single cast and snagged the stricken fish in the back, then staggered to shore, where its tail dragged a track in the sand all the way to my campfire. No fish I ever touched seemed as wondrous or otherworldly.

A bright chinook salmon of unremarkable size is worth more than a barrel of crude oil, and this, at least, is as it should be. Still, the price of salmon-the-product does not reflect the value people place on salmon-the-animal; it reflects only what someone is willing to pay to eat salmon rather than other food. Such market prices are distorted, because they do not account for many other values of salmon in human society that are difficult to compare or measure. Salmon are ecological capital, and one way to describe the salmon problem is to say that the value of the Pacific Northwest's salmon-capital asset has depreciated. The ecological fabric that once brought forth such enormous populations of salmon that they seemed to have been provided by God and generously sacrificed themselves for human benefit has been rent. Logging, damming, farming, fishing, trapping, irrigating, ditching, draining, filling, spraying, and even grazing are a few of the reasons salmon are not having a nice day. Near harbors and industrial facilities, juvenile salmon ingest enough contaminants to suppress their immune system.

Almost anything done on land—living in a house containing wood, buying a potato grown in Idaho or rice grown in California (or a score of other crops), turning on a lightbulb in much of the western U.S.—adds to a salmon's troubles.

Since 1800, the European invasion has added about ten million people to the region, a trade-off of about two salmon subtracted for every sapient *Homo* added. Spawning people now outnumber spawning salmon. In the next hundred years, an additional fifty million people will attempt to enjoy the place and will no doubt find, or feel they have found, some measure of success.

Some—in fact, many—wild salmonid populations throughout the world are in decline. The Atlantic salmon is having trouble because of everything from dams to overfishing to food shortage following depletion of its prey by commercial fisheries. In the Northwest, salmon are protected to varying degrees under the Fishery Conservation and Management Act, the Endangered Species Act, the Northwest Power Act, and other federal and state statutes, but these constitute a tangled web of good intentions so diffusely focused, so impenetrable to even their human sympathizers, that the salmon can hardly hope to persevere.

Not *all* salmon populations are declining, and some are even increasing, but the declines are widespread. Pacific salmon runs range from very strong—for instance, in much of Alaska—to extinct. Alaska is touchy about being lumped with the bad guys. In 1996, faced with a glut of salmon, the Alaska legislature offered to promote salmon consumption by adding the fish to prison menus.

Along British Columbia's vast coast, the situation is generally best in the north, where some large, healthy runs still riddle the rivers. The really battered runs are to the south. On the central coast and in the southern part of the province, hundreds of small breeding populations have been extinguished and over six hundred runs are faltering and at risk; and in eastern B.C. all salmon populations in the Canadian reaches of the Columbia River were completely cut off by U.S. dams and are now extinct.

In Washington, Oregon, California, and Idaho, more than three hundred salmon populations are at moderate to high risk of extinction in the region, and one hundred major populations of salmon and anadromous trout have already been snuffed. Only 16 percent of the runs are *not* known to be declining. Reflective of how bad things have gotten, a recent study defined salmon runs as "healthy" even if they had declined by up to two-thirds but were now stable. But nearly all of the hundred or so "healthy" populations face habitat degradation.

There is a pattern. Two patterns, actually. One, the summer runs—those that come during low flows and wait for months to spawn—are faring worst. Two, the situation generally deteriorates the farther south you go. Alaskan runs are healthiest. California is hurting the most, with only one "healthy" run. A wave of extinctions is spreading up the West Coast of North American from the southern part of the range, traveling in a northerly direction like a bad infection.

More patterns: Populations breeding near the coast tend to be better off than those running into the far interior. Populations from larger rivers, like the San Joaquin–Sacramento, California's Klamath, and the Columbia-Snake, are extinct in a higher percentage of their former range than those from shorter, smaller rivers. Populations where juveniles stay for extended periods in freshwater are worse off than those that go quickly to sea after hatching. Efforts to reverse the declines have been numerous, expensive, and generally ineffective.

Many "interlocking sets of debilitating causes," as the Canadian fisheries scientist J. R. Brett said, devastated the Columbia River's great salmon runs. Overfishing was the first. Soon, river diversions for irrigation began not only competing for water but drawing hundreds of millions of salmon onto farm fields (some farmers liked the free fertilizer). This continues even today. Then there are dams, most notably those that remade the Columbia Basin. Pollution—from pulp mills, agricultural pesticides, silt, and stream-putrefying cattle—and extensive forest destruction round out the salmon's major problems.

Consequently, efforts to restore, reestablish, or even just conserve salmon runs confront the preeminent big-money interests of the region. Not surprisingly, the prospect that people would resort to the Endangered Species Act to help balance the prevailing trend for salmon has spawned a great deal of, shall we say, anger, over the act itself.

The main problem with the Endangered Species Act and our normal way of thinking is that most attention and money go to saving the most at-risk populations. This is the highest-cost, highest-risk strategy. Waiting until that point, rather than cherishing and shepherding those in the best shape, helps ensure both that the best runs will eventually join the worst and that some of the worst will be lost. But human nature includes the strong tendency to remain in denial until things are undeniably bad. And the Endangered Species Act is fixated on extinction instead of abundance. So, crisis management of the region's salmon has begun.

Along the road stunted, wind-blown, and salt-burned pines, looking like natural bonsais, grow thick and dense. The car radio says, "We need your pledges. Yesterday the governor declared the Oregon coast a disaster area because of the salmon situation. He is seeking federal disaster-relief funds. We don't take corporate money that influences what other radio stations can tell you. So we can tell you the reasons there are no salmon anymore. But we can't do it without your donations." After the news and the fund drive, back to music. Jimi Hendrix, in that liquid wail of his, is singing, *There must be some kind of way outta here,* as I drive into Yachats, Oregon.

I have a reason for driving past a dead-end sign. The little gravel road breaks out of the pines overlooking the beach but then turns sharply left. Among a small row of modest homes, a weather-beaten pickup truck rests beside a ramshackle cottage. If you have a good pitching arm, it is a stone's throw from the beach. Nice spot. I walk up to the slatted wooden porch, which sports two dangerously dilapidated rocking chairs.

On this Sunday midmorning, the whole small house smells of pancakes. Mary Scully, a fine woodworker who makes extraordinary cabinets with inlaid designs, is home, along with her son Kaegan, seven. Kaegan is stroking a precocious six-month-old cat that has two blue-eyed kittens. In the kitchen, paintings, photos, postcards, and woodcuts cover almost every available bit of wall space with depictions of people, animals, and flowers. Hanging pieces of driftwood cover all remaining interstices. A hand-powered coffee grinder is clamped firmly to one end of the counter, and in the middle of the kitchen stands a plain wooden table, unfinished, thrown together by the master woodworker herself. The house is loaded with plants, including jade and blooming bird-of-paradise. A small wood stove provides the living room its center of gravity.

Kaegan's father, Paul Engelmeyer, is sitting near the big corner window in the living room before a stack of pancakes loaded with homemade yogurt, apple sauce, and honey from his own beehives. His thick, dirty-blond hair piles forward over his forehead, almost shading his pale, blue-gray eyes. He looks relaxed in a blue cotton shirt over a black T-shirt, and he is sucking tea under his mustache.

Paul is a rare commodity these days: a rural conservationist with a connection to the landscape. Because most environmental-policy decisions are made by politicians, most environmentalists, rather than working close to the land, work at politics and law in urban centers, near the seats of power. They succeed in playing the political processes, but they are less successful at inspiring people to action and at earning the trust of those inclined to be adversaries, or the respect of those who decidedly are adversaries.

No one is likely to mistake Paul for a lawyer anytime soon. Engelmeyer grew up in St. Louis but felt hemmed in there. After studying psychology and then doing drug-rehab work with kids, he headed out to the great Northwest in 1975.

"I had always felt good about doing social service work, but if you're telling underprivileged kids to tackle things they find challenging—and you say that long enough—pretty soon you ask yourself, 'Well, what do *I* really find challenging?' For me, accepting challenge means going into untouched forest, putting myself at the base of a tree that is ten feet across and two hundred feet tall, and climbing to its canopy."

For fifteen years, he climbed in national forests all over the region, collecting seeds used by the Forest Service for replanting logged areas. "It was intense labor. And it was fast money. You'd have a chunk of money that lasted weeks, and between jobs I found myself trying to save these last great places—funding my conservation work by climbing the remaining giant trees." Later he worked as a climber on a research team studying a small seabird called the marbled murrelet, which nests in huge old trees and is threatened by overcutting.

Paul finally landed at Ten Mile Creek, and by then he knew a lot about the woods. Ten Mile Creek Basin had fifty-four hundred acres of continuous forest, much of it old-growth and "still gorgeous." Big-butted, eight-foot-diameter Douglas-fir, western redcedar, western hemlock, and Sitka spruce rose from the ground. Elk, spotted owls, deer, black bear, eagles, and the largest concentration of nesting marbled murrelets left in Oregon inhabited the forest's three-dimensional interior. The creek itself still nurtured wild runs of coho salmon and steelhead.

Paul learned that a privately owned, 116-acre parcel in the middle of the Ten Mile Creek Basin was scheduled for clear-cutting and subdivision. Following Paul's tip, the National Audubon Society, with local folks' support, initiated an intensive negotiation to acquire the property for wildlife protection and education. Hands shook in 1990.

When loggers began pressuring to clear-cut adjacent federally owned parts of the Ten Mile Basin around silt-sensitive salmon spawning beds, two hundred members of the community formed the Ten Mile Creek Association. Paul found himself being point person. "I think my skills as a social worker helped me deal with the agency people—finding who is receptive to the way I'm posing questions. And of course I had enough tree experience to go out with foresters and call their bluff about the effects of cuts they were planning. So that's how I kind of got into this conservation thing."

What Paul refers to as "this conservation thing" includes, besides brokering the salvation of Ten Mile's forest and salmon streams, his courage in being the first to show—and say publicly—that coho salmon reproduction had dropped so low that fishing should be suspended, and his current work to direct federal disaster funds into programs for employing out-of-work loggers and fishermen in restoring stream habitat for salmon.

My main reason for visiting Paul today is to get a look at the great salmon forests, and he takes me to a place he knows well, perhaps better than anyone, called Cummins Creek.

Walking in from the beach—the route of a spawning salmon—setting footsteps into streamside gravel, we enter a realm among the bases of enormous ferns, massive Sitka spruces, towering western hemlocks. By the time sunshine penetrates to this forest floor, it has been sifted like light in deep water. The trees' canopies, interlacing hundreds of feet overhead, filter out the sky. Forests—especially those of this vertical magnitude—are not places familiar to me, and I have the benefit of first impressions. Among the huge ridged trunks and limbs cushioned thick with mosses, the main impression is of silence, a silence so resilient you can almost press it with your hand and feel its flex. Rain is filtering through the giants as we walk, but the silence somehow rises to envelop the droplets. And the running stream. And the bubbling call of a wren. And the sound of our footsteps along the elk trail we are following. It is a dense web of silence, a silence that includes sounds, a silence that hums with the body electric of an ancient community of living beings.

The spiring height and sentinel age of the trees imbue these forests with a solemnity so deep it seems spiritual. One explorer described the rivers moving in deep shade through these brooding forests as "dim aisles in ancient cathedrals." The first white men who cast eyes upon this coast were awed to find the world's tallest, densest rain forests, bathed in continual drifting mists. In 1792 explorer George Vancouver marveled, "I could not possibly believe that any uncultivated country had ever been discovered exhibiting so rich a picture." Settlers wrote of trees "so thick tall and straight that it must be seen to be believed." Of the Willamette River, a traveler named Theodore Winthrop raptly wrote, "In no older world where men have in all their happiest moods re-created themselves for generations in taming earth to orderly beauty have they achieved a fairer garden than Nature's simple labor of love has made there."

A great, intricate diversity and profusion of living things—that is another impression. The power and vigor of life. The mysterious way the inanimate organizes itself; the rearranging and ordering of air, light, and soil that thrusts itself so massively skyward as cells of wood and leaves; the crystallizations that we call trees—these living things.

While I soak in these impressions, Paul explains how the forest creates its own rain by reaching into the sky and capturing passing clouds. He also points out a nondescript bit of nothing named *Lobaria oregana,* an epiphytic lichen with the rare talent of capturing atmospheric nitrogen and turning it into a form needed by plants for making proteins. *Lobaria* grows only on trees over a century old.

As we gain a little elevation, Paul points out the first Douglas-fir, the tree that dominates most salmon forests in the region. Higher up come true firs and mountain hemlock, and ponderosa pines and others. These trees are exceptionally long-lived. Five hundred years is common here. The Douglas-fir reaches more than a thousand years of age. One species can live a life spanning thirty-five centuries, a long time to stand in one place and feel the world spin. (There may yet survive a few Alaska-cedars that were minding their own business as seedlings while Moses was floating down the Nile, and some of the trees here were already half a millennium old when Christopher Columbus discovered the New World.) While the age can be sensed, it is the scale—the size of everything—that first imposes. Western redcedars can attain twenty feet in diameter. While the tallest tree in eastern North America (eastern white pine) reaches two hundred feet at most, at least thirteen species in the Northwest blow past this height. Coast redwoods, the world's tallest trees, approach four hundred. The tallest recorded Douglas-fir was itself just shy of four hundred feet.

The exceptional size and longevity of the trees creates diversity among other living things between the ground and the utmost canopy. As trees grow and break, an exceptional array of life forms shuffle into the layering light gaps. Just for example: More than one hundred mammal species live in the forested Northwest coastal region, an unusually high number, including peculiar creatures found nowhere else, such as the only mammal that eats mainly truffles (the western red-backed vole). And of course there are the salmon, hundreds of different, diversely adapted, genetically differing, finely tuned local runs, running the forest streams.

We continue up along Cummins Creek, gaining a little more elevation. Looking up at a tree so tall that it disappears from view is an unusual experience. During the Middle Ages, some of these trees were already gripping soil here. If there were no money to be made—if the trees were like stars—I am sure the nearly universal consensus would be that they are impressive in a way that quiets one's mind and gives a twinge of involuntary reverence.

The coastal Northwest salmon forests have been called "the most magnificent forest on the continent and the greatest conifer forest on earth." Compared to tropical rain forests, the Pacific forests have far less variety but support a far greater mass of living things. The most productive tropical forests contain 185 tons of plants per acre. Pacific rain forests average about 400, and some redwood forests sustain *1,800 tons* per acre. Such forests once carpeted the whole Pacific slope, from northern California up through Oregon, Washington, British Columbia, and the Alaskan panhandle, like green fuzz on the western crust of North America.

Though people had been moved by the profuse power of Pacific forests, all most foresters thought they needed to know about them was how to cut them down. In 1952, a Forest Service silviculturist called them—of all things—"biological deserts." It is said that humans are defined and distinguished from other animals by our ability to use tools and language, but often I wonder if the most uniquely human trait is our ability to deceive ourselves.

Touch a huge tree's skin with a running chain saw and you are about to create a gap in the forest several yards wide and a thousand years long. Take out a five-hundred-year-old tree and you have removed five centuries of the past, at a minimum replacement cost of five centuries of the future. An old tree is a pucker of time on the surface of the earth. Time you can climb.

The tops of the biggest trees—those that emerge from the canopy to have a look at the world at large—eventually get their heads blown off in cracking winds. It's often the beginning of the end for them, but in the years-long interval before the call of death and the crash of gravity, as the upper limbs widen with mosses in the newfound light, the broken trees become nesting habitat for that odd little seafarer that Paul studied, the marbled murrelet. A large and growing segment of the coast no longer has ancient forests or, consequently, the now-threatened marbled murrelets. (And at sea the birds sometimes carry their last gulp of air into a gill net set for salmon.)

Upon finding a long-fallen tree, Paul says, "This is an exciting gap." The tearing crash of a giant brings instant opportunity for renewal, and direct sunlight may strike the forest floor here for the first time in hundreds of years. In these forests, downed trees are not merely recycled into soil. They become "nursery logs." All along the trunk of this big fallen tree, dozens of seedlings have sprouted and sprung to life in the sunlight, sending their roots into the moldering wood. Where better for a seedling to draw the stuff that will make it big and strong than from an ancient fallen giant that may well be its own grandparent? Anyone who thinks trees that fall are wasted should see this wild nursery. This is direct inheritance, an heirloom of five hundred years' accumulation of ancestral wealth and wisdom. Dead trees are essential to the health of the forest, because the bulk of the nutrients are not in the thin soils but in the wood. Remove a tree and you cut the seedlings off from their hereditary endowment, their head start. Decay is the executor of the tree's estate. The forest feeds itself. This is part of the reason why successive generations of planted trees—poor orphans that they are—grow less and less vigorously.

A standing dead tree is called a snag. It takes a forest five hundred years to begin to produce large snags, and a snag itself can last over a hundred years. Many birds need such snags, and many a salmon has reached the literal high point of its existence in the great platform nest of an osprey or eagle in the broken-off top of a very old tree, long since dead.

Eventually and inevitably, the gravity of the situation proves irresistible, and the tree falls. When it does, 163 species of birds, mammals, reptiles, and amphibians (plus more invertebrates than you can drop a tree on) move in, under, through, and around fallen logs. And fallen logs are critical for salmon.

On a tiny side pocket of the stream, in about a foot of very clear water, water striders cast shadows like animate lace on the bottom. Two warblers are talking in an adjacent patch of maples. We step into the sunlight of a gravel bar. On the cobbly stream bottom rests a thin and broken blanket of algae and some sand. Several very large, root-bearing trunks, swept downstream during floods, lie grounded fast here. The rooty tangle arrests the streamrush, and through the logjam slides very slow water that pools up like time after lovemaking.

Paul shows me how pebbled gravel fragments of uniform size have collected in the slower current behind the fallen trunks—a good site for spawning salmon to dig a nest and lay eggs. And, pointing out something so obvious but so subtle I had not noticed it in the shining, moving water, he shows me a large group of baby salmon—dozens—in the sheltering eddy around the massive fallen wood.

I crouch to gaze more closely. Surprised not only by the sight of them but also by how thoroughly they captivate me, I stare a long time. And eventually I remember the philosopher Alan Watts:

> A floor of many-colored pebbles lies beneath clear water, with fish noticed only by their shadows, hanging motionless or flashing through the liquid, ever-changing net of sunlight. We can watch for hours, taken clear out of time and our own urgent history by a scene which has been going on just like this for perhaps two million years.

At times, it catches us right below the heart with an ache of nostalgia and delight compounded, when it seems that this is, after all, the
world of sane, enduring reality from which we are somehow in exile.

In the mud of the bank, an elk's sliding hoofprint.

Even after—especially after—you have seen the young salmon, their continued
presence in these streams may strike you as utterly remarkable. Young salmon
confront you with living proof of the reality and, yes, the *endurance,* of a life cycle
so seemingly heroic as to appear mythical. The presence of one delicate little
young salmon not only implies but indisputably confirms the ecstatic victory of
all that has gone before: the struggles against death, the driving and striving for
life, the unquestioning devotion to the future that brought their parents back
from so far away.

When it comes time, adult salmon that have ranged into the ocean as far as
twenty-five hundred miles from the mouths of their birth rivers turn toward
home for the first and final time. There is no equivocating; an adult salmon's
homeward migration is rapid and direct, averaging about thirty miles per day.
Fish that have spread out over thousands of square oceanic miles converge with
alacrity, arriving at their natal rivers within days of each other.

Visibility in the sea is extremely limited, and the fish live and travel with no
reference to visual markers—a tremendous disadvantage compared to, say, a
migrating bird. Yet in its migrations a salmon can maintain homeward direction
for mile after mile—though returning by a route it has never before traversed. It
is traveling by means of extraordinary internal navigational systems that remain
one of the most intriguing mysteries of animal migration. Aside from the hundred million bits of magnetite arrayed into chains in a salmon's brain, the fish
have revealed few of their navigational secrets. Scientists are still guessing. To
accomplish its migrational feats a salmon must be able to form a "map sense."
Salmon are probably using the inclination and declination of the earth's magnetic field, backed with a celestial compass, and then comparing a sense of how
daylight varies with latitude against an internal annual clock containing rate of
daylight change throughout the year. They must also be able to call up some
sense of their position relative to the location of their home stream.

However they are doing it, a salmon certainly knows where it is going. Homing rates are as high as 99 percent. Homing to the correct stream is important for
salmon because different streams are continuously forming the fish for the best
fit. Homing brings the keys back to the locks they are made for; it brings a
salmon back to the stream that suits it, rather than to one in which the waterfalls
are too high, the gravel too coarse, the diseases too virulent, the water temperature too warm. Those streams have their own adapted fish.

Yet when they arrive near the rivers of their birth and impending death they behave as if they may be having second thoughts, wandering erratically, drifting, moving toward and away from the river itself.

Here, the whiff of odors from their childhood streams, suddenly familiar again, take the helm. Not only do salmon smell their way home, their olfactory sense is extraordinarily acute, allowing them to find tiny natal springs flowing into major rivers.

Now the salmon that, as a youngster, transformed for life in the sea changes again for surviving freshwater. Accompanying this are changes to nuptial colors (including the spectacular coloration of breeding sockeyes, with their bright green heads and cherry-red bodies afire), the greatly enlarged teeth, the grotesque hooking of the males' jaws for breeding combat, and the monumentally humped back of breeding male pink salmon.

Once in the river, the fish must trick the current. In fast rivers, they must travel against water flowing more than half again as fast as the salmon's fastest sustainable swimming speed. Choosing paths of least resistance, they use bends, irregularities in the bottom, rocks, logs, and other objects that break up the flow or even produce eddies where pockets of water are flowing upstream.

Salmon have usually ceased eating by the time they enter natal streams. They depend on energy reserves for maturation of sperm and eggs, migration upstream, spawning, and nest defense. This may seem unremarkable for those runs that breed within sight of the sea. But for those that must ascend rapids, leap waterfalls, climb nearly a mile above sea level into mountains, and—boring into the current at rates of about twenty miles per day without anything we would recognize as rest—penetrate a thousand miles into the continental interior (and in some cases then wait for months while fasting until river conditions are right for spawning), the feat approaches miraculous. It marks the extreme adaptive edge of the ability of a creature to endure. Yet they have flourished.

But the toll involves extensive biochemical and physiological changes, immune-system failure, and total exhaustion of bodily reserves. In a sense, the fish becomes a delivery system for offspring, its fuel and infrastructure calculated to get it to the spawning grounds—and no further. Systems not needed for spawning are used to fuel the travel. The throat and digestive organs degenerate as the fish consumes its own body. Protein is broken down and metabolized until, by the time they are ready for spawning, their muscles are mush. But enough water replaces the burned-up tissue to keep the skin plumped and streamlined. All other things are sacrificed for one: In the male, that sperm is healthy and vigorous; and inside the female, that eggs are well-endowed with nutrients to carry them through hatching, then months of early development.

When, finally, the tributary of their own birth is attained and the time has come, they will seek out suitable gravel—clean and of the appropriate size—to dig their nests, called redds. The female turns on her side, presses her tail to the bottom, and with powerful flexes lifts sand, debris, and gravel into the current.

Her vigorous digging is interspersed by periods of resting, while she evaluates her progress with her fins. Her nest-making activities attract suitors. Other females, undesirable males, and potential predators of eggs, she drives away.

The accepted male fights off other males, though some may continue to hover nearby. While the female continues to excavate, the male courts her with repeated touches—his snout to her flanks—and by crossing over her tail and then quivering his body against hers. Eventually the pair will lie side by side with their bellies close together near the bottom of the nest. They go through the motions a few times, then their backs arch, bodies tilt to bring bellies closer, mouths gape open. Eggs and sperm gush forth.

Satellite males often rush in, strafing with sperm, fertilizing enough eggs to perpetuate their behavior in the species' repertoire. The female must soon cover the eggs, lest they be swept away. Afterwards, she rests for several hours. Over several days she will lay more eggs in the same redd, which may be fertilized by the same or another male. With laying completed and the redd fully covered, the female will guard the eggs for as long as two weeks, driving off other salmon who might accidentally dislodge her nest, until her death.

Males also often combat intruders near their nests, or they may continue courting until they become too weak to stem the current, and then they drift downstream.

By the time a salmon is near death, its fins are frayed, its skin battered and broken, its body host to white fungus. Internally, its cardiovascular system, pituitary and adrenal glands, stomach, liver, and kidneys are degenerate and wrecked. The creature is consumed and consummated.

A time to live, a time to die. "The death of a salmon," wrote Roderick Haig-Brown in 1946, "is a great gesture of abundance." Salmon bring the wealth of oceans—transformed into their own animate bodies—into mountain streams, feeding eagles, bears, and their own children with their carcasses. When we eat a salmon—when we put its body into our own—we have allowed the fish to do the mysterious work of gathering the wide ocean's sparse nutrients together for us in the form of their very flesh.

The thin soup of the whole North Pacific Ocean, strained and condensed into decadent muscle, is now delivered to the scavengers. Many there are. To the list headed by bears and eagles, add the insects that will feed the baby salmon that are incubating in the gravel. Add more than twenty species of birds and mammals: raven, dipper, jay, wren, shrew, skunk, raccoon, otter, bobcat—even squirrels and deer may nibble the cadaverous fish in search of some trace nutrients delivered from the deep and distant sea.

The dead propel the living. Something like half of the carbon and nitrogen in stream insects, trout, and young salmon is of marine origin. In other words, much of the bodies of young salmon are composed of the resurrected bodies of their parents, the new salmon assembling themselves from the disassembled molecules of the old. One thing follows: The fewer adults that return (and the more that hatcheries insist upon removing and discarding carcasses), the fewer of their children the stream can support. If adult runs decline, the fertility of the stream declines. Its production potential drops, an ever downward spiral that can fall much faster than it can rebuild.

In the gravel, eggs are developing, protected there from predators, freezing, desiccation during low flows, and scouring during high flows. Salmon gravel must be porous and silt-free enough to allow a continuous stream of oxygen-rich, waste-removing water. Fertilized eggs develop in the gravel for about three months—often during winter—before they secrete an enzyme that weakens the egg membrane. Hatching with attached yolk sacks, the tiny salmon—called "alevins" at this stage—remain in the gravel, growing, for another two to three months or so.

When the alevin's yolk supply is exhausted, it wriggles itself through the gravel, alternately working and resting, emerging in the streambed after night-fall during the darkest hours of the month's darkest nights. Their first need is to surface for a gulp of air. The little salmon bites a tiny bubble out of the atmosphere, munches, swallows it. When it has swallowed enough air into its swim bladder to achieve neutral buoyancy, it is now a swimming fish, no longer an alevin—now a "fry." First food usually consists of larval midges, mayflies, caddisflies, and stoneflies, and adult insects that fall into streams. When the growing fry develop markings, they are called "parr."

Into this idealized stream, a little rain must fall. When fry emerge, the hungry mouths of trout, sculpins, larger juvenile salmon, leeches, whitefish, sticklebacks, terns, gulls, kingfishers, snakes, crows, mink, herons, otters, mergansers, and many others are ready to apply their superior experience. Any fish that emerges cautiously for its first glimpse of the dark world has about a 10 percent chance—sometimes better, sometimes worse—of surviving the freshwater phase of its life. Still, any salmon that survives long enough to get a look at the inside of another mouth can count itself lucky. Eggs are killed by dislodgement, infection, predation, and (in droughts) desiccation. If all goes well, most eggs will survive and develop. All seldom does. Often 80 percent are killed for one reason or another. A "lucky" nest will often suffer 50 percent mortality before eggs even hatch. Unlucky can mean virtually complete mortality. Those youngsters lucky enough to survive their entire freshwater phase and smoltification, of course, must eventually move into the ocean to try their luck anew.

On the road, looking out at the ocean as we drive along, it is both easy and impossible to imagine those fish out there, the young ones that have moved out into that great immensity, the adults on their way home. The waters look leaden under an overcast sky, while the west slope of the forests still lie in early-morning shadow. Paul Engelmeyer and I turn off the coast highway and onto a loose gravel road.

The tires come to rest in a little cul-de-sac next to a copse of blackberry bushes bent with the weight of fruit and heavy dewdrops. A few steps away, Ten Mile Creek is mumbling incoherently to the early-morning mist. A mallard lands, quacking happily in the light drizzle just begun.

Filling the space between a pair of muddy boots and a blue cap stands Steve Johnson, early for work in the heart of the most beautiful spot left on the central Oregon coast. He is already examining some young fish swimming in buckets on the tailgate of his pickup, producing a nearly endless stream of numbers generated by measuring each almost identical fish, already engaged in the meditative tedium and peacefulness of doing science.

A gaunt and mustachioed man, Steve Johnson earns his bread as a fisheries research biologist with the Oregon Department of Fish and Wildlife. His truck is a laboratory on wheels, filled with buckets, coolers, backpacks, and electro-shockers, used for counting fish by stunning them.

The creek has grassy banks, overhanging hemlocks, sharp meanders, gravel bars, and a muted green tranquillity. Near where we stand, the stream water comes around a bend and pauses as it eddies, then shoots past a riffle where a shunt puts most of the stream through Steve's fish trap.

Steve's assistant Bill Wornakie, wading ashore from the trap, holds aloft a bucket of little fish, saying, "Lunch!" The raftlike trap, held in place in the current by guy ropes, is a clever affair, its main operating component a large, auger-like aluminum screw through which much of the streamflow is being funneled. Recent rains have swollen and quickened the stream, and the creaking, cone-shaped screw is slowly rotating in the current. Like a revolving door, the screw prevents fish from going back upstream after they've entered, and a perforated holding box at its end retains the young smolts.

Steve is piecing together a picture of the life and times of young salmon in this forest. Despite the importance salmon have to people, astonishingly little is known about their survival in various habitats. Downstream migration is now at its annual peak, and the trap—one part of a much larger project—is helping him understand how many have survived freshwater and are leaving for the ocean, which pounds the beach just a few hundred yards downstream. Steve wants to find out how many salmon this stream can support, and what the limiting factors are. "And if we can get funding to count adults coming back, we could really understand both the fresh and the marine survival rates."

Paul says that should have happened decades ago.

This morning, his trap has caught eighty-seven little coho, thirty-one baby steelhead, and a six-inch coastal cutthroat trout that has become all silvery-soft for the sea. As Steve and Bill confer, I bend to look into the newly arrived pailful of small fish. They spook, racing in fright around their confines. Seven pails and tubs, with different kinds of fish sorted into each, sit on the tailgate of Steve's truck. One bucket has seventeen two-year-old steelheads. Another has smaller steelheads. Young cohos similarly sorted by size await their involuntary contribution to science in different containers. Many are halfway to turning silver. Some rest in the bottom of the plastic tubs, some hang at mid-depths.

They seem a frail but independent lot, all pointing in different directions, not schooling up like team players. They project no hint of their strength, latent determination, or ability to migrate far into the ocean and return years later. These little fish that have in them such power to survive look only delicate, vulnerable.

Steve is painstakingly measuring and tallying them, one and all, taking a few scales from some fish in each size group for microscopic analysis, so he can learn the ages at which they are entering the sea. Length alone does not reveal age, because growth depends on food abundance, which varies.

Not all the migrating fish find their way into the trap, so Steve and Bill are marking some by clipping tiny pieces of fin. They will release the marked fish upstream, and from the proportion that get recaught, they will estimate the number the trap misses. Steve is saving the fin slivers that he is clipping, explaining, "We're using these little pieces of fins to look at mitochondrial DNA and the genetics of salmon stocks in streams up and down the coast." Steve works with an appealing economy of effort that I have noticed in the best field science, an attempt to learn the most from every action that disturbs the wild creatures under study, so as to minimize stress to them.

Nonetheless, I ask how much this entire treatment might harm all these little fish, since Steve wants to catch and handle most of the juvenile salmon that are leaving this drainage for the ocean, and I am noticing that the ones that have been on the tailgate for a while seem sluggish compared to the newly caught smolts in Bill's pail.

Steve explains, "These guys are under a mild anesthetic, so they don't beat themselves against the buckets, so we can work without hurting them."

At a little past nine o'clock, more crew—mostly men in their twenties and early thirties—arrive in another gear-filled truck. It is Monday morning, and they are a few minutes late. One yawns, "The coffee has worn off." Two of them immediately urinate next to their truck.

Steve says, "Stan, there's a couple of lamprey ammocoetes here. Do you want them?"

"Sure, I haven't had breakfast yet."

Steve says to me, "I see it's going to be a long week."

I haven't had breakfast yet either, so I pick a few of the many surrounding blackberries and lob them into my mouth. Stan, wearing a T-shirt bearing a skull and two white crossed salmon, with the words "Spawn Til You Die," comes to collect the ammocoetes: larval lampreys several inches long, still lacking the eyes they will have when they become eel-like adults that fasten themselves to other fish, parasitically rasping flesh with jawless, tooth-festooned, sucker-disk mouths. In the sweet dream of the natural world, nightmares can sneak up on you.

After a brief discussion of the day's plans, the newly arrived crew members—including Stan and his lampreys—go farther upstream to work.

When Steve has measured and released his little fish, he and I go to another site. Steve's research requires counting juvenile coho, steelhead, and cutthroats throughout this entire drainage, so he can begin understanding how survival relates to habitat quality in different areas. In most sites, he counts fish by snorkeling in pools.

As he readies his gear, Steve tells me about the fishes' personalities. "When you get in the pool, the coho practically come to greet you. Cutthroat are much touchier. If you don't spot them right away they're, like—Poof! Gone. Usually you'll see a lot of tiny trout and maybe a few coho at the very back of the pool. There may be a big middle stretch with few fish. And when you get right up to the pool's head where the riffles flow in, all of a sudden you'll see a congregation of small fish again. What's interesting is that in a pool with a lot of fallen wood in the middle, you'll also have fish in and around that wood structure. So you've added a lot of fish to a pool if you add wood."

Though the water runs only a few inches deep, reflected sunlight and the current's muscular ripples make it almost impossible to see fish. And so Steve dons his dry suit and snorkeling gear and enters the cold water in a stream section flowing just about deep enough for him to slide through, but not deep enough to float in. Moving on his belly like a seal, he works upstream. He looks absurd.

I carry Steve's notebook to the end of the pool, standing by to record what he sees. Meanwhile, I look up. A luxuriance of ferns grows from the high rock wall along the bank. With the canopy of trees closing overhead, most of the stream lies shaded or sparsely dappled with light. Moss hangs like drapery. Everything seems quiet and lovely. Salmon are fish—ocean fish—and they live in water. But when they are spawning and living their childhoods in streams, they are truly forest animals.

Steve calls, "A dozen little coho, four really nice ten-inch cutthroat, a couple of steelhead, and about a half dozen trout too young to identify." He places his mask on his forehead and wipes his face. "Not big numbers."

Steve glances up appraisingly, explaining, "See, this all looks very nice around here, and it's not bad habitat, but the problem is, there's gotten to be so *much* habitat like this—mostly shallow riffles. No pools, no gouges, no scours behind big logs. Hardly *any* fallen wood to shelter young fish from the current." In the 1930s and '40s, timber companies came in and took out a lot of the large wood. That wood was important, for adult salmon as well as juveniles. "A consequence of losing the big trees is that nice spawning gravels are now confined to the lower drainage, where the streambed flattens and the smaller stuff settles out.

"If we had more wood there would also be better places for young fish." Steve explains that in summer, young steelhead prefer fast riffles, rapids, "and trenchier sections of water like scour pools." Coho like quiet pools instead, because they feed on forest insects falling to the surface. But when November rains begin, all the young fish must seek shelter and protection from high-velocity winter flows—in deep pools caused by large trees fallen across the stream or in scour pools behind big root wads.

We walk on to a place where several logs block half the channel. The stream now swerves around them, but in the spill and scour behind the wood the swirling waters have gouged a deep, quiet pool aside the main current. Sure enough, several juvenile coho salmon, which were holding quietly in the clear, slow water above the clean gravel, move off to hide in the shadows of the wood at our approach.

"Unfortunately, these are the kinds of pools that we don't have a lot of anymore. We've found that one of the main problems for young salmon is getting swept out of the river during high winter flows because there's no wood to hide behind." The winter deluges are like hurricanes, and the area behind a huge fallen tree is like a bunker, where little fish can hunker down and wait for the storm to pass. "In Cummins Creek, which still has a fair amount of wood complexity, winter survival is well over fifty percent. A lot of our streams have over-winter survival rates of only ten or twenty percent. But in streams where we've put a lot of wood back in, we've seen those overwinter survival rates jump up to forty or fifty percent." For baby fishes, deep pools formed by wood also offer cover from predators. In small streams flowing through healthy ancient forests, dead wood often covers half of the channel. Perhaps no other part of a stream except the water itself is as important to salmon as large fallen wood.

I follow Steve upstream, stepping over raccoon droppings packed with crayfish shells. A couple of dippers fly upstream, calling, and land with a heavy splat to stand upon gravel in an inch of water. They step in deeper and disappear, prowling along the bottom while walking underwater, unlike any other birds in the world.

And here before us upon a log half-fallen into the stream sprawls another living icon of the Northwest, neither salmon nor elk nor owl but an eight-inch banana slug. The wood of this log itself is habitat for the food of salmon, such as larval caddisflies (with their odd, Friar Tuck heads), stoneflies, craneflies, riffle beetles, and mayflies.

For many people it might seem a waste to let a valuable dead tree that could yield thousands of board feet of lumber die, fall, and get moved downstream to become a refuge for voles, truffles, salamanders, insects, and salmon, but it is a necessary, life-giving death.

Nothing like the great masses of wood that once characterized salmon streams remains today. In former times, the sight and bulk of a fallen tree could be shocking. Many trunks ten feet in diameter spanned two hundred feet of forest floor and river channel in the crumbling rigor of their repose. A single fallen tree could challenge a high-jumping salmon, and turn back a party of men.

When the U.S. Army Corps of Engineers was first set loose on western rivers in the late 1800s to improve navigability, they removed nearly ten thousand trees from the lower twelve miles of the Tillamook River. In those days, many "rivers" comprised a messy network of sloughs, islands, beaver ponds, and drift-log dams, with no identifiable main channel. In 1850, what is now "the" Willamette River flowed in five separate channels. In such river systems, tangles of trees and drifted limbs became entities with names like Wood Island or Snag Island, moving as a single woody raft during floods, sometimes entering the sea looking, indeed, like islands afloat—complete with bushes, trees, and flowers.

Conversely, after loggers removed trees from steep slopes, rains washed great masses of branches, bark, and other logging debris into waterways, choking streams and blocking salmon. Then, from the 1940s to the '70s, fishery managers aggressively removed such debris, viewing wood in water as unnatural. Stream "clearance" became dogma, consuming millions of dollars annually, sometimes 90 percent of funds allocated to habitat restoration. People wishing to help salmon overzealously removed even the larger trees that fish needed. Where all the logs were removed, spawning habitat immediately diminished, and fish populations declined.

Some of the "clearest" streams are artifacts not of intentional clearing but of old-time log transport. In the early decades of logging, lumbermen backed up streams behind temporary "splash dams," to float logs down toward mills. When enough logs had been brought into the pond (some impassable dams were in place long enough to obliterate salmon runs), lumbermen removed the splash dam and the logs rushed downstream. The resulting wood-filled torrent could scour stream bottoms to bare rock, wrecking salmon habitat. Thousands of splash dams operated over decades, and many stream bottoms are still slick bedrock for significant stretches, devoid of gravel for would-be spawning salmon.

We break for lunch. Steve scans the trees appreciatively, saying, "This watershed hasn't been hit as hard as some have. It doesn't have major water-temperature problems. A lot of people don't understand how serious temperature is." As stream water warms in direct sunlight after clear-cutting, increased temperature increases the oxygen needs of fish. But warmer water holds less oxygen. When oxygen need exceeds oxygen content, fish begin dying. "When you start getting seventy-five-degree water flowing through streams, you're just not going to have salmon. These streams here can still raise fish, but without the big wood they can't raise as many as they used to. There are between six and ten thousand juvenile coho in Ten Mile. It could have twenty to thirty thousand if the habitat was improved."

As he unpacks his food, Steve says, "We've got big habitat problems here in freshwater. And changes in ocean conditions have lowered salmon survival."

An abrupt change in ocean conditions in 1983, for instance, had drastic effects on salmon. The density of zooplankton eaten by salmon dropped two-thirds. Competing species such as warm-water mackerel invaded from the south. Normal prey species like anchovies and herring declined, and predation on salmon themselves by larger fish, mammals, and birds probably intensified. Nearly 60 percent of adult coho salmon died in the ocean off Oregon and Washington that year, and those that survived were the smallest on record, laying fewer eggs before they, too, completed a difficult life and died.

These changes in oceanic conditions result from large-scale changes in a cold current called the West Wind Drift, coming from the vicinity of Japan and hitting North America around Vancouver Island. If a lot of the current's cool, nutrient-rich water then goes to the south, you get more plankton and good fish survival off the West Coast. When the bias pushes to the north, as in recent years, the opposite prevails here (but fish in Alaska benefit). Driving this bias is a weather system called the Aleutian Low, and helping drive the low is the Southern Oscillation (also called El Niño), an atmospheric pressure wave moving back and forth across the Pacific Ocean that affects weather worldwide. If a shift in air pressure intensifies the Aleutian Low, southerly winds are drawn up the west coast of North America, pushing warm water northward, deflecting the West Wind Drift to the north. This warming reduces plankton production in Northwest coastal waters, and for salmon there, the world turns from tough to inimical.

The temperature shift influencing the Northwest from the early 1980s through the late 1990s has been the most prolonged on record. For nearly a decade a very intense Aleutian Low has pulled a lot of warm air into here, bringing poor ocean conditions for salmon and causing drought, affecting the streams. So these temperature shifts affect both juveniles and adults, both in the ocean and in streams.

Steve says, "They get it going and coming. But salmon have coped with changing ocean conditions for millions of years. The problem is, we've known these warmed ocean conditions can happen—even if we couldn't say when—but catching seventy-five percent of the fish out there each year left no margin for error. Then, when the water warmed, we tried to continue fishing at a rate we'd gotten used to. And what happened? Coho spawner numbers this year are one-fourth of the previous all-time low. I mean, it's just fallen off the charts. Some of the hatcheries are afraid they won't even get their brood stock back. As of this year commercial coho fishing may already be a thing of the past. Maybe it's just all caught up with us."

We are seated on a log and I am listening with my head down, idly scratching at the forest floor with a stick. I ask whether the salmon can come back after all this.

Steve pauses for a thoughtful bite of his sandwich, then says, "You can make it complicated or you can make it simple. The fish need three things: one, cool clean water; two, clean gravel to spawn in; and three, physically complex stream structure. And you can't have just two out of three. Then, if you don't catch too many in the ocean, you'll have fish in the streams."

He takes another bite and ruminates a moment, chewing things up finely in his mind. "To directly answer your question about whether they can come back: We don't have to lose the salmon in these streams if we don't want to. We know what we need to know to have salmon. But the damage that was done to these basins isn't going to be cured overnight." He looks at me with an expression that seems somehow both declarative and inquiring. "So how's that for a wishy-washy answer?"

"As a scientist, that's what I expect from a scientist."

Steve has work to do, and I, too, must get going. I walk out alone downstream, stepping from stone to stone, splashing mindfully around pools I now know are populated with salmon children, noticing the sizes of nearby trees and the variety of gravels, and feeling rueful about the lack of dead wood in the salmon forest. Live and learn.

Valley of Giants, Mountains of Gods

Fran Recht's modest hillside house features an immodest view. Through the telescope on her kitchen table, you can sweep the Pacific looking for whales, but the telescope is often unnecessary. Fran is on the phone, and my gaze drifts out the window, beyond the kelp patches, as a gray whale blows a tall column of vapor. The gray's recovery is one of the most spectacular successes of the Endangered Species Act and CITES, and the new whales make a joyous sight. Recht works for the Pacific States Marine Fisheries Commission, and her job is to make people understand that fish need habitat. By now I understand that many of the salmon swimming the Pacific Ocean somewhere out beyond those whales were spawned in shaded streams in deep forests, so I understand her T-shirt, which says, "It's a little-known fact that fish grow on trees."

Fran and I arrive at Gleneden Beach Airport just as Jane Nickolai and her passenger are landing. Our plan is to get an aerial view of a bit of ancient salmon-friendly forest known as the Valley of the Giants, and I am excited about seeing it. If you talk to people in New England about fisheries, they tell you about netters, long-liners, rod-and-reelers; they tell you about *fishing,* mostly. In the Pacific Northwest, if you talk to people about ocean fisheries, they tell you about salmon, and about forests, about timber exports, about farm subsidies, about cows, dams, grain barges, about almost everything *except* fishing, because all these other things—*more* than fishing, it seems—affect salmon. Come here seeking the sea, and you will soon find yourself inland seeking to understand the forces transforming it. It might seem as though you had stood upon the beach and asked of the ocean, "Tell me about your salmon," and in response an enraged sea hurled a great tsunami, sweeping you off your feet and depositing you high in the coastal mountains.

Jane, a tall, athletically built woman in her midthirties with a brown pageboy haircut, emerges from her blue-and-white plane. A silver eagle ring adorns one hand. Her leather belt is tied in front, holding green jeans snugly to her hips. Jane is a graphic designer but is working as a full-time mommy for a while, describing her two-year-old boy as "the most wonderful person I've ever met, right up there with my husband." Jane's husband, in fact, got her into flying. "I wanted to learn how to fly," she recounts, "but it cost a thousand dollars. I never thought I would see a thousand dollars. And I never thought I could be smart enough to do the math involved. Then I met my husband, who was a glider pilot. He was full of life, and he never asked, 'Can we?' With him it was always, 'Let's do this, let's do that.' I decided I wanted to have enough money and be smart enough, and so I did it." Jane's vivaciousness is instantly appealing and infectious.

Less exuberant than Jane is a forester who doesn't want to tell me her name or who she works for, because, she says, "I'd be fired before I got back from lunch if they found out I was here with you all."

Okay, enough said.

I ask if I can call her Ann, and she manages a worried smile.

We lift off and swing out over Oregon's central coast. A wide line of foaming breakers edges the dark Pacific, giving the continent a creamy border. Houses dot the banks along a blue-ribbon river. From this perspective, the visual impression is of patterns, quite pretty. From altitude, the finished works of humanity always seem placid.

A checkerboard patchwork immediately appears on the mountains as we fly inland. In some directions, more than 50 percent of the land has been cleared of its trees. Many of the clear-cuts are so recent that only the brown of newly exposed topsoil shows. I see no evidence of selective cutting, and when I ask Ann, she says, "It's basically clear-cut or nothing."

I haven't seen anything yet. We come over a ridge, and the world changes for me forever. I say only, "Good Lord."

"Take a look at *that*."

"Good Lord."

Behold an endeavor of destruction so great as to first confuse the mind, a far-and-wide landscape of mud, stumps, slash, bark, and a few green sprigs. Over twenty-three thousand acres—nearly forty square miles—every tree has recently been cut down. The women say the land has been "slicked." The visual effect is quite startling. I'm searching for a word that does not sound hysterical, but, actually, the sight is shocking.

Jane, who I can hardly pay attention to, asks if I'd like to take pictures.

I decline. I won't need pictures to remember this, unfortunately.

Ann, looking down, quietly breathes, "All brown and bloody. This was trees not long ago."

Quoth Shakespeare: "O! pardon me, thou bleeding piece of earth, that I am meek and gentle with these butchers."

We go over a stream. On private lands such as these, tree cutters logged right down to the water's edge until recent laws—which they fought—required them to leave standing "buffers" along waterways. The buffer below looks ridiculous—a narrow, grudging, Mohawk of trees, in brown surroundings. Parts of the stream have no buffer at all, their silted bottoms warming in the sun.

But look over there; the *highways* are lined with nice trees—called beauty strips—left as screens. Screens to hide the nudity. It is false modesty. From your car, you see the forests of the Great Northwest. From the air, you see the land forcibly stripped naked, the stump-studded hills standing in goose bumps, suffering from exposure. The cutters won't willingly leave trees along the streams to keep the water cool and clean for salmon, but they will voluntarily leave trees along the roads, to fool us into complacency.

Jane says, "I've been flying all up and down the countryside for about six years now, watching the trees disappearing. I feel responsible, because my father worked for Weyerhaeuser and raised us by cutting down the forest. Maybe I can help put something back by letting people see just how little is left."

Just how little is left is what I am seeing. Jane, ostensibly so we can get a good look at this cut, is circling a bit too enthusiastically. I look at her and she says, "I love this feeling of standing on a wing as we turn." It feels like the kind of fairground rides I won't go on anymore. Fran's face is getting pale, while Ann, not looking too good herself, falls silent. My stomach starts bubbling. I notice the airsickness bag. It says, "Suggestions to reduce airsickness: Regulate vent for more air. Concentrate on a distant object." The only "distant" object I can concentrate on right now is the all-too-distant airport.

Jane straightens out. After a few seconds of deep dizziness the world comes back into focus, and I am looking at stump fields zigzagged by logging roads. Certain slopes are so truck-trod, denuded, and eroded, that they superficially resemble new strip mines. I am getting agitated. I recall an article quoting one forester saying, "Simply put, clear-cutting is deforestation." Another forester said, "Generally, if logging looks bad, it is bad." Well, this sure looks bad.

This deforestation is not forestry. I have visited commercial forests in Appalachia where logging is so exquisitely managed that it takes an expert to point out and explain where they cut. There, foresters select trees with skill and planning and remove logs from a forest. After logging, a forest remains. Here, the forest is removed from the hillsides. Afterward, the forest is gone.

Ann explains that when lumber companies remove the forest, they replace it with a tree plantation, not a forest. The replanted trees will all be the same age and species. Species not lending themselves to commercial tree farming are not replanted, and she says that despite what we hear about planting trees forever, "by the third rotation we're seeing a big difference in quality because of soil exhaustion." Trees that begin to mature at about three hundred years of age are taken at one-tenth that, cut the way a lawn is mowed. "If they want pulp, they cut at thirty years. If they want boards, at forty."

In that brief interval, Fran says, "no habitat will develop for all the interior forest species that need old trees, like the pileated woodpecker, the pine marten, flying squirrel, spotted owl, salmon—"

Can't we just worry about salmon for now, kind of take one thing at a time? The answer is no, because everything has been taken *away* together.

At twenty-eight hundred feet, we are flying just below a cloud ceiling that is whiting out the highest peaks. Over a clear-cut several square miles in extent, Fran points out a draw where the land has been sliding into a creek, saying, "It hurts fish by clogging the gravels."

Oh, yes, fish. I had almost forgotten about fish while I was looking at this. Silt can be murder on salmon eggs, slowing water circulation and thus strangling salmon embryos. Much of the silt comes from log roads. No one in the world builds more roads than the U.S. Forest Service: 360,000 miles of roads (and building) lace and filigree our national forests—seven times the aggregate length of America's interstate highway system. In northwest California, western Oregon, and western Washington—salmon country—thirty million acres of commercial forestlands are spaghettied with about a quarter million miles of roads (at last count, more than enough to circle the earth nine times and occupying twice the area of Delaware in road surface alone). Crossing streams many hundreds of thousands of times, logging roads can cause frequent mud slides, increasing the amount of silt and sand entering streams by as much as a thousandfold.

A deep green spot draws our attention and we hook toward it. As we near, a patch of gigantic trees comes vaulting up as though reaching to catch our plane, the way they snatch the sky's very clouds and turn them to their own purposes. These trees absolutely tower far above anything green on the surrounding land— anything that passes for trees in normal conversation and commerce. We are all looking not only *at* them, but down through them, through the overarching canopy into deep shadows many shades and layers of green, into a plush organic sponge of Life, holding itself up vertically off the mountain. Seeing these trees rising up from the land and really reaching for you brings a surprising solemnity.

Jane breaks our silence by saying almost belatedly, "Oh, that is some *nice* old stuff down there."

Ann adds, "This is a nice little pocket of old growth. This could be it—the Valley of the Giants."

That is the impression. Not a huge area. Not a whole valley. A pocket—a remnant of the forest that once blanketed this entire coastal region of the Great Pacific Northwest. It is very striking. But part of what makes this grove so striking is how small it is.

Timbermen of business refer to such old trees (typically they do not refer to entire forests) as "overmature" or—my favorite—"decadent fiber."

As Emerson wrote: "To speak truly, few adult persons can see nature. Most persons do not see the sun."

We fly on.

The rare and occasional skeleton of an ancient tree stands dead—spared the cutting crews' saws through virtue of its own deformed body or disfigurement, such as those forked by lightning. They impart a comparative scale for metering the sticklike plantation trees surrounding them. These are 4-F trunks, having avoided the export draft to Asia in the Northwest's undeclared forest equivalent of the Vietnam War.

Fran says eagles and ospreys like the big dead standing trees. "There's a nice old snag over there."

Jane turns, saying, "What did you call me?" Still smiling, she says she doesn't want to continue north and east, because the ceiling is dropping.

The clouds suddenly fall down right on top of us. Now Jane looks a little worried. Which means I feel very worried. We descend rapidly to just beneath the clouds, with decent visibility of the scarified land below—unfortunately.

Jane slows the plane and straightens out, then heads us out toward the coast. The ceiling lifts, bringing our moods up with it.

We've all had enough of forest destruction for this bright afternoon, and we head toward the Drift Creek Wilderness Area, which appears dark green before us. Ann says that the 630,000-acre Siuslaw National Forest has set aside about 20,000 acres—3 percent—as wilderness areas, along Drift Creek, Rock Creek, and Cummins Creek, the spot I visited with Paul Engelmeyer.

Jane climbs through light clouds to reach the altitude legally required over the wilderness area. After all, we are not allowed to disturb the trees.

This wilderness is a respectable chunk of forest. The clear-cuts are in the distance now, and even from the air, you can scan unbroken forest for a fair interval here. Thank God and the people who fought for it. Ann says this is one of the nicest areas of the Coast Range.

"What's it like farther along the coast, up in Washington?" I ask, afraid to find out.

Piles and piles of logs awaiting export occupy nearly a full mile of waterfront docks and yards at Weyerhaeuser's facility in Aberdeen, Washington. From the air, it is an impressive sight.

Rich McDonald, himself a former logger, is pointing out the window at it, telling me over the headphones, "See this? This is why more log trucks than I've ever seen are running on Washington's Olympic Peninsula. This is the first time I've seen this yard full, and look at it—it's plugged."

As I try wrapping my mind around the number of logs I am looking at, McDonald is saying, "When they say environmentalists should shut up because they use the wood and paper, they're pulling your leg."

Cranes are busily loading ships bound for Asia, as trucks steadily deliver more fresh-cut logs. McDonald continues, "We will never *see* wood or paper from all *these* logs. We're just exporting our raw natural resources and all we get at home is the unemployment that results. I don't understand why society sits back and lets these companies ruin all these communities. And then when environmentalists say, 'Save the last ten percent,' they're made out to be the enemy of the worker. In America, we've been conned to thinking it's the God-given right of industry to giveth and taketh away whenever they feel like it. In the end, they've left the rural Northwest empty, with little future."

Toward the end of a time when people could grow up in a part of the landscape and call that place home forever, Rich McDonald grew up on the South Fork of the Coquille River in southern Oregon's Coos County. The Coos Bay Lumber Company, which Rich's dad worked for, sold out to one of the lumber giants. "Once they took over, they closed up the mill in a matter of a few weeks, and then took off everything that was still standing and said, basically, 'We've got all your logs. Bye-bye, and you can kiss ours.' Thousands of truckloads of logs came out, and I noticed the fish runs slowly declining. Now, the salmon, the steelhead, the sea-run trout, they're just—. My brother is still in the logging business, and he agrees that the logging went way overboard."

Rich himself no longer works in logging. Sharing Jane Nickolai's feeling that he "needed to give something back," he returned to school for law enforcement, and after stints with the state police and National Marine Fisheries Service, he now works for the United States Fish and Wildlife Service. He looks the part: a stocky man, wearing the law enforcer's mustache and straight brown hair that seem as much a part of his uniform as his sunglasses.

This airplane is owned and piloted by Sydney Schneidman, M.D., head of the emergency department in the naval hospital in Bremerton, Washington. Today, wearing blue jeans and leather sandals, he doesn't look very clinical, but he brings an interesting emergency-room perspective to the landscape below, as though he just can't stand to see it hemorrhaging without proper intervention, care, and a chance at recovery.

Accompanied by the engine's buzzing drone, we are meandering generally north along the Olympic Peninsula of coastal Washington, across rivers and valleys that tilt mostly west to the Pacific Ocean. The writer John G. Mitchell has said, "It was and is the sort of place that inflates a person's expectations. It seems to promise more than any place should. Look first to the names—Olympic, Olympus. What a mythic scale those words imply. A sanctuary of the gods. A temple of Zeus. A showcase for the superlative."

Yes, but sensible people understand that there must be limits to every expectation, even in the shadow of a mountain named Olympus on a peninsula named Olympic.

Mountains in clouds dominate the peninsula, one twisting ridge after another, leaping from sea level to eight thousand feet in a god's wink. All year, glaciers and snowfields weep rivers through deep valleys. The rivers follow the maze toward the sea. And in that dark maze live the beings reaching closest to the heavens and the gods themselves. The world's largest surviving Douglas-fir resides in the Queets River drainage. Down the Hoh stands a western redcedar more than twenty feet in diameter. In the Quinault Valley's pantheon repose the biggest Alaska-cedar anywhere (including Alaska), the biggest silver fir, the largest vine maple, and a western hemlock and a Sitka spruce as tall as any other. You'd think the throne room would look like the Parthenon at the Acropolis, but it's a disheveled place, full of moss, fallen wood, and the sprawl of baby trees, and sometimes, in places, it still reeks with dead, spawned-out salmon. (The Hamma Hamma River, meaning "stinky stinky" in the native tongue, is nowadays nearly devoid of the multitude of salmon whose rotting carcasses once raised such a holy stench.)

Dr. Schneidman says into our phones, "When we cross this river here—the Skokomish—just *wait* till you see all the silt!" Where clean cobbles belong, a slug of brown mud, too easily visible from the air, clogs the riverbed. "Look at that landslide going right into the stream. People wonder why there's no salmon?"

Dirt and shining mud roads lace the visible clear-cuts, etching and engraving the land like age wrinkles and worry lines, leaving the earth's surface looking frangible, fissile. A road crew is working its way farther up a ridge beyond the cut, pushing a dirt swath through the trees, into a hitherto roadless area. In velvet mists day and night, this forest into which the bulldozer is digging like a heartworm stood for ten thousand years. The road will carry tree-cutting machinery and log trucks up the slopes and into the forest like an insuperable infection in the blood. And down these slopes along these trails the forest will flow off the land in the beds of trucks like rain finding its way into streams. Off the land with them will come the jobs. Down the forest will flow, like the last young generations of doomed races of salmon from warmed and silted rivers.

The Olympic Mountains rise abruptly alongside. Below lies the open expanse of Olympic National Forest. "Look at this." Dr. Schneidman gestures with his chin around us. "Totally denuded." At every point of the compass for several miles around, no living trees stand. In places so steep that the cost of roads would make logging unprofitable, $4 million helicopters that burn three gallons of fuel a minute will fly out four-ton logs. "Your federal government at work, managing our lands."

As John G. Mitchell wrote in the late 1980s, "I had always held the Redwood cuts of northern California to be the worst of the worst, until I saw the view here in Olympic Doug-fir country. These weren't cuts. These were landslides. Battlefields and moonscapes. Scylla and Charybdis, the far flanks of Hell. We're talking harvests that are five, ten, or fifteen years old, maybe, and most places hardly sprouting a weed. This is what the Forest Service calls sustained yield."

California congressman George Miller has also been disturbed by national forests in the Pacific Northwest. Said Miller: "In spite of repeated assurances by the Forest Service, the forests we've cut down are not growing back. The Forest Service does not check whether new saplings are growing after they are three years old, they do not check forest inventories against actual on-the-ground surveys, and they have not stopped cutting in forest areas that they know will not grow back."

The Forest Service manages public lands, our lands, and the relationship between public and private lands has a history reaching back over a century. In the sepia-colored, top-hat times of yesteryear, Honest Abe's Congress dangled a thirty-nine-million-acre carrot upwind of the Northern Pacific Railroad as an incentive for it to lay tracks from Lake Superior to Puget Sound. It was the biggest giveaway of public land in U.S. history, and no one could have guessed that it would have a profound effect on salmon in the vast Pacific Ocean. The railroads then sold much of it to private timber companies, who amassed millions of acres.

It did not take long for western timber barons to acquire the appetite for excess and contempt for public interests that have become their culture, and as early as the 1880s officials in federal and state governments and nascent citizen conservation groups began trying to defend themselves from an appetite out of control. In 1891 Congress gave the president the right to establish forest reserves "to preserve the forests therein from destruction," and Presidents Benjamin Harrison and Grover Cleveland drew lines around forty million acres. Theodore Roosevelt added millions more in the interests of the public and the future, and he created the Forest Service to manage these lands.

The lands were not the choice cuts. Higher, rockier, snowier, and farther from river transport, these lands had, on an average square mile, half the good-quality timber of privately held lowlands. They became our "National Forests."

These were not parks; they were set aside for the wood. But when and how that wood would be taken out would be under the say-so of a government of, by, and for the people.

That was the idea, anyway. And it enraged the timber companies. In 1907, they pressured Congress into wresting from the president the authority to create national forests. The bill passed and landed on Roosevelt's desk. At the urging of Gifford Pinchot, the Forest Service's founding father, Roosevelt stuffed another sixteen million acres under the public mattress the week before he signed the law.

Pinchot was a user. He believed parks were "sentimental." Nonetheless, Pinchot believed deeply that it was up to the Forest Service—this is important—to replace the rootless, boom-and-bust, cut-and-run logging on private lands with stable timber economies supporting stable communities, by virtue of a continuing supply of timber from the national forests. "In the administration of the forest reserves it must be clearly borne in mind that all land is to be devoted to its most productive use for the permanent good of the whole people, and not for the temporary benefit of individuals or companies."

Through the 1950s, the timber industry had lobbied to keep the federal timber uncut and off the market, to keep prices up. The national forests were long considered to be set aside for the timber famine that would ultimately result from the kind of overcutting that was being done on private lands. Now the predicted famine was here. The annual timber cut from federal land quadrupled between the mid-1940s and the mid-1960s.

This fathered a new era, in which major logging corporations were born with a congenital dependency on publicly owned old-growth forest. Some big logging companies came into this world without a stitch of acreage—no timberlands of their own, at all. The federal government became their supplier. Cutting on public land by private companies began exceeding cutting on private land. By the 1980s, virtually all the lowland ancient forest that had stood for millennia (except the pockets in national parks and legally designated "wilderness" areas) was gone or marked for elimination.

When a recession depressed wood prices, the timber industry laid off thousands of workers and lobbied to be released from contracts so it would not have to pay for trees it had once lobbied to cut. Even then, between 1980 and 1985, the cutting in national forests was 60 percent faster than the rate of tree growth. When the economy picked up, the wood industry lobbied this time for more federal trees to cut. And, again, they got what they demanded.

Trees on public lands are a good buy. You should be charging more. In most of the National Forests, the Forest Service loses money on timber sales. We pay more to oversee the sales than the tree buyers pay for the trees. The White House Council of Economic Advisors admitted that the Service lost $234 million in 1975. According to forester and retired Congressional researcher Bob Wolf, the Forest Service lost $5.1 billion between 1983 and 1996, averaging losses of nearly $400 million per year. Other loss estimates have ranged to over $700 million a year in the public forests of the United States of Amerrycut. As the poet William Blake said: "A fool sees not the same tree a wise man sees."

On certain recently clear-cut hillsides lie woodpiles of "slash" tens of yards in diameter, like enormous beaver houses. They await the torch.

I mentally estimate the cutting to be 90 percent of the land in view and, without telling Rich my estimate, ask him for his. He says, "That's a bit hard to figure. I would say, uh, about ninety percent."

Our visual impression here reflects the region. Satellite maps show that between 85 and 90 percent of the lush ancient forests of North America's Pacific Northwest have been cut down. Most of what remains clenches federal soil.

I ask, "Why such thorough deforestation in such a short time?"

Rich answers, "A lot of the remaining timber on federal land was tied up to protect the remaining spotted owls." When the owl got listed under the Endangered Species Act, logging near their nests was restricted. Enforcement was spotty, and the Forest Service issued lots of exemption permits so logging could proceed near nests anyway, but fear spread that further protections would reduce the supply of logs. "So," Rich explains, "prices are spectacular right now—we've *never* seen prices this high—and the thinking is, 'Let's cut it *now!*' They're laughing all the way to the bank. Financially, the owl listing was the best thing that happened to them. The spotted owl has made some people extraordinarily wealthy. Beyond-comprehension wealthy."

Schneidman adds tersely, "The owl gave timber companies the perfect cover."

Throughout the 1980s, timber companies cut lands owned by the American people at record rates, while selling more and more raw logs overseas. Oregon and Washington lost about twenty thousand lumber jobs to exports and automation. A 16 percent increase in wood taken off public lands accompanied a 15 percent drop in logging and milling jobs. While wood prices—and company profits—rose to record highs, management exacted pay cuts up to 25 percent.

Rich says tightly, "They should be giving the processing jobs to people in mills here. Allowing them to export raw logs makes no sense to me *at all.* As far as those big lumber companies that show no obligation to the mill workers and have gone entirely to exporting, well, I have no respect for them. I grew up in the woods, and I saw towns decline because companies came through and moved on. Many of the mills closed for reasons that had nothing to do with the spotted owl. This has been happening since day one. It's not because of the *owl.*"

By the late 1980s, when less than 15 percent of the tattered ancient forests remained, several environmental groups put this soft-plumaged bird into their sling and confronted the Goliath. They argued that the northern spotted owl needed ancient forests and was becoming endangered by their disappearance. There is no endangered habitat act, so in a legal sense the remaining federal ancient forests needed the owl.

The approach worked. Sort of. After legal eagles locked talons several times, the spotted owl was listed as threatened in 1990. In a sense the federal government was forced to acknowledge that the spotted owl had taken a number and was seated patiently in oblivion's waiting room.

Implications of deforestation went far beyond the owl, but the owl attracted more than its share of headlines and attention. Many species suffered from forest destruction—salmon included. Yet in the din over the owl even conservationists almost totally overlooked the salmon who were quietly blinking out in run after run, stream after stream.

Part of the reason the owl got airplay was that it was the perfect scapegoat, handed to the timber industry on a silver platter. Hyping the protections provided on federal land for the owl, the companies were able to dodge responsibility for job losses due to mechanization and exports, and pin the blame on environmentalists. The northern spotted owl became the biopolitical punching bag of the 1990s, the snail darter of the air.

Using owls instead of salmon as the flagship species for trying to save the remaining ancient forests might well be the largest single tactical error the conservation community has ever made, even though the case was on very firm biological and procedural ground. Biologically, the owl could carry all the other values associated with ancient forests. Politically, it could not.

The spotted owl fight engendered a fomenting backlash in which all the arguments over forests, salmon, other creatures, ethics, aesthetics, and social responsibilities could be cast aside and one bird could become the lightning rod for a public-relations caricaturing that pitted owls against people, and environmentalists against jobs—against the ENTIRE ECONOMY! This pitch would have been much more difficult to sell had a threatened salmon been hurled at Goliath instead of an owl. With salmon, it would have been jobs versus jobs—at least a level playing field on which to argue the biological and legal merits of protecting remaining forests.

Rich whistles. "Look at these steep-slope clear-cuts!" Landslides dripping like paint off logging roads are slouching into streams. The Wynoochee River slides beneath our wings. A red-tailed hawk sails by below us. Most of the clear-cut hills bear scattered, bleached bones of trees: leftover slash and some abandoned damaged logs. Some hillsides are light green with a thin veneer of new vegetation. Others are dense with "dog hair"—young, planted coniferous trees seven to twenty-five years old, growing tightly together on wildlife-unfriendly plantations sprayed with herbicides to kill off hardwoods that might try to sprout.

Juvenile salmon and the creatures they eat are sometimes killed by herbicides and insecticides that get into streams. Sometimes the effects are subtle, such as a reduced ability to capture food, avoid predators, or hold a place in the current. These effects can be caused by spraying at recommended levels, and a salmon living in a thin soup of toxic pesticides might not feel quite right, like a person on chemotherapy—but bed rest is not an option for a salmon. The Pacific Fishery Management Council wrote, "We are concerned that coastal salmon runs may be suffering injury from . . . the widespread use of herbicides." Herbicides have been banned in national forests since 1984, after they were strongly implicated in cancers that had begun appearing among people taking drinking water from seemingly pristine forest streams. But they are widely used on private lands and commonly detected in stream water.

Just past the Humptulips River, huge trees suddenly leap skyward toward us. Rich says, "This is real old-growth. Probably an owl pair saved this piece."

The owls don't always win. A colleague of Rich McDonald's, another logger turned law-enforcement agent named Ed Wickersham, told me a story recently: "A while back, I initiated an investigation for an Endangered Species Act violation. Weyerhaeuser had apparently destroyed a spotted owl nest. I'd gotten a call from a logger on one of the cutting crews. He described the site and said, 'You're investigating that, aren't you?' I said I was. He said, 'Well, I got some stuff you need to know. I want to meet you.' I'm getting old enough to know that maybe meeting him wasn't such a good idea. So I arranged to meet him in a public place, and I sent another officer in first in plainclothes, and he said it looked safe and hung around while I was in there. The logger told me, 'Hey, look: It ain't that I love spotted owls. But I hate the effin' Weyerhaeuser Corporation. All they're doin' is tryin' to get the money as fast as they can. They don't wanna pay nobody anything for it. And this is what happened: The cuttin' crew I was on, we seen two spotted owls sittin' on limbs right where we were cuttin'.' I showed him a map and asked where this was. He put his finger right on the spot where the biologists said an owl pair lived. 'There was a lot of talk about the owls, because we were afraid it was going to delay the cuttin'. We told the Weyerhaeuser rep, and everybody was talkin' about them owls being there.' He gave me the name of another guy who'd seen them. We went to his house. He said, 'I could lose my job over this, but I'm fifty-five years old and I haven't lied yet.' I took out the maps. He pointed right to the site center and said, 'I saw two of them here. I was fifteen feet away from them.' He also told me they had told the Weyerhaeuser representative.

"We had a good case. The Weyerhaeuser guy would never admit to having been told, but a good prosecuting attorney would have let out little pieces of his informants' information and backed Weyerhaeuser into a corner, and we probably would have gotten a plea of no contest. But the U.S. attorney kept looking for ways to get the hell out of it. Do you think appointed attorneys are going to go after those who got the people who appointed them into office? A good prosecutor would have pushed them much farther. But they weren't going to push the biggest logging company. They didn't want to prosecute Weyerhaeuser, because Oregon is Weyerhaeuser and Washington is Weyerhaeuser. And eventually, they stepped out."

The sky is alive with moving puffs of water vapor and heavy curtains of distant rain. We meet some clouds head-on and they briefly white out the world.

When patchwork land comes back into view, I ask, "What are we looking at here?"

Rich replies, "Right now, the heavily cut-over land on our left is Forest Service land. All that mud was forest a few years ago. On our right is the Colonel Bob Wilderness Area: uncut. Straight ahead, up the drainage is Olympic National Park: uncut."

Rich continues, "On this river below us—a tributary of the Quinault—there's no major logging from here upstream. This is what a river should look like." The riverbed below is all clean gravel in clear-running water, with none of the mud slugs we've seen most everywhere else. These slopes have never been cut, and they bear a thick, deep mantle of very tall trees.

"Magnificent," Syd says.

"Yes," echoes the former logger who was brought up on trees that were brought down. "Magnificent."

Most remaining big trees preside in exile in a few protected showcases, wherein the ancient monarchs, the decadent overmature fiber—or whatever metaphor suits the beholder—live under house arrest. As Joni Mitchell sang, *They took all the trees, put 'em in a tree museum.* Around here they haven't paved paradise—just removed most of it and left mud.

We reach the Olympic National Park boundary. From the air, the park border is as clear as on a roadmap. The forest has been removed right up to the park's edges. The cut follows assiduously the zigzag boundary. A clear-cut that runs along both sides of the road for about five miles comes to a screeching stop at the boundary to Olympic National Park. As though the saws hit a wall. They can slice through a thousand-year-old tree, but they cannot cut through a little line drawn on a map, on a piece of paper made from trees (not yet, anyway; some people have been trying). But for the moment the little line is drawn like the doors of a church, where one can almost hear the besieged trees and creatures wailing, "Sanctuary! Sanctuary!" like Quasimodo, with his twisted, bewildered face, on the threshold of the great Notre Dame cathedral.

We were lucky to get this park. When the proposal was floated in the 1930s, antipark forces charged that the idea was the work of misguided idealists who couldn't tell a hemlock from a cedar and who would sacrifice jobs and investments of local residents to provide scenery for effete tourists' "individual pleasure." It is amazing how little the rhetoric has changed in sixty years, and how consistently this rhetoric is applied from one issue to another, from parks to sharks.

A park could not be discussed without the Forest Service doing its best to portray park supporters as sentimental and—worse—"emotional." They predicted the usual economic catastrophe. The usual worst-case calculations were made: Either you can save six hundred loggers, six hundred mill workers, five mills, or you can have a park so people can come and just *stare*.

But Secretary of the Interior Harold Ickes saw it differently, saying, "If the exploiters are permitted to have their way with the Olympic Peninsula, all that will be left will be the outraged squeal of future generations over the loss of another national treasure."

Actually, the fight for the park had long antecedents involving numerous U.S. presidents over four decades. In 1897, there was the president—Cleveland—suddenly saying half the peninsula was designated the Olympic Forest Reserve. Well, the people wouldn't stand for it. Just wouldn't. And they made the president—McKinley, this time—return a third of that land to the unprotected domain. Just as things were settling down, the president—Teddy Roosevelt—comes yanking another six hundred thousand acres and saying this is Mount Olympus National Monument, to protect *elk*. Well, the people wouldn't stand for it. So the president—Wilson—sawed old Teddy's elk monument in half (*This land is your land / This land is my land*), saying this was to mine manganese for the war. Miners found very little manganese, but—lo!—loggers mined all those big trees. Cutting on the private lands had been intense, and more outsiders began thinking it might make sense to turn Teddy Roosevelt's bisected monument into a National Park. And that was when the president—Franklin Roosevelt—after much haggling and struggle, signed a bill creating Olympic National Park, including a narrow strip of land along the wild ocean coast, in 1938.

The beginning of the Second World War in Europe and Asia in 1939 distracted attention from the park fracas. Timber interests greeted even this development with their usual cold calculations. The dominant industry journal, the *Timberman,* strenuously opposed U.S. military involvement, pointing out that the military involvement of *other* powers would result in "an extended period of prosperity, occasioned by the flow of European gold into American trade channels." U.S. participation in the war, they said, would disrupt business activity and therefore be "a national catastrophe."

Slipping by below just north of the Hoh River in Olympic National Park is the preserved part of the spectacular Hoh Rain Forest. Just outside the park, the unpreserved part of the rain forest is missing, bringing forward the question: If we cannot maintain our own rain forests, whose rain forests can be maintained?

Rich breathes almost to himself, "What's left are fragments."

Syd says, "And look at the highway." Lined with trees.

The great forested Pacific Northwest has somehow disappeared. It should be here, but it is essentially gone, absent, deleted. And it still looks pretty from the road.

Sheets of rain again pelt the windshield. Droplets slither around the curving glass.

It isn't long before we reach another recently cut-over watershed. In the Queets River, more silt. Dr. Schneidman says, "It isn't hard to tell when you've left the park, is it?"

Sprouting horns, I posit, "But we all *do* use wood and paper."

He snaps, "We don't need to cut any more ancient trees. We can use the regrowth, and new kinds of things like hybrid cotton and hemp for paper, and save the little bit that's left. No one is saying, 'No more logging,' just, 'Save what's left.'"

What's left: In nice round terms, a century of logging eliminated 90 percent of the ancient salmon forests of Oregon and Washington. About 5 percent is protected. People are still fighting over another 5 percent or so. A quarter century into the new millennium, any unprotected ancient forest remnants will be ancient history. *All* the remaining ancient forest on U.S. soil in the Pacific Northwest will be gone by 2025 unless specifically protected (as in several national parks). The last stands in Olympic, Gifford Pinchot, and Siskiyou National Forests will be gone before 2010 and are already reduced to bits that can no longer hold together the watershed ecosystems for salmon and much of the other wildlife.

The fate of North America's remaining ancient forests has engendered intense controversy, a rage over trees, a war in the woods—as ugly as it can get just short of bloodshed. The wood companies have largely won. Frantic, would-be protectors of trees have sometimes underexaggerated economic concerns and sometimes overexaggerated biological risks. Others, at a loss for words, have laid

themselves across roads, buried themselves up to their necks in the paths of bulldozers, chained each other to tree trunks, or bivouacked in slings from branches
high above ground for days. Some resorted to vandalism, pouring sugar into
machine fuel tanks. Yet others moved one step closer to violence, driving spikes
into trunks, arming the trees to shatter the mill saws, with possible collateral
injury. Such impassioned actions, while perhaps understandable from one point
of view, are inexcusable.

The timber companies, for their part, were content to lie or apply deformed
logic. While they increasingly exported raw logs, they blamed environmentalists
for loss of mill jobs. While they cut thin young trees at record rates with
machines that replaced muscles, they blamed environmentalists for loss of logging jobs. While the ancient forests were whittled toward 10 percent of their
original extent and their elimination was well in sight, the timber companies
pled that they could not survive without cutting ancient forests they were
rapidly eliminating.

What is being done with the last of that superlative, ancient wood? Fine fur-
niture builders, master woodworkers, musical-instrument makers, wooden-boat
crafters, and even high-quality door and window framers would like to know.
Wood for these purposes that require it is becoming scarce. Douglas-firs centuries
old are splintered into two-by-fours that could as easily come from forty-year-old
pine. Planks of rare cedars are used to line throwaway concrete molds in Japan.
Ancient hemlocks are pulped into rayon, cellophane, wrapping paper, or disposable diapers. "That's just plain wrong," said Bart Koehler of the Southeast Alaska
Conservation Council in a *New Yorker* interview. "When a four-hundred-year-old
tree ends up on some baby's ass, it's an insult to all that's good and right."

Buildings appear ahead. "Here's the town of Queets. Don't blink."

The town is tiny. "I see a lot of cut-over land and very few people," I say.
"Who's benefiting?"

"The timber brokers, the Japanese, and the Koreans," answers Rich.

The land abuse, worker dislocation, and subsidized below-cost timber sales
that are pushing salmon, other wildlife, and communities off the map are not
limited to the visible landscape below us. This is the pattern from California to
southern Alaska. There is scant refuge from it for either salmon or people.

Up in British Columbia, timber companies have inflicted clear-cuts of up to
180 square miles—visible from space—upon the coastal salmon forests. One
thousand square miles of ancient forest are being flipped on their bellies and
turned to dirt every time Earth circles the sun, and many fail to regenerate
because of the short growing season, the poor soil, and the lack of shade that
leaves would-be seedlings overexposed. The best coastal sites, most valuable to
salmon, will be history by 2005, and virtually all the unprotected forests there
will be gone by 2020, according to University of British Columbia researchers.
For those of us whose image of British Columbia is dark forests and dense
salmon, we can think of B.C. as standing for "Before Clear-cutting."

Up on Alaska's panhandle, the seventeen-million-acre Tongass National Forest remains the continent's "great reservoir" of ancient timber. Fifty-year contracts signed in the 1950s guaranteed two companies (one is Japanese-owned, one is Louisiana Pacific) access to large quantities of ancient timber for an average price of a dollar and a half per thousand board feet. The Forest Service would charge you more for a road map of the Tongass. The wood is *worth* about seven hundred dollars per thousand board feet. The Tongass sells more timber and loses more money than any other national forest—forty to sixty million dollars a year. In some years, it has lost ninety-nine cents on every dollar it spent to sell trees. The ostensible idea of these massive subsidies is to save local jobs. Said jobs declined from twenty-seven hundred in 1980 to seventeen hundred in 1990, largely because of automation. Each remaining job costs us taxpayers about twenty-four thousand dollars a year. The biggest employers on the panhandle, tourism (two thousand jobs and growing) and fishing (twenty-six hundred), are threatened by the subsidized forest destruction that loses money and loses wood to foreign markets and does not save timber jobs. Not surprisingly, some of the salmon runs on the Alaska Panhandle are starting to decline. In 1990, Alaska passed the Forest Practices Act to protect streams "from the significant adverse effects of timber harvest activities on fish habitat and water quality." But in 1996, Alaska Departments of Fish and Game wrote that its staff members are "uniformly of the belief that the implementation of the Forest Practices Act remains seriously deficient . . . particularly for fish habitat." Researchers Mary Willson and Karl Halupka of the Forest Sciences Laboratory in Juneau write that the salmon decline "resembles historical patterns of decline in the Pacific Northwest and British Columbia."

Up ahead, clear-cuts stretch across the land as far as the eye can see, all the way to the ocean. In places, all the bodies of downed trees are fanned out in a circle, as though flattened by a bomb. Rich says what I am thinking: "This whole thing looks like an atomic blast."

This is the Quinault Indian Reservation.

Schneidman says, "This is how these Indians treat their land. This was our American rain forest. It became ground zero for our children's heritage and theirs. Totally raped."

If the clear-cutting on the private land seems thorough, the clear-cutting on the Indian land seems vehement. Having come steeled for anything and imagining the worst, I had not imagined such wreckage or industrial violence on this scale—this forest holocaust.

Rich says, "Last year we tried to stop a timber company from cutting eighty acres it owned on the Salmon River here in the Quinault Reservation. It was right around a pair of spotted owls, so we sought an injunction to prevent the logging before a violation of the Endangered Species Act occurred. Most of the trees in there were cedar and Douglas-fir. Big. Spectacular ancient growth, thousand-year-old trees—just unbelievable. They were going to log right down to the water's edge and right up the other shore. Because they were inside an Indian reservation, the state and federal laws couldn't touch 'em. We lost."

That sounds weird. A timber company owned land inside the Indian reservation?

Under the Allotment Act of 1877, male Indian heads of household were given ownership to a chunk of reservation land that they could then sell. These tracts contained extensive and valuable ancient forests. Impoverished Indians, plied with booze, were pressured to sell their allotments to whites. In Oregon, by 1900 the Siletz tribe had gone from owning more than a million acres to fewer than three thousand. Nationwide, Native Americans lost two-thirds of their lands—if you don't count the whole continent. Allottees refusing to sell their trees were declared "incompetent" by the federal government and had their land effectively taken from them (*This land was your land / This land is my land*).

I think back to travels in Central America, where some of the best places left are Indian lands. I traveled part of the Caribbean coast with an extraordinary man named Armstrong Wiggins, a Miskito Indian leader who, during Nicaragua's civil wars, was forced to dig his own grave and came within a hair's breadth of having his brains blown out. Wiggins is now with the Indian Law Resource Center in Washington, D.C., working for indigenous peoples' rights throughout the Americas. As we visited villages with no electricity, no plumbing, no telephones, not even radio contact with the outside, he insisted that poverty is mostly a Western notion related to money and material, and he was adamant that the people were not poor but rich. Suspecting he might be ideologically dogmatic on the subject, I asked if he had *ever* seen Native American territory that struck him as poor. "I equate poverty with the destruction of natural resources," he said. He mentioned Haiti and the state of Washington. There, yes, true poverty. "In the Pacific Northwest," he said, "they went berserk."

We hook back north, coming soon to the mouth of the Queets River, which widens hesitatingly before relinquishing into a receiving line of foaming breakers and the deep blue ocean. Farther north lies Destruction Island and its lonely lighthouse. We head that way, screaming along the beach. The tide, feeling the pull of a full moon, is at lowest ebb. A wide band of white breakers rolls in along a ribbon of wet gray volcanic sand. The shoreline is heavily loaded with immense wood debris, some of it natural, some from logging, some probably having been blasted into the sky when Mount St. Helens exploded, then floated downriver. Out over the ocean, a large flock of birds is into a feeding frenzy over a school of fish. From up here, the white seabirds, streaming into and concentrating on one area, look like a dandelion puff. With the salmon closure, there are no fishing boats anywhere in sight.

Exquisite, columnar boulders, rocky islets, and patchy kelp beds spice the coast. The offshore rocks, encircled by the ocean surge as though draped in bolts of bridal lace, are attractive to seabirds. Atop a pillar of rock a quarter mile off-shore shines an adult bald eagle, and I am surprised to see four brown pelicans gracing over the ocean's surface this far north. Along sixty or seventy miles, spectacular rock formations and big trees confront the Pacific coastline. For anyone approaching by boat, this is still a wild and beautiful coast, untouched.

But from a thousand feet overhead, it is a fronting facade, intended to deceive, backed by clear-cuts that recede into the haze as far inland as a salmon can swim.

Sidney says, "See? The park boundaries make the coastline look beautiful for all the tourists. You go a mile or two in from the beach, and, man, it's just *bald!*"

We have stopped those who would kill the last great whale on this coast, and the whales have recovered. We have yet to stop those who would take the last great tree. We can bring back whales in our lifetime, but when a stand of five-hundred- or thousand-year-old trees is killed, it's pretty much over as far as we, personally, are concerned.

We fly over Cape Alava, and from here we can see Tatoosh Island, the north-westernmost part of the contiguous United States, named after a monstrous thunderbird who brought terrible storms from the ocean, shot lightning from his single eye, and ate whales as if they were herring. Beyond, at Canada's Vancouver Island, a line of low, bosomy clouds presses the coast. Under us, large, ragged, violent-looking clear-cuts—the Makah Indian reservation.

Sidney says, "Man, we got lucky with the weather today."

Maybe. But the gloom and sodden overcast have moved into my chest and mind, and the forecast is for more rain.

On the Ground

Beauty strips no longer line the road here, along Route 101 from Quinault to the town of Forks. The lumber companies no longer need them, since they have finished cutting the natural forest right to the roadside. Now, a large public-relations effort via billboards replaces the beauty strips—hardly an improvement. One of the companies most visible on the signs here is ITT Rayonier, a quintessential example of forest agribusiness writ corporate. Every little while a sign tells motorists when this place was cut over, when planted, and with how many seedlings: FIFTY YEARS OF PLANTING. FIFTY MILLION TREES. They don't want us to see the forest for the trees.

A common road sign adjacent to the clear-cuts features a picture of a flaming fir tree and the message USE YOUR ASH TRAY. Apparently, the companies don't want fire to destroy the trees before they do. Another road sign, in the middle of a clear-cut, announces that the forest-fire danger—because of the drought—is moderate. Perhaps the forest-fire danger would be higher had they left some trees here. When that avuncular ranger Smokey Bear kept reminding us that forest fires burned more than just trees, I worried about spotted fawns and nestling birds and believed that only *I* could prevent forest fires. But it turned out that what Smokey was afraid would burn was money. Smokey lied to us. He was just another lobbyist, one of the slickest.

Just past Jimmy-Come-Lately Road, near the peninsula's north coast, I turn at the mailbox marked Lichatowich. Jim Lichatowich is a taciturn scientist in his midfifties, notable as co-author of a paper titled "Salmon at the Crossroads." An instant classic upon publication in 1991, "Salmon at the Crossroads" gave the world—for the first time—a unified picture of the status of salmon south of the Canadian border. Unfortunately, its main message was that over one hundred major populations had already vanished and extinction stalked two hundred others.

Lichatowich works and writes at his home, backed by clear-cut-checkerboarded mountains. His garage-sized office, crammed but orderly, reflects a methodical man hard at work. From where I am sitting, Jim is framed by part of his immense book collection. "The habitat a salmon needs, going out to the Pacific Ocean, can be thought of as beads on a string," he says as he stands and searches for a volume. "A salmon needs to connect those beads. Some rivers have great habitat for a long distance, but then you hit a stretch where part of the stream has heated up or silted in, or there is no longer cover from predators. The bead chain has been broken."

"If we allow the rivers to heal, the salmon will know what to do," he continues. "Salmon have coped with catastrophic habitat changes for thirty million years, and they carry those lessons in their genes. We've never let them show us what they have learned in all that time."

While Jim is talking and rifling the books for the one he needs, I notice several awards hanging on his office wall. For a time, Lichatowich's natural-born scholarly aptitude had remained latent. Not the best student in high school, he went to summer school every year to make up for the Fs. As a kid in Indiana, Jim spent many a long night along the shores of lakes, casting in the dark for bass among lily pads. It was a solitary thing, and if he went with anyone it was usually his uncle, a man of such quiet countenance that fishing with him was the same as being left alone with one's own thoughts.

After a stint in the Marines just before the big Vietnam buildup, he worked two years at a pulp mill—"a depressing place to work; smelly, dirty, dangerous." He resolved to work toward a career in wildlife management. Studying at Purdue and Oregon State universities, he completed postgraduate studies in fisheries. Jim credits his major professor with teaching him to think independently. But one senses Jim hardly needed instruction in independent thinking.

"The government says the salmon situation is a natural disaster," Jim says as he settles into his desk chair. "That's like blaming the sunrise for your hangover. True, salmon abundance has been rising and falling for hundreds of thousands of years. But now the troughs are deeper and the peaks are lower than they would be naturally, because we've taken all the resilience out of the system."

I have come to see Lichatowich to learn more about the natural ecology of salmon, and to put politics aside. I am too hopeful.

"Decisions made coming out of the last trough determined the depth of this trough. We let the commercial fishing fleet expand very rapidly and we slacked off on protecting habitat. Now the habitat damage that we did is *really* starting to show."

Lichatowich's persona encompasses a broad mind, a broad face, and a grave bearing. Normally, his mouth turns down at the corners. When his broad face broadens more, and his mouth simply flattens to a straight line, it means he is smiling. He smiles not too terribly often. He is not smiling now. "The awful reality of salmon is that they're in a world of hurt. Salmon are in continual decline. If I were a betting man, I'd bet on more extinctions during the next trough. I'd bet on the end of salmon as we know them."

I glance at him appraisingly, hoping to find a way to discount what he is saying, running his argument through my mind, searching for a weak spot to probe, evidence to the contrary, a counterargument based on something—anything—I have read, heard, or seen for myself. I remain quiet.

Jim continues, "Salmon penetrate the Northwest ecosystem like no other animal, going from the mountains all the way out to the Japan Current. They are the silver threads that tie together the whole system. And when they unravel, it means the system is on a trajectory that is changing our society. One measure of that change is job loss. I feel just as bad about losing a fishing community from one of our coastal towns as I do about losing a stock of salmon. Something about working as a primary producer on the land or the water is healthy for society. There are not a lot of professions where the child follows the parent's and grandparent's footsteps. I've seen four generations of loggers from great-grandfather to the youngest boy. Same with fishermen. I don't think you're ever going to see four generations working at McDonald's." For a moment, his mouth flattens just a hint. "But loggers and fishermen are falling victim to an imbalanced economic paradigm they've supported."

I ask if he wouldn't mind explaining the imbalance as he sees it.

"The globalization of markets is one of the biggest problems I see," he says. He explains that in the Indians' original, very local economy, the feedback between the resource and the user was felt very directly as food or starvation. As we have moved to a more regional economy, then to a national, now to a global economy, those feedback loops have first lengthened, then disappeared. "The companies are no longer tied to regional areas or local communities. The markets creating demand certainly are not. Local loggers and fishers still have direct and personal ties to regional resources, but when the corporation cuts all the trees around those people and moves its logging operations elsewhere—perhaps Borneo or the Philippines—it continues to feed the same market at a profit." In a sense, it uses people as fuel.

Jim continues, "It's always seemed a real irony for me that the political party that most touted families also touted the global economy that has devastated families in our local communities. The two are totally incompatible. When communities no longer control their resources they no longer control their destinies, and they become caught in these boom-and-bust cycles that demolish families. Throughout the history of logging, the owners have treated the loggers like crap. Yet when it came down to it, the loggers supported the owners."

Jim says that around the now depressed town of Forks the owners could have logged on a sustained rotation forever, but they boomed and busted. Coos Bay could have supplied the local mill for eighty years—two working lifetimes—and then been ready for the next rotation, but the owners logged it all off in twenty years for export. The companies have the money earning interest, but the loggers are out of work.

Jim believes local resources should be managed to support local towns. We both know he's dreaming. "But with the emphasis on the global economy," he insists, "many decisions about using our fish and logs are not even being made in this country anymore. Having people in Tokyo and London deciding the fate of our resources right here is one of the scariest things that has ever happened for our communities and for our landscapes and waters. It removes the decision-making process from our entire national framework and our democratic institutions. The two-thousand-acre clear-cut right down the road was logged because of decisions made in London." One Sir James Goldsmith of Great Britain bought tens of thousands of acres on the Olympic Peninsula and in New England. "And he was knighted for figuring this out: That if the companies he bought logged their lands on a sustainable rotation—say a hundred years—to supply their mills, their stock was valued on the basis of what their mills were putting out, not on the basis of their standing inventory. So he went in with leveraged buy-outs, sold off the mills, fired a few thousand foresters whose services were no longer needed, then liquidated all the timber—clear-cut everything. In three years, he made a profit of half a billion dollars and retired. He got a hell of a lot richer by managing irresponsibly. The local people got poorer."

By now I am wondering whether talking about Pacific Ocean salmon without talking so much about logging is simply impossible.

Apparently. Jim takes me to see a small clear-cut. While we are looking at a weedy expanse full of broken branches, with a sunlit stream running through it, Jim explains, "This clear-cut probably earned fifty to a hundred thousand dollars profit, after expenses. The salmon that were destroyed weren't worth that—not to the landowner, anyway. The salmon and the trout won't stand a chance as long as you're worshiping at the altar of economic efficiency. A purely profit-oriented thought process is incompatible with healthy environments, healthy resources, good strong communities, the nuclear family. If we are going to have livable communities, we need to rebuild a sense of loggers, farmers, and fishermen caring for each other, and we need to rebuild economic inefficiency."

The more I think about it, the more upset at government I am getting. Where, I demand to know, are the official people paid by taxpayers to look out for the long-term public interest? Maybe it is time to see someone inside government who is actually employed to manage fisheries. I have decided to hunt down Randy Fisher, executive director of the Pacific States Marine Fisheries Commission and former head of the Oregon Department of Fish and Wildlife. Fisher was much disliked and widely regarded as a failure when he was in charge in Oregon. Conservationists referred to him as Dandy Randy, describing him as a cardboard-cutout bureaucrat who cared neither about resources nor people—other than himself. People say he made a mess there and then skipped out to take a more prestigious job at a higher salary. I find him in his office, an odd-looking man with puffy, blow-dried hair and a thin, flat body, like a government-salaried Gumby. I tread onto his carpet with hostility in my breast, and I am looking forward to pinning him down with some embarrassing questions. The only problem is, from his opening remark, I begin to suspect that everything I'd heard about Randy Fisher was wrong.

"The reason why I left Oregon?" As he repeats my question he crinkles his forehead to look at me with eyebrows raised, and then says flatly, "Burnout. In the last legislative session, the timber industry and cattlemen went at the agency, trying to change its mission. They wanted to eliminate such words as 'to protect fish and wildlife for future generations.' Incredible things. And I spent a lot of time trying to stop that kind of activity. It was a very difficult time. The timber industry was being fronted by a lobbyist who works for Weyerhaeuser. I had a friend inside the company, and I called and said, 'Is your Oregon lobbyist nuts, or what?' And he said, 'No, the things he's conveying represent a corporate decision.' Also, there is a conglomeration of smaller timber people, called OFIC; I can't quite remember what the acronym stands for— I guess I'm trying to block it out of my mind for as long as I can—Oregon Forest Industry something-or-other. And the cattlemen's association from eastern Oregon. It was a concerted effort. It was well organized. They were really making a run this time."

Now *my* forehead is crinkled and *my* eyebrows are raised.

He leans forward, speaking intently as though the pain of recalling makes it difficult but he wants me to understand. "They spent a *lot* of time with legislators, especially those who didn't have a lot of money, calling their chips in. They worked a lot on fear, saying the world was going to fall apart if they didn't get what they wanted. There were a lot of personal attacks on me and people who worked for me. And they ended up getting two of our—this is just disgusting— two really, really good biologists fired. Two really good people." He glances down at his blotter for a moment. "They went to the legislature and fixed it so that these biologists' salaries would have to get legislative approval, then the legislators denied the funds." He sits back, fiddling with the tip of his tie.

Then he continues, "The timber industry has gotten hired guns to come in and say, 'The *real* problem is overfishing.' Or, 'The *real* problem is sea lions.' Well," he says, leaning forward again and drilling his desktop with his index finger, "the REAL problem is a combination of all of the above, *plus* all the habitat destruction, *plus* seven years of drought, *plus* warming ocean conditions. You add those together, and you're just stretching it to the breaking point."

I am wondering how the conservationists who complained about Fisher could have so misjudged him. Perhaps they evaluated him solely on the basis of what he did and did not do, rather than what he could and could not do. Could that be it?

Fisher shifts his weight and settles back again, saying, "The timber industry knows full well that if lots of salmon runs are declared threatened or endangered, they're in deep—you know—trouble. But the loss to them is that they may be forced to accept three-hundred-foot-wide no-cut buffers along streams to protect salmon habitat from silt and higher temperatures from direct sunlight. They just can't stand that. The cattle industry—same type of thing—they're concerned that they'll have to fence their cattle away from stream banks."

Fisher surprises me again by saying, "But they are not bad people. The *whole issue* underlying a lot of this stuff is: What are private-property rights? Number one, they are concerned about government telling them what they can do on their own land, and, number two, they are trying to figure out, 'Well, if I've got to increase my no-cut buffer area' or, 'If I can't graze cows out there just so some jerk can go and fish on the weekend or some commercial fisherman can make money off that, *what do I get out of it? THAT'S* the problem."

I say that if things done on private land—so *much* private land—affect the public communities and public resources like water, whole industries like fishing, and the very existence of certain species, doesn't it suggest that this is a particular kind of "private" property, and that other considerations apply?

Fisher says that the legislative sessions in Oregon are now almost entirely about these kinds of property-rights issues, and recovery of salmon will be a test of wills to see how much restriction we are willing to put on private land.

I ask whether the public can afford that; can salmon compete against the price of wood?

He says, "My fear is that by evaluating everything so completely in financial terms, we have the possibility of losing it on economic grounds. There are other values. Knowing that salmon are running these rivers is a way of understanding that the world is a good place. People feel better about their life here if there are salmon. It's that basic. That's my view as a white person. Certain Indians' religious feelings run much deeper than that."

Fisher continues, "But if you consider all the decisions that affect salmon survival, then yes, we've failed, obviously. Why? Because we don't have an agreed-to understanding of what our goal is for salmon and how to get there. That's been a *huge* failure. And I was part of that failure.

"If a plan for all the resources of the Northwest was done and done right," he says, "it would look like a large land-use plan based on the natural boundaries of the watersheds, with the ability to make decisions and take coordinated actions within those natural boundaries. And it would deal with the expanding human population. We've had some huge successes that prove we could succeed.

Willamette spring chinook: Huge success. They were down to two thousand a few years ago, and we now have adult runs of over a hundred thousand. We *know* enough now to restore salmon, but that is *totally* different from having the political courage or the desire in our hearts to do it."

I ask whether he thinks good compromises between the competing interests can be reached.

"With natural resources, you can compromise to the point that, next time there are bad natural conditions, you lose everything. You've got to have enough leeway in natural systems that when nature turns harsh or unfavorable, there is enough to allow the resources to survive through those times. Call it margin of error. Otherwise, we find ourselves saying, 'Well, we must have allowed too much fishing, because there aren't any left.' Or, 'Well, we must have allowed too much logging, because these streams can't raise salmon anymore.' That's why salmon are going onto the endangered species lists. The tendency is to compromise to a level that is too low, and not recognize it until it is too late."

Not everyone has been in a mood to compromise while the list of endangered species has been lengthened by the names of salmon species. Facing wholesale listing proposals for forest-spawning salmon under the Endangered Species Act, apoplectic over President Clinton's plan to reduce logging to save the remaining federally owned ancient forests, and finding it increasingly difficult to convincingly claim the need to cut the last publicly owned ancient trees, the timber industry gave up on the public front. There had to be a way around all these obstacles.

Big timber decided to give up on attacking the laws or trying to change them, and they took a novel approach: Leave them on the books. Just write a little ditty saying, "The laws and regulations don't apply to us," and tack it onto something much hotter for the president.

The budget was much hotter.

In 1995 Congress sent President Clinton a budget-cutting appropriations bill that carried, on its coattails, a rider that would have seemed to corporate loggers made in heaven—if they hadn't written it themselves. Conservationists barraged the president with pleas for a veto and even organized a twenty-one-chain-saw salute outside the White House. He vetoed the bill. But when it came back a couple of months later it carried not only the budget cuts and the loggers' rider but also tacked-on packages of financial aid to victims of earthquakes and the Oklahoma City bombing. Congress was making the president sweat over the public-relations implications of vetoing a bill containing aid to disaster victims, and rather than sending the bill back again, he caved. Because the logging rider threatened to void Clinton's own painstakingly constructed Northwest Forest Protection Plan—a compromise plan the president said would preserve jobs in logging and fishing—some people could not help wondering what Clinton was inhaling when he signed it.

The logging rider was called the Emergency Salvage Timber Sale Program. It was sneaked onto the budget cuts and aid package almost surreptitiously, and many members of Congress had not read it when they voted on the budget bill.

For those Congress members who did not get a chance to read the 1995 salvage rider they voted for, here's part of what it said: "Notwithstanding any other provision of law . . . all timber sale contracts . . . shall be deemed to satisfy the requirements of . . . all applicable Federal environmental and natural resource laws."

Bear in mind that we are talking here about federal land—*public* land. Logging companies could already do pretty much as they wanted on their own land.

Opponents called it "logging without laws." That, it was.

Washington's Senator Slade Gorton, the transplanted New England codfish-cake heir who could never understand salmon, said this rider would provide wood for American mills. Japanese mills were practically gagging on American wood from private lands in Washington State, while in that self-same state the local mills' ribs were showing like a starving dog's. But that was *business,* just following the market. Can't touch that!

Gorton knew a lot about private business, having received forty thousand dollars from five timber companies. That's quite a bargain for the companies, when we're talking about billions of dollars worth of wood. Louisiana Pacific, a big player owning no lands whatsoever and heavily reliant on public timber, gave money to Gorton—who was also quite active trying to gut the Endangered Species Act—and Senator Larry Craig of Idaho, who was already busily sponsoring a bill that would extend for a decade or more many of the logging-without-laws provisions. Three California congressmen also caught contributions from Louisiana Pacific, and those three threatened the Forest Service with budget cuts unless it increased levels of logging in the state immediately (one of them, sounding like the timber goon he had become, demanded that the service "get creative"). Around the time of the logging rider, Louisiana Pacific shoved money at twenty-five lawmakers, bringing its six-year total to 160,000 well-invested campaign-contributed lip-smacking bucks.

The provisions of the logging-without-laws rider force the Forest Service to allow logging, even if it is losing money on the deal: "Salvage timber sales . . . shall not be precluded because the costs are likely to exceed the revenues derived." No problem; the service has lots of expertise in losing money.

The process by which citizens appealed illegal sales is ended: "Timber sales . . . shall not be subject to administrative review. . . . No restraining order, preliminary injunction, or injunction pending appeal shall be issued by any court of the United States."

Promoters said the bill was to allow removal of trees attacked by insects. "The term 'timber salvage sale' means . . . the removal of diseased or insect-infested trees . . . or trees imminently susceptible to fire or insect attack." But "such term also includes the removal of associated trees." If you want, you can cut 'em all. And the phrases "imminently susceptible to fire" and "or trees affected by fire" are interesting in themselves. What better way to make fire-damaged trees available than to set fires? In 1995, after an area designated for owl conservation had been torched, an Oregon district court had issued an injunction against the sale of the timber, saying that "the effect of selling arson-fire-damaged timber could be future acts of arson." The so-called salvage rider wiped out that court injunction, too.

Lest I forget: Because it also suspends the National Environmental Policy Act, public comment and environmental impact statements are no longer required.

After all that, it seems almost minor that the rider also exempts logging from a requirement to leave a three-hundred-foot no-cut buffer along stream banks to protect salmon habitat.

When a shrouded law gets in through the back door with no hearings by a Congress bent on distorting democracy, this is what we get. Make no mistake. This was nothing minor. It suspended a quarter century of lawmaking, and it applied not just to the Northwest but to the entire nation. It warranted an open discussion. It warranted one—just one—of the umpteen-hundred hearings that Congress ordinarily loves to hold. And that's why such pains were taken to prevent hearings.

In an extraordinary move, eight members of the House of Representatives and one senator filed a brief to the court stating that they had been intentionally misled (that means lied to) by their congressional colleagues. They said they'd been given "a significantly different view" of the legislation.

The president tried to contain the damage, saying, "We do not believe that this extreme expansion of ancient timber sales was authorized by the law. . . . This could jeopardize the livelihoods of thousands of people who depend on the Pacific Northwest's fisheries."

But a judge said it was pretty plain that all federal timber sales ever offered in Oregon and Washington had to be released at their originally offered price, and that they needn't comply with environmental laws. Every sale of timber ever offered on federal land *had* to be cut. And that was the heart of the matter: This "savage" rider was the timber industry's successful attempt to grab every public-land timber sale ever canceled for environmental reasons. At Depression-era prices.

They now had a window of about a year and a half to buy up those trees (the sales provisions would then automatically expire if ongoing efforts to extend the rider were unsuccessful). Having fantasized about such a golden opportunity for years, the timber industry began buying and cutting as fast as possible. They were in a big hurry, and they even tried to have two Forest Service officials jailed for not selling them trees fast enough.

Things were, in so many words, out of control. The Endangered Species Act, the Clean Water Act, the Clean Air Act—virtually every major federal environmental law was simultaneously staggering under sneaky, debilitating amendments, or all-out attempts at their evisceration. Mother Nature was getting no respect, and the ideological fervor of the Congress seemed almost bizarre. In 1995 the new Republican leadership in the U.S. House of Representatives changed the name of their Natural Resources Committee by dropping "natural"; the very word itself seemed to make them uncomfortable, like saying "breasts" at the family dinner table. The new name—Resources Committee—seemed awkward and self-conscious, seemed to imply less than its full charge, seemed as though something important was missing, like eunuchs guarding the palace.

By now it was evident that we were suffering one of the most atrocious raids on public property in U.S. history, and both Congress and the president were probably surprised at how many people really cared about it. People did. The *Des Moines Register* wrote that Congress should revise the law promptly, "on behalf of the taxpayers, who own the trees." The *San Francisco Chronicle* said, "We strongly urge the president to seek repeal of the entire salvage rider." The *Seattle Post-Intelligencer:* "It has become painfully clear that the salvage logging rider was a piece of stealth legislation that despite its label was designed to open to chain saws the clearcutting of old-growth timber otherwise protected in the 1994 forest management plan."

Letters. Lots of letters. The president was earning pen pals. There was the City of Portland Office of Public Utilities: "We urge you to seek outright repeal." Nineteen Indian tribes wrote to the Great White Father in the East, expressing "our dismay" over the "greater risks for the survival and recovery of salmon." Washington State's commissioner of public lands tapped out, "I urge repeal. . . . The ill-conceived rider threatens to again ignite timber wars." Oregon's governor called on the president and Congress "to heal the wounds caused by the passage of the timber salvage rider." Lots of other people had the same message: Somehow, get rid of this law to end all laws.

Oregon representative Elizabeth Furse, at an outdoor rally to repeal the rider, said, "America is a nation of laws. But the salvage rider has put logging outside the law. By setting aside all due process, it has forced confrontation and violence." She went on to say the rider was described to her "over and over again" as an emergency measure to remove dead or dying trees, but it was being used to cut healthy, centuries-old forests. "Giant, irreplaceable treasures," she called them. She'd been told the rider "wouldn't harm the Northwest's efforts to revive our fast-dwindling salmon runs and the billion-dollar fishing industry they once supported." But that was proving equally untrue. She added, "When we're slashing vital programs like Medicare and school lunches, it's unfair to ask the American taxpayers to subsidize corporate welfare programs like this."

"This rider requires fishermen to subsidize their own destruction," said Glen Spain of the Pacific Coast Federation of Fishermen's Associations at the rally. Spain was hot-mad. He excoriated lawless logging as "a disaster for the region's remaining wild salmon runs, and a disaster for salmon fishermen all along the coast." Spain said, "These illegal sales will—not *may*, but *will*—extinguish or severely damage some of our last best salmon runs outside Alaska." Spain added that over the last two decades the salmon fishing industry has lost seventy-two thousand family-wage jobs in the Northwest, "much of these losses caused by the destruction of the region's last remaining old-growth forests." He railed, "We cannot and will not support raping the last of this region's old-growth forests, which the salmon need for their survival."

Then the pictures started showing up, some of them taken furtively and "illegally" on public lands by photographers wearing camouflage and risking arrest, showing salmon streams turned into mud pies.

Meanwhile, it was, "Gentlemen, start your chain saws." The Forest Service's timber director wrote a memo to his staff that said, "I encourage you to take advantage of assistance offered by the timber industry. . . . They only want to help."

They only want to help themselves. Environmentalists were in mourning. Andy Stahl, director of the Association of Forest Service Employees for Environmental Ethics, sadly said his members were "very distressed at being told by Congress to ride roughshod over the lands they are charged with protecting." Awkward, melodramatic phrases tried to express a true sense of grief. "The rider passes like a shadow across the sun," said one group's newsletter. "The sales are popping up like evil mushrooms," wrote another. Not all of the newsletter and e-mail language was awkward, though. A noted (and heartbroken) defender of America's forests, Brock Evans, wrote, "Whatever we have succeeded in making safe of our forest heritage these past decades has been won in the open, fair and square, with public debate. And always by the rules. Now industry's allies are in office, and the rule of law is gone in all the nation's public forests."

Private citizens began lying down on logging roads on public lands. In Siskiyou National Forest, three hundred people—young children to the elderly—entered a logging road in a section of public land off-limits to the public, where Boise Cascade would be mowing the massives. It was seven hundred acres of seven-hundred-year-old trees. The roads had been blocked with armed guards. The people began to sit in the road their tax money had built, to hamper the log trucks whose presence they were subsidizing. Among those people was a former congressman and reporters. Fearing bad press, law officials made no arrests—until some of the protesters got out of sight of most reporters. Those who walked up the road were met by less friendly enforcers. A news cameraman shortly found his head between the road and the sole of a police boot. A sixty-two-year-old woman who tried to get between the policeman and the reporter was promptly maced. But she provided diversion enough to allow the reporter to flee, and he did so at high speed, past an applauding crowd who gave him a sitting ovation from the middle of the road.

Eventually, nearly a hundred people—business-suited environmental leaders (including Brock Evans), the former congressman Jim Jontz, a fourteen-year-old girl, a decorated war veteran in his uniform and carrying an American flag, old men and elderly women—were made to sit outdoors for eight hours in chains that did not reach to the snack shop or the rest room. Some were still chained there when the chill of night fell. The indignity and petty harassment ended when they were released from jail in the morning with light fines. But there were the many lingering effects and ill feeling—or, in the case of one man whose handcuffs had been too tight, no feeling. At arraignment, one protester sentenced to community service amused the judge by asking to work with an environmental group protesting the logging.

The roads were clear again for the trucks. Freed by the grinding saws, the great trees—thousands of them—began their sudden and thunderous descent to earth as though nothing but the defiance of gravity had been holding them upright all these centuries. It was happening all over now. Publicly owned ancient forest areas that had been set aside for spotted owls came down, and places with endangered salmon were cleared to proceed and proceeded to clear. Around what has been called *the most productive chinook salmon stream left* in the Lower Forty-Eight, the North Fork of the Elk River in the Siskiyou National Forest (which had been painstakingly protected through repeated challenges in the 1980s), many trees fell. Some were saved—again—in eleventh-hour swaps of other federal lands with the timber companies (reminiscent of the way some governments ransom hostages) and because of a court decision that—again—protected tree tracts where marbled murrelets (those odd little seabirds officially listed as threatened) were nesting.

The National Marine Fisheries Service's Northwest director, William Stelle, wrote that "remaining high-quality areas, these 'last best habitats' critical to the long-term survival of salmon, are most at risk." He went on to say that the imminent logging will "increase the likelihood of a species becoming listed under the Endangered Species Act." Ah, but Congress had fixed that, too, with a nation-wide moratorium: No new endangered species could be added to the list, for an indefinite time.

The Fisheries Service made its own list, checking it twice, for species of particular concern. Sea-run cutthroat trout and coho salmon—threatened throughout Oregon—would suffer from increased logging in Umpqua National Forest, Siuslaw National Forest, Siskiyou National Forest, and Rogue River National Forest, they said. On the Rogue, steelhead were also in for trouble. In the Wallowa-Whitman National Forest, chinook listed as threatened and due to be "promoted" to endangered, were probably going to slip further.

Conservationists and fishers knew that the spotted owl and the salmon need the forests that spawned them. But they also realized that the forests were becoming thin and frail, and just as the child becomes caretaker to the parent, the ancient forests now needed the spotted owl and the salmon, children of a New World gone prematurely old.

But as trees that cannot be seen again for a thousand years struck the duff, the Senate voted forty-eight to forty-six to keep the rider, then did so a second time. The *Wall Street Journal* called this vote a "show of strength" by the timber industry. Considering all the sneaking and lying, the artful deception and pains to conceal, I call it a show of pathological cowardice, a dark, compulsive, festering greed that cannot bear direct sunlight, born of that spirit Henry David Thoreau named the "blind and unmanly love of wealth." The mark of all that has already happened will be upon the land for a long, long time, until millennium-old trees stand again, if they ever do. In that meantime, the timber industry of the Northwest has ensured itself a thousand-year Reich.

Astoria

Before Europeans arrived, people of the Northwest were largely dependent upon the salmon. Soon after Europeans arrived, salmon became dependent on people.

Now, people who depended on salmon are depending on the government. Tonight, federal representatives from Washington, D.C., will be coming here to talk to townspeople about options for distributing millions of dollars in disaster relief to the fishing community.

The seaport town of Astoria lies near the mouth of the great Columbia River, and since before the United States touched the Pacific it has been (and remains) an active hub in the history of human exploitation of fish, furs, and wood. With both accumulated wisdom and present-day urgency, Astoria bears living witness to the network of effects people, rivers, and salmon all have had on one another. The relationships are not simply linear; it's not just a matter of "people affect forests and rivers, which affect the ocean's salmon." No. What goes around comes around: Salmon have helped shape part of the social fabric, and many people have come to depend on the fish. Yet many people have also had effects on salmon—mostly negative ones, unfortunately—and those changes affect many of those people. That's apparent by now, but less obvious is the lengthy history that has ultimately brought me here to where the Columbia and Pacific mingle, on the approach into downtown Astoria. The mouth of the Columbia, with dilapidated, broken pilings still standing along miles of shoreline like decaying teeth, immediately whispers of a long and changing story of human use and exploitation.

The first West Coast salmon cannery opened in 1864 near Sacramento, California, founded by people from New England, where dams had already largely demolished Atlantic salmon. Within two years, sediment from hydraulic gold mining so devastated Sacramento River runs that the company moved here, to the Columbia River. They canned about a quarter million pounds of chinook salmon—caught by just two gill-net boats—that first year. More canneries followed. Targeting only the vast chinook runs, catches rose quickly, peaking in

1883 at about three and a half million fish weighing forty-three million pounds (about 170 times the first year's canned catch), the largest chinook catch ever. After that, chinook (which had come to be called king salmon) declined quickly, catches slipping by more than half by 1890. Other salmon species that had up until this time been discarded wholesale when the nets stopped them—coho, chum, sockeye, steelhead, pink—were pressed into service.

Concern about overfishing had already led to the opening of a "salmon-breeding station" (a hatchery) in 1877, and its brief eleven-year history presaged that of the entire Northwest. Livingston Stone, a member of the U.S. Fish Commission, wrote of the hatchery, "mills and dams, timber-cutting on the upper waters of the Clackamas and logging in the river, together with other adverse influence, so crippled its efficiency that it was given up." Stone, a former Unitarian minister, revered salmon. He saw to the placement of a dozen hatcheries on the Columbia River. He also saw that these could not save his beloved fish. In 1892, Stone urged the establishment of a salmon national park, patterned after Yellowstone's role in saving the buffalo, saying prophetically, "The helpless salmon's life is gripped between these two forces—the murderous greed of the fishermen and the white man's advancing civilization—and what hope is there for salmon in the end? . . . Nothing can stop the growth and development of the country, which are fatal to salmon. . . . Provide some refuge for the salmon, and provide it quickly, before complications arise which may make it very difficult. Now is the time. Delays are dangerous."

By 1894 the U.S. Fish Commission reported to Congress, "The number of salmon now reaching the headwaters of streams in the Columbia River basin is insignificant in comparison with the number which some years ago annually visited and spawned in these waters."

By the early 1900s, about forty canneries were doing a job on the salmon. An articulate fishing industry spokesman named Miller Freeman emerged, writing, "There can be no compromise with conservation . . . if you use your fish wisely you can have them forever." Freeman focused on the future.

But most people live in the present. Fishing intensified. More than twenty-eight hundred gill-net boats strained the Columbia, and total catches maxed out in 1911, at just under fifty million pounds. A closed season was introduced to allow more salmon spawning. But to get around the closed season, boats rigged to troll the ocean just outside, using new gasoline-powered internal combustion engines and equally new refrigeration.

By 1926, five hundred Columbia River fish traps were intercepting salmon coming upstream from the ocean. More than a hundred seine-net crews were exerting their muscles. Salmon catches fluctuated between forty-five and twenty-five million pounds until the early 1930s, but the runs were declining.

Then the catch fell apart. Fishing was belatedly restricted. Fishwheels—Ferris wheel-like traps that scooped salmon out of the river twenty-four hours a day—were banned in 1935; there had been nearly eighty of them, each catching up to fifty tons of salmon a year.

Columbia River salmon began an almost uninterrupted nosedive lasting three decades, as catches fell from thirty-five million pounds to about five million. Not wholly coincidentally, these were the decades during which all the big dams were built. Plans to build the Columbia dams had been announced in the late 1930s. The lowest dam on the river was planned without a way to get fish past it, dooming the salmon and twenty-five thousand fishery jobs. Public outcry was considerable. Bonneville Dam—with the world's first fish ladders—was completed in 1938. But in 1941 Grand Coulee Dam—without fish ladders—blocked more than eleven hundred miles of habitat, extinguishing those runs. For the Columbia runs, overfishing yielded the mantle of leading salmon-killer to dams.

Most hatcheries had ceased operations by the 1930s because of poor returns of adults. The U.S. commissioner of fisheries pronounced hatcheries a waste of public money, saying the key to having salmon was letting enough fish reach spawning areas. But to help clear the way for the era of monumental dam building, Congress had in 1938 funded construction of forty hatcheries, despite their earlier failure. Most salmon interests were willing to grasp at anything by then.

Seine nets were banned in 1950.

In 1955 another fifty-two miles of river were blocked to salmon by a dam named for the great Nez Perce leader Chief Joseph. (Nearly a century earlier Joseph had said, "Rather than have war I would give up everything." And he did. In 1877, after a tactically brilliant thousand-mile flight to Canada through the Rockies, his freezing, starving followers—by then mostly women, children, and the elderly—were stopped thirty miles from the border. Though they were praised by U.S. Army generals and townsfolk for their "bravery and humanity," their surrender terms—that they be allowed to live on the reservation from which they had been driven—were quickly violated. All Chief Joseph's children and most of his band died of privation in later years. Lieutenant Charles E. S. Wood, who had been present at the capture, later wrote, "I think that, in his long career, Joseph cannot accuse the Government of the United States of one single act of justice." If only Wood could have known that the great chief would one day have a dam named after him—and that it would stop the salmon from entering the chief's beloved country.)

Columbia Basin salmon catches had by now fallen from more than forty million pounds in the 1920s to five million by 1960. Brownlee, Hells Canyon, and Oxbow dams were plopped into the upper Snake, also without fish ladders, wiping out 96 percent of the Snake River sockeye's rearing habitat. By this time concrete blocked or caused flooding to a third of the spawning habitat in the basin, bringing extinction to the largest race of salmon—chinook up to a hundred pounds, once known as "June hogs."

More closed fishing seasons were added.

Catches climbed a bit in the 1960s and '70s, before crashing to a new low—under two million pounds—as abnormally warm ocean temperatures took the last bit of stretch out of a system strained beyond its limits.

The last Columbia River cannery closed in 1975.

In 1983, fishing was prohibited on the upriver chinook runs that a century before had supported a catch of forty-three million pounds.

Catches struggled upward in the mideighties to about fourteen million pounds as another, sharper, shorter round-trip ticket was bestowed upon the fishery by fate and human hands. The next crash was—predictably, some said—to an all-time low.

The number of commercial fishing days allowed in the river below Bonneville Dam was by now down from 270 in the early 1940s to 18.

The original Columbia River runs of ten to sixteen million salmon dwindled to under one million. By the mid-1990s, Snake River chinook numbers had dropped to under two thousand—a decline of 99.88 percent.

Times have indeed been rough. Only half the currently registered trollers are still fishing. Those that are have had their income halved. Though courts had increased the Indian relative share of the catch tenfold in the mid-1970s, Indians in the 1990s were catching half as many fish as Indians in the 1940s.

The decline in income in the salmon fishery is much greater than in any other natural resource industry in the Pacific Northwest. Society, saddled with the loss of salmon and their habitats, is paying to grow fish unsuccessfully in hatcheries and paying for lost jobs from all the aforesaid blunders, miscalculations, and calculated misanthropy.

A large wooden Indian head carved from a sizable log stands next to a sign saying WELCOME TO ASTORIA, the small city— ten thousand—at the mouth of the mighty Columbia River. It takes only five minutes to drive clear across Astoria, though it feels distinctly urban. Astoria is old and feels old, but not badly run-down. At least not yet. It has a well-worn, comfortable feel, like an old denim jacket. I pass Dollar Mania, the Liberty Movie Theatre, Owl Drugstore, the Columbia Christian Supply, Trudy's Treasures, and The Workers' Cafe. The town, like most, has its seamier side: a topless bar, a porn shop, and a men's bathhouse. A couple of trucks go by, laden densely with logs of unremarkable size.

I turn into the performing arts center of the Clatsop Community College, an old church building. I had driven fast for a couple of hours to get here on time for the hearing scheduled to start at five P.M., and I am twenty minutes early. I pull into the empty lot and check an empty auditorium. Is this the right place? The building sits upon a hill with a fine, close-by view of the Columbia's mouth, some five impressive miles across, sea green, carrying oceangoing freighters. I leave to find a quick snack. Returning to the center at precisely five o'clock, I cannot find a parking space in the now jammed lot. In a town this small, everyone knows just how long they need to get from point A to point B, and they arrive exactly on time for the public meeting with the people from D.C., the nation's capital.

John Bullard, a former mayor of New Bedford, Massachusetts (a town that is no stranger to fishing problems), gray-suited, looking very much the politician, is on center stage. Because of the salmon famine, a state of crisis has been declared by the governors of Oregon, California, and Washington and the secretary of commerce. The result: Some sixteen million dollars of federal tax money has been loosed, mostly from a fund earmarked for "naturally caused fishery disasters." And Bullard, head of the new Office of Sustainable Development, formed explicitly to do *something* about the fisheries collapses in New England and the Northwest, has come here to listen to the people's advice about how the money should most wisely be spent.

There are about 150 people at the meeting, many of them longtime friends. Many fishermen, and many women, and some quite elderly couples, make up this graying group. No one looks under thirty-five. Most young people have known better for quite some time than to go into fishing. A man near me overhears someone telling an anecdote and asks him to repeat the beginning of it. The storyteller says that it's just an old fish story. "Well, of course," the man says. "There aren't any *new* fish stories around here."

As the meeting comes to order, Mr. Bullard has everyone's hushed attention. He addresses the assembly, saying this is the first time any presidential administration has acknowledged that there is a human impact to the degradation of fish populations. This hardly rocks the hall as news; it seems only to underscore that all through the incubation of this calamity government has held a position of extreme remove.

The congressional representatives, granted an unearned deference, are asked to speak first. The local congresswoman has sent a staffer to recite, "We need to bring back the salmon, who for so long sustained our unique way of life." She carries no proposals for action. Her crock of empty platitudes is only the first in a litany of phony sentimentality from elected officials who stay well fed no matter what.

Another congressional staffer reads, "These are sad times. What will it take to bring back our treasured salmon?"

What will it take? For decades, Congress was *told* what it would take—was warned that this train wreck was coming—and ignored those warnings, changing neither course nor speed. They deserve no credit for acting concerned about the victims. Both U.S. senators have sent women here to read statements not worth repeating.

Spare us the indignity. So much for the national "representatives." They are too out of touch to realize how much they've embarrassed themselves in front of authentic people.

After being forced to endure the vapid patter of the Washingtonians, who scurry hastily from the meeting, the real people are allowed, finally, to step up to the microphone.

A fisherman says, "We've been down to the floor in the past, and we've come back up. But we've never seen it like this before, when everything came together and took it all down at once, so there was nowhere to turn. I want you to know I have an awful high regard for the resource, and I want to see it come back. We're ready to work with you."

A radiant blond woman from Tillamook Bay, projecting a striking presence at the microphone, says she, too, still has faith in the system, and is likewise prepared to do whatever it takes.

A harbormaster tells of the layoffs at his marina. Gillnetters rise one by one, many self-conscious at the microphone, to try to put their fishing heritage into words. Some are coarse and some highly articulate. Some are brave and some clearly frightened of the future. Some talk of their pain. Many ask that the federal government buy their boats so they can afford to exit this way of life. Most speakers express the fear that the disaster money will be eaten up by administrative bureaucracies and ask that the money to go directly to the neediest fishing families.

But there is scarcely enough money to make a difference. With a rare blend of wisdom, pragmatism, and emotion, a local official says, "I recognize a lot of faces here, and I want to see us all remain positive. But we have to be realistic and think long-term. This could take twenty years to turn around. If we give a little of this disaster money to everyone, it won't help, and it won't solve the problems."

Another official says to Mr. Bullard, "The town of Ilwaco will lose two and a half million dollars this year. If you add up all the ports in Pacific County, that's six million. If you add the fishing-related commerce, it comes to twenty million. In all of Washington State, about four hundred million dollars will be lost. Your sixteen million dollars will not go very far."

"If you divide the money equally," says a woman representing charter sport-fishing boats, "every salmon-dependent family would get about twelve hundred dollars, about enough to pay the bills sitting on the dining room table."

Willow Burch, a thirty-seven-year-old grandmother who is part Cherokee, part Czech, walks up to the microphone in a "Salmon for All" sweatshirt and says brightly, "I know a lot of you all here." She pauses. "I hear people who are afraid they'll lose their house. Well—" After an awkward pause, she looks directly at Bullard and says, "I lost my house." She looks down for a moment, then back at Bullard. "I'm not in the habit of asking for help. I've done a lot of things by myself. I raised my kids by myself." Her voice becomes a bit shaky. "I used to fish by myself, too. But this year I couldn't afford the permit. Now I mend nets by myself—when there's nets to mend, which there's not so many anymore. I don't have any schooling. I'd like to take some courses and get some training. That costs money I don't have. I've heard people here asking to be bought out." She wavers a little. "The only thing I have left to be bought out—are dreams." Her voice cracks. "I've lost everything. I have nothing left." She's crying softly now, at the microphone, in front of the entire assembly of her neighbors. "Please go back to Washington and tell them I'm out here. I didn't cause these problems. Don't let them forget about me. Please don't let them forget that I'm here. I'm not a number. Please don't let them forget my name." Before she steps down, she regains just enough composure to add, "I want to say I really appreciate your coming here." She takes her seat in the back and I can still hear her sobbing softly.

Bullard is visibly shaken as he steps up to the microphone and asks simply, "Who's next?"

Unable to endure this massacre of human dignity, I am gripped with an urgent need to leave the auditorium.

In the lobby, as at a wake, people are milling and talking and getting caught up on news and gossip. I overhear a man who runs a charter boat saying, "I have two sons who love fishing. I'd like to get *that* out of their heads."

Willow Burch has come back here, and she says, "Mr. Bullard looked so sad up there, I felt so sorry for him." Up close, Willow has a ruddy face. Her dark, wavy hair is pulled back, but a little of it spills forward over one eye. She is slight of build and pretty, but she looks like she's been through a lot.

A fiftyish woman with fluffy hair and red lipstick is saying, "Ninety percent of my business was salmon. Our charter boats did a half-million-dollar business. We had eleven boats each doing two trips a day. In Depoe Bay, they were doing three trips a day. People came from every state. Most of the people who worked with us are no longer fishing. Our captains can tell you the devastation of no salmon."

Her husband says, "I don't understand how policies are made, but everything is working in reverse, opposite to how it should go, and it's killing us."

His wife, almost too exasperated to continue speaking, inserts in a pinched voice, "People are *so* angry at government. These are the people—. They're—. They're ready for a revolution."

A guy named Don says, "Environmentalists are our biggest problem. Even five years ago, we had plenty of salmon. I don't understand why they're scaling back hatcheries when the ocean conditions are bad. The enviros are into saving everything—these sea lions, which are such miserable nuisances, cormorants, everything—even down to some little bug or animal that we never even heard of. Why didn't the environmentalists save the dinosaurs?"

I have to pause to consider just how bad things really are when the word "dinosaur" slips into a discussion on salmon.

The woman with the fluffy hair adds, "Westport had three hundred salmon charter boats five years ago, with all kinds of shops along the docks. There probably aren't twenty boats left. It looks like a ghost town. In Ilwaco, there is total devastation. Those people are *very* angry.

"We can't make it on salmon anymore. We're trying seabird watching, whale watching, halibut fishing. But they just announced closure of the halibut season here after thirteen days. And a lot of those people that used to come for salmon are not interested in whale watching or anything else. Without salmon, this isn't the Northwest."

Randy and Brenda Wall are both about forty. Their kids are home tonight. Randy says, "It brings tears to your eyes, what's happening to people. This year, my fishing income is down seventy-five percent. *We're* not going to be fishing anymore, *that's* for sure. I'm throwing in the towel. We'll stay and survive, because we are blessed with a good family support system. With all the problems it's a wonder there's any salmon left at all. With thirty-three walls of concrete in the Columbia, how can you even call that a river?"

Don Riswick, age seventy-seven, says, "We fought the dam builders tooth and nail. But we were the only ones fighting. We lost."

A woman of about fifty wearing a large cross around her neck, adds, "Behind the ecological disaster is a whole way of thinking: We do not cherish the gift we've been given." This is Irene Martin—the *Reverend* Irene Martin, Episcopal priest, married to a man whose sole source of income for their family has always been fishing.

Les and Fran Clark have been listening quietly. He is sixty-five and wields his fifty years of fishing experience with crusty authority. "I just heard everybody get up and say how much they're hurting and how they're starving to death, but nobody got up to talk about what we're going to do for the fish! Nobody asked, 'How are we going to salvage the resource?' If you get the resource back it'll take *care* of all these crybabies.

"With hydroelectric dams, irrigation, transportation, and everything else, we've hammered 'em. *Boy,* how we've hammered 'em. Now, I've got the ninety-thousand-dollar boat I always dreamed about, and no fish to go with it. It's not worth five cents. And if they buy us out, who is gonna fight for the fish?"

Reverend Martin responds, "I, too, am really torn on the idea of using this money to buy people out of the fishery. The people need money, but the very real thing I see is, if fishermen sell out, the fish are gone. The people with the most invested—the guys that have been in this all their lives—are the ones that would sell out in a heartbeat, because *they* are the most desperate. Then, you've lost the fishermen's associations, you've lost those people. Then—I agree—who will speak for the salmon?"

Ivan Larsen, a muscular, compact, dark man with black hair, a black beard, and a black shirt over a black T-shirt, says he doesn't think there will *be* any buy-outs, because bureaucracy is going to eat up all the money. "Sixteen million isn't even a Band-Aid. It's not enough to do *anything,*" he says with a disgusted wave of his hands.

"There's been a tremendous insensitivity to the lives and livelihoods of the people here," says Steve Fick, a beefy thirty-seven-year-old who runs Fish Hawk

Fisheries in Astoria. "It makes me sick to think of what was here, and what they did with it. Our coastal economies lost over a billion dollars because of the dams built for the aluminum industry. It was a stupid trade-off. Here we had a free, renewable resource that people want, and some fast-buck artists cut a bunch of deals. Fishing is a way of life; is aluminum a way of life? I have eighty-five-year-old retired people who come and help me out because they want to be part of fishing. How many retired aluminum workers go back to the smelters?"

Every cityscape offers its most innocent aspect at dawn, even in towns with a mean history. I have a long day ahead, visiting some of the people I met only briefly last night.

I drive south from Astoria over the long causeway bridge, past the rotting pilings of old docks that once lined the shore. A ramshackle driveway marked by a black fifty-five gallon drum, an old blue boat, and a rusting car is where I'm supposed to turn. Fragments of nets, dredges, and other bits of fishing equipment are scattered about. Willow Burch and a woman named Tammy are sitting on low plastic stools among extensive heaps of new netting in a big shed, bent diligently to their work. Two big panels of net part at Willow's lap and flow past her faded pink shorts. Using a net needle, she is sewing a seam to join them. She holds the net stretched with her bare toes, while dexterously weaving the two panels of netting into a shrimp trawl. "What's happened to the fish is one of the saddest things, but I have faith in the salmon. They could come back. We could all come out all right. But I don't have faith in the people that are in control. And for that reason, I think we could lose the fish."

She pulls each panel to bring more of the unsewn seam into her lap. "I never wanted anything but to be a salmon fisherman. Something about it is in my blood. It's clean, healthy. You feel that you're providing excellent food for people. I banked my whole future on it. Now I'm sitting here sewing. For a fisherman like me, do you know what this is like?"

She cuts a piece of sewing twine against her thumb with a knife. I ask if that makes calluses on her thumbs.

"Not really. There's not enough work for me to get calluses."

When Willow first started working on nets, it was ten hours a day, eight days a week. There were ten people working here. Now she works one or two weeks a month, and Tammy and she are the only employees.

"I really loved fishing. I can't imagine giving up my boat. But I have to be realistic. I bought the boat in the nineteen eighties, and I was doing really well fishing for a few years. The Bonneville Power Administration promised to double the runs. Now I have no house. I guess Bonneville Power wasn't really serious."

Willow keeps a bag of clothes in her car. "I live wherever: at my sister's, or at my friend's house. I have a room here at the net shop that I can use as well."

Again she tugs more netting to her lap. "I'm not educated. What I'm trying to do is set myself up so that if any money for schooling comes out of this disaster relief I can learn how to be an electrician. I figure that if I can become an electrician I could work on boat electronics. That way I wouldn't be far from fishing."

The shop's owner shuffles in. John is a very old looking sixty-seven, a hollow-faced, imploded man, resembling a recently liberated concentration camp survivor. His face carries a stubble of beard and his stiff yellowed fingers hold a cigarette as he squats on his haunches to confer with Willow. He jokingly tells her that if she could sew as fast as she talks, he could make some money. It is said in jest, but it seems an unkind and bullying remark and it makes me feel self-conscious. Willow has scarcely taken her eye off her work the entire time I've been there; mostly I've been looking at the part in her hair as she talks. And it's not as if the work is backed up.

He leaves, and Willow continues stitching and talking. "My first commercial fishing trip was on my seventeenth birthday. I had my baby with me. I went at night with my husband. In the morning as I was sitting on that deck with the sun coming up, the calm, the sounds—it was so pretty. Something just reached into my heart and caught me. I said to myself, 'This would be a good way of life.'

"I fished with my husband until 1987 or so. We were married for fifteen years. He was an alcoholic and eventually we got divorced. He used to yell a lot, and I don't like fighting and I don't like yelling. I feel bad, though, because I really cared about my husband.

"After my husband, it was such a relief to fish with my son. My son was my steady deckhand and was ultimately going to take over the boat. We used to fish near a place called Eagle Cliff. Every year the eagles come back there. They're so beautiful. It was so peaceful."

She pushes a heap of finished netting onto the floor and draws more of the unsewn panels across her knees. "I was doing really well in the eighties, but then my income kept dropping, until this spring I couldn't afford the three-hundred-and-eighty-five-dollar fishing license. And you can't renew the license if you don't deliver fish on it."

In 1985, Willow could have sold her salmon permit for forty thousand dollars. People who wanted to buy permits took out want ads in newspapers or paid permit brokers. People who turned down the opportunity to sell then are kicking themselves now. And boats built for gillnetting cannot easily be converted for much else.

"Five years doesn't seem like a long time," she continues while stitching, stitching. "You have a bad year, but you're O.K. Then you have another bad year. You begin to wonder. Then you start losing things to creditors. The only easy thing to do is get drunk. Alcohol gets a lot of people. Then you lose your car. Maybe you lose your house."

She stops sewing for a moment.

Then she picks it up again, saying, "My house was *beautiful*. It was on ten acres. It had a big grove of cedars. There was also a grove of the most beautiful fir trees you ever saw. Those firs were eight feet across at the butt. They were huge. I used to go sit by them, in awe of how gorgeous they were. And when it got stormy in the wintertime you could hear them howling in the wind." She stops, looks at me, and says, "You heard about trees howling in the wind? Well, these trees would do that." Back to stitching again, she continues, "And my daughter would get scared and she'd cry because they'd make such a beautiful howling sound. And I'd tell her it was just the trees talking. It was the most beautiful place. We had a creek running through the property."

"Sounds like heaven," I offer.

"Yeah. It was. But we bought it from a private party and they foreclosed."

"That must have broken your heart."

"Oh, I could deal with losing it. But what *did* break my heart was what I saw when I went back to visit. They had sold it to a guy who logged it off. *That* broke my heart." Her eyes well up. "Sometimes I feel angry, or desperate, or embarrassed. The stress can get to you. I have a lot of pride and it isn't easy to tell someone how bad it is. When I started, I was told not to be on the water. 'A woman should know her place.' 'It's unlucky to have a woman in the boat.' I was close to tears many times, but I wouldn't go away."

As I pull into the parking lot at Fish Hawk Fisheries in Astoria, a large container full of shrimp slips off a forklift and spills all over the ground. I walk upstairs to Steve Fick's office, which is continually vibrated by the rumble of machinery below. A large mounted crab splays upon the wall, and a box of bumper stickers promoting dolphin-safe troll-caught albacore awaits distribution. Two old pictures of Celilo Falls, that famous salmon fishing spot on the Columbia River now lying buried underwater behind a dam, decorate a shelf.

Steve greets me in the reception area and invites me to have a seat in his big-windowed office overlooking the sprawling river, saying, "In three years it seems like I haven't had enough salmon in here for a barbecue. When I first started my business, I was in the salmon business. Now, it's maybe twenty percent of my volume."

I take that to mean that, unlike most people I've met here, Fick is pretty well buffered from the declines of salmon because he has diversified.

"I'm not buffered, I'm looking over my shoulder. I don't feel comfortable about the situation. We need more money to make money now, and the profit margin is thinner. I've had to take hundreds of thousands of dollars of hard cash and throw it back: reinvested it in my shrimp- and crab-processing equipment, for example. It's a different business. I would have had thirty more employees than I do now. And I've adjusted just to maintain some kind of employment for a number of people, but I can't pay them as much as I could with salmon.

"The lack of salmon takes you from a situation where you're making money, and you're prospering, and you're contributing, to a situation where you're just existing—and there's a big difference." He glances out the window at a passing barge. "When there was a good salmon season, you could feel the difference. There was activity, money being spent, people smiling. Now, it's just not there. We used to be able to contribute more to Little League, to scholarships, things like that. I used to be able to pay college students three thousand dollars for six weeks' work, processing salmon. They could count on that for school. That's not there, either. So when you look at the decline and you see that people like me are still here, that doesn't mean it's O.K."

He leans forward, his beefy forearms upon his desk, saying, "There are people in the electric-power industry running the dams on the Columbia River who do not care one bit about the salmon, and they would like to see us gone. If there is really no chance of saving this, then please tell me, so I can get on with my life."

Les and Frances Clark live in a place not quite a town, called Chinook. In their kitchen, where we are sitting, hang two pictures of Celilo Falls, where Les used to fish until water backing up from The Dalles Dam flooded and buried the falls in 1957. He'd started fishing in 1943, just a few years after Bonneville, the first and lowest of the big dams, went in on the Columbia. In those days, there were neither sportfishermen nor environmentalists. "The region was young. The farmers liked the young salmon comin' through the irrigation ditches onto the fields because they said they made good fertilizer. The smolts came out of the ditches into the fields by the *millions*. They *still* do."

Les's perspective is that of a hunter of wild fish who has seen society overtake him in his lifetime. "Once, all our challenges had to do with the tide, the wind, the weather. Now, sometimes it's one-tenth fishing and nine-tenths politics."

Fran nods her emphatic agreement.

"Well, you've got to look for the light at the end of the tunnel," he adds.

"Yeah?" his wife challenges. "What if that light's the train comin' at you?" Then, to me, she says, "I think there's just too many people now. Man is responsible for destroying everything. I don't mean men. I mean man generically. I don't want a sexual-harassment suit here." She winks at me.

Referring to the old days that were the best times of their life, Les says, "The river community and the river people were like the Indians. We always lived right along the river. You can learn something new every day on the river. When we caught enough fish to save enough to move uptown into a house, we lost all the fun days."

But it wasn't always unalloyed fun. "A lot of times we were broke for several years, but there was always some little scrap you could salvage, some little part of it that was still working until the runs came back. Now we don't have any cards to play or any other place to go fishing or any healthy stock to fish on. Everything is coming together, going down at once. We're just up against the wall."

Fran says, "I know families who are down to their last hundred dollars. They're hard workers, but they are in a bad situation. My youngest son, good fisherman—single parent—was within a week of losing his house recently, before a refinancing came through. Almost every fisherman I know barely got through the winter, hoping to have a good season in Alaska, hoping that this year would be better here. Now we see it will be worse. I don't know what some families are going to do."

Les, waving his hands in disgust, offers, "We've had a lot of agencies and a lot of interagencies working in the Columbia Basin for years. Stacks and stacks of papers and draft papers and all kinds of stuff and studies. None of it has ever borne any fruit. You've got Washington Department of Fish and Wildlife, Oregon Department of Fish and Wildlife, Idaho, the tribes, the U.S. Fish and Wildlife Service, National Marine Fisheries Service, the U.S. Army Corps of Engineers, the Bureau of Reclamation, the Forest Service, the electric industry, the logging industry, the farming industry, the ecology people, and on and on and on. And you can't get them to sit down and decide to do something. They're all protecting their turf."

He adds, "There's big predation by seals and birds and sea lions. The birds are just absolutely eating us out. We sometimes get seals tangled up in the net and they drown, or we'll kill him and dump him overboard."

Now here is something I have a problem with—this disdain for other living parts of the system. After all the problems they are suffering because other people abused parts of the system *they* didn't care about, you might think the salmon fishers would realize that all the parts matter, even the ones that don't seem to matter to *them*. Most of these people are gillnetters, and gill nets fish dirty a lot of the time, catching birds, seals, and prohibited fish. Some fine people happen to be gillnetters, and I hate to see what is happening to these folks as the salmon have been destroyed. But the fine people who are gillnetters would be equally fine as trollers, or better yet, operating fish traps where specific runs can be selectively targeted as they enter tributaries, and fish can be sorted selectively while they are alive so protected ones can be released instead of dumped. It's a thought, anyway. And we can't entirely blame fishers for their by-catch as long as we buy seafood caught with dirty gear.

I say my good-byes to the Clarks, feeling torn allegiances.

Don Riswick also lives in Astoria. His twenty-eight-foot cedar gill-net boat, *Shoofly*—one of the few wooden vessels left—is a neat, pretty craft, capable of holding a ton of fish.

He's pushing eighty, smallish, roundish, and baldish, with a well-lined face. Don has reached the age where many of his friends and associates have died. He lost his wife six months ago, after a long illness. He's not feeling too great either. A large, fresh scar from recent open-heart surgery shows over the top of his shirt.

Don was an active fisherman right into this year. He started fishing in 1930, when he was twelve, as a boat puller, or oarsman. By the time he was seventeen, he had his own boat, with a four-horsepower, one-cylinder engine that "barely bucked the tide."

Don has done more than his share of the fighting. He fought the dams and the pulp mills. "Logging started in the eighteen hundreds, but the pulp mills didn't start until the twenties, so I was around near the beginning of the pulp era. When the pulp mills started taking over, they'd pump their liquor into the river once a week. The bacteria adhered to the sawdust and it creeped down the river. It made a floating mass and it clogged our nets. Every Saturday we had to soak our nets in copper sulfate to kill the bacteria, then clean them with a high-powered hose. You could walk across the Willamette on a mat of pulp waste. Fish were floating upside down for lack of oxygen. I mounted a campaign against it. I helped set up stations to sample water up the river. But you know, you're fighting city hall when you're fighting Boise Cascade Lumber and James River and those other lumber outfits. It took us nine years, but we got the dumping stopped."

Riswick's small suburban home sits on a little hill with a magnificent, sweeping view of the river. Birdhouses and a birdbath, well-tenanted, are situated outside a picture window and backed by the blue river. His house is loaded with war memorabilia: pictures of planes, photos of him with the bombing crew he headed in the Pacific. Airplane models hang from the ceiling and from doorways, as they might in a fifteen-year-old boy's bedroom. There are numerous photos of boats and fish and people, going back to 1934 (how many businessmen and lawyers have photo albums of their life of work on the coffee table?), as well as an honored photo of his recently deceased wife.

Don pops into the VCR a video called *Work Is Our Joy,* a history of Columbia River gillnetters that features many people Don knows—or knew while they were alive. Don talks to me throughout the film, but he is at least as interesting as the narration. He tells me, "In 1938, Bonneville Dam went on line. The fishermen opposed it. They were going to sacrifice all the fish in the Columbia Basin for electricity. The guy in charge told us, 'I haven't got time to play nursemaid to a bunch of fish.' But they did put in ladders to help the adults get past the dam. [Grand] Coulee Dam was the big killer. It was finished in 1941—no ladders— and it wiped out a big race of salmon. You'd catch twelve salmon and have six hundred pounds. That's right. Those were monsters. They went clear up to Canada to spawn. They were big because they needed the strength to get up there. When the dam closed, those big salmon just went up there for six or eight years, beating themselves to death against the concrete, until they died off forever."

When the video is done, Don kills the VCR with the remote, and, in the moment it takes for him to turn off the television, the TV jumps to life with a local station running *Casablanca.* Humphrey Bogart, with those eyes, that voice, says to Ingrid Bergman, with that face, "It's pretty bad timing. Where were you, say, ten years ago?" Don clicks off the set.

Ivan Larsen owns a small commercial fish dock and the adjacent convenience store. He sells some groceries, gas, beer and wine, engine parts, meals, and ice. He runs food and gas around to gillnetters in the bay while they are fishing. "Anything for a buck. I've got a pretty large operation here, but my clientele is going broke." His customers are loggers and commercial fishermen. He has had up to 140 boats docked here. Now he has nineteen. He himself is paying mortgages on boats he can't use. "I have a lot of customers in the store, but now they buy coffee for lunch instead of a sandwich, and business is off forty percent. We're going downhill real bad. I need to buy three hundred thousand pounds of salmon off the boats to offset my debt service. Last year I got sixty-six thousand pounds. I bought more salmon from one guy six years ago than I bought last year from everybody combined."

His fourteen-year-old son comes in. He's having problems trying to remember how to write a receipt for gas.

"You know how to do it. I don't have to tell you again." The boy leaves, still confused, and looking hurt. Ivan says to me, "I try to teach him to be self-sufficient because the self-sufficient ones are the only guys who can make it anymore."

Randy and Brenda Wall live in the kind of floating house working fishermen tow up and down the river with them as they follow their prey, and they plan to stay in the house even though they will no longer be fishing.

Randy takes me to his grandparents' home. Grandfather Oliver and Grandma Nora have been married sixty-eight years. This is a fishing family: Nora's Gran'pa Hansen was one of the first white men to fish the Columbia River.

A huge set of antlers from an elk Oliver shot in 1938 dominates the living room. Next to the rack is a photo of the elk itself, with Randy's mother, then a little girl, standing on the animal's head, her arms spread to the antler tips. Pictures of kids, grandkids, great-grandkids, and amateurish but very attractive paintings of the river line the walls. And, off to the side, the votive photo of Celilo Falls. No one says as much, but with all these pictures of Celilo in everyone's homes and offices, it seems as though the heart of the river was killed when the thundering falls drowned.

Grandfather Oliver, age ninety-six, has a surprisingly bright and open face, though it is sunken as if with a great sigh at the end of a long life. Oliver is dressed in jeans and suspenders, wearing a blue shirt. He has wispy hair and a wispy voice and is reclining in a chair in front of the TV, watching reruns of *The Rat Patrol.* Oliver started fishing in 1913, when he was fifteen. He says whisperingly, "There were good and bad years. The price varied. Once, the price was half a cent a pound. A ton of fish got you ten bucks. I was around forty when Bonneville Dam went in. We had good runs for a few more years. There were thirty-six canneries on the river. There are none now. After the canneries left, fishermen basically lost their political power."

Grandma Nora, a thin woman ten years Oliver's junior, says, "They wasted a lot of fish in the old days. The canneries didn't want the very small and very big ones, and they wasted 'em."

After a pause, Grandma pipes up again and says, "This spotted owl thing is nuts. Old-growth does not matter. It'll fall and rot if you don't cut it."

Randy says, "Well, they should leave some of it standing for my kids."

Grandma laughs. "Ha! By the time your kids are grown, them old trees'll all be rotten."

Grandpa whispers, "There seemed to be so many trees and so many fish, I didn't see the end coming."

The river near Skamokawa, Washington, is so full of islands that it does not seem so much a river as a system of rival sibling channels, all braided and trying to see who will be first to find the sea. The Reverend Irene Martin's home is a neat blue house with red trim.

Reverend Martin has shoulder-length sandy-blond hair and a soft-featured face, with clear, insightful blue eyes and a thoughtful bearing. Her family includes two adopted daughters from India. Her husband of twenty years, Kent, is a gillnetter whose ancestors came here as fishermen to escape the famines in Sweden in the 1860s. Kent's fishing has been their sole source of income; Reverend Martin receives no pay for her ministry. She has written a book, *Legacy and Testament,* portraying the passing of the life and times they have known.

Leading me into a small living room, she thinks out loud, "How can I summarize what I've seen happening?" We sit, and she pauses to gather her thoughts, then offers, "I'm seeing the internal collapse of a community that's had its major sources of identity removed. I see people who believed they were society's surrogates in nature—the fisherman catching food for society—being told that what they have known all their lives no longer counts for anything positive. When people have been proud of what they do and pride turns to self-blame, it is extremely difficult to deal with. And I see very troubled people—the entire community—who can't understand what is happening.

"What I've seen as a clergyperson is, first of all, families that come to our child-care facilities because they have no money. We've had a run on the food bank over the last few months. I'm seeing an increase in people with drug, alcohol, and mental-health problems. I also see the kinds of stresses that is putting on families."

She sits back. "In the old days, we had a real social life around the fishery. That's all collapsing. The economic life is *certainly* collapsing. And as the men are gone longer and longer stretches, leaving women alone with their families here, some marriages break up—especially the younger ones. It's harder on the children than anything else. I think this is just the beginning. There will be more. And now even when the men go away to fish they can't make enough money. Most of the gillnetters already figure it's over. They're looking for a way out. Not just because of power companies and what the dams have done to fish, but because the ecosystem has changed to the point where it is inimical to salmon."

She leans forward, hands clasped in her lap. "I see this as a moral, theological, ethical, and religious issue. The role of the priest is the care of souls. And what I see"—her eyes narrow—"has been *powerfully* destructive to people's souls. *Incredibly* destructive. Tremendous damage has been done to people. And—" She pauses and begins again hesitatingly, as though this is the hardest part for her to admit. "I—have—*no way*—of healing that."

She sits back again, as though from the exertion of speaking these troubles. "The power companies have characterized fishermen as the big killers, not their dams. To blame is human nature. But when you degrade and revile people whose services you have used, it is the end of any possibility for communication.

"In my community, the loggers are suffering along with the fishermen. The logging companies pulled out with no show of social responsibility. They had told people they were going to be here permanently. Based on those kinds of promises, people put down roots, took out mortgages on homes, started families. And then the company was gone. That was reprehensible. Have we no social contract? No social fabric?"

Her eyes widen as though searching me for the answer.

"I went as part of a delegation over to Weyerhaeuser when they bailed out of here a few years ago. We asked whether local people could at least be put to work in doing things like tree planting, brush clearing, maintaining roads. And we were told—" Her voice cracks and for a fleeting moment the dignity of her presence seems to crumble, and she is just a woman looking small, a bit scared, and cold from inside. "He said, 'We're going to hire cheap crews from Mexico.' "

Until the moment her outer armor cracked, I had not sensed the depth of her strength, nor just how much strength is required, in these times, to forge the dignified comportment she carries.

In her very next breath, she comes back reforged and strong of voice. It is a locked strength that only hatred can carry, priest or not. "I can *still* remember that man's face as he said, 'Forget it,' looking right at me, smiling smugly."

She tilts her head back a bit, looking somewhere past the ceiling, and swallows hard. "And the logs that they are sending to Japan to be milled, instead of milling them here? I don't comprehend the export of jobs. I can't cope with this. I never have understood it. So, should the company be forced to do something for our community after our community helped make them rich? You bet. *Everyone* should care about this.

"When you look at the story of Adam and Eve in the Bible, when we misuse our resources, we fall out of Eden. And like Adam and Eve, we're blaming everybody else—the loggers, et cetera. But it's *all* of us. None of us put those forests here. But we *all* use them.

"Heart and soul, I see this as a religious issue. Eleven out of twelve of Jesus' disciples were fishermen. That was no coincidence."

"He asked them to leave fishing and follow him, did he not?" I say.

"He asked them to become fishers of men. What does that mean? This may seem a silly question, but for a religious leader whose community had found God in a gill net, it must seem that anyone who asked fishermen to leave their profession would be viewed with extreme skepticism, unless God had given them some reason to doubt the future. What kind of fishing community follows a messiah? One that is under stress. I want to know: When those fishermen decided to follow Jesus, had there been some kind of change? A lack of fish?

"My husband is a very moral man. The hardest thing for him is that he has dealt honorably and we have lost. I can leave that with God. My husband cannot. We feel like we are giving up. The nagging question is: Have I done all I can? Is there something else I could try?"

It has rained every day I've been in Astoria, quite as if a cloud is hanging over the city, and as I leave, it is pouring.

Columbia Gorge

The road into Oxbow Park is beautiful with foxgloves, snapdragons, and Queen Anne's lace. The park itself, on land that was once heavily cut-over, is sanctuary to what might be called "young old-growth": trees ranging in age to more than a century, now just beginning to re-create their natural structural complexity, rebuilding habitats for other forms of life, slowly becoming a forest again. Despite its proximity to Portland, this park on the Sandy River retains much of its wilderness feel. The airplanes and the highway traffic are mostly unseen, but the velvet murmur of not-so-distant engines reminds that a major city churns nearby.

A blacktail doe tip-hooves across the road. The path, thick with ferns, threads through trees thick with moss, then out to the riverside. Three flying trios of hen mallards, with flat, quacking faces pointed upriver, are making fleet progress to who knows where or why. Five mergansers, with heads underwater and scanning for fish, are spreading chevron wakes as they prowl a slick pool. It is a pool of some size, bounded on either end by riffles slipping over cobbles that range from fist to fist-times-two and larger. Between the riffles, the still-looking water runs, as they say, deep.

This river, part of the Mount Hood watershed, still works like a real river, with high winter flows and flood scouring. It is wide, more than a hundred yards across in places, a reclining, almost Rubenesque river. The flow carries a small load of glacial powder, giving the deeper pools an emerald cast. Importantly for the fish, the Sandy enters the Columbia below the first dam, so the fish have a clear shot to and from the ocean, like salmon are supposed to have.

On the opposite ridge stand Douglas-firs, and, in succession down the slope, cedars, hemlocks, bigleaf maples, and along the banks, alders. On the gravel bars, where their timidity in the face of competition from other trees forces them to take the most courageous, flood-defying stand of all, are willows. Some trees have greatness thrust upon them. Each tree species portrays its own shade of green, which is darkest in the sentinel firs that line the ridges, then grades through color changes to lightest in the willows on the river bars. As I am admiring the hillside, Bill Bakke says, as if narrating my thoughts, "Nice texture, nice species composition to the vegetation."

Bakke bears the unmistakable field marks of a former hippie ripening toward middle age, mellowing toward something not too closely resembling perfection, blending into society a little better, one suspects, than he has in thirty years. A light-green shirt covers a spreading midsection, and his sandy-brownish hair is graying.

Director of the Native Fish Society and formerly with the conservation group Oregon Trout, Bakke was for many years the only person in the Northwest arguing that, as he is telling me now, "Without wild fish you don't have a future for salmon. If the hatcheries worked, we'd be up to our butts in fish, but we have fewer now than ever." Millions of dollars were—are—being spent on hatcheries, but for a long time no one had been willing to do the simple division to figure the cost per individual returning adult salmon. If they were afraid of knowing the answer, their intuition was good. Bill Bakke and economist Hans Radtke did the math and found that most fish cost ten to twenty-five dollars apiece, and some much more—up to hundreds of dollars per salmon. Has the spending helped salmon? Congress's General Accounting Office found that the $537 million spent on hatcheries between 1981 and 1991—the single largest chunk of money spent on the fish—bought "continuing decline of salmon."

As we walk, Bill bends occasionally to pick pieces of trash from the mostly clean trail. He has a sense of proprietorship here in this public park. The Sandy grows three seasonal runs of chinook, winter and summer steelhead, coho, and sea-run cutthroat trout, and Bakke has worked for the recognition of this river— and particularly this stretch—as important for spawning and worthy of protection. "This is one of the only places you can assemble a crowd to see wild salmon spawning, and you have to imagine the early days, the interactions between a hundred and fifty people who'd arrived for a morning 'salmon spawning walk,' and a guy standing alongside a pool, snagging egg-laden salmon with a treble hook. But the draw these fish have on people is really remarkable." Indeed, in a few weeks, when fall-run chinook salmon ascend this river to spawn, Bakke's annual salmon festival will draw ten thousand people.

If Bill has given many thousands of people something to see and some things to think about and learn from, it is because he has been thinking and learning about fish himself for a long time. When he was five, he was intrigued by his neighbor's goldfish pond and frequented the place. "My dog and I were so effective at capturing goldfish that my neighbors gave up and cemented the pond over. So I learned a most important lesson: When you abuse the fish you lose them *and* the habitat as well."

Later, as an avidly fishing teenager, he visited the Oregon Department of Fish and Game, looking for information that would help explain something puzzling—

why there were big fish in small rivers and small fish in big rivers. A couple of gentlemen there opened their libraries to Bill. When that door opened, the light fell
upon, as Bill puts it, "the ways flesh and the physical world are connected. The
salmon are not just fish. They are the forged product of millions of years of geologic
history, erosional history, hydrologic history, evolutionary history.

"Over the geologic time that these animals have evolved," Bakke says, "they
have faced fire and ice, surviving everything from volcanism to periods of glaciation. That has made them fluent at adapting to change; that's why they're so
tough in coping with the changes we've heaped upon them."

Surviving so many changes for so long bred tremendous diversity into salmon
populations up and down the coast, a varied fine-tuning to the local conditions.
Shaking the stem of his pipe at me for emphasis, Bill says, "Unless we do a better
job of understanding that diversity, our children will be poorer than we were."

He explains how different parts of rivers are suitable at different times of the
year, and how the various salmon have adapted to exploit the changing suitabil-
ity in place and season. Take chinook salmon. The fall chinook spawn in rivers'
main stems, in October and November. Spring chinook climb high up in the
tributaries, entering in spring but spawning in late September. Summer chinook
colonize midsections of the river. So the whole river is colonized and productive,
with different genetic strains of salmon using the whole range of the river from
the bottom to the top, throughout the year, as water flows and temperatures
become most favorable.

So, too, the juveniles have their times and places. Young sockeye spend their
freshwater youth in lakes, young chinooks in the upper main-stem rivers, coho in
smaller tributaries, pinks and chums in the lower reaches close to the tidal areas.
Some leave for the ocean right away, some stay in freshwater for several years.

Size also evolved as a variably adapted trait. For chinook in the Rogue River,
thirty pounds was large. But on the Elwah River they sometimes attained more
than a hundred pounds—before dams made that stock extinct. Steelhead can
reach thirty pounds in some rivers, though they do not top ten in some others.
These are a few of the diverse ways salmon adapted to their streams.

They adapted to the ocean's characteristics as well. Some stay in nearby
waters. Others migrate to the central Pacific (their life history, taking them from
mountain brooks to the deepest ocean and back, gives each individual perhaps
the widest ecological niche yet evolved in any species, present company
included).

"But we are taxing that resiliency and diversity," Bakke says as we settle
down on a log at the water's edge. "The Columbia River Basin had the largest
chinook and steelhead runs in the world. With Grand Coulee Dam, and the
Hell's Canyon Project on the Snake River, we intentionally made about two-
thirds of the Columbia Basin's salmon habitat inaccessible. With Grand Coulee,
we lost the populations adapted to breeding in forested uplands. With Hell's
Canyon, we lost fish adapted to an arid ecosystem. Those two groups were very

different." Bill stands up, as though agitated. "When we lose fish that were genetically adapted to specific conditions on specific rivers—as is happening up and down the coast—we may not be able to reestablish runs with hatcheries in those rivers even if we try."

When a logging dam that had blocked and destroyed a six-million-fish sockeye run on a tributary of the Fraser River in British Columbia was finally removed, sixteen attempts between 1949 and 1975 to reintroduce sockeye all failed to establish a run. In a 1995 special report, a National Academy of Sciences panel wrote, "The long-term survival of salmon depends crucially on a diverse and rich store of genetic variation . . . not only on abundance."

So finely attuned are some populations that it astonishes. In laboratory experiments, sockeye hatchlings, in their first movements, traveled along compass headings that would have brought them to their specific nursery lakes in their native river systems, had they still been in the wild. In some cases the correct heading was north, in some cases south, and the young swam along the right heading in their tanks, depending on which river had shaped the evolution of their behavior.

Relatively few of the local breeding populations of salmon that existed a century and a half ago in the Pacific Northwest exist today. In 1880, ten to sixteen million salmon spawned in the Columbia River Basin alone. By 1980, this number had been ground to 2.5 million, 80 percent of which were raised in hatcheries costing more than the value of the fish they produced, and causing other problems. Less than 5 percent of the natural populations remain, and even with hatcheries about 75 percent of the original number of runs in the Northwest are either going or gone.

Finely tuned salmon runs, genetically adapted to local conditions, evolved independently many times in the Northwest since the glaciers retreated. So for those who don't mind waiting another ten thousand years, the current crash is less of a problem—especially if we preserve enough healthy runs. I myself tend toward impatience in such matters, believing that it is more practical to hang onto something that has taken millennia to form than to abuse the privilege of free will that God is said to have been wise to endow us with. When things of great value that are irreplaceable in human time are knowingly destroyed, it can only be because we have elevated and venerated the worst we are capable of, and we have all conspired with our actions and inaction in a great dishonesty and debasement of ourselves and our descendants.

Bakke says, "The salmon heart has beaten for so long in so many rivers. They convey a sense of being connected to something larger than yourself, and at that point, they become holy—holy because they are so ancient."

I ask if that feeling can be called religious. He shrugs, appearing to feel the question is unimportant. "Call it what you want," he says. "I don't call it anything. It's just how I feel."

We continue walking along the bank, Bill with hands in pockets, head bent thoughtfully. "Human cultural history with the salmon spans thousands of years. That's an awful investment in time to just kiss off with hardly a thought. When the coho went extinct in the Snake River in 1986, you didn't see it in the paper, you didn't see it anywhere. I called the Oregon Department of Fish and Game and said, 'Are you going to put out a news release that coho are now extinct in the Snake River?' and the guy said, 'Why?' I cannot accept such terrible disregard for the extinction of something so old. It just wasn't important to them.

"Well, by God, I was going to *make* it important to them." He runs his hand through his graying hair, as though the thought of that time still makes his head hot. "And once we filed to list certain salmon runs under the Endangered Species Act, all of a sudden salmon became important. Now, you're not going to see the Snake River chinook go extinct—which they probably will do—and you're not going to see the Snake River sockeye go extinct—which they probably also will do—without a great deal of public awareness that we are not adequately responding to an enormous problem."

He stops and turns to me, his feet suddenly planted in the gravel as though he has chosen to make a stand on this very spot. "I have a kid, and if he chooses to live here I want him to be proud of it and not suffer some sense that it is less than it was. That's the stake you make when you start a family. That's the fight I'm trying to wage right now.

"But we really haven't done anything significant to recover salmon," he admits a bit forlornly as we continue walking. "Salmon management is still a widget-making program, commodity-oriented and completely external to the ecosystem, as though we were making shoes."

We find another comfortable drift log to rest upon, with a new view of the water. Bill continues, "Shifting from a failing, short-term commodity focus to a long-term ecosystem focus might take closing the hatcheries, logging less in stream corridors, not grazing cattle along streams, obliterating old logging roads and restoring the forest landscape, revamping dam operations, and having the whole fish-management program aimed at rebuilding wild salmon."

"Will that be politically feasible?" I ask.

"One thing that is different between politics and nature," he replies, stabbing the air with his pipe for emphasis, "is that you can change politics." We sit quietly for a few minutes, as time and the river pass.

Bakke rises to his feet, and we resume walking. A light breeze comes up, the shimmering white noise of running water infusing that of air through aspens. We step onto a wide bar at the confluence of the river and a large side channel, watching as a spotted sandpiper lands, its tail bobbing.

Bakke relights his pipe. "When hatcheries got started," he puffs, "it was assumed that a salmon was a salmon was a salmon." Hatchery managers usually took all the eggs they needed from one run in one geographic location at one time. So, a few fish from one place parented much of the next generation. "That immediately cuts out a lot of the genetic variability," Bakke says, gesticulating his frustration with a wave of his pipe. "Particularly when habitat is deteriorating or marine survival is suffering, the more genetic diversity you have, the higher the chances that some fraction of the population will persist and perhaps adapt to new conditions. We have to pay attention to evolution, or we'll lose the fish." Hatcheries took fish adapted to particular water quality, temperature, spawning gravel size, diseases, and waterfall conditions, and put them into streams where they were not well suited. "Local adaptation wasn't understood. But now that we do know about it, people are still doing it. *That's* a problem."

I had once been mistaken about hatcheries, and so I understand how other people might be. The first letter I ever wrote to an elected official was asking that our local trout hatchery not be closed as planned. I was twelve. The hatchery stayed open. Hatcheries instill a false sense of security that a solution is at hand, and this distracts attention from the real problems and potential solutions.

Hatcheries started with the best intentions—to greatly increase fish numbers by rearing young in safety. Soon, they became excuses for excesses. In the U.S., early fish culturists claimed artificially stocked fish would "negate the need for regulating commercial fishing." A revealing thought. It reminds me of the promise in the 1950s that atomic energy would produce electricity "too cheap to meter."

In the 1880s Spencer F. Baird, the first U.S. Fish Commissioner and founder of the federal hatchery program, concluded that stocking salmon was not working, and he halted it. Still, people demanded hatcheries, and they resumed. Canada went through the same revolving door. Because most hatcheries were evaluated only on the basis of how many young fish they put out, not on how many adults resulted, they were flying blind for decades.

Hatcheries went hopelessly wrong when they were asked to make up for— and thereby implicitly condone—intentional, planned destruction of habitat. More than eighty hatcheries—federal, state, and private—were built in the Columbia Basin to mitigate anticipated damage the dams would cause to the world's largest steelhead and chinook salmon runs.

It is now clear that hatcheries themselves have also caused declines of wild salmon populations. That might not be as much of a problem if hatchery fish simply replaced wild ones, but hatchery fish generally don't survive well after they are released. They have numerous abnormalities of behavior, health, and physiology.

Because they are usually selected from a small subset of all available fish, hatchery fish are often inbred, sometimes exhibiting physical abnormalities. There are also behavioral problems. Hatchery fish lack stream smarts and are easily scarfed by predators. In nature, fish must make complicated decisions. As conditions change, they must decide what to do to maximize food intake while minimizing energy expenditure and their exposure to predation risk. You just don't get taught that kind of stuff in hatcheries, and during the period young wild fish learn these things or suffer the consequence, hatchery fish live in the aquatic equivalent of a greenhouse. These unschooled fish, released to the real world, are at a loss. Suddenly deprived of nutritionally balanced pasteurized pellets falling from heaven, they often cannot find food. (In some hatchery-stocked waters, fishers use lures designed not to imitate insects but to resemble hatchery food pellets.)

Adult fish returning to spawn in hatcheries do not engage in courtship. They are merely killed, slit, and their eggs and sperm mixed in buckets. The bright breeding colors, the hooked jaws, the competition for mates by which salmon prove themselves worthy of immortality, the knowledge of how to dig a nest— all are rendered pointless at the hatchery. Use it or lose it. Some hatchery salmon are losing their ability to dig nests.

In the U.S., massive hatchery increases in the 1980s were followed by declines to new historic lows. The more coho hatchery smolts have been put out in the northwestern states, the fewer adults have returned. The fewest returned when the most were released, raising the distressing implication that hatcheries actively hurt even themselves.

On the Columbia, many populations declined precipitously despite massive hatchery production increases. On the Snake River, hatcheries went from a million to fifteen million released fish per year between the 1960s and the late '80s, and adult populations crashed. When more than eight million hatchery chinooks were being pumped into the Strait of Georgia in British Columbia, catches declined. And on the Rogue River, while the number of hatchery adults rose from near zero to about half of all fish, the size of the population declined to a quarter of what it had been in the late 1970s.

One of the biggest recurring problems: Hatchery fish out-compete local fish and then themselves die. In an area where salmon must migrate to distant oceanic feeding grounds, coho from two nonmigratory populations were bred and released wholesale, and they died wholesale. But before those hatchery-released fish died, wild hatchlings in freshwater were forced to compete with swarms of them. In streams where densities as low as one juvenile fish per square yard can deplete available food and depress growth, hatchery releases packed streams with five fish per square yard, starving both wild and hatchery-hatched salmon.

Watersheds with few or no hatchery fish make up fully 85 percent of the Northwest's stable salmon populations. The scientific literature bristles with articles critical of every aspect of hatcheries, appearing at an average rate of one every three months. Despite it all, the public still wants to pay for hatcheries, like a new $40 million complex being planned on Washington's Skagit River. Oregon and Washington commonly spend about 40 percent of their fisheries budgets on hatcheries (compared to about 3 percent on management of natural production). The public pays about $50 million dollars a year just for the Columbia River's hatcheries. Virtually no one dares do cost-benefit analyses, but one such analysis of Alaska's hatcheries in the early 1990s showed that the greatest positive net economic benefit would come from eliminating hatcheries entirely. The greatest economic detriment would accrue from increasing the hatchery program.

Anyway, hatcheries may soon be old news. In a step beyond hatcheries, salmon endangered in the wild are plentifully pen-raised for the market, mostly in Atlantic and North Sea rivers, but some Atlantic salmon pen-rearing operations have come to the Pacific coast, where escaped Atlantic salmon are raising concerns that they may compete with, displace, or infect native species. One of those native species is human: "The issue for us is about home, about how we're dying," said Chief Simon Lucas of the British Columbia Aboriginal Fisheries Commission. Salmon farmers there have refused to release records of disease outbreaks and drugs used on farmed fish despite repeated requests by the provincial government.

Farmed fish are grown and harvested in the same spot, like tomatoes. They are never released, and ultimately, the evolutionary pressures that made salmon salmon and keep salmon salmon in the wild are relaxed or removed by captivity. To see the logical conclusion, one need only compare the wild, fleet-footed animals of the plains to the stupid, fat, waddling domestic creations that we raise for meat. Turning the roaming, leaping, celestially navigating, river-defying salmon into a barnyard flesh package that no longer exists in the wild is one of the great crimes against nature. But that is the trend. And rather than take pressure off wild fish, the salmon farms pollute adjacent waters, and diseases spread by escapees are killing off more wild salmon runs. Worst, perhaps, fish farming kills some of the incentive for conserving free-swimming fish and the environment that brought them forth, and further undermines fishing as a viable economic activity.

Once, in a restaurant overlooking the ocean on the central Oregon coast—in the heart of salmon country—I inquired about the featured salmon special.

"Is it fresh?" I asked.

"It comes frozen," the waitron said.

"Where from?"

"Iceland. It's farmed. The supply is much more consistent, so it's much better than local."

For most people, the disintegration of the North America's wild salmon is just no big deal at all. They are in the enviable position of having nothing to lose. Blessed are the passionless, for they need not painkillers.

A fish rising for an insect spreads its ripple effect. The cobbly bar yields four crows to the blue and cloud-puffed sky, and a kingfisher flies upriver, rattling its odd voice, perhaps at us. Bill Bakke draws thoughtfully on his pipe. Then he tells me about an experience he had on the Marble River, on Vancouver Island in British Columbia. "Above falls that seemed too high for chinook to jump, were pools so full of salmon all you could see were tails and backs. Eagles were hunting there, and bears. The sand bore the prints of wolves. I was in a system that was *working*. It's very hard to have those experiences now. So we forget what we are supposed to have, what the world is supposed to look like. You lose the benchmarks. Ecosytems are now like history books with many of the pages ripped out. And when people come along there is no way for them to know what was on those torn-out pages. Their values are not constructed around the abundance that once filled those holes. They accept the blank parts as though they've always been there."

It is dawn, Saturday, the day of the Clark-Skamania Fly Fishers' annual snorkel count on the Wind River, a tributary of the great Columbia. Under alders filtering shafts of sunlight, various tents, canoes, prams, and vehicles throng Gifford Pinchot National Forest's Beaver Creek Campground. The vehicles' bumpers exhibit an unusual collection of stickers (SALMON = FOOD + JOBS + TAXES and WILD SEX FOR WILD FISH—FREE THE SOCKEYE!). Camping and snorkeling gear fills the trucks and presses the windows for more space.

Footsteps in gravel sound somehow lighter and brighter in the morning-cool air, as people are carrying cups of coffee from the fire, walking to and fro, chatting while readying gear. Leashed by a long rope to the trailer hitch of a red pickup that holds a green fiberglass canoe, a friendly springer spaniel gets a pat on the head from each passerby. Everyone seems relaxed. It is even starting to affect Ed Wickersham.

Wickersham, a former logger, has for the last twenty years worked as a special agent for the U.S. Fish and Wildlife Service's enforcement division. He loves fish and flowing water, and he keeps a photo of Celilo Falls in his living room. Yesterday, Ed took me patrolling on the Columbia River with him, bucking the four-knot current below Bonneville Dam in his twenty-three-foot, aluminum, jet-drive enforcement boat. Where a sheer rock wall entered the river, two fishermen were casting for bass, and Ed checked licenses before wishing them a nice day. Putting the boat into reverse and backing away, he said to me, "The government would have us pester the average citizen to death."

"Where does that leave you, as part of our government?"

"I have to be very careful to avoid pushing around unconnected individuals. If the average citizen benefits from something that government does, it's an accident. Government is a shell game to allow rich people to move money to other rich people so they can continue to do what they want."

Today, Wickersham is off-duty and he's in a mellower mood. He hands me an elk-sausage sandwich to fortify me for the morning ahead. We divide up in groups to survey twenty miles of river. Brian Blair, a U.S. Forest Service biologist, joins our segment, and we gradually assemble prior to the ride toward our starting point. Everyone is eager, but preparations are methodical. Right now the important things are making sure each group has their data forms and checking that everyone has all the equipment they need—and hasn't left their mask or snorkel or wet-suit booties in their tent.

It looks like it will be a while before we get to the river, and when we eventually do, our job will be to identify and count all the salmon we see, juveniles and adults. The native adult steelhead are quite large here, up to twenty pounds, having evolved the size and power requisite to overcome the ten-foot falls confronting would-be spawners. Some adult chinooks are in from the sea now, too. For the adult fish in this river, it has been a long, strange trip back. They have been lucky to get home, and the young fish living in the river can count themselves fortunate as well. Many did not fare as well as those still resisting the current. We are here to tally the lucky ones.

At the appointed spot we park and walk in our wet suits through the alders to a small side stream surrounded by woodland, then leave the blue sky behind and enter the water like so many muskrats. Everyone floats oddly in the shallows. I put my head under and immediately the surface sounds of the stream are silenced. My first visual impression is that the bottom is absolutely alive; mostly with caddisfly larvae dragging protective houses of glued wood and sand on their backs, but also with sculpin fish and other creatures. Ed Wickersham's son, Jeff, walks along with the data form, recording what people tell him they are seeing.

We drift a ways, until, near the tangled roots of a grounded log, twenty small fish are placidly hovering along the shadow line. Ed motions for me to surface and says, "See these in here? See how their tails are forked? And with the big dark spots? Those are young chinook. That other one with the rosiness along its flank is a steelhead."

We place our snorkels back into our mouths and immerse our heads again. I see a crayfish, pick it up, show it. A rivulet enters the pool near a steep-cut bank walled with embedded stones. We float along, over, and through gravel bars, riffles, and small pools. Each pool hosts between six and thirty young chinook or young steelhead. They hold facing into the current, some in golden sunlight, most around wood and in the upstream ends of the pools.

Once underwater, you can see them grabbing little bits of food that come by in the breeze of water. In a deep gouge beneath a toppled alder trunk, several dozen young steelheads and juvenile chinooks are hiding. Ed stirs the bottom with his hand and the little fish rush from their cover, gobbling stuff disturbed from the sediment.

The current flows through a small rapids and tumbles into a boulder pool, as do we, amid a blizzard of silver bubbles. Looking upstream, we see dozens of fish heading into the flow and the shimmering fizz. It is an unusual perspective, watching fish from behind, their tails quivering while the little steelhead move up and down, left and right, picking through pieces of potential food in the bubble blast. These little fish have dash, vitality, and no fear of us.

By now we've become accustomed to looking under each boulder, log, and root wad. At the base of a large rock nearby, a blue-green bit of a broom-shaped tail is showing. A large adult steelhead, perhaps twenty pounds, resting on the bottom. How hidden and still! Enormous. I touch its tail, detonating a shocking explosion of power, the creature ricocheting off boulders in its tiny little cave, then rushing me, jumping out into the pool, and vanishing completely in the churned cloud of bottom, leaving my heart pounding.

Deep in one pool, a dead beaver, hideously covered with white fungus, lies motionless on the bottom. In a shallow pool an adult steelhead is moving along slowly over sunlit cobbles, its smooth skin spotted, its nose showing faint whitening from wear. As this fish moves from my underwater field of vision, I stand to watch it go upstream, which brings me back into the world of topside sounds. If a young salmon is lucky to be alive, a surviving adult has received miracles. Brian, also offering a standing ovation, says, "He's eagle food, if he stays out here." He adds, "This amount of exposure is not natural. We should have only ten to thirty percent sunlight. See all the small trees? There's no big wood in the stream. No velocity modulation from old-growth deadfalls. Bad bank stability: The banks are eroding sharply, causing a large width-to-depth ratio here. Very little stream sinuosity: This river just blows through here." Brian says this area was clear-cut in the early 1920s. They removed the cover structure and nutrients. "See those Doug-firs downstream? That's how it used to be here. It looks real pretty here, but it's still recovering from that logging."

My riverine bliss is shattered by this minilecture on unnatural ecology. Perhaps I should have kept my head underwater, like some aquatic ostrich. Why is it I always end up next to the person who knows the most? This odd and continual stroke of positioning, and the unfortunate fact that I respect informed people and want to learn what they have to say, has been the tragicomic irony of my life.

To reconstruct how it used to be, Brian and his coworkers have installed pieces of timber—large pieces—just downstream of here, and we float down for a look. At the first log that Brian has placed, held in the channel with cables, he says, "You'll see how the finer gravel drops out behind the timber, forming good spawning places."

The water is deeper here, and I inhale fully before diving to poke around in the shadows under the big logs. A huge bronze chinook, hooked jaws formed for spawning combat, arrests my attention and makes no outward response. There are also many juveniles, but the presence of this big chinook renders the juveniles momentarily invisible.

I rise for air and Brian adds, "These have become very nutrient-poor streams. Each salmon, when it dies, is a big fertilizer ball—bringing from the ocean carbon, nitrogen, phosphorus, and calcium—and if there is no wood they just get flushed right out again." I pack my lungs and dive into relative silence again, under and along a five-foot-diameter log that Brian's crew implanted. Seven additional big adult chinooks are resting on the bottom, tucked into the shadow and gouge under the log. I can see for myself now that without logs in the stream there are few places where these pre-spawning fish could hide or rest. In the areas where there were no logs there were very few fish compared to here, and those were swimming in the channel and vulnerable, with little cover to hold in and be still.

Jeff alerts us to an elk moving off the bank, but it is into the shadows by the time we look.

Onward we float. At its confluence, Tyee Spring spills a cold white torrent into a sizable pool. The pool contains a root wad and a steelhead of sufficient size to be called huge. I turn into the current to watch the fish, and for several seconds we are both stemming into the buffeting inrush. Co-equals, we, bucking the river. The fish cuts to the left a few feet, in the blast of silver bubbles rushing at us like a universe full of stars on a movie screen. Then it holds position like a pointer. I am holding too—onto a rock—and rather clumsily, trying not to get swept downstream. I need to breathe, but I am four feet underwater, and I don't want to end this moment, this joy and privilege of watching a wild steelhead. It is a fresh fish just in from the sea, silvery, without the broad rosy side. It is sculling this way and that in the current with sinuous grace and slide. For a moment, I am lost in pretend; I am a steelhead, and this other steelhead is my friend. I really need air.

By the time I inhale and am set to dive I am already being pushed out the tail end of the pool and into the next riffle. I bob along.

Because my eye for young fish is so inexperienced, I have been spared the responsibility of being an official counter, and I allow the river to sweep me away from the rest of the group. It is a mild stream, without the overwhelming rapids or irresistible current that almost claimed my life on a different river, far away, when my raft overturned in heavy rapids and the river ate me alive, sucking me deep within a recirculating whirlpool beneath a roaring hell of foam. Here in this gentle watercourse, though, I have no apprehensiveness about finding myself alone, afloat in the current, with fish below and forest—recovering forest, anyway—to either side. Hey, go with the flow—how unlike me! It's an interesting sensation. I could get used to it.

Several redds where eggs have been laid are obvious because the cobbles and gravels are turned upside down, creating a patch of bottom with no algae cover. An adult chinook is moving up the stream, already partly covered with fungus.

A terrific logjam blocks much of the channel. It is a wild, disheveled array, a three-dimensional Jackson Pollock in wood, wrought by an exuberant river gushing the high flood of springtime. I inhale my deepest breath and take my leave from the world of air. Five big steelhead and three large chinooks, one an enormous hook-jawed male, watch from a protective cage of thick roots. They are in a safe place, and they know it. I may be the first person they have ever seen, and it would be as well for them if I am the last.

Downstream I go, floating the pools, hunting the boulders, and scouting very closely the few root tangles and the logjams. Where the water is too shallow to scrape along, I resume my upright gait, walking the gravel intermittently and reentering the aqueous medium where the water is just deep enough to float an otter.

Too soon, the stream has delivered me at the camp's edge. This *is* a dilemma. Should I continue on and into the Columbia and then the Pacific and beyond, traveling, perhaps, with the other young steelhead, to the center of the greatest ocean in the universe? Or should I stay for some of the forty pounds of ribs and twelve whole chickens sizzling on Ed's three-hundred-gallon grill and worship at the smoking altar like everyone else? I will probably always regret this decision—and if it weren't for the problem of getting myself past the dams it might be otherwise—but I am going to stay with the humans.

Smoke, lots of it, is rising into the shafts of sunlight around the camp. As the food cooks the team captains report today's counts to the compiler. Twelve teams covered about twenty-two miles of river. Some saw only one adult steelhead. Other groups saw more than twenty. This survey has been performed at the same sites on the same rivers since 1988. The survey's highest numbers were seen that first year.

Everyone else is talking about fishing in different rivers in North America, especially Alaska. Ed is telling someone, "The salmon are so thick there you can't put your foot down without stepping on fish, and they're too packed to get out of the way. Every fishery manager should go to Alaska and see salmon the way they are supposed to be. They think reality started when they came on the job. This area right here was as rich as Alaska, a hundred and fifty years ago. The difference is that in Alaska, for the fish that get past the nets, once they hit the river there is nothing ahead of those salmon except water, tundra, mosquitoes, and a few native settlements." The immense value of Alaska is as a measuring stick.

Protagoras said, "Man is the measure of all things." Thoreau said, "In wildness is the preservation of the world." If I may combine both thoughts, it is that wildness is the measure of all things human, vital for distinguishing progress from excess.

In the late 1800s the famed Chief Joseph (a.k.a. Hin-mah-too-yah-lat-keht—Thunder Traveling to Loftier Mountain Heights) foreshadowed much of the future progress and excess of the Columbia by saying, "The white men were many and we could not hold our own with them. . . . We were contented to let things remain as the Great Spirit made them. They were not, and would change the rivers if they did not suit them."

The Columbia spills more water into the Pacific than any river in the Western Hemisphere, and it seems almost designed by Providence to be dammed. Before any person thought of holding back the river, the Columbia was repeatedly dammed by natural forces, and it repeatedly broke free. About twenty million years ago, volcanic basalt extrusions forced the river to the north. For millions of years, the river filed a groove through successively applied layers of volcanic rock: the Columbia Gorge. Toward the end of the last great glaciation, about ten thousand years ago, an ice dam thousands of feet high blocked part of the great river, backing a lake hundreds of feet deep into Idaho and Montana, over an area the size of Lake Michigan. The dam broke suddenly and catastrophically, spreading a tumult as wide as the state of Indiana, gouging canyons overnight. It is possible that humans were already in the valley. If so, they would have heard a curiously building rumble for about an hour or so, followed by the roar and sight of a scouring wall of water ten times as great as the combined flow of all the world's rivers, sweeping them to oblivion far, far out to sea. The river has been blocked many other times by ice, lava, and landslides. In the most recent natural blockage, seven hundred years ago, much of Greenleaf Peak and Table Mountain slumped into the main channel (probably triggered by an earthquake), shoving the river over a mile and backing a five-hundred-foot-deep lake up to what is now Umatilla. The river immediately set to tearing down this dam, and its remains formed the Great Cascades of the Columbia, a stretch of whitewater that survived until the arrival of the U.S. Army Corps of Engineers in the 1930s.

But that is getting ahead of the story. In 1848, the Oregon Territory constitutionally prohibited any dams that would interfere with the travels of salmon. In 1934, a dam built on the Salmon River in Idaho met with a dynamite-laden raft and was blown to splinters. Elsewhere in the basin, though, irrigation and hydropower dams were built on tributaries beginning in the late 1800s and early 1900s. And, by the end of the same decade that saw that exploding raft, the most audacious complex of big dams the world has known was being built in the Columbia River Basin, providing hydropower, flood control, navigability, and irrigation. The rate of progress was phenomenal—one major dam completed every two and a half years on average—and by 1975, eighteen major federal concrete walls spanned the Columbia and its major tributary, the Snake.

It was said that the Columbia River had "died and was reborn as money." Three-fourths of the electrical power in the Northwest now came from falling water, at the lowest prices in the nation. The dams are operated by the U.S. Army Corps of Engineers. To market the enormous output of electrical power, the federal government created the Bonneville Power Administration. BPA's electric power is sold as far away as Los Angeles, but a big chunk goes directly to large aluminum refiners along the Columbia, who account for nearly half of the aluminum made in the United States. This makes Bonneville and the aluminum makers potent economic and ecological forces.

For a long time everything about the dams conspired against the Columbia's salmon. Salmon can overcome a lot, but they could not overcome the combined forces of the concrete, the slack warm water behind the concrete, the economic power of billions of dollars in revenues from electricity, government bureaucracies of the United States, and the apathy of most of the country's citizens toward fish. The results were commensurate with the problems. The problems were commensurate with the boldness of dams. The fish were going down the tubes.

The promise of a new era of balance for beleaguered Columbia River salmon arrived in 1980, with the Northwest Power Planning and Conservation Act—a revolution. Before, Bonneville and the Army Corps held all the cards. Now, the rules changed. The act actually made healthy runs of fish a goal equal with power production. And the act requires that salmon numbers lost because of the dams be restored. This was to be carried out by a body called the Northwest Power Planning Council, representing the four states through various governors' appointees. If it all sounds dreadfully complicated and ponderous, it is.

Even people intensely interested in salmon could not afford the expense and time required to attend meetings throughout four states. And so the "public" was soon replaced by organizations representing polarized interests—electric utilities, consumers, tribes, and the like. Finger-pointing by these interests predominates, substituting blame for analysis and yielding lowest-common-denominator accommodations. The government reps who make up the Power Planning Council, dutifully listening to the expressed advice of widely divergent interests—and coming to believe that mere listening is their job—have done little to move everyone beyond consultation and into collaboration. And that has largely accounted for the council's failure.

In the 1980s the Power Planning Council adopted a goal of doubling the runs of anadromous fish, though it tidily neglected to set a deadline for itself. Nonetheless, the council determined that the dams are responsible for fish losses on the order of eight to eleven million salmon per year. It also, laudably, adopted a goal of no further loss of biological diversity to the fish populations. And the council identified measures to be taken.

On these measures, Bonneville Power spends about $50 million a year and claims costs of another $200 million in forgone power-generation revenue because it has to use water for fish instead of electricity. It also claims other expenses, for a total of roughly $400 million, about 1 percent of Bonneville's annual revenues. Bonneville says that the cost of salmon is the major factor affecting Pacific Northwest electric utility ratepayers.

This is a peculiar accounting, though. The forgone power revenue figure tripled between 1991 and 1994 because of the combined effect of drought-induced low flows for electricity generation and poor power markets. But salmon got "charged" for it. When the Los Angeles earthquake of 1994 damaged the long-distance power transmission lines through which Bonneville sells electricity to L.A., Bonneville's bean counters added the $8 million repair bill to the "cost of salmon." For interest, amortization, and depreciation, salmon get a bill for $60 million. To Bonneville Power Administration, salmon are the ultimate "little guys" to whom all costs get passed along. Bonneville's total salmon charges doubled in the first half of the 1990s, but the power administration is loath to mention that drought and soft markets are making electricity more expensive.

And while salmon are charged for electricity that could have been made from the water they need for their declining existence, irrigators, barge operators, and flood-control measures are never "charged" by Bonneville's accountants—though these things, too, use water that might have made electrical power.

The cost of running hatcheries and getting the young fish past dams ($150 million a year), activities that exist because of the damage done by dams and irrigation, are charged to salmon. (Though most of the lower dams were, as an afterthought, designed to let adult salmon get upstream, no provisions were made to safely allow for the young coming down.) The National Research Council gently asked, "Why should salmon be charged for flaws in the design of the hydropower system?" The research council went on to say that Bonneville uses shadowy assumptions about interest, amortization, and depreciation rates. Take-home message: Look behind the curtain and you'll see Bonneville's wizards trying to make salmon look very expensive.

And though salmon get "charged" the maximum for "using" the river, no Columbia water is legally allocated for wildlife (unlike on some other rivers). Salmon have no rights to Columbia River water. To their credit, the long-suffering salmon have ignored the bills they have been sent. They have had no comment. If I were them, the whole situation would seem as though I had returned home to find that the government had turned my house into a hotel and insisted on charging me exorbitant rates to use my own bedroom.

Where has all this hassling and stinginess gotten us? To the lowest salmon population levels in Columbia River history—despite all the "money" Bonneville "spends" on those water-swilling fish.

"They would change the rivers," Chief Joseph had said. And was he ever right. Thousands of smaller dams clog the arteries of the Northwest's rivers and streams from California to British Columbia. The many small dams here have caused many small extinctions. The big Columbia dams are something else again. Before those dams, salmon had access to 163,000 square miles in the Columbia River Basin of the U.S. and Canada. More than half the basin area and a third of the stream miles were eliminated as salmon breeding habitat by impassable dams.

Even "passable" dams with fish ladders stop 5 to 10 percent of the adults. At 5 percent mortality, fish that have to pass, say, seven dams, face about a one in three chance that they will not make it.

But probably the biggest problem is volts versus smolts: The water must go *either* to making electricity *or* to moving young fish downstream. Interference with the young salmon's downstream migration is the worst problem posed by the big dams. Young salmon are evolutionarily timed and tuned to sweep seaward on the surge of spring snowmelt. Before the dams, a trip from Idaho to

Columbia's mouth took three weeks. The dams upped it to seven. Delays upset the biological window of opportunity for proper physiological transformation for saltwater. The dams also killed the current, forcing the fish to swim with energy they were not designed to use up. And some of the cues that got their bodies stirring—temperature and stream-flow changes—were greatly altered.

Each dam poses hazards for young fish trying to pass it. Smolts from the whole width of the Columbia can be gathered into a dam's bypass and delivered in highly concentrated chaos to predators gathered at the tail end of the pipe. Alternatives involve going over the dam or through turbines, hardly an advantage because fish get hurt or suffer from excessive dissolved nitrogen in the plunge pools. Another alternative is to collect the fish, put them in barges or trucks, and deliver them past all the dams. Once upon a time, fish used the river and grain was shipped by truck. Now, grain goes in river barges and fish travel in trucks. This is done wholesale, but it has its own problems because, again, the fish are handled and their timing disrupted.

Transporting baby fish eats up about $30 million a year. Large numbers of young salmon have been barged each year since 1981, and the only things that have changed in the Columbia Basin during the interval are the addition of several salmon runs to the Endangered Species List and the extinction of the Snake River's coho.

Researchers working back in the 1970s proved the obvious: The faster young salmon got downriver in the currents, the better they survived. That's what they were engineered by evolution to do. Water spilled past the dams would take young fish with it—just like a river. But engineers and power advocates refused to let young fish have the water for migration out, because that's water that could instead make electricity.

Fish advocates kept looking for more ways to argue for more water. By the early 1990s, the industrial users of the river were getting worried that increasing communication between environmental groups and fishing interests would refocus the salmon debate on the loss of fishing-related jobs and economic activity. The argument could become one of jobs versus jobs, and control of the debate and the public sentiment might begin slipping away from the industrials. If that happened, they might have to pay electric rates that were not the lowest in the country. (Bonneville's electricity costs less than three cents a kilowatt hour, compared to nine in the Midwest, eleven cents in New England, and fifteen cents where I live on Long Island).

In March 1993, a number of utilities, aluminum companies, and irrigation districts went public with a strategy that the fishing industry immediately began to call the Final Solution. The industries' bombing raids consisted of large ads in newspapers blaming fishing for the salmon declines, coupled with lawsuits arguing that, since endangered runs mixed with others in the ocean, the only way to protect them fully was to stop all fishing.

They had a point. But the judge saw it this way:

If the plaintiff's ultimate goal was protection of the listed species . . . then conspicuously absent is a claim for a reduction in hydroelectric activity or correction of those aspects of the dams which overwhelmingly destroy more juvenile migrants . . . than all the harvests combined.

By 1993, Bonneville Power Administration was suffering the effects of a six-year drought that limited the dams' ability to produce power, and BPA was actually buying electricity. Plus, the aluminum makers' electric rates are tied by law to the world aluminum market price, which was in a slump. In the preceding two years, Bonneville had watched its cash reserves drop 90 percent.

Bonneville Power proposed to save one-half of 1 percent of its revenues by cutting out funds for development of an inventory of the region's wild and naturally spawning salmon populations and by cutting out the development of rebuilding goals and monitoring for weak runs. Of course, doubling the runs and preventing the loss of additional biological diversity—the Power Planning Council's two main goals as updated the year before—could not be accomplished without that kind of information.

Some people were saying that if BPA really needed to find an extra $15 million or so, why go after fish? Why not hit the $13 million electric-rate subsidy the irrigators were getting?

This is the ongoing tone of the relationship between the dam interests and the fish interests. But I had a feeling that individual people inside the day-to-day dam operations would have a variety of perspectives not seen in official reports and policies.

Rising from both banks in imposing, reposeful power, the Columbia River Gorge's vertical cliffs and escarpments climb straight up out of the forest, while the countervailing outpourings of several streams fall a hundred feet or more into the trees along the river. At the gorge's rim, clouds brush a stubble of trees, and viewed from a cloud's face the mountains themselves would seem to plunge into the Columbia.

I confront the monolithic visage—the scene—of the river's first and most downstream dam. A roaring, almost frightening, twenty-five-foot wall of white water is shooting from underneath guillotine gates, raising a continual, drifting mist. Gulls ceaselessly patrol this massive tumbling froth, picking off confused or injured fish. High-tension wires carry fresh electrical power up the adjacent mountains and away into the clouds.

The sign at the gate says, WELCOME TO BONNEVILLE DAM. A fountain featuring a bronze leaping salmon sprays water outside the gift shop. Work crews are mowing the lawns and tending attractive flower beds. At a hatchery maintained primarily for tourists, a young woman hurls fish food into the cement ponds, and thousands upon tens of thousands of juvenile salmon are frothing the surface to get at it.

The bottom of the sturgeon pool is tiled with coins spent on penny-ante wishes. Above the loose change, in a sluggish current, wallow rainbow trout so obese that their backs bulge from behind their skull, making them misshapen. At a person's approach they come laboring over like fat old dogs, looking for more of the only thing they've learned about in their confined lives—being fed.

A man of about forty, with gray-blue eyes and chiseled features, wearing cowboy boots, jeans, and a blue shirt with cigarettes in the pocket, pauses but makes no wish. His name is Dan Daley, and he's a fish biologist with Bonneville Power Administration. He asks if I have heard whether the Snake River chinook's status has been changed from threatened to endangered; the decision is due today. I have not.

Daley's job is designing ways to regulate water flows to minimize harm to fish. He is working on new water-manipulation strategies, seeing if they make sense for salmon and for business.

He explains that you can let water flow downriver evenly all year, generating electricity at a constant rate, or you can "shape the water into the migration season to benefit fish." By letting more water past the dams in spring to help young salmon migrate downstream to the ocean, you generate surplus power that can be sold to counties in California, enabling them to reduce their fossil-fuel use. Using that kind of creative tinkering, Daley believes salmon can make the system more efficient.

Sounds simple, but there are problems. "This year we used all the water for juveniles, and now we have none extra for getting more adult fish over the ladders. You can use all the water for juveniles, knowing ninety percent are going to die, or we could reserve the flows for adults—if we think it is more beneficial to get adults back than to get the juveniles out. You have to make those difficult decisions."

If I recall my biology, it seems that getting the adults up and the young down are equally important. Any either-or approach seems doomed to fail.

Other problems: Farmers balk at letting stored water be used for fish. But irrigation itself takes plenty of water that never reaches crops. Putting two feet of water on a one-acre potato field requires taking ten or more acre-feet of water out of the river, because of waste from seeping ditches, evaporation when watering under a desert sun, and other inefficiencies.

Daley draws on his cigarette, squinting. "But start talking about changing irrigation in southern Idaho, and they'll run you out. Even if we buy land from a willing seller to get the water rights to use for salmon, we run into tremendous opposition from seed sellers, fertilizer sellers, and pesticide companies. Don't get me wrong: I'm not trying to focus the attention away from the hydropower system. Because of logging, agriculture, *and* the dams, fish have problems."

Difficulties aside, Daley believes that if changes toward efficiency are made with salmon in mind, salmon will benefit greatly. "So, yes, one could say it's going to cost billions to save the salmon. But I would argue that we can save billions by saving the salmon."

I mention to him that by some estimates, modifying the dams to save Columbia River salmon would require merely that the region's millions of fairly comfortable middle-class households pay two to three dollars more per month for their household electricity.

He looks up suddenly and fixes me dead in the eye, saying testily, "It doesn't just mean a couple of dollars a month for the guy at the aluminum plant who loses his job when their costs go up. As someone who grew up poor, it strikes me as very snobbish of the environmental community to talk about three dollars per month. That's not their place."

But is it the place of the aluminum industry to expect and demand the country's cheapest electricity?

The logic of the market favors liquidation of nature (if you prefer, natural resource capital). The illogic of public policy has been to aid the liquidation with massive government subsidies that artificially inflate pressures on forests, fish, and water by lowering operating overhead and increasing profitability. Taxpayers and ecosystems are stuck with the true costs.

Behold the electric utilities. They receive subsidies that have been called "among the costliest anti-environmental handouts in the Pacific Northwest" because of the dams' effects on salmon. Floated by subsidies, Bonneville undercharges its customers more than $200 million a year compared to private utilities in the area. That is quite interesting from a salmon's-eye view, considering Bonneville's claims that using water for fish instead of electricity costs it $200 million annually in forgone power-generating revenue.

And that doesn't include the fancy stuff. If Bonneville had to repay its loans for construction of the dams at government bond rates or the market rates you and I would have to pay, Bonneville would have to charge its customers $1.2 billion more per year than it does, to earn the same rate of return as private utilities. Presidents Carter, Reagan, Bush, and Clinton tried to refinance Bonneville's debt at more realistic (higher) interest rates. But the Northwest's members of Congress consistently blocked them.

Of all the beneficiaries of the Columbia's subsidized salmon-killing system, aluminum smelters make out best financially. They buy about a third of Bonneville's electricity. BPA's cost of providing electricity to the aluminum makers exceeds revenues by around $100 to $150 million per year—possibly higher, but let's say $100 million. The average household pays two dollars a month for this subsidy, about the calculated cost to rebuild salmon populations by reconfiguring the dam operations. The slop in the system encourages the Northwest's smelters to be 14 percent less efficient than is average for aluminum smelters elsewhere. Salmon, and people who fish for or like to eat salmon, suffer the effects of all these subsidies on the Columbia.

Farmers make out O.K., too. Idaho farmers divert the entire flow of the Snake River in certain months in certain places. All the water—a public resource if ever there was one—is absolutely free for the taking. "The subsidies are so wide and so deep that, basically, farmers are farming the government, not the land," said one observer.

In 1902, the Bureau of Reclamation was created to help small farmers settle the arid West. They built irrigation projects with public money, but the law said that only small farmers could participate and that they would have to repay the costs in ten years. Well, by and by, that was a hardship, and Congress lengthened the payback period from ten to fifty years. By and by, lots of big farmers got in on it. By and by, the original decision not to charge interest became a valuable long-term subsidy in itself. If your "ability to pay" is low, the all-merciful government defers your payments further. And by and by, close to 90 percent of the government's (i.e., your and my) costs for the projects are never repaid, and taxpayers cover 90 percent of the cost of delivering the water to those farmers.

These are the same farmers who do not have money to screen irrigation diversions so baby salmon don't end up in their fields along with the diverted river, the same ones who yell that, if the river is drawn down to let young salmon past the dams, they'd have to extend their pumps, *which would cost money!*

In the Snake River Basin, some farmers are paid not to grow the same crops that other farmers in the basin are growing in surplus with subsidized water taken away from salmon. To grow, and not to grow, that is the farmers' answer. Whether 'tis nobler to suffer slinging a fortune to outrageous farmers is the question for the rest of us.

Up the Columbia, Grand Coulee Dam and associated canals and pumps get water to some of the most lavishly subsidized big farms anywhere, farms benefiting from $3 billion in construction and interest subsidies and around $275 million a year in operating subsidies. To get more personal, the average subsidy to a thousand-acre farm in this area is about $2 million each year. Farmers here pay less than $1 million for water that could generate $25 million worth of electricity, though when you read about how much salmon "cost" the hydropower system, you don't read about how much farmers "cost" it—but they certainly do cost it. And—my favorite part—the farmers get so much water so cheaply that they have built their own hydroelectric plants and sell about $1 million worth of electricity annually.

Bargers pay none of the Army Corps of Engineers' costs for operating and maintaining the locks they use. Nor for the dams. Nor for the dredging (about $30 million in the mid-1990s) so their ships can float.

Enter cows. Cows that overgraze the range and destroy the banks of waterways and help make streams hostile to salmon. Want to feed a cow on federal public land for a month? You'll get change back from two dollars. In exchange, you'll get eight hundred pounds of forage, and the bureaucrats will build and maintain watering tanks for your animal. In 1994, Interior Secretary Bruce Babbitt tried to raise the fee to around four dollars. He met so much resistance from welfare cowfolk and their legislative representatives that he backed down. If my calling the rugged range men welfare boys seems harsh, I'll take it back. Let's call them shrewd, because they pay so little they often sublease—at a profit, of course—their permits to put habitat-destroying animals on this land that belongs to you and me. On state land, the system is different and the prices higher. But don't talk about changing the state system, either. When one guy in the Northwest outbid local ranchers for grazing permits and said he intended not to put animals on the land but to let the habitat recover, the state refused to give him the permits.

All these salmon-killing subsidies originally intended to help poorer businesses may in fact be hurting the poor. The Columbia Basin Project, for example, takes more money from low-income taxpayers than it gives to low-income farm families. Below-cost public handouts for timber, water, and grazing rights in salmon country go to an increasingly shrinking number of propped-up farms and enriched corporations that are hurting the habitat. Real free enterprise would be better for the fish. A number of people in this region have come to the same conclusion.

Andy Kerr, who gained notoriety as the conservation director of the Oregon Natural Resources Council, has been called by the timber industry the most hated man in Oregon. It was a good enough recommendation to make me want to see him. Kerr is a high-voltage guy with two cellular phones and a nonstop travel schedule. During conversation his hands have two positions: listening (crossed and pressed to lips) and talking (flattened like blades thrust forward and moved rhythmically back and forth as he speaks). "Here's my argument," he told me a little while back. "Eighty percent of the problems we work on are related to federal subsidies. Why do we have subsidies? Because the private sector wouldn't do these projects. My point is this: Apply a market test first. And if the market test shows that it doesn't pay, don't do it. If the test shows that you can make a dollar, then it should be looked at more carefully to see if it is desirable. To the side that wants to exploit things, it's just money. So if it doesn't pay, their interest evaporates. But if it doesn't pay in simple, current dollars and cents to save a living resource like salmon, it is still possible that the market analysis does not fully reflect the social values of salmon, or clean air, or other things. Then, I argue, we can still have our debates. But we'd have a lot fewer debates if the federal subsidies were first removed. I'm very market oriented. I want free enterprise, with regulations to protect long-term public interests. But instead of free enterprise, hundreds of billions of dollars in taxpayer subsidies have killed off the great salmon runs."

• • •

Dan Daley introduces me to Jerry Bouck, a large man and a professor emeritus from Oregon State University. Bouck spent an earlier decade in the employ of the Bonneville Power Administration. Like the Columbia itself, Bouck has a lot of energy. Bouck says overfishing in the early years has a lot to do with the present declines. You had twenty-five hundred commercial gillnetters on the river. You had fish wheels going day and night. You had haul seine–net crews. You had dipnetters, and so on. "If you wanted to declare war on the salmon, you'd have had to go about it the way they did. This year I just tore up my salmon fishing stamp. I just felt I didn't want to hurt one anymore."

Daley has to leave, and Bouck and I stroll toward the Bonneville Dam visitor center. This is a power plant complex that is expecting company. There are carpets, plaques telling how a generator works, an information desk, and, on the floor to guide your progress among the exhibits, yellow arrows with salmon painted in each one. Any visitor who sets foot here is in a great and continual public-relations hammerlock. Part of the exhibit says, "For centuries, Indians have waited for the fish to return to Celilo Falls. Treaties now guarantee their fishing rights." This is as close to misleading as it gets. It doesn't say that the falls are now gone, under the reservoir held behind a dam. There's a photograph of a salmon leaping up a falls, and it says, "Salmon return to the place of their release." It doesn't say they return to the place of their origin; they are subtly inculcating a salmon-are-made-by-humans perspective.

We take the elevator up and out to the fish ladder. The floors, instead of being numbered 1, 2, 3, bear only their elevation above sea level. After I figure out what all the numbers mean, I find it amusing—almost charming— but Jerry huffs, "Only the Army Corps of Engineers would do something that confusing."

Bonneville was the first and lowest dam on the river, and closing it would have eliminated 90 percent of the Columbia Basin as a habitat for the world's largest chinook salmon and steelhead populations. Because of the outcry from the fishing industry, something never tried before—a fish ladder—was designed at the midnight hour before construction. Jerry has postulated a reason why the dam was designed without ladders, and it is the first and only one I've heard that blames fishermen: "Since only ten percent of the fish were left by then because of overfishing, maybe everyone figured salmon were on the way out even without the dam." Then, as if to be fair, he adds, "Or, maybe they just didn't care."

Some fish are visible in the spilling water in the ladder, which is sort of a flight of concrete stairs for fish. Each step is a foot of elevation, and there are sixty steps in the ladder. The ladder zigzags its way down the dam in a series of switchbacks, and the fish labor up like Sherpas tilting toward Everest. Thoreau:

Still patiently, almost pathetically, with instinct not to be discouraged, not to be *reasoned* with, revisiting their old haunts, as if their stern fates would relent, and still met by the Corporation with its dam. . . . When Nature gave thee instinct, gave she thee the heart to bear thy fate? Still wandering the sea in thy scaly armor to inquire humbly at the mouths of rivers if man has perchance left them free for thee to enter.

Roughly a hundred yards downstream of the dam, the river's surface is a-boiling. This is the exit of the smolt bypass system, designed to move the young that pile up behind the concrete as they are trying to migrate to sea and shoot them out the other side of the dam. (They are unable to use fish ladders to get down.)

The scale of the powerhouse—twelve hundred feet long with an eighty-five-foot ceiling—is very impressive. Inside, a glass observation deck overlooks the machinery. A row of eight immense generators is visible. Beneath them and not visible are turbine propellers, each twenty-seven feet across. Every second, twenty thousand cubic feet of water—624 tons of river—pass through each turbine, generating the power of 105,000 horses. There is no question that the dam and the generating facilities are a marvel of engineering on an audacious scale. There is beauty here, too—a magnificent boldness of concept.

The facility is managed by the Army Corps of Engineers. Jerry says, "For a long time the corps was an arrogant bunch of bastards. They didn't give a damn about anybody."

He doesn't mean that as a pun. Over its history, the corps has alienated some people. In 1951 Franklin Roosevelt's Interior Secretary Harold Ickes lambasted the corps, writing that they had been "working hand in glove with monopolies," that they were "willful and expensive . . . a self-serving clique in contempt of the public welfare" that "wantonly wasted money on worthless projects." U.S. Supreme Court Justice William O. Douglas called them "public enemy number one."

Jerry is saying, "Now the corps is sensitized, but no one trusts them."

I'm getting all choked up at the thought of the U.S. Army Corps of Engineers, so misunderstood.

Jerry continues, "Engineers can do amazing things. That's why I think they can fix the problems they've caused. We just haven't given them the right orders."

Jerry wants to take me into another big concrete building, where the public is not allowed. This is the fish-processing facility, where, periodically, the migrating fish are shunted through the building for researchers conducting wild-versus-hatchery survival studies, age and growth studies, things like that. But, he explains, "I'm no longer really authorized to enter, and I don't have a key anymore." We circle the exterior looking for a weak spot and slip through a door left ajar.

The building's interior is filled with grated steel catwalks over large-gauge plumbing, with panels of electrical circuits and metal lockers against the concrete walls. A barn swallow is fluttering around inside the big, open intrados. I hope it knows how to get out.

We stumble upon Bruce Monk, a biologist working for the National Marine Fisheries Service. He looks like a fisheries biologist, in fact like a commercial fisherman, as though some human genetic complexes are just destined to work with fish. One can instantly imagine him behind the wheel of a salmon troller, his beard rustling in the breeze like a salmonberry bush and his dirty-blond hair stuffed under a knit cap instead of the hard hat he is wearing. Fortunately for us, he knows Jerry.

In the building are a series of sluices with metal detectors for sensing the wire tags that are placed in some hatchery fish when they are very young. As the fish slide through the sluices, if metal is detected a gate shuts automatically and an automatic shunt is engaged to channel the tagged fish into an anesthetizing pool for measurements and scale samples.

Once, there was just a river here.

Jerry and I don hard hats. Bruce leads us down into a concrete catacomb, an engineered cave system inside the dam, and I have to tell myself that it's a good thing I'm not claustrophobic. The air dampens, turning cool. We walk down and then up several flights of concrete stairs, toward a loudening rumble of moving water. We come at last up to a level where an intensely roaring mass of rushing water is running through a dimly lit channel reminiscent of a subway tunnel. Water is sloshing up through the steel grate we are now walking over. This is a freakin' scary place. Because of the way the water is diverted, it is running parallel—not perpendicular—to the dam; that is, it's running along the dam's length. Monk informs me that right now we are ten feet below the river's surface. The tunnel is for conveying salmon smolts around the turbines. Feeding into the tunnel are thirty open gates, with lights near their apertures for attracting the fish, whereupon the smolts are caught in the current, blasted upward in the forcing water, and shot into the angry maelstrom running under our feet. Bruce, practically yelling in an effort to be heard above the ferocious noise, says that there is basically no damage to them despite the force of the water—they sample 10 percent of them to be certain.

I know that fish are built for water, but the artificial force seems incredible. Jerry shouts, "Yes, it's a lot of force, but if you go with the flow it's not too bad."

How does he know, I wonder; has he tried it?

The smolts are shot through hoses and then separated by size through grates to keep the different species apart so they don't nip each other while being held. Bruce says that the number of fish passing the dam without going through the turbines has increased from 25 to 50 percent.

Jerry reminds me that about 15 percent of the young salmon going through the turbines at each dam are killed. If you're a baby salmon, the farther upstream you were born, the more dams you have to come through, and the lower your odds of surviving to taste saltwater.

I had not realized that the fish are so handled and manipulated. But in other words, three-quarters of them used to go through the turbines, and half do now. Interesting.

Bruce says he believes that the efforts to shunt more smolts around the turbines is actually helping save the fish.

I am wondering, Save the fish compared to what? I had not envisioned any of this until I saw it a moment ago, and I am still trying to let it all sink in.

Referring to fisheries technicians like Bruce, Jerry says, "These guys are heroes. Once you get past the politics, the workers are very dedicated."

Bruce adds, "And even the Corps of Engineers has changed a lot in the last ten years. The dams are being operated very differently now. Now, there's not so many of the old troops, and the new people are thinking about the fish."

I refuse to dance to the violin music. I refuse to get fluttery about the Army Corps of Engineers, which for decades has destroyed wet habitats with almost inexplicable zeal. But what if Bruce and Jerry are right? What if I'm being too harsh? Well, if these guys are right, if the corps has suffered a conversion, I will wait until Dick Good, Willow Burch, Irene Martin, and everyone else tell me everything is all right, and that it's O.K. to hug the Army Corps of Engineers. Until then, I'll tend more toward the sentiments of Harold Ickes, who also wrote, "No more lawless or irresponsible group than the Corps of Engineers has ever attempted to operate in the United States either outside of or within the law. . . . It is truly beyond imagination."

We enter Bruce's office, which is cluttered with books and papers and hard hats. A photo of Celilo Falls hangs on the wall. I ask Monk for his opinion about other methods of getting the young fish around the dams, such as catching and trucking them or drawing down the reservoirs and simply flushing the fish through, which has been proposed by some conservation groups. He answers, "When I started ten years ago, we had ten percent hatchery fish and ninety percent wild, and that's totally flip-flopped; now we have ninety percent hatchery fish, and they're just not making it. If you ask which would be better for the fish—drawing down the river or transporting them in trucks—to me, with such a high percentage of hatchery fish, the only difference is in how they would die."

Buoyed by those encouraging words, Jerry and I hang our hard hats and exit to the viewing area inside the visitor center, where people are sitting at glass windows looking into the side of a fish ladder. A big steelhead goes by. A chinook also passes.

And here we are, watching fish as we are accustomed to watching them in an aquarium. The setting—fish behind glass—seems so deceptively familiar that one has to remind oneself that we are really looking directly at the salmonic phenomenon. We watch so casually, as though they had not traveled thousands of miles into the Pacific Ocean, survived for years under hostile conditions, fought their way back in surviving triumph, up this concrete ladder to right here, still fighting their way to their single, culminating chance at procreation, their one opportunity to maintain the great and mysterious chain of generational continuity that each fish has brought forward to this fragile point from the beginning of its ancient lineage. We assume our seats as spectators almost nonchalantly, as though these fish can imagine expending anything less than the blind determination to complete a miracle—a difficult miracle that these fish unthinkingly comprehend, yet so incomprehensibly difficult for us to recognize, and embrace.

Jerry says, "I'm much more scared of the genetics than the dams. For one thing, we can't turn the dams around quickly. It's just possible that these salmon populations are in a death spiral brought on by excessive fishing."

There it is again: the "death spiral." Only, why does he keep talking just about "fishing"? Aren't we forgetting a few other things?

"In the fishing era, everyone believed that God wanted us to go forth and multiply, have dominion over the earth; in other words, 'It's all yours, kid, go take everything.' In *that* era, the same thing was going on in Alaska, in the Great Lakes, on Cannery Row with the California sardine—"

Has something changed dramatically for the better in *this* era that I've missed?

"And we're just now reaping the debt, and you and I and our kids will pay for that debt. I'm not trying to defend dams—"

Of course not.

"But I think overfishing took a lot of the genetic diversity, and that removes a lot of the fishes' adaptability and resistance to diseases. If that's true, it will either take a very long time for them to come back, or they will just continue a death spiral. I don't know."

Death spiral. Death spiral. What would it feel like for the world to be caught in an irresistible *life spiral?*

Nearby, kids are making sounds like barking dogs.

Several lampreys and some squawfish come into the window, and the first kid to notice says, "Whoa, what are *they?*"

Jerry says to me, "These lampreys, by the way, used to be in here by the thousands."

Now that poses an interesting situation: No one has ever fished for lampreys, and yet their numbers are going down.

Jerry explains, "Bad ocean conditions. Just like the coastal coho. There are no dams on those coho rivers."

"But those streams are very degraded."

"I'm no expert on those streams, but I've paid for an awful lot of habitat restoration. A peer review said we threw the money away and that the best thing we could do was to fence the cattle out. One thing's for sure, you've got to have water to have fish, and there are a lot of streams that used to flow year-round that now go dry intermittently because of abuse to the land."

A big chinook has come into view briefly, and a kid turns, calling to his friend, "Come *here!* Look at *this!*" His friend comes running, and when the kid turns back to the window he says frustratedly, "Hey! Where did that big one go?"

Jerry continues, "And I think that we've got a much worse disease problem than people want to admit. It used to be that you couldn't find fish with ceratomyxosis upstream of the John Day River. Now we find it hotter than anything clear up to the Snake. Hatcheries may have created reservoirs for disease and helped it move upstream. There's a pretty delicate balance between this disease and water temperature; if the water temperature gets a little bit warmer, the disease would progress a little faster and many fish wouldn't live long enough to spawn. So it isn't just one thing, there's so many things."

"O.K., but why does it seem so difficult to do fairly simple, commonsense things to address these contributing problems?"

"The Columbia River is run by committees. Plural. And it's run by governments. Plural. And it's run by agencies. Plural. Often we get people appointed who really don't have the time. All the agencies are too territorial, and I don't have a lot of hope until we shed that burden. But what causes that? The human condition.

"Among these agencies, there is a fight on for control. The control of hundreds of millions of dollars that would go into their budgets under their personal influence. There is no narcotic in the world as addictive as personal power."

Jerry says he's very discouraged about the salmon, says fishing in the ocean has beaten the tar out of them. You can get depressed just thinking about it. "Even if we decided to blow all the dams out, think how long it would take to do the environmental impact statement." The only thing we could do quickly is to stop fishing, and that's what he thinks we should do.

Jerry has to be getting home, and he extends a gracious and unexpected offer for me to spend the night at his place. But we're headed in different directions.

When I get into my car and turn the ignition key, the radio jumps to life: "This year's numbers amounted to a virtual collapse of the fish. The Snake River chinook now joins the Snake River sockeye salmon as an endangered species. The chinook had been listed as a threatened species for two years. But it's unclear how the more urgent listing will further protect the fish. Salmon advocates variously blame dams, overfishing, logging, and grazing along streambanks for the chinook's near extinction. In the past, conservation plans have favored limiting fishing, and more recently logging and grazing, over regulating dam activity. In the past, though, all efforts to bring salmon runs back to the Northwest—have failed. For Oregon Public Broadcasting, I'm Patrick Cox."

John C. Ryan has written interestingly that in a region once dominated by biological giants, "the natural endowment of the Northwest has been belittled, made small." There is some literal truth to this. Chinook salmon off Oregon and

Washington average half the size of their ancestors of the 1920s. (The largest races were made extinct by the dams, and heavy ocean fishing stacks the odds against fish spending more time growing large at sea before they return to spawn.) The largest trees on the best sites were cut down decades ago. The nineteenth-century Scottish botanist David Douglas, who fell in love with the tree that now bears his name, reported that they *averaged* seventeen feet in diameter in the rich lower valleys. The largest known Doug-fir today is fourteen feet wide as you face it, and today's average is around two feet. *Seattle Times* reporter Bill Dietrich has said, "We have downsized our vegetation and are living in a pygmy world." But Ryan says we need not bemoan irretrievable losses. He points out that the Northwest has yet to entirely liquidate its natural inheritance. It has come pretty close, but ancient temperate rain forests stand here still, more than anywhere else in the world. And if you go up into British Columbia and Alaska, all the species still exist. For all the endangerment, and the loss of several hundred salmon runs, for all the depauperization, none of the *species* has gone extinct. Not yet, anyhow. And on Alaska's salmon rivers the densest populations of grizzly bears and eagles on the planet still thrive. So if you're willing to reach up to the northern end of the Pacific Northwest, you can still find peerless conifer forests and carpeting runs of salmon. All face threats as never before, true, but what remains represents options. Options long ago lost to the rest of the world still present themselves along this coast. Options to restitch the worn and tattered ecosystem, and perhaps quilt together a durable economy. And what better, brighter thread to begin to patch the holes and to tie the seams taut again than the silvery salmon—the fleets of fleet salmon—in a fleeting opportunity for healing the whole.

Don't mistake this for hope; I'm just stating the options.

The Dalles and Umatilla

The arid West's heart pumps a dry summer heat. Short grass and scattered sage-brush struggle forth upon sere soil, leaving one feeling far and disconnected from the ocean. Yet the great Columbia rolls on through here, too, helping drain the desert, giving the dry country's sparse water to seagoing salmon.

Nearly a hundred miles inland from the ocean coast, at a vantage point several hundred feet above the water, I've pulled over to a road marker, which reads:

Celilo Falls.
A historic waterfall, fishing ground, and annual gathering point
for untold generations of Northwest Indians, and always an
obstruction to water travel on the Columbia, was buried deep
beneath waters of The Dalles dam in 1957.

Traffic dusts the dry air. This spot so distant from the sea is where the inter-mingled history of humans and Northwest salmon is oldest; this dialogue spanned ten millennia, from about 8,000 B.C. until 1957. Lewis and Clark passed this way, walking. And writing: "Here is the Great fishing-place of the Columbia. In the spring of the year, when the water is high, the salmon ascend the river in incredible numbers."

The natives called the Columbia River Nch'i-Wána, Big River, and for a length of time no one can really conceive of they had caught the fish at Celilo Falls, standing on makeshift platforms over the roaring white curling cataracts and whirlpools, and dipping salmon from the maelstrom with long nets or spear-ing the leaping ones midair.

The salmon were plenty enough to draw tribes from a wide region into trade. Alexander Ross wrote of the many "foreigners from different tribes throughout the country, who resort hither not for the purpose of catching salmon, but . . . for other articles." Coastal people brought whale and cedar products, clams, shells, beads, and canoes to trade. Southern tribes brought baskets, obsidian, water-lily seeds, tobacco. Buffalo robes, meat, pipestone, and feathers were carried from farther east. The Celilo Falls area became a major communications center where diverse cultures made alliances, exchanged stories, and spoke about religion and their history, in peace. What days those must have been, trading fine crafts and feasting and sharing tales and dances.

When The Dalles Dam backed up the river in 1957 and Celilo Falls was being submerged, Indians stood on the bank, watching. Some wept.

Celilo Falls was the navel of the Columbia, a birth scar, the pull and tuck cinching water, salmon, and humans tight together, a center of spiritual and defining power for the people, and of evolutionary challenge for the fish. Its removal deforms the figure almost too hideously to look at directly. Perhaps that is why, although there is a black-and-white photo of Celilo Falls in almost every home and office I enter, I have never seen it hung as the center of attention. Usually it is off to one side, or on a mantle with other memorabilia, perhaps next to a dusty porcelain figure or an antique coffee grinder or sepia photos of salmon in horse-drawn haul nets on the beach.

Just north, the prairie begins to undulate, wrinkling and crimping the earth until it resembles a tawny velvet cloth hiding some veiled sculpture. Enormous stanchions and high-voltage wires follow those undulations and wrinkles, radiating energy across the belly of the sky.

This landscape strikes me as stark and isolating. I can feel at home on the ocean—which is hostile to human life as any desert—but I've always found enormous *arid* spaces vaguely threatening. That feeling arrives now on the wind that has just begun whining through dry grass, carrying feelings of alienation and real discomfort. As a visitor from a well-watered part of the world, I can understand the urge to irrigate the brownscape, and how beautiful things can look to the lonely, homesick human eye when so unmerciful a place turns green.

Farther east now, about 210 miles from the sea, the sun strikes enough bare rocky ground that the word "desert" easily applies. The river is an unlikely blue ribbon sandwiched by two brown, dry plains of land. But here is yet another dam that salmon must cope with, the John Day. The Columbia has indeed been backed up into a series of lakes—no longer a river, some say. Columbia Aluminum Corporation has a plant here. Again, from this dam, the radiating high-voltage wires transmit power across the desert and out of sight. An ocean-sized barge sporting a huge and ludicrous smiley face is making its way westbound, from the "seaport" of Lewiston, Idaho, some five hundred miles from the ocean.

By the time I am roughly 270 river miles from the ocean, the land reclines and agricultural country first becomes visible from the highway, as does another dam—McNary—and the surrounding town of Umatilla. Just uphill from the lake behind this dam are places with names like the Desert Inn and the oxymoronic Desert Marine Supplies. Seldom has so short a drive brought such sense of extreme transport. Toward dusk, nighthawks float in the sunset. At the dam, lights begin sparkling in the gathering gloam.

I have come not to see the desert but to meet a man of considerable notoriety, about whom I have heard sharply differing opinions:

"I've known Ed Chaney an awfully long time. This is not your run-of-the-mill person, and it would be pretty hard for me to say that he's not a zealot."

"Ed Chaney is the most moral man in the salmon picture. He has personally given up money, health, and marriages, to deal honorably with everyone. Ultimately, his failure makes him a tragic figure."

"He's so fixated on the dams that he's lost sight of the whole picture. That doesn't mean he doesn't raise some good points. I just don't pay attention to him anymore."

"Chaney is just the best."

"Ed Chaney is not a fisheries biologist. I can't accuse him of violating professional ethics, because Chaney is just not qualified to make those kinds of judgments."

"Chaney? A legend in his own mind."

Ed Chaney, all six feet, six inches of his lean corporeal presence, is seated before me, wondering how he will consume the enormous breakfast just served him—but he will. He is given to excessive eating while he's on the road. He has other imperfections: He smokes an occasional cigarette, and if it's been a rough couple of days and he knows he's not driving, he might have one drink too many. But while he's never been called a saint—at least not to my knowledge—Ed *has* been called "the holy man of salmon."

That descriptor seems to hang awkwardly upon him when you try to apply it. Chaney just does not come across as a spiritual presence. Sitting here behind his food, with his sunglasses tucked into the top of his short-sleeved black shirt where a puff of gray chest hair emerges, he is all too real. And his eyes are quick to twinkle with an unsaintly relish for mischief. Ed's unangelic physiognomy bears testament to having survived past five decades; his bald head reflects the desert albedo, and what little is left of his sandy hair is graying. Chaney is thoughtful, but he likes to talk—he's good at it—and his voice flows as smoothly as the syrup in which he's drenching his pancakes and sausages.

Ed Chaney started this life in the Missouri hills and began his long biopolitical struggles in the mid-1960s, in Indiana's natural resources department. "You either paid two percent of your gross salary to the Republican Central Committee, or you left. So I left. By accident, I went to Oregon in 1966."

Chaney started working with the Oregon Fish Commission and soon ran headlong into the U.S. Army Corps of Engineers on the Columbia River. In the waning days of the 1960s, when Vietnam was hot and the country tense, John Day Dam was nearing completion. At the time, it was the largest hydroelectric powerhouse in the world, and Vice President Hubert Humphrey was to make the dedication speech. The builders were behind schedule with the fish ladders, but the corps considered it unthinkable that the vice president might dedicate a finished dam that was not already holding back water. So they closed the dam before the fish ladders were ready. The entire run of surviving adults coming back ready to spawn encountered the barrier, hurled themselves at the concrete, and died by the scores of thousands.

"Two hundred thousand adult salmon and steelhead. Dead. Littering the shores. The corps denied there was a kill." He waves his knife at me, marking time while he swallows. "Those were the good old days, when you knew who the bad guys were because they acted like bad guys. I went up to that dam, shot a bunch of photographs, and took 'em to the *Oregonian,* the daily newspaper."

Pushing his eggs around with his fork, Ed continues, "I was under a gag order from the governor's office. I'd expressed concern about what was going to happen to the fish, and I was told to shut up. I was—to use my supervisor's phrase— 'jeopardizing the good working relationships between the state of Oregon and the Corps of Engineers.' So I said to the paper, 'You're welcome to use the pictures, but don't put my name in the story, because I'll get in big trouble.' The next morning, the lead story is 'Ed Chaney Says This and That About the Corps.' I open up: There's a full page of photos and a little box, 'Photos courtesy of Ed Chaney, Oregon Fish Commission.' Well, I was in deep doo-doo, and I left for a job with one of the big conservation groups in D.C."

Chaney is impressing me by being able to speak so animatedly while conveying a constant stream of fried potatoes, sausages, eggs, and pancakes into that same mouth.

He goes on, "The John Day Dam closure was a revealing experience. The corps had told the state that they were going to close the dam without the fish ladders working and asked what the state thought. Our state director—who later became director of the National Marine Fisheries Service—wrung his hands for about a month, saying, 'Oh, oh, *oh,* what am I gonna do?' I said, 'What do you mean, what are you gonna *do?* Tell 'em *No!*' He just couldn't bring himself to do it. And we've had a series of people stamped right out of the same sheet of dough. Perfect example is the person now heading fisheries in D.C. They never upset anybody, so they can get appointed to their next political job. The turds always float to the top of the punch bowl. They steal the public's money by filling chairs. They are nice folks, except they are largely responsible for the disasters we've got."

More eggs vanish while Ed keeps talking. "All the agencies dealing with natural resources are part of that culture: the Army Corps, the Bonneville Power

Administration, the United States Bureau of Land Management, the United States Forest Service. Interchange the names; they are captives of the same pattern. Corporations that profit from the nation's resources—here it's the aluminum companies, the big pump irrigators, timber companies, the utilities—learn to protect and abet their own largesse through the political system. They are personally benefiting by depleting the public estate, and enriching themselves with billions of dollars of subsidies given to them through these government agencies. Then they invest those profits in political influence to control government. When that happens, the regulated control the regulators, and the whole purpose of government becomes co-opted. Government becomes the handmaiden of the companies that they've been forking the pork to. Then instead of looking out for the public interest, government serves a private mission."

Ed engulfs a forkful of potatoes, synopsizing, "The Army Corps has built these dams, creating waterway transportation, irrigation, and hydropower. Bonneville Power Administration markets the electricity. So the government owns the infrastructure that produces income for people that don't pay the true costs. Very much like the Soviet system. We have here in the Northwest a politburo of vested interests that—by God—are going to try to hang onto their iron grip."

He bites a sausage in half, continuing, "These giant public-fund suckers all have penis envy of true private enterprise. They all want to be CEOs of actual businesses, but they couldn't *make* a living in the real world. They've been on the public tit from Day One, mining the public's funds and resources for private gain, privatizing the profits while commonizing the costs, and no matter how badly they screw up, they get paid."

One might come away with the impression that Chaney is not fond of the U.S. Army Corps of Engineers or the Bonneville Power Administration. "The Corps has slaughtered more salmon than fishermen have ever caught. What's extraordinary is, they're *still* getting away with it, because they've gotten a lot smarter." Ed mops up the last bit of syrup with the last half piece of toast, swishing it all down with some coffee. "You will not find anyone in the corps today who doesn't *love* the salmon, and you won't find anyone in the Bonneville Power Administration who doesn't want to *save* the salmon," he bellows mockingly.

Ed pushes back heavily from the table, daintily wiping the downward-turning corners of mouth under his short brush of mustache. "I'm sure glad I ate all of that."

Today we will be going to see a river—the Umatilla—where salmon had been extinct for seventy years. A government irrigation project had dried up the lower three miles of river in summer. Places where the Indians were guaranteed by treaty to be able to fish turned to dry gravel. "That's as bad as it gets—no water. The government had sold the same horse to two people, promising the Indians and irrigators the same water. The irrigators *got* theirs. And the Indians wanted what they were promised."

Chaney advised the tribe's lawyer to claim their right to the salmon. The lawyer responded, "Salmon! There's not even any *water.*" "Exactly," Ed said, and laid out his plan: "to put some fish back in the river and make water for the tribe." So while the river was dry down below the Three Mile Dam, Chaney got the Oregon Department of Fish and Wildlife to put in hatchery-raised fall chinook upstream. The young fish went downstream during spring floods. "Then I went to the irrigators and said, 'In a few years there's going to be a whole bunch of big fall chinook trying to get back into the river, but there's no water there, so we've got to *do* something. What *they* wanted to do was lynch me, but it shows-t'-go-ya that if you want water, you've got to put fish in a dry river."

Our first stop on tour of the Umatilla project is McNary Dam. All of the Umatilla River had been diverted into irrigation ditches. Chaney's plan called for bringing water from the Columbia River—taken at McNary—for the irrigators, and putting the Umatilla River back into its riverbed. "The water comes out of the reservoir, goes into that ditch, goes around to the Umatilla River, is siphoned under the river and into the irrigation ditch. So that irrigation district is now getting its water out of McNary Reservoir, and not taking any water from the Umatilla River at Three Mile Dam. They're letting river water go past their diversion, and they're getting the same amount of water out of this ditch from McNary."

We get into my car—leaving Ed's at the dam—and head out. Ed instructs, "Go straight up the highway, then we'll be taking a right in a couple of miles. Watch your speed through here. It's a favorite speed trap." Chaney has not been back here for a while, but he's driven these roads—as he says with some pride—a thousand times.

Chaney continues, "We were very lucky with the Umatilla River project that a fix was possible. Not every place has that. But it took years of just *awful,* gut-wrenching persuasion, even though it was in their own best interest—as though the horse that is dying of thirst simply will not allow itself to be led to water."

An early indication of what Chaney and the tribe were in for came at an informational meeting at the Stanfield Fire Hall. "It was packed with irrigators who were out for blood. And they *got* quite a bit. By the time I got out of there, I was shaking at the knees. But I come from a farm background—I was president of an irrigation district for a while—and I know you can't give them an inch, because they're like dogs that can sense fear and dislike people who are afraid of them. When we started, the irrigators asked, 'Why don't we send the lazy Indians to the ocean to fish?' I said, 'Why don't we send you pork-barrel farmers down to the Willamette Valley to farm, where there's water, and the government wouldn't have to subsidize you?' I think you want to bear right up here to catch the old highway.

"And it got rougher. I took verbal abuse beyond belief. The anti-Indian racism was very hard to bear. I had to keep explaining that, 'This is not trouble—

you can avoid trouble here.' It took years of fighting. The only thing that made it work was the irrigators' fear that the Indians would go to court and get *all* the water. I personally don't think there was a snowball's chance in hell of that happening, because politics dictate how the law is allowed to work. But I didn't offer that opinion at the time. Still, they might have lost an expensive court fight. This way, they get their water. Take a left here; here we are."

We have arrived at Three Mile Dam on the Umatilla River, and we walk down to the willows growing along the shoreline. New fishways and fish ladders for the new fish now stand at the old, two-hundred-yard-wide dam. It is late morning, and a Swainson's hawk circles the half moon hanging out to dry in a moistureless desert-blue sky. A gently sloping hayfield recedes from the opposite bank to form the horizon. Until the Bureau of Reclamation built the dam, circa 1915, salmon had spawned here for millennia. Their absence, which might have gone on forever, lasted only until Chaney had his idea three-quarters of a century later. When Chaney first came here this time of year, he walked on desiccated riverbed all the way to the Umatilla's mouth. Until 1990, this river was dry from here down—three miles—except during big spring floods. "All we're doing so far is putting some flow back in the lower three miles of the river, but after ten years of bloody battling, the sound of that running water sure feels good. And coho, fall chinook, and spring chinook have all been restored to this river—and Indians are fishing here again now for the first time since 1914."

Brian Zimmerman, a fisheries biologist working for the Umatilla tribe, is at the dam site. Thinking he is helping me understand something, he says, "There's a C and S fishery on the rez for spring chinook."

"C and S on the rez?"

"Cultural and subsistence. On the reservation. It's quite significant to the tribe."

"Why don't the Indians have Indians working on these projects?"

"Right now most of the tribe's biologists are W.G.s, but—"

"W.G.s?"

"White guys. But our technicians are tribal members. Hopefully, there'll be more of them going to school to get the technical training to run these projects."

Zimmerman's job is assisting the fish in getting up and down the river around dry stretches. "Basically, we catch all the adult fish here and take them upriver about thirty miles, past a dry area, then they spawn naturally there—not in a hatchery. When the little ones are coming downstream, if there's not enough water for them, we catch them up above and haul them down here."

I'm a bit confused. Chaney has for years insisted that trapping and hauling fish around the big dams is the main thing killing Columbia River salmon. I want to know why he's doing the same thing here that he's been crusading against on the main river.

"All the details differ drastically. Here you're hauling them twenty miles. There you're hauling them up to *four hundred* miles. We haul only when there is no water, and the goal for this project involves getting permanent flows; this is a temporary part of the program. On the Columbia, it *is* the program."

And who is paying?

"Bonneville Power Administration, to belatedly begin doing what they were supposed to do in the first place, which was to mitigate for the damage caused by the federal Columbia River power system." For Ed, this is one seamless thought, and Bonneville will not be off the hook merely because they funded his project. If they restored the salmon runs throughout the entire Columbia Basin, one suspects that Ed Chaney would see it, pronounce it good—as good as before the dams—and forgive nothing.

"Bonneville had no intention of having these fish here. I have documents that show in tedious detail how Bonneville Power Administration fought this project to the *death*. In the end, we kicked their ass. Our senator finally told them to shut up. Then Bonneville immediately put up signs and made a video showcasing their 'model project.' But that's O.K. That's success, when you've got them doing pirouettes to claim credit for something they fought for ten years. Fought it bitterly. And in the process, blacklisted me. If anyone tries to hire me for any Bonneville-financed project, Bonneville won't give them the money. So I make a living working for people who aren't afraid of Bonneville, and that basically means outside the Columbia Basin." Ed's work has taken him to Arizona for the Navajo nation, to Puget Sound for tribes there, and to France's Loire River, in all cases working on master plans for restoration of river watersheds and fish runs.

We continue through irrigated country, with farms and cattle on the open, rolling plains under a wide sky.

Impressed at Chaney's ability to survive and thrive under challenging circumstances, I say, "Well, it seems like you've gotten into a position—even if you were forced into it—that many would envy. You can say what you want, you are a prominent defender of what you believe in, you've been hired by the government of—"

"Yes, it's true. And all of that plus sixty-nine cents will buy you a candy bar at the corner store. I'm fifty-two years old. I've been around several blocks. I don't expect to buck the economic and political forces in a *death* battle, and kick 'em in the butt daily, and have them not exact the kind of retribution they are capable of. I expect them to dry up the monies that might be available to me for consulting work in the Northwest. They have done that. And they put out the word that I am not professional, not a thoughtful person. Get in the left lane here."

"They say you're a zealot."

"The bigger question is, am I essentially correct or not? I think I can make a convincing case that they are ruining people's lives and costing the nation billions by destroying a major natural resource. So if a zealot is a person who persists at not letting them get away with it, you can call me a zealot, I guess."

"They also say you're not a fisheries biologist and so are not qualified to be in these debates."

"Ha!" he just about roars. "These debates have *nothing* to do with biology. Anyone who wants fishery biologists can hire fifty of them. They're everywhere. Thank *God* I'm not a fisheries biologist. I hear that all the time from the bureaucrats: 'He's not a biologist.' Oh yeah? Well you're not an engineer and you're arguing to me that the dams can't be modified. Left turn, I think. Oh, sorry; take a right. I think I really screwed us up; I've only driven this a thousand times, but—"

Chaney describes himself as a generalist. The degree he wanted did not exist, so he cobbled together an education—a bachelor's in English, and a bachelor's in natural resource science—that he thought would prepare him for what he calls "strategic planning in natural resource management."

Ed pauses as though considering whether to divulge more, then allows our discussion about his professional history to lead just a bit into his personal life. "There was a time—long time ago—when I burned out. I just wanted a normal job with no political implications. I tried very hard getting a job in agriculture, even in office work in the food industry, but they wouldn't hire me because they were afraid I was overqualified and wouldn't stay.

"I was desperate. I had a three-year-old kid, and I was just about out of money. Finally, the guy at the state employment office felt sorry for me, and he removed everything from my résumé except my work in construction, on farms, and for the railroad—which I did for two years when I dropped out of college. Everything else—all my professional experience—he took off. Everything.

"He finally felt he'd lined something up: feeding sheep for a rancher. It paid three hundred and sixty dollars a month plus room and board. I told the rancher I'd take it. I told him I couldn't live in the bunkhouse because of my young son, but that I'd rented a little place and I'd just come to work every morning. He looked at me. He was a real cowboy type—nice fellow—and he said, 'Well hell, room and board comes with the job.' I said, 'That's O.K. I'll just eat lunch. You won't have to pay me any more money, and I'll just go home at night to be with my son.' He scratched his chin and looked at the floor. He said, 'Well, I dunno, I never done it *that* way before.' I needed this job bad. He said, 'I guess I'd better pass.' And I thought, 'I can't even drop out.'

"I took my son, my books, my three dogs, and my three hundred dollars and moved to Boise. I thought, 'Holy smoke, *now* what am I gonna do?' I used all my money to make the rent and security on a little place, and I hit the streets trying to find work. I didn't find squat. I borrowed money on my car. I hocked my shotguns. I was down to the wire. And I finally got a job doing a fifteen-hundred-dollar consulting project for the Bureau of Land Management. If a big consulting firm had taken it, it would have been about a ten-thousand-dollar job. But it allowed me to pay some bills, and it led to a steady job turning their scientific reports into English. Okay, up here you have to go left."

A couple of years ago, the Bonneville Power Administration—which Chaney has fought, as he says, to the *death*, and which has blacklisted him—tried to hire him. Thick in the middle of Senator Mark Hatfield's much-touted—and failed—

"Salmon Summit," there was an interesting sideshow: "Bonneville wanted to blame everyone—and thereby no one—for hurting the salmon. I tried to focus on the agent of extinction—the dams—as opposed to all the things that have ever affected salmon. I think we want to take a right up here.

"I essentially failed, but I had no money and of course Bonneville had millions. But they knew facing us in public was a problem. Okay, right turn here.

"I was tired. I had been up all night as usual, fighting these bastards across the table. I was sitting in the bar of the hotel in Boise, and the Bonneville troops, including the one who was their spear carrier at the summit, came over. They said I could be a lot more effective at changing—" Chaney cracks a broad smile. "I can't even repeat this with a straight face now, after all this time, it's so bad. That I could be much more effective at changing Bonneville from the inside"— he is laughing now—"from the inside than from the outside. I began to laugh. I was exhausted. I hadn't had any sleep. My back was hurting. But I couldn't stop laughing. I had tears running. This guy just went right on with the canned speech he'd been sent to deliver, even after I just broke out laughing in his face. Can you imagine? He said, 'And of course, once you are on the inside, you could no longer be a public advocate for the salmon. Well, what do you think?' I was so tired, I *couldn't* think. I was watching everybody straining to see what my reaction was gonna be. So I just said, 'I'll get back to you.' Imagine what agony they must have gone through to offer me a *job!*"

At the time, Chaney was borrowing money on his house to attend the conference. "Driving home, I thought, 'I should have taken the job, then given half the money to someone to do what I'm doing now.' I went home and told my then wife that maybe I should think of some way that I could take this job, and she said, 'If you do that, I'm leaving you.' Yet it was my continual work that led to the dissolution of our marriage. Take a left here. Wait. No. Go straight."

"Bitter breakup?"

"Oh no." His voice softens. "No, it was tragic. I was living a life that was not conducive to a good relationship—or to my health. She was right, of course, about the job. I've watched a lot of good people who went to Bonneville, trying to work from the inside. I don't think it's possible. The resource agencies won't allow it, really. You've got to decide which side you're on. That doesn't mean that one side is all right and one is all wrong, but you have to pick the side that you'll be on."

A channel appears alongside the road, exposing a thin vein of water. "See the little trickle right here running alongside the road? This is the river below two diversions. Pull in up ahead."

A cloud of dust envelops us as I stop the car near a chain-link fence. "This is the diversion for Westland Irrigation District. You can see that they totally divert the entire river right out of its bed into this dirt ditch, then onto farms."

Ed peers into the ditch, then calls me over. There are a lot of little fish on the downstream side of the diversion. "See these fish here? The bulk of them are spring chinook. Some fall chinook, coho, and steelhead. All the juvenile fish go into the irrigation ditch, obviously, because the whole river goes into the ditch. But, of course, the river in the ditch runs not to the sea but onto farm fields. So here the young fish are screened out with these big round fish screens that are turning. They rotate so as not to clog with debris."

The system is a surprisingly high-tech affair, entailing copious concrete and steel and numerous chains driving different rotating cylindrical screens that are each about fifteen feet long. A pair of barn swallows that have affixed their nest under a catwalk are feeding their young. This is an expensive birdhouse; the cost of this 150-foot-wide screening plant was around a million dollars.

There are still thousands of unscreened agricultural water diversions. In the mid-1990s, more than 80 percent of the sites pumping water from the Columbia River for irrigation still failed to comply with requirements designed to protect salmon. The subsidized farmers who caterwaul about providing food for our tables don't seem to mind removing it from the tables of salmon fishers and their families.

I go down to the stone-lined bank. The operator tells me to watch my step: "Listen for rattles." A mink, the first wild one I've ever seen, slides off a log and swims toward shore.

Ed reminds me that when phase two of this project comes on, supplying water to these irrigation districts out of McNary Dam, the river water will be allowed to bypass the diversion and the Umatilla will be flowing again all the way down to the Columbia. "Usually, if you are at a place saying, 'This will never look the same again,' it's because it is about to be built on. But here I can tell you it will never look like this again because next year this river will be flowing—straight out of the mountains."

When we next glimpse the river from the road, we have gained some elevation and the land feels different. About ten miles back we started ascending. Ten miles upstream of here, the gradient increases into the Blue Mountains, and timber country begins. We are driving alongside the Umatilla River above the irrigation diversions now and can finally see what the Umatilla looks like before it's dried up.

Ed tells me to turn left and pull over. We get out and walk to the center of a small bridge spanning the riverbed. The river is wide and shallow, flowing steadily. Cottonwood trees line the banks with shade that contrasts with bright green irrigated fields nearby. A truckload of some of the biggest, juiciest-looking onions I've ever seen thunders over the rattling bridge. Chaney says, "This is extraordinarily productive country when you add water. Corn, potatoes, alfalfa, wheat, melons—this area is famous for melons."

After a moment's contemplation of the moving river, Ed, leaning his forearms on the bridge, looks out at the broad landscape, saying, "When you think about what a hostile environment this was for people, trying to make the desert bloom was really quite an extraordinary vision for the technology of the time. I can understand those irrigators that fought me so desperately over water and salmon. To them, I was questioning the whole concept of what human progress is. We have to remember that a lot of lives have been burned up trying to create something here that these people see as civilization itself. To give that less than its full due understandably disturbs people who have been part of that."

I glance at the man some call a thoughtless zealot. He is looking into the water again.

Most water withdrawn for irrigation—two-thirds of it—does not return to the rivers. What does return is often warmer, less oxygenated, saltier, siltier, and of course carrying fertilizers, pesticides, and other toxins. And remember that so much water is lost into the ground in irrigation ditches or evaporates into the desert sky that it takes ten feet of river water to put two feet on a potato field. So much water is taken from the Snake River (a major interstate tributary that gave rise to genetically unique races of salmon) that it goes completely dry at times. This is seen as a good thing, since none of the water is "wasted" on fish or let out for other users. It appeals to a certain fractured sense of thrift—something like "Waste not, want not" but with a lot of waste, and excessive wants.

"All a salmon asks," Ed says as we head back to the car, "is, 'Let me get to the ocean in reasonably clean water, and I'll just keep producing wealth for people forever.' That was the deal humans had with salmon for thousands of years. People have a hard time imagining the numbers of Columbia salmon—between ten and sixteen million spawning adult fish annually. And in fifty years, we've brought our options for having salmon down to a very bare minimum. That's quite an accomplishment, and it could only have been done without any concern for the future. Out of sheer stupidity, we have virtually annihilated one of the world's most valuable and productive systems."

"When you say 'stupidity,' you're acknowledging that honest mistakes were made," I point out.

"There were a lot of honest mistakes. The mentality at the time was non-malevolent: a nation out to prove it was biggest and best. However, the Corps of Engineers knew that salmon must go upstream to spawn, yet as you know they designed Bonneville Dam without fish ladders. They were willing to write the salmon off.

"We could absolutely have had the dams *and* the fish. The Columbia system wouldn't look a whole lot different than it does today, and would produce nearly as much irrigation, transportation, and hydropower as it does today, and we could have virtually all the salmon we once had."

There would be a few differences, Chaney explains. You wouldn't have built the Grand Coulee Dam or the Snake River dams as they are—totally blocking about a third of the basin to salmon and destroying the giant chinooks. You would have built a different kind of dam, or two dams, where Coulee is.

Damming the Snake was a giant pork-barrel project to make Lewiston, Idaho, a seaport five hundred miles from the ocean, so they could barge grain—which is shipped by railroad from everywhere else. Ed says, "If they'd built a lock-and-dam system like on the Mississippi, Lewiston would have their pork-barrel waterway, we'd have a flowing river, and we'd have the salmon. But other than that, the other Columbia dams could still be there; they would just look a little different.

"So," Ed continues, "we did not fulfill the early vision of the Congress: to realize the power potential while ensuring the salmon's survival. And what used to be the world's largest salmon and steelhead runs are now teetering on the edge of extinction. This is not the inevitable price of progress. It's the inevitable price of stupidity. The place is up here on the right."

The man we've come to see is seated and waiting in the roadside restaurant. His long braids, snaking out from under a cap, are joined at their ends over his belly above his big silver belt buckle, producing a stethoscopic appearance. Antoine Minthorn is no W.G. This guy is a real Indian who looks and sounds it. He speaks with the soft, inflectionless, laconic tone typical of American Indians, and his voice has a hint of gravel in it. For the last thirteen years he has served as the Umatilla Tribe's general council chairman.

Antoine is explaining some of the tribe's political history under United States occupation. "When we signed the treaty of 1855 we signed away six point four million acres. Just like that. That was the economy of the tribe." Sitting with his arms crossed over his lavender shirt, he continues, "The treaty gives us fishing rights in all streams running through and adjacent to the reservation. Our rights were violated with the building of the Three Mile Dam on the Umatilla, which affected our subsistence, in other words our life, being, existence—however you want to say it—by destroying the salmon.

"They didn't leave us with much to work with. I came to understand this one day in the 1970s, when I went with my son up a creek on the Lostine River, where in the 1960s there had been plentiful salmon. We went way, way up before we found three salmon, two males and a female. My son gaffed out the female. We didn't fully realize what we were committing. But when that female came ashore trailing a stream of eggs, I suddenly understood the seriousness of what we had just done, and I have never forgotten that moment."

When the first adult salmon returned to the Umatilla in 1988, Minthorn went down to the river, and he stood in the shade of streamside cottonwood trees, watching them a long time.

Ed and Antoine are old and close comrades in arms, and Ed is in the mood to reminisce about the wars, telling Antoine, "At one meeting, Bonneville Power Administration was complaining about the cost of the Umatilla project. That's when they were fighting it to the *death*. And one of them said to you, 'Well, Antoine, how much are these fish worth to the tribe?' I'm sure his next move would be to say, 'O.K., here's a check, now go away.' "

"Basically, that's right, he'd have said, 'Here's money, now cease to exist.' "

"And you just sat there for a long while, until the silence was getting embarrassing, and then you said exactly these words: 'How can I tell you how much the fish are worth? The salmon define who I am.' That was one of the most powerful and interesting things I've ever heard in thirty years in this business, and I immediately wrote it down. You will be known for having said it."

Antoine turns to me. "You can put a dollar value on it, but it's your being. I don't know how to explain it in English terms. It's just like the land. I don't know how to explain that either. The land is there. The land is being. Without it, we just don't exist. The fish are our being. I don't know how else to say it." He gropes for a word and finds one so fundamental it needs to be stated twice: "Reality. Reality. So with the fish. It's just the way things are. Genocide. That's the other word. Genocide. They did to the fish what they did to us. Genocide. Part of you goes."

As we head back down the road to the Columbia, Chaney says, "A decade and a half ago, Congress passed the Northwest Power Act, which unequivocally states: 'Thou shalt give fish equal importance as all other uses of the river. Thou shalt provide adequate flows. Thou shalt not study this emergency any longer. And thou shalt develop a plan within sixty days that will restore these fish runs.' That is the law.

"You know what's happened? Nothing. Why? The Power Council—the Powerless Council—created by the act turned into a dumping ground for out-of-work politicians and former legislative assistants, a crowd whose whole culture was that *the process was the product.* They have processed the salmon to *death.* No yawning absence of progress is enough to humiliate them. The jobs are too cushy. For complexity that will create inaction, anything will suffice. 'Oh! But it's just so *complicated!* There's the commercial fishermen, the killer ocean, land use, too much dissolved nitrogen—.' Everything but the dams. Their favorite is: 'The science we have is not conclusive.' They're just like the tobacco-industry lobbyists who say the link between smoking and cancer isn't proven. Until the salmon are all gone—even *after* they're gone—they'll say, 'You can't prove conclusively, absolutely, that the dams did it.' Left here."

Something seems missing in Chaney's interpretation, and I decide to press it. "You seem to dismiss logging, fishing, ocean temperatures, and a lot of other factors, but salmon are hurting outside the Columbia, too."

"Those things all contribute, but I dismiss them as agents of extinction in the *Columbia* system. Ocean temperatures have been bad only during the last few years. But we have *measured* how many fish the dams killed annually."

"But the runs were way down before the dams went in," I point out, "because of habitat problems and overfishing."

"We had enormous numbers of fish until recent times. Yes, there was horrible overfishing in the old days. Fishing has been restricted. But remember—sockeye salmon were not fished for, and *they* are all but gone. And there are thousands of miles of pristine spawning habitat in the Snake River system, yet salmon there are on the lip of extinction.

"The main problem in the Columbia drainage," Chaney declares, "is the dams' effects on juvenile fish that need to migrate downriver. On average, it's fifteen to twenty percent mortality per dam, and most fish have to pass several. They've been barging young fish around the dams for decades, and the results are in: The salmon are going extinct.

"Barging assumes that these animals don't need to migrate downstream, only to arrive at Point B. It eliminates a whole portion of their life cycle. It's like catapulting cows from the pasture to the barn, and then wondering why the herd has thinned. Their thinking is not that catapulting cows is a problem, it's that we need a better catapult. It goes against everything we've learned about living organisms. Salmon typically have a window of time to make the transition from fresh- to saltwater creatures, triggered by environment and genetics. If they make the migration within that window, the system works. If they don't, then the system doesn't work and they either become saltwater animals before they get to saltwater, or they get to saltwater while they are still freshwater creatures. You can't continually remove these fish from their environment and expect them to survive. The results *are* in: It doesn't work."

Invoking a small amount of knowledge, I counter, "But in nature you have fish spawned close to saltwater and fish spawned a thousand miles inland, so they must have tremendous flexibility in that window."

Ed reminds me, "The different runs' particular timing is evolved and adapted to their local environmental conditions and challenges. One size does not fit all. Yet, the thinking behind all their pipes and ducts for moving fish around is that we just have to build a more intricate collection and barging system—an advanced catapult—to fix it. They have diverted the debate away from the real issue of allowing the river to simply act more like a river again.

"To fix the problem," Ed concludes, "the laws of nature reduce the options to one: If you're going to leave the dams in place, you have to draw the reservoirs down periodically to mimic a natural river."

I ask how.

"All we need to do is to modify—*slightly* modify—this gargantuan system, to allow most of the young fish to get downstream. Your goal is to speed the young fish through the reservoirs and spill them past the dams without going through the turbines. You can draw down the reservoirs temporarily, from mid-April to mid-June, when the majority of the fish would naturally go out on the spring snowmelt. This would speed up the water. Once you get the fish to the dam, you can spill them through ports that could be opened. So you speed up the fish and get them past the dam.

"It's so simple that the most difficult thing to understand is why anyone is resisting it." A fly is buzzing annoyingly and Ed is wiping at the air to get rid of it, but he doesn't lose his cadence. "The modifications are straightforward. The military engineers tell me, 'This is easy, we can do this.' But the administrative boys won't willingly let it happen."

"What other effects would there be?"

"Fish ladders would need modification. About fifteen irrigators would have to extend their pump intakes to reach the lower water. While the reservoirs are drawn down the barges can't travel the river. The other impact is reduced electrical generation for that ten-week period. The total annualized cost of making these modifications, including the forgone amount of electricity, fixing the pumps, and additional subsidies to the waterway transportation people, is about fifty million dollars a year."

"Coming from where?"

"It would represent a *savings*. Salmon can make the system more efficient. First of all, much of that fifty-million-dollars-a-year calculation is money the dams won't make because of reduced electrical revenue. But the forgone value to the salmon fishing industry—the money real people will *lose* because the fish are disappearing—is *never* figured into their equation. I tried to get them to do it. They won't. So I did. We calculated the costs to the fishing industry at three hundred million a year during the last twenty years. Present value, it calculates at one point eight billion a year. The utilities put together a team of economists to shoot down my study. I kept waiting for the attack, but it never came. You know why? Because I was conservative in my estimates. So on an annual basis, grinding the salmon down is costing much more than the fifty million they claim it would take to get the fish back!"

"You said that's just annual costs. What's the up-front cost for all the modifications?"

"Capital costs? The worst-case estimate is a billion dollars. The low-end estimate is six hundred million."

"*Ouch.*" I wince.

"A billion dollars *is* a lot of money. But spread it over the region's rate base, over a hundred years of the project's lifetime, and it gets lost in the rounding errors. The utilities admitted it publicly. I pressed them, saying, 'Don't you agree that in fifteen or twenty years the price of energy here is going to be the same whether we have salmon or not?' And the head lobbyist for the utilities—the Darth Vader of salmon—said, 'That's right. But it's the costs right now that we're concerned about.' Well, we should be thinking about more than tomorrow's subsidized-aluminum-industry balance sheet. *Government* certainly should be. But thirty-some-odd years after John Day Dam closed, we haven't changed anything, really. The only difference is, the corps has killed the Snake River's coho, sockeye, and fall chinook, and it's about this far away"—he demonstrates with fingertips almost touching—"from killing the Snake River spring and summer chinook. That's why we need the drawdowns. *Now.*"

"But what if drawdowns don't work? You can't really be sure—"

"We've got ten thousand years of empirical evidence saying, 'If you let me get downstream, I will come back.' That's very conclusive. Saying, 'It's not certain, it's not technologically feasible, it's not politically feasible, it's not economically feasible, we don't have enough good science'—all these phrases simply mean we've slipped our moral and ethical moorings."

"But, Ed," I counter, "other people's belief in taking natural resources and converting them into electrical power and products *is* a moral and ethical belief."

"Yes. We *share* that belief. I'm absolutely bought into that. But we're just asking those people living and gorging at the public trough to back up an inch. Let them gorge—just back up an inch. But they're willing to sacrifice the fish, the tribes' cultures, every commercial fisherman, everyone tied to sportfishing, every boat, motel, and restaurant operator—everyone who buys and eats salmon, every person who wants to see salmon. They're willing to sacrifice all those people and these resources just so they don't have to give up one crumb at the public trough."

Back at McNary Dam, the fish-viewing facility's sliding glass doorway bears two signs:

CAUTION: STAND BACK

CAUTION: DO NOT STOP IN DOORWAY

I ignore the first sign and obey the second. Inside, a continuous blasting of shining bubbles is whipping whirling vortices behind glass panels that form a window into one rung of the fish ladder. A squawfish is wavering unsteadily in the current, and a lamprey holds onto the glass with its bizarre, jawless, rasp-lined parasitic sucking disk of a mouth.

A boy says, "Those eels are *cool!*" Most people come into the viewing room with children, the generation to come, as though they should know something about salmon but it is not something adults need take a real interest in. Like piano lessons, perhaps.

A man with two kids tells me he'd like to take the lampreys and throw them out into the parking lot. I say to him, "Well, we eat fish, so do they." He says, "Yes, but somehow it seems more sporting when I eat fish."

Sporting?

A chinook salmon bores its way into the swirling silvery maelstrom. So they really do come up hundreds of miles from the ocean! I had intellectually understood this; now, here in the desert, I can *feel* it. A second chinook enters, turns back as if undecided, then reappears a moment later. Transformed by the time and effort they have expended in their river journey, the chinook have become deeply colored, charcoal-bronze animals. At the window's exit port, both fish are delayed by the buffeting current. Engaging a burst of power, their tails speeding to a blur, the creatures suddenly overcome the seemingly insuperable torrent, propelling through. I stifle an urge to cheer. Ed does not.

"God! *Look* at that guy!" If you had not just spent the day with Ed, you might think he was a ten-year-old, seeing his first salmon.

Another chinook—large, going on thirty pounds—comes before us.

Every salmon seems to perform open-heart surgery on Chaney. "Jeez, what a fish! These creatures absolutely inspire me. Anything that can take this kind of abuse, can take everything that the government and the pork barrelers can throw at them—everything!—over and over, year after year—. The fish aren't gonna give up. That's why we're gonna beat the bastards. These fish are just *not* gonna go extinct. They are not gonna go down. They're just—. They're not. These creatures are gonna defeat everything. It's corny, but I think it's a matter of right versus wrong. It is not right to destroy benign things. Civilization is a very thin veneer. This is really a battle of civilized people against uncivilized people. Intelligence against—. Who in the hell *knows* what motivates me. I don't think I want to. It'd probably scare me."

I'm looking at Ed, who is transfixed by the sight of the fish. He pauses a beat, and to redirect my attention to what is important, says in a hush, "Look, here comes another one—a steelhead. So beautiful."

This fish looks a little tired, laboring and struggling against the current. Ed says with intensity, "Not surprising, when you think of the thousands of miles it has come. Come on," he says, encouraging the fish. "There you go!"

As the lonely steelhead drives into the current, a toddler named Dakota, holding her father's hand, has her large brown eyes opened wide at the sight of such a big living thing. She says to it, "Go bye-bye. Go bye-bye."

Ed must be thinking the same, in even fewer words.

It struggles through. "It was just pausing," Ed says, as though trying to deny that the fish was unwell.

"I think it was ailing," I say.

"It's unbelievable; that one *was* really laboring, but rather than take a rest it just drove itself onward."

Another, much more vigorous fish enters. Ed says, "Boy, that is a big steelhead. God! isn't that a *beauty?*" With its rosy blush, it certainly is. Not even Solomon in all his glory was arrayed as one of these. Chaney whistles in appreciation and wonder at the profound mystery of it. It shoots right through.

When the next big chinook makes its entry, someone who has come to stand behind me, a cowboy sort—hat, black jeans, boots, picking his teeth—says too loudly, "Oh man. *Yeah! That*'d be a nice fish to play with on the end of your line. I'll believe we've got a shortage of fish when they stop them Indians from gill-nettin'."

I address the gent, seeking clarification on his point: "You don't think there's a shortage of salmon?"

"Oh, there's a salmon shortage all right. But Canada is catching them all. *Ooh!* Look at *that* big fish."

His buddy says, "I'll tell ya, the way they're managing, it just doesn't make sense." This guy really has his volume turned up, and I suspect there's a recently emptied six-pack or two in their pickup. "You get some *eco*-freak—and there's a difference between a conservationist and an environmentalist: You've got to have your common sense removed from your brain before you can become an environmentalist." Beat. "Bee-*cuzz,* you can't just let humanity suffer. There's got to be a balance between man and nature."

Ed is already outside smoking a cigarette when I find my way into the sunshine and fresh air, and he says: "It's important to know what the average guy thinks, because it reflects the information he's exposed to. This is a measure of how successful the boys are. This guy said we have to deal with everything—Indians, Canada, nets. And we do. But the basic premise of the disinformation program is that you have to solve all the problems at once. And solve the *other* problems first. Until we deal with everything, we can't stop killing the fish at the dams. It's like saying, 'Until we have world peace, we shouldn't have peace efforts.' "

We stroll toward a building labeled NEW PERMANENT JUVENILE FISH FACILITY. Referring to the facility, I say, "For all your dissatisfaction, Ed, you have to admit that an unbelievable amount of money and effort has gone into trying to save the fish."

"No, it's gone into avoiding changing the way the projects are operated. The dams killed the original population, and they're unchanged."

"But look at this new facility—"

"This is much cheaper for them. And it looks good. I mean, aren't you impressed?"

"I *am* impressed."

"Oh, it *is* impressive," he says. "But it is a search for a technological fix to an ecological dilemma. They have angled screens tacked on to the turbine intakes. Young fish dive for the current and are diverted up, inside the dam. There they go into this pipe, and they sort them, handle them, stick tags in 'em, and then take them two hundred and fifty miles downriver in barges and trucks. And remember, these are fragile creatures. You pick one up, and the scales come off in your hands. How can we treat these wild animals like this and expect anything less than catastrophe? But, hell, if it worked, I wouldn't care if you FedExed them to the coast. What's interesting is that they've been barging the fish for the last twenty years while the fish are going extinct. At some point, results have to count."

Ed halts abruptly at the sight of a small sign hung across a path. "Oops, no trespassing."

I am game to proceed.

"No," he warns, "they'll come and get you."

I look at him inquiringly.

"They will. I can't afford to risk it."

We turn and walk slowly toward our parked vehicles. "Well," I say, "what is this guy Chaney really advocating?"

"It's really quite modest: Just do the right thing and obey the law, and I'll go home. I'll make a living, have a family again. I'd get a life. Ah, but that is the talk of a zealot." He's smiling, his eyes shining mischievously.

"What would a life be, if you got one?"

"More time to spend with my kids. With my bird dog. Find a mate. Do some writing. It'd be nice not to worry about working all the time. Save a little money. I don't have a dime in the bank.

"But," he says, debating even himself, "I can't remember a day that hasn't been interesting. *That's* been worth a great deal. I don't know if it's worth the price I paid, but I can't remember a day that I didn't wake up charged, thinking, 'God, I've gotta get this, I've gotta do that.' The older I get and the more I see what other people have to do, or have chosen, the more I'm realizing it's not bad to get up with a fire in your belly every morning and delay going to bed because you're thinking, 'If I stay up a little while longer, squeeze a few more hours, I can finish this or that.' I didn't always realize this. But that's worth a lot. I've convinced myself that what I'm doing is important. Cosmic scheme of things, of course, it means absolutely nothing."

"Is anything important in the cosmic scheme of things?"

Ed shrugs. "Who knows. Probably not. So, relatively speaking, this is *very* important."

Ed pauses in thought, as though gathering a grand summation. "Stripped of everything, it comes down to people who don't care and people who do. They're not going to win this. I'm not quite sure how we're going to whup 'em, but we are. I'm confident we are."

"You *are* confident?"

"I am. I have my dark moments. I mean, the greed and corruption run so deep you have to wonder how to avoid drowning, but I feel more energized than I did twenty years ago, because now people are starting to listen. I can smell the final battle, and I know it's do or die. And the fear that the stakes are high—it's scary stuff. So it's got my adrenaline running. And you know that the boys you're up against have no moral or ethical foundation; they're really dirty fighters. They've lied. Deliberately. They are conning and propagandizing themselves as much as anyone. They have to, because who really wants to be responsible for wiping out the world's largest chinook salmon and steelhead runs? There are laws on the books to stop them; they have not been followed. The political onslaught is just so overwhelming. We have no congressional champions right now. It's hopeless. And the Idaho congressional delegation is just the worst of the worst, transmitting the propaganda of Bonneville Power and of the aluminum industry. I'm hopeful that when this is all over, the people in Idaho will see how our senators have sold them out, and—"

"Wait a second! Hold it!" I'm waving my hands in front of his face, signaling time-out. "You say the propaganda is overwhelming. It's hopeless. You have no congressional champions. The governor of Idaho can't get his delegation to move. What is getting you pumped up? Where's the palpable smell of victory?"

"They've run out of excuses. The politicians can't ignore that the fish are going to go extinct on their watch. I think at the final hour the public will rise up and smite them, and Congress will be forced to take action. I think at the final hour the system is gonna work. I think this country is not going to stand by and let the pork-barrelers destroy this resource for no reason. You've gotta believe this, or you just say, 'To hell with everything.' The law is clear that the fish are to be preserved. I think the public is smart enough to see through the con at the eleventh hour. I can't believe they'll watch the buffalo hunters do to the Northwest what they did to the Plains.

"This was half of the world's chinook salmon and steelhead runs. I mean, this was on a scale—. Animals whose individual range goes from the Continental Divide to two thousand miles out into the ocean. We're talking about something that makes the great herds of Africa look piddling. In sheer numbers and economic value, there's just no parallel to this. Anywhere. I mean, this is the Big One. If you can't prevail here, then the whole system is bankrupt. And I won't believe it; I will not accept that.

"And I do smell fear. Goliath is sweating. These people are scared. Their lies are getting more and more shrill, more and more desperate. And there's nothing more heady to me than to see a bureaucrat who was out to harm the public interest starting to sweat. To smell fear on these people is intoxicating.

"They're gonna get the blame. And that scares the hell out of them. And I like that. The Nuremberg defense—'I was just following orders'—is not going to work here. My job is to kick that rotten door in, and I hope I can break it down before the fish are gone. It won't be much longer, because they're vanishing right now before our very eyes. Extinction on a scale that's unprecedented is happening. So these are interesting times."

Ed pauses. The sudden silence is awkward. I am looking at my shoes. He says calmly, "Wow, I *do* sound like a zealot this morning, don't I?"

"This morning you do, Ed, yes."

"Well," Ed says, glancing at his watch, "I need to get out of here."

Golden State

"In the Northwest, they still believe that agencies and experts will find the key to salmon recovery. Here, we're way beyond that." The expert telling me this is a consultant to an agency, so he should know. Bill Kier, a big ruddy-faced man, works in a small office outside San Francisco, near where the waters of the Sacramento and San Joaquin rivers—what's left of them by the time they get here—first meet the bay. Zeke Grader, executive director of the Pacific Coast Federation of Fishermen's Associations, is here too, looking around for a place to sit. The exfoliating piles of paper in Kier's office, spilling under the weight of gravity and the march of time, suggest some attempt at order, but for the most part the place is an exceptional mess. I've always thought a messy office is a sign of an active mind, anyway.

The disarray reflects the region's turbulent history—both distant and recent—regarding salmon. Jack London wrote of central California's bustling salmon fishery even before Joltin' Joe DiMaggio and his brothers pulled their first gill nets from these waters as young men. But colorful eras have a way of being short-lived.

The problems and promise for salmon in California are complex but can be synopsized: Along the coast, coho salmon have declined 95 percent, primarily due to irresponsible logging, as in Oregon and Washington. In the Central Valley, where coho are already gone, chinook face an uncertain future because they must compete with agriculture for water.

But what had been a showdown with agriculture that the salmon seemed sure to lose has become an unexpected opportunity for civility, compromise, and the hope and goodwill of some unusual people.

California's very existence, as Marc Reisner wrote in *Cadillac Desert,* is predicated on epic liberties taken with water. Water from formerly prime salmon habitat now irrigates bodacious farmlands growing a third of the United States' fruits and vegetables. That's only part of it. Seventy percent of California's rain falls north of Sacramento. Eighty percent of the demand for water is south. Sustaining the urban growth, suburban sprawl, and farms of the arid south means taking water from salmon country *and* from northern farms—precipitating bitter agropolitical civil war.

The middle of California—the Central Valley—is drained by the San Joaquin River running north and the Sacramento running south. The big wet kiss formed by the mouths of both rivers is called the San Joaquin–Sacramento Delta, emptying into San Francisco Bay and then, beyond the Golden Gate, the Pacific Ocean.

Control of these major rivers and their tributaries was accomplished through a dazzling system of dams, canals, pumps, and reservoirs: the Central Valley Project. "A vicious blow to nature," rattles Kier from somewhere behind his piled-high desk where he has vanished in a deep dive to retrieve another document he wants to show me—if he can find it. The Central Valley Project is a Depression-era public works extravaganza, by far the largest water project in the world at the time. It remains, as Reisner says, a project of absolutely breathtaking scope, still the most mind-boggling public works project on six continents, and "without question the most magnificent gift any group of American farmers has ever received."

The project's exemption from interest payments was alone worth billions. Then the U.S. Bureau of Reclamation allowed farmers to pay illegally low prices for the water. According to an investigation by the Natural Resources Defense Council, the bureau wasn't even charging enough to cover operating costs. Some farms pay one-tenth the delivery costs of water, amounting to subsidies on some individual farms of a half million dollars annually. And $1.5 billion of taxpayer niceness in the form of capital costs that was supposed to be paid back will not be.

So, parasitizing public funds allowed yet another welfare industry to destroy a free-swimming resource gift and a way of life for fishing communities over a vast expanse of coast and ocean.

The closure of Friant Dam on the San Joaquin River in 1944 wiped the slate for that river's salmon. *No* water—not a drip—was released from that dam into the lower river, explains Kier, reappeared from behind his desk, his ruddy face deepened in color. Up on the Sacramento, Shasta Dam's six-hundred-foot wall of concrete blocked the northern part of the river, creating a solar water heater called Shasta Lake, in which snowmelt warmed to temperatures fatal to salmon eggs. Additional dams were plopped into nearly every tributary of the Sacramento as the Central Valley Project grew to fulfill a grand vision of irrigation, flood control, and water transfer to southern California.

Six thousand miles of salmon spawning habitat was reduced to three *hundred*. As elsewhere throughout the irrigated Northwest, hundreds of diversion intakes—mostly unscreened—turned millions of young salmon into farm fertilizer. In addition, such massive quantities of water were being pumped from the river delta to arid southern California that the current sometimes flowed upstream into the pumps. In the entire geological and evolutionary history of the river and the salmon, the current had always flowed downstream. While the river was flowing toward wealth and political influence instead of the ocean, adult fish coming from the ocean to spawn became disoriented. Juveniles, who normally ride the current to the sea, became hopelessly confused and, as the fishermen all say, "lost in the delta." In wet years when the signal from the currents could still be read by fish, more of them made it to where they were going. In dry years, when the pumping's insistent pull drew them across the delta, they died like salmon.

In and around this mess still swim a few surviving fish. The Sacramento River has steelhead and four runs of chinook salmon. The winter run is now endangered. Spring chinook, which spawn in foothill streams, are now at numbers as low as the winter run was when it was listed. Once the most productive run in California, producing about a million fish annually, the spring run fell to a few hundred—a decline of 99.99 percent. The fall salmon run—still the strongest of a diminished tribe—once spawned in thirty tributaries in the drainage and now spawns in ten.

Central Valley rivers that had major salmon runs—such as the Shasta, the Feather, the Mokelumne, the Tuolumne, the Merced, the American, the Stanislaus, the San Joaquin—are blocked by dams. From the air, you can follow the Sacramento's tributary rivers with your eye up to the far distance, and in each a dab of concrete backs up a blue lake into the mountains. The huge Sierra snowpack, ten times the volume of the Colorado River running in dozens of streams, is entirely under human control; not one drop goes anywhere unless someone approves it. Comparing the tiny vein that is the Sacramento River with the huge amount of land that is irrigated, it is hard to imagine that the river and its tributaries can donate enough blood to nourish all those pears, plums, peaches, nectarines, tomatoes, melons, walnuts, and rice (half a million acres of rice). From the air, the entire width of the Central Valley, from the Coast Range to the Sierra Nevada Foothills, appears as farms. The Sacramento River itself looks bound and gagged, hemmed between levees, its meanders frozen in place for all foreseeable time. The river water is a bright, eutrophied green, and water that has been borrowed for irrigation is returned to the river as an opaque emerald plume, warmed and laden with algae and silt and some chemicals, rather worse looking for the wear.

Yet much of the control of nature here is less visible. Once, inside Folsom Dam, I was shown into a small control room—hidden like a fallout shelter—in which a guy with a gray ponytail, wearing a T-shirt, black jeans, and sneakers, was eating a fast-food take-out lunch from a paper bag while manipulating a computer panel. It took me a while to understand that he was simultaneously controlling all the water and all the dams in all the rivers throughout the entire Central Valley Project via instruments, managing unseen flood waters, and tracking unfelt earthquakes.

Before the Central Valley Project was built, about twenty to thirty million acre-feet of water had carried young salmon to the sea. Droughts in the late 1980s and early '90s meant only nine or ten million acre-feet were making it to the delta, and more than half of that was being pumped away to sunny southern California. The salmon spawns of those dry late-1980s years were disastrous, but from 1987 to 1989 exports of freshwater from the delta to the south *increased* as reservoirs and river levels kept dropping—as though half the state had stuck a straw into northern California on a hot day and was in full suck.

While the farms were glistening, the salmon lost nearly 90 percent of their water. When fishers protested, fishing was restricted. Signs of collapse were otherwise ignored.

By 1991 the reservoirs were so depleted that they had two months' worth of water left in them. Now, everyone who needed that water began to hit the wall they had been speeding toward.

Farmers—who had gotten full deliveries for the first years of the drought as though nothing was amiss—suddenly got an education about rain. Lucky ones got a quarter of the water to which they had grown accustomed. Others were cut cold turkey. Hundreds of thousands of acres were idled, as were tens of thousands of farmworkers. In some counties, unemployment tilted toward 30 percent.

By this time, fishers and biologists outnumbered the last gasping troops of spawning fish trudging in from the Pacific. The 1.5 million fish that had hit the decks of seagoing boats in 1988 became a skeletonized catch of 150,000 in 1992; down 90 percent. But these were vast numbers compared to the tatters that were making it upstream. Only a couple thousand springers reached the spawning grounds. The fall runs were nearly shot, too. The winter "run," limping along with four hundred spawners in 1990, halved the next year, as 191 surviving winter chinook salmon leaped onto a page bearing the heading "Threatened," later promoted to "Endangered." (In 1985, the National Marine Fisheries Service had denied a petition to list the winter run under the Endangered Species Act, saying various agencies would fix the problems.)

From 1980 to 1995, the number of people that salmon employed in California was, like the water, "headed south," dropping from fifty thousand to ten thousand, from nearly six thousand boats to just over two thousand.

The situation was far out of balance and the state's water was out of whack. Bill Kier and Zeke Grader had been trying for decades to put some balance into the Central Valley Project, but they had been swimming upstream against the flow—until the drought and the endangered species listing changed the pivot point of the debate. It was becoming clear to everyone that water was badly managed in California, and farmers throughout the country were getting tired of competing with California produce grown with such heavily subsidized water. Fishermen plying the ocean and rivers were screaming. Conservation groups were suing. Even the scientific community was going public on the salmon problem.

Congress finally passed the California Valley Project Improvement Act on an October day in 1992. It was a dizzying victory for its proponents. The act gave about half of the water on the Sacramento—eight hundred thousand acre-feet—to fish, with the goal of doubling the number of salmon. Where, when, and how to apportion such a fundamental change is taking years to fully sort out and implement, but it signals the end of a long era in which the desires of agriculture and big water interests held all sway. The winter chinook salmon's "listing" forced other changes in the use of water, giving fish interests their last hope that remaining salmon would be conserved and restored.

But these changes only provide a window of opportunity. They ensure nothing except that the people involved in the old water interests will challenge both the Improvement Act and the Endangered Species Act. At this momentous crossroads, a few people have undertaken to seize the opportunity by doing some things differently, because on the Sacramento there are enough salmon left to fight over. And that was what I had come here to learn about.

Zeke Grader, resigned to standing up amid the clutter, is explaining that the Federation of Fishermen's strategy entails using the Endangered Species Act as leverage to bring salmon back, by working with farmers and timber interests to increase salmon numbers enough to avert more endangered species listings. "We call it our Three-F Initiative: Fish, Farms, and Forestry. We're building a coalition of opposites. Farmers want to keep farming, loggers want to keep logging, and we want to keep fishing, and to do those things we all need to prevent more fish from going onto endangered lists. The big dilemma for us is that most of what they believe in is absolutely in opposition to the things we need, because they generally see private-property rights as sovereign to other considerations, and salmon and water quality can suffer from things done on private lands, like overcutting or pesticide use. So the trick is designing a program that can restore the fish while being sensitive to the other users, because if more salmon go onto the lists and that results in more restrictions, private-property advocates will try to eviscerate the Endangered Species Act. And without the Endangered Species Act we'll probably lose the salmon. It's a fine line to walk, and we are doing a lot of hand-holding with the farmers and timber people. With the threat of an ESA listing you can get more accomplished voluntarily. When you actually list the animal, you've already pulled the trigger, and people will resist you. But we are clear that we want to avert a listing by recovering the fish, not inventing a scam to get out from under the ESA."

Kier says that by aiming to avert more listings, the Three-F plan short-circuits the tendency for denial. "And it takes away the stink of confrontation."

"But, honestly," Grader adds, "I don't think the other industries would have talked with us if it hadn't been for the spotted owl experience and the water restrictions following the winter chinook listing."

Salmon are the first species with substantial monetary value that the Endangered Species Act has been applied to. Says Kier, "For twenty years, we have been using it to conserve snail darters, louseworts, and other obscure life forms, and have brought a megadose of abuse on the act. But with the salmon we have an industry, an economic resource, and all the things that most people see as real."

Zeke opines that this should have been done much earlier. "It's really too late to prevent major damage."

Apparently, it is still possible to breathe a whiff of that confrontational stink Kier had mentioned, because he himself remarks, "Farmers say that if they can't pump the rivers until their bones stick out, we'll deprive the world of food. I say that rivers produce food. A nice, balanced meal of rice and salmon would result from a nice, balanced distribution of water. The system is badly out of balance from the standpoint of social justice because it unfairly favors irrigators over fishermen and does not recognize the role that rivers and estuaries must play in the survival of human life here and around the world."

"But if we can stay alive and fighting for a while longer, the runs might increase," says Grader, who is leaning against a file cabinet. He feels they have made progress. They got cold-water releases out of Shasta Dam (at a cost of $80 million to retrofit the dam). "That will help." They got the gates lifted at Red Bluff for a longer period to let salmon pass. "That should help." And if they can get some restrictions on spring irrigation pumping to allow for juvenile migration, "that would help" too.

Kier agrees, and he thinks the endangered species listing that required modifications at the delta pumps is starting to show some early dividends in the form of increased numbers of fish. "Even though the action was designed for winter salmon, it is helping some other runs by interrupting the pumping."

"But there are a lot of real problems," worries Zeke, with his brow wrinkled like a stream riffle. "I don't know *how* we're going to deal with the coho situation," he sighs. "We're going to have to talk with some timber people and some ranchers, but coho are going to be listed."

I am sorry to hear Zeke say that about the coho salmon. But Zeke is being realistic; the coho will be added to the federal list of threatened species. There are real problems, both along the coast and in the Sacramento Valley. The salmon need more water in the rivers for breeding, and they need it colder and cleaner. They need a riverbed that is receiving spawning gravels now held behind dams. They need wetlands along the river that can produce enough insects to feed young salmon. As one state biologist had told me, "Much of what we see as the Sacramento River are the physical remnants of a dying system. That system had been maintained by dynamic processes which are no longer functioning, because the river has been stabilized for flood control and agriculture, and it cannot at the same time preserve salmon." But he had good news too, and hopefulness. He said that the new system can be manipulated to bring back some of the support systems that fish need. And then he said something surprising. "I'm optimistic, and this is the source: seeing people realizing shared responsibility with the public for their land and resources." And Professor Peter Moyle of the University of California at Davis had told me something similar: "A whole bunch of interconnected things have begun happening at once because a few people decided it was better to find solutions themselves than to pound each other with the Endangered Species Act. This is a real switch, and it is very positive. The only caution is that all the cooperation upstream will not succeed by itself unless the problem of fish being killed in the delta pumps is also solved."

Opportunity cannot be exploited without hope, and hope can be squandered if applied without caution. Grader's and Kier's introduction has left me armed with both hope and caution as I venture to explore the efforts now gathering momentum in the Central Valley.

It is time to get a glimpse inside the belly of the beast, those delta pumps, Great Satan to salmon interests in the valley. Mike Parks, a hydroelectric engineer, is my personal guide. He explains that the positives of the pumping and water transfer include irrigation and municipal water for the people of southern California and flood control.

"What are the negatives?"

"I'm not sure there are any."

Having gotten an earful about the facility's effects on salmon, I presume this place must buzz continually with talk about the changes the Central Valley Project Improvement Act is causing as the system is compelled to adjust and conform to its mandates. I ask Mike his opinion of the act.

"I don't really have any idea what it is."

"That's the law that gives eight hundred thousand acre-feet to salmon, with the object of doubling the runs."

He says, "Giving water to fish is semilogical. The native fish are almost extinct already. And I don't think the salmon's problems have anything to do with water management anymore. My personal opinion—which doesn't stand for much—is that we're overpopulated. They've appropriated six times as much water as they have. Nobody gets their full amount. People don't understand that our water is limited. I'm amused at how our urban development is allowed to happen."

Getting back to the engineering and operations topics with which he is most comfortable, he explains, "We only pump when the tide is incoming. Otherwise, we could reverse the river's flow."

"A lot of people have told me these pumps actually do reverse the river's flow out of the delta," I say, "and suck small fish back upriver when they are trying to migrate out, but you don't really reverse the river's flow?"

"Not intentionally. We're very careful. This facility is managed with a lot of thought to how it affects the wildlife in the delta. We've got more Fish and Game biologists watching us than anybody."

We pause at a sign on the wall that brags about the use of power. On a per-hour basis, each of the eleven pumps uses an amount of energy equivalent to forty thousand homes. Another sign reads, "Brackish water is drawn upstream into the San Joaquin River and other channels by the pumping plants, actually reversing the river's flow."

I turn to Parks. "I thought you said that's not allowed to happen."

"It is not *permitted.* We try to prevent it. It does happen. When it does, we have an unscheduled shutdown for a few hours. It's embarrassing when we have to do that."

"How many times this year has that happened?"

"I don't know," he says. "I'm not trying to avoid your question; I just don't know."

We get into Mike's vehicle and drive out toward the pumps. Fish are now screened out before they reach the pumps, but the pumps themselves are of interest.

The pumping plant, built in the 1960s, does not look like much. It is essentially a big, rectangular corrugated-aluminum barn, 510 feet long by 100 feet wide and 50 feet high. Fronting it is a canal three miles long and about 160 feet wide, crossed by gas and petroleum pipes, coming from an artificial, lakelike forebay, which draws water from the delta itself. The incision in the landscape that creates the canal reveals ocean-originated sedimentary rock thrust at a forty-five-degree angle. Ground squirrels are burrowing into the diked canal banks as we drive past. The opaque green water in the canal hosts ducks of several species. Behind the plant is the ridge over which the water goes, headed for sun-drenched southern California.

Every day, the plant pushes nearly seven billion gallons over that ridge, enough to cover twenty-one thousand acres—thirty-three square miles—under a foot of water, enough to keep twenty-one thousand families in water for a year.

The plant's sole and lonely operator, a rotund, mustachioed man in his thirties wearing a baseball cap, is on the phone to the outside world at a bewilderingly large bank of controls, dials, gauges, and switches. Mike tells me that management is in the process of fully automating this plant. It will then require no attendant at all.

I ask why, and Mike replies, "Payroll." After a longer than usual pause, he says, "But the trouble with automating is that you have to foresee all your problems. The benefit of an operator is that it puts a human mind in the facility that can receive inputs directly."

It seems that to Mike, a human mind is another piece of equipment in his engineering flow chart. But that is more value than his monolithic employing entity is willing to concede.

I pause at a spot-lit oil painting. It is Harvey L. Banks himself, first director of the state water project and the man this facility is named for. When the plant is fully automated and one salary is "saved" by eliminating it, the portrait can look out over the activities of the almost-living machinery day and night without the air being tainted by a human exhalation.

Mike continues to show me around. "This is just a big aluminum barn with eleven electric-driven pumps in it. Really quite simple. The water is just pumped through this penstock, out these gates, and up into the San Luis Reservoir."

Pump heads in diameters measurable in tens of yards dominate the plant's interior. Each pump motor is housed in a hexagonal structure about fifteen feet high and thirty feet in diameter, with a pump below packing the power of forty thousand horses.

Each unit has a bedazzling jumble of graphic monitors, dials, checklists, and flow diagrams with electrically lit green and red dots signifying "normal" or "problem" at each key point. Each machine is monitored by hundreds of relays. Failure at some of the relays would signal an alarm; at others it would trigger automatic shutoff. A sign on each pump motor door says:

CAUTION

HIGH PRESSURE CO_2 SYSTEM

ISOLATE BEFORE ENTERING

The currently installed motors are made by General Electric. Awaiting installation are several new motors in crates from Japan. "We haven't had an American bid on an engine for eight years," Parks comments. "The government apparently doesn't want anything to be made in America anymore. Even the Westinghouse and G.E. stuff we are buying is made somewhere else."

One motor has been opened for servicing. Parks shows me the intake valves far below. Only then do I realize the vertical depth of the facility; it is 120 feet from the rim of the motor to the impeller and inlet. The entire plant is five stories—the vast majority of it underground, and some of it underwater.

Mike describes the pumping process. The inlet is well below sea level. Here water receives energy, which is converted to velocity. The velocity is then converted to pressure, and the water comes through the impeller and is shoved up the penstocks with so much force it is thrust almost two hundred feet higher and discharged over the ridge outside and into the reservoir above.

Parks guides our descent down metal stairs through the so-called exciting generators and the motors, then an intermediate level with the shafts and bearings, then the pump heads, then the impeller level and cooling water gallery, then the discharge valve and door to the pump suction, above the inlets.

Here, among working machinery several levels below ground, Mike Parks is in his element, and for the first time he is walking and talking much faster than I, his apparent stiffness gone, passing easily among the plumbing and the catwalks where I now feel out of place and physically awkward.

"As far as devices go," he says, "this is pretty simple—a vertical pump with a vertical motor. Everything attached to it is to safeguard the lives of the machines and the public." Never have I met anyone who makes so little distinction between humans and hardware.

Two pumps are pushing enough to cover eighty acres with a foot of water—eighty acre-feet—per hour right now, and I ask under what conditions would all eleven pumps be operating.

"When the river is trying to flood, we do our best to suck as much out of it as possible."

The penstocks are capable of accommodating a lot of water. Parks tells me that if control of the discharge valve were lost and the water backed up, the entire aqueduct and reservoir would begin to siphon backward, a catastrophe so great that the valve controls have five layers of backup systems. "If the water reversed, it would turn the pump into a generator. It can go faster in reverse than in forward, and if this happens, things come apart."

"How frequently have you had it fail?"

"Never. Of course, we do a lot of maintenance in here. And there's a visual inspection every three hours."

"None of the backup systems have ever had to kick in?"

"Backup systems have come in, yes."

"First level only?"

"We've been into the second backup system."

"But there was never a total system failure?"

"No."

It is plain enough that this is a massive tribute to the human ability to manipulate nature on a large scale. What is less clear so far is how this plant interacts directly with salmon, and that is what we are about to see.

"This is where we do our best to strain all of the fish out of the aqueduct before we pump it," says Mike on our way to the Skinner Fish Facility. Here fish are screened and shunted away from the aqueduct before the water goes through to the main pumps. Mike explains that the fish come in under this parking lot, into a secondary set of screens. Most of the water is sucked out, but some of it stays with the fish, and they go into the building. Inside the building, the water containing the fish is diverted into seven cylindrical concrete tanks, each about thirty feet deep and twenty feet across, each with a cylindrical screen in the middle and a well in the center of that screen. The cylinders fill quickly via a large valve. Once the tanks are filled, the water is drained off and the fish, retained by the cylindrical screen, end up in the well's removable bucket. The bucket is extracted mechanically and travels via an overhead tram to a waiting tank truck, where it is emptied. The fish are then trucked to sites in the delta, fifteen to forty miles from here, and turned loose. Depending on who you are talking to, either all of them or none of them or some of them will survive.

The numbers of fish going into the concrete tanks are sampled for a minimum of ten minutes every two hours, twenty-four hours a day. An organic-looking, young bearded man named Randy, from the California Department of Fish and

Game, is removing samples for identification. A ten-minute sample will yield anywhere from zero to a thousand fish, depending on the time of day, time of year, amount of pumping, and wind direction—all of which affect the fish's orientation and distribution. Randy reiterates that the main objective here is to take all the fish out before the water goes through the pumps. I ask how well that works.

"Don't ask me," he replies with a laugh and a shrug. "I just handle the fish. *He'd* be the guy to ask." He is motioning to a young, scraggly-bearded man wearing a T-shirt and back supporter. His name is Dan, and he is employed by the state Department of Water Resources, in charge of this facility.

"We *do* try to save the fish," Dan answers. "I think we do good. I'm into saving fish and saving the environment. Of course, some of the fish are a little too sensitive. They got those—what do you call it? the endangered ones?—delta smelts, for instance. They die if you touch them. I feel we put a lot of effort into this and a lot of people just don't appreciate it." He flicks his cigarette butt into one of the concrete tanks. "See, when the fish come into the aqueduct and go through these screens and stuff like that, I determine the flows here. If we get a lot of fish, we slow the pumping down. If anything happens to this facility, Banks pumping plant has to stop."

I say, "Fishermen and farmers call this place the Black Hole of Death. They say no matter what they do up there, it won't matter as long as this place is killing so many fish."

"This facility right here is *protecting* the fish. We're not killing the fish. Banks pumping plant over *there*, where you just *came* from, is the place that supposedly kills the fish."

"Isn't this all part of the same operation, and isn't the point of this building to screen out all the fish so none of them get to the Banks pumps?"

"Right, right. But. . . . O.K., it's still the same operation, but what we do here is—O.K.—we divert the fish from going to Banks. We might do a little damage to the fish population, but we support the hatcheries and we put in many more than we kill. We bring them back to the delta. They drive them about thirty-five minutes away and dump them in a pool, like they was out there all along, and they monitor the fish to see how they survive."

"What do you find?" I ask.

"Well, you find out the mortality."

"I know that, but what is the mortality?"

"Well, that's what you want to find out."

"What's the answer?" I'm tempted to ask him, Who's on first?

"Well," he replies, "the answer is, uh. . . . We're doin' good! We release fish every day. But you don't know, see, once you release the fish, if all of the predators are hiding there waiting for them."

"Overall," I ask, "what is your opinion about people saying that until something is done about the fish killed in operations here, we cannot restore the salmon?"

274 SONG FOR THE BLUE OCEAN

"As far as we know, between what we save here, and what we put out from hatcheries, we do a lot. When a lot of young salmon come down, we haul them out twice a day. Every day. Sometimes, three times a day. Even if we get only one salmon, we haul it out in the truck. He's outta here. That other one—what do you call that?—delta smelt?—that's another thing. When the delta smelt start to show up here, they haul them out and release them three times a day. They mark them and offer a reward."

"What do you find out from that?"

"Oh, I have no idea. They've been doing that experiment since the 1960s or so. My understanding is, they do different kinds of studies. With salmon, they get four hundred thousand from the hatchery and mark them and put them in the forebay and see how many will come here. Almost less than fifty percent will come here. So, what's causing the loss of the salmon? Preditation. Striped bass are eating them. Just like candy. So when people say that we are the problem, well, there could be a lot of problems: habitat, preditation—. Fishermen are another predator. Then you got poachers. But since we're such a big outfit, everybody points to us. But we do try. Like I said, this is a fish protection center. We *protect* fish."

"If you go through all this effort and the fish—as you say—get eaten by predators, are you really accomplishing anything? Is it worth it?"

"Well, you know, there is no question that this is worthwhile. The question is whether it's worth the money we're spending on it. But it's doing its purpose. The critters would have been eaten by predators anyway. Right? Right. We're giving them a second chance. And when the baby salmon come, we rotate release sites so the striped bass won't get as many. Striped bass were put here from the East Coast; they're not really supposed to be here. We used to have a striped bass hatchery right out in the parking lot. We stopped because striped bass eat salmon. Plus, there's other people that can raise striped bass better and cheaper than we can. Some people want the salmon, some want the stripers. So, we gotta save them both."

I ask Dan how he got this job. He says he first started off as a janitor. Then he took the apprenticeship program. He's worked for the department seven years and been the head of this thing two and a half years. He's twenty-eight now.

"You seem pretty into this whole idea of trying to save the fish," I observe.

"Oh yeah," he replies earnestly. "Yeah, definitely."

As we're saying our good-byes, Mike says, "We're kind of proud of the old place. Of course, I think everyone is proud of what they do."

There are at least two ways—perhaps from two polarities—the Central Valley may be viewed. Driving through the intensive agriculture and the great mountain-hiding haze of dust and smoke kicked up by tractors and burning fields, near the immobilized riverbanks, one can get the impression of a land oppressed, enslaved, forced to work, never allowed to recoup or rest, squeezed for absolutely everything it can give up. Or conversely, one can see it as people working hard together in unlikely circumstances to bring from harsh earth a banquet of good food to help fuel a great nation. As one person put it to me, "Most of this valley was just jackrabbits and sagebrush, and now it is some of the most productive agricultural land in the world. A lot of honest work went into it, and a lot of lives were made here. It was a wonderful thing." My mind ranges between these two extremes as orchards, farm stands, and the bright yellow-green, flooded fields of irrigated rice country whiz past the car window.

A sign in the coffee shop in Maxwell, California, reads, I HAVE PMS AND A HAND-GUN—ANY QUESTIONS? Across the street, another storefront window says, EVERY DAY IS EARTH DAY ON THE FARM. Colusa County produces more rice than any county in the United States: ten thousand pounds off each acre. This is serious farming, and it requires a dependable supply of water. A *lot* of water. And this storefront houses the offices of the three-year-old Family Water Alliance. Mark Twain said, "Whiskey's for drinkin' and water's for fighting over." These people fight over water.

Bill Kier and Zeke Grader had said these folks are involved in the Three-F Initiative—Fishermen, Farms, and Forests—and I should talk to them. But the reception when I called this office was downright hostile: "Why should I talk to a cold-caller? Outsiders should best mind their own business." Nonetheless, an appointment was granted, and here I am, hoping for the best. I've been led to understand that the person who will speak with me is a Sue Sutton. I take a seat near the front door for a minute, and a gentleman comes in and says to me, "Haven't I met you before?"

"I don't think so," I say as I rise to shake his hand. "I'm not from around here."

"Oh. I guess your kind of people just all look alike." Momentary pause. "No offense meant, of course."

"None taken. Of *course.*"

Sue Sutton emerges. She is pretty, well-dressed, fortyish, with a cool and businesslike manner—a huge improvement over all previous impressions from this office. Her husband, John Sutton, dusty from the farm, comes in the front door as Sue and I are still exchanging introductions. This is the guy I spoke to on the phone. He has decided to come and talk.

Sue looks like she could be a Washington, D.C., lobbyist, and she talks it, too, launching directly into her main argument with a spitfire delivery. "Regulations made in Washington are affecting people. When the Sacramento River's winter-run salmon got listed under the Endangered Species Act, a judge said we could not have water from August through November."

John, sitting upright with his sunburned arms on the table, says, "You invest in seed, fertilizer, machinery, all the work you put in, and if you have no water to finish out your crop, you go bankrupt. We were in culture shock. I was emascu-lated. I had no way of taking care of my family. If I can't have water, I'm worth zero. We're dead."

After the judge's decision, angry farmers went after the fish, the fishermen, and the Endangered Species Act. "We had seventeen people at the first meeting; next meeting, thirty-five; next meeting, about a hundred, and by the end of Feb-ruary we had four thousand people on the capitol steps," says Sue.

"First we felt it was the fish's fault," John says. "Then we began reading about overfishing. So we had a salmon troller come here, and we talked for six hours. It's interesting: Steelhead are not caught in the ocean, but they've declined like the chinook salmon. So that *tells* you that it's not overfishing. Then we met Shel Meyer, a Sacramento River fishing guide. We've met with him eighty-eight times in the last year and a half, and I now understand that there are communi-ties dependent on fishing just as there are on farming. Some of us even have rela-tives in the fishing communities."

"Now, look at this," says Sue. She shows me graphs demonstrating that the declines correlate strongly with water exports to southern California. The more water pumped in the spring, the fewer fish from that year appear later as adults. "It's not just the farmers or fishermen. It is water transfers, ocean temperatures, toxic pollutants, timbering, all these things."

"All these things. But we realize," John says, "that if we hurt the fish more, there'll be no water for farming, and that's the end of everything."

"So we came up with the idea that, 'If there's fish in the river, there'll be water on the land.' It's our goal to do whatever we can do to stimulate those fish."

John adds, "Resource-based industries are going to have to find ways to accommodate each other, whether it's fish or farmers or hunters. Colusa County gets twenty-six million dollars a year from waterfowl hunting—everything from shotgun shells to motel rooms."

"Twenty-six million, from hunting," reinforces Sue.

"Millions of ducks from as far as Siberia migrate into the rice fields in the winter. I've developed five duck clubs and sold them. I took those lands out of rice production and put them into permanent, year-round flooded condition. I sold some very low value land for an awful lot of money."

I am thinking, "In other words, making permanent wetlands for duck hunt-ing can be worth more—at least for a certain percentage of one's acreage—than agriculture? And these landowners are profiting by killing wintering wild ducks, from populations breeding as far away as Siberia?"

Sue darts him a baleful glance that seems to hiss, "Don't spill the beans; this guy's a stranger." Aloud she says, "Let's get back on the track about people and fish: It's really very exciting, because when other farmers are saying, 'Just say no,' We're saying, 'O.K., we have to *live* with the endangered species law; let's work with it and with all the people who have a vested interest in recovery of the fish."

The front door opens, and Shel Meyer joins us. He is a retired fishing guide in his midsixties, and his voice is just taking on the creak of age.

Sue tells him we were just talking about how everyone is working together, and Shel says, "Only problem is, we can save all the fish in the world up here. Doesn't do us any good if they just get slaughtered in the delta pumps."

John adds, "I'll tell you another thing we can't control here: the human population. Even with all these farms, we don't produce enough food for all the people in this state. And they all expect water."

Shel was born and raised in Redding, "before they even dreamt of building Shasta Dam," he says. "I saw and knew those days of a million fish, so thick you could walk across their backs. Before they built the dams—" He pauses, as if watching a black-and-white movie running in his mind. "In the summer, this river ran so low, you could wade it in many places. In the winter, it *roared.* Now they've reversed that, because they hold the water back. So it's a hundred and eighty degrees from what nature intended. Plus, they've shut off miles and miles of spawning habitat with dams. They used to go way up to the cold water. When they built Shasta Dam there was so many fish in the river, nobody even give 'em a thought. Shasta blocked everything above it. If you tried to build Shasta Dam today you'd never get it approved, because of the changes in thinking. *All* the dams: Today, they'd never be allowed, because those are the things that are destroying a whole way of life. Those dams are bad. I wish those dams had never been put in, or had been put in with thought given to the fish. But if the problem is man-made, we ought to be able to find a man-made solution. If we can put a man on the moon—"

"So now," I ask, "in terms of backs-to-walk-across, what does thirty thousand remaining fish look like compared to a million?"

"Like nothing. You hardly never see them. Can't find 'em. Gravel riffles that I used to see two or three hundred pairs spawning on just five or six years ago, now I see one or two pairs on." Shel tells me in very simple terms that their goal—which is now required by the Central Valley Project Improvement Act—is to have a total of three to four hundred thousand fish of all four runs.

"That sounds extremely optimistic," I say skeptically.

"Well, we're very optimistic people," he says brightly. "And we've gotten a lot accomplished in the last three years. For twenty years, we slid backwards. Now I see a turnaround. Spring-run numbers climbed from two hundred to twelve hundred adults over one year. Right now we have double the number of returning fall-run fish that we had last year. Numbers are still low—thirty-three thousand, down from a million—but it's at least a step toward the right direction."

Heads nod appreciatively as this good news sinks in.

"But those delta pumps are the biggest fish killers in California," Shel reinforces. "Every fish that gets sucked out of the Sacramento River and into the delta is as good as dead; they never get out of there."

Sue goes on the offensive, speaking rapidly and agitatedly. "*We*'re not allowed to kill a fish, but the delta pumps can kill plenty; that's selective prosecution. That's only *one* thing wrong with the Endangered Species Act. It also violates the Constitution. The Constitution clearly states that the federal government must compensate people when it takes their property." Hammering the table with her index finger, she says, "It is used as a threat. Environmental groups said, 'If you don't let us get protection for these rivers, we're going to list the spring run.' That's a fear tactic. I don't go for that. And I tell you, there's a *major* backlash headed their way.

"And," Sue rails, working up a full head of steam, "the *absurdity* of a law that puts some of these weird animals over people. Kangaroo rats. *Fairy shrimp!*"

(The Riverside fairy shrimp really is endangered, but it would be hard to find a less compelling endangered species. Discovered in 1990, it is very similar to the brine shrimp sold in pet stores for tropical fish food. They live in southern California, and though the vernal pools they need are being dried up quickly—95 percent of that habitat is gone—not much is known about the historic status or distribution of these little beasts.)

Shel says, "Just putting an animal on a list isn't going to do anything. If you're going to list something as endangered, you have to take the steps necessary to recover it, or else why list it? I want to see the availability of funds to recover it. Even something as important as our winter-run salmon doesn't have a recovery plan yet; we've been waiting for years. They just say, 'It's coming, it's coming.' "

"When you list a fish," Sue says, leaning forward, "it's *people* who are affected. I'm committed to the people in these communities. Those people have families. So it's important to bring those resources back so we can continue a *way of life* that's based on those resources."

"Well," I say, "the goal of the act is to bring resources back."

"Just to bring them back," Sue says pointedly, tapping a middle fingernail on the table. "Not to bring them back because there's people connected to them. The Endangered Species Act does *not* care about people. It has no compassion."

I ask whether letting the fish go down, and letting the fishing communities go down with them, has been compassionate, and whether they all would be involved in these efforts now if it were not for the Endangered Species Act.

Sue answers, "I admit, I would not have probably been involved, because everyone is concerned about their own working world. Only after this outside force came in and hit us so hard in the head—"

"So is there some silver lining, because it got you so motivated?"

"It is a *bogus* law," Sue fires back. "Congress originally had good intentions, but now the bureaucrats and the agencies and the environmentalists have gotten hold of this law and use it to shut things down. If they wanted to recover things, the environmentalists would put money in—to put in new fish ladders; to put water-temperature-control devices in Shasta Dam; to do things on the ground.

Not just shutting things down and saying, 'See, we're saving the fish,' because shutting things down does *not* recover the species.

"This fish is worthwhile saving," she continues. "It provides value to man. It is one of California's oldest industries. But are we gonna spend this kind of energy saving fairy shrimp? God put millions of animals here, and if He intended everything to live forever, we'd still have dinosaurs. So it's just part of evolution that—"

"Sue," Shel interrupts, "the things that's destroying the fisheries are not God-made things. It's all man-made things that's what's destroying it. I believe there *is* a silver lining—it motivates us to do something. When they took six months of my fishing season away, I sat up and took notice."

"Yeah," John allows, "I do think that at some point a wake-up call is needed."

Shel adds, "If there was no Endangered Species Act, the fishing industry would probably have went extinct before the salmon. And now we've got the attention of all kinds of everyday people. It has drawn people together in a way that has never happened before, and nothing but good can come from that. We went to Washington, D.C., and spent ten days in negotiations over allocations of water from this valley. We kept inviting the corporate growers from the San Joaquin Valley to talk with us. They said, 'We don't need to talk to you. We've got the money. We've got the power. We don't have to talk to you.' Well, when it was over, they wished they had talked to us. Because this time it took more than their money to buy those votes. When we walked into those congressmen's and senators' offices, and we had environmentalists, farmers, cattle people, and fishermen, arm in arm all asking for the same thing, it blew their minds. They'd never seen such a group before. They couldn't turn us down."

"Sue," I ask, "do you think the Endangered Species Act helped bring all these people together, as Shel is saying?"

"I think the biologists can't even show that there's four distinct runs, and—"

"Sue, there is," Shel says definitively. He turns to me, saying, "Well, like, John and Sue, they were busy farming. One day they found themselves with their water being taken away, and, next thing, they're in federal court. All at once, they woke up to the fact that there was something wrong, and they better get to the bottom of it."

John, making a point, says, "Carl, if the agencies had done their jobs in the first place, we wouldn't even *need* an Endangered Species Act. Where were the agencies?"

"Where was anyone?" I ask. "Where were you?"

John shoots back, "We were too busy trying to make a living and—"

"We were raising our kids," says Sue. "Going to PTA meetings—"

"Coaching Little League—"

"Teaching swim lessons so kids don't drown in the irrigation canals—"

"Boy Scout meetings—"

"Keeping our libraries open—"

"That's what *we* were doing," declares John, quite convincingly. Counting on his fingers, he says, "You've got National Marine Fisheries Service? You've got Fish and Wildlife? That's *their* job. I did *my* job. Now I'm doing *their* jobs." He is jabbing the air next to him with his finger. "I'm doing *their* jobs." He settles back in his chair as though from the exertion of getting worked up, takes off his cap, wipes his brow with the back of his wrist, and sets his cap firmly back in place.

"The problem is," Shel says, "they like to study the problem. I like to *attack* the problem."

John says, "There is some tremendous new technology out there. But it's gotta help you in the pocketbook, or why do things different?" He says to Shel, "Take him to see the screen that's saving thirty million young salmon a year." Then, to me, "The screen at our irrigation district diversion is so simple, it's stupid."

Shel glances at his Mickey Mouse watch and says that if we're gonna go north, we'd best be heading out.

John adds a parting thought: "We're gonna get this job done. Whatever it takes. People will scream and tears will flow, but we're gonna get the job done."

I'm following Shel north up I-5. He had warned me that his speedometer doesn't work, and I am trying to keep him in sight. Our speeding vehicles evade detection and Shel Meyer and I come to pause at the intake of the Glenn-Colusa Canal. One of the largest diversions on the Sacramento River, Glenn-Colusa pumps up to three thousand cubic feet per second—taking as much as half the river at times, I am told, irrigating 170,000 acres.

Shel tells me that this one diversion was killing thirty million young salmon a year. The screen system that now prevents young salmon from being diverted out of the river and onto farm fields is the fix that John Sutton had described as "so simple, it's stupid." But Shel says, "National Marine Fisheries, Fish and Wildlife, California Fish and Game, and the Army Corps fought us tooth and toenail to prevent this screen from going in. They want to build a fifty-million-dollar, state-of-the-art screen—though they can't say *when;* it may be ten years down the road. And Lord knows what it'll cost by then. They didn't want us to build our million-and-a-half-dollar interim screen, which has not let one fish through! They didn't want to work with us. But ten years at thirty million fish a year, that's a lot of fish we're saving."

The river is diverted from an oxbow off the main channel, and here the riverbank offers the beauty shared by all flowing water. The screens themselves are stationary, formed of stainless-steel wedge-wire in three-sixteenth-inch meshes. An automated sweeper continually travels back and forth, cleansing them of debris. Above the hum of the screen motors, I can hear a few songbirds. From a perch on the hardware, a hungry black phoebe is launching sorties against flying insects.

Gino Romano, who helps operate the dam for the Glenn-Colusa Irrigation District, opines that this project is a big success. "We were going to have nothing but problems if we waited until the federal agencies were ready to build something. And meanwhile, they could have shut us down because of fish mortality."

The screen was paid for by federal money appropriated through the efforts of the local congressional representative (motivated by Shel and others), proving definitively that pork can complement salmon even better than a good white wine.

We continue north, following the river, until we reach the Red Bluff diversion dam, erected in the 1960s to provide irrigation water to a couple of hundred thousand acres of farms and several wildlife refuges.

We park and walk to the 550-foot-wide dam—only thirteen feet high—where the water is diverted into a large irrigation canal. The fall run—the largest remaining run—has been arrested by its confrontation with this structure, and bronze-colored salmon, some large, are jumping just below the dam. Salmon always orient into the strongest current, because in nature that is the surest way upstream. Here, the strongest current is created by water being spilled through gates in the center of the dam. The fish ladders are at the ends of the dam, away from the current, so after swimming thousands of miles in the ocean and finding their way hundreds of miles upriver, these poor salmon may take days or weeks to find ladders at the ends of this dam.

A male salmon, its flanks flush, leaps and falls away. I see a fish struggling in a white, swirling froth at the partially opened gate where the water rushing through has too much "head"—too much hydraulic pressure—for the salmon to pass into. An eddy curls in behind the adjacent, closed gates. Caught in the flow reversal, the salmon are oriented into the current but facing downriver, pointed in the direction of the 250 miles they have just struggled to ascend. The dam costs them not only valuable time: They are using up energy fighting a current that is misorienting them. I hear Thoreau again, bearing up with more lamentation: "By countless shoals loitering uncertain meanwhile . . . awaiting new instructions, until the water itself tells thee if it be so or not . . . In this backward spring . . . perchance knowest not where men do *not* dwell. . . . Armed with no sword . . . armed only with innocence and a just cause . . . but still brave . . . reserved for higher destinies. . . . I for one am with thee . . . against that dam."

An engineer from the Bureau of Reclamation says mockingly, "Ha! Look at them pointed the wrong way: They think they're headin' upstream."

He seems to soil himself with his own disrespect for something so alive.

Shel says to me heavily, "This dam was *death* on the winter run. The salmon are programmed to go up into the high, cold foothill reaches, wait till summer, then spawn. Because of the dam, most of them got stuck way down here, and when they tried to spawn in the summer, the water was so hot here that their eggs cooked."

Overhearing Shel's complaint, the engineer from the Bureau of Wreck-the-Nation says, "Part of the economic justification of the dam was that they were going to not only compensate for the three miles of inundated stream, but enhance spawning over and beyond the natural amount, by building spawning channels. They did not operate as planned, though they were operated for twenty years or so. Another problem was fish passage. Those were both problems."

In plain English: The fish couldn't get through, and they couldn't spawn. Meanwhile, the ocean grew less populous, and fishers on the wide and shining sea went bankrupt. "Pardon me for asking a silly question," I say, "but this thirteen-foot-high dam is a joke compared to the giant Columbia River dams, and they have huge fish ladders that let the adult salmon get up many, many yards of vertical rise. This piddling dam is a major factor in the decline of Sacramento salmon. Why wasn't it designed better? Why isn't it being made to work better?"

"Ask the people who designed it," the engineer says. "They were concerned with diverting water, not spilling it. So they built the ladders with low flows that don't attract fish very well. It's a costly process to redesign it. You have to basically rebuild the whole dam."

Thoreau's haunting voice answers again: "Others say that the fish-ways were not properly constructed. Perchance, after a few thousands of years, if the fishes will be patient, and pass their summers elsewhere meanwhile, nature will have leveled the dam, and the factories, and the River run clear again, to be explored by new migratory shoals."

But maybe we and the salmon won't have to wait millennia because, now that the fish have come under the auspices of the Endangered Species Act and the Central Valley Project Improvement Act, the whole dam is, in fact, being rebuilt. Cranes, various heavy equipment, and lots of moved earth occupy a big construction site framed by the brown hills and the dam. A battery of rotary-drum screens a hundred yards long have been installed at a cost of $15 million. No one has calculated the cost that the fishing people out on the ocean and here in the river have absorbed over the decades of decline.

In a few days the gates will be opened up for eight months, and the fish will be allowed to pass, because they are endangered. If the spring run gets listed, that would add another month to the gate opening. That one additional month would be a killer to agricultural supplies of water.

At the fish ladder on the east bank, we watch an underwater video monitor as salmon who have found the ladder streak past the camera. Yesterday, a heart-warming 1,599 fecund adults passed here. The total this year so far—and it is early—is nearly ten thousand, almost twice the number at this time last year.

"Right now, we're still on the verge of losing the whole thing," Shel says. "But I'm hopeful, because in the last few years, we've made some progress." Like Bill Kier, Shel is convinced that changes mandated at the delta pumps are largely responsible for recent increases.

Every few minutes, a fish comes slicing and sputtering its way up the ladder. Each fish makes the truest leap of faith, coming once and for all time. No dress rehearsal, no curtain call. All bravura performance and grand finale.

A big buck salmon with a rosy belly jumps up the ladder, gorgeous even against the framing concrete and metal, a stand-out specimen, like a celebrity in a crowd. "Oh! What a fish!" Shel calls. Directing his next comment less to the universe at large and more to me, he says, "I want to see these fish around for my grandkids." In 1988, Shel had a quintuple heart bypass. It did not go well, to say the least, and a doctor signed his death certificate. But he hung on in intensive care for sixty days. "I started praying for help. I don't know; maybe this is why God saved me—to come out and help save these salmon. Look! There's another fish." Apparently, Shel has not yet seen enough chinooks in his lifetime.

Although Shel quit guiding a few years back, he still enjoys taking people fishing. "I get a lot of satisfaction in bringing people out, taking eight- and nine-year-old kids out and watching their eyes get *this big* when they hook a twenty-pound salmon, knowing it's something they'll remember all their life." Now comes the part I was bracing for, hoping he wouldn't tempt me: "It's too bad you don't have time, or I could show you the most beautiful river you've ever seen in your life. We see deer, turkeys, eagles, otters, beaver, and we catch fish."

"That would be great," I say, "but the way my schedule is set up, there's really no way I could . . ."

Even before the sun reaches the river valley, it is casting a golden glow on the distant blue ridges and the snow- and ice-pocked Mount Shasta. We have great trouble launching Shel's boat from the trailer, and when we do get it into the water, the battery is dead. Shel's brother-in-law Roger goes to look for jumper cables. People regard us as if to say, "This old man is out of it. He doesn't have his act together anymore." I have to admit, it's starting to seem that way.

The riverbed is lined with gravel, and the current is running like gazelles. Like acacia trees upon the Serengeti, live oaks prickle the surrounding browned-out grasslands. In the predawn, vultures flap heavily off their roosts and beat over the river in the dead-cool air of first light. But for the smell of sage, this could be dawn on an African river; it has that feel to it.

Finally, we get a jump start, and soon we are moving upon the waters. A hundred and fifty yards upstream from our launch site, the first houses and power lines appear, purging all comparisons to Africa. Twenty-five boats, kissing-close, crowd the preferred fishing hole. Shel tells me that a few years ago, when the fishing was better, a hundred boats would often cram into here. Hard to imagine. He maneuvers carefully into position in the current, and when he judges us to be at the right spot, he nods the signal to drop lines. Despite our bungling late start, the trouble launching, and the looks that we got, Shel gets a small salmon instantly, as if he has dropped the hook right into its mouth. People who have been here for an hour (and, for what they've caught, might as well still be sitting in their trucks) look miffed. Shel, trying to look matter-of-fact, suppressing a smile, says, "They forget how many years this old guy has been on the river."

The very next drift past the hole brings another fish, a heavy one. Acting tired and looking tired, this fish does not fight. It is wearily seeking only to flee, to get on with the critical climax to its life. So many odds beaten, only to be tripped up here near the triumphant finish line, by some dumb, halfhearted mistake. Such old warriors, so near their end, are heroes meriting decoration, celebration, not execution. An orderly prisoner in the net, it deserves pardon for its mistake. About twenty pounds, this is an old-woman fish, in her second childhood, the color of her back again the color of the riverbed, as it was years ago when she was a fingerling in this river, fleeing in fear under a flying kingfisher's shadow. She has endured and experienced all a salmon can—save the shivering act of procreation. She has lived, surviving each daily challenge, year upon year. She is venerable, and timeless, and deserving of having her sentence commuted.

A sudden blunt smack to her head renders me speechless.

Roger, excited by the fishing, asks me rhetorically in his deep, country twang, "These salmon are worth saving, ain't they though?"

"Saving?" I barely mumble. "Yes."

The club again strikes the fish's head, and life dims from her eye. The loss of her quiets me. Shel removes her eggs to use as bait.

I need to rationalize our actions here, and I think of us as replacing eagles and bears in this system; the grizzly bear, which is so famous a fisher of Alaskan salmon, is extinct in California, surviving only on the state flag. We are replacing their predatory activity, taking a few salmon as they near the spawning beds. But it doesn't work, even in my own mind. It is too forced to fit.

On our third drift, a third salmon offers itself in sacrifice to Shel. People in other boats are staring dumbly, exasperated. What I was willing to chalk to simple luck, I must now attribute to the accumulation of superior skill that comes with time and the insightful evaluation of past luck. Only the cows on the bank seem unimpressed.

We leave the crowd dumbstruck and ride upriver for a break. There, we begin drifting alongside another guide who knows Shel. The man says he used to work as a guide eight months out of the year. Now, maybe a couple. The rest of the time he patrols a ranch and gives natural history tours of the river. And he means *history:* "I take people out and try to explain what it used to be like here." After a short silence, he says, "We need another kicker. They should list the spring run."

For a long moment, you can hear a pin drop all up and down the Sacramento Valley. If that's an exaggeration, maybe it is just the impression I have, because the deafening roar of Shel's glaring silence seems to reverberate from the Sierra foothills to the Coast Range. "That would shut us down," Shel says, incredulous. "There'd be no more fishing."

The other guide says, "But if it would save the salmon—. The bottom line is the salmon. Right?"

Shel is silent. But the selfishness that is now silencing him is what keeps him fighting. Facts are, Shel refuses to give up fishing, refuses to stop struggling, refuses to give in to defeat, has been breaking his back to do something positive, and has racked up some significant wins on behalf of the fish and everyone else on this river. The other guide, for all his earnest caring, is only watching the fight from the sidelines. Only a few fishermen like Shel have actually fought to save the fish and the fishing, and this counts for more—even from a salmon's point of view—than just wanting to see another run listed.

Large runs of springers once swarmed out of the ocean and into twenty-six rivers in the valley. Now, about the only places they still breed are Mill and Deer Creeks—about the only undammed rivers left. Chris Leininger spearheads a property owners' group called the Deer Creek Alliance, formed to prevent protection of these key streams. I'm headed to meet Chris now because I can't understand how people who worked to defeat a proposal to protect critical spawning streams could be considered friends of salmon and part of the Three-F Initiative. But I figured I was in for some surprises when I phoned her out of the blue and she said, "I'll look forward to seeing you, because we've never met a person who didn't become a friend for life."

Chris's house is virtually impossible to get to from wherever you happen to be, so I first glimpse Chris in her pickup on the roadside in the town of Vina, California, where she is patiently waiting for me. After the briefest of hellos, she is leading me up into the hills. Turning onto Leininger Road, we travel about seven miles through darkening pasture country, with the day's last light silhouetting the Coast Range across the valley. As night falls, one star and half a moon come to grace the stage. When we arrive at the ranch in the dark, Chris ushers me and my overnight bag into an adjacent bungalow and offers a seat between the wood stove and a green piano.

Chris Leininger is a thin woman in her forties—friendly as can be—and though she's a cattle rancher, her grandfather was a salmon fisherman on the Columbia. "So it certainly is appropriate that I help bring salmon back," she says. As she's preparing a tray of pretzels and root beers, her friend and neighbor Sue Knox—a sturdy, compact woman—arrives out of the clear night. Chris says that Knox "was born in this canyon, raised in this canyon, and has lived in this canyon, and if *anybody* knows these resources, she does."

Sue says, "Of all the streams in California, Deer Creek is the gem. And that's what the university professor told us, too."

Then why fight efforts to protect it?

The women explain that an environmental group had campaigned to have Deer, Mill, and Antelope Creeks designated under the Wild and Scenic Rivers Act. "But parts of that legislation are just not compatible with private-property rights," says Sue. "What really bothered me was they were coming into our territory to protect the streams and the fish. We said, 'Why?' They wanted to prevent dams—we don't want dams, either—but they also said, 'Grazing is a problem.' We said, 'No, it isn't; we want to know why you think it is.' See, I don't understand why farms can be paved over, but some people throw a fit if you put a cow on the land. They've gotten away from common sense!"

Chris says, "They could've used the Wild and Scenic Act to litigate against cattle ranchers and timber companies. And, you know, making decisions in the courtroom doesn't do anybody any good but the attorneys. You can litigate in courts," she says, locking my gaze with hers, "but the eye is the gate to the heart, and you can tell by who will look you in the eye, who are the straightforward people who will make the difference." People had figured out all these plans to try to help fish by managing private lands, she says, "but no one ever figured out how to walk over and talk to the landowners."

Sue knits her brow, tilts her head thoughtfully, says, "I see where the environmentalists are coming from, the more articles I read. But the people who want to 'protect' the stream want recreation also. They want to be able to *come* here. They say this area would be good for white-water rafting. I say—for *this* area—you need to keep people out in order to preserve it. When we have people trespassing, the mess they make—as far as trash—is worse than anything our cattle do."

Chris adds, "My husband's family has lived here for five generations, and if they hadn't taken care of the land, there wouldn't be this pristine watershed that outsiders want to 'protect.' So we've been trying to figure out why some environmental people are so upset with us. *We*'ve been taking care of it. We want to protect it from *them!*"

Of all the Sacramento Valley streams, Deer Creek has the greatest potential for increasing naturally spawning populations of steelhead and spring chinook salmon. The upper reaches have thirty-eight miles of spawning and holding habitat with undercut banks, deep pools, cold springs. Consultants hired by the state of California to evaluate the creek wrote that the whole stream, from its source to the Sacramento, comprises "extraordinary resource values." The consultant recommended that consideration of the Wild and Scenic River designation be deferred for a year and a half to allow the landowners group to craft their own alternative. Chris says this is a major step toward planning a watershed strategy that would give even *greater* protection than could be achieved by bringing the river under the Wild and Scenic Rivers Act, because the landowners' plan includes the *whole* river, not just the nicest parts.

"Judge us by what we've actually done," Sue asserts. "Don't lump us with other people who might not have done the right thing."

Chris adds, "Those people creating the hype tarnish the honest environmental groups. Then *we*'re guilty of lumping people. And that's not right either. Though it *is* true that some environmentalists just haven't been brought up well." She cracks a smile and giggles, "I hear some of them don't wear underwear."

Sue gives Chris a quizzical smirk and says to me, "If you let people in every-where, there's no place for animals. You see all the pavement, the crowding, development pressure, all the people under stress, and then the same people are angry at us because we don't want people from town here."

"We even have the family-owned timber companies on board with us," Chris adds. "They started meeting in the Quincy library, to discuss our community, and they said, 'Okay, now here's an area with timber, and we have to live with these mandates about the spotted owls, so we're going to selectively log this area, and the logs we take out are going to remain here to be milled. They aren't going to go out of this area. It's going to be community based, so that the local pro-ductivity stays within this area.' And that way, you don't go beyond what your resources are."

This Quincy Library Group, it turns out, comprises about forty loggers, min-ers, merchants, environmentalists, and county officials, and it also turns out that they meet regularly to work out common-sense, nonlawsuit, voluntarily agreed upon plans and proposals for 2.5 million acres of land, including public lands. It seems they have this almost unheard-of idea that if people accommodate one another's values and concerns, a well-managed forest can protect fish, water-sheds, and endangered species. In their plan, lands set aside to protect owls, pine martens, and goshawks would be opened to logging, but the loggers have agreed to go to a two-hundred-year rotation—a huge concession. Are they serious? When the logging-without-laws bill hit town, a timber tract in the Deer Creek watershed went up for sale. No one bid on it. "A deal's a deal," said Tom Nelson of the family-owned Sierra-Pacific Industries. "We had agreed this sale was off-limits." The *Economist* magazine called the Quincy Library Group "the future of federal land-use planning."

"We've got something that works here, and we want to keep it that way," Sue continues, biting into a pretzel. "What's important to us, what makes us so suc-cessful here in the watershed, is family. Many people have forgotten that old Jew-ish idea of family. We have people who are related to each other throughout this watershed, and that makes us a community from the top of the canyon to the bottom."

It is becoming clear that I have never met women quite like these two. Their backgrounds and their generations-old, bloodline relationship with family, com-munity, and the land is a way of life and upbringing unfamiliar to me. When Chris was a small child, her mother would take her into the hills and sit her on a rock while she stalked a deer and steadied herself for the shot. Sue, at age fifty, still goes hunting alone, and that means gutting and dragging out the deer. The experiences in this valley, while not geographically broad, are deep. They have connection, a strong sense of place, roots from which they are still growing. Like boulders left by ancient glaciers, they have been here long enough to settle into the land a ways. And that means they understand who they are and what is important to them. They are not searching for meaning; they are trying to protect what is meaningful. And trying to understand the motivations of people "from away." People like me.

"I've been reading a lot about other places recently," Sue says, "and I think we're lucky here because we *are* a community. Like, if somebody's cow is out and needs to be put in, not only do we phone the neighbor, we put it in—we do it. If our neighbor has a cow giving birth and we know they're not home, we go pull the calf. We still like to work together and help each other."

"When we first started on salmon, we'd get a different story from every government agency," says Chris. "They never talked to each other. We said, 'If your neighboring agency needs help, don't you help them? Don't you work together?' They said 'No, that's their territory.' That's why they say 'things fall through the cracks'—the cracks at the borders of the territories. We didn't understand it. But now the agencies are working together better with us. I believe that if we all work together the salmon will come back. But it's gonna take a while because this is a new thing."

Chris takes a sip of her root beer and says, "It's new for all of us. Until recently, we just didn't really understand about the salmon. Now, we understand. I'm not a fisherman, but Sue's seen the salmon when they were plenty."

"Yes, that was in the fifties, not too long ago," Sue says. "There should be salmon and steelhead spawning in *all* these streams. When I was a kid, you—literally—you *could* walk across 'em. They were comin' up to spawn, them fish, there were just—I mean it—*thou*sands of them. You didn't have to *look* for a fish like today. You simply watched them all. That's just the way they were. They started declining after my daddy died, about thirty years ago."

I ask why, if they have lived and ranched cattle here all their lives and the fish started declining thirty years ago, have cattle people just suddenly begun to care about fish?

Sue responds, "Well, we woke up, you might say."

"Before it went under the Endangered Species Act," Chris says, "we'd think, 'Well, gosh, the salmon aren't like they used to be.' But neither are the deer like they used to be, and the birds aren't like they used to be. I've seen herds of two hundred deer running across a hillside. I've seen bears up there. We don't see those things too much anymore."

Sue says, "Anybody who is already making a living off their land—and I'm talking family-oriented anybody—wants to take care of it to hand it down to their children. So they are already in stewardship of the land, and the majority want to be left alone. With the salmon, it's like anything else; unless it really hits you, you don't deal with it. And now we're dealing with it."

Chris explains, "Some of the people feel that the healthier our fish runs are, the healthier our water rights will stay, because the only way anyone will ever take our water rights away is if the fish are on the verge of extinction. I think we're real lucky here because I feel confident that we can coexist with the fish.

And old-timers consider the fish part of our community—*our* fish. That's not the case in some other places. For several years the Fish and Game people have asked the irrigators to leave water in the stream in amounts and times the fish need it. It's voluntary. It's always been on a handshake and their word. And it has worked. It's hard for the environmental community to accept that, because everything has to be signed on the dotted line."

"You're fortunate," I say. "A handshake alone doesn't work in a lot of places."

"I know," she says with a thoughtful frown. "Well, here, it still does. And that's the way we like it, because we're so busy making a living, it's hard for us to get to all these meetings. I went to a meeting and an agency man come up to me and said, 'Where's your husband?' And I said, 'He's got to be back home, makin' a living.' And women, going to all these meetings; it's a stress on our family work, because we help in the ranching. And I'll tell you something about the women here: We don't have to deal with that kind of thing that women in the city deal with, because our husbands respect us. When the fellas mark calves out there in the springtime, we fix the food for around thirty men. And them men don't eat little-bitty bits! That's a lot of *food*. And sometimes I get up at three in the morning to start cooking so all the meals will be ready in time. And these big guys come and put their arm around you and say, 'Hey, that was a great lunch.' We are appreciated as partners. These men respect us for who we are. And we work! Sue irrigates. We pull calves. I ride. I rope. We're out there in the elements. We're tied to the weather. And when you're out in the weather, you get a certain rounded personality that people in climate-controlled offices downtown don't have. People from town lose perspective, and they really don't understand wildlife, and they really don't understand nature.

"Give you an example: There's a program here where the teachers take kindergarten kids out and plant a tree along the stream, and then they're supposed to visit that tree every year until they graduate high school. Well, that's a wonderful idea. But what if a beaver gets it? What if a flood takes it away? Have they prepared the kids for that? No, because the teachers don't understand nature. They're giving kids the wrong idea of how nature is. Nature is great; how could you *not* love nature? But nature changes.

"You know, lots of things are going to change. But if we can hold onto things for the next ten years I think we'll see some *good* changes. And if we do, it's going to be because we've stopped fighting and started talking.

"And I think it will be the women that will bring the men to the table, because women can think with both sides of their brains and talk at the same time. I think women are more emotional, and maybe we will see a hole in the heart that needs to be filled. A man may not want to come to the table just for a fish. He might be willing to come to the table because of something deeper down inside that matters more than fish, but maybe fish will be kind of the excuse. You know what's the motivation for me? My kids."

"I have three grandkids," Sue interjects.

"They've grown up loving the land. Your Jewish families know this better than any—"

"I'm not Jewish," I tell her.

"You're not?" She seems almost disappointed.

"I'm Italian. But Italians know something about families, too, so go ahead."

"O.K., well, the people here that live this life, we *love* the land. You can't get that out of a book. You get it by living with the wildlife. Like, recently we had a mountain lion in our cemetery; one got a cow last week. And this is a major migratory area for blacktail deer migrating to the high country in the summer and down in winter. I got to thinking about how we don't see as much wildlife as we used to, and I said to my husband, 'Let's not allow hunting on our land anymore.' We made a lot of people mad. But so what—you know? Our neighbors have hunts, and—I wouldn't want them to know this, but—it's O.K. with me if the deer come over here and be safe. So when outsiders came in to 'protect' this area, we were wondering why everybody was so darn excited!"

Sue says, a bit entreatingly, "We always thought that people understood agriculture, because our nation was based on agriculture."

Chris adds some insight to help me understand, saying, "Picture this, too: We live in an isolated area, and we live kind of an isolated life. My husband, Tod, is totally focused on his ranching and almost completely out of touch with the outside world. He's probably one of the few people in the United States who hadn't heard of Oliver North by the time he ran for Congress. My husband is really limited in his options, because cattle's all he knows. Most people can pick up, move, change jobs. We can't. If my husband lost his cattle tomorrow, he would not know any other way of making a living. We do things like we did years ago. We still drive the cattle over the mountain, and it's long days. You get up in the morning and you don't turn on the radio, you don't have time to read the newspaper, you're just workin' all day long and then you go to bed and get up and do it all over again."

"Very true," Sue says, listening carefully with her head bowed, nodding so deeply she is almost rocking. "And most of what we know and see is our own valley right here."

"Where we are," Chris explains, "we don't see some of the problems you have elsewhere. I had never seen big clear-cuts until I took a trip to Seattle last summer. Up there in Oregon and Washington—those severe clear-cuts?—that's pretty provocative. I had not known about them. Here, the timber companies never clear-cut. One company did a little clear-cut near here, and the ranchers here were up in arms. None of us want to see *clear-cuts!* And we're real thankful that we've got two timber companies in our watershed that are really environmentally sensitive, because they are oriented toward the community."

Chris takes another sip of root beer, then continues. "We didn't know about the delta. When we went to see the delta pumps, it was overwhelming. There is so much killing down there. I looked at Sue and I said, 'Sue, how did this *hap-*

pen?' And even though we are ranchers, I have never seen stream banks kicked in and collapsed by cattle, though now I've seen pictures of it. And now even Tod is getting up to speed. We were sitting in the truck talking one day and he says, 'You know, darn it, this is no good. We aren't gonna have any of them salmon left, the way we're goin'.' And I said, 'That's right, and that's why they have the Endangered Species Act.' He said, 'Well, maybe some fella oughta tell 'em to *list* that salmon out there.' Now he is helping to fence off Battle Creek to keep the cattle away from the stream. Other cattle people now are coming on board in a stewardship program that is being fostered by the cattle industry, with fencing off riparian areas, making more places for waterfowl. Our cattlemen's association is giving an award and publicizing things ranchers are doing on their land to improve wildlife habitat.

"So now our kids also know about fish. And they know that fairy shrimp need vernal pools, and—"

"Ah," I interrupt, "what do you think about fairy shrimp?"

Sue's head jerks up. "I think it's bogus. The way we understand it, there was this little gal biologist, and her heart was set on these vernal pools and these pretty flowers—you ought to come back in the springtime and see these pools with these beautiful rings of flowers around them. Well, she liked flowers. But you couldn't get flowers protected, so she got the shrimp listed under the Endangered Species Act to protect the part she wanted to protect, because if the shrimp got listed then the pools and their flowers would stand. This isn't just my story. This is the story from everybody in California." Sue, emphatically, does not believe the fairy shrimp is endangered.

"What if the shrimp *was* endangered?" I posit. "Would you care?"

Sue considers the scenario, then responds, "To a certain degree, but probably not much more than I care for the dinosaurs. If there's ever a reason to list a species, salmon would be it."

I ask whether she means that some species are just not important enough to care about. I explain that some people in the Central Valley feel that if a species is in the way, it's a natural part of evolution to let it go extinct.

Chris is already shaking her head before I've finished speaking. "Naw, I don't think you'd find anybody here that feels that way. I bet the person you were talking to was making a living using the water. As far as extinction being part of evolution, now, I don't believe in evolution, and I've read quite a bit about it. I did not come from a monkey, O.K.?"

Sue comes on with, "I don't believe in evolution, either. I feel we ought to protect any species because God made a balance. We care about the resources; we don't want anything to go extinct. But we're always going to have some species go extinct, and we have to face that. Thing is, we have to distinguish between natural problems and man-made problems. It isn't my fault if it didn't rain enough for the fairy shrimp."

"That's interesting," I say.

"Nine times out of ten," Sue asserts, "the people who administer the Endangered Species Act are from town. They don't understand agriculture. We have to take government back, and control of our land back. We've put our heart and soul into this land. I'm not totally against the Endangered Species Act like so many are, but I think it needs to be revised."

"How?"

"I'd have to read up more before I can make an informed statement about that," Sue says.

I ask whether the Endangered Species Act creates a lot of problems for them.

Sue considers this. "No," she says. "The Endangered Species Act, it don't panic me, for some reason. We been livin' with it, so I'm not scared of it. Because, if it's an endangered species or not, it's important to its habitat. If it's declining, it's important that we see what we can do to help."

Chris follows with, "I was reading the Endangered Species Act today before you came. And from what I was reading, there's a lot of language in there that gives us a lot of leeway."

Somehow, it's gotten to be midnight, and we have a long day ahead. Through the bedroom windows comes coyote music. The songdogs are a couple of hundred yards from the house in oak-shadowed pasture, not too far beyond vision, out near the moon.

In the earliest morning, when I step outside, the sun is not yet over the Sierras, and the Vina Plains stretch before me, partly revealed by daylight, partly hidden by night, as though harboring some secret expectation. The sky above is cloudless, and the morning holds a hint of fall. Every so often, a bird calls in air so clear and still that its voice seems to dissipate in space and be absorbed into the silence. Although it is fenced for cattle, this country, with its oak-freckled grasslands, conveys a sense of open parkland. It still seems intact, authentic, and original, and as the sun pierces the horizon you can feel the land's age and agelessness under your feet.

Setting the truck into four-wheel drive, we venture across the plains, a broad expanse of surprising scale, and up to part of the family's ranch. The grass under the oaks is California brown. The soil, thin. The earth's surface here is exceptionally rock strewn: souvenirs of the Lassen volcano.

Toward the Sierra foothills nearby, we drive up-country. Chris, forging bumpily up bouldery hills of forbidding incline, occasionally has the wheels spinning, producing a hail of flying rocks as we go ramping up the land. This is no milk-and-honey Sharon. Chris says that homesteaders came up here mainly to get away from cholera and smallpox in the lower valleys. Sue reminds us that those homesteaders included her ancestors.

Though Chris sometimes introduces herself by saying, "I'm a farmer; I raise cattle," this is no farm. This is landscape. The earth's surface, even if it has borne and supported human activity, has not known a plow, has not been broken into.

She says, "If you live in town and there's an endangered red-legged frog on your lawn, and you run over it with the mower, no one is going to say anything. Well, my lawn is twelve thousand acres. Ranchlands may constitute some of the last remaining unfragmented habitat for rare species. It's the truth. How many people do you know who own twelve thousand acres?"

She's got me there.

Chris continues, "I have to accept the responsibility of a habitat for all these living things. People who own big pieces of land have a special responsibility. That's what I want to teach my children: 'O.K. now, you have a ranch. But let's call it a habitat.'

"I want to hand this habitat down to my children. The enviros want to preserve it. They don't know me, and the fella down the highway may have sold his land for condominiums. So I can't blame the environmental community. They have a place in all of this. They've been a good thing. The strong stands they've taken have really gotten people's attention on salmon. And in a way, the push that the conservation community has given us is helping me provide for my kids later on, too. Tell you what I mean: I want to find a way that my kids can have this and not have to sell land off for development to pay an inheritance tax. That's an incentive to me. This year we learned about conservation easements. They are an encumbrance to the land that goes on the deed, permanently. They're better than laws. Laws can be changed by all kinds of people. They can't change deeds. For instance, I may put on the deed that there is a wild and scenic corridor, and that the land cannot be broken up for subdivisions. It devalues the property, and if the property is devalued, then the inheritance tax is less. Several of the landowners here are up for conservation easements. What the environmental community doesn't realize is, we're on the same page. We want this preserved as much as they do. I want the environmentalists to feel good and I want to feel good."

That's interesting, I tell her, because the leader of the private-property-rights political movement in the U.S. says his objective is to destroy the environmental movement. He says, "I'm not kidding; I won't be satisfied with anything less."

"He sounds very angry," Chris says.

Sue agrees. "Nobody's going to get anywhere like that."

"He needs to be better educated."

"I would need to understand his family background," posits Sue.

By and by, Chris is turning the Deer Creek Alliance—formed to fight a perceived threat—into the Deer Creek Watershed Conservancy—to cooperate for common goals. The conservancy comprises property owners in this drainage, "formed to protect the unique ecological values of Deer Creek," it says in writing, "in the entire watershed, from ridge-top to ridge-top, from its headwaters to its confluence with the Sacramento River." A watershed approach. Just like the scientists up in Oregon recommended in vain. Just as both Randy Fisher and the National Academy of Sciences say is needed. Just like the Clinton Forest Plan that Congress scuttled with the logging-without-laws rider.

The conservancy has been fencing cattle away from the creek. Its members have been assisting the state Fish and Game department in studying spawning salmon, young salmon, and stream conditions; they have been giving Fish and Game free access onto their private land—the private land that everyone in Oregon and Washington says will be the hardest to get cooperation on. (And they didn't just give them the gate keys. Tod Leininger also guided a team of biologists plus his two children in along the creek, looking for the best study sites for counting young salmon.) For the last four years, they've diverted little or no water during the peak migration season (they used to divert most of it). Now they are digging wells to replace the water given to the fish (in most of the rest of the state water had to be torn from farmers by an act of Congress).

The conservancy's Deer Creek Watershed Management Plan has been submitted to the state of California, and it's fair to say the bureaucrats must have been blown off the chairs they were stuck to, because nothing like this has ever happened before. It is sheer good faith, an agreement among plain people who know what they are talking about because they have lived it and they understand their options. And they decided that losing salmon was not something they would opt for. One conservancy member said they saw the watershed strategy as "part of our estate planning for our grandchildren." The plan has a lofty aspiration stated in its Overall Goal:

> Deer Creek Watershed Conservancy is dedicated to the continued preservation of the Deer Creek watershed ecosystem through cooperative efforts between landowners in the watershed area and various public and private agencies that are also dedicated to such preservation.

The California Department of Fish and Game presented Chris with a plaque, recognizing her for "Outstanding Wildlife Conservation Achievement." She tries to tell me she just got her name on it; it *really* represents the work of a bunch of people. She is being way too modest, but in one sense she is right. Private-property owners elsewhere are waging war on nature. Here, property owners are the Deer Creek Watershed Conservancy's Board of Directors:

Tucker Baccala, rancher. Family arrived from Switzerland in 1848. Grandparents homesteaded and reared eighteen sons and daughters. At grandfather's death, ranch passed to seven surviving children.

Bill Howe, forester with Collins Pine Company—entirely family owned. Family has been in this valley since 1907. "A lighter touch on the environment has always been a guiding principal and hallmark of the company's forest management philosophy." Company uses "sustained yield and single tree selection practices that are compatible with fish and wildlife." Company has been noted by the Sierra Club and was the first industrial forest to receive the Green Cross label for environmentally sound forest management. Collins Pine has agreed to donate and maintain split-rail cedar fences to keep cattle away from the stream.

Somebody, pinch me.

Julie Reynolds, wildlife biologist, Sierra-Pacific Industries—also family owned. Responsible for providing wildlife, biology, and habitat information to the company's Registered Professional Foresters (so much pride they capitalize those words), for use in planning environmentally sound timber cutting.

Tod Leininger, rancher, Chris's husband. Doesn't know who Oliver North is, in addition to other enviable attributes. Family arrived here from Nova Scotia in 1850.

Jim Gaumer, president, Baldwin Construction. Owns eighty-five-hundred-acre ranch, in family for fifty years.

Fred Hamilton, rancher. Shares ownership with brother and sister.

John Edson, orchardist. President of the irrigation district, school board member, volunteer fireman.

Bill Berens, orchardist. Family here since 1860s. Taught high school agriculture for four years. Grandmother served thirty years on school board. Has managed family's farm since 1975.

Butch Anderson, orchardist. Family from Denmark. Has grown walnuts all his life in Vina.

Bob Ramsey, orchardist and farmer. Carrying on family operations started in 1920s. Owns land along upper Deer Creek near Ishi Wilderness.

Brother Paul Bernard, Trappist monk. Columbia University alumnus. Joined Carmelite order in 1955. Manages monastery in Vina on six-hundred-acre farm and orchards cared for by thirty-five monks. Serves on irrigation district board.

Cheryl Silva, rancher. Fifth generation.

Sue Knox, rancher. Family here since 1870s. Grandchildren are sixth generation and committed to good stewardship and living with "amiable management" in the watershed.

When this board believes they need another opinion, they bring in academics, conservation groups, and other people whose opinions they have grown to trust and respect. The state has written to thank the conservancy for "prompting" its agency's "much needed" fish studies.

Somebody, say Amen! Somehow, a pocket of sanity has taken hold along Deer Creek and is flourishing here.

Meanwhile, the conservancy is not relying on goodwill alone. The most concrete (actually, unconcrete) thing that a legal Wild and Scenic designation would do would be to preclude by law the possibility of a dam or new water diversions on Deer Creek. The conservancy has gotten a bill through the legislature that does just this, prohibiting—it says right here in the law—"any other water impoundment facility that could have an adverse effect on the free-flowing conditions of Mill Creek and Deer Creek, or on their wild runs of spring chinook salmon." A group called Friends of the River, which first proposed the Wild and Scenic designation that led to Chris's forming the opposition Deer Creek Alliance to fight that proposal, wrote an enthusiastic endorsement of the bill prohibiting any dam or diversion and of the Deer Creek Conservancy itself. Other surprising support for the bill that would have been unthinkable in the war zones of the states to the north comes from the California Cattlemen's Association. "Not only will the lands be maintained in perpetuity for fish and wildlife," wrote the association's government-relations director, "but also for the future generations who will be making their living off the land." *That* he says, is "common sense," which seems to be the highest category of endorsement bestowable by cowfolk.

Chris is taking us toward Ishi's cave, an overhanging rock ledge at the bottom of the canyon along Deer Creek. Ishi, a Yahi, is considered to have been the last "wild" Indian in the United States. In 1911, Sue's great-grandfather and the survey group he was with had discovered and removed all of Ishi's family's belongings—including their food cache—from the cave. What the history books don't tell you—what Sue is telling us now—is that the booty came so heavy with guilt that the party brought it all back the next day. The books do not mention it because by then Ishi's family's cataclysm was well along and irreversible. The strand had been broken, and in the vertigo following the loss of all worldly possessions and their winter food stores, the center could not possibly hold. Ishi was found nearly starved to death on a ranch in Oroville, and he spent the rest of his unnatural days living in a museum.

Chris tells us that, before that episode, "they had a bounty on Indians, just as they do on coyotes. People would come up hunting the Indian people like animals, and they'd collect the bounties. They did! It's sad. It's *very* sad." Everyone seems to fall silent while the truck rocks and lurches upward into the Sierra foothills, toward the rim of Deer Creek Canyon.

Suddenly Chris applies the brake. Here we are. She tells me to go on ahead while she calls her husband on the cellular phone. "These phones are great. They saved our marriage, because when he's running cattle up in the high country in the summer he stays in an old cabin that has no electricity and no phone. But now, there's no excuse."

I crunch through the dry straw and across the grainy soil, spotting two quail and a fence lizard along the approach to the canyon's yawning lip. The sun is hot, dry, enervating, the kind of desert-strength sun that opens your pores, reaches in, and drains the fluid from you. Stepping up to a vantage point on a flat lava rock, feeling the drying wind and the heat reflecting off the stone, I survey the fifteen-hundred-foot plunge that follows gravity from the escarpment. The canyon is surprisingly deep. And wide. The canyon bottom is greener and more vegetated than the surrounding plains and foothills. Deer Creek, somewhere down among the trees lining the distant river corridor, is not visible. But, cupping my hands to my ears, I *can* hear it! "Who hears the rippling of rivers," wrote Thoreau, "will not utterly despair of anything."

Chris and Sue walk up and point out the cliff, many hundreds of feet high, at the base of which Ishi and his family slept the last night's sleep of the uncontacted North American native. I pull out my binoculars. The overhang that sheltered them remains, with bright yellow-orange lichens on the jagged, broken lava. A prairie falcon, like Horus himself, presides impassively from an outcrop in the striking sunlight. When a shadow crosses the rock upon which I stand, I look up to see a vulture pivot on the wind and swirl around, coming by at eye level on motionless wings, its own black eyes making appraising contact. Why the curiosity, friend? I *am* still alive, aren't I?

The women want to show me the clear-cut that everyone was up in arms over. We go to four thousand feet as the salmon climbs. Here the valley grasslands have yielded to broken forest and sage amid rock outcrops, and the canyon is narrower and shallower. Up-canyon, with elevation, the forest closes in, becoming more densely vegetated. Deer Creek is running below, and a short stretch, bearing white water, is visible. A blacktail doe crosses an opening. Chris points out the clear-cut on a distant hillside. Compared to the horrors of Oregon and the hellfire of Washington, it's tiny, probably under five acres.

Chris tells me their cattle are in the upper meadows beyond the timber in the summertime. As soon as it rains and the grass starts growing, you bring the cows down. "Environmentalists call this a watershed. We've always managed it that way, only we called it a range. Some people here are so afraid that if we call it a watershed they're gonna get another law slapped on them. But I'll tell you this: there's no way you can run this business and not realize it's an ecosystem in a watershed. The ranchers knew it before there were environmental consultants in the Yellow Pages.

"Remember last night, when I told you about all the things we'd never seen before—big clear-cuts, stream damage from cows, the delta pumps—because we'd spent all our time in this valley? Well, I have also never seen bad overgrazing. In our pasture—as you can see here—the grass is up to your knees, because a fatter calf brings more money, and that's the only money we make."

"But that can't be the reason," I point out, "because if it was, everybody would do it that way. There'd *be* no overgrazing."

"Overgrazing is bad cattle management. You have a lot of doctors and lawyers who own cattle and hire someone to manage for them."

"But they all want to make money."

"A lot of them want to lose money—and they have invaded our industry. If they lose money here, they avoid taxes. I can't go out and be a doctor. But a doctor can come into our industry and bring all the cows he wants, and run them any way he wants. There's a lot of insurance companies that own cattle ranches, and they want to show a financial loss. That's the way the tax laws work. And the way they manage or abuse their land affects our reputation. People who manage cattle poorly make it bad for everyone."

Sue chimes in. "Like I told you: Don't lump us all together. There *are* areas where people—because of money, basically—have crowded too many cows in one area and degraded the streams and the land. But not in this canyon. We have good cattlemen here. That's why I don't like to be bunched with other people."

Chris reminds her again that the admonition about lumping cuts both ways. "In the publication *Western Livestock Digest,* a rancher called environmentalists 'nature Nazis.' This not only offends me, it embarrasses me for my kids. My kids were raised to respect cattlemen, so now what do I tell them about cattlemen? We are cattle people, so this tears at our sense of community. He's tearing down these values and our own culture. That man is on my list of people we need to educate," Chris says with an affirming nod, pressing her lips together.

She tells me that this year, because of the drought, they had to sell their calves early, to prevent them from ruining the pasture. They weren't worth as much, so they had to accept less than they'd budgeted for. "We slid backwards this year," she sums. "Speaking of money, I have a question that I like to ask people, and I'd like to ask you. I've asked the big bosses there at the Department of Water Resources, and I've asked the bosses in Sacramento, and no one can give me the right answer."

I'm getting nervous already. I don't like to look stupid, I say, but it happens, so shoot.

"So here it is: Where does money come from?"

"Well, now, mind you, I'm not a businessman, but I think—this is just my opinion—that money comes from the conversion of natural resources into products."

"That's right!" she shrieks. "That's *right!*" She's practically jumping up and down. "That's exactly right! And do you know, you are the *first* person that ever answered that question correctly? The *first!*"

"What did other people say?"

She is grinning ear to ear and almost unable to keep herself from laughing. "Ready? They said, 'Money comes from the Federal Reserve,' or, 'It's printed in Washington,' or, 'It comes from the bank.' I said, 'You *guys!*' "

"Nobody ever said that money comes from natural resources?"

"Nobody. You're the *first* one. You are the first *one!* It's *embarrassing,* Carl. Natural resources are where it *all* comes from. And if you have a community that is regulated by the supply, you're not going to survive if you try to go past what's available. And in California, we've gone way past what was available. We've mined out the water and other resources. The resources can't handle the development and the numbers of people. But people just don't want to make the economy fit the resources. How do you tell people to make the economy fit?"

We go back down the valley and then up the east side of Big Dry Creek, which, despite its name, is running. We can see all the way across the Central

Valley, about forty miles to the Coast Range. Beyond that blue ridge is the unseen ocean that has, seemingly ironically, sent me here.

I almost have to remind myself that the things these people do here, way up in the hills and creeks and apparently so far from the sea, have a great and continual effect on that ocean and the people plying it. Gravity everywhere exerts itself, drawing downhill the consequences of our actions and values, so that they flow as the very waters, into the sea.

We climb to high meadows. Chris points out a place where cows are being fenced away from the creek. One rancher's wife convinced them to use split rails for aesthetics. The rails were donated by the local timber company—a twelve-thousand-dollar value—and erected by prisoners (at considerably more expense; tax money very well spent, for once). "We're doing some good things around here to help wildlife," Chris says. "I don't know why the people in Oregon are so polarized. From what I've been reading, a lot of people outside this valley can't get past their nose.

"We're not *totally* against people coming in here. Don't get that impression. We just don't want people in here that will trash it. On the other hand, I'm working on a deal through the Deer Creek Watershed Conservancy where we can begin to manage some visitation, so outsiders can learn about the watershed and about us as people. And when they come here, they're going to see land the same way it looked five hundred years ago. And hopefully they're going to have salmon to see, too. I hope someday my kids get to see the salmon the way Sue was telling. They would *love* that."

When I get to Roger Thomas's sixty-foot *Salty Lady* at about five-thirty A.M., stars are still lining the dark bowl of sky. A variety of people are arriving, nearly all men in their sixties. One has his grandson along, a boy in his early teens who will soon be shown how to shave his upper lip. The boat begins to feel crowded.

The mate, Michelle, climbs aboard saying, "Jeez, look at you all." One old geezer says, "We're gonna have just as many people here today as when we had forty-eight people here one day." By actual count, there are twenty-three paying customers by the time Michelle loosens the clove hitch and Roger pulls the *Salty Lady* from her slip. Many customers know one another and know the captain and mate on a first-name basis, and vice versa. Dawn begins bringing the shadowed hills into contrast with the morning, blinking out the fainter stars in a cloudless sky.

Inside the cabin in the sink, a bucket of anchovies is defrosting next to the coffee and Danish pastries.

Captain Roger Thomas, president of the Golden Gate Fishermen's Association, has been fishing here for about thirty years. His receding white hair is combed back; his eyes are deep blue. The captain says, "I don't feel too secure, but we may be able to keep this fishery if we do everything we can."

We move into the harbor past Alcatraz, the skyline of San Francisco on our left and the headlands of the Golden Gate Recreation Area on our right. Two jaegers are chasing Caspian terns that are diving for fish in a tidal rip at the mouth of the Golden Gate. The bridge itself is packaged in a cloud, with the tops of its suspenders breaking through the sky.

Roger says 90 percent of his association's boats rely on salmon. "If there was a sudden downturn from what we have left of our salmon, ninety to ninety-five percent of boats left fishing in the Bay Area and central California coast would be out of business. The customer or resource base just isn't there for other species, and some of those are already overfished anyway."

The mouth of the Golden Gate, as river and sea are getting acquainted, is a marbled swirl of brown and clear waters. We enter thick fog just outside the bay entrance. Roger turns on the radar, and ghostly green spots remind us that we are not alone in the mists.

Near me, enveloped in a fog of his own, stands a California state senator. He is a blowhard, habitually interrupting civil conversations, his jowls rattling as he touts his own activities in the state capitol with a burdensome stream of sentences starting with "I." He bellows continually like the sea lions he detests: "I SUPPORT FISHING. I KNOW THAT FISHING OUT HERE PUTS *A HELL OF A LOT OF MONEY* INTO THE ECONOMY." Except for Roger and Michelle, who seem understandably pleased, all these old retired guys have *paid* money today to have a nice pleasant experience, but the senator is too boorish to realize how uninterested in him the surrounding people are. Now he is railing against seals for eating fish, and complaining that sea otters "wiped out the abalone fishery," as though overfishing didn't, as though the otter did not exist abundantly along with huge numbers of abalone before fishermen and fur trappers tore into both species like the senator is tearing into the first of his several ham-and-egg sandwiches.

It is still early morning when we put the lines down to troll in the dense fog. They are let down with two-pound weights, and the depths are staggered, allowing all twenty-three people to troll simultaneously around the boat without tangling, something I would not have thought possible. When a fish bites, it pulls a release, which frees the line from the weight so the angler can better feel the fish's "fight"—its struggling being the source of our perverse enjoyment. But this sends the ball of lead, all two pounds of it, to the bottom. Roger says it would be too much trouble to rig the toxic weights on separate lines so they could be retrieved after they are released from the fishing line, but I don't think so.

After trolling only three minutes, a miracle occurs: My rod bounces with the boat's first salmon of the day. It's a small chinook, and I am grateful that though it is a keeper it was too small to trip the release that would have freed my lead weight. Another two have been hooked as I was bringing mine in. Suddenly there are more fish than Michelle can net. They are bright young chinooks, two years old and two years shy of spawning. Their sides are bright silver, their backs emerald with black flecks. After the initial flurry, the fishing slows to an irregular pick. The fog opens up. Land appears. We now see that sooty shearwaters, glaucous-winged gulls, and handsome Heermann's gulls share the grounds with us. Sunlight breaks through onto the rocks of Pedro Point; the city of Pacifica reflects light back.

A little before ten, I get my second fish. Two is the legal limit per person to take home. Though we can keep fishing until there are twice as many fish in the boat as there are people, I decide to reel in, sit back, and relax. For the moment, life is good.

Captain Thomas is pleased that I have caught my limit. He says, "Years ago the sportfishing people from Oregon and Washington would say to me, 'What are you doing, talking with that commercial guy? They're stealing all your fish!' Now all those folks are out of business and I'm still fishing, because these groups around here are pulling together."

Enough people catch more than their limit that everyone aboard, even those who did not catch one themselves, gets at least one salmon to take home. Upon receiving his fish, the senator, who has caught none, says, "Now, when I lie about my catch, I will have credibility."

BOOK THREE

Far Pacific

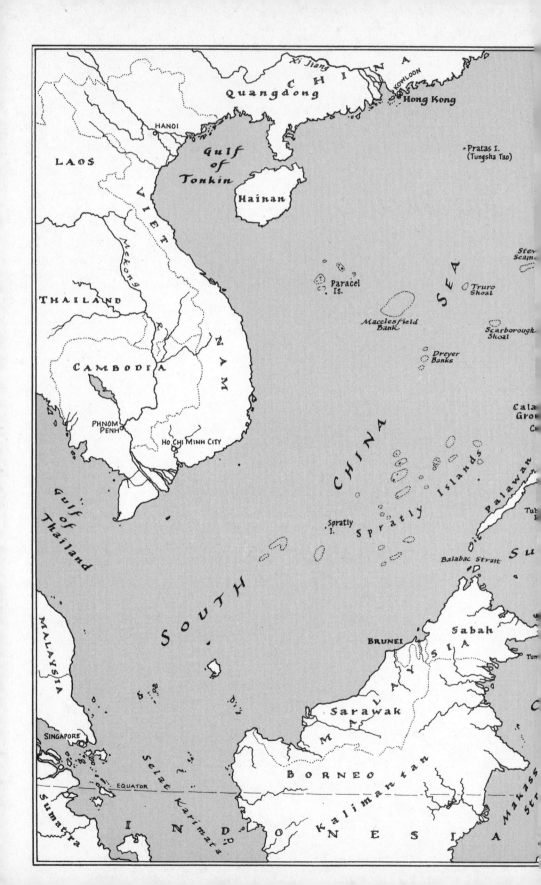

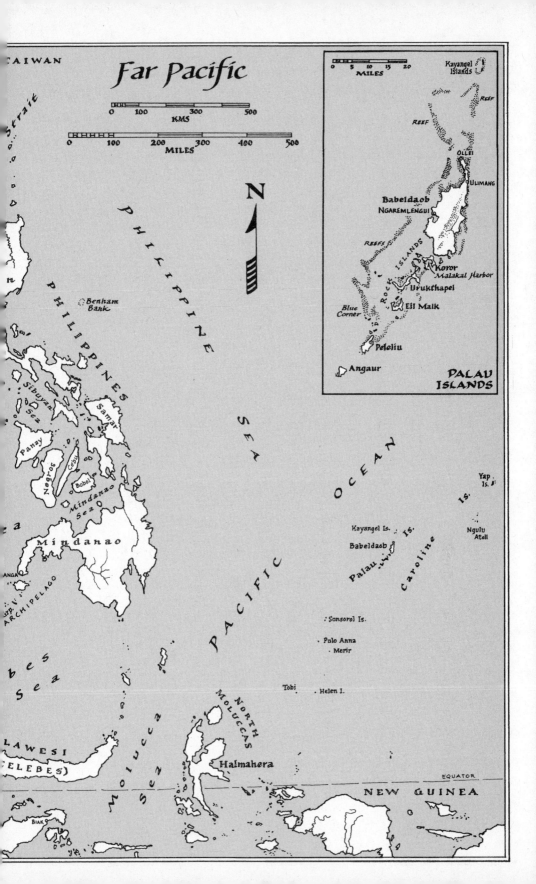

Nowhere on earth does the word "paradise" roll off the tongue as easily as in the tropics. "Arctic paradise" doesn't work. "Temperate paradise" doesn't work. Tropical paradise.

Even if you have never visited tropical shores, you have your images. What images come to mind in your tropical paradise? Palm trees, surely. Bright, faintly pinkish coral-sand beaches. Waters glistening all hues of blue. Jungles tangling volcanic slopes. Towering clouds reflecting the turquoise tint of lagoons. Coral gardens blooming multicolored fishes like fantasy flowers.

Let us drift among those fishes. They dart and flutter, they graze and munch, they confuse us with color and dazzle us with fabulous forms. Why such an explosion of fishes, so brilliantly adorned in pattern, so famously varied in contour? No one knows. Sharp minds have blunted themselves on the question of why or how there came to be such profusion of fishes on coral reefs—nearly 40 percent of all the world's fish species. Maybe the secret is the tropics themselves. Safe from the periodic deep-freeze ravages of ice ages, tropical evolution can run like a trip meter that never gets reset to zero, endlessly branching in bewildering variation.

The ordering of species into neat niches, easily seen and understood elsewhere, seems blurred and confused on the reef. The sensible evolutionary radiation of salmon, for instance, into every available place and season in their rivers, so elegant and so comprehensible, seems to have scant parallel among reef fishes, where multiple similar and competing species have piled up on one another's niches like multicar accidents. The coloration for camouflage and warning that makes eminent sense on animals from other places seems tossed to whimsy on the reefs. *Humuhumu-nukunuku-a-pua'a,* meaning "grunts like a pig," is the unadorned Polynesian name for Hawaii's state fish, an abundant creature westerners call the Picasso triggerfish. That it is named after the most celebrated modern painter suggests the impression a first glimpse of coral reefs gives. Indeed, *so many* of the animals seem to have been colored by children that you want to ask: Who painted all the fishes?

If you have never seen these creatures rioting the reefs in nature, perhaps you have seen them swimming behind glass in a pet shop or an aquarium. In Hong Kong, you can see coral reef fishes—groupers, parrotfishes, surgeonfishes, and many others—in numerous locations throughout the city, swimming to and fro in glass tanks, looking almost like aquarium displays. Their proximity to restaurants hints otherwise. Looking at them, you would never guess that getting them here entails ecological disruption and human suffering on faraway reefs, nor would you likely guess the staggering sums of money involved.

The Philippines and Indonesia—where many of these animals come from—are the very center of living diversity in the world's seas. Nowhere else do more kinds of corals, fishes, mollusks, and other sea creatures exist in any area of comparable size. The southern Philippines and western Indonesia lie in the "Fertile Triangle," having the richest, most diverse marine biota in the world—more than 2,500 fish species of 165 families. Plus, more than 3,200 mollusks, nearly 500 species of coral in almost 80 genera, algae and sponges enough to boggle the human mind, and a higher number of animal phyla than anywhere else. All in all, the most spectacularly complex diversity of life in the known universe. And the triangle is only the core of a larger region of living riches known as the Indo-Pacific, a vast reach of the tropical world stretching from the Red Sea to Polynesia.

I traveled to the center of the seas' living diversity to see some of the best remaining reefs in the world. Amid the biological chaos of our times, I wanted to find a place still full of abundance, and to search my heart for hope.

Dreamland, dreamland, goes the refrain of a song about the tropics. But imagine that in this dreamland you had a nightmare. You went to Paradise, a heaven lush with the living beauty of Creation, and slowly, one by one, the decorations started coming down the moment you arrived, until it finally dawned on you that you were really in Paradise Lost.

An expanding fishery that poisons reefs with sodium cyanide is engulfing this richest one-third of the world's coral habitats, across an area spanning a quarter of Earth's circumference. Ironically, cyanide that is used to stun fish so they can be delivered to markets alive leaves reefs dead in its wake.

But while the best remaining areas are beset by problems, the worst places are drawing the inspired, hopeful efforts of a few remarkable individuals. Such people—from scientists to villagers—now labor heroically in some of the most challenging places, where doing anything positive requires determination of uncommon scale.

Some things run in cycles. Perhaps everything does. Change is the most inevitable part of life, yet change is what many of us fear most. What is good can go bad. But what is bad can become good again. Scattered throughout the Philippines, for instance, where the reefs have a well-earned reputation as the world's most devastated, several dozen fishing communities have now established coastal reserves banning habitat-destroying fishing methods. Where the villagers persist in protecting previously wrecked reefs, a profusion of small, young corals begin colonizing after only a few years, fish numbers begin again to build toward abundance, and the whole protected area assumes a striking, hope-inspiring aspect in contrast to the adjacent devastation. Local reefs are now getting some much-needed protection in a few other places, too, in the Pacific, the Indian Ocean, and the Caribbean. It has been said that these protected areas constitute "specks in a sea of environmental degradation." Exactly, but I prefer to think of them as "a start"—the beginning of a cycle of renewal.

The greatest mystery of nature is its power to generate life, and life's regenerative power responds generously wherever people find within themselves the will to allow it. The only requirements: heart, hope, and unusual courage.

Malakal

Bob Johannes, a mountain of a man, is hauling both his diving gear and his large frame into a boat that looks too small for him. White-haired and fifty-eight years old, Johannes has worked as a coral reef ecologist for most of his life, returning again and again over the last two decades to labor lovingly in the tiny island republic of Palau, his heart's home. His classic 1981 book, *Words of the Lagoon,* documented in attentive detail the old ways of Palauan seafaring traditions, now mostly passed. Through Bob's nomination, a few years ago an American association of scientists, educators, and divers designated Palau as Number One Underwater Wonder of the World.

A first glimpse of the place affirms the title. Pastel-colored parrotfishes, black surgeonfish, and steely-sided jacks are cruising over corals. This natural aquarium begins immediately beyond my toes, yet I am still merely standing on the fuel dock at Francis Toribiong's marina, handing equipment to Dr. Johannes.

As it does each morning, the place bustles, with six boat crews readying to take American, Australian, Japanese, and Swiss tourists out to Palau's famous dive sites. Palau—six hundred miles east of the Philippines in the Caroline Islands—leads nearly every scuba diver's list of most-dreamed-of destinations. *Scuba Diving* magazine's readers recently bestowed upon Palau ten first-place awards, including Favorite Reef Dive, Favorite Site for Photography in the Pacific, Favorite Shark Dive, and Favorite Place to See Big Animals. The favorite among favorites, a site called Blue Corner, was described as "electrifying," "mindblowing," and "sensory overload, because of the amazing numbers of large fish which can be spotted here at any dive." A vertical reef wall jutting into the ocean, Blue Corner, so I have heard, forms a virtual wind tunnel for the Pacific currents, concentrating food and attracting dense numbers of big fish.

Bob Johannes grew up in Vancouver, British Columbia. Upon receiving his master's degree, he sent for applications to three Ph.D. programs. A palm tree decorated the application for the University of Hawaii. He thought, "I've never seen a palm tree; I'll go there." Johannes never filled out the other two applications. Following his graduation from Hawaii, Dr. Johannes embarked upon two decades of work in the U.S. and Australia, during which, he says, "I was a conventional ecologist."

But not too conventional. He'd been reading anthropological literature of the Pacific Islands. "These islanders seemed to know a lot about marine biology that we didn't. So I thought I'd go someplace in the Pacific and find out just what the people *did* know." He got a Guggenheim Fellowship and a year's leave from his job with the Australian government's Commonwealth Scientific and Industrial Research Organization, and went to Palau.

Dr. Johannes lucked out doubly. He got to Palau just in time to chronicle the old coastal culture. And he went to a village where the first person he asked turned out to know more about the old ways than anyone still alive in the country. That elderly fisherman, named Ngiraklang, possessed extraordinary observational powers and exceptional energies—a bona fide genius, according to Johannes. Bob evinces his feeling of lifelong debt to Ngiraklang by the esteem in which he holds his memory.

Ngiraklang's grandson Francis Toribiong—now nearing fifty, a dark, strongly built, and solid-looking man with four kids and a wife from Indiana—is handing me gear, explaining, "When people come here for the first time, they are really excited—like you today. For us there have been a lot of changes. My grandfather was a fisherman. I am not. I am now fighting for the fish. Tourism—like the diving business I'm in here—gives us a financial incentive to conserve. The customers will be pleased if the reef is excellent. During the World War II Japanese occupation, they fished almost everything out of this place. Everything came back. In the late fifties, fish and turtles were everywhere. So there is still a good chance to get it right for Palau. That is what I am saying."

Once we get all our gear aboard, Francis tells us he has invited one other person, Devon Ludwig, to join us. When Toribiong goes into the office to attend to some customers, I ask Bob if he knows this Devon person. Bob rolls his eyes ever so slightly—almost involuntarily—and says he knows of him mainly by reputation, as the American biologist for Palau's capital state of Koror who is said to be unduly fixated on outflow into the harbor from the federal government's sewage plant. Some problems exist, sure, but Ludwig, according to what most say of him, exaggerates them in his mind and amplifies them when he talks to people. Even if there are some effects from the small sewage plant, Johannes says, they would probably be local and insignificant. Koror, after all— the capital "city"—is really just a small town with a single main street, no major intersection, and imminent plans to erect the country's first traffic light to regulate its sleepy automobiles (about half of which are right-handed cars from Japan, and half left-handed models from the States). Johannes tells me that Ludwig's sewage problem was proved more imaginary than real by an independent expert, brought in from Guam, who checked the outfall and gave it a clean bill of health. "My advice is, take what he says with a grain of salt, and enjoy the scenery."

Enjoying the scenery is indeed what I plan to do. Palau's many steep, jungled islands, set like faceted emeralds into a sapphire and turquoise sea of expansive coral lagoons, compose perhaps the most visually stunning realization of Paradise in any ocean.

Fifty thousand U.S. troops attacked Palau on September 14, 1944. The U.S. was fighting its way across the Pacific, and Palau, with its enemy air base, was pivotal. Not until the U.S. took Palau could it advance westward, struggling doggedly toward Japan. So ferocious was the fighting that local Palauans say blood from one battle reddened the water for days, cartwheeling in a tidal eddy off the tip of a reef. When the Japanese retreated into the jungles, the U.S. decided to starve them out. For months American troops thwarted all attempts at farming, reportedly starving many Palauans in the process (though locals say most knew the islands well enough to survive).

The richest and most diverse collection of marine life in the world lives among the tens of thousands of islands of Indonesia and the Philippines. Standing closest to this biological hot spot, tiny Palau harbors a richer species assemblage than any other single oceanic island group. In the 1970s, two of Bob Johannes's colleagues found thirteen species of fish that were new to science during a two-hour dive. Another colleague later recorded 163 species of corals during a four-hundred-yard swim in water less than twenty feet deep: twice as many species as are known from the entire Caribbean to a depth of three hundred feet. That survey was done in Palau's main harbor, slated at the time for dredging to construct a U.S. submarine base during the Cold War.

Few places in the world have more than two species of sea grass. Palau has nine. Hawaii has thirteen species of damselfish. Palau, about eighty. One tiny cove in Palau holds all seven of the world's species of giant clams. Palau has fringing reefs, lagoons, patch reefs, barrier reefs, mangrove communities, and more than twenty marine lakes holding delicate forms of life not seen elsewhere. A greater variety of marine habitats pack Palau's waters than in any area of similar size anywhere else in the world, and more than most places regardless of size.

Devon Ludwig arrives: late forties, balding, with a serious scientific bearing that might strike you as affectation. A devoutly Christian vegetarian, he explains that he no longer eats fish "in order to help protect the resources here," saying that his protein comes from trees: "About fifteen percent of an almond is protein; about the same as beef." Don't argue with him about almonds, because he is, it turns out, a farmer who still has people growing almonds on ranchland he owns in the Sacramento Valley—not too far from John and Sue Sutton's rice fields— where he will someday return. He has worked as Koror's state biologist for five years. But because he considers his stay in Palau temporary, he and his family are squatting in an abandoned hospital, a small, windowless, cement-block building. The master bedroom is a former operating room, with an enormous, movable overhead light, measuring about six feet across, above the bed. On the whole, as I am hearing about it, his seems a peculiar existence. Devon first came to Palau with a Navy research expedition in 1967, studying venomous marine creatures. When I express surprise that the Navy was researching sea creatures while the Vietnam war raged, he says, "Far be it from me to explain military logic on anything, but it was an undeclared war, and they couldn't very well put all of their efforts into fighting it."

A young boat driver named Troy climbs in and starts the engine. A Micronesian with long coarse hair and a few wisps of beard, he sports a gold earring, a tattooed skull and crossbones over his right pectoral muscle, and a marijuana-leaf necklace. A second young man, a deckhand, has finger- and toenails painted bright red. He looks rough and remains quiet, leaving me unsure what to make of him.

We push off from the dock into Palau's watery Shangri-la. Spectacular high islands draped in jade jungles ring the harbor beneath blue sky.

Devon says, "The water clarity you'll see right here is degraded because of unmanaged construction of a channel. Out a little farther we have the big sewage problem."

Bob shoots me a "What did I tell you" glance, and I move nearer to the outboard motor, where I can't hear as well. I'm the first person to shout "Pollution!" but I came here to see and enjoy the world's *best* reefs, and if the harbor has some little problem, I don't want to hear about it today.

We slip through a narrow channel between vertical cliffs that—when you look straight up—frame a sky where swifts are skimming along the rock ridge. We emerge among the famous Rock Islands archipelago.

Tree-covered boulderheads pepper this shallow region, rising fifty to a hundred feet from the water. Eroded at the waterline as though a drawstring were pinching each one at the sea's surface, the rocky islands look top-heavy. On some, grottos hold the visible remains of ruined Japanese anti-aircraft guns and fighter planes. The water's complexion varies with depth and shadow, running to blue, turquoise, lime green, and aquamarine. Two graceful white terns, gliding and zigzagging in close courtship maneuvers, pass directly over our boat. Over the lagoon sail other tropical seabirds—studies in elegance, all: brown noddies, black-naped terns, startlingly bright white terns, and the masterpieces of this exquisite gallery, the streaming white-tailed tropic birds.

Our boat planes up to top speed as forested islands rise in an abrupt maze around us. Uplifted limestone of coral origin, the islands sit like bright green loaves of land. Most are bread-shaped, but some are formed like heads of broccoli, or tree-topped cupcakes, or eggs set on their narrow end, about to topple. Some are mere rocks, but even the quite large islands show no sign of human settlement; all the surrounding land is too steep for people. The jungle along the cliffs clings mostly to bare rock, and many of the trees and other plants have long tendrilly roots, spilling over the rock faces, trailing down toward the waterline.

In places, the islands undulate in and out of the sea: fat, spongy, rounded lands looking like the backs of a colony of sea serpents.

Undercut, sheer, eighty-foot rock cliffs cast cool shade on clear water, in which rose corals form expansive gardens. The cliffs' rocks are hued light gray, lighter gray, and pinkish. A few black-naped terns perch on the rocks themselves, revealing the subtle but striking blush of peach-colored breasts.

We cross an open lagoon, then plunge into a new maze of vertical land forms and islets. It seems impossible that such scenery can go on so long, but we travel twenty miles through this heaven. I find myself thinking, "If I died right now—." On reconsideration, experiencing this seems better than any description I've heard of the Celestial Kingdom. Forbear the apotheosis, then, and *live!* Bob hands me a cookie. Perfection.

Seeing my beatified look, Bob shouts over the engine, "The beauty of Palau creates an aesthetic dilemma: I find myself constantly torn between taking in the glistening rain forest—with the sounds of birds and insects—or diving to enjoy the silent visual feast of fish, corals, sponges, and jellyfish." Nicely put.

Devon, as though jaded to the beauty around us, persists in lecturing Bob about Palauan ecopolitics. Despite my efforts at remaining soundproof, I'm catching such snippets as, ". . . desecration of water quality. . . ." I hum to myself and watch the fluid flight of a noddy that is pacing the boat. It shears off to join a flock of about a hundred others diving over a school of predatory fish—probably jacks—exploding at the surface as they pulverize a group of silvery prey fish caught vulnerably in the open channel.

Troy, the boat driver, may look crude, but he certainly knows this boulder maze. I am profoundly lost. Here, the cliffs have caves, the rocks have arches, and a few of the islands have deserted, palm-lined, white-sand beaches set perfectly into jungled amphitheaters. I have wet the soles of my feet in many a tropical "paradise," but I've never seen anything like this. Devon's voice intrudes: ". . . which is why gastroenteritis is now very common, and the chances for cholera and other epidemics—like the first dengue fever outbreak we just had—is increasing." I snuggle closer to the roaring outboard and focus toward the distance.

Our boat rockets through a narrow, turquoise pass, and we zoom into open water seasoned with whitecaps. The expansive, almost lime-green coral flats here spread many square miles to distant islands. We are crossing a shallow, two-mile-wide lagoon separating the main islands from the fringing reefs that confront the deep ocean beyond.

We run through a blue channel dug across a wide reef flat by German engineers in the early 1900s. Thirteen live-aboard luxury dive boats bob at anchor along a wall at the end of the flats here. We pass them, go outside the reef, and turn north along the deep dropoff. For the first time, the shoreline to landward looks typically "South Pacific": a sandy, palm-lined beach atop the fringing reef on our right, enclosing the wide lagoon we have just come through, with the larger islands in the distance. To seaward, open ocean stretches to the blue horizon, and far beyond.

Dive boats anchored about a mile ahead mark Blue Hole. Several dolphins suddenly blast exuberantly into the sunshine alongside us, and bunches of them begin breaking the surface around our boat: dolphins of all sizes—adults, adolescents, little babies.

Devon turns to me, asking, "Do you want to get in the water with them?"

With fumbling fingers I hurry to put on mask, snorkel, and flippers. Troy keeps a steady pace and many of the animals are now riding the bow wave. Others are surfing our wake.

I'm afraid they'll depart before I can get in the water. We stop the boat and I slip in. By the time my bubbles clear, they have vanished.

Devon throws me a rope, telling me I'll have a better chance of seeing the dolphins if they pull me through the water, because the animals like a moving boat. With my body boring through the surface and cool water rushing past my ears, I look down into the endless blue, watching shafts of light disappear beneath me through clear water into bottomless ocean. I am having a blast. Until I feel I am being watched. The words "tiger shark" seep in from a corner of my mind, and along with them comes a barely manageable sense of panic that something large and hungry, something that can see me clearly silhouetted against the sky while it is hiding its perfectly countershaded body in the deep dark blue below me, will come rocketing out of the depths and tear off my legs.

As I stream along at about five knots, my horrifying reverie is broken by the sound of my watch beeping. I look at my wrist. I am not wearing my watch. What's that sound? Several sleek dolphins materialize ethereally from below. Like the tiger shark I had imagined, these dolphins *were* watching, and talking about me. Now they have moved in for a better look, their electronic-sounding voices growing more distinct. None of them are surfacing—the people in the boat can't see them. The dolphins pace along effortlessly, turned on their side, making eye contact. Their beauty overwhelms. What extraordinary luck for us all—how *wondrous*—to have such creatures share and grace our world.

While the sight of them is emblazoning itself into my mind forever, their whistle-and-squeal talking intensifies excitedly. Though curious about the odd sight of my being towed along on the line, they keep a cautious distance.

After some unmeasured interval of hypertime, they descend from sight, though for a while I can still hear them and see plumes of bubbles rising. No doubt they maintain a clear view of me against the sky. Then their talking trails off and they vanish from my perception altogether. Now that the novelty of a person on a rope has worn off and they realize I am less fun than I might at first have seemed, the dolphins have become bored with me and wandered on to see what else the world will bring them today.

I clamber back into the boat, leaving the dolphin pods breathing at the surface in the near distance. As Emerson wrote: "I have enjoyed a perfect exhilaration. I am glad to the brink of fear."

We plan to drop in at Blue Hole and work our way toward Blue Corner. Devon says something about the crowd of eight boats. We tie up to another boat, to avoid breaking even more coral with our own anchor (though it strains credulity to think that the bottom right at the drop-in site is not already powdered by anchors). We bob in the swells a few tens of yards off the sandy beach, over a flat shelf in about thirty feet of water. A few yards farther offshore, the shelf breaks at a vertical wall dropping into oblivion. The open sea radiates to all points past that.

The water here is so blue it looks purplish. Devon, Bob, and I will dive, with Devon—who knows the site—serving as divemaster. We have all brought large bags full of dive gear, and as we unpack, equipment quickly clutters the deck. Suiting up takes a while. I do not scuba dive often, and I must do everything slowly and deliberately. Scuba can be wonderful, but it is fraught with subtle dangers requiring attention to details. I pull on a thin wet suit and booties for insulation; don my weight belt; attach my breathing regulator, air-pressure gauge, depth gauge, and calculator-sized dive computer to a tank of compressed air; and open the air valve and check to make sure the tank is full—which it is, at three thousand pounds of pressure per square inch. I strap and latch the tank to a vest called a buoyancy compensator, also known as a B.C. The deeper one goes, the less buoyant one gets because of pressure, and by shooting or releasing quantities of air into the vest one can maintain neutral buoyancy throughout large changes of depth (fish have evolved an organ that does this, called a swim bladder). At depth, it eliminates the need to work at avoiding sinking; at the surface, an inflated B.C. can become a life preserver. I make sure the inflator button works and the B.C. does not leak. I test a couple of breaths off the regulator. The flow of air is smooth. Everything is in order.

Flippers on, I flop and stagger to the boat's gunwale, sit, place my right hand on my mask, and tumble backward into the ocean. Devon and Bob await, clinging to a rope. The water greets me with a surprising chill. The current's immediate, insistent pull again evokes the uncomfortable memory of nearly losing my life in the river, and the overwhelming, sweeping power of streaming water still frightens me. We will be drifting in the strong running tide during the dive, and the boat will pick us up at the surface later. That is the plan, and it is infused with hazards. I have never before attempted a drift dive in a strong ocean current. The knowledge that this is the most physically challenging dive I have attempted has given me an augmented case of predive jitters. I remind myself: "Disrespect your fear but remain careful."

Devon says to me with set seriousness, "This is going to be the best dive of your life," and he drops below the surface.

I exchange my snorkel for my regulator mouthpiece, empty my buoyancy compensator, and drift down slowly without swimming. Devon and Bob descend quickly. They don't need to stop to equalize the pressure in their ears, but I have to stop my descent, pinch my nose while "blowing" into it, and try to get my ear pressure equalized to the increasing water pressure, which increases most rapidly when you first descend from the surface. I fall a bit behind the more experienced divers and have to hurry to catch up.

Visibility is about fifty feet. We swim along the flat reef shelf to the lip of a large cylindrical opening, about forty feet across—the Blue Hole. Devon interrogates us with the "O.K." sign, and we sign back affirmatively. We slip over the hole's lip, sinking passively amid our bubbles and the sound of our breathing. Life encrusts the hole's walls. At about sixty feet, a blue gloom envelops all.

A window large enough to swim through appears in the wall, but we continue sinking. I am getting reacquainted with the feeling of being in and under water, breathing off the clicking mouthpiece, committing myself to the equipment, and trying to relax. I check my depth gauge. So little light penetrates here, my gauges are glowing luminescently as though it is night. Normally nocturnal soldierfish, at home in the gloam, are foraging along the wall.

At about eighty feet, one side of the cylindrical hole opens into a great archway, lit from without by a cosmic blue glow like the last moments of daylight streaming through a cathedral's stained glass. We swim forward now through the arch, where the scene abruptly transforms and we emerge into brightness at the reef face.

A rainbowed blizzard of butterfly fishes and a multispecies fusillade of fusiliers are fluttering in the running tide like bright flags on a holiday. We swim strenuously into the current—which is part of a large eddy circling counter to the tidal flow nearby—laboring along the wall against the streaming water for about twenty minutes, using too much air. At one point I notice that, several yards out and away from the wall, the fish are suddenly facing a different direction, indicating a flow reversal—the end of the eddy. We swim together out toward the fishes, and there the countervailing current picks us up abruptly and begins moving us along. Now we drift effortlessly. Breathing slows. We glide deeper.

A hundred feet down, the natural light has attenuated to a bluish gloom; other colors cannot penetrate so much water. Big, flat plates of coral dominate the wall we are traveling along. (Devon is busy with his video camera, indulging his fixation by poking at and filming a drifting bit of algae, evidence, he believes, of nutrient pollution from sewage. The idea that any pollution from Koror's sewage pipe could affect things all the way out here seems preposterous.) Bob pauses in the current, poking his head under some of the coral shelves and crevices, looking for hidden creatures. Copying the expert, I look into a dark hole—directly into gaping jaws of a large green moray eel. O.K., enough of *that!*

Along and just off the wall, less startling fishes flit, flutter, and swish by in superabundance: the peculiar unicorn fishes—large ones—with their ready-for-jousting heads, and Moorish idols with their elegant streamers, and black surgeonfish carrying two scalpels and trailing long pennants from half-moon tails. Two big jacks with neon-blue side slashes come prowling along the wall. Tiny, feisty, territorial damselfish—the little nippers—attack Bob, who ignores them while pointing out a feather star clinging to some coral.

Too much to look at! On the spectacular wall itself, thick coral plates, whips, and fans stand silhouetted as I scan up toward the light. A little past a hundred feet, most hard corals are starved for light, and when I drop to a hundred and ten, they thin noticeably.

The black void beneath us is the color of absolute night, the black night of outer space. I shoot some more air into my vest with the power inflator to neutralize my buoyancy and drift along in the tide, awestruck. Suspended, weightless, and relying on life support, I am spacewalking. I have landed on the only planet in the universe known by earthlings to harbor life. I check my instruments yet again. My air supply remains ample, my depth steady. My computer says that I have four minutes left at this depth before I must rise to a shallower depth to avoid the need for decompression. Breathing compressed air forces excess nitrogen into the blood. Beyond a certain concentration, this nitrogen will seek to come out of solution in the form of bubbles when pressure is released as the diver surfaces (like the fizz in a carbonated drink). This event, known as "the bends," can cause paralysis, permanent nerve and joint damage, and death. Better to pay attention and stay within limits.

A big grouper appears briefly below me, and an extralarge parrotfish emerges from cover. Several dogtooth tuna, a species prone to patrolling the walls of Pacific reefs, stroll slowly by. One is a big, old, scar-faced individual. Their Latin name, *unicolor*, well describes bodies the hue of galvanized trash cans. The tuna are utterly unhurried, but the shape of their bodies suggests enormous power potential.

A towering tornado of barracudas—hundreds of them—in a stacked school about forty feet high is moving in a slow cyclone, their bodies shining like flexing sheets of metal. Nearby, a big swirling school of jacks and herds of humpback snappers swim along the reef slope, followed by a small group of rainbow runners with their pastel-blue bodies and bright tails. The numbers of animals and the activity is almost beyond belief. I could never have imagined such a blackened-blue aquatic madhouse.

The first gray reef shark I have ever seen that is not on television looms into view from behind a facade of fusiliers, which prudently part to let it through. The shark passes, heading slowly up-current, and I pivot to watch it. Two remoras are hitching a ride on its belly, and a jack closely accompanies it at the shoulder. Something suddenly bumps my leg. I swing around, startled, to find

Bob, merely pointing out the shark to me, in case I hadn't seen it. *Thanks, Bob. Yes, I see.* Bob drifts off.

Two, three, four more sleek sharks weave slowly into view. A terrible inhuman beauty. Three of the animals move up-current, but the fourth, its mouth fixed in a taut half moon, circles for several appraisals as I back against the wall and begin using more air. It is the largest of the four, perhaps seven feet—not awfully large as sharks go, but large enough. Large enough to evoke a response from a very old part of a person's brain. It appears to be flying on instruments, sifting scent, searching for a thin reading of voltage indicating an encounter with another life form. Though it confronts me closely, there is no sense of eye contact; its unblinking, unthinking gaze is calm as the eye of a storm, blank and pitiless as the sun.

It moves slowly up-current and I, pivoting further, watching it, continue being swept along downcurrent, backward. Belatedly I realize the current is sweeping me farther away from the wall. I begin turning to face forward, into the direction I'm heading, to see where going with the flow is getting me. Hardly is the thought formed when, as the poet Yeats wrote, "a vast image out of *Spiritus Mundi* / Troubles my sight." The flow is carrying me directly into a pack of eight sharks stemming the tide. My body is vertical and slightly feet-first—as though I am water-skiing toward them. Pacing the current like lazy trout—on second thought, like nothing but sharks—some of them edge closer. They are indolently curious, self-assured. The water connecting us seems to thicken.

Some divers rate the gray reef shark as the world's third most dangerous, after the great white and the tiger. Virtually all attacks result from a diver's intruding into the shark's territory, violating the animal's sense of secure space. From the shark's point of view, such attacks are defensive. The sharks are not trying to eat the person, merely to drive the diver off with their teeth. They would prefer that the intruding human leave peacefully and without contact, so a warning display precedes the attack. When displaying, a shark comes on with back arched and pectoral fins down. This is the shark's polite invitation to please leave. Divers who do not recognize this, who fail to back off immediately, may get hit with one devastating bite that usually makes the point.

I am wondering just how close the current has to carry me before I begin to infringe on millions of years of customary etiquette. They say old habits die hard. One large shark veers ever so slightly toward me at an oblique angle, that reaper-grim mouth inching closer. I am riveted to its body's every flexion, and I see its pectoral fins drop ever so slightly, just enough to suggest strongly that in that pea behind its eye an evaluation of space and motion may be going on in superior confidence.

Some people meditate for years before achieving the focused presence and clarity of concentration I am now experiencing. As I begin to suppress a degree of attention that is escalating toward fright, the gray velvet creature angles slightly away, passing me and continuing up-current—just as the scientific part of my brain was virtually certain it would.

Another shark glides above me, silhouetted against a cloud of black surgeon-fishes and angelfishes quivering in the current like leaves in a breeze. I look at my computer. One minute left at this depth. I rise slowly to fifty feet. The air in my buoyancy compensator expands as the surrounding pressure lessens, floating me toward the surface. I pull the release cord, letting air out from the top of the B.C., resuming neutral buoyancy.

Bob and Devon are rising with me. Despite vastly superior experience, Bob is having much difficulty with a new B.C. He cannot clear the air out. The shallower he floats, the more the air expands, and the faster he goes toward the surface: a potentially dangerous situation if he loses control of his ascent. He suddenly turns feet-highest, strenuously swimming downward just to hold himself in place. He is pulling his air-release cord, but now he is in the wrong position to dump the air, which has moved away from the valve. I get in his face and mime an alternate way to release the air from his vest: by holding the inflator hose over his head and pressing the purge button. He understands and does this. We are now all back in control.

As we rise higher into more and more light and our surroundings brighten, colors return. Corals resume their full spectrum of blue, red, green, and beige—mostly subtle, muted tones. The fishes' colors, anything but muted, get wild. And the diversity of fishes explodes as we approach the well-lit zone, with more species of damselfishes, butterfly fishes, parrotfishes, tangs, surgeonfishes—. The most varied group of vertebrates on Earth is in full bloom around us, galaxies of living stars burning brightly in this blue universe.

A Napoleon wrasse—its body the size of Bob's—looms into view like a huge blue-green apparition materializing from the waters and light. In fact it has done just that, as has every living thing in the sea, as have we all. Bob had told me that these creatures—among the largest of reef fishes—may live up to a hundred years, reaching more then seven feet and four hundred pounds. Its softly barred flanks, prominent forehead, and big, soulful lips give it a splendid, distinctive bearing. Those gibbous lips—for feeding on deadly poison-spined urchins, armored boxfish, and crown-of-thorns stars—seem poised as if to speak to us a message from the Ocean Kingdom. But the fish maintains a silent countenance, circling us warily at safe distance, content to observe. Yet it engages. It appears calm, reserved, almost distinguished. Its eye—alert as a bird's—is swiveling like a chameleon's, watching our faces, not just our forms. Never have I met a fish whose gaze conveyed such sense of comprehension. With its imposing size and that incredible alert curiosity, it has an enchanting and soothing effect, the encounter not so much a sighting as a visitation.

We rise toward the lip of the wall, where it meets the flat shelf in about thirty feet of sparkling water. A stiff current is flowing off the shelf like a strong and steady wind. The moon will be full tonight, and it has the tides blasting. Bob is grasping a boulder to hold himself in place, and as I come over the top of the wall the scene widens my eyes. Hundreds and hundreds of jacks, the largest angelfishes I have ever seen, sharks, and just about everything else are defying the current. When the fusiliers get nervous, a four-foot mackerel comes rocketing through like a thrown javelin. On the bottom rest three white-tip reef sharks, lankier and more lethargic than the densely muscled gray reefers. Several jacks vigorously rub their flanks along a shark's sides. Whether they are trying to scratch themselves or to drive away the shark, I don't know; I have never seen or heard of this behavior. Bob shrugs; he apparently hasn't either.

Holding a boulder in the buffeting current, I look at my air-pressure gauge. Five hundred pounds: a safe time to surface. Watching the fish, I am thinking that Bob, being so much larger than I, must be nearly out of air.

Devon is alongside with his camera pointed at the fishes, filming something exciting for a change. Even with all the hype, this scene surpasses the billing. Beyond spectacular. But I have a nagging thought about my air supply as the minutes melt. I look at the gauge: three hundred pounds left. I've used 90 percent of my air. The surface looks close. With all the surrounding action, breathing air seems an unimportant detail at the moment.

Bob gives me the low-air sign and starts upward. Devon follows almost immediately. Bob breaks the surface first, and the boat, which has been drifting in the current, swings around to pick him up.

I realize that I can squeeze a few more moments if I drift along under the boat, and I rise ever so slowly while Bob and Devon remove their gear at the surface and climb aboard. I let go of my boulder, and the strong current immediately sweeps me over the reef shelf like a leaf in a prairie wind. The shelf ends suddenly where the wall drops away, and once again the open ocean frames me against bottomless blue-blackness. I feel suspended against a giant movie screen on which the background is cutting abruptly from one scene to the next. I am perfectly weightless, feeling sublime. When the last pair of legs have disappeared into the boat, I realize that I have run out of excuses and must surface. I kick gently upward, slowly twirling, being careful not to rise faster than my smallest bubbles. I glance down for my last glimpse into that bottomless blue, only to see a thousand barracuda flowing like a river beneath my feet. Fluid and unified, they collectively move as one, like iron filings being led by an invisible magnet dreamed idly along by an unseen hand.

Above, through the wavy surface, I can see the boat's orange canopy. My head enters the atmosphere, and so ends the fastest, most slow-motion forty-two minutes of my life.

Lightly spitting raindrops fleck a surface that has turned from purple to windy gray. I hear Devon talking excitedly about some unusual algae he has seen and how its presence here might suggest a source of excess nutrients—perhaps sewage— that he doesn't think was there in the past. After everything that we've just seen, I can't believe he is still talking about sewage. As for me, I am speechless.

Nearby, on a boat full of Japanese tourists, the crew has speared several sur-geonfish. Many Japanese starved in Palau in World War II, and the tour com-pany seems determined not to let that happen again. As we head back toward Koror, a fierce squall comes pelting across the water, its rain advancing in slith-ering sheets. When it hits us, the wind-driven droplets strike hard enough to sting. The rain lasts just a few minutes before the sun burns through again. Between bouts of intense sun, another tropical squall snaps through, and I revel in the dramatic changes of light.

We reenter Malakal Bay, which contains Koror's main harbor. At the base of one cliff, Devon points out a derelict Japanese fishing boat that finally sank yes-terday. He says there was oil all over. Although a floating containment boom now surrounds the boat, I can clearly smell the oil from half a mile away.

Devon insists on stopping at the end of Koror's sewage outfall to show us the outpouring particles. This is the last thing I want to do, look at, or think about. Maybe tomorrow. Please, let's not ruin this day. But he insists. He says the treat-ment plant ceased functioning months ago, and that the particles billowing from the pipe are raw, untreated human sewage.

We go to a spot about half a mile away. Devon says this was once a dive site, says the corals here started dying ten years ago and are now dead. The glory of the day fades. In about thirty feet of water we snorkel down to look at dead coral thinly covered with algae.

Bob Johannes remains skeptical. Treading at the surface, he explains various reasons why corals may die and various reasons why they may have some algal cover. Devon Ludwig points out a subtle green tinge on the shoreline rocks. "You only see that in the bay, because of the outfall pipe. That algae would not be growing here." I must admit he has a sharp eye.

We get back into the boat. Ludwig takes us to another place about a mile from the outfall—a shallow flat covered with a sea-grass bed. It doesn't take us long to see that coarse, streaming filaments of algae, like green hanks of mer-maid's hair, heavily overgrow the sea grass. A bit farther on, the algal cover thickens to a dense mat.

We wade into the thigh-deep water. Devon shows us how you can dig below the algae and find all kinds of coral, virtually all dead. Not long ago, living coral covered this flat. Picking up one piece of coral, he says, "See, this is this year's mortality. See here? The algal bloom cut off this early coral growth." For several square miles around, he claims, dead corals are what you'll find. The green algae looks lush and beautiful, but if in fact it does represent what Devon is saying, the implications do not bode well.

Bob, who has maintained a quiet skepticism about Devon all day, is under-water, pulling up algae and turning over pieces of dead coral. He surfaces, say-ing, "O.K.—this is unnatural. Now I'm convinced. This is a mess. I would never have thought the eleven thousand people in this town could cause this."

"So I'm not crazy?" Devon says sarcastically. "Everybody thinks I'm full of crap."

I feel suddenly ashamed of myself for my attitude toward Devon all day, and for prejudging his analysis of the situation. I so deeply wanted to believe this was one place we did not have to worry about.

In this paradise, in the number-one underwater wonder of the world, what Devon is showing us is not a good sign, especially when he says the present government has explicit plans to expand the population of the tiny country from about fifteen thousand to sixty thousand people, by encouraging development and attracting immigrants. Why would the government want to quadruple the population? "In order to build more tourism infrastructure," he says. "It costs a lot of money to become president, and a president has four years to recoup his million-dollar investment and try to make a profit. The best way to do that is by expanding the constituent base, opening up new business and investment opportunities for yourself and others. So in the near future we will double the volume coming out the end of that pipe every day. It will only hurt more of the harbor's seabed to do that. Responsibility is something new for Palau. Before they got independence in 1994, it was always, 'Blame the Americans.' If the population increases like the government wants, nutrients from the sewage will act as fertilizer and grow algae that will kill the corals miles and miles from here, and then you'll start seeing its effects on some of Palau's premier dive reefs."

If that happens, it would be a choice, not an accident, because Devon has warned them. Devon continues, "Near Blue Corner, where the lagoon flushes out, I found a few broken pieces of algal wool drifting on the current." The image of hanks of filaments that might attach and begin growing elsewhere brings to my mind the image of the pods from *Invasion of the Body Snatchers*. Devon says, "There's not enough nutrients—so far, anyway—for the algae to survive there, but when those pieces of broken algal streamers snag and tangle on coral, especially if they become clogged with silt after they snag, the shading and killing effect is the same, whether the algae is alive or not. Of course, living algae will start spreading on its own."

Bob says he is very surprised that this problem has extended this far into the bay.

Ludwig says, "The place is wasted all the way to Airai," a place about three miles from the outfall. "That's as far as I've looked so far. Because of the way the current runs, I can show you pristine reefs in one spot and two hundred yards away, reefs covered with algae and thoroughly dead. You have to understand the current circulation to understand the pattern."

Johannes asks, "What about the guy who came to independently evaluate the outfall? Why did he miss all this?"

Ludwig says, "He only looked right near the mouth of the pipe. You need to look down-current, where the sewage plume has spread and had its effect. He never sampled the miles of dead areas. When I asked why, he said no one told him to look there."

This situation reminds Johannes of Kaneohe Bay in Hawaii twenty-five years ago. That time, it was Johannes no one wanted to believe. "They were saying there was no pollution in Hawaii. I couldn't get anyone on the faculty to take me seriously. They wouldn't so much as put on a mask and snorkel and simply look. After a six-year battle we finally got an appropriation of a few million dollars to redesign the sewage treatment plant, and the change was dramatic. The water cleared, the coral started growing again. It can be done."

It would be good if Palau were the only place facing such problems, and it would be good if every place had Hawaii's resources for dealing with them.

Devon, glancing panoramically at the ringing islands, cliffs, and jungle, says to no one and everyone, "I love this bay." Then he turns to us and says, "Environmental quality goes down fast, but comes back very slowly. Right now, with the current administration and the emphasis on business and development, the physical beauty of the landscape will remain but the environmental quality will decline. Restoration will happen eventually, I think, but not in our lifetimes."

A large school of silvery anchovies, tens of yards long, comes rapidly along the flat, right over the algae. A flock of terns moves in for the attack over the shallows, and they begin diving right in front of us. I duck underwater and watch as they plunge through the surface in silver clouds of bubbles. The fish can run, but they can't hide. I know the feeling.

I turn to Devon, whom I've been trying to avoid all day because I didn't want him spoiling my fantasy of Paradise, and say, "The place you mentioned—with the pristine reefs in one spot and algae-snarled reefs two hundred yards away— would you have time to take me there tomorrow?"

Devon pilots his little aluminum outboard skiff through channels between islands that stand up from the water like eighty-foot muffins, then out onto the open reef flats. He cuts the engine and we drift over shallow water clear as gin, looking at sea grasses interspersed among small corals, delicate of feature. He says, "See, this is healthy here."

A few hundred yards farther, Devon gets out of the boat in knee-deep water. He bends down and picks up a diminutive coral—still alive—snarled with algae. "Algae is a wonderful thing. It has its place. But when I discover it in a new spot, I see it as a flag. A little patch of algae like this is not a problem, but when it spreads and goes on and on and begins to kill everything it covers—"

Devon moves us to a deeper channel. We are about three-quarters of a mile outside the landmasses but still in the wide lagoon, inside the fringing reef that defies the ocean. The water here is about thirty feet deep, the coral-covered bottom clearly visible. As we put on our snorkeling gear, a sudden plosive expiration of air behind us startles me. A big green turtle has just surfaced; it breathes again and dives glidingly away. Devon says, "This is right at about the point of transition. There are dead corals here, but this is about the edge of it so far."

We snorkel down among an unruly extravagance of corals that, in quiet competition for space and light, are trying to outbid each other as if at a silent auction. The unusual, bright-blue corals here look lovely. I snorkel past a giant clam with its thick, sensuous-looking, indigo-colored mantle. The many small fishes here, of colors aplenty, are busy feeding and cruising. A faint, green algal tinge colors much of the coral. Some of the coral is dead, but what killed it remains unclear. This small amount of algae is not enough to block the sunlight or smother the corals' polyps. At the surface, Devon says, "You see this green algae? In a couple of months when the currents shift and the sewage nutrient plume hits this area, this algae will grow out in long strands."

Devon announces break time. He motors us to a small beach set into a rock theater, completely shaded by coconut trees except for a bright ribbon of powdery coral sand right along the waves' lap line. A shimmering chorus of insects, the occasional whistle of a bird, and the melancholy cooing of doves emanate from the surrounding jungle and reverberate from the rock. "This is my favorite beach," Devon says. "Joanne and I love to come here with the kids. It's a great pleasure to be able to share it with you." He finds a ripe coconut and sits on a log. As he removes the husk, we see that the coconut is just starting to sprout. "Right behind the sprout on the inside of the shell is what we call the marshmallow."

This is new to me. Devon finishes removing the husk. He opens the coconut itself by hammering around its edge with a piece of coral, then takes a knife and cuts off big pieces of meat. The sweet coconut is so rich it feels greasy. What he calls the marshmallow tastes like a lichee nut.

"Without the coconut," he says, "I think most islands in the Pacific would have been uninhabitable when people first arrived. Coconuts provided instant food and water. They're loaded with nutritious fats and sugars. It's an odd fruit that you pick from the sky and that comes in different styles. In my family we each like them at different stages. My daughter likes them green, I like them ripe and uncarbonated, my wife likes them carbonated, my son Bradley likes them when they're just sprouting. So when my son goes up the tree—he climbs like a native—he has orders from us for coconuts in different stages of development."

Having now spent the better part of two days with him, my take on Devon Ludwig has changed. Far from having a fixation on the negative, he is continuously impressed with the physical beauty of the islands. He loves Palau, and he combines the unusual freshness of a child's enthusiasm, the insights of a keen investigator who can still really notice details years after arriving, and the insistence that things could be done right and should be done better. In Paradise, this *appears* like a fixation with the negative, because Paradise is nothing other than the fantasy of perfection we bring with us to temporarily escape our troubles in our own lives and villages.

I glance at Devon sitting on the log, barefoot, surrounded by shards of coconut husk, and I try imagining him in California, tending his almonds. And I think back to the people I met in the Sacramento Valley. I ask, "Have you ever thought of your farming activities in terms of the water quality of the Sacramento River?"

"About twenty years ago, we made the choice not to use insecticides or her-bicides. It was unusual when we started. Now everybody's doing what they can to see how close they can come to that line."

"What's the incentive?"

"Relatives dying of cancer is a good incentive. Basic human health—people close to you—that's the strongest incentive."

I rise to explore the grotto backing the beach. Deep in the shade of tall, buttress-rooted trees, the burrows of coconut crabs almost completely under-mine the lush foliage and the ground. Their entrances are—many of them—bigger than my fist. With almost every step the riddling warrens collapse underfoot and the ground sinks several inches. An old taro patch whispers of human lives once lived here. Standing near the edge of the overgrown garden, looking up at the trees, watching birds flitting among the dense green, listen-ing to the sounds of the jungle, I feel as if I'm forgetting something. Then I realize that what I'm forgetting is my life—that artifice most people euphemistically refer to as the real world.

I turn and walk back toward the beach. For a few long minutes Devon Lud-wig and I sit quietly in the shade, looking out at the sunlit turquoise waters and the blue horizon beyond. Devon breaks the reverie by saying, "You can stay in paradise too long. You can start out with all the right reasons and all the best intentions, and let it eat up your life."

Koror

Larry Sharron runs the Palau field station of the Coral Reef Research Foundation, a four-year-old organization partly funded by the National Cancer Institute, a division of the National Institutes of Health in the United States. He collects marine invertebrates such as sponges and other creatures of unassuming bearing, for screening as potential drugs for cancer, AIDS, and other afflictions. Centers of high biological diversity such as tropical rain forests and coral reefs have yielded many important medical discoveries, and Sharron's work is a deliberate effort to sift the biological trove, prospecting for precious nuggets whose value to humanity may prove invaluable. If we are lucky.

I have come to Larry Sharron's office this morning to learn a little more about coral reef biology and the different values of reefs, and I am telling him about my outing with Devon Ludwig. Sharron tells me that when a visiting algae specialist wanted to see the most algae species on one dive, Larry took him diving near the end of the sewage outfall, and he agrees that the plant is clearly behind on maintenance. Sharron cautions, "Sewage is *a* problem for corals, but not *the* only problem. The crown-of-thorns starfish, which eats coral, has only two predators, the Triton's trumpet snail and the humphead wrasse. Both are overfished. Even the guys who work for me want to collect Triton's trumpets if they see them. That's why we have so many starfish killing coral."

A dive guide who has just arrived to drop off some scuba tanks chimes in, saying he believes he now sees excess algae caused by sewage way out in German Channel, more than ten miles from the outfall and a favorite dive site for seeing manta rays. The dive guide continues, "The increase in the number of tourists also means feeding that many more, and they all want seafood."

Larry agrees, saying, "I was amazed at how many lobsters the big resort had on steak-and-lobster night. Where did they all come from?"

Larry Sharron is forty-one. He looks twenty-six. For a guy who spends most of his time out in the punishing sun and salt, his youthful appearance is especially striking. It might be his unconventional approach to living. A yo-yo rests beside the computer on his desk. A big Mickey Mouse clock waves away time. And in a big cage Larry keeps a large and friendly pet fruit bat, whose mother was shot for soup by locals.

But Sharron has a serious side as well. Larry's office at the station is loaded with computers, electronic equipment, and aquariums harboring toxic fish and venomous sea urchins. The more poisonous, the more promising. The idea behind his work is that some of these animals' chemical poisons may make good compounds for drugs. "Many of the animals on reefs that we are very interested in—for instance, sponges—are soft-bodied, brightly colored, and living out in the open; yet many of them aren't preyed upon, and that is because they have chemical defenses. The defensive poisons in many organisms kill cells indiscriminately. The National Cancer Institute is looking for chemicals that are not poisonous to cells in general, but might be specifically poisonous to cancer cells or viruses. The odds are about one in ten thousand that the people working with us will find a chemical with drug potential in any one of these samples. Still, with the tremendous biodiversity around this region, that's not bad odds."

Larry was born in Morocco and raised in New York. He began his professional career at age thirteen, with a part-time job at the Amazon Aquarium in Sheepshead Bay, Brooklyn. He went to California in his late teens, to work for an aquarium-fish importer and wholesaler. The importer wasn't happy with fishes he was getting from Indonesia, so he sent Sharron there to oversee some of the collecting of fish from their natural environment. Larry says, "With each move, I was working my way toward the source." He remained on the Indonesian island of Biak for about a year, building and running an aquarium-fish collecting operation, and did another such stint on the Pacific island of Ponape, catching small bright reef fishes with fine nets and exporting them for the living room aquariums of the developed world. With that experience under his belt, he met a tropical-fish wholesaler who was interested in setting up an operation in Palau, and Sharron drew up a plan and went to work.

He had been in Palau three years when the foundation job opened, putting Larry's skills and considerable knowledge within immediate reach of a different clientele. Though he is based in Palau and works here much of the time, his work now takes him throughout the entire tropical Pacific and Indian Oceans. When he is not traveling, other people come to him to avail themselves of his guidance. An erasable calendar on the office wall shows that this month his visitors will include various scientists from several continents, the world-renowned underwater photographers Al Giddings and Stan Waterman, and Jean-Michel Cousteau (a chip off the old Jacques).

Ultimately, millions of us might benefit from Sharron's work. Many of us have seen, on television, underwater footage for which Larry was the photographers' guide. And it is possible that one of the creatures he collects will hold the key to new drugs that we might use.

This morning Larry is scheduled to bring a visiting German scientist from the University of Heidelberg's Zoologisches Institut out to observe and photograph two types of coral communities. The gentleman's business card reads:

PROF. DR. DR. HAJO SCHMIDT

Dr. Dr. Schmidt has come here to photograph sea fans and intertidal corals. Larry's two assistants lug our dive gear and photographic equipment out to the dock, load it into the foundation's outboard skiff, get the engine started, and untie the lines. The morning sun is already hot and strong. I smear myself liberally with sunblock. So does Larry. Hajo (pronounced HI-o) says he'll do without it. Hajo shows a strong set of tendencies toward doing things his own way. In fact, Larry's supervisors on the island of Chuuk consider Hajo's diving practices so reckless they have given Larry strict orders not to dive with him if his plans are dangerous—despite the first rule of diving: Never Dive Alone.

Larry has in mind a place that he thinks will satisfy Hajo's needs. As we leave the harbor's island maze, Sharron points to a channel between two landmasses and says to Hajo, "There is a place in there called Ngerkuul Pass that you might be interested in seeing sometime. It has possibly more ascidians than anywhere else in Palau." Larry explains that the very narrow pass forces the currents to make such a tight squeeze—thereby increasing their velocity—that organisms in the pass experience higher than normal nutrient bathing. In addition to numerous and diverse ascidians (sea squirts), the lovely and venomous rainbow urchin lives there. If your skin merely touches its spines their venom will sting you. Larry had one in a tank at the field station. Its spines, which appear to be strung with alternating yellow and purple beads, moved constantly as though powered by motors gone haywire. "There are also some pretty unusual sponges and a coral called *Stylaster* that normally grows in dark holes, but here it is all over the bottom in the open. That's the only place I've ever seen that. There is also a bull shark that lives there," he adds. Though usually not aggressive (like most sharks) bull sharks have nonetheless been the source of numerous attacks on humans in other parts of the world. "We've seen it twice, it's a very large one, and very . . . thick."

We run out into the open across a wide expanse of lagoon. I ask Dr. Dr. Schmidt about his area of interest. In his German accent he says, "My special field is the Anthozoa, and within the Anthozoa, the anemones." Hajo wants to see colonies of sea fans and black coral (a CITES-listed species). He has come to Palau—as we have, as has every tourist—because of its very high diversity of living things. He says Palau's physical configuration is unique: So many islands make for a highly structured and physically diverse lagoon system of greatly varying depths, not a simple shallow one as for most islands.

We approach some rocks exposed to air on the reef as the tide drops. Though we are still inside the lagoon, an underwater gorge runs from here to the ocean via a break in the fringing reef. Larry chose this site for Hajo because the drop-off goes down, in steps, to eight hundred feet. Hajo wants to dive deep to observe and photograph assemblies of the gorgonian (soft coral) communities. The rest of us have less ambitious goals. Matt, Larry's Palauan right-hand man, whose main job today is to prep equipment before the dive, wants to spear some fish for dinner, and Larry and I will go to moderate depths to collect a particular sponge species and photograph its natural associates.

Sharron, perhaps revealing another part of the secret of his youthful looks, is in no hurry. Time abounds for what is needed. Though Larry grew up in New York, he operates on Island Time. He has also adopted the South Pacific custom of chewing betel nuts, and now he is sitting and taking a few moments to prepare a nut and enjoy its salubrious effects. With the nut wadded up in his mouth, he says—if I hear him correctly—that this place is named Babalukes, "lukes" meaning—if I understand him—reef, in Palauan.

While Larry spits a red slug of betel juice overboard and watches it get swept toward the greater Pacific, Hajo and I begin prepping our gear. Hajo, apparently a minimalist, has in fact almost no gear, only mask, fins, tank, and camera. No wetsuit. No buoyancy compensator. No dive computer. Even his bathing suit is so brief that the creamy-white part of him it reveals conjures the phrase "Crack kills." His butt is sunburn bait if I've ever seen it. Much more hazardously, he consults no dive tables for safe duration at intended depth, nor does he have a preplanned dive profile. Dangerous. Dangerous as hell.

Hajo has been diving for four decades, and one day, years ago, he came very close to having his diving career, his scientific career, and his life significantly shortened. The release valve on a new buoyancy compensator stuck closed and would not allow the escape of any air. It ballooned him to the surface uncontrollably in a great rush from a great depth. Nitrogen that had been dissolved in his body under pressure began bubbling out of solution, fizzing his bloodstream and jamming his joints with excruciating pain. After he got to the surface he took another tank and—though people are told never to do this—immediately dove again to repressurize and gas off some of the nitrogen. He believes this saved his life, and though he became temporarily paralyzed from the neck down, his paralysis eventually dissipated, leaving him with only a slight limp, a distrust for equipment, and a perverse disdain for precisely the precautions that can prevent another attack of the bends. "I have learned that, for *my* body, the important thing is just to come up slowly." Let's hope so.

We slip over the side. I stick my head underwater and take my first look at a china shop of corals, including many expansively spreading and intricately structured table corals—all very delicate, all intact. Breathtaking. I raise my head and look at Larry. My reaction to the sight of the corals must be easily readable even through my face mask, because he simply says, "No one dives here."

Hajo quickly swims out to the edge of the shallows and disappears immediately, diving alone. Larry, Matt, and I swim out along the surface to the edge, where the flat plane of the reef transforms into a vertical wall. We stop for a moment, treading. Larry and I exchange our snorkels for our regulators, and prepare to dive. Remaining vertical, I slip below the surface, pushing up with my hands until I'm about ten feet down. At this point, the water pressure squeezes me just enough to negate my buoyancy, and I begin a slow freefall along the wall. At thirty feet I turn and swim headfirst, following Larry and keeping an eye on Matt. Matt, snorkeling without scuba gear, splits off and levels out when he spots a yellow-dot trevally approaching. A medium-size bumphead parrotfish trails the trevally by a short distance as they both approach Matt. More desirable for eating and once common, bumphead parrotfish are now rare because they had the unusual habit of sleeping in very shallow water, where they were easily speared in the moonlight. I'm pleading telepathically for the parrot to be spared rather than speared this time. As soon as the trevally gets within range, Matt pulls the trigger, the spear glides through its head and brain, and the trevally stops dead. Larry, through his mouthpiece, offers a muffled, "Nice shot!" Matt surfaces. I follow Larry down about another sixty feet before he stops.

The reds on my equipment have gone black. Some sponges and encrusting organisms are showing pale, murky yellows. At ninety-nine feet, the only bright colors are blues. Some of the more delicate corals appear as a bright blue filigree. I check my depth gauge, air, and remaining time. I'm feeling fine and everything seems fine.

Larry finds the sponge he's looking for, takes some photographs of it growing in place, and begins collecting. He needs two kilograms—about four and a half pounds—and the sponge is tiny. It is not a sponge one could use in the tub. It grows thinly, encrusted on shells, and only a little bit can be scraped at a time. Slowly the samples in the plastic collecting bags accumulate. I'm really enjoying this dive, feeling perfectly comfortable and riveted by the subtle life growing around me. Larry points out a long, thin, neon-blue nudibranch called a Chinese dragon, a kind of shell-less marine snail with fringelike external gills. Cool!

As little bits of the sponge accrue in the bags, I am trying to take a closer look around and become more observant in these unfamiliar surroundings. I begin noticing that although very subtle, the soft corals here are highly varied and much lovelier than I had previously realized. Also quite interesting, now that I'm seeing, are organisms looking like clear tubes and tiny glass vases, and others like shriveled fingers, belonging to a group called tunicates. Colonies of clear cylindrical tunicates bearing thin blue stripes and yellow rims remind me of a picture in a book that I had as a child, depicting some of Earth's earliest life, in ancient seas. This flashback brings a strong and pleasurable wave of nostalgia. Virtually everything I am seeing is new to me, stuff I've seen only in books, if at all. Larry continues to pick and glean, traveling slowly. At first this place looked nondescript and gloomy, and I am delighted now that I have made the mental transition to being focused on the life around me instead of on my gear. I am breathing easily, floating, feeling rhapsodized. Look at these little tubes growing! This is so-o-o cool! This is *way* cool! Forget Blue Hole; I think *this* may be my best dive. This is wonderful, and I've never felt better.

The sudden sound of beeping is calling me to a somewhat confused attention. It is Larry's computer. I check my mechanical depth gauge. It says 60 feet, but I'm sure we are deeper, around a hundred. I look at my computer. It's depth display reads: "160 FT." Slowly I realize that the circular dial on my mechanical depth gauge, which maxes out at 100, has gone completely around once, passed 0, and gone on to 60. My computer is correct; we are at 160 feet. My depth gauges are functioning properly. My brain isn't. I had not checked my instruments for the last sixty feet of descent! It slowly dawns on me that I must have nitrogen narcosis, or "rapture of the deep," the dangerous euphoria produced by too much nitrogen in the blood, a fairly common symptom of being deep. I've never been this deep, so I'd never had it. Now I am this deep; now I have it. Certainly I have one of the main symptoms: not realizing I am "narked." Diagnosis complete. This rhapsody is about the closest I've come to killing myself.

My computer says we have one minute to get out of here or we'll have to make a decompression stop near the surface later. I show Larry. He is fully aware. Unlike me, he has been monitoring his instruments while working. He closes his sample bag and we begin rising, coming up slowly. The pressure lessens and I must readjust my ears and dump some air from my buoyancy compensator. We spot Matt, who has been hunting near the surface along the drop-off. He strikes another fish—a small grouper—and it pinwheels in frantic circles around the spear skewering its middle.

We continue ascending slowly up a wall adorned with spectacular fans, dusters, whips, white globular sponges, red, blue, orange, and yellow spreading crusting organisms, coral plates, and small fishes, especially damselfishes. We kick and rise steadily, up over the wall and onto the shelf, only about thirty feet deep, among a massive display of intricate corals. Larry begins pointing at some coral rubble, trying to get Matt's attention. I'm staring right where he's pointing, three feet away, wondering what he's pointing at. Matt dives to us and fires, and a smallish fish explodes on the spear. It is a crocodile fish, about fifteen inches long. Its camouflage is extraordinary—as are Larry's eyes.

A few minutes later, Matt zeroes in on a cowfish about a foot and a half long, with its odd, boxy, armored body and little bovine horns. Caught up in the hunting moment, I hold my breath, hoping for a hit. His spearpoint strikes the cowfish just above its right eye and rams in along its spine, coming out near its tail. The fish, nowhere near dead, jitters on the spear, breathing rapidly as though hyperventilating. With its fused teeth, it looks as though it is saying the letter F over and over. As would I, if I were this poor fish. Enough of this.

Back on the boat, Larry puts onto the deck three plastic bags full of slimy stuff that might eventually save millions of lives. While various parts of the reef have various values to various creatures, this unprepossessing bit of the reef might prove priceless to humans. Odds are against it, but when the magic day comes, this is how it will start.

I wonder out loud what might have happened to Hajo. Matt says that he surfaced briefly for another tank, and went back down again. No surface interval, no dive table, nothing. Dangerous as hell.

About ten minutes after we board, Dr. Dr. Schmidt surfaces, still alive and kicking. Larry asks him how deep he went.

He says, "Eighty."

Larry says, "Feet or meters?"

"Mee-tahs," he replies in his German accent. He continues, almost wistfully, "There were the gorgonians" (*Zhere were ze gorgonyanz.*) Then he volunteers, "I haff only been diving here twice on this trip, but since my last trip twenty years ago, my impression is that the place has much more algae. And I can state that the fish are much smaller. And fewer."

We head toward the next location, a tidal flat along a shoreline. As we are nearing some shallow patch reefs, Larry says to Hajo, "This place right here has a lot of *Goniopora stokesii*." Dr. Dr. Schmidt, replying with engaged comprehension, says, "No kidding! Right here?" Larry explains to me that this hard coral is among the very few that reproduce by budding. I nod, trying to catch up to the flow of the conversation. He promises to show it to me.

With the boat near shore under a spectacularly fractured rock grotto in a steep jungled slope, we relax for a few minutes before snorkeling on the coral flats. Then Sharron and I slip into the water with our masks and flippers, leaving Hajo on deck. Hajo wants to wait here for the shallower flats to become exposed at low tide, because he is interested in the adaptations that allow some kinds of corals to withstand periodic air exposure under the hot tropical sun. Mostly, he explains, they seem to survive by exuding a mucus that traps water, keeping them moist. What I am interested in is how *he* plans to survive *his own* exposure.

I kick along the shallows and stop to watch a sea urchin walking along at a surprisingly rapid boogie. While looking at the corals and the damselfishes, I notice some persistent, faint, grunting noises. Suddenly something strikes my forehead and I'm amazed to see that it is a four-inch damselfish of uncommon courage. Watching this distressing damsel in astonishment, I realize that the sounds I've been hearing might be the damselfish themselves. I surface and ask Larry, "Are these damsels growling and barking at me?" He takes the snorkel from his mouth and says, "Yes. They are."

Soon Larry is busy collecting a small sample of a certain kind of fine-leafed algae. I say to him, "You have an entire tank full of that at the station."

"Same genus, different species."

I continue kicking along, moving into slightly deeper water, and a minute or so later Larry comes over and places into the palm of my hand a soft, slimy creature. He says, "This is the species that's been found potentially active against cancer. You might be holding a cure for cancer right here." He plucks a feather star off its coral perch and searches it visually, telling me he is looking for a crab-like crustacean called a squat lobster that changes its color depending on what species of crinoid it is living in. I begin to realize that Larry Sharron is one of the finest naturalists I have ever met. Perhaps the finest. And I have known some fine ones. Here in the center of marine biological diversity, where heavyweight academicians specialize in particular subgroups of obscure organisms, Sharron's working command of taxonomy across such a mind-boggling diversity of living things is profoundly humbling.

I am drifting in seven feet of water with my attention focused on something squirmy when Larry kicks over and says, "A big black-tip shark just swam by. You didn't see it, I guess."

"No, I didn't see it at all. What was it doing?"

"Sizing up your butt, I guess."

Larry and Hajo and I spend the next couple of hours in the desiccating heat, watching the tide drain and photographing the adaptations of the corals.

When we climb back aboard, Hajo bends over under the hot sun to put his camera into its bag, revealing for those of us behind him an angry-looking half "moon" the color of a broiled lobster. That looks painful. Sharron stifles a laugh. I quickly snap a candid close-up.

As we are heading back to the dock, Larry points out several long-line boats and a large building owned by a tuna fishing company. He's worried about the ability of long-liners to deplete large areas. He had been on an expedition to a place off Papua New Guinea called Eastern Fields, a sunken atoll more than a hundred miles offshore. The person who took them there said that there were once so many sharks that as soon as the Zodiac stopped, they came up to investigate. A year after Taiwanese long-liners worked the area over, Larry dived there for six days without seeing a single shark. I tell him of the damage long-liners have done in my own waters to swordfish and marlin, that tuna longlines are catching enough albatrosses to endanger some species of the great birds, that leatherback turtles appear headed for extinction in the Pacific because so many die on longlines, that I've heard China is building a thousand new tuna long-liners, and that France and Spain are also putting immense new long-liners onto the world's oceans.

When we get back to Larry's lab, he and Matt process the sponge sample, dividing it into subsamples and logging it on data sheets. Larry's eye is exceptional. Matt brings out the sponges from the bags he has collected. Larry looks at one bit of encrusted shell and says to him, "Scrape this part away. It's another sponge species." When I express disbelief at how he can tell one small encrusting bit of sponge from another, he says, "Look here, if you squeeze this one, it's sticky, but not mucusy. And only this sponge has symbionts, mostly small brittle stars like these." He is pointing to a couple of small wriggling creatures.

He makes up several sample bags and vouchers: one for the taxonomist, a woman from the British Museum; one for the Smithsonian; one for the National Cancer Institute; and one for the collection here at the laboratory. Depending on the type of creature, samples are sent to different parts of the world for identification: sponges to London, ascidians to Paris, and so on, wherever the leading taxonomist in that field is located. The taxonomist will either identify the organism or, if it is previously unknown, formally publish a description of it as a new species in a technical scientific journal. Larry collects each species only once, but the diversity here is so enormous that this alone is a full-time job. "Our work will probably double the number of known invertebrate species from this area."

The National Cancer Institute people will grind up the sample they receive and, with the aid of a computer, test extracts of the sample against sixty types of cancer cells and the AIDS virus. Larry says, "We enter into an agreement we call a letter of intent, between the governments and the National Cancer Institute. We're only the collecting agents, and we can never financially gain from anything we collect. Let's just say—best-case scenario—that I collect something here and it turns out to cure AIDS. The Coral Reef Research Foundation gets *nothing* for that. And the host country—in this case Palau—*must* receive economic benefits from any discoveries made in their territory."

Larry has photographed each species he has collected, and as he and Matt are working on today's samples I look through the voluminous albums of color slides cataloging each species whose acquaintance they have had the pleasure of. I express my surprise that there seem to be more than two hundred sponge species and close to the same number of other invertebrate animals. Larry answers, "There are a lot more sponges than people thought." That's an understatement.

Incapable of understanding how Sharron can keep them all straight, I blurt out, "If you collect this fairly nondescript-looking sponge one time, and you go through hundreds that look similar, how do you know you hadn't collected it before? How can you remember that you collected—. I mean, you have to have hundreds and hundreds of species in your head and—"

"It's like anything else."

Somehow, I don't *think* so. I pause at one slide of exotic-looking creatures that seem slightly familiar. "Are these nudibranchs?"

"They're pleurobranchs. Their gills are under a flap here. Nudibranchs have external gills."

"Right. Of course."

When I leave Larry, my head is full of images of strange creatures, of the astonishing diversity in healthy reef communities, and of the importance of these living treasure troves we have yet to unlock.

Strolling the waterfront some time later, I bump into Gerald Heslinga, a minor hero across the South Pacific, a brilliant aquaculturist who, while working at the

Palau government's Division of Marine Resources, developed a method for raising giant clams in captivity. His work has attracted attention in numerous magazines. Thanks to Heslinga's methods, cultured giant clams had replaced the
overfished and severely depleted wild giant clams for the local markets. And for
every one sold by the project he ran, they transferred clams to the wild or
donated them to breeding projects in other countries around the Pacific. It was a
model program, filling a real conservation need both locally and over a large
region, while making its own way in the commercial market, attracting investment, providing food, and turning a profit.

Heslinga has recently been fired in what seems like an ethnic purge within
Palau's Department of Marine Resources. Palau's new, pro-Japan government
appears less than fond of what it seems to view as Western notions of conservation. It has installed as new head of the Division of Marine Resources a man who
seems to disdain most foreign conservationists. Heslinga was the first and most
prominent of the Western marine conservation workers to be sacked by the new
administration, and his termination caused the immediate withdrawal of several
hundred thousand dollars in overseas grants that had been made to the Palauan
government in support of his work. This was not viewed as a loss, because the
new division chief wanted to end the project anyway. The new chief also terminated the country's memorandum of understanding with the U.S.-based Nature
Conservancy. Volunteers, who couldn't really be fired, were simply pushed out.

Heslinga says that the Marine Resources people are now selling off the breeding stock of giant clams to Hong Kong for meat, for a quarter of what they are
worth. With the supply to Palauan restaurants cut off, the locals are starting to
go after wild clams again.

I'd been told that, as a result of Gerry's work, Palau has more clams than anywhere else in the Pacific. "Here you see giant clams all over the place now, even
at the end of the dock," one person told me. "If you go anywhere else, there's a
lack of clams." One man told of being in the Caroline Islands recently when the
person he was with came across a clam and began exclaiming, because it was the
first clam he had seen in a long, long time. He proceeded to cut the meat out.
"Although Palau still has more clams than anywhere else, I've been seeing a lot
of newly emptied shells recently while I'm out diving."

Heslinga is now planning to establish a coral gene bank in Hawaii for commercial cultivation for the aquarium trade. Listening to him, one might con-
clude that the new division chief is a one-man anticonservation force.

But perhaps conservation really is a Western perspective. Most of the complaining
I have heard so far has been from westerners, in fact. Maybe it's time I hear what
the local Palauans—those of them who don't cater to foreign tourists—think.

After dark, Larry Sharron takes me to see a man with an unpronounceable
Palauan name whose nickname is Angel. Larry describes him as "a one-man fish-

ing army," the son of a legendary fisherman. He has gone completely around Palau in the vessel he wrests his living with: a twelve-foot boat with a fifteen-horsepower engine. He has been a commercial fisherman in Saipan as well as Palau, worked on tuna boats, and spent three years with Larry collecting aquarium fish. He's now forty years old, and has been fishing, as he says, "for a long time."

I ask what makes him such a formidable fish killer. He says, "My mind is with the fish. When I am line fishing, my mind is on the bottom with the bait. I know which fish is at my bait by how it is biting it." He says, "Like the big red snappers, they take slowly. If you strike too quick, you will miss them. Some other fish, you have to strike very quick, so you have to know what kind of fish is at your bait."

Nowadays his main form of commercial fishing is free diving to spear fish at night. He usually fishes a tide—six hours. "If there are not so many fish, I will fish till morning," he says. But if there is a big low tide at about nine at night, and no moon—"*That* is the best."

I ask him to compare the fishing today with that when he was a child. After a long, uncomfortable pause, he says, "Every year, less fish. Going with my father was fun, we fished with line only and never dived. There were plenty. We used to fish right in front of Koror town. The corals are dead there now. There are still places with plenty of fish like before, near Ollei, near Kayangle in the far north, and near Angaur. I usually fish outside Ngemelis and Ulong. There are not so many fish there and the coral is dying there also, but I go there because of shelter and closeness."

I ask why the coral is dying and the fish are fewer. He says, "In some places, some people are still using dynamite. Each blast makes a hole in the coral about ten or fifteen feet in diameter. Fish come up stunned or dead. Some Palauans are expert at it, and are too smart to get caught. And they are still using chlorine to poison fish down in Peleliu." Bob Johannes had also told me about the problems in Peleliu.

Devon Ludwig has arranged an audience with Yutaka M. Gibbons for me. His title is Ibedul, "the head," paramount chief—Palau's traditional king, essentially. He is fifty-one years old, of medium height and a tad hefty, dark-skinned, curly haired, wearing a newly pressed blue shirt. Devon had told me that the Ibedul is "the shrewdest, smartest Palauan that I know, although he doesn't come across that way."

He certainly doesn't. For the entire hour and a half that I am talking with him, he has a pair of sunglasses dangling off one ear.

As he sinks into a big, gray, fake-leather chair, he is ranting. "The rich are going to be very rich, and the poor will be fighting over crumbs, the people cheating each other, like in Philippines. Young people have problems with alcohol and other drugs. In our own culture, was peace and respect. The most impor- tant cause of all these problems is that leadership doesn't pay attention to its own people. We grew accustomed to handouts from the United States. Now, elected officials are only concerned about lining their own pockets, increasing their busi- ness connections in the U.S., Japan, Taiwan, Hong Kong, Australia, and Arabia. So, conservation and preservation for our beautiful culture and land and ocean is going away every day. I don't want us to become like Japan and America. There, the oxygen is less than the carbon monoxide, and there are no trees. They have to be planting trees inside their house, and on their balconies. These tourists come here because they're frustrated in their homeland with the corporate jungle. So the future of Palau for tourism is very much connected to our resources. But now in Palau, everything is money, money, money, money. Very bad attitude. This place is going to get like Hawaii and New York. Greed is turning Palau into an ugly place."

Devon had told me that as a teenager the Ibedul was such an accomplished chicken thief that people began moving all their chickens under their houses, figuring they could hear anything that happened through the floorboards. But he became so crafty at it that he was able to sneak under a house, slide his fingers under a chicken, and lift it out so gingerly it would not wake up. He was ban- ished to Ollei, to live with his uncle. It was a three-hour boat ride up the coast, and he felt that he had been deposited at the end of the world. After a year he became so homesick and repentant that he wrote home, begging forgiveness. To make amends and show respect for his mother, he began volunteering to help women in all of their tasks and chores, and he has become a champion of women's causes. Women are traditionally very powerful in Palau's matriarchal society and, to this day, his reputation as a helper of women is the root of his support among the diminishing pool of traditionalists.

And the erosion of tradition worries him. "Just because the U.S. has imposed a legislative system of government doesn't mean it can replace tradition," he says. "In traditional leadership, life tenancy of a chief provides consistency—as long as he continues to have the community's support and doesn't do anything to get himself removed. I believe that system has a lot more to offer the people than the revolving door of Western politics, where elected office is used to gain choice positions at the front of the business trough."

Maybe this guy is shrewder than he looks, after all.

Another Palauan perspective comes from Minoru Ueki, a man of culture and refinement. "In Palauan society, before money, we always had enough from the ocean or the land," he says. "Now, people can make money by taking more than they need, by cutting down all the trees or catching all the fish. Money is threat- ening our cultural stability. We are choking off our future, including our future options *for making money.* Your country is so developed that it has no places left as beautiful as Palau. Your people come here, so our conservation is not just for us and not just for our generation, but for many people throughout the world. When Japanese schoolkids come here for the first time, see fish swimming in clear water, see the beautiful colors of the waters and the islands, they get very excited. Their only view of fish before has been on a plate. Also the sense of space for overcrowded Japanese is impressive. In Tokyo, it is dizzying. Too many people. What are they all doing?"

Ueki, a retired physician, born in Palau of Japanese extraction, seems quite aware of major influences in other cultures. On his desk is the *Oxford Book of Quotations,* the *Executive's Book of Quotations,* the *Book of American Proverbs, Great Ideas Today* (last year's edition), and the Victoria's Secret catalog.

"One thing is certain," he continues. "Twenty years ago, I could go out and in one day catch enough fish for my family for the week. This is now impossible." (A government biologist with the Division of Marine Resources, Theo Isamu, had told me much the same, saying, "Fishermen younger than I think I am exaggerating, but in high school twenty years ago I could catch big bumphead parrotfish right near the dock. I could get two hundred pounds of fish in one day. Now you would be lucky to catch fifteen.")

Ueki continues, "Yet the government wants unlimited growth and unlimited tourism. The businesspeople want more direct flights, bigger planes coming, and more big hotels. We now have about thirty thousand tourists a year. The government wants to expand this to three hundred thousand. It scares me! There will not be enough to go around.

"The key to our culture is thinking about others and sharing. We have no beggars here. But today a gap is opening in Palau with the rich getting richer and the poor, poorer. Just like in big developed countries. I've been to Washington, D.C.—a beautiful city with the monuments to the history of the young country. I drove from New York through Connecticut in the fall when the trees were their most beautiful colors and I thought, 'How beautiful; how can an American want to come to Palau where it is so hot all the time?' And the snow: I loved walking in snow. But to see such poor people among the rich, it's hard for me to comprehend the United States, with people homeless in rich cities."

"Dismal," mutters Bob Johannes. The utter downpour pelting us is raising a hissing white noise from the water's surface along Koror's waterfront this morning.

Dismal in more ways than one. The boat is late. The new Division of Marine Resources chief—the same bureaucrat who fired Heslinga and others—has prohibited Dr. Johannes from using the government dock alongside Johannes's research-equipment locker and office, so all the research gear has been tediously trucked to this distant pier. We hope that the boat driver can find us standing here, soaking up the scenery.

With nothing to do but wait in the rain, I tell Johannes that I am not sure how to reconcile the teeming schools of big fishes I have seen with the locals' assessments that the fish are down in numbers. I'm trying to understand, I say, whether the world is better or worse than my impression of it.

Dr. Johannes says, "Probably both. There are still some great places. But many knowledgeable people with deservedly weighty reputations are reporting a virtual absence of big fish where they were abundant a decade or two ago. As a scientist, I can tell you this: It pays to listen to the locals on these islands."

Listening to locals is why we are here. During Bob Johannes's first visit to Palau in the mid-1970s, local fishermen taught him about fifty fish species whose spawning migrations are linked to moon phases. The amazing thing was that this was more than *twice* the number of lunar-spawning species then known by biologists for the *entire world*.

Some Pacific Island cultures accumulated encyclopedic practical knowledge about marine life, which Western science has generally studiously ignored. For a decade and a half, Bob Johannes tried unsuccessfully to get the Australian government fisheries agency he worked for interested in following up on what the Palauans had taught him, studying spawning migrations of commercially important reef fishes. But the very notion that reef fish migrated to spawn went against a firmly established and dogmatically held misconception that reef fishes were sedentary.

Fishermen all over the region didn't have to be convinced of the practical importance of understanding breeding movements. They knew. Many reef fishes converge from wide areas and gather in large groups to spawn, and targeting spawning aggregations can get you an awful lot of fish in a very short time. Because almost all the large reef fishes spawn in groups, understanding spawning behavior is key to understanding their vulnerability to overfishing, and to successfully managing fishing for these species.

Though Johannes's insights failed to convince his colleagues at the time, his writings won him the Pew Charitable Trusts' Scholars Award in Conservation and the Environment in 1993. He used the cash prize as start-up money, resigning his post with the Australian government's scientific and research organization to begin working on issues he'd yearned for so long to explore. Now he focuses his research on helping local people learn the breeding biology of important food fishes, thus arming villagers with knowledge they need for determining how many fish they can take consistently over the long term, without depleting the population.

The need is urgent, because there is a new international trade in live fishes driven by demand from markets opening in south China. "And," says Johannes, "the live-fish traders understand breeding biology far better than the scientific community. I feel it's *really* important. Fishermen complain the fish are much scarcer than in the past. What we're learning will translate into application within a very short time, not just in Palau, but in villages and countries throughout the Indo-Pacific region.

"Handled right, the live-fish trade could be wonderful for Pacific islanders; they make three or four times as much money for each live fish as for a dead one. But right now this trade is devastating reef fishes in Micronesia, the Philippines, Papua New Guinea, Indonesia, Australia's Great Barrier Reef, and elsewhere, before anyone in the scientific and management community even knows where they breed. But the fishing interests sure know."

There are two main problems: overfishing in spawning grounds, which depletes populations, and fishing with cyanide. Johannes works on both problems in several countries. Palau has so far been spared the devastation of cyanide fishing, and Johannes concentrates intensive field efforts here.

Today he needs to move equipment to a village called Ollei (the place to which the Ibedul had, as a boy, been banished). There, Johannes's assistants, government collaborators, and villagers are cooperatively studying grouper breeding populations at important fishing sites.

The project encompasses several modest objectives that are virtually unique in the world. One, estimating local population size, entails actually counting breeding groupers on their underwater spawning grounds during peak lunar mating periods. In addition, by tagging fish, the workers can learn whether the same fish spawn each month, how far the animals disperse between spawning, and whether they visit other breeding colonies. "We designed quick and easy methods we can leave with fishermen to monitor their own sites," Johannes says. "Some scientists take information and give nothing back. We wanted to give control and independence to the local people by helping them get the knowledge they need."

Johannes's work is inspired partly by sheer scientific curiosity and partly as tribute to his mentor Ngiraklang and other Palauan fishermen who taught him so much about the biology of tropical fishes. "One thing Chief Ngiraklang said has always stuck with me: 'The trouble started when the chiefs forgot that the most sacred thing of all is the people.' "

Bob Johannes is leading up to something: "There is more to be concerned about throughout the Pacific than its natural environment. There are its human inhabitants. Nature is capable of considerable healing, but I know of no shattered culture that has repaired itself. There are tens of millions of species of plants and animals on the planet. There are only a few thousand human cultures. When we lose a culture—for instance, when we lose an island culture because of industrial overfishing—we are losing something more precious even than a species of plant or coral. But westernization, militarization, and industrialization are erasing human cultures proportionately much faster than we are exterminating species."

Johannes sees time running out. And his patience is going with it. "The days are past when you could afford to be the kind of elitist researcher I was when I got out of school. My attitude was, 'Why do *I* need to get into conservation? That's not science.' Well, the world changed. Reefs are collapsing all over the

Pacific and Southeast Asia. Dynamite fishing is a picnic compared to the effects of cyanide fishing for the live-fish markets. While we are producing nice, neat, well-documented articles for our fellow biologists, another thousand reefs have been wiped out by cyanide."

Most aspects of the cyanide fishery Johannes is referring to are too bizarre to be guessed. Divers armed with squeeze bottles chase fish into coral crevices and caves, then squirt "medicine" into the holes. In a few moments, crazed fish start looping out. This medicine is not the snooze juice Steve Johnson used to calm young salmon and steelhead, nor the quinaldine used by researchers for mildly anaesthetizing little damselfish on coral reefs so they can be marked and let go. This "medicine" is the same sodium cyanide used to execute prisoners. Think of cyanide as "the death penalty," because its use amounts to execution of the reefs.

If a particularly desired animal the diver has dosed does not come out, the diver begins ripping away pieces of live coral, widening the hole enough to grasp the stricken creature. Valuable fish are brought quickly to the surface. Others—one study says 90 percent of those overcome by the clouds of cyanide—are unmarketable, and they sink or float away, missing in action and presumed dead. Of those captured, many revive and are held in floating net pens on quiet, remote island reefs under the dazing, dozing tropic sun. Here they remain for days or weeks, awaiting sale to exporters who come around periodically, buy the fish, and provide divers with the "medicine" or "magic powder" that works a sorcerer's spell.

Day by day, diver by diver, quart bottle by quart bottle, hundreds of tons of cyanide are poisoning reef systems. Cyanide is widely available, though at more remote outposts fishers say the potency is lower, indicating that the middlemen are cutting it with inert filler, like the drug dealers they are.

Cyanide is a broad-spectrum poison that acts on enzyme systems involved in respiratory metabolism. Exposure to it damages the liver, stomach, intestines, and reproductive organs. Fish that do not die right away from the acute toxicity usually succumb from complications several months later. One reason colorful tropical aquarium fishes from the Indian Ocean or Pacific often die a few weeks after they arrive in your living room tank is that many of them, too, were taken with cyanide.

Even worse than the fish it kills, cyanide—as fishers who use it will invariably tell you—kills the corals. Laboratory tests show cyanide can be fatal to corals at concentrations *two hundred thousand times lower* than those in the fishermen's squirt bottles. Within seconds of exposure, coral polyps begin emitting a thick mucus, trying to purge the irritation. After a few hours the mucus disappears, and all seems well. A few weeks later, the corals are dead, their skeletons bright white. Soon they are greened over by algae. Because big coral heads can be several hundred years old, we can expect to see living corals of this size again no earlier than the year 2300, if recovery commences immediately. In geological time, that's not very long, but for us as persons, it's greater than forever. Killing corals, say Bob Johannes and fisheries economist Michael Riepen, has the same effect on a reef's fish and invertebrate community as clear-cutting trees has on forest animals: It destroys their habitat and they disappear. Another gold-laying goose lately gone.

Large transport boats take the fishes from their tropical Paradise-turned-prison-camp, winding through island channels out to open sea, where they often steam for weeks before the glassy tips of skyscrapers first tickle the horizon. From some islands, the fish are heavily sedated and flown to market. The big profit margins amply cover the costs of airfreighting the large volumes of sea-water needed for keeping the animals alive. By air or by sea, the captured fishes are destined for distant markets, primarily in the "People's Republic" of China (especially Hong Kong and the mainland's Special Economic Zones, getting their first nip of real capitalism and booming like supersonic cash boxes). Other big markets are Taiwan, Singapore, and countries with large, affluent Chinese population centers (such as Indonesia, where the 4 percent of the populace that is Chinese accounts for an astonishing 70 percent of the country's private economic activity).

Like the moon's effect on tides, these markets exert tremendous pull on the world's oceans.

An active cyanide user doses fifty coral heads a day, about 225 days a year. In the Philippines alone, some three thousand cyanide users squirt tens of millions of coral heads each year. At this point, just stopping cyanide fishing would be a victory. Never mind catch limits. Never mind quota restrictions. An unrestricted hook-and-line fishery—what we consider uncontrolled, unmanaged fishing in the West—would seem a blessing in the Indo-Pacific, compared to what's now happening here.

Perversely, trade in live reef fish could be an economic blessing to many small island communities if done without destroying the coral habitats. But meanwhile, coral reefs collapse under the poison pressure, and small, family-owned boats are being shoved out by larger, more seaworthy company vessels able to steam several weeks to distant grounds, stay at sea for months, and return with up to twenty tons of live fishes swimming in their holding tanks.

Driving this "vast and expanding ecological tragedy," as Johannes puts it, is a market in which consumers are willing to pay over eighty dollars a pound for certain prized fishes. For the ultimate, consider a plate of Napoleon wrasse lips—just the lips—at $250 per serving.

Hong Kong, as I've mentioned, is the largest live fish importer. Until recently, the animals involved were from freshwater or local coral reefs. As Hong Kong and south China's population has grown increasingly affluent, a taste for the exotic and the new ability to pay for it has created insatiable demand. And the fishery seeking to serve and exploit that demand is ranging ever farther afield. In the late 1960s, Hong Kong fishers, using mostly hook and line, began bringing back live reef fishes from the South China Sea—practically their backyard. Consumer response to the colorful new varieties of live fishes was favorable in the extreme.

In the next few years the fishers expanded south, to the Paracel and Spratly Islands. Someone in this fishery started using cyanide around the early 1970s (aquarium-fish collectors had been using it since the early '60s).

The trade in live reef fishes continued expanding outward from its Hong Kong epicenter, as closer reefs were fished bare and laid waste. By 1975, boats fishing for this market were thick among the Philippines' seven thousand islands, heavily using cyanide, causing extensive destruction to the reefs. By the late-1980s, the disease of cyanide addiction had spread to Indonesia, rapidly depleting fishes and inflicting major reef damage. In the early 1990s, the poison fishery invaded Papua New Guinea's extensive coral wilderness, with several Hong Kong companies systematically targeting grouper spawning colonies in a country utterly unequipped to monitor them. Then it spread east to the Solomon Islands. Then, like a strange coastal wildfire burning out of control, the immolation radiated more than three thousand miles west, to the twelve hundred islands of the Maldives archipelago off India. The fishery (including companies from mainland China) first got to the Maldives in 1993, and some fish populations began to crumble within a year. Though regulations there restrict fishing to hook and line, three Hong Kong cyanide boats were caught poaching in 1995.

No slowing of this expansion is in the cards. Increasing demand is coming primarily from southern China. Guangdong Province near Hong Kong is already a major market for live reef fish, and this trade will likely continue expanding throughout China. Until recently China had remained like a huge head at the edge of the ocean, resting its chin on the shore; but now the enormous, hungry mouth that is China is opening, tilting all the world's oceans toward it.

Indonesia now produces more than half the live reef fish in this commerce. But not all of Indonesia is still productive. The Indonesian Institute of Sciences says that only 7 percent of the country's coral reefs remain in good shape, 30 percent have been ruined, and the condition of the rest is critical. Dive boats report favorite reefs destroyed by cyanide. One dive operator returned to find his "most favorite reef in the world" dead and vacant. He told Johannes, "Not one nudibranch was moving." With many reefs already picked over, the poison fishery is rummaging through the remotest of the nation's seventeen thousand islands. Even some of the buyers, now having difficulty obtaining large Napoleon wrasses (freely exported, illegally) and big groupers, think Indonesia will be played out in just a few years. The presidents of both the Philippines and Indonesia have personally taken steps to stop the cyanide, but bribery and corruption of local officials is as common as dead coral.

Cyanide is extremely toxic when inhaled, ingested, or absorbed across the skin, and predictably, this fishery from hell claims human souls. It has killed fishers' family members who ate fish brought home in bags that had held cyanide. It has killed divers who swam through their own clouds of the stuff.

Cyanide divers also have other problems. As Johannes reminds me, in almost all these fishing communities, diving "accidents" cause additional suffering: "So many untrained, brutally exploited divers are dying to supply this growing market." People are given poorly maintained equipment and simply told to dive. No one bothers explaining the safety procedures that can keep divers healthy. Nearly every community involved in cyaniding has victims of the bends, which always involves pain, often entails paralysis, and can kill. In the Philippine town of Marinduque in 1993, thirty of the two hundred divers got the bends. Ten died. The killing and maiming mystifies most divers. They blame their aching joints on cold water or "ghosts of the sea" and say, "Either we go deep or starve." The very air divers breathe often carries contaminants. Antiquated compressors taken from paint sprayers generally have intake ports adjacent to their own exhaust vents, feeding divers a toxic mix containing carbon monoxide and unburned oil. One Philippine community worker saw divers spitting blood into the water, from which rings of oil began spreading on the surface (precisely the same problems torment many Caribbean fishers diving for spiny lobsters destined for U.S. restaurants). Some cyanide-fishing companies "insure" their divers, paying widows fifty dollars—less than the price of a pound of Napoleon wrasse in Hong Kong.

Let's get off cyanide a moment, because there are other things going on. People have long driven fish from cover by shattering corals, especially by fishing with explosives. During World War II, people began using hand grenades. My father did it as a G.I. in Fiji and on Bougainville Island, and the way he told it, you just threw the thing in, waited for the blast, and—*voilà!*—fish came bobbing up. What could be easier? A lot of people started using explosives, and doubtless they never thought that what they were doing to the coral below could possibly matter. When the war ended and grenades got scarce, a number of fishermen blew themselves up trying to pry the business material from abandoned explosives. Subsequently, bombs made from fertilizer, dynamite stolen from mines, and a variety of other volatile substances have been applied to the task of fishing.

All over the Pacific, waters have shaken, rattled, and rolled: Fiji, Micronesia, Chuuk, Vanuatu, the Samoas, the Marshall Islands, Ponape, Tonga, the Philippines—you get the picture. Over the years, while large numbers of dead and dying fish came floating to the surface, a lesser number of fingers, eyes, and arms went sinking to the bottom when blasting caps and bombs jumped the gun. In one survey, every fisherman interviewed had been injured by explosives.

But as long as people are willing to buy the fish, fishers with slim options consider it worth the risk. Don't think the answer is banning these things; they are already illegal in most places. The problem is detection, enforcement. The problem is apathy, ignorance. The problem is poverty, hunger. The problem is *too many* hungry mouths.

The lucrative live fish trade, if nothing else, is at least putting explosives out of favor because they kill fish that fetch more alive. But—catch-22—the cyanide replacing it is even worse for the reefs.

But let's put all these things in perspective. A lot of coral gets destroyed by natural events. Storms break up a *lot* of coral, though storms tend to ravage some areas repeatedly and leave others untouched for thousands of years. Coral can't tolerate freshwater, so heavy rain runoff can kill it. That happens more now as a result of bad logging, but some of it is natural. Coral *can* grow back. As long as the dead coral doesn't get so overgrown with algae in the meantime that recolonization and regrowth is precluded, a moderate amount of living coral cover may be back in as little as four or five decades.

Fishers aren't the only ones working the reefs. Some human activities are directed at extracting coral itself, for building roads or houses, or for shipping it to aquarium fanciers or jewelry makers or people who want a piece of coral on the bookshelf.

Added to all these other things, cyanide is triggering a new wave of deterioration for reefs throughout vast reaches of the tropics. Like fishers everywhere, cyanide users are endlessly creative. Some tuck a cyanide tablet into bait trolled for large fish such as tuna. Quickly immobilized after taking the bait, the fish can easily be hauled in. Another variation: Mix cyanide with a chum of finely ground fish, and when large numbers of fish that have eaten the poison come jittering to the surface, spasming and vomiting, they can be quickly netted. On the reef, regurgitated bait, still potent, may be taken by other fish. Or poisoned chum may sink to the bottom, where it settles on the coral, diffusing a deadly dose of cyanide to the tender polyps.

Despite the price to divers and the reef, fish taken with cyanide appear to be safe to consumers, so the trade flourishes.

By the way—a footnote here—cyanide is not the only modern, industrial poison. Chlorine bleach is also used, as are pesticides like paraquat from sugarcane farms.

Using cyanide and industrial chemicals for fishing might seem bizarre, but it's only a better mousetrap in many cultures. Throughout the Pacific, people have for centuries used poisons made from seeds, bark, leaves, fruit, roots, and the internal organs of strange, sluggish, bottom-dwelling animals called sea cucumbers. A girl might, for instance, place bundles of beaten derris bark (the active ingredient is rotenone) in holes in the coral, then easily spear the stunned fish rising toward the surface. She might squeeze the guts of the black sea cucumber *Holothuria atra* into coral crevices, with much the same result. So modern poisons are not really a *new* thing—just improved! In some places, new poisons go by the same name used for old poisons.

But as a recent study from the University of the South Pacific in Suva, Fiji, concluded, "although the use of destructive fishing methods is not new, nothing done before can compare with the intensity and magnitude of the impact of human fishing activity of recent times." Neither can anything in the past compare with the increasing numbers of people for whom fishing—any form of fishing—is an attractive alternative to starvation.

The Philippines, with the longest history of cyanide use, provides a clue to the logical outcome of all this. Its minister of agriculture and food has said, "The rapid depletion of our fishery resources due to destructive fishing practices, particularly explosives and poison, is threatening to aggravate problems of poverty." Small-scale rural fishers, the poorest people in the Philippines, have seen their daily catch drop from about twenty pounds of fish to about ten in the last few decades, and more and more are malnourished.

The rain intensifies—something I would not have thought possible. The boat is quite late. Bob Johannes gestures to the plume of red soil running into the harbor off a hillside road, saying, "You can see these islands bleeding from the air, all over the Pacific. Bad land clearing and bad road building take soil from being the basis of life to being a pollutant that kills corals." It's true elsewhere, too. In many areas throughout the Indian Ocean and Caribbean, for instance, reefs have been smothered and killed by silt following irresponsible logging or bad road building. Johannes is convinced that such sedimentation does more damage to coral reef communities than all other human activities combined. In the tropics as on the salmon rivers—as everywhere—erosion rates increase sharply when land is cleared. What we do on land affects the coastal ocean. Gravity is the enemy of the sea.

The red plume of rainwater wafts far into the harbor in the current, its mud contrasting with the blue-gray of the raindrop-pocked lagoon. Johannes looks down for a moment, and water runs off the tip of his nose and onto the pavement between his feet. "When I fly over an island that was solid green twenty years ago and I see that it's bleeding red because logging and roads have caused such enormous soil erosion, when I look at the rate at which the reefs are crumbling, and the tuna fisheries, the tropical forests—it's really depressing. But I don't stop and think about it too often. And I keep remembering, things can change in ways that no one could predict. Who would have thought that the Soviet Union would come apart the way it did? Once in a while, you make a gain here and you make a little nudge there and you feel you're at least not squandering your life away, accomplishing nothing."

Johannes strongly believes that the breakdown of local traditions abetted depletion of the reefs. Some Pacific Island peoples had a strong traditional conservation ethic that we would easily recognize: an awareness that they could deplete or otherwise damage their natural resources, coupled with a commitment to self-restraint. In many of these places, these traditional practices and proscriptions have weakened or been forcibly abolished.

As Bob says, a vast store of orally maintained information collected and used over centuries "has been hemorrhaging into oblivion because of a lack of appreciation of its value" by islanders themselves, as well as by Western scientists. Traditional knowledge is vanishing throughout much of Oceania as its possessors, unable to find anyone interested in receiving it, die out.

Johannes cites two interrelated processes: the imposition of new laws by colonial powers, and the introduction of money. Before Western contact, fishers throughout Oceania shared their catch with their fellow villagers, fully expecting to receive products of their fellows' labor in return. This may sound simplistic and primitive to people like us, whose most basic assumptions about the flow of goods and services refer to the exchange of money. We in developed countries have difficulty understanding the fundamental importance barter can have in cultural and societal cohesion. Think of it this way: Barter *was* their money system. Replacing barter with money was as disruptive to their culture as would be replacing our own use of money with trading fresh fish. Go into a grocery store and tell the clerk you'd like some lamb chops in exchange for two red snappers, and get her reaction on video.

Money does one thing that snappers—even red ones—can never do. It greatly extends the reach of markets and takes the insularity, circularity, and recycling of wealth out of local economies. It throws trade open to vast areas of geography. Bob Johannes has written,

> The introduction by Westerners of this money economy, the development of distant markets (i.e. district centers, foreign countries), and the consequent growth of the profit motive started the process of environmental decay around many Pacific islands. Under this fundamentally new economic order goods are bought and sold, not shared; the fisherman finds himself competing for money, and therefore for fish. In order to compete effectively he must buy better equipment and fish harder. This process is self reinforcing. The need to spend more money to get more efficient gear to harvest more intensively increases as the numbers of fish decrease. As equipment becomes more sophisticated, its price ultimately rises beyond the means of the average fisherman. A new profession, money lending, arises. The fisherman borrows to finance his purchases and he often falls into debt. Employment opportunities diminish as more efficient modern boats drive out native craft. The fisherman becomes further impoverished, and profits, such as they are, end up largely in the pockets of a few entrepreneurs. This pattern is all too familiar in tropical artisanal fisheries. It is part of the oft-repeated sequence of events whereby self-sufficient, internally regulated subsistence economies are converted to money-based economies, governed ultimately by decisions made in market centers thousands of miles away.

Under such conditions, Johannes says, a conservation ethic cannot thrive. No longer will a fisherman let some of the fish in his nets go, or refrain from catching all the turtles he sights. His income is now proportional to his catch. Restraint on the fishing grounds now constitutes self-denial. Some individuals defend traditional laws, but with diminishing success as modern-style governments usurp power and prestige. The resources dwindle, and eventually the reef harbors too few fish to satisfy even local needs. Johannes has seen it throughout Oceania. I had heard precisely the same analysis when I traveled the Caribbean coast of Nicaragua with Dr. Bernard Neitschmann, who, like Johannes, has worked at the confronting interface of ancient (long-term) and modern (new and untested) perspectives on nature for a couple of decades. And now I'd also gotten a firsthand primer from some of Palau's native old-timers.

"I've seen an awful lot of coral destruction," Johannes says as he tries to wipe the water from his forehead with the back of his soaked arm. "If we're gonna try to bring it back, let's get going."

For anyone who might still ask, "Why bother?" I pass along one reason offered me by Smithsonian scientist Héctor Guzmán, who works in Latin America: "If we restore the reefs, we restore the whole food chain. In one word, as far as people are concerned, we restore protein."

Ollei

The boat we are waiting for finally appears, piloted by a taut, solidly built young Palauan man. The boat carries the British ichthyologist Yvonne Sadovy, currently a professor at the University of Hong Kong, who is collaborating with Johannes on the grouper project, and an elderly couple hitching a ride to Ollei. The wizened old man is breaking betel nuts in a pestle with a hammer—the cracking method used by people who lack the requisite number of teeth. We load the gear and bid Johannes farewell as we head to his study site (he'll stay office-bound, tending to budgets and reports).

We leave behind the red plume bleeding off the road and pass close by some of the rock islands on our way out. I notice that wherever a torrent of rainwater is spilling out of the densely vegetated jungle and into the sea, it is as clear as the rain itself, not carrying soil.

Rain yields to hot sun and a fresh breeze, and we plunge up the coast, plowing and slamming into a stiff, white chop driven by a blustery quartering wind. Spray is not the only thing rising before our bow. Frightened flying fish are getting up high in the buoying breeze—well above eye level—as though the spray itself was sublimating into birds, as in an Escher drawing.

Dr. Sadovy and I are enjoying both the spray and the flying fish. In her field clothes—red cap over short dark hair, sunglasses, red T-shirt, and culottes—Sadovy seems, well, different than I remember her from scientific conferences where we have previously met. She is trim, bright-eyed, energetic, harboring a reserved but ever-so-slightly mischievous British sense of humor. She has the kind of indeterminate looks that could place her anywhere in her thirties, though I suspect she would thank me for saying so. The precise age at which she became a marine biologist is more certain. When Yvonne was eight, her family went on a holiday to the Mediterranean coast of France. All the other kids used to dive off a particular rock, but Yvonne was scared to jump for fear of what might be lurking below. Her dad bought her a little mask so she could look under the surface, and when she saw what was there, she forgot about the rock. "All I wanted to do was keep looking."

Sadovy went to an all-girls' school. Virtually all the students were encouraged to become bilingual secretaries, and she was good at languages. She didn't know how to go about becoming a marine biologist, and her headmistress said it didn't make much sense for a girl anyway. At age eighteen, realizing she would need an advanced degree, she enrolled in zoology at Manchester University—against everyone's advice. "My mom was very concerned that I have something I could fall back on, so I took shorthand and typing, and French and English, all of which have been fantastically useful."

One day, someone gave her a paper describing fish that change sex based on cues in their environment. It captivated her. "I had been a tomboy, and I was already interested in the idea that your perception of who you are is based partly how society views males and females. And I'd just read a book by an Englishman who had been an army man, climbed Mount Everest, married, and had children. In his forties, after having felt for a very long time that—I mean an absolutely crazy thing—that he should have been a woman, he underwent a sex-change operation. And the thing that struck me most was that his—now her (James Morris having become Jan Morris)—ability to do certain things, little things like opening a bottle with a corkscrew, was very much affected by what people expected her to be capable of. All this was mixing in my mind, and the question of what determines sexual identity got really interesting to me."

Yvonne decided she wanted to do research on the actual factors that induce sex change in some fishes. Some species change sex based on social cues rather than at a fixed age. Yvonne wanted to observe behavior; she didn't like manipulating animals. She also wanted to spend a lot of time in the water, and that meant working in the tropics. Money was a limiting factor, and the marine research station in Puerto Rico was the least expensive of several possible options. "I think life's a little bit like that: You have a particular combination of events that culminate." The culmination of Yvonne's early set of events was her research on groupers in Puerto Rico and a Ph.D. dissertation on determinants of sex change in fishes.

Sadovy did not expect to return to Puerto Rico, but then she was offered the directorship of the Department of Natural Resources Fisheries Research Lab. "Here was this female-male thing again. They had never previously considered a woman for that job." She nailed it. "It was a really unique opportunity; I mean, at my age—early thirties—to have a job like that in England or in the States would have been impossible." Sadovy's ecological research on groupers led her to realize that fishing was taking enormous numbers of these fish, and she became concerned. A stint with the Caribbean Fisheries Management Council followed. She got to realize "how the people involved in management really know so little."

The situation with groupers was particularly troubling to her. "Groupers are incredibly vulnerable, and they provide an example of how quickly we can do damage." Yvonne has done a sort of postmortem on the Nassau grouper; her published papers add up to a lengthy obituary on an age of plenty that many living people can still remember. The Nassau grouper had been among the most valuable fishes in much of the Caribbean and nearby Atlantic. Breeding colonies had been fished in many areas since at least the beginning of the twentieth century. In 1900, the ichthyologist Barton Warren Evermann, writing the first United States government survey of Puerto Rico's fishery resources, stated that the Nassau grouper was "a common and very important food fish, reaching a weight of fifty pounds or more." For decades, at about the time of the full moon each December and January, a small fleet of sloops and dories would set sail well before dawn from the fishing villages of western Puerto Rico. With their wicker fish pots and their handlines, the fishermen easily took as much as they could possibly need to their homes and villages. But eventually, of course, they took more than they needed, because that is how human nature and the market often conspire. The Nassau grouper is now effectively extinct for fishery purposes in Puerto Rico. You will never see one even suggesting a weight of fifty pounds.

The Nassau grouper is also commercially extinct in the U.S. Virgin Islands and Bermuda. It's not doing too well elsewhere, either. Yvonne documented declining trends for Belize, Cuba, the Dominican Republic, Florida, Honduras, Jamaica, and the Netherlands Antilles. In Belize, Nassau groupers made up fully a third of annual marine fish landings in the 1980s. At that time, fishermen caught them from breeding colonies using hand-held hook-and-line tackle, landing around a hundred tons each year. Fish traps, a technological "improvement," were introduced in 1986, and by 1991 landings plummeted to twenty-three tons. Onward and downward. In Bermuda, Nassau grouper landings plunged nearly 95 percent between 1975 and 1981. Cuba: down 97 percent between 1960 and the early '80s. In Florida, Nassau grouper landings dropped 80 percent during the 1980s. Honduras: Where ten thousand fish had spawned at a newly discovered site *one year earlier,* five hundred breeding fish were counted in 1991. In the Virgin Islands, known breeding colonies vanished completely by the 1980s. Throughout its range, almost a third of all the Nassau grouper's spawning aggregations have disappeared.

While fishermen knew the whereabouts of many breeding sites for decades, only in 1972 was a spawning colony first seen from underwater. That was off Cat Cay in the Bahamas, and while C. Lavett Smith of the American Museum of Natural History was documenting the extraordinary sight of a hundred thousand individuals gathered for breeding, fishers were removing thirty-five thousand to forty thousand fish. Today, the closest you can get to experiencing that spectacular site at Cat Cay is reading Smith's description. By 1992, a mere twenty years after that account, the Nassau grouper was one of the first two fully marine, commercially important fishes named as candidates for the U.S. Endangered Species List (the other is also a grouper, the huge jewfish *Epinephelus itajara*).

Almost invariably, the introduction of fish traps, spearguns, and intensified fishing preceded these declines. Breeding colonies can withstand light levels of fishing for extended periods, but as soon as efforts intensify, they go bust. Most other animals become progressively harder to catch as they get rare, because their densities decrease. The aggregating behavior of breeding groupers, however, means that even if only a few adults remain, they continue showing up vulnerably at the same spawning sites. And if the population is dwindling, and fishers take the same number of fish each year, the catch becomes a higher and higher percentage of the remaining breeders.

It is "certainly striking," Yvonne writes, that various kinds of groupers are unusually vulnerable—not just in the Caribbean, but in many places around the world. In Puerto Rico the tiger grouper has one fin on a banana peel. In Bermuda, landings for the whole grouper group suffered a fifteenfold drop from the 1970s to the '80s. In the Mediterranean, the grouper *Epinephelus guaza* (also called the giant rock "cod") is in serious condition because of fishing and pollution. In the Pacific as in the Caribbean, the introduction of intensive commercial exploitation driven by new distant markets and the arrival of new tourists from distant places swarming new local restaurants have severely depleted several species. In Australia, the spotted black grouper, *E. daemelii,* is depleted and classified as "potentially threatened" because of spear fishing, and Malabar and giant groupers are already protected in New South Wales.

Groupers are a large family—three dozen species in the Pacific alone—of mostly tropical coral reef fishes. Many spawn in dense aggregations at highly predictable times, places, and specific moon phases—behaviors have been shaped by evolution to maximize survival. But in an age in which books are given titles like *The End of Nature* and *The End of History,* I can tell you this: For many wild animals worth money (or standing in the way of money), our age is basically the end of evolution. The groupers' complex breeding behaviors bring them together in ways that, instead of continuing to maximize reproduction and survival, now mark them for easy elimination. Their own finely tuned evolution now betrays them. When fish from tens of miles in every direction gather in one consistent spot during a certain month's full moon, you can bet a plate of wrasse lips that someone on the deck of a boat is salivating about payday. The proof that these breeding colonies are supremely vulnerable to overfishing comes in the form of the formerly enormous, now demolished grouper populations throughout the world.

We are passing the village of Ngeremlengui, where Bob Johannes lived for a year in the late 1970s while working on his book. Heavy rains over the last several days have so thoroughly washed out part of the new road-construction project that a tongue of red sediments more than a mile long is hemorrhaging into the lagoon.

A few days ago, I came here with Johannes, his research collaborator Lyle Squire (whom we are now headed to see), and Noah Idechong (the "ch" is silent, denoting a glottal stop: Ide'ong). Recently the acting director of the Division of

Marine Resources, Idechong became the new administration's first native casualty. He was replaced by the new division chief—the "one-man anticonservation force"—when he began questioning the country's development plans to build roads and hotels for ten times the current number of tourists ("No one was asking how much development the resources could support"). Idechong is now director of the Palau Conservation Society, the only native nongovernmental conservation organization in all of Micronesia. (Idechong is not without other geographic points of reference. He had lived on a Minnesota farm as an exchange student, and for this sun-baked islander it was a wondrous year filled with untropical experiences like snowmobiling and skiing. He later studied in other places where in winter water turns hard enough to walk on—England and Canada—training in fisheries management and administration. And the world has recently come to him as well. Noah recently won the Goldman Prize, a prestigious environmental award.)

Noah, Johannes, Lyle Squire, and I had come here to go spear fishing, and as we were preparing to enter the water, Noah said jokingly, "Go berserk. No bag limits today." The joke is, there *are* no limits.

Coming here that day had been a mistake. After snorkeling along this channel for only about fifteen minutes, Bob came up looking visibly shaken, saying, "This used to be a coral paradise. Now it's a silty mess." Palau is building its new roads cheaply and carelessly. When an American working for the Division of Marine Resources showed that road work was silting and killing some of the corals, he was relieved of his duties.

On the day we'd come here, Noah went hunting far from the channel, where the corals are still alive. But by the time he got back to the boat with only palm-sized fishes on his stringer, he was shaking his head importantly, saying, "Not good. This area is very much fished out. We are becoming part of a bigger overfished region because of exports for the live fish trade. Palau is getting pulled into that vacuum."

Though coral grows in less than 2 percent of the oceans' area, coral reefs are the most economically important natural resources in more than a hundred countries, relied upon for fisheries, seafood, and tourism. But many—most—reef areas worldwide are degrading, some seriously. Reefs are resilient and can bounce back from major shocks like cyclones, but they begin withering under the combined, steady stresses of fishing with poisons, overfishing by other means, siltation (caused by deforestation, dredging, road runoff, and agriculture) coral mining, pollution, and ship groundings. By some scientists' estimates, 10 percent of the world's reefs are now doomed, 30 percent are in critical shape and may die by 2020, and another 30 percent are under such continual stress that they may not last beyond 2050. I hope those estimates are wrong. Jeremy Jackson, a paleobiologist with the Smithsonian Tropical Research Institute, a cautious and methodical researcher who does not come across as a sentimentalist, has said, "I used to be reluctant to say the sky is falling. I'm not anymore. Today when I go for a swim on a reef in Panama, I cry." Jackson studies large-scale changes in corals over millions of years, and when I expressed surprise that he, of all people, is worried about recent changes in reefs over just the last couple of decades, he answered, "We live only seventy or eighty years if we're lucky, and our children not much beyond that. Since we care about ourselves and our children, the quality of our lives and the stability of the world is of some real interest. And it's not very satisfying to a tourist operator in Jamaica to tell them that their reefs will come back in a hundred thousand years."

Fishing is one of several major sources of stress. Jamaican coral reef ecologist Tom Goreau told me, "We've had catastrophic overfishing, no question about that." Most reef researchers agree on a few points. If fishing is at all intensive the system gets simplified. Big fish get very scarce. Sometimes, whole groups of species essentially drop out of a local area. Callum Roberts, a reef specialist at the University of York, wrote in the science journal *Conservation Biology,*

> Fishing has caused massive reductions . . . throughout the tropics. . . .
> It can be argued that reefs can afford to lose a few species here and there, and with some justification. But I believe we are no longer tinkering . . . , adjusting a surgeonfish population here, removing a grouper species there; rather, we are in danger of fishing reefs into oblivion.

Indeed, when the National Academy of Sciences brought together many of the world's leading marine biologists at a workshop in Irvine, California, in 1994, the scientists concluded that fishing—not global warming, not pollution: fishing—was the single greatest threat to the diversity of life throughout the world's oceans, coral reefs included. This is not necessarily an irreversible catastrophe. Like other activities, it's a matter of scale and intensity. But on the world's reefs the scale is increasing and the fishing intensifying. Poisons, dynamite, fine-mesh nets, and other destructive fishing practices create an overfishing spiral in which more and more people attempt to feed their families off fewer and fewer fish. Increasingly intensive fishing driven by increasing human population pressures is called "Malthusian overfishing." Masses of men leading lives of desperation. In the worst cases—like the Philippines, Haiti, and Jamaica—edible species have been eaten nearly out of existence, leaving empty holes in people's stomachs.

And creating holes in the reefs' living communities. Some effects are straightforward, some are not. Overfishing not only directly depletes fish, it can rob other fish of food, lowering overall abundance across many species. Fishing can lead to shifts in the community, rearranging the neighborhood by pulling out key species, causing cascading effects as the rest of the species adjust. This is called "ecosystem overfishing."

Behold, for example, the urchins. Sea urchins seem, to the casual eye, to be pincushions rooted in one place. But in fact they graze. Slowly. But efficiently.

They scrape algae off reefs. So do some reef fishes, and these compete with urchins. Other fishes, like triggerfishes and puffers, prey on urchins. But triggers and puffers are highly vulnerable to fishing. When they are removed from an area, it's party time for urchins: no more predators. Boom! Urchins everywhere. Eating every speck of algae. In studies off Kenya, urchins were *one hundred times denser* in areas with fishing. In areas protected from fishing, fish densities and fish predation *on* urchins were four times higher than in areas with fishing. So heavy fishing makes the urchins explode, and they graze off all the algae. When predatory fishes were holding urchins down, grazing fishes could compete. But now, the grazers starve and crash. The urchins, meanwhile, keep scraping away the algae, and pretty soon they are scraping away the coral itself. It has happened. Only one part of the community is directly disturbed—the predatory fishes that were caught by hungry people—but the whole reef community suffers domino effects.

Here's another real-life twist: In Jamaica and other parts of the Caribbean, the fisheries took not just the fishes that preyed on the urchins, they took every fish they could, including the urchin-competing, algal-grazing fishes. Then an epidemic of unknown origin killed most of the urchins. No predatory fishes, no grazing fishes, no urchins to speak of. Now it was the *algae* that exploded, growing over everything. It grew in filaments. It grew in fleshy blobs. It coated the coral, killing it. New coral larvae had no place to settle and recolonize. New fish coming in to gain a foothold found no sanctuary, either; the fish traps were relentless. The reefs went from coral-and-invertebrate-dominated systems abundant in fishes to algal-dominated, fish-poor systems. They seemed to get stuck like this. They remain so. The system does not appear headed toward repair. It seems like a new system. Ecologists call this a phase shift or state shift. Callum Roberts, again:

> The appalling rate of tropical rainforest destruction has captured public concern in a way the destruction of reefs has failed to do. Yet the crisis of habitat and biodiversity loss is probably no less acute for the most diverse ecosystem in the sea than for that on land. Just as wholesale destruction of rainforests for timber and ephemeral agriculture has been criticized as a terrible waste of biological riches, so extractive fisheries on reefs may be a poor way of using these resources.

Roberts went on to make a point that caught me by surprise. Both rain forests and coral reefs, he explained, are very productive. But their productivity is based on very efficient *recycling* of nutrients. When nutrients come in, they get captured and reused very effectively. But few nutrients come in, so the amount you can remove without depleting the system is actually very low. Because of this, Roberts believes fisheries should concentrate not on reefs but on upwelling areas (mostly offshore), where loads of new nutrients are brought in from the deep ocean, resulting in large net productivity. But he acknowledges that because so many poor people are so reliant on them, "reef fisheries are the most difficult in the world to manage." It will not be easy for poor fishing communities to reduce the amount they take from reefs. Unfortunately, they will ultimately suffer the same fate—without options—unless they *do* find ways of going easier on the reefs and the fishes, and soon. That will take work, commitment, vision.

Fortunately, a few people out there have what it takes. We are about to visit some of them.

We are approaching a dock bearing a sign reading,

OUR SWEET HOME IS CLEAN,
LET'S KEEP IT CLEAN AND HEALTHY,
WELCOME TO OLLEI.

Ollei is the settlement—not quite a village—at the far northern end of Palau's main island of Babeldaob. Yvonne Sadovy and I thank our boatman, Asap Bukurrou (who is a technician with the Division of Marine Resources), for delivering us safely despite the blowing bellows of nature, and toss our gear up onto the concrete wharf.

Anticipating an exciting week of team fieldwork, we practically trot the hundred yards to the field station, awkwardly toting our stuffed duffels of clothes and scuba gear.

Sitting in the shade outside the doorway, relaxing and chatting amiably among themselves, are several Palauan fishermen who have been participating in this project. It has taken Bob Johannes and his collaborator Lyle Squire more than a year to earn their confidence. The confidence is not transferable, though, and as we approach and say hello the mere presence of two new white strangers is enough to end the siesta. The men leave quietly for another spot where they can feel more at ease. Their departure leaves me feeling intrusive, uncomfortable.

Inside the station, Lyle Squire is upset. Last month, spear fishermen from outside Ollei (no one knows exactly where from) got into the nearby spawning site at Ebiil Channel and shot about a hundred fish. Though the chiefs have declared the site *bul,* or off-limits, the village is not yet organized to guard it.

Lyle says this village needs someone sitting out there to police against outsiders. In each of Palau's municipalities, chiefs can control access to local fishing grounds, for the benefit of the people they represent. By extension, the chiefs are partially responsible for their people's behavior; the chief of a poacher's village loses face. Fishermen who cause such embarrassment may be made to pay for it in cash, though nowadays traditional responsibilities are breaking down. Formerly, offenders—if caught—forfeited their lives, the prescribed punishment for poaching throughout much of Oceania.

By current law, the five most important grouper species cannot be captured or sold during most of their spawning season. But enforcement leaves much to be desired, and many restaurants in Koror continue blithely serving these fish to tourists during the closed season.

Groupers are once more arriving and gathering for spawning, and Lyle says irritably, "If that site gets hit by fishermen again this month, we should pack our bags and leave." Lyle, who is just recovering from dengue fever (he contracted it during Palau's first outbreak of the rapidly spreading tropical disease), pops a pain pill. Lyle returned here two days ago, but he looks as if he should still be in bed. Nevertheless, he insists on going out for his daily count of fish on the spawning ground.

After a quick drink to rehydrate from the desiccating boat ride in the brutal sun, Yvonne slips into her wet suit and is ready to have a look at the breeding site. Lyle dons his bright-red, full-body Lycra suit and hood.

"Ugh," he groans, straining and stretching to pull the suit on. "You know you're getting old when your feet seem so far away." With his white hair and beard, Lyle in his hideous red suit looks like a cross between Santa and Satan. The suit is designed for protection against jellyfish—Lyle calls it his stinger suit— but he also wears it in the boat all day against the sun. "Over the years," he says, "it's not the stingers or the sharks or the bends that'll get you. It's the sun. Always, the sun."

Lacking a stinger suit of my own, I slather sunblock onto my forehead. From the wharf, with binoculars, you can actually see towering ocean waves smashing the reef crest four miles away. It is to a gap in that reef, amid all those exploding white geysers, that we are headed. Lyle says wearily, "Yesterday was bloody terrifying." He does not scare easily. He usually downplays the ocean's dangers with typically Australian bravado. So when he says they nearly lost the boat in breaking seas, I believe him. But he says he can't afford many holes in the data at this critical period while the fish are arriving. Inevitably there will be days when wind precludes work, so while it is at all possible, we must push ahead. The wind is gusting still, but Lyle thinks conditions have been slowly improving since morning. After loading scuba tanks, drinking water, and other gear, we motor out across the wide, white-capped, blue-and-turquoise lagoon toward the seaward face of the reef. Halfway across the lagoon, I look back. The main island's verdant, jungled, mountainous outline is framed by high-rearing, pink-bellied clouds.

The marker buoy at Ebiil Channel is bobbing fitfully in the roughened heave. Lyle assesses conditions as much better than yesterday's. The wind has slackened considerably since we left the dock, and waves are no longer breaking as violently over the reef.

We are over a spit of corals jutting out into the channel that leads from the reef edge. It is here that the fish gather for spawning, which will peak in a few days, with the fifth new moon of the year. Fish scientists call these gatherings "spawning aggregations," but they are basically the same as seal rookeries and bird colonies, with animals coming from a large area to find and fight over mates and to reproduce.

We don our dive gear and check each other out. Lyle says, "All me mates who've been hit by reef sharks were bitten just after they noisily jumped overboard, before the bubbles cleared, so enter the water slowly."

Slipping quietly into water of an overwhelming blue, we descend sixty-five feet to the bottom. The fish we have come to see are marvelously camouflaged, difficult for my inexperienced eyes. Though Yvonne is pointing, the males holding territories blend vanishingly among the bulky corals.

Why, of all the different places on the reef, do the fish come and congregate *here?* Reef fishes needed a solution to the dilemma challenging their reproduction. A reef—rich as it is—is an impossibly dangerous place for small creatures like baby fishes. Remember: Corals are not flowers. They sit there, polyps open, tiny stinging tentacles scratching the watery breeze, just itching to snag anything small enough drifting by. Think of corals as water filters, straining whatever they can for food. Add the planktivorous fishes, by the billions or trillions. More than half of the zooplankton—such as fish eggs and tiny, just-hatched fish larvae—that drifts onto a reef is nailed before it has gone more than a few hundred yards. The surrounding open ocean, while safer, is a desert. The dilemma, then: Which is better—having your offspring eaten on the reef, or having them starve away from it? How can you reproduce when the only options for your youngsters are near-certain death on the reef or near-certain death in the deep-sea desert?

Native Pacific islanders, to whom the ocean meant everything, were keenly observant of events and patterns in the sea, and they provided the first clue. Charles Nordhoff (co-author of *Mutiny on the Bounty*), writing in 1933 so modern marine biology could catch up with the natives of Tahiti, penned:

> The natives say, and I believe with reason, that nearly all of the fish
> that haunt the lagoon and reefs of their islands, spawn at times when
> the currents sweep the eggs far out to sea. The result is that hundreds
> of different kinds of fry hatch out in the open Pacific.

The Tahitians were pretty good scientists, but neither they nor Nordhoff understood *why* fish that need coral habitats would let their eggs be swept away. Now we know they do it to get those tender offspring away from all the waving tentacles and open mouths on the reef. But now what? There is very little plankton for the larvae to eat in the open ocean, and many starve. But the danger of starving is just slightly less than the danger of getting eaten on the reef—and those were the only two options evolution had to work with. Natural selection favored, of course, the better evil, and survival accrued to genes encoded to express a certain behavioral tendency. And so, many fishes, when the time comes, go to the outer reef, to spots where currents sweep seaward, to the points of extreme land where the water moves fastest, wait until the moon exerts its most powerful pull on the locomotive tides, and then: Spawn! Spawn when and where the currents take your children far from this vale of tears.

Eggs hatch in blue desert. A few larvae find enough to eat, and they grow until they are ready for transformation into baby reef fishes. But there is no reef in sight, nothing but blue sky above a bottomless, ink-black floor. What happens next is something science began figuring out in the 1970s. The Japanese researcher S. Hattori perceived that spawning places of reef fishes are "especially frequent in gyral areas near peninsulas and islands." Gyral currents make slow, circular, sweeps (like that place off the tip of one Palauan island where American and Japanese blood is said to have cartwheeled in a tidal eddy for several days).

Bob Johannes pulled together the ethnobiological, behavioral, and oceanographic information, formed the evidence into an argument, and published "Reproductive Strategies of Coastal Marine Fishes in the Tropics" in a science journal called *Environmental Biology of Fishes.* He said, essentially, that the fish put their eggs into a conveyor belt that first gets them off the reef, then returns the youngsters to the coral habitats when the time is right and they've grown a bit. Johannes went on to explain that not only do the fishes tend to spawn on full and new moons, when the near-shore tides whisk the eggs away from the reef as fast as possible, they also give them a head start by spawning in a rapid upward rush toward the surface, exploding high above the dangerous reef with gushes and clouds of eggs and sperm. And spawning occurs at times of the year when prevailing winds are at their weakest, so, once offshore, eggs and larvae are generally not transported long distances, improving their chances of being returned to the reef rather than lost at sea. (Yes, fish can be lost at sea.)

Johannes emphasized and reemphasized the importance of intense predation. The evidence was circumstantial, but the logic was substantial. In temperate oceans, fish tend to spawn where their young will have the most food. In the tropics, there is more potential food for young fishes on the reefs, yet here are all these species traveling to special places with transporting gyres that take their offspring away from the reefs and the food. Conclusion: Predation pressure outweighs food supplies in determining larval survival on tropical reefs and has driven the evolution of reef fish spawning behavior.

Johannes also noted that while planktonic food for the larvae was sparse offshore, it was in fact just slightly denser in gyre currents than elsewhere in the open sea, because the circular motion gathered and held it more than currents that moved linearly. Evolution had made the best of bad circumstances. It was all commonsensical (evolution excels at practicality), but discerning the patterns and the underlying driving forces and pulling it all into focus took unusual insight. Johannes was quick to try to give the credit away. "Much of the 'new' information on spawning strategies in this paper," he wrote, "did not originate with me, but with the expert fishermen of Palau who have accumulated it, tested it, and passed it on over a period of centuries. They provided the knowledge; I simply 'verified' it through observation." It was a surpassing gesture of generosity and affection toward the fishermen he'd grown to love and respect. Regardless of how much credit belonged to whom, the paper was a great advance for our (Western) understanding of coral reef community ecology.

We are moving along the edge of the reef slope. Yvonne, hugging herself as though feeling a slight chill, tarries, observing the groupers closely, occasionally making notes and drawings on her underwater writing tablet. These are square-tailed groupers, *Plectropomus areolatus*. The Palauan name is *tiao*.

Lyle is steadily pumping along into the current, counting fish, showing no particular effort. I am straining to keep up with him. On land, Lyle walks with a waddle as a result of being crushed under several tons of steel that slipped off a crane hook when he was in his twenties. His spine is wrapped with metal wiring, and five operations to do and undo various procedures have not quite fixed his problems. Lyle is only forty-two, but he moves with the stiffness of someone much older. With his white hair and beard and his large scarred abdomen, I would not have blinked if someone had told me, while we were ashore, that he was closing in on sixty. But when he gets into the water, Lyle is an altogether different animal.

A small hawksbill turtle, the first I have ever seen alive, glides past and disappears into the gloomy distance. Here in the Pacific, as in the rest of the world, the hawksbill is overhunted for its appealing shell. As I watch it glide a curious but cautious half circle, I think back to a woman in a rundown Central American coastal town, offering me lovely combs and earrings of hawksbill shell. I explained that these turtles were in danger. With weary patience and an indulgent smile I had not earned, she replied in Spanish, "I have four children and a dead husband. That is all I can think about." Everywhere, it seems, such need confronts, confuses, pits compassion against compassion. But I come again and again to the same place of reference: If the last are taken, the people with least will be left with none.

Lyle and Yvonne are gesticulating enthusiastically to each other. They see so much that I am missing. I catch up to Lyle, look over his shoulder at his clipboard, and see that he has already counted fifteen groupers, mapped them on a waterproof sheet, and noted their sex and size. I have spotted just four.

I feel that I'm just swimming around among a seemingly chaotic profusion of life, while their eyes and minds are probing into the riot of input on the reef, perceiving an ordered system that they have largely helped discover and explain.

After a while, I begin seeing more fish. Through the eyes and guidance of my companion scientists, the reef begins coming into focus. I begin differentiating males from females. The males are aggressive to each other. The females are preoccupied with going into caves and under sheltered spots in the coral, prospecting for safe sites to hide in while their eggs ripen.

Science, like love, can be blind, inspired, glorious, or brutal. The piercing ability to perceive order within apparent chaos is, to me, the great, elegant power of science. Not to impose order, but to perceive it. To begin in confusion and by endeavor to gain a sense of how the world works. To turn the seamless picture into a jigsaw puzzle, and by seeing and understanding how each pixel fits, to stand back again and gain a much deeper appreciation of the magnificent beauty of the unified whole. And to wonder how it is that part of the universe—ourselves—can delve into the rest of it. The most incomprehensible thing about nature, Albert Einstein said, is that it is comprehensible.

An observant person sees things overlooked by others. A scientist sees things going on and then asks how these goings-on array themselves into patterns, patterns that are reliable and predictable. A really *good* scientist—or a really good artist for that matter, anyone whose mind and soul are capable of some extension—sees what is going on, sees the patterns, and asks, "Why?" What underlying forces are at work? How are those forces exerting themselves? How may we understand? Once pried from the universe by a great mind or a discerning heart, the hard-won understanding may then be conveyed and conferred upon humanity at large. A painting is nothing more than light reflected from the surface of a pigment-covered canvas. But a great painter can make you see the depth, make you feel the underlying emotion, make you sense the larger world. That, too, is the power of science: to sense and convey the depth and dimensionality of nature, to glance at the surface and to divine the shape of the universe around us. It operates on many scales.

Fish scales for instance. Back in the boat after the dive, Lyle says, "Much more interaction among males today than yesterday. And quite a few more females, with some ripe ones." Lyle quickly tallies his notes, announcing 135 *tiao* total, with two males per female today. "That's the highest count we've had here. Look at this," Lyle says, holding up the waterproof notepaper on which he's mapped the males' territories. "Doing this day after day, you slowly get an appreciation of the importance of this one little tiny underwater spit to breeding fish coming from miles around. We already know it's important for at least three species of groupers, but we're seeing other kinds of fishes here as well."

Back at the station, Lyle enters today's numbers on data sheets and reviews the last few days' information and figures, looking at trends and hunting for patterns. The numbers have been building and the sex ratio changing slightly.

The field station is not much to look at. Besides three tiny bedrooms with double-decker bunks, and a shower and toilet, it is just a single large room. Food stores, stove, and sink occupy one wall. A table and chairs sit in the middle, rounding out the spartan luxuries. Along the main room's walls sit boxes of diving and tagging equipment, clipboards, and fresh data sheets. Everything must be thought of—tags, all the scuba gear, fishing gear, tagging kits, linens, data sheets, everything that we need. There are no supplies to be bought here. Not fuel, not even food.

A fat photo album sits prominently on the table. Every photograph is a picture of Lyle and fish he has speared. Lyle uses his spear fishing skills and knowledge to break the ice with Palauan fishers. Some of the photos are old, and in them Lyle is young, taut, muscular—a tanned and sun-bleached warrior. Some photos feature only Lyle and one enormous fish. In other pictures the fish are numerous, and friends are gathered around—some now deceased. Talk to Lyle for just a few minutes and you quickly discover a person who, for many years, cultivated a compulsive devotion to the art of hunting while holding one's breath.

Lyle entered the world of competitive spear fishing as a teenager, and he holds more than twenty standing world records. "Spearing took over my life early," he admits. "To go deeper, longer, on a single breath—you push yourself to extremes that you don't know."

It was a dangerous dedication. Lyle lost five "mates" (Australian for "friends") to what he calls "the hardest sport I can think of." None of them succumbed to sharks, sea snakes, venomous octopi, or deadly jellyfish. Those hazards—always present—can be dealt with.

Something far more deadly killed Lyle's friends and nearly got him one day. The cause of death in each case was a sudden loss of consciousness that was *not* preceded by any urge to breathe. This insidious killer is called shallow-water blackout. When snorkelers hyperventilate at the surface with more than three or four deep breaths to enrich their blood with oxygen prior to a dive, they blow off too much carbon dioxide (CO_2) in the process. Carbon dioxide is a metabolic waste product, so starting a dive with as little of it as possible would seem desirable. But that is exactly the lurking danger, because it is the level of CO_2 in the blood, *not* the level of oxygen, that signals the brain about the need for air. Unless the carbon dioxide level is normal, the diver will feel no urge to breathe, even if no oxygen remains in their blood. Without warning, the diver loses consciousness. When Lyle passed out underwater and began drowning, he was fortunate that someone nearby had enough oxygen left to drag him to the surface by his hair.

"The Polynesians have never had a spear fishing champion beaten," Lyle says, "because each Polynesian champion has died before losing his title." Shallow-water blackout seems the only aspect of diving that scares Lyle, and he no longer hyperventilates. "Deep divers rely on finding dumb fish, but once I stopped going deep, I had to find smart fish and out-think them. So I became an ambush specialist, going into caves."

One time, Lyle entered a small cave after a large Napoleon wrasse. It was a tight fit. He found the big frightened fish pressed up against the ceiling, doing its best to hide in the tiny space, facing him directly. Lyle was young and impetuous, but he also knew it would be dangerous to spear the wrasse head-on because it was likely to bolt out of the cave, and Lyle's soft, penetrable body was blocking the entrance. "It was a big fish. I wanted to bring it home, but that eye was looking at me."

He shot it anyway. When the spear pierced its head, the terrified animal charged forward like a knight on horseback armed with a jousting pole. An instant before the big creature hit him full force, the spear shaft struck Lyle a glancing blow in the face, shattering and ripping off his mask, though not impaling him. The last Lyle's diving companion saw of the wrasse, it was headed into blue water, with Lyle's mask hanging from the spear lodged in its head. Lyle still bears the scar. The fish, in all likelihood, soon died.

Yvonne seems visibly disturbed by the story, or perhaps I am just projecting.

Lyle once entered a cave so narrow at its opening he figured no one else was likely to have been in there; it would probably be loaded with lobsters. Holding his breath, he squeezed in, looked around, and saw lobsters backed into every crevice. He reached out and grabbed one, then a second. It had been a tight wriggle in. And now he couldn't back out. He tried to force himself backward. He seemed stuck. He continued trying to work his way out. He could not move. He thought, "I need to breathe." He decided it might be prudent to let one of the lobsters go. But only one. He thought, "If I'm going to die anyway, I'm not letting go of this lobster." He could feel that the tips of his flippers were probably outside the cave, but he was wedged tight, stuck, expiring.

Just then his diving buddy found him and immediately planted both feet on the coral outside the cave, grabbed Lyle's ankles, and gave a mighty pull. Lyle suffered severe lacerations all along his side from the coral and rock and lost much skin and blood. He kept the lobster.

But all that was two decades or so ago, and Lyle is almost sensible now. If confronted with the same scenario today, my guess is he'd let both lobsters go.

Lyle can talk about his spear fishing heyday forever. I cannot. Exciting as those exploits were, by today's lights the thought of killing so many big, old creatures does not rest comfortably on my mind. But, truth is, nowadays even Lyle spends much more of his time talking to schoolchildren about the importance of protecting their reefs than he does spear fishing, and when he's in the water he is much more likely to carry a clipboard than a speargun.

I ask Yvonne about peak experiences of her own. She tells about a time in the Red Sea, where dusk-spawning surgeonfishes migrate along the reefs to assemble by the hundreds in particular places. "I settled down at the bottom. There were *so* many fish, *so* much activity, it was like an electricity in the water. I swear I could feel the water *vibrate.* Some kind of signal started them off. And *then*," she says, looking up at the ceiling, painting a picture with her hands, "with the sky darkening and the fish shooting up towards the surface and spawning—just exploding with bursts of eggs and sperm—the fish seemed like fireworks. Watching this absolute *show* of animals, I actually forgot I was underwater."

But enough about the past, she says. What about this momentous event unfolding in Ebiil Channel? Lyle was here before any of the males arrived, so he has seen the entire buildup and now understands the way the spawning fish establish themselves. Lyle says the males arrive first, fighting to establish territories of about four meters square.

Yvonne asks, "Can they keep holding that large an area?"

"Yes, they can," Lyle replies. "But the males fight tooth and nail to do it. You'll see scars and tattered flanks."

Yvonne asks what the females do, and Lyle says they come in after the males are defending territories. "The biggest males are at the front, near the slope, holding the best real estate, with the most caves in the coral for the female to sit in while her eggs ripen."

"So, if I'm a female and I want to be clever about it," Yvonne says, "I would just go to the front and select the male based on his territory. What do you see the females actually doing?"

Lyle says, "When a female comes in, she changes from black to yellow and green. Then the males begin courting, shimmying and dancing with her. The females are outnumbered five to one here. They're very popular. They have their pick. But I don't think this sex ratio is natural."

"It's more usual for the females to outnumber the males," Yvonne agrees. "Perhaps, outside the breeding season, fishermen on the reef are hitting the smaller female fish. Males may be out in deeper water and not getting caught as much. In the Gulf of Mexico, in one species, *males* now constitute only two percent of the spawners, and many females can no longer find mates."

"Here, we've got just the opposite," Lyle responds. He thinks understanding spawning is critical for managing fisheries in tropical countries. "You'd think there'd be more scientists trying to jump in on it. But it's put in the 'too-hard' file." It's *not* too hard, he insists. Awkward and inconvenient, maybe, but workable. "I'm not the best scientist in the Pacific, but I know this is do-able—and we're here doing it. We've got twenty countries saying, 'We'll use your information,' but they're not willing to put their hands in their pockets. Bob Johannes is willing to put his own money into it. That's why I can't get over him. No one else in the Pacific is willing to do that. Every day that passes makes it harder to understand what 'natural' was, even here in Palau."

Yvonne agrees. "We still don't know the very basics, like how many eggs they lay, how often. Palau is one of the very last places where one can attempt this work. Most of Southeast Asia is already too overfished. The Caribbean is too overfished. When I worked in Puerto Rico, my supervisor instructed me never to say the word 'overfishing.' By the time I left five years later, it was so undeniable, *he* was saying it! The time to do this work is ticking away. In a sense, I'm desperate to start."

Around dusk, a rough- and tense-looking Palauan man suddenly fills the open doorway. Conversation stops cold. He enters the room. He is looking for Lyle, and he has found him. He blurts out agitatedly, "My baby is seven months old. When she grows up, I want to show her the fish. Not just tell her about them. I went spear fishing a few nights ago. We left the *tiao* alone to make their babies. Before you came, we would have shot them all. The work you are doing: It is very important."

The tense moment transforms into a watershed for Lyle's mood. As the man accepts our invitation to join us at the table and he visibly relaxes, Lyle says to me, "He's just made it worth my trip, my troubles, and my case of dengue fever."

With the moon nearing new, the nights are growing progressively inkier. In this part of the world, night still knows how to be dark. Not a single light appears along the coast, and with clouds screening the Southern Cross and blocking the starlight in tonight's stormy skies, the effect is absolute blackness. A driving wind is spitting cold rain through the window next to my bunk. I am too tired from the travel and the diving to reach up and close it.

Dawn brings a clear sky, but the air is gusting with a decisiveness that removes the burden of decision making from Lyle. No way. Lyle is pleased that he pushed it yesterday, when he could. Today is much too blustery and rough for us to venture out to Ebiil Channel.

So I spend the day exploring part of the island. No road yet connects Ollei to the capital, only thirty miles away, but this village is connected to several other villages. One of them is called Ulimang.

When I get there, the tide is well out on the adjacent reef flat. A night heron flies in with something wriggling. I fix binoculars upon it. A sea snake. Landing on the exposed flat, the heron shakes the snake violently, pounding it against the coral sand, attempting to scarf the fighting serpent alive. The snake, highly venomous but small-mouthed and small-fanged, is trying to forestall being swallowed by wrapping itself around the bird and frantically but ineffectually attempting to deliver a bite through the heron's dense neck feathers. Culminating a struggle lasting more than five minutes, the heron breaks the writhing snake in two and downs it.

In the tiny village, a compact young man named Philip offers to take me to meet the chief and to act as interpreter. I can't imagine anything better. The chief, clad only in a yellow-flowered bathing suit, a waterproof yellow watch, and a day's stubble, is an old, chocolate-skinned man of seventy-six, sparse of hair and round of shoulder. He is sitting cross-legged—showing a large scar on one leg—on a wooden bench outside his tin-roofed bamboo home, which is built on stilts about fifty yards from the beach. His smile shows surprisingly good teeth, their whiteness amazing in a place where so many dentitions are stained red from chewing betel nuts.

Through Philip, I ask how many people live here. The chief says, "At least thirty-two people live in this village. Young people prefer to stay here if there is opportunity, but jobs and money are forcing them to Koror. There are half as many people here now as during World War Two. Many things have changed."

Like what?

"Now there is less respect to older people. My concerns about the land are not respected now. The new governor has more power than the chief. Lack of respect will cause a lot of pollution. Now, also," he says, shaking his head deeply with eyes closed, "much, much fewer fish. In the 1960s I could light a coconut-leaf fire, walk out in the shallows at night, and get more than one hundred lobsters. Now, that would be unheard of." About all the changes, he adds, "It is too late for my personal life. I hope only the best for the children."

I ask Philip to ask the chief, "If I were a young person here, what would you want to teach me?"

"I have nothing to teach young people now, because my knowledge is from ten years ago, from twenty years ago. Teaching the young is hard now."

I ask him what is causing the changes. He replies solemnly, "Most people think it is boats with motors. But I am a Seventh-Day Adventist, and the Bible teaches that things will slowly fade away."

While he is saying this, a wasp suddenly flies into the baggy leg of my bathing suit. I control my first urge and somehow get the wasp to come out of its own accord, managing to remain an unstung hero.

The old man continues gravely, "Kids now will not listen. When they are told to clean up the trash and to keep the village neat, they will not do anything unless they are paid money. They want to be like in the States—no more voluntary works. And young people don't eat the coconut."

Philip, who is thirty-three, adds, "This is true. I'd rather eat bread in the morning than go out and husk a coconut. In the evening, though, I do like Palauan food, like taro and canned corned beef."

Canned corned beef? Philip, apparently a connoisseur of canned corned beef, says the best corned beef is from Australia. Islanders don't like corned beef from the States: too dry. But Philip dutifully adds that the chief would consider tapioca or fish to be Palauan food, *not* canned corned beef.

I ask if the chief has ever been outside Palau.

He says he worked on ships and he has been to many places in the South Pacific and to Hong Kong, Thailand, Indonesia, and San Francisco. Picking up on San Francisco, I ask him how he liked the United States.

"I did not like the United States, because I could not see the other side. I'm comfortable when I can see the ocean on both sides. My favorite place is Palau. Other places, you can drive for miles and not see the ocean. Other places, you need too much money. Here, you don't need money for food or shelter. Other places, if you do not have money, you cannot sleep well. Here, we can think about tomorrow with no problem."

The chief has seven children: two in Koror and the rest in the United States.

"Where in the States?" I ask.

"Guam."

I ask their opinion of plans to bring a road here from Koror. The chief shakes his head negatively. Philip also doesn't want it. "It will make it like a metroplex."

Somehow, I don't think anyone will look at this sleepy village of thirty-two people and see a "metroplex" anytime soon, road or no road.

Philip has noticed that I am watching him prepare a betel nut and he asks me if I would like to try. Apprehensively, I say O.K. I am not adventurous with substances. He reassuringly says, "This is a good time to try betel nut. The setting is good, sitting with the old man and wishing each other luck." He puts burnt limestone powder on half a nut and wraps it in a leaf, advising, "At first it will taste very rough. I've been chewing enough all day to kill the feeling in the skin in my cheek, so I'm much more comfortable with it right now."

He adds educationally, "Sometimes instead of the burnt limestone, we put half a cigarette on it, which makes the spit turn yellow instead of red, so it is not so noticeable. The students at the Protestant School like it this way, so people won't see red spit all over the place and suspect that the students have been chewing."

With some hesitancy I take the nut, crunch it, begin chewing. Philip and the chief watch closely. In about two minutes my head becomes very hot, starting from the top, moving down toward my neck. My saliva thickens. I feel slightly dizzy, and a slight pressure builds in my skull.

Philip is extolling the practice in a sincere voice reflecting his now-heightened sense of community with me, saying, "It gives a sense of relaxation, it is good for any situation."

Ready to expel my first betel juice, I momentously spit a big, thick, gooey, red glob, like phlegm with tomato juice. Revolting.

Philip is exceptionally pleased, and he continues his exposition on expectoration. "In a serious conversation, if you feel that you are locked looking at someone, spitting gives you the opportunity to turn away. It's good when you're in a touchy situation. You are relaxed and can respond much better if you are getting a bad talk from someone. It gives a lot of edge, a great advantage in conversation."

The chief says, "And the reason we spit everywhere: It's a good spit. Without chewing, spitting is dirty, not sanitary. But with chewing it's a good spit that helps fertilize the plants."

I'm glad to hear this, because I am now spitting up a storm, enjoying the wonderful social and horticultural advantages, and spitting very well, thank you.

"So how do you like it now?" Philip asks. "It should be at its best now."

I nod enthusiastically. "Mmm-*hmmm!*" I'm horrified by the stuff. The chief seems delighted.

Philip says, "It's pretty much good for all occasions. A long time ago, we sprayed the spit, now we spit one bunch of spit but not in the same place twice, so we spread it out, so it's neater."

"Mmm-*hmmm!*" Neatness counts!

"There are many good situations for chewing," discourses Philip. "It is good for the presentation of ideas. When I'm not chewing, I go straight to the point. People think I am not patient. My tone may get people angry. When I chew, I take my time to say what I want. I do not appear to be abrupt. I am much more myself.

"Americans don't understand our need to sit and relax and chat before we come to the business," continues Philip with cosmopolitan insight. "The Palauan way is to chat first, talk about planting, talk about the houses. The old men like to talk a little bit about sex before we get down to whatever is the business, maybe talk about the fishing."

This house of the chief who likes to see the water on both sides has a fine view of the lagoon and reef edge. From where we are chewing we can watch the thundering waves that kept Lyle ashore today, pounding the reef in a line of pearly white breakers, snaggle-toothed and wild. But the lagoon in the island's lee is calm as a clam. The scene is heartbreakingly beautiful, almost hypnotically relaxing, an altogether convincing rendering of the Isles of the Blessed—a spitting image of Paradise.

Field preparations this morning have already taken fully three hours. Today, in addition to underwater counting, we will attempt to catch fish for tagging, aided and abetted by several Palauan participants in several small boats. Loading tagging kits, bait-catching equipment, diving gear, clipboards, various forms and data sheets, pencils, food, water, and the fishing gear seems to take forever. But we finally appear ready to go.

Lyle boards a boat captained by a man named Nimrod, assisted by a fellow called Mike. Yvonne will ride with a Palauan named Harvey Renguul who, like Asap, works for the Department of Natural Resources, and a bushy-haired, ponytailed, scraggly-bearded fisherman named Franzier. I'm tagging along with Asap and a fortyish fisherman named Joe, who is introduced as one of the village elders. What remains of his missing and broken teeth are stained blood-red by betel nuts, like the one he is now chewing. He's wearing a purple T-shirt and a red cap bearing the logo of an American football team.

Most of these guys have worked with Lyle and Bob Johannes before. And they are dedicated. Harvey refuses payment for use of his own boat. Lyle tried to give him $150 for two months' use of it, but Harvey wouldn't take it. Harvey and Asap have both refused the dollar per fish that the taggers earn. They think the project is too important and would rather see the money spent directly on needed equipment.

The other fishermen get twenty dollars a day. With three boats outfitted for today, and plenty of drinking water on board, we run under the sky across the broad lagoon, then along the reef to Ebiil Channel.

About a minute after the baits go over from Nimrod's boat, Mike hooks a grouper. He tries to bring it up rapidly, hand-over-handing line as fast as possible. I am wondering what the hurry is when a shark—a gray reefer—appears behind the struggling *tiao* and quickly ends its terror with a bite behind the gills. Mike is still shouting "Shark!" when Nimrod hooks another grouper. Within a moment they are yelling, "Sharks everywhere!" Nimrod's shark begins ripping the straining 150-pound-test line through his fingers. Our boats are anchored within shouting distance of one another—and the men are shouting plenty. After a brief contest with the husky shark, the line parts.

Things go quiet. The tide slacks and changes. The current rushing out the channel swings our sterns to windward and we bob pleasantly in the light chop. Our bow is pointed back toward the green mainland—if the island of Babeldaob can be called that. A line of white breakers along the nearby reef top separates the azure ocean from the turquoise lagoon. We are in a stream of outgoing lagoon water, blue-green, carrying some coral silt. Less than twenty feet away is deep ocean water, abruptly dark blue.

About half an hour passes before Joe brings a small *tiao* to the boat intact. It is a surpassingly beautiful fish of golden radiance bejeweled with sapphire dots. Asap swings it into a round tub of seawater, which it rapidly circumnavigates several times before settling down. He covers the fish's eyes, calming her and preventing the sun from burning her retinas, and prepares the tag. She is thirty-seven centimeters long, about fifteen inches. Because this species changes sex, there are no males this small.

Asap inserts the harpoon-shaped tag into her back, pushing it under her skin and past her central row of bones to anchor it, an indelicate procedure. The end of the little plastic tag streams out, with a serial number on it that will always identify this *tiao* as an individual with a history, plus a phone number to call if the fish is recaptured. Acting as Asap's assistant, I dutifully record the details of length, sex, location, and tag number. Asap returns her to the water. A strong swimmer, she bolts for home upon release, so she earns a "condition one" designation on the data form.

Joe has just hooked another grouper that is in considerably worse condition, having been bitten in two halfway to the surface. I am disturbed that we've gotten several fish killed, and I ask Joe if he thinks this is really such a good idea.

Misunderstanding the thrust of my question and focusing more on the project's goal, he says, "In our village, we need to understand more biology of the fish, so we can have a good management. Six years ago, you could catch ten or twelve fish in thirty minutes, then go home with all you needed for food. Now you try all day for maybe two. We have seen it really go down. So we need this knowledge to gain control."

Joe brings another fish to the boat alive. I notice for the first time its gold iris and sharp white canine teeth.

Harvey's boat, which has moved alongside because Joe is doing well, catches a larger grouper, sending Yvonne scurrying for her clipboard. At this size it could be either sex, so Yvonne inserts a small tube into its vent and sucks gently to see if she can pull out a few eggs as a way of determining sex. A few tiny, unripe eggs come into the tube. It takes a trained eye to see them, and the Palauans, interested in learning everything they can, crowd in close.

Some interval of tropical time passes. The sun, set on "scorch," seems dangerously close, slowly broiling us. Joe wraps his wet T-shirt around his head against our punishing star, but otherwise the Palauans seem unperturbed. We with white skins adopt unusual-looking ways to ward off the excessive insolation. Yvonne has only her hands unclad, and she keeps them shaded; her face is wrapped lightly in a white towel, only her sunglasses showing from beneath her hat's brim—a chic mummy. Lyle is covered head to toe in his bright-red suit. After about an hour with no bites, Asap says he wants to have a look at what the fish are doing and slips quietly into the cool relief without a splash. The water looks irresistibly inviting, but it is—empirically verified—shark-infested. I strive to remain intact by staying in the boat, suffering the heat under a towel, gulping water.

"Lots of grouper here," Asap calls from ten yards away. Joe whirls his line around, heaving it out to where Asap sees the most fish. But they are not biting. Even they must feel this heat. Our three boats have collectively tagged six fish. Nimrod's boat, with Lyle, has tagged none, only fed three sharks their tithing.

To conserve enthusiasm, we break for lunch. Afterward, Asap, Lyle, Yvonne, and I prepare to go down for the afternoon count. This time, as we drop to the bottom, I am constantly checking above, around, and behind me for hungry sharks. I'd like to know what's eating me. By prearrangement, I will accompany Yvonne while she observes and sketches interactions and color changes. Lyle will be making his standard circuit while teaching Asap to do the count himself.

The coral heads—"bommies" in Lyle's Australian—grow here in distorted plates shaped like mushroom caps, or like Dali's melting clocks. They afford the fish plenty of cover. This time, when I stop to look, groupers slowly take shape all around. I am learning to discern the splotchy camouflaged fish amid patchy coral and shadows, and I am feeling better about it. On the prime real estate with the best coral cover for females, the males are quite dense. Their territories abut so closely that any individual who moves off at our approach is almost immediately rushed by its territorial neighbor. Aggressors blush darkly, looking charcoal-colored at this depth, while the fleeing fish blanch and—lo and behold—their blue spots appear. The color changes are instantaneous. The flushing and blanching and spotting flash as quickly as we would signal with our eyebrows.

We are on an underwater field of fierce and intense silent communication. And, I suddenly realize, when fish come into the boat, pale golden and blue-spotted, they are in full submissive blanch, scared out of their wits and pleading for mercy! An artist painting a *tiao* on deck or from a photo of a fresh-caught fish would be illustrating an emotional state. It is as though, if fishes had their own field guides, the illustration representing all humanity would depict someone with a look of shocked terror, like Munch's painting *The Scream*.

With their undershot jaws and canines, the guarding fish look like bulldogs. So alert, interactive, and emotional are they, they might as well be birds on their territories. Like birds, they chase across boundaries invisible to us but well understood by them, then turn and glide back to their respective home turfs. Their colors immediately resettle, though sometimes with lingering aggression showing in their blushing flanks. If I ever again decide to eat such a complicated creature, it will be a different experience for me.

We watch two baited hooks fall into territories where they are promptly ignored. Suddenly Yvonne points at a fish and signs the letter T. I look again and see that the fish is tagged! It is a data point—the first resighting in the history of this young project—and it begins to answer one of the most basic questions: Do the same individuals congregate at the same sites in consecutive months? This fish was tagged here last month, when Lyle and the fishermen were first experimenting with the technique. So now we know that at least some do return. An exciting sighting!

We watch the tagged fish intently, as though expecting it to do something special. It takes so long to piece together an understanding, bit by little bit.

Despite the hammering they are taking from fisheries, the fishes' basic movements are virtually unknown. Suppose a species uses a spawning site four times during the year. If during one spawning you catch all the fish present, have you taken one-quarter of the population because each fish spawns only once, or have you taken it all because all the fish spawn in each of those four months? Another fundamental question: How far do fish come from; how big an area of the reef is affected by catching spawning fish at one breeding site? In the Bahamas, a tagged Nassau grouper traveled a hundred kilometers (more than sixty miles) to get to a breeding colony. That means the entire population of fish over a large area might be vulnerable to fishing at one small site during one short period. As fishing and human population pressures increase, we cannot hope to manage fisheries and maintain future options for either the reef or hungry people without such knowledge. That is precisely why we are here, studying the fish outside this little village that at first seems so inconsequential.

This tagged fish we are watching provides one of the first clues to the natural movements of groupers anywhere in the Pacific. The only other similar study I know of was conducted in Australia, where Lyle and a graduate student named Melita Samoilys did some preliminary tagging work and showed that one grouper returned not merely to the same aggregation, but to exactly the same tiny self-defended breeding territory—as birds do—in two consecutive years (it was caught by a fisherman before the third breeding season).

How much effort it takes to shove the door of knowledge open a crack, and what an enormous and extravagant room it is when you glimpse its well-lit interior! This little, average fish, with its special tag, is nudging that door a tiny bit.

Our scuba tanks now short on precious air, we must ascend to the surface.

Today, Lyle and Asap counted about the same number of males as yesterday, but fewer females. Lyle thinks yesterday's ripe females have spawned and left, but

Yvonne believes many females might be hiding under the corals, waiting to complete several consecutive days' spawning.

The afternoon fishing session produces as many fish as did the morning. But the sharks are absent or not hungry—which is good for us *and* the groupers, and more are tagged.

Late in the afternoon, we haul lines and anchors and start the engines. While we are running homeward, more than a hundred spinner dolphins sweep in to engage us, zigzagging our bow waves and wakes, leaping and shining. Leaning over the bow of our running boat like a figurehead, I shoot a roll of film. They are frolicking in the pressure wave almost close enough to touch, pumping vigorously, streaming along glistening, surfacing in unison for breath, then trailing bubbles.

They say you can't have everything, but this is close enough. Over the noise of the engine and rushing water, Lyle calls, "These spinners are the horniest animals I've ever seen. I've *never* been diving in a school of these guys when it wasn't nonstop fornication going on." Is this the meaning behind the dolphin's enigmatic, Mona Lisa–like smile? If so, I can't help smiling at the thought of what might have been behind old Mona's.

At the end of a wonderfully exhausting day in the sun and salt, we settle in to discuss the day's data and share a cold, rehydrating drink. But Harvey and Asap, who have just finished doing the lion's share of unloading all the scientific and scuba gear from the boats, head out again, without supper, toward the setting sun. They will sit vigil throughout the moonless night, guarding the site from spear fishermen before tomorrow's all-day scientific efforts under the broiler.

By the third day, certain things seem routine: the Palauan fishermen straggling into the kitchen before breakfast, the readying of lunch and filling of water bottles, the leisurely preparation of bait. I admire the easy morning joking and teasing between Lyle and the men. While they are readying the supplies, he says to me, "Last year, these guys didn't take me seriously. When I came back this year, did some spear fishing with them, and talked to the schoolkids, they began to see we were serious and we care for them." He winks. The fishermen roll their eyes in affectionate jest.

Soon after we start fishing, Asap hooks something heavy. It yields reluctantly. He puts his back into it. Several long, sweaty minutes later, we realize he has hooked our own anchor. By noon, with only three groupers tagged, we go underwater to count the fish, and I again join Yvonne to watch them on their own turf.

This afternoon we are going to check another breeding site, far more remote: an extra hour up the coast, where the reef makes a jag out to the west. As we are running, several fins break the surface slowly. I am thinking marlin. Lyle thinks manta ray "wingtips." We pass and hook back around. Now the fins resurface. They are some type of dolphins, but *large* dolphins: gray, with high, blunt foreheads. Lyle says in a hushed and wondrous tone, "This is a species I've never *seen* before."

That is saying a lot. I already have my mask and flippers on. I would love to meet these animals eye to eye. Seeing that I am prepared to enter, Lyle with a nod says, "Go ahead. *Don't* splash." I slide overboard into the deep ocean, knowing that sharks often shadow a large pod of marine mammals. I tell myself the calculated risk is just like getting into an automobile, but without the numbing familiarity. It doesn't work. We're not talking about a fender bender. We're talking about being eaten. The imminent sense of unseen threat clenches my gut like a fist, and I, relying on luck alone, feel as utterly vulnerable as I am.

The animals' large backs and dorsal fins are rolling through the calm surface, moving slowly and effortlessly away. Determined to get a look at the creatures, I swim after them with all I've got, splashing and silhouetted against the sky like a struggling fish, defenseless, fighting the press of panic. Curiosity killed the cat, after all. The mystery dolphins elude me. The closest I get is a swim through a cloud of fresh dung: endangered feces.

I look around for the boat. It is more than a hundred yards away, bobbing in and out of view in the swells. The water I am in is probably more than a mile deep. I want to get picked up *now!* When the skiff comes around, Lyle has his mask and fins on. We get ahead of the animals, which have reappeared on the surface. Lyle reminds me again, "Just slip in; no splash." I slide in after him, and he's off like a balloon in the breeze. In the water, this guy with the belly and the baling wire holding his spine together is *fast!* I struggle unsuccessfully to keep up. Just as I am totally winded and almost unable to continue, Lyle, thirty feet ahead of me, points directly beyond him. A large, light gray creature is swimming off at the edge of vision.

At the surface, we can still see their fins, moving away. Lyle got a much better look, and he says that the animals whose fins we had seen were only a fraction of a pod of several dozen, extending down into shafts of light disappearing into the infinite deep.

At the sound of the approaching boat, all the creatures at the surface throw flukes into the air and the mysterious animals slip below for good.

As we approach our destination, our other two boats become visible up ahead, fishing at anchor. While we are still over open water I ask Lyle to slow down so I can troll the last couple of hundred yards to the site, and I toss a lure overboard on a hand line. Shortly, I have a bite—a jobfish of about fifteen pounds. It pulls hard for a few moments, but after one particularly energetic tug it comes in quite easily, and soon its head appears—without a body!

Harvey, Franzier, Nimrod, and Mike have already tagged about ten fish. Lyle slides off our boat with mask and fins to reconnoiter. "Right here: plenty of big *tiao*. Drop the anchor here." We suit up with scuba gear. I am thinking we are all crazy to keep doing this with so many hungry sharks around. We slip gingerly into the water.

Even from the surface, we can see groupers. We descend. The bottom here is tongue and groove: coral ridges and sandy channels. And the site, thanks to its remoteness, is *loaded* with groupers. The square-tailed *tiao* are chasing one another and guarding territories everywhere we look. Lyle, wide-eyed behind his mask, looks at me and writes on his slate, *"Grand Central Station!!"* Thirty to fifty *tiao* are in sight within the limits of our fifty-foot visibility. We pause and watch. A school of large unicorn fish, some blue and some black, dreams in upon us and splits, enveloping us. Slipping over the lip of a steep slope, we go to a gloomy ninety feet, paying our respects to a large Spanish mackerel and a small shark in a gray flannel suit. Lyle writes on his slate, "I feel that this is the end." What? Is this a bizarre suicide note? Oh—he only means this is beyond the limits of the grouper breeding colony. We head back and surface.

Once again in the atmosphere, Lyle's enthusiasm uncorks. "Did you see that! *Tiao* all *over* the bloody place! The number of fish chasing around was unbelievable! Two hundred and ten females and a hundred and fifty males! There seems to be a female under every bloody rock and bommie! *This* is more like a real population. *This* population is still in good condition. The ratio of males to females is right. Plenty of young females are entering this population. This is *great* to see. This is what fisheries management people still don't seem to comprehend: the large number of females there should be. Now we can compare population numbers and sex ratios between this site and more exploited spawning aggregations. This site makes each other site much more important."

Lyle's enthusiasm infects all of us, even the laconic Palauan fishermen. When the next fish comes into Nimrod's boat for tagging, there is such a scramble for buckets and equipment that, from all the excitement, you would think they— and we—were all twelve years old. Yet Lyle had told me earlier that Nimrod's first reaction to the proposition of tagging was, "Hey, I'm not here to waste my time throwing fish back. I'm in this for the money. Why should I bother?" Could this be the same person, dancing around the deck?

Lyle is shaking me awake. By the time I finally stop dreaming of sharks, it is already first light. What day is this? Today, I calculate, is the fourth day of this lunar spawning cycle. I step outside. Dawn is spreading a breathless crystal silence over mirror-still waters. The soles of clouds reflect the great lagoon's turquoise in an openhearted sky. The poet Rupert Brooke: "It is sheer beauty, so pure that it is difficult to breathe in." I dream each night of sharks and morning. Each morning, I awaken to a dream. Henry Thoreau: "Behind every man's busyness there should be a level of undisturbed serenity . . . as within the reef encircling a coral isle there is always an expanse of still water." Emerson: "In their eternal calm, he finds himself." Lyle, in his thick Australian accent: "Come on then! It's just another bloody day in paradise."

The early-morning routine has taken on a sublime quality rarely achieved in life, where the mere making of a sandwich for lunch resonates with anticipation of a day cloaked in the glory and mystery of living, shimmering with thoughts of dolphins playing in the blue ocean. In a few days, the passage of the new moon will send the fish back to where they came from—and will do the same to me. This knowledge fills me with a rare sense of full-focused presence.

We glide on a sheet of glass to the site Lyle called Grand Central Station and start fishing at eight-thirty. Things go well, and with the aid of fresh bait and much shouted enthusiasm, we tag and release eight *tiao*, mostly females, by ten o'clock. The sharks, bless them, are off elsewhere and do not charge their tariff.

Catching slows as the day's heat intensifies. At midday, the boats draw together, tied up and bumping gently in the rocking swell. Fried moray eel and taro root supplemented with peanut butter sandwiches and soft drinks are our lunch on the hottest day yet. Now even the natives cover themselves head to toe against the sun. Yvonne reveals her visage just long enough to eat, keeping the towel draped over her head like an Arab.

The bushy Franzier, wearing shredded, cutoff jeans and a shirt of indeterminate color, comes aboard our boat. He says, "Tagging here is fun. Up north a little, it's *dry!* Hard to catch! The Hong Kong boat comes, they hire Palauans, and they take *everything*. Fish this size!" He shows us with his thumb and forefinger. "They could clean it *out,*" he says, shaking his woolly ponytail. "They sleep on the boat, and early, early, they are fishing. Catching *everything*. Three years ago, and today—it's going down very much, very fast."

Nimrod, who has fished on the Hong Kong boat, argues, "The Hong Kong boat is good. I fish there for money. Never in my life in Palau have I been paid so much money for grouper. A dollar sixty for one pound. They pay you right from the ship. If we use our own boat, gas is cheap. If we use their boat, gas is free. The boat is air-conditioned and fishermen can wash clothes on board. They give free coffee. They pay the most. Now, because the elders have declared the *bul,* the Hong Kong boat cannot be here and it has gone south. But August first they will come back, and I will be there."

I ask, "So they are respecting the *bul?*"

Nimrod pauses and says, "I don't know."

Yvonne, who will return to her job in Hong Kong in a few days, says dryly, "If they had a choice, they wouldn't cooperate." It is a cut so out of character that I involuntarily glance up to appraise the look behind her sunglasses.

"They are cooperating because they have no choice here," opines Harvey. In Palau, as on Australia's Great Barrier Reef, fishing for the live market is restricted to hook and line, with apparent success despite rumors of some cyanide poaching.

Palau has had problems with outside fishing interests in the past. In the mid-1980s, an agreement was reached between the Palauan government and a Hong Kong–based company exporting live reef fish. Palauans would be trained for six months in fishing techniques, then they would replace company fishermen. This was not honored. The company's fishermen continued doing the fishing.

Lyle, who fully understands just how great a pressure the Hong Kong trade is exerting on this entire Indo-Pacific region, says, "The way the Hong Kong boats work in places like Indonesia or Papua New Guinea is that they first ask permission from the villages to use the reef. Often they bribe the chiefs and promise to employ young men. Unemployed young men are a major problem in many villages. Once they get permission, their first questions are, 'Where are the spawning aggregations; at what months?' That's all they talk about. They use the local fishermen's knowledge to find the spawners. Then they begin complaining that the locals are not working hard enough or catching enough. It's all planned. And in a week to a month—that's the longest I've heard of them keeping locals on a payroll—they have found out where the fish breed, and they drop the locals."

One of the fishermen says, "That's why this project is so important."

The first Hong Kong operation in Palau depleted a major grouper spawning population near Koror (which has not recovered), then went after the splendid, giant Napoleon wrasses. Eventually the company was banned. They resorted to poaching in Palau's remote southwest islands. Their vessel was finally apprehended there with about 24,000 pounds of live wrasse and groupers aboard. A Palauan businessman who has a joint venture with the currently operating Hong Kong interests in Palauan waters claims the decline of groupers is caused by boat exhaust and global warming, not by overfishing.

Lyle was once hired as a consultant by the Queensland Department of Environmental Heritage and National Parks to look into the live fish trade there when a Hong Kong company was allowed in. Lyle learned that the money behind these operations is phenomenal. He says it's a billion-dollar industry, the underworld is heavily into it, and it generates corruption at high political levels in countries all over the vast Indo-Pacific region.

The afternoon diving count reveals roughly the same number of males and about half as many females as yesterday. Lyle had predicted yesterday that most of the females from this site would spawn and leave during the night. It appears he was correct. By late afternoon, we end a very hot, very long, very productive day with twenty-one fish tagged and none lost to sharks.

When we get back to the field station, Asap has just returned from a trying day in Koror getting fuel, food, and air. Three of our precious rented scuba tanks were taken back by the dive shop because they were having a busy week with the tourists. That's roughly nine fewer dives, which will require another day spent making the round-trip to get air that much sooner. That's not all—not nearly. The second largest known grouper spawning aggregation in Palau—after the one we were at today—is in Ulong Channel. An American research technician employed by the Division of Marine Resources has been monitoring the Ulong grouper rookery as part of Dr. Johannes's studies, much as Lyle and Asap have been doing here. Asap gives Lyle a note informing him that the new division head, the man who seems to be doing his best to make life difficult for meddlesome Western conservation biologists—has forbidden the American technician from counting the breeding fish, invoking a long-standing law against taking or "harrassing" fish there during spawning season and interpreting visual counts as constituting "harrassment." The new division head seems to be poking at soft spots here at the field station as well; his underlings have expressed displeasure at my presence here and have forbidden me to use any of the government-owned boats, equipment, or facilities. (Anticipating this, I have brought my own roll-up mattress.) There is another problem: The money Lyle was expecting is still not in the bank, though that money was supposed to be wired in from Bob Johannes's account in Australia. So there is no money for salaries or supplies, none to pay the taggers.

At eight P.M., only a minute or two after Harvey and Asap have left to guard the dark channel against spear fishermen, a stranger—a fisherman—comes through the doorway. He is clearly agitated, maybe a little drunk. "I don't normally come in here," he says. "But I know what your problems are. I saw three boats on Ebiil a half hour ago. I saw the lights. They were diving with tanks and spearguns. They are gone now. That's your problem. Your guys were here while people are spearing your fish."

Lyle, tight-faced and oddly unwelcoming, says that when the fish show up in the markets in Koror the identity of the people who poached them illegally will rapidly spread along the grapevine.

The stranger laughs, "The fish will never show up in the markets in Koror. They are not being eaten in Palau. I am talking on reality here."

Lyle asks where they are being sold.

The fisherman answers, "I cannot say."

I ask the obvious: Hong Kong?

"Find out yourself." He turns to Lyle, saying, "They have your map because you are explaining your work to the people. And that really bothers me. What you are doing, it is good. But times have changed and it's going to screw you, your project, and the fish—excuse my language. We're gonna lose our everyday life to people who live in Koror and have government jobs and come at night and get our fish illegally. The new division head is there because someone wants him there."

I ask who, but the stranger laughs and exits melodramatically into the darkness. I look inquiringly at Lyle, who says, "The division head has family in the president's office. He is connected and reconnected."

But Lyle thinks the stranger knows less than he implied. He is much more upset that the American research technician can no longer work at Ulong. "I've got an ulcer called Government Bureaucracy," Lyle says, and he sighs with discomfort and swallows a couple of pills. Lyle is almost always in physical pain, but you would never know it. He gains superiority over his affliction with his enthusiasm for helping people and his belief in the importance of this project. But the new division head has just shot a large hole in Lyle's ability to cope with his pain.

"His decision to stop the technician from working at Ulong is stupefying!" Lyle says angrily. "We're the only people in the country who can't go to Ulong. Tourists can go, illegal fishermen can still go. Just not us. Just not the people who are trying to help."

Out on the dock, a group of socializing locals has just started playing a tape of "Hotel California" and a line from it pops out at me: *This could be heaven, and this could be hell.*

The luster that had greeted each new day has been replaced this morning by a leaden, awkward silence. Lyle's attitude, once infectiously enthusiastic, is now infectiously sullen. Everyone is wondering when the new division chief will find a way to shut down the entire study and the cooperative work with the Palauan fishermen. I feel like a liability and offer to leave. Lyle sidesteps the question by asking me how, precisely, I would cross the water or find my way thirty miles through the jungle. Good point.

As we prepare the day's equipment, everyone seems to be treading on eggshells. Lyle is so distracted that I hear him ask Asap three times whether the fishing lines and tagging kits are already in his boat. Three times Asap patiently tells him, yes, he has kept the lines onboard and the tagging kits have been brought out to the boats.

Lyle, Asap, and I cross the lagoon and reef and anchor up at Ebiil. The familiar process is now suffused with tension. I feel very bad for Lyle, who seems so hurt by the division chief's undermining of the project as to be ailing. The fishermen, too, seem dismayed. Why, they wonder, would their efforts to learn enough about the fish to ensure their own future not be supported by their government officials?

When it is time to begin fishing, we discover that someone has borrowed the fishing lines out of Asap's boat. Despite Lyle's repeated questioning before we left the dock and Asap's repeated assurances, Asap never actually looked to make sure the lines were still *in* the boat. Nor did he actually look to make sure new data forms were inside the tagging kits.

Because we can't fish, there is nothing to do for the next two hours, until it is time to go down for the visual count. But Lyle needs nothing less than to sit around for hours brooding on the project's many small problems and on the new division chief, who has already cost him a night's sleep. Lyle sits in dejected silence, trying to contain his aggravation and giving an occasional sigh of exhaled air, like a big, exhausted sea turtle. Asap, for his part, is so mortified with embarrassment that he goes off idly snorkeling across Ebiil Channel, as if hoping to get eaten. "He won't be that lucky," Lyle says. "He'll have to live with himself today."

While Lyle and Asap are feeling miserable, I sit in silence, looking through my binoculars, watching a distant school of high-stepping dolphins transit the lagoon between two palm-clad islets, gleaming and glistening in the sparkling sunlight.

Asap returns even more deeply disturbed than when he left. He has worked himself into a state and is now every bit as sullen as Lyle.

Yvonne and a new fisherman named Rodas arrive with fresh bait and fishing lines. Fifteen minutes later, the first grouper, a big male *tiao*, is clipped off behind the head by a shark within seconds of being hooked. Asap, in a festering anger, seeks comfort in revenge, taking out a rope and affixing to it a large shark hook. But the bleeding head of the *tiao*, dangling overboard on the hook, just sits there soaking. The sharks may be ravenous, but apparently they are not dumb.

Unable even to draw one of the ubiquitous sharks, Asap has silently wound himself into a most foul distemper. He refuses to dive with Lyle today for the underwater count. Lyle, though annoyed, decides not to press it. I stay topside because of the shortage of air. Lyle dives solo.

Lyle eventually resurfaces, a bit renewed by his sojourn beneath the sea. "Far fewer groupers than yesterday," he says. "They've peaked and are on the way out." But he's just seen several big male Napoleon wrasse chasing each other. He believes they are going to breed here too. "Always something new happening. Down there is my office, and they change the pictures every day."

That sounds more like Lyle. He, Yvonne, and I put our things together in one boat, haul anchor, and go to Grand Central Station for the count there, leaving Rodas and Asap behind to try to tag a few more fish.

We have timed our arrival to coincide with slack water. Eager to dive before the tide starts running and produces a strong current to contend with, we hurry into our gear and slide over the side.

Almost immediately upon reaching the bottom, we notice two Napoleon wrasse—eighty-pounders at least—slipping slowly and shyly out of our field of vision. Lyle is right: They are moving into the same spawning sites, as the groupers are leaving. As at Ebiil, many *tiao* have spawned and gone, dispersing back throughout the reefs.

Something grayish in the distance materializes into the first manta ray I've ever seen. With breathtaking grace it sweeps in on big, slow-flapping, rippling, winglike fins, eyeing us curiously. It is a smallish one, with a seven-foot wingspan. Banking past and changing course, it comes back for another look at us. It is an utterly benign presence, and its superiority in this regard is disconcerting. I want to be able to say—or even to honestly feel—"We come to your home in peace." But while we have come to help the groupers, we have cost the lives of several. "We are double-edged blades," Thoreau observed, "and every time we whet our virtue the return stroke strops our vice."

While Yvonne and I stay on the bottom, Lyle signals that he is now returning to the boat. One of the main reasons Yvonne came to Palau is to collect gonad samples from fish that have died during tagging. She is eager to examine sperm and egg cells under a microscope to learn if the groupers spawn all at once or over several days. Only a few fish are needed to learn something this fundamental, but she has gotten no samples all week. All of the fish that have made it to the boat intact were handled well and survived, and those that were taken by sharks were taken whole or right behind the head, gonads and all. So by prior arrangement Lyle will go back up to the surface now and trade his clipboard for his speargun, and go off alone to hunt for science. Considering the losses to sharks that we have caused, all of us have mixed feelings about intentionally killing any additional fish to examine their gonads, but the information is sufficiently important to make the sacrificing seem justifiable.

Lyle heads for the sky. Yvonne and I continue watching the fish and see four tagged groupers, which we find tremendously exciting. The resighting of a few tagged fish can be used to estimate the total population. It works this way: Say you have tagged fifty fish, and then, on a dive, you see five tagged fish plus a hundred other fish. You know that there are fifty tagged fish, and you know you've seen five, so you figure that you've seen one-tenth of the population. So you multiply the number of untagged fish you've seen by ten to get an estimate of the total population. Perhaps, if this project is allowed to come to full fruition, tagged fish will eventually be sighted throughout the reef system. Perhaps we will learn that when they are not breeding they return to the same home sites time and again. Perhaps we will learn how far they travel, whether individual fish usually spawn once or several times per year, how fishing along the reef affects the numbers and sex ratios that appear on spawning sites, and, ultimately, how many fish can safely be taken over the long term, perpetually. Perhaps we will learn all these things we've been talking about and hoping for.

Or perhaps the project will suddenly be terminated the next time we get word from Koror.

The tide starts running. We'd better leave now. Yvonne and I surface about a hundred yards from the boat, across the tidal flow and slightly upcurrent, as planned. The current is stronger at the surface. We try simply crossing the flow to where the boat is anchored, but we are swept past too fast, missing it by a wide margin. We must now turn directly into the current to reach our boat. It is all we can do to make forward headway. The tide, under the influence of the new moon, is picking up power by the minute and starting to run harder. Yvonne, a stronger swimmer than I, moves ahead, working strenuously but making slow progress. We are kicking hard and augmenting our kicks with breast strokes. With fifty yards yet to go, I am tiring. The tide is building rapidly. With each pull of my arms I cover less of the remaining distance. The drag of the tank and the vest and the weight belt are all adding to my mounting exhaustion, but I don't want to start ditching expensive gear. By the time I can see the propellers ahead of Yvonne, they are turning like windmills in the current. She finally reaches the boat, pauses to catch her breath, pulls off her tank and vest and shoves them up and onto the deck with one hand. By this time, I'm about thirty feet behind the boat, struggling but barely moving forward. I am remembering again the river I nearly drowned in, the mounting exhaustion then, too. A rope hits the surface near my head. Perfect! I grab it, yell a quick thanks to Yvonne, pull myself to the boat, and act calm. Yvonne says, "That's one of the worst things in diving: a long surface swim in strong current after a dive." I nod. I'm O.K. but winded and still trembling with the overexertion of my arm and leg muscles.

But this is nothing, not even worth mentioning, compared to what Lyle is dealing with right now. His bubbles appear near the anchor line and in a moment he surfaces with his speargun and three groupers on a stringer. Two of them are deeply slashed.

I take his tank, asking, "Shark?"

Still in the water, hanging off the boat with both hands, Lyle takes a deep breath, blinks, and says declaratively with a deep nod, "Yes." He spits into the sea and hoists himself aboard. "I've just spent the last five minutes trying to fight off the *biggest* damn gray reefer, *beating* him on the head with my speargun. Usually you smack them in the snoot and they ping off! But this bloody monster was dogged. He was *huge,* and just about trying to crawl into me suit with me." Lyle holds his hand out flat, fingers spread. "Christ, look at this." His hand is shaking.

He's really rattled. It is a good ten minutes before Lyle can calm down enough to want a gulp of water. But Yvonne is immediately effusive in her pleasure at having the samples, and she gets to work immediately, removing and preserving them.

Lyle says, "I almost got seriously eaten for your bloody gonads."

"Yes, Lyle, but—they're great, just great," Yvonne says. "It was worth risking your life. I'll give you, uh, I'll give you some *really great* information from them."

"I'm not sure it was quite worth getting them that way. That was bad. I'm still shaking."

I say, "It could have been worse, Lyle: It could have happened to me."

He squints at me. "Right. Anyway, Yvonne, of these three fish: This one was being actively courted by a forty-five-centimeter male. This male was courting a thirty-five-centimeter female. This one that got raked so badly by the shark was just guarding his territory when I saw him." After a deep breath and a couple more sips of water, Lyle says, "God, that was a big shark."

Yvonne says, "Big? I thought you said it was *huge!*" Her eyes are twinkling.

Lyle says, "A few minutes ago, it was huge. Now that the adrenaline is wearing down, it was big."

A distant cloud of seabirds catches my eye, and with binoculars I see that a few hundred yards offshore a large school of yellowfin tuna is churning like a hail of bullets into shoals of flying fish. Herman Melville referred to the yellowfin as "the superb albicore, with his glittering sides." One of these superbly glittering yellowfins, streaking through the surface just under an airborne flying fish, takes its prey in a smother of foam the instant it touches back to the sea. It is a war of well-matched, co-evolved adaptations, an evolutionary arms race that has brought both contestants near perfection. And today, as every day for thousands of years, the slowest flying fish will be eaten and the slowest tuna will go hungry.

The future is never assured. Within the year the Division of Marine Resources will prohibit the grouper tagging entirely. Catching and releasing the tagged fish will be deemed illegal under a new law designed to protect the groupers by barring their capture, sale, and purchase during the spawning months. Thus efforts to gain the knowledge necessary to manage the fishery for the future will be thrown out with the bathwater despite what—on the surface, at least—seem like good intentions.

Hong Kong

Although it has not been raining here in Kowloon, the street is wet. Trucks with beds converted into holding pens for live fishes are lining up, their aerating compressors continually growling and pumping bubbles. The air *we* are breathing—Ian Collier of Hong Kong's Agriculture and Fisheries Department and Yvonne Sadovy are here with me—is heavy with the breath of diesels.

This market—Lei Yue Mun—is situated between the busy wharf (packed with boats delivering fish) and the busy street (packed with trucks hauling the fish away). Because all the animals are alive, they must be kept moving fast. They are the ultimate perishable product. And so the place itself, like its operating style, is flow-through: open-sided, under a high metal roof with skylights.

Unlike Tokyo's massive, world-of-its-own Tsukiji, the markets in Hong Kong are decentralized. This market's corrugated roof covers an area just eighty yards long and thirty yards wide, with only ten or so large wholesale businesses here. But if Hong Kong's many markets for live fish are not as large as Tokyo's singular Tsukiji, the fact that *everything* here is alive gives a heightened sense both of fast, almost festive action and of impending doom for the stress-shocked prisoners in the tanks and tubs.

Guys in rubber aprons, walking quick-step through the puddles, are yelling rapid-fire Chinese into cellular telephones. The din of barely organized chaos—truck doors banging, people shouting, pumps and aerators incessantly whirring—make conversation difficult, and we ourselves are forced to shout to one another, too.

Along the wharf, boats are unloading in a hurry. Their decks are jammed with tanks and confused with vinelike tangles of air tubing dangling from above and snaking from below. For outsiders like me, who aren't supposed to be in here anyway, the action is best observed from a safe, unobtrusive distance. Everyone walks in quick, splattering steps among, between, and on top of tiers of square pens—crammed with fishes—through which pumped water is cascading and running over, out, and off the wharf. Everyone else is wearing boots or rubber sandals; my new white sneakers are quickly soaked and as quickly speckled black with street grime and the sputtering carbon from the tails of trucks.

Parrotfishes, calico-patterned crabs, various wrasses, snappers, emperors—wild creatures from all over the southern Pacific and South Asia crowd the concrete runs and glass tanks. In one pen, several moray eels gasp toward death. Though the fish represent familiar families, neither I nor Yvonne nor Ian Collier can identify many of the distinct species. This says as much about the vast area from which the fish are coming as it does about the diversity of this region's reefs—as well as about how scientifically and managerially out of control all of this fishing and trading is.

While Dr. Sadovy can at least offer well-educated guesses on the fishes' identities, I am quickly reduced to utter ignorance. Here are red fish, yellow fish, pale fish, dark fish, fish with small blue spots on a tan background, black-spotted groupers of some kind, groupers with blue scrawled markings on a beige-saddled background, venom-spined scorpionfish, rabbitfish, blue-spotted red coral trout, various morays and other eels, fish that are black-spotted on red, and red-spotted on pink—virtually all unknown to me.

Here, indeed, is just about anything that swims near coral reefs. Notably absent are the open-ocean species so prized in Japan. The tastes are almost inverse: While the Chinese are enamored of the white, flaky flesh of colorful reef fishes, the Japanese prefer the oily, meaty flesh of tunas and other denizens of deep and chillier waters. Nowadays, virtually nothing that swims or crawls underwater is lucky enough to be unloved.

A narrow walkway and tunnel separates the high-priced side from the rest of the market. Emerging from the tunnel and walking up a wood-planked ramp, I find myself within the domain of Wingsang Sea Products, where men wearing rubber aprons are walking the edges of cement pens, netting expensive fish from the river of water flowing through. One pen holds tiger groupers. At an adjacent tank two guys are struggling to contain a large and frightened Napoleon wrasse in a too-small net. One worker boasts, "These are the best fish." He kisses his fingers with his eyes closed, like a French chef. "*Very* good."

A Taoist shrine, illuminated by red lights, with offerings of strange Oriental fruits and burning incense, presides over the office overlooking the operation from above. This company sells eight hundred tons of fish per year. Fish on this side of the market average about four pounds, so that's about eleven hundred fish each day. The modest man in charge quickly points out that he is by no means the biggest dealer here. He tells me the fish are from Indonesia, the Maldives, the Philippines, Papua New Guinea, the Solomon Islands—and Palau.

Making a solid estimate of the volume of the live reef-fish trade in the region—or here in this one city—is not possible. Bob Johannes and his collaborator Michael Riepen have tried. Governments don't keep good statistics. Oddly, Hong Kong counts only dead fish as "fish"—not imported live ones. Collier himself says he considers this a trading operation, not a fishing operation. (Talk about losing sight of the forest for the trees!) The fishing industry underreports for tax purposes—or because they've been poaching or fishing with illegal methods. The less they say, the better for them. The best estimate—the best *conservative* estimate—is from Johannes and Riepen. They figure twenty to twenty-five thousand metric tons of reef fishes from throughout the region are involved. (The average fish weighs about a kilogram—a little over two pounds—so that's about twenty-five million fish.) By "involved," they mean the ones that make it to market. It is nearly impossible even to guess the numbers that die before arriving at their destination. In many cases, fatalities en route account for about 10 to 50 percent of those shipped. And remember, some observers say that for every fish shipped, about ten have been killed underwater by cyanide.

Collier, Sadovy, and I walk a few blocks from the wholesale market to a large retail district, where some sixty brightly lit stalls are all selling live fish and shellfish to consumers: lobsters, clams, scallops, cuttlefish, mantis shrimp, chitons, and many others. At one stall with particularly large tanks, giant groupers and potato cod await their fates. The shopkeeper proudly indicates their high prices by explaining, "These are protected in Australia."

From these stalls, shoppers can buy live fish and immediately take them to adjacent restaurants. It is an amazing system, really, the pinnacle of a culinary ideal flawlessly executed: to have access to live wild fish swimming the reefs hundreds or thousands of miles away, and then to eat them absolutely fresh, just moments after they gasp their last.

People in Hong Kong love to eat. They spend half their disposable income on food, and in this business-friendly city where the people pay only minimal taxes, many have high disposable incomes indeed. They use food to celebrate. To socialize. To entertain VIPs. To show off. When they sit down to eat in a fancy place, they don't get up for hours, not until they have dealt with a dozen or so courses. And for the Cantonese who make up most of Hong Kong's populace, food means seafood. The city's six million residents burn through three hundred thousand tons of seafood—about one hundred pounds per person—per year (Americans eat about fifteen pounds). Seafood symbolizes prosperity and luck, and the word "fish" itself suggests abundance and good fortune. So, having just made a killing and wanting to celebrate, an investor might glance at his Rolex, drive his Mercedes downtown to meet some friends, and splurge by treating them to a dazzling procession of exquisitely prepared reef fishes. If the fish is red, for good luck, so much the better. The main thing: Either it's freshly killed or forget it. Eating fish that were alive until moments before cooking has been a Chinese custom for centuries, the ultimate way to ensure freshness. Fish gourmands here pay four to eight times as much for live fish as for dead ones. If the fish is too big to be sold whole—a large Napoleon wrasse, say—retailers carefully slice it open so freshness-minded consumers can see reassuringly that its heart is still beating even after large portions of its flesh have been removed.

Collier's contacts being what they are, we receive an invitation to lunch with six men involved in the fish business, plus two fisheries agency people and Michael Riepen, who is Bob Johannes's recent collaborator and an economics adviser for Fisheries Development Associates, a consulting firm based in New Zealand. We are summoned to one of the many restaurants immediately adjacent to the live-fish stalls.

Our principal host is a Mr. Yung, from Wingsang Sea Products. He is introduced to us laughingly but not jokingly as the "Big Boss," one of the many millionaires in Hong Kong. He confers long instructions upon the waiters.

Another host, the one with the best English, is Ricky Lau, a Chinese yuppie who earned a law degree in Great Britain and now works with a company called Fisheries Holdings, Ltd. Ricky has been in the fish business for ten years. Before that, he was in government service working for the crown prosecutor. At the large round table, Ricky takes a seat to Yvonne's right, and I settle in on her left. Lau finds it very interesting that we have just come from Palau, saying, "Really! We have fishing activities in Palau."

Ah, something in common. It's a small world after all. And shrinking. Perhaps some of the groupers we will be eating today are even individuals we saw underwater. In my mind I flash back to Lyle scrawling *"Grand Central Station!!"* across his slate when we landed amid the dense colony of spawning groupers at the remote site; I remember the look in his eyes—and the taut excitement I felt at seeing such a large and healthy group of animals carrying on as they have for millions of years. What a sappy sentimentalist I am.

Hearing that Lau is also heavily involved in aquaculture, Yvonne asks him about the availability of fry of the red grouper—a particularly popular fish because, as one person explained, "In Chinese culture the color red means happy, means luck, means wealth." She is asking because it turns out that many species "raised in captivity" cannot be bred in captivity. The supply depends on wild babies—called fry—caught in nature.

In response to Sadovy's inquiry, Ricky Lau describes at length the spawning behavior of the red grouper, holding forth a discourse that reveals an understanding more thorough than many scientists'. Ricky concludes with a telling answer to Yvonne's question: "The supply of wild fry for many species that we are unable to breed in captivity is getting scarce and increasing in cost. There is no problem with the demand for our fish captive-reared. The supply is what limits our aquaculture business from expanding. So actually, mariculture is a declining industry."

Mariculture declining already? Most people still believe that aquaculture will be the wave of the future, and in fact aquaculture is off and running worldwide. But it poses some problems that might trip it up. Many areas with intensive aquaculture have seen productivity tumble because of chronic problems with disease (despite heavy use of antibiotics and antifungal chemicals) and water fouling. It's no friend to nature, either, eliminating natural habitats, introducing diseases fatal to local wild fish and shrimp, and often causing water pollution—so much pollution that in 1996 India's Supreme Court ordered closure of all large shrimp farms—hundreds—along India's west coast. Aquaculture can be done better; for instance, if it is sited on land with lined ponds to prevent leaching and if its outflow is treated as the industrial wastewater it is. Better still if the creatures raised are one of the few vegetarian fish species and breed easily in captivity. But these approaches are seldom taken. The way it is usually done now, aquaculture is poised to do to natural coastal habitats what agriculture did to prairie habitats. It will occupy, simplify, convert, and replace natural systems, as it has done in much of Asia and other parts of the world. On land, most of our wildlife problems are caused by habitat loss due to conversion of natural areas for human uses. Aquaculture will do that. Right now, overfished wild fish can come back quickly if we ease up on them, because their habitat is still there, so the potential for their recovery is excellent. Intensive aquaculture in certain areas will end that and will—and has—cause the local decline of wild fish.

By the mid-1990s, fish farming and "ranching" (growing wild-caught fry to marketable adults) was supplying a third of the demand for live reef fishes. However, most reef species cannot yet be bred in captivity, including the most sought-after and expensive fish: the Napoleon wrasse. One Napoleon wrasse at Hong Kong's Ocean Park aquarium took nearly twenty years to grow from one pound to seventy pounds. And this is a well-cared-for fish fed a good diet. On the reefs this species grows to over seven feet and four hundred pounds. How old is that? Johannes had said he thinks they may live more than a century. They are the old-growth of the fish world, and fish of these sizes are becoming extremely rare over vast areas. But not one Napoleon wrasse has ever been spawned in captivity, and virtually nothing is known about their reproductive biology. So don't count on aquaculture to do the trick. Only ten species of reef fish valued as food have spawned in captivity, and only two—the malabar grouper and the orange-spotted grouper—have yet been successfully raised on a commercial scale. The rest of the reef fish in aquaculture must be raised from wild juveniles, supplies of which are faltering in some places.

Raising wild-caught baby reef fish is not exactly a snap, either. Despite what some people think they taste like, they are not chickens. Grouper larvae are among the smallest and most delicate things anyone has ever tried to raise. Vigorous artificial aeration of their water can destroy them. Their food needs are extremely complicated and demanding, requiring various kinds of plankton. Each individual stage of their early life cycle can require a different food. Some may need algae at first, then perhaps rotifers, then copepods. Growing all these organisms takes money and personnel, and artificial diets can be prohibitively expensive as well. Because of this, the cost of raising young can be very high. So even for fish that *can* be bred in captivity it is often more cost-effective to find young wild fish that have already undergone the earliest stages of development, bring them in from Thailand, the Philippines, or even North America, and raise them to market size in captivity.

Raising fish does not take pressure off wild fish. Fish are not cabbages; they do not grow on sunlight. Feeding most of these species requires continual fishing. Tons and tons of immature and undersized fish are being strained from open waters with fine-mesh nets to be ground into food for aquaculture operations. Here, most of this fishing for fish food is done by trawlers from the forty-five-hundred-boat fishing community that forms a veritable floating town occupying about a mile of Hong Kong's harbor.

Regardless of considerations about the problems of aquaculture, consumers still prefer—and will pay more for—wild-caught fish, whose texture and appearance they regard as superior to farmed. So demand for wild fish will continue as long as there are any to be had.

A platter of spotted snails arrives and goes around the table, followed immediately by pickled scallions and jellied quail eggs called "thousand-year-old eggs." Yvonne assures me that they're not a thousand years old—just a few months.

Lau has ideas and plans for improving marine aquaculture. He wants to upgrade this industry so more knowledgeable people will join it. But there are many constraints on fish mariculture in Hong Kong. The young don't want to go into it: "How can you expect a well-educated person to want to work on a fish farm when there are so many opportunities to make a great deal of money?" Money is becoming more important everywhere, but it is particularly important here. Like most Southeast Asian countries, Hong Kong has no social security system. So making and saving money is a major objective. As one resident explained, "Making money is the whole object of life's meaning in Hong Kong, because there's very little social welfare. So if you don't work, you don't live."

The waiters come with a bigger platter, bringing a spontaneous round of appreciative "Oohs" at our table. "Come," Ricky invites with a gesture of his hand, "enjoy our famous Hong Kong seafood. Look at these beautiful giant prawns, caught in the South China Sea."

The mood is relaxed and festive. I am struck with the warmth of the Chinese, how easily they laugh. With their hearty approach to eating and their expansive enthusiasm around food, they remind me of my Italian relatives. The shrimp before us are truly jumbo shrimp—in this case, *not* an oxymoron. Unfurled, these monsters are fully seven inches long. While I struggle with my chopsticks, Ricky is using a knife and fork to deshell and dismember his creature.

"Ricky, what's your favorite fish?" asks Yvonne.

Ricky deliberates thoughtfully for a few moments while chewing, then answers, "Well—Napoleon wrasse, coral trout, red grouper—I love them all!" Ricky tries explaining to us what eating fish means, saying, "Chinese way of eating is very, very refined. Here, the texture of tuna is said to be too coarse."

Because of the exacting emphasis on texture and taste, cooking methods here differ from those in other Southeast Asian countries, Europe, and the U.S. Baking changes the texture. Frying affects the taste. To get the full, unadulterated pleasure of fine fish, steaming is the way to go in south China. "With raw fish, the Japanese know what they're talking about. For cooked fish, the Chinese are the tops. Chinese people can tell by the taste, texture, and color whether it's a cultured fish or a wild fish. I can't define the taste for you, you've got to have eaten. It's subtle, so subtle. It's almost an art form. It's so refined that people will only eat certain portions of the fish: the lips, or cheek, and not the rest of the body. Certain very, very affluent people, to maintain face amongst their peers, or to show off, will entertain their guests with a plate of just Napoleon wrasse lips. That plate is maybe ten or twenty lips, and that costs a fortune—even one Napoleon fish may cost one thousand Hong Kong dollars. That is one way of showing, 'I'm a very rich person, an affluent person.' "

"Have you tasted the lips?" Yvonne asks.

"They're a totally different kind of eating, which means it is difficult to comprehend at first. They are like jelly."

Once, in Palau, presciently anticipating that I would perhaps be partaking in just such a conversation as we now are having, I myself tasted the lips of a small Napoleon wrasse. A local fisherman had speared it and given it to Lyle Squire. At my request, Lyle circumcised its lips from its face, in a perfect circle. In the pan, the lugubrious lips shriveled to a buttery pucker, and they sat on my plate poised as if ready to speak intimately. I can't vouch for the cooking method, or the presentation, but to my unrefined palate they tasted like nothing so much as a slug of the slightly crunchy fat that one might trim off a steak.

"Come, Yvonne, one more prawn," Ricky urges.

Yvonne leans back, hands protesting the thought. "No, I can't."

"Sure you can." Ricky enthusiastically thuds the intimidating shrimp onto her plate. His cellular phone rings. In Hong Kong a cell phone seems only a minor convenience, because this restaurant—like most places—has a bank of free phones. All telephone calls within Hong Kong are free, to stimulate business activity.

Noticing that the restaurant has the same shrine I saw in the fish market, I ask Ricky who the statue represents. He replies, "Kwan Tai, our hero of justice, who lived twenty-five hundred years ago and was a person, and is now a god. It is like your statue of the Lady of Blind Justice. But he is more powerful. He can fight, he can kill. She represents justice, but he fights for it."

A heaping plate of steamed coral trout arrives. "How is *that!*" Ricky gushes proudly. "Beautiful! Now you can really taste the difference of live fish." With each course, the waiters flick new plates around the table as though dealing cards. In the short intervals between courses, they hover over and around us, pouring bottomless glasses of beer and tea.

"We are pioneering a new industry for live fish," Ricky says. "It will take a generation to really learn the techniques." He pauses to enjoy a bite. "But I am very optimistic. As more people get rich, they will demand better quality food to increase their standard of living."

After I am indecently stuffed, another huge platter arrives. This is the same species of fish, but different parts—cheeks and heads—and fried this time instead of steamed. A huge platter of shrimp and rice comes to join it.

Reminding him of his earlier comment that supply of wild juveniles is limiting his declining mariculture business, I ask if he is concerned that there will not be enough wild adult fish to fill the demand for food.

"Many people exaggerate," Ricky says. "Only a very small fraction is depleted."

A heaping platter of crabs hits the table, steaming. I can hardly bear the sight of more food.

The waiters remove three-quarters of the crabs, three-quarters of the shrimp and rice, and three-quarters of the fish from the table, uneaten.

A plate of stonefish is delivered. The stonefish is the baddest of the venomous Scorpaenidae—scorpionfishes—a family of well-earned ill-repute. This hideous creature may well be the world's most venomous fish. It uses its venom—injected through sharp dorsal spines—strictly defensively, but its excellent camouflage and habit of burying itself often render the stonefish virtually invisible. Wading the shallows, you might step on one, and its spines will easily penetrate a tennis shoe. The excruciatingly painful wounds may result in the loss of toes or fingers and, occasionally, in death. Fortunately, the stonefish has a habit of cramming itself up against or under rocks, out of the way. Also fortunately, an antivenin has been developed. The antivenin to the poison is made from stonefish venom itself by an outfit called Australian Serum Laboratories. Stonefish are really abundant in only a few locations, and the lab has for years relied on a population near one village in New Guinea. But now the lab is competing with the live-food fish trade, which is exhausting the stonefish population, and their supply of stonefish is faltering. Unfortunately for anyone who needs the cure, the ugly, poisonous stonefish is quite tasty.

I am munching curiously on one as Ricky offers, "The countries are beginning to restrict fishing, so I think the resources will not be exhausted. A lot of the resources are not being touched. The waters around Papua New Guinea have hardly been scratched. I anticipate no shortage of future supply. Technology will help us grow fish better in the future."

Ricky estimates that domestic Hong Kong aquaculture grows three thousand tons of live fish per year, 40 percent of all fish production. Wild caught fish, he estimates, supply forty-six hundred tons of high-value fishes per year to Hong Kong, with an approximately equal amount also going through Hong Kong into mainland China.

Michael Riepen, the fisheries economics specialist who has collaborated with Bob Johannes, is seated on my left. Though he's been engaged in other discussion up to now, he has also been listening to what Ricky is telling us. He whispers into my ear, "The amount of disinformation in this business is incredible." He tells me that fifteen thousand tons of live wild fish are coming into Hong Kong by boat and air each year. That is about 60 percent higher than Ricky's estimate of forty-six hundred for Hong Kong plus an equal amount going through to China. Riepen says there are about fifty boats, each with ten tons of holding capacity, working out of Hong Kong, making ten to fifteen trips per year, bringing about ten thousand tons. Another two to five thousand tons are brought in by the hundred or so small airfreight importers. And Riepen reminds me that Hong Kong is just one destination. There is also Singapore. Taiwan. Mainland ports. And so on. Ominously, China has doubled its fish consumption in the last decade, according to the United Nations—a trend that continues.

Regardless of whose numbers are more accurate, I opine aloud that it's a lot of fish coming off the reefs, essentially uncontrolled and unmonitored at the sources where the fish are caught.

At the words "uncontrolled and unmonitored," Ian Collier perks up defensively, saying, "It is not an issue for our department. I can't see how Hong Kong can do anything about it. The Hong Kong people are simply going to other countries and buying fish caught in other countries' waters. If a country won't police its own fishery, we certainly cannot. It's a trade issue, not a fishing issue."

The proposition that all that we have witnessed and heard—all the live fishes, the boats, the platters of seafood, my distended belly—is not a fishing issue surprises me into silence. I have learned that very surprising statements usually betray either brilliance or stupidity. One or the other. I need to think about this.

With further eating out of the question, Yvonne, indulging an idle scientific curiosity, dissects an earbone out of a steamed stonefish head. She counts its growth rings, learning its age. Bowls of steaming soup are set before us. Inattention allows them to cool. It has been approximately two hours since we first pulled the snails out of their shells and had our initial sips of beer and tea. The snails seem a distant memory now.

Ricky says, "By giving fishermen good money, we help increase their living standards so that people won't treat the fish as rubbish."

Speaking of not treating the fish as rubbish, I'm wondering whether all the seafood we—with *our* high living standards—are not eating is going into the garbage. I'm afraid to ask.

Ricky continues, "We are concerned, and we have told the local islander people not to use explosives or cyanide to catch the fish. If the coral is killed, there will not be enough housing for fish in the future. We tell them to use hook and line or grab fish underwater using flashlights at night."

Changing the subject slightly, Collier says something to Ricky about the possibility that some of the places that they are getting fish from might have problems with ciguatera, a poisoning of the fish's flesh caused by a naturally toxic, one-celled dinoflagellate called *Gambierdiscus toxicus.* The dinoflagellate attaches itself to dead coral and marine algae, and its toxins are passed up the food chain from herbivorous to carnivorous fish, concentrating in their flesh. Though the fish seem unaffected, ciguatera can be fatal to humans. For reasons yet unknown, ciguatera outbreaks are usually associated with coral reefs that have been damaged, either by natural events such as hurricanes or by human activities. Collier says no spot checks are done, and it is quite likely that sooner or later a fish carrying ciguatera toxins will get through and someone will be poisoned. In fact, he says, this is almost inevitable.

The loquacious Ricky suddenly falls taciturn. "No," he laughs, shaking his head and looking into his lap, "No poison."

"But it is a possibility in the future," presses Collier.

Yvonne whispers to me, "I think Ricky knows exactly what the thrust of the comment is and I think he's worried that the department might develop a way to start checking. Imagine the chill it would throw on the industry if some of the fish show up as poisonous?"

I tell her I think that if the industry was smart they themselves would ask for more rapid development of screening techniques. If the fish are unscreened as they are now, and a couple of people get poisoned, it would demolish public confidence and make the trade seem like Russian roulette.

But Lau clearly doesn't like the topic. Suddenly acting as though his English is not quite as good as it has seemed all along, he repeats, "No poison."

On that note of discord, we waddle painfully out of the restaurant.

"You know," Riepen says as we wander back among the live fish stalls, "I have noticed indications that this industry might be getting into a squeeze. There are some boats tied up for three or four months. The business chatter is conflicting. Some new investors are still looking around, other people are saying it's a good time to get out. I always think of the bluefin tuna. In New Zealand there were so many bluefin tuna twenty years ago that they were used for lobster bait. They were just all over the place. How fast things can change!"

Indeed.

Riepen motions with his chin to a tank holding a couple of platter-sized wrasse. "All of the Napoleon wrasse are cyanided. Look at all these juveniles here. The boats are going into Thailand and Indonesian waters and grabbing all these young fish. It's criminal. That would be the easiest thing to regulate."

At the word "regulate," Collier pipes up defensively again, saying, "We haven't had one complaint from another government. It would be presumptuous and arrogant of us to try to regulate this trade when the countries that are selling the fish are not complaining about it."

I am now forming an opinion as to whether the surprising nature of Collier's comments constitutes brilliant insight or its converse. "Ian," I say, "you've contradicted yourself. You told me earlier that South Africa complained that boats from Hong Kong were buying unlimited amounts of abalones caught in South African waters, and that this market was driving the depletion of their abalones. You said, 'How are we supposed to do anything about fishing in their waters?' You said that South Africa would have to deal with that itself. So, taken all together, what you are saying is that when other countries do not complain, there is no reason for you and your department to act, and when other countries do complain about boats from Hong Kong, it is up to them, not you, to act. When, in fact, would you take it upon yourself to do anything at all?"

Collier tries evading, but he does so clumsily, saying, "The fish are all caught within the national waters of other countries."

"But the fishing is driven by Chinese markets and Hong Kong business interests," I persist. "This whole system is nailed together with Hong Kong money across the Indo-Pacific. And the people in your agency are the ones who are paid with public funds, to work without profit motive, to have the big picture and the long-range view, so that these businesses and these resources can have a future. And you're saying there's no way for your government agency to be involved in all of this business that is drawing from millions of square miles of ocean and bringing it here?"

"I don't see how we can be," he says.

Our host at lunch—the Big Boss—is now asking Riepen, "How can we get access into Australia for our business? What do we need to do to set it up? I could sell as much fish as I can get, into China."

With the usual hand-wringing failure and impotence of fisheries management literally standing before me, I dart a frustrated glare at Collier. He too has overheard Yung, and in a soft, powerless, ominous voice, he says to me, "The bottomless pit of China is now opening."

A large, struggling Napoleon wrasse is brought out and put on a killing block. Yvonne turns her back as the cleaver comes down.

Dr. Sadovy had joked that I would be "allowed" into Hong Kong only if I was prepared to lecture to the Marine Biological Association at the University of Hong Kong. Tonight is the night—in fact, I have only a few minutes left—and I am in her office hurriedly going through my slides of photos, charts, and graphs, trying to select—mostly by guessing—the best ideas to present to an audience I am thoroughly unfamiliar with.

Yvonne tells me, "As you've seen, food is a quite sensitive issue here. It is very important to culture, social status, and tradition." I am holding slides up to the light, sorting, and trying to concentrate, as my prep time is running out. Yvonne is continuing her interesting distraction: "It's amazing, the misconceptions that persist even among the university students. Many still think you can't overfish the sea. Conservation is a Western concept. You can't try to sell people on your values; you have to *show* them why."

Based on that bit of helpful perspective, I decide to stick to the facts, putting the slides of data and graphs in the tray for the lecture, leaving the slides of concepts and ideas in the box.

The thing is, I believe large parts of our oceans are depleted mainly because we treat marine creatures as commodities, forgetting that they are wild animals breeding in natural habitats. In reality, marine creatures are the *only* wild animals still hunted on a large scale. The language used in fisheries amounts to a forced attempt to induce amnesia on this point. Fisheries people talk incessantly of "harvesting" fishes, and even of "harvesting" whales—trying to impart a sanitized and agricultural tone, as though hunting the largest creature ever to live on earth by firing bombs into their bodies is analogous to picking watermelons that have been planted and cultivated. Fish populations are referred to as "stock," like shoes in a warehouse. And when sea turtles that have drowned in nets wash up on beaches, they are referred to as—of all things—"stranded."

The language is intended to confuse and mislead, and it is selected carefully. I have, for example, been in meetings with fishery managers who did not understand that all the "stranded" turtles the fishermen were dismissing as "not a problem" were, in fact, *dead.* They are no more "stranded" than a person killed in a plane crash is "grounded." Boat captains speaking among themselves over their radios talk of what fish they are catching, but the moment they step up to a microphone at a public hearing, they speak only of "product" they have been "harvesting." To conceal the fact that these are living wild animals, some people promoting the fishing industry choose words for public-relations objectives, even if they must force the fit. Consider this grinding line from a report by the United Nations' Food and Agriculture Organization: "A shortage of tuna raw material continued to overshadow the market." They really mean the fishermen could not find enough wild tuna to satisfy the demand. Why not say so? Because that would give a different—and more accurate—impression of the pillage going on in the world's oceans. Since fish roaming the oceans are wild creatures, fishing differs fundamentally from agricultural production. We can catch the fish, but for the vast majority of species, we can't make more. Ironically, refusing to acknowledge this for business reasons leads to financial ruin. Rather than stewarding living, renewable ocean resources for continuity, long-term wealth, and well-being, we have approached fishing more like mining. Because the animals are taken rather than manufactured, supplies of marine resources cannot be raised at will to meet demand, and attempts to force indefinite increases in supply by fishing more intensively can result in collapse. And in some areas, it has. Catches in the Atlantic, Pacific, Mediterranean, and Antarctic have all fallen from highs reached in the 1970s and 1980s, in some cases by 30 to 50 percent. Fishing has become so uneconomical in many places that massive government subsidies are required to keep it going; the U.N.'s Food and Agriculture Organization estimates that to land annual catches worth $70 billion, world fisheries incur $124 billion in costs. Ironically, the overemphasis on short-term economics and viewing wild fish as merely foodstuff has caused depletions resulting in losses of billions of dollars to businesses and coastal economies, widespread unemployment, and real threat to the food supply for many people around the world. It's O.K. to use the oceans, but not to use them up.

Deciding at the last moment to include conceptual "Western" ideas anyway, I put two of the previously discarded slides into the tray and hurry into the lecture room. At worst, the perspective that fish are wildlife will strike the audience as absurd and I'll be a flop—but an honest flop. It's a risk I'm well acquainted with. I've learned that you can't please everyone, and that it's best not to try to. My feeling is: Know yourself, and allow yourself to be known, and you will have lived. Anyway, they've asked me—a voice from the other side of the world—to speak to them, so in a sense I owe them my thoughts; they'll form their own reactions. Of course, I still have trepidations as I stand to face the audience.

Yet it seems go over well. In the lounge after the lecture, Dr. Joe Lee, the chairman of the Marine Biological Association, says, "I *loved* what you said about the need to realize that fish are wildlife. So many of us, even after years of working with them, have never thought of it that way. As a Chinese, I am interested in changing the attitude of seeing fish as only something to eat. Someday I want to end a lecture on how biologically wonderful a marine organism is without a student asking immediately if it is good to eat!

"When you have money, you feel you have a privilege to taste. And the rarer the fish, the more you're willing to pay for it, because the more prestige is associated with the distant, exotic, and rare. But I hope that by getting rich, people will become more civilized; I hope for a gradual change to increasing respect. We have the beginnings of environmental awareness. But we also have expanding consumption by sheer population growth. If we realize too late, there may be little left, it could be beyond remedy. But I am hopeful."

Another professor says, "There's no way you can control it. Too much money is involved all over Southeast Asia, Australia, now even Canada and the U.S. A species may be dirt cheap where it lives, but when it's marketed right, it could be one of the most highly priced fish here, as long as the texture is right. As species are depleted, fishermen move on to new ones. Who ate stonefish five or ten years ago? No one would have considered it. Now it is one of the most high priced. Ten, twenty years from now, no more of certain species. They'll just be wiped out, then another type of fish will be popular until that's wiped out, and another one, until that's wiped out. I'd like to see many species of fish put on the Endangered Species List immediately."

Dr. David Dudgeon, the head of the Department of Ecology and Biodiversity, has a different angle. "Taking full-sized Napoleon wrasses off the reefs is like killing tigers. And they suffer appallingly before they are killed, as do all these reef fish that are kept in crowded conditions."

Yvonne, supporting Dr. Lee's hopefulness, counters with, "But people here *are* getting the idea: There is much more about this in the newspapers, with recent articles about overfishing, shark-finning, and such."

Dudgeon shrugs. He's not convinced either. He glances at his watch and tells us he has to get going. It turns out that Dr. Dudgeon plays bass guitar. He happens to be performing tonight at a nearby rock-and-roll establishment, and he invites us to go along. The band also includes two of his recent students, upon whose Ph.D.s the ink is hardly dry.

The club is a two-story affair, the second built as a balcony around the stage. The place is profusely decorated with electric guitars, a big American flag, at least one American motorcycle hanging from the ceiling, and more psychedelic posters of Jimi Hendrix, Frank Zappa, Elvis Presley, and a variety of present, former, and long-fossilized British and American rock stars than I knew existed on the continent of. . . . Are we really still in Asia?

Over the sound system, Carlos Santana's wailing guitar is ripping classic solo lines from the chords of "Black Magic Woman." Perhaps 95 percent of the faces in the pressing crowd here are round-eyed. This seems a kind of haven for young and youngish *gweilos*—Westerners—coming to pull a piece of their cultural identity around them like a security blanket, simultaneously feeling closer to their roots and, by doing so, underscoring how far from home they *really* feel. Mostly, these are expats, the distantly assigned yuppie businesspeople from Europe and the States who make, as Yvonne says, far too much money. They are nicely dressed, a bit stilted looking. Some of the young males, with their short haircuts, freshly shaved faces, and neatly cinched ties, are already half-stewed—which I interpret as a strong indication of sexual frustration.

When the band plugs in, the sudden, ear-splitting surge of feedback sends chills of nostalgia up the back of my neck, reminding me of the days when I would be looking at the pretty back of the lead female vocalist from behind the drums. As the walls reverberate, Yvonne, smelling like a beer, is shouting in my ear: "People like Ricky Lau really worry me. I've seen people like him in the Caribbean. Bright, educated, sincere, a good businessman. But he has another profession—law—that he can fall back on. He has no real financial need to secure the resources for the long term. If it doesn't work out in this business—or if they overexploit for a fast buck—he has very lucrative options."

Shouting back over the noise, I say I'm not worried about Ricky. Worrying about resource management is not his role. And his views against fishing with explosives and cyanide seem to make him a relatively responsible exploiter. Self-interested, maybe, but responsible. If we had a world of more responsible exploiters, we might be preserving our future options. Yvonne is nodding the way I do when the music is too loud to hear anything, but she is hunched forward at our little table, looking intently at my face, seemingly filling in what she can't hear by watching my lips, squinting just enough to make me think she is understanding me. Convinced she comprehends, I continue, "I'm much more worried about people like Ian: given the authority and doing absolutely nothing—believing there is nothing that can be done."

"I don't believe there is nothing that can be done," she yells.

"No, I said that's what *Ian*—Ian Collier—. He seems to think nothing can be done."

"I don't believe that," she yells. "Do you?"

"That nothing can be done, or that Ian thinks that?"

"That nothing can be done."

"I agree," I shout back.

"That something can be done?"

"Yes, I think so." I am losing the thread here.

"So do I."

I never *could* understand how people can talk when the music is so loud. The band finishes its set and the song "Stairway to Heaven"—inevitably—comes on over the sound system in the bar.

Yvonne recognizes a student in a tie-dyed blouse who has been here only a few weeks. The student tells us she has finally found a place to live, an hour outside the city. It is getting rather late, and Yvonne asks, "Are you going home all that way tonight?"

"Well, um, that depends," she says, glancing sideways at a male graduate student who is chatting a few feet away, seemingly oblivious to her.

She is living at a wildlife reserve called Mai Po, at the extreme northern end of Hong Kong. It is a place I visited with Yvonne and some other university people, searching for a rare wading bird, the black-faced spoonbill. We found it, but the exquisite birds—and even the throngs of mudskippers on the vast mudflats—were not the most impressive of the sights there. The wide Sham Chun River separating Hong Kong from the rest of China bore an endless procession of enormous barges carrying construction material. I counted thirty-five barges going upriver at one time. On the north bank, the city of Shenzhen, China, was growing explosively—ferociously—as we watched. Along ten miles of riverfront, the sky was crammed with the outlines of cranes throwing up new high-rises. Through our birding telescopes we could also see a theme park featuring a replica of the Eiffel Tower. But no Statue of Liberty.

The young woman wanders away from our table to stand by her man. The blaring song seems to be offering her encouragement: . . . *with a smile she can get what she came for.*

Yvonne's husband, George, has arrived, fought his way through the loud crowd, and found us. I ask him about his work. Mostly, he says, he is working on artificial life systems—characterizing life in terms of computer-programmable functions. Are, for example, the processes of evolutionary adaptation to changing environments reducible to easily programmable rules and algorithms? Some work suggests they are.

As a biologist and an unabashed lover of living things, I am horrified at the thought. His line of work strikes me as filled with Frankenstein-like implications. I ask, "What about emotions? Don't they suggest that living is, at the very least, awfully complicated?"

"If you look behind profound experiences," George says, "you find they are empty, like the three-D effect in a movie. Behind the movie screen there is ultimately nothing."

"But you don't go to the theater to look behind the screen. You go to experience the movie. Satisfaction, joy, and fulfillment are found *within* the human experience, not looking for ultimate and absolute meaning standing disembodied somewhere outside ourselves." This conversation is a clear sign that it is too late. It has been a long and interesting day, and it is time to bring it to a close. We get home at two in the morning. I am stone-cold sober, as usual, but exhausted.

In the morning, I open my bedroom door at about nine o'clock. George, at work in his home office, says, "I was tempted to bang on your door at seven."

"I was awake," I say, "but determined not to get up until nine."

"That's good," he says approvingly. "It's good to have goals."

Rob Parry-Jones is a tall young man—midtwenties—with shoulder-length brown hair. A Brit with the unusual distinction of knowing how to speak *and read* Cantonese, he is a research consultant with TRAFFIC East Asia, an affiliate of the World Wildlife Fund.

In a city in which almost every kind of business seems to have its own "district," Parry-Jones is taking me walking along Des Voeux Road, a decidedly organic quarter. We pass a variety of specialty shops selling various grains, then shops selling various mushrooms. We eventually come to the shops selling sea creatures: dried scallops, dried abalones, dried sea cucumbers, load upon load of these animals, stacked and stored, bundled and proffered, from the far reaches of Earth. Most of these shops are small, barely too big to be called stalls. Their displays are neatly arranged, well presented, and all brightly lit.

An adjacent pharmacy shop features parts of many different types of creatures, everything from dried sea horses and pipefishes to seal penises and testicles. Virtually every kind of creature that moves in the sea, it seems, is killed and offered as salubrious, believed—or at least touted—to promote health and vigor in various ways.

"Potency" is a big ticket. Rob asks about the seal penises. In Cantonese, the shopkeeper tells him that they are tiger penises. As we are walking out and onto the street, Rob translates for me, adding, "It was certainly dumb of him to say that those were tiger penises, especially since he was lying. Selling tiger parts is highly illegal under CITES, but for somebody to lie about it to a foreigner, and say that something that is not tiger is tiger, gives you an idea of the fear of enforcement they are feeling—none."

In another shop's window hang a large number of dried sea snakes and starfishes. The sight of them causes me to remember Devon Ludwig telling me that he used to see far more sea snakes, and Larry Sharron's remark that starfish are being tested against cancer because their chemical defenses are so well developed that *almost* nothing eats them. But here they are. The storekeeper, patting his chest, explains, "Good in soup for the lungs."

Yeah.

We continue walking past the rubble of the world's seas. Feeling that old sinking feeling, I wonder again whether I am overreacting. I probably am.

Maybe not: Here are the shark fin markets. Shark fins, shark fins, shark fins, shark fins. Stall after store after shop, block after block, on both sides of the street. At any given moment, the fractional remains of hundreds of thousands of sharks must be moving through these markets.

We look around, trying to be unobtrusive, but the shapes of our faces and our presence here says a lot to the shopkeepers. They eye us suspiciously, sullenly. Rob says, "They've heard about the furor over shark finning. It has been in the papers here. They believe Americans want to close the shark fisheries. They have heard of the CITES resolution."

Based on a formal petition that I had put forth, the United States Fish and Wildlife Service in 1994 proposed to the world's 120-plus CITES-signatory nations that the CITES authority collect information on the world's shark fisheries and the biological status of sharks. The idea was simply to recognize a need to put together a better world picture of sharks. Japan objected, precipitating a series of negotiations over several days.

Japan's delegates (some of the same faces I had grown accustomed to at the tuna shoot-outs in Madrid and Kyoto) said it was inappropriate for CITES to gather information on species not listed as endangered or threatened, that it was too impractical, too expensive, too unimportant an issue on which to waste valuable time. In other fisheries meetings, Japan is constantly citing inadequate knowledge and insufficient statistics as reason to delay taking action for conserving species and frequently argues for continued and increased commercial exploitation under the guise of gathering "scientific information"—such as the crude fiction of "scientific whaling" and the "scientific monitoring" of bluefin tuna. "We need more data," seems the favorite English expression of most Japanese government representatives.

Their arguments against simply gathering and analyzing known facts on sharks seemed a bit hollow to most other counties, who are familiar with Japan's more usual script of "Not *enough* information to take action at this time." Japan then tried to water down the shark resolution's wording. This did not work well either. Japan could not gracefully and convincingly argue against the idea of collecting data. This time, the Japanese government did not get what it wanted—earning instead only an "A" for effort in the negotiations. When the resolution was brought back to the floor for a vote later in the week, it was still pretty much intact, its preamble reading in part:

> NOTING the increase in the international trade in parts and products of sharks;
>
> CONCERNED that some shark species are heavily utilized around the world for their fins, skins, and meat;
>
> NOTING that levels of exploitation in some cases are unsustainable and may be detrimental to the long-term survival of certain shark species;
>
> NOTING that, at present, sharks are not specifically managed or conserved by any multilateral or regional agreement for the management of marine fisheries;
>
> CONCERNED that the international trade in parts and products of sharks lacks adequate monitoring and control . . .

The resolution ended with a commitment by CITES to work with the United Nations and other organizations to gather information and to prepare a discussion paper on the biological and trade status of sharks. This time, the resolution sailed through.

Sharks thus became the first fishes embroiled in big-money, high-volume, industrialized commercial fisheries formally brought under CITES's purview. Japan and its satellites wanted to avoid exactly that precedent—lest it suggest a trend.

This international struggle is on my mind as I stroll the street. Each shop has multitiered display cases of fins sorted by size, from large sacks stuffed with tiny "chips"—the fins of small species and very young sharks—to the enormous fins of whale-sized, forty-foot-long basking sharks. The dorsal fin of a basking shark, approximately three feet tall and corrugated like the bark of a tree rather than the skin of a fish, is selling for about $200 per pound.

Of the nearly four hundred species of sharks in the world, the global fin trade exploits about a hundred—most of the big ones. Between 1980 and 1990, the volume of shark fins in trade doubled.

Sharks make up only about 1 percent of the world fisheries catch, but that 1 percent is a lot of sharks: forty to seventy *million* or so each year by the late 1990s. That's conservative; estimates range up to one hundred million annually. By contrast, sharks kill only ten people each year on average—fewer than are killed by bee stings or even hogs. Your chances of getting struck by lightning are thirty times greater. In fact, of all the things that kill people, sharks kill fewer people than just about anything.

Commercial fisheries targeting other species catch many sharks incidentally. Longlines set for tunas, underwater minefields that they are, snag most of the sharks killed. Because shark meat is often worth too little to warrant taking up onboard space reserved for more valuable species, fishers often slice the valuable fins from the living animal, then dump it overboard. Bleeding and unable to control their swimming, they wriggle to the bottom of the sea, where they die. So long as large predators of ancient lineage are thought of only as commodities convertible to cash, it will be an especially auspicious time to be a hungry crab or a scavenging hagfish.

The U.N. reports that the "tragedy of sharks" is that, while their valuable fins make them targets, sharks contribute so little economically compared to other fishes that their research and management is a low priority, even if shark populations are depleted. This means "little hope for viable management consistent with both economic and conservation interests."

For millions of years, sharks cruised the seas as the top predators—like lions and wolves on land—and they were not expecting much trouble. Designed by nature to be long-living, slow-growing, and late-maturing, they bear only a few young per year. Some breed only every other year. Heavy fishing exerts so unnatural a pressure, such high mortality in the face of such slow reproduction, that sharks are simply unequipped by evolution to withstand it.

In almost all cases where sharks have been targeted by commercial fisheries, they have been depleted within a few years, yet global shark fishing and trade are expanding virtually unregulated and uncontrolled. Only three of the twenty-six major shark-fishing countries have any management and research programs. In addition to the fin trade, shark meat is increasingly sold as other, more desirable species become depleted. People also catch sharks for skins that can be tanned into valuable leather, for oils, and for cartilage used to make the bogus "anti-cancer" pills now sold in many Western countries. Because of all this, shark populations in most areas of the globe have declined rapidly.

In the backs of many of the shops here, workers are drying and skinning the fins, then soaking them to get the fibers used in making soup. (A bowl of shark fin soup can cost $90.) One shop displays a sign in English:

> We import all kinds raw shark fins,
> make all kinds shark fin products,
> selling shark fins, shark fin fiber.

This might be a world record for the number of times the phrase "shark fin" appears in one sentence. The unusually enthusiastic and friendly shopkeeper, showcasing his inventory, explains: "This, pectoral shark fin. This, dorsal shark fin. This, shark fin tail. Here, this shark fin stomach."

Rob asks this shopkeeper about volume. He says he moves about ten tons per month. Fins are about 5 percent of the animal's weight, so it takes about two hundred tons of live sharks to supply ten tons of fins. If the weight of an average shark is, say, eighty pounds, he is moving about 170 sharks' worth of fins each day. A more realistic average weight is probably sixty pounds: 220 sharks daily.

Hearing that I am American, he says, "I get many from America." Small world and shrinking fast. Hong Kong, in fact, gets more of its fins from the U.S. than from almost any other country in the world. This street was undoubtedly the final shipping point for many of the sharks that Captains Joe McBride and Billy Campbell no longer see off Montauk, New York. And what of the shy sandbar sharks I used to see basking at the ocean's glistening surface, their dorsal fins lazing along, making chevrons? All summer long we used to see them; I have not seen *one* in the last few years. The sandbar shark's East Coast population fell more than 80 percent in just ten years of heavy finning and export, with many pulled from the ocean just a few miles from my own home. Same with dusky sharks, with the hammerheads whose high dorsals we also often saw, and others. Here is where lots of them—their fins, anyway—ended up. Here or Taiwan or Singapore. The shopkeeper continues, "I get many, many from South America, Europe, Australia, Africa, India, Arabia. Many, many from the Fiji Islands now." I am wondering if there is any place where he does *not* get shark fins from. He adds as an afterthought, "And now Indonesia. Indonesia, too."

Of course. Word has reached me that shark finners have gotten into Palau, too, and when I heard that, I felt a sick feeling in my stomach. I pick up a package of shark fin fibers packed in cellophane, and in the directions on the back the secret of making shark fin soup is revealed to me for the first time:

> Cook two hours with ham or chicken, in chicken stock.

I stare at this for a few moments and read it twice. I can't get over this! We are demolishing sharks worldwide to make ham-flavored chicken soup? I had heard that the fins add texture but no flavor. Apparently, this is true. In my own wasteful throwaway society, we do not appreciate the real value of so many things. Here, so many things are wasted because they are valued in ways that are not real.

In every restaurant we've been to in Hong Kong, various soups featuring shark fins are an entire section in the menu. Just as buffalo tongues, passenger pigeons, and cranes once graced the menus of fancy restaurants in America.

I am having some trouble keeping Yvonne in sight amid the jungle of sidewalk markets and advertising along Tung Choi Street in the Mong Kok section of town. Multicolored neon signs jut perpendicularly from the buildings, so far out over the street that they overlap overhead, visually screaming for attention, blocking one another off in crowded, aggressive competition and practically enclosing us. On the street and sidewalks, between buildings old and new, hurry carts, cars, pedestrians, trucks, and bicyclists with grocery-laden baskets crammed with meat and vegetables, all crisscrossing among clothing stalls, electronics shops, food stands, alleys jammed by sellers offering live birds and exquisite, hand-made bird and insect cages, and probably a lot that I am not noticing as I hurry along.

Hong Kong is a modern metropolis of six million busy souls, a comfortable, clean, safe, hustling city, with dense morning mists, workers on bamboo lattices building skyscrapers, and businesses and products with names like Very Good Trading Company and Double Happiness Cigarettes. In Palau, Dr. Dr. Hajo Schmidt had told me that Hong Kong was his favorite city in the world. And now Yvonne, leading me through the crowds and confusion, is saying over her shoulder, "To me these markets are like a reef—I just love all the color and movement and stimulation." Afraid of getting lost in the throng, I am practically trotting after her as she slips and weaves through the humanity and among the dry goods.

"Come on! This way!" Yvonne is calling. A few paces ahead, at the corner, she is flickering in and out of view within the moving crowd.

Ah! The place we have been looking for. Baskets and tubs of live frogs, turtles, salamanders, and aquarium plants clutter the sidewalks. Shop after shop of live aquarium fishes line the street.

Narrow stalls and larger shops, one after another, offer a spectacular array of ornamental fishes. Goldfish and carp in dozens of varieties are displayed by the tens of thousands. As I am trying to step carefully, lest I trip and splash into a basket of amphibians, Yvonne is telling me that traditionally the carp, in image and in life, has borne the fish's symbolic meaning—fecundity, abundance, and financial prosperity—but access to new kinds of fishes is stimulating new interest in aquarium-keeping in homes. The freshwater fish shops yield quickly to the many side-by-side saltwater aquarium shops, purveying brilliant reef fishes and corals. But the competition must be stiffer than a catfish spine.

We step tentatively inside the Wave Aquarium, where the elderly proprietor is shakily practicing Beethoven's "Ode to Joy" on an old violin. Bright red-and-white shrimps, seahorses, small skates, flounders, anemones, and other living beauties I have seen on the reefs enliven his crowded shop. Baby specimens of high-backed groupers, a very popular and expensive food species, huddle nervously inside tanks labeled DON'T SCARE FISH.

Back to the sidewalk.

At the entrance to the Yat Wong Aquarium, the shopkeepers are unpacking a new shipment, removing plastic bags full of live fish from foam shipping containers. Wet newspapers separate the bags. I unroll one: the *Manila Bulletin*. These fish are among the many coming from the Philippines. This shop is neat and bright, and the "stock," well displayed for quick appraisal by potential customers, is separated by types: all the triggerfishes there, all the surgeonfishes here, all the butterfly fishes over there. One tank holds only Picasso triggerfish; another, young sharks. Little mandarinfish, aptly named *splendidus,* from a family known as dragonets, fill one tank. They are fantastically colored, as though a child had crayoned their scrawls, spots, and stripes. In one brightly lit tank, corals, anemones, and baby giant clams are presented on Plexiglas pedestals. There is no habitat or cover in any of the tanks, and the fish seem agitated and stressed for lack of hiding places.

Calling my attention to one tank, Yvonne says, "These are Caribbean: the rock beauty, *Holacanthus tricolor;* the gray angel, whose Latin name is *Pomacanthus arcuatus.* Here is *Gramma loreto,* the fairy basslet. Puerto Rico is the most important source; Haiti used to be. This one is *Centropyge argi;* I will remember the English name in a moment. Oh, yes! The cherubfish. There's nothing quite like these in the Indo-Pacific." She bends down, putting her face near the glass, observing closely, saying softly and almost to herself, "I'm always amazed to see fishes all the way from the Caribbean here." She turns to me, adding, "But that's how vast the aquarium trade is."

On the sidewalk fronting Happiness Aquarium, workers are unloading a new shipment of corals. Fifteen huge tanks of live corals occupy much of this shop's interior. Another tank displays four-inch-long sturgeons—babes of the monsters that once ruled large rivers, now reduced to remnant populations. In floating baskets that are too shallow for them, wide-bodied angelfish are struggling continually to get upright. Other tanks are filled with poisonous lionfish, and still others feature shrimpfish, porcupinefish, boxfish, frogfish, and ribbon eels.

Yvonne says, "I'm afraid I see this street as a kind of death row. Mortality is very, very high because so many of the fish were caught with cyanide. The idea is to move them quickly. Some of these shops don't even feed them."

They know better. If captured with cyanide, the effects of the damage to a fish's stomach, intestine, and liver may appear shortly after active feeding resumes. Occasionally, cyanide-caught fish die immediately after eating their first large meal.

I want to inquire about cyanide without accusing anyone of anything negative, so I ask this shopkeeper if he has any problems with cyanided fish dying and thereby cutting into his profit.

Instantly annoyed with me—and fully comprehending the thrust of my thinking—he says agitatedly, "Americans' understanding is totally opposite! Cyanide fish *best.* Only piece of coral get killed. But fish get medicine and go quiet. They not scared. Not damage. Perfect. Fish caught with medicine worth most money. When hand-caught, fish scared; bangs into coral, bangs into net, scales come off, fins ripped. Caught with medicine is best. Americans not understand."

Back out to the sidewalk. Yvonne says, "For the sellers, cyanided fish are fine. They don't have them long enough for them to die."

The Universal Beau Idéal Aquarium Center is busy packing an outgoing shipment, loading bags of fish into polystyrene boxes. In the window of the nearby Red Coral Marines, an odd sign reads:

> Nature's Reef.
> Better than real underwater scenery,
> by top American artist.
> A U.S.–Hong Kong joint production

We step up and in, passing another sign saying, "We create lifestyles for the fish and famous."

To my surprise, Red Coral Marine is pushing fake molded coral from an American acrylic manufacturer. A salesperson explains, "Artificial coral better; never die."

The proprietor, who seems to think I'm a bit too nosy, glides over. He asks me what I'm interested in. Still reeling a bit from the dressing-down I precipitated with my gentle inquiry over at Happiness, I blurt out clumsily, "I wonder if you are having problems with cyanide?"

He suddenly straightens, clears his throat, and says in fine English, "We are the only business in Hong Kong to use only hand-caught fish. Cyanide is suicide. The strain on nature in this business is unbelievable. It is a sickening, sordid trade. With healthy fish and good husbandry, you can keep fish alive for a long time. *That* is a hobby; otherwise, it's just useless killing. For what? You and I are on the same wavelength."

So surprising is his response, I merely nod speechless affirmation.

He continues, "The Philippines are hopeless—bombed out and cyanided. It has now spread to Indonesia. I don't know how long this can last."

He believes the food-fish trade is the real problem. "It is like cocaine," he says. "You can get three hundred U.S. dollars for a single Napoleon wrasse this big," he says, indicating with his hands the size of a dinner plate. "With fleets from mainland China, Hong Kong, Taiwan, and the Philippines, carrying drums of cyanide, this is big business. Huge money is involved, attracting some bad people. And the average Chinese, the last thing they're thinking about is the health of coral reefs in other countries."

He walks me to his wall-sized display tank and proudly says, "Ninety percent of our fish survive more than a year. You need good, net-caught, clean fish to start with, otherwise forget it. The problem with cyanide is the fish are not killed right away. In a few weeks' time, though, you see it's got a sunken stomach even if it is eating well, because its liver and digestive system have been destroyed." He puts his hand up to the glass and several fish approach with unhurried curiosity.

I tell him how surprised I am by the contrast between him and the proprietor of Happiness.

He says, "I can't blame the other shopkeeper for what he told you. He sells only cyanide-caught fish. He's just trying to make a living.

"But—" he laughs "—the problem is, no one cares! You see all the hard coral by the tons on the street? All smuggled and illegal. They say they had the stock before the law. They haul the whole bottom up and sell it very cheaply here. It is so competitive, the profit is tiny; but the destruction is colossal.

"In my view, we are running out of time. China's markets are opening up. That is worrisome. The reefs are going so quickly. At this rate, there will be nothing for my kids to see. Forget my kids; there will be nothing for my own generation. We need government regulation."

Thinking back to Ian Collier's statements that he could not see how the government could become involved when the fish are caught in other countries, I suggest that improved regulations are probably not imminent.

He answers, "You could control all the cyanide fishing at the final destination, by chemically screening for cyanide-caught fish." He looks at me hopefully, saying, "Perhaps the U.S., the largest market in the world for aquarium fishes, could set an example."

"Perhaps," I offer. I hate to quash hopefulness, but we have plenty of deadwood bureaucrats in the States, too. And now we have the new global religion: Free Trade. In the United States of Amerchandise no less than many other countries, trying to protect distant resources and other people's futures—while their governments and multinational corporations are stuffing their shorts—is considered all but treasonous.

We wish each other luck.

Yvonne and I go in and out of several other shops on our way out of the aquarium district. In one shop is a fish about a foot and a half long. It is selling for 25,000 Hong Kong dollars, but that's only about 3,400 U.S. dollars.

Sulu

I have been to the edge of human existence before, but this will prove different from anything in my experience. For the moment, though, I have no way of knowing what I am getting into. After a sleepless night of harried travel, I am still too wound up to doze as the first tint of dawn outlines the Philippine horizon outside the airplane's window. When I was in Palau, Larry Sharron gave me a copy of a letter to his father, and he told me to read it when I got to the Philippines. Now I pull the envelope from my bag.

> Dear Dad,
>
> Well, I'm back from the Philippines now. And what a long, hard trip it's been. After 5 weeks there I was ready to come back to Palau. I'll tell you a little about the trip.
>
> Palawan is the most southwestern large island in the Philippines, and we went there because we felt that the marine life would be different from other places we had been. Our first few days were spent diving from shore. I must admit the invertebrates were interesting. The species we were looking for had no food value, and were abundant. But I couldn't help notice the absence of larger fish. Like in other parts of the Philippines the pressures of the large populations of people have taken their toll.
>
> After about a week we chartered a refitted freighter to take us to a large reef system called Tubbataha, 100 miles offshore, out in the middle of the Sulu Sea. We dove all around Tubbataha for a week. The reefs were beautiful, though some dynamite fishing had occurred. Again, no large fish, and not a single shark. The crew on the ship said the Taiwanese fishing boats had been coming there and caught all the sharks for their fins. I went out several nights looking for various invertebrates. But here, there were very few. And live

shells were almost non-existent. The crew of our ship explained to me that the shellers had also been out here in large numbers, but they do not frequent the area anymore. No wonder they don't, they've picked it clean. The seagrass areas in the center of the lagoon were the same—beautiful habitat, no animals. We did observe a large sea turtle leaving her nest one night. Perhaps there is hope for this area. The water was very clear and we did manage to find several new sponges and other invertebrates for our project.

We returned to Palawan for the next phase of our trip, out to San Salvador Island in Zambales Province. What we saw shocked us. The reefs in the area had been decimated and covered with silt. On one entire dive we saw only two fish. Local divers attribute it to dynamite fishing and the use of sodium cyanide to capture fish in and around coral heads. Both these methods have gone on unchecked for the last 20 years. They discovered that cyanide could be used to collect fish when they observed that the runoff from a nearby gold mine was killing fish in the river and eventually the sea. Cyanide is commonly used to remove gold during mining or to dissolve it. It wasn't long before everyone was using this deadly compound to fish with. And for those who don't dive and cannot spray the reef directly with a poison, there is dynamite. When exploded underwater it stuns everything in a 100 ft. diameter, while blowing the reef to bits. Every day that we dove off San Salvador we could feel and hear blasting underwater.

We wondered what they were catching, since we hadn't seen too many fish worth serving up. A trip to the local fish market answered our question. There were no large reef fish for sale, but there were thousands of one-inch baby rabbitfish, dried and salted like potato chips. I guess they just can't wait for them to grow up.

The divers of San Salvador Island are aware of their plight and know the damage they have done. Many are seeking employment in other countries to support their families. At present, if they make 100 pesos ($4.00 U.S.) a day, they can survive. But even their island is fast becoming overcrowded from the growing population. Their fate is gloomy at best. Since I know many of them personally, I feel for them. In an effort to try and return the reefs to their original state, they have set aside the reef on one side of their island as a refuge. No fishing whatsoever. We dove there and found that there may be hope. We observed a few large fish on those reefs. It's a beginning. They say that the hardest part is policing the area for fishermen from nearby islands. They've set up a small house on the beach in front of the sanctuary and someone is always there watching for illegal fishing activity.

We spent a few days in Manila, working out of the National Museum, and then shipped our stuff off to Washington, D.C., to the National Cancer Institute. We needed dry ice for our samples, and found it at a nearby ice cream factory. But they made us buy one gallon of ice cream for every 2 blocks of dry ice we purchased. We ended up giving the ice cream away to the various museum personnel that had been so helpful. Well that's my story. I hope that wasn't too lengthy or boring. Take care of yourself and stay well.

Lawrence

My gaze drifts out the airplane window at the islands below. Sleeping soundly in the next seat is Dr. Vaughan Pratt, director of the International Marinelife Alliance. At Bob Johannes's suggestion, I had contacted Pratt about his work to end cyanide fishing in the Philippines, and he had invited me to accompany him on his first trip to one end of the world. Situated between the Sulu and Celebes Seas, the island of Mindanao, and Borneo's Malaysian Sabah region, the predominantly Islamic islands of Basilan, Jolo, and Tawitawi and their many out islands form the southern tip of the Philippines—the Sulu Archipelago. There, the country jags and shatters into splinters, geographically and politically.

Though the Philippines were endowed naturally as part of the world's richest marine region, years of abuse have turned them into perhaps the world's most ravaged coastal ruins. By the late 1980s, the condition of a third of the reefs in the Philippines was poor, 40 percent were fair, a quarter good, only 5 percent excellent. Over the long haul, habitat destruction poses more of a problem than overfishing in the tropics. Most effects of overfishing, if corrected, can be reversed in ten or twenty years, if the habitat is there. But coral recovery takes many decades.

Much of the Philippines' coral reef destruction followed forest clear-cutting during Ferdinand Marcos's reign. As tree cover declined from 80 to 20 percent, deforestation caused major soil erosion. Sediment runoff quadrupled. Eroded soil, carried by rivers out to sea, settled on the coral reefs, smothering them in places. The fisheries and tourism destroyed by logging had yielded higher total profits than the logging itself, according to the coral reef specialist Don McAllister, who published several technical papers on the Philippines. And the use of explosives and cyanide by fishers destroyed much of the coral. These practices are illegal, which doesn't count for much. It just means that everyone doing it is in violation of the law. A conservatively estimated 330 tons of cyanide per year, year after year, waft over Philippine reefs. Forget the number. Take-home message: It's hit virtually everywhere.

But some of Sulu's remote reefs remain more intact than most, and Sulu is where we are headed. Pratt himself has never been to Sulu. His mission here: to help establish a program training cyanide fishermen to instead use nets for collecting aquarium fishes.

High-priced angelfishes, emperors, tangs—especially the blue tang—and several species of damselfish and basslets found nowhere else haunt the islands and offshore reefs of the Sulu Sea. Groupers, which also inhabit these areas, often end up in the live-export trade and, eventually, on dinner plates in Hong Kong. Fishers here receive five times as much money for live groupers as for dead, and many have turned away from blast fishing, which kills fish, toward sodium cyanide, which stuns them.

It is not an improvement. I once spoke to a former cyanide fisherman from the village of Nasugbu, south of Manila Bay. He is now a provincial fish examiner and leader of a three-thousand-member group formed to end destructive fishing. He knew the horrors of cyanide firsthand, having known fishers who died underwater when they swam through milky clouds of cyanide they had squirted. He'd also known a fisher who died after eating with cyanide-contaminated hands, and several children who died after eating cyanide-contaminated fish. I asked whether he could catch more fish with cyanide. He answered, "Yes! Yes, of course. You catch plenty in a short time. But when we went back to our fishing areas there were dead corals and no fish. The snails and shellfish we collected for food disappeared. We are our own victims. Now we want to help ourselves."

Vaughan Pratt is trying to help people help themselves. Vigorous and energetic, Pratt is in his early forties, tall, square of jaw, his slightly graying, wavy hair swept back. Pratt first came to the Philippines from the U.S. in the 1970s for graduate studies in veterinary medicine, inspired by a childhood desire to help animals. After completing his doctorate he returned to the States for several years, going into private veterinary practice. "After a while," he explained, "it got obvious that killing fleas on Mr. Wilson's dog was not saving the world." So he got into rehabilitating injured wildlife: animals hit by cars, birds that had hit wires or become tangled in fishing line, geese with broken wings, those sorts of cases. "Soon I realized you can't quite save the world one animal at a time. It's too slow that way." He moved on to entire groups of animals and their habitats. "And what habitat," he says, "is larger than the oceans?"

If that seems idealistic, it is. Idyllic, it is not. Pratt has bitten off a difficult, dangerous chunk of work. He now lives in Manila with his Philippine wife and their three children. To me, ending the use of cyanide in Philippine fishing seems nearly impossible. For one thing, the chemical is widely available. As Pratt once said, "In addition to fishing, cyanide is used in pesticides and to fumigate. So we have cyanided vegetables, cyanided rice, cyanided fish, and now they've legalized the death penalty, so maybe we should donate all the cyanide we confiscate to the gas chambers." More to the point, cyanide fishing is already illegal, and has been since 1974. It is done out of sight. It is ingrained. Cyanide was introduced in the 1950s, so three generations of fishermen have a tradition of using it. But Pratt says, "Our slogan is: 'Toward a cyanide-free fishing tradition.' "

That slogan is his guiding vision. For a visionary, Pratt is extraordinarily practical. His strategy for achieving the impossible involves a comprehensive plan of action so simple and pragmatic I think it could work: 1) Teach fishers how to use nets and hook-and-line setups. (Nets and hooks might seem pretty basic to fishing, but many Filipino fishers who use explosives or cyanide have never learned to use them.) 2) Spot-check all live-fish shipments for illegal cyanide, using a chemical technique he helped develop. 3) Make authorities ready—and willing—to seize shipments that test positive.

Envisioning such a plan of action is an impressive first step. Implementing the vision will take a lot more than imagination. It will take networking, establishing credibility, securing agreements with government, obtaining funding, building and staffing testing labs, and being reachable by phone at all hours to catch stuff when it falls.

Vaughan's group now has five offices, with four cyanide-detection labs and fifty staff members on the payroll. ("On the payroll" is more accurate than "paid staff," since many of them go unpaid at times when government contracts get hung up or private contributions from the U.S. lag.) The whole operation is running on a shoestring of about $200,000. Salaries are very low by American standards; most workers earn $200 to $300 per month. Vaughan himself relies on income from his wife's hair-bow manufactory, which occupies a room adjacent to their kitchen.

Vaughan's commitment to his work stems from his belief that destructive fishing contributes to human misery, displacing thousands of former fishing families to urban slums. "The reason we're here," he told me, "is that exporters were exploiting people. The cyanide trade is like drug pushing. You hook the fishermen and then you sell it to them. As the reefs die, the exporters get rich and the people get set up to go hungry. The corals are food factories. The fish supply for three hundred thousand Filipinos is already insufficient. Malnutrition in children ranges up to seventy-five percent in places." Vaughan's commitment is shared by his staff. Never have I seen an office where so many of the staff cheerfully stay so late and the phone so frequently rings on Sunday. I have seen Vaughan on his hands and knees at nine P.M., cleaning the floor with a rag, while the chemists patiently awaited the delayed arrival of some grouper samples that had to be tested by morning. They sometimes conduct analyses late into the night, napping on the couches while the tests run.

But commitment, patience, and sacrifice are not enough. In this country it takes unusual courage. Tangling with illegal big-money fishing can be more hazardous to your health than handling cyanide. Recently the cyanide-detection labs have been generating about fifty court cases a year. They have also been generating death threats.

Pratt once told me, "It's been dangerous for us because in places we've eliminated the middleman who bought the fish and supplied the cyanide. I don't want a lot of news coverage. I don't want to let the bad guys know what I'm doing or what I look like. It's too easy to get blown away here. People who got kickbacks to look the other way are not too happy with us. It bothers my wife when government people come to my house at five in the morning with guns to 'investigate' us. But what are you going to do, quit? What would that accomplish?"

The net-training project Pratt is taking me to see, "Net and Let Live," is a joint endeavor of the Philippine Ecology Foundation—a local group—and Pratt's International Marinelife Alliance, in collaboration with the local and national governments. The program is brand-new; the first training session was concluded just last month. Training includes catching fish without poison; techniques for handling, decompression, and shipping with maximum survival; and safe diving using compressed air.

I am flipping through a report by one of the local trainers, which says,

> The approach is through community enterprise for the greater benefit of the fisher folk in our country's most depressed areas, particularly in remote and farflung island reef systems, in which our government is unable to monitor or enforce rampant illegal fishing operations because of the lack of resources. These depressed areas have been deprived of much economic and social services in the past.

The thick mud outside the airport in the city of Zamboanga (population several hundred thousand) keeps forming heavy balls on my shoes, and I keep stopping to scrape it off. It is dawn on the island of Mindanao—our stop enroute from Manila to Jolo—and the streets, such as they are, are beginning to swell with pedestrians, bikes, taxis, and peddlers. We are considering breakfast among the peddlers' carts. Vaughan says, "As you can see, here everyone eats fish, and if there are none, people will die." That seems a bit melodramatic. Having had an hour of sleep, I am groggy and not fully attentive. Vaughan tells me to stay alert and not to get separated. "This is not the safest place in the world."

After breakfast, we board a midmorning flight in a small plane to the town of Jolo on the island of the same name, in the Sulu group. I sit back and read a newspaper account of the murder of a member of a local conservation group in Zambales. That's near where Larry Sharron had been when he wrote to his father. Shot several times in front of his family while having supper at his residence, the victim was vice president of an organization of civilian volunteers, deputized to protect a local bay from illegal fishing activities. After apprehending a number of fishermen engaged in cyanide and blast fishing, he had received threats of physical harm from these groups. Wow, this is scary.

Pratt says, "Yeah, but the country as a whole has improved a lot."

Another article says Islamic terrorists are targeting American and Saudi Arabian nationals in this area. This jogs my memory. When I was in Palau, Devon Ludwig had told me, "In Sulu in the Philippines, the Islamic extremists look upon Americans as potential hostages."

Vaughan says, "They're always saying that Americans are targets. Let 'em try. I haven't heard of any real trouble for a while." Unfazed, he points to a computer ad on the same page and shows me the hardware he's saving up for.

The door of the plane opens. I step out and the sun leans forward to plant a kiss on my forehead. We walk across a dusty runway to the tin-roofed shed that functions as the terminal. It is hot inside, too, but at least it's shady. Our host is not here to meet us as planned, so we sit on the wooden benches along with air-port loiterers of uncertain intent, watching chickens pecking at the dirt in the glaring light outside the doorway.

The place seems sleepy. Vaughan says, "This region is the most peaceful it's been in twenty years. I haven't heard of much trouble since a missionary was kid-napped a year and a half ago. Back in 1974, the Moro National Liberation Front, battling government forces, burned this town to the ground."

What?

"Oh, yeah. There are three active political movements: the MNLF—which wants more autonomy, more local control—the National Government, and Abu Sayyaf." Vaughan suddenly looks up above my head, saying, "Hello, Pete!" We rise to meet our host.

"Ah, yes. Abu Sayyaf! Hello, Dr. Pratt!" He greets Vaughan, then takes my hand, saying, "Extremists. Terrorists. Fundamentalist Muslim separatists who espouse their cause through kidnapping and killing." Then, to Vaughan, "They have again become active, Dr. Pratt!" Perfecto (Pete) Pascua has a turban wrapped around his head and is wearing military fatigues stenciled "Philippine Ecology Foundation," the name of the local group of which he is president. Several men stand behind him—all armed with rifles except one. The exception is wearing a white T-shirt and black pants. "Dr. Pratt, Dr. Safina, this is Bishop DeJesus."

The bishop, a middle-aged Filipino with a hint of Chinese features, extends his hand, saying cheerfully, "Congratulations, you are still free! We were a bit concerned. Two Americans and two Australians were kidnapped while they were waiting for the plane here a few weeks ago."

It takes me a moment to process this. Before I can ask Vaughan why the hell he has brought me, blundering ignorantly, into a war zone without briefing me, Perfecto changes the subject, saying breezily, "The Catholics and we Moslems are working together."

"Yes," the smiling Bishop DeJesus says. "During mass, I mention that we must take care of nature so it can take care of us. I have been here thirty years, and I have seen how cyanide and dynamite fishing are disastrous for our people. So when Pete told me about the arrival of the training program, it was good news. We Catholics are only four percent of the population, but I have offered our classrooms."

We walk outside, where a pickup truck bristling with guns awaits us. I am not used to this, *at all*.

Vaughan shrugs and says, "It's a war to save the oceans. If the rest of the environmental community only knew what's happening—"

"If *I* only knew," I interrupt. Simultaneously apprehensive and annoyed at being unprepped, I throw Vaughan a dirty look.

"You're from New York. It's probably more dangerous at home."

"I'm from *outside* New York."

We climb into the truck and head toward Jolo town, population one hundred thousand. Sunshine gives way to drizzle, forming puddles, making mud. Snack stands, thatch-walled tin-roofed huts, bougainvillea flowers, turkeys, cows, goats, chickens, and staring kids line the roads, many of which are unpaved.

As we bounce past small stands of sugarcane, coconuts, bananas, papayas, and unusual forms of eggplants, the bishop explains to me clearly and simply, "If you are an outsider here, you are subject to kidnapping."

Nice.

He tells us several Belgians building a hospital were kidnapped, as was an American priest while saying mass a few months ago.

I'm feeling this is just a tad too late to be getting clued in on this.

The bishop says gravely, "Somewhere along the line, someone must take the risk and be brave, and end the vicious cycle of violence."

I'm from the suburbs. I can't imagine what that kind of bravery would even look like—much less what it would feel like. I ask, "How might someone possibly do that?"

Father DeJesus, looking a bit surprised at my asking, answers, "Well—what you are doing here: to train the people about sustainable fishing, because the problem is that the people are poor. If they can have a more secure income and future, the problems will begin to go away. Of course, some of the military who receive bribes from the cyanide suppliers will be displeased with what you have been doing, but risk is part of progress."

Whoa! I am thinking, "Hey, I haven't been *doing* anything. You're confusing me with heroes. Don't make *that* mistake! I'm just visiting. I don't know anything about this. I'm not part of this. If I had known, I wouldn't have come here. My house is on the other side of the world. I'm not from around here. I just came to watch the experts and maybe learn something—that's *all*. Don't you or anybody get the impression I'm with these guys. I'm going home in a few days. I'm interested in fish, not politics."

And I can almost hear his reply. He'd say, "Fishing, politics—it's all the same here."

Clearly, I *am* involved just by being here, like it or not. And I don't. Not one bit. Adventure is fine, but this is too rich for my blood. I have a cold feeling. I whisper tersely to Pratt, "Did you *know* about this? You said this place has been peaceful for years."

"I didn't hear about *all* those kidnappings," Vaughan says. "They must have kept them quiet."

"I hope they keep *our* kidnapping quiet, because if I hear about it, I will be upset."

The bishop says to Vaughan, "They know that if they bother you they will be tangling with the congressman's family forces. That's the word that has gone out."

I say, "What does *that* mean: 'family forces'?"

Vaughan explains, "The local congressman—the guy we are headed to see—is also a warlord. His family is one of nearly two hundred Philippine warlord families listed in a recent newspaper article."

"A warlord. Meaning *what?*"

"He has raised his own private army. That's who all these guys are."

"And all this armed escort is to protect us against whom?" I inquire. I am beginning to feel I have a right to know.

"Abu Sayyaf," Perfecto says. "Or anybody that would think of harming us. But not necessarily the government or the MNLF. The MNLF is very well aware of this project, but they like what they have heard."

We stop to drop the bishop off. His bodyguard goes with him in the rain.

None of us can know that in a few days the newspaper will report that Abu Sayyaf has swept into a town north of Zamboanga, mounting the region's largest attack since Jolo was burned in the mid-1970s, killing dozens, including a police chief and an army commander, and wounding nearly a hundred people while robbing banks, setting fires, and turning the town into a battle zone blanketed with thick smoke. The entire four blocks of the town's commercial center will be razed.

A heavily guarded driveway into a walled property marks the home of the Honorable Bensaudi O. Tulawie, member of the Philippine House of Representatives from the Sulu District. The congressman has invited the Cyanide Reform Program here—the project Pratt and Perfecto's people are collaborating on. Several additional people, wearing Philippine Ecology Foundation flak jackets and "Net and Let Live" T-shirts, are present, awaiting us. We are led to a spacious veranda outside Tulawie's residence, a large, open-sided, tile-floored area with a big tiled roof over it. Very gracious looking. An adjacent global communications shop features a large satellite dish. Pigeons coo softly from a loft beside the house.

Mr. Tulawie himself is seated on a wicker couch on the veranda when we arrive. He rises to meet us. He is wearing jeans, a T-shirt advertising sneakers, and Western-style sandals. At age thirty-four, Tulawie is one of the youngest congressmen ever elected in the Philippines. He is serving his first term, but the look of his surrounding army does not invite the label "freshman." Fatigue-clad gunmen carrying automatic rifles stand casually or idly pace the veranda's perimeter. They seem bored. An automatic rifle laid carelessly across a bench is pointed directly at the congressman's back.

We are invited to sit. Tea and cookies are brought. The mood seems stiff. A moment of pregnant silence hangs over us. Searching for something to say, and thinking a little flattery can't hurt, I try, "You look very young to be a congressman."

"I'm old enough," he says tersely.

Feeling awkward, my eyes wander to a portrait hanging on one of the pillars. It is a photograph of Colonel Muammar el-Qaddafi—Libyan "Strongman," international terrorist.

Seeing my eyes pause, the congressman says, "When I was young I looked up to him. But now he has mellowed."

"Oh." Mellowed. Of course.

He turns to Vaughan, which takes the pressure off me. "So, Dr. Pratt," he chuckles just as I am raising my teacup to my lips, "maybe to get the U.S. government to fund our project, we should kidnap Dr. Safina?"

Everyone is smiling. Everyone *else*.

What does Miss Manners advise in situations where your teatime host turns out to be a warlord and is joking about kidnapping you? I can't remember. I believe I'll have a cookie, while that remains possible.

Tulawie tells us that he has recently set up a pharmacy with free medicine for people holding prescriptions. Good idea. I am going to need some muscle relaxants and anti-anxiety drugs pretty soon.

The congressman then launches into a short, semiformal speech. "In five years, we want the Philippines to be the number-one model in the world for marine resources. We will have marine parks and reserves."

This is too weird. For the first time ever, the term "environmental terrorist" makes some sense to me.

Tulawie continues, "Countries in the region are distorting their resources with cyanide fishing. We are in the last virgin islands in our country and we want to preserve them: our reefs and corals and other creatures underwater. Our local people will make use of this project for their own sustenance. Cyanide does not only kill marine resources, it could contaminate our own bodies. Now we need training to divert this into good things. Instead of carrying around firearms, loitering, and plotting to kidnap or murder, our people will be making a living in a nice way."

I especially like that last part.

Sensing that our audience with the congressman is over, we all rise to exchange farewells. The congressman says warmly, "You will be staying overnight in a wonderful place." As we are departing he adds, "Don't worry, be happy. Everything is normal."

I want to believe him. Vaughan and I are shown to a capped pickup truck where a driver is waiting, and we climb into the back. Perfecto will be coming later. We will be driven across the island of Jolo to a small village, from which we will be ferried to the boat that functions as headquarters for the fish-netting training program. In an open vehicle ahead sit six gunmen corsetted with cartridge belts, fingering automatic rifles: our escort. Vaughan says sarcastically, "I'm glad to see we are keeping a low profile."

As we bounce along the heavily potholed dirt roads, I notice that several of the wagging guns in the lead vehicle are pointing directly at our windshield. Each time the escort vehicle hits a hole hard, I brace myself for the possibility that a gun might go off and one of those bullets might poke a space through my brain.

We pass three schools (nice to see a government that values education, anyway) and one absolutely huge lone remaining rain-forest tree towering over what is now a large banana grove. I wonder why that one tree was spared. Many of the houses we see are on stilts, suggesting that flooding might be a problem here during typhoons. And many of the people we see occasionally walking along the road or passing in trucks are carrying guns. I say something to Vaughan about all the guns. Our driver laughingly informs us, "During the elections time, there is a ban on carrying guns. Elections time is now."

Vaughan says to me, "Don't worry, nobody ever gets shot here accidentally." Vaughan tells me the Moro National Liberation Front is active right in this area. He says, "Peace talks are ongoing. They want an autonomous Muslim region."

Autonomy is looking pretty reasonable right now. I say, let 'em have it if it means that much to them. Because, you know what? I'd like to keep mine.

Clouds sweep across forested slopes of distant mountains. We travel on. After penetrating deeper into Jolo Island for about an hour, we turn off the "main" road onto an even smaller one. But this road is better, with a smoother surface of clay.

The sky is thick with clouds, vapor, and passing rain, and for the next few miles we travel through still jungle as though into the very heart of darkness: an implacable hostility, brooding over an inscrutable intention.

We have seen only an occasional dwelling after turning onto this road. The few houses are mere huts constructed entirely of bamboo. Vaughan says a little ominously, "I haven't been in an area *this* remote in a long time." Then he adds brightly, "That's why it's good to work here: You can bring something new."

A drizzle begins falling—pretty steadily—and the road that seemed so smooth acquires a slick, slippery coating as the wet clay turns squishy. We weave and career down declivities, occasionally spinning our wheels when the need to climb presents itself.

After a while, this track narrows, becoming potholed and washboarded as well. The flesh on our driver's thick neck shakes as we vibrate along. The wetter the road gets, the more difficulty he is having preventing the vehicle from sliding and skidding. Our armed escort vehicle, appropriately equipped with four-wheel drive, is doing better, pulling farther ahead, occasionally disappearing from view around curves. Losing visual contact with our escort makes our driver look even more worried. He seems to be getting nervous, and he has begun sweating.

Our driver mentions something I don't quite get, something about cosmetics people. This is not exactly the place I'd expect to see the Avon lady, and I ask Vaughan what the driver is referring to. Vaughan says, "He thinks this is near the place where the four cosmetics company people—seaweed buyers—were kidnapped. They were held hostage for about three weeks. One was killed but the others escaped."

My humor is altogether gone now. I am scared. This is a bad place. I don't know why I am here. I fall silent, wishing—hoping—for this trip to be over.

Suddenly, the narrow road pinches sharply as it dips into a hollow, at the bottom of which a stream runs through a couple of culverts. Beyond the stream crossing, the road rises steeply out. Our escort vehicle is already climbing the other side, but with some difficulty. We begin sliding down the slope into the dip, fishtailing through the clay, our driver spinning the steering wheel left and right, trying to keep the truck from slipping off the side of the road and flopping over into the stream.

At the bottom of the decline, we hit thick mud.

While our wheels spin hopelessly, our escort up ahead is about to disappear from view. Our driver leans on his horn for about four seconds to get their attention.

I wish he hadn't done that. They don't seem to hear us—or have decided to ignore us—and they drive away, never to reappear.

Vaughan says nervously, "Not a great place to get stuck."

For a newcomer, I must be catching on very quickly, because I already know this.

We all get out. The tires are in mud up to the bottom rims. I am in to my ankles. I notice for the first time that our driver has a handgun tucked into his belt—despite this being elections time.

Vaughan says agitatedly, "I can't believe we're standing out here in the jungle. The whole idea was: Come quickly, go to the island quickly, unobtrusively. Now everybody knows we're here. If my wife knew about this—"

For a few moments, no one says a word. The shallow stream, about six feet below, is gurgling under the road and running off through a quiet forest—a forest silent but for the white noise of raindrop upon leaf times infinity.

The truck itself is in a very tricky position, angled sideways and only a few inches away from sliding off the road and into the stream, where it would lie half-submerged on its side, with no hope of recovery by us. The first order of business, then, is to straighten the truck. We line up on one side of it. For the congressman, and the people we are scheduled to meet later today, I am wearing the best clothes I have with me: new shirt, new sneakers, new pants.

One! Two! Three! On the first push, the spinning wheels splatter me with mud. Three pushes later, mud is clotted to our feet. Our legs have achieved full encrustation. It is raining on and off. We are wet and hot. A few mosquitoes are annoying us. But at least the truck is straight, no longer in imminent danger of slip-sliding away. This will have to pass for progress.

We chock the wheels with rocks from the stream bank. With hope springing eternal, and fear being the great motivator that it is, we break pieces of bamboo and palms and woody branches and shove them under the wheels. Pratt and I rock the vehicle to inch it forward, while the driver splatters us with more mud. The truck wants to tail out sideways, and we shove with everything we've got, keeping it straight. I slip and fall and come up chocolate-coated. Pieces of bamboo fly as we grunt and shove the vehicle three feet forward until the wheels begin drilling holes in the mud and the vehicle starts rapidly sinking.

"Whoa! Stop! That's enough!" We explain to our driver that the trick is: Don't give too much gas. No spinning the wheels—O.K.? He hasn't done the rock 'n' push routine before. Vaughan and I grew up in places with lots of snow, and lots of sandy beaches to get pickups stuck in, and rockin' 'n' pushin' makes us feel like teenagers again. All right. Chock those wheels. Move the bamboo and everything. Let's not lose any ground here. Let's keep it going. We'll get there, little bit at a time. O.K.—once again. Ready?

The first barefoot gunman appears like the first shark in Hemingway's *The Old Man and the Sea*. His mere arrival, a bad event in itself, is a sign that things are likely to get worse before they get better. If they do get better. Padding cat-like, silent, he regards us poker-faced. I look to our sweating driver the way a child looks at you when they've fallen, to see by your reaction whether they are hurt. He is clearly alarmed. He is standing on the other side of the truck's hood, and the gunman cannot see that his hand is on his pistol.

The gunman is holding his rifle across his chest. His demeanor seems calm. He is assessing things. He looks to be about forty years old. Lord knows what he is thinking, or why he is here.

Vaughan is behind me. We are all just facing the man, and he is facing us. I am trying to keep a grip on my nerves. In New York, they say it's worse if you act scared. I don't know about here. I have no idea.

Three teenagers about fifteen years old, two armed with rifles, the third carrying a long, crude, homemade pistol, come filing down the slope. Their brows are knit over wide eyes. I don't like the looks of this *at all*. They seem tense and unsure of themselves, looking to one another as they advance, as though this is a game of chicken. These armed kids are in their prime fanatic years, and this could be their chance to prove themselves. When really bad things happen, this is how they start. My knees turn to rubber. We are outnumbered. We are outgunned. Our "bodyguards" are God-knows-where. For all I know they might have sent these guys. They might be drinking up the payoff right now, chuckling as they chug. Who knows? I'm not from around here. I don't know how any of this works. I'm understanding less and less as the day wears on.

Our driver—bug-eyed, beaded with sweat, tense as a cocked trigger—seems on the verge of freaking. None of the gunmen can see his pistol from where they are standing, and if he decides to start shooting we are all dead. Especially me. I'm way out in the open, standing closest to the strangers. I'm the front-liner. We'll end up facedown in the mud, in the warm rain.

But the thing is, no one has made a move either hostile or friendly. Maybe they are still deciding what to think of us. Maybe just scared of the consequences of mistreating us, not knowing who we are or who might seek retribution. Maybe they know who we are and they like what they have heard about why we are here. Maybe they fear the congressman's army, or think we are all armed, and that is making them hesitate.

In the suspended-animation uncertainty over what is about to happen, I'm trying to think of something that might possibly lower the tension. I decide to smile submissively, wave hello. By my motions I indicate the stuck vehicle, tentatively inviting them to join us in freeing it. My legs are jelly.

With deadpan faces and inscrutable intentions, they decide to help, slinging the guns across their backs. That's one giant step for mankind. We work for a few ineffective minutes while I am calming down. Things seem O.K. but the driver is nerve-racked and fumble-fingered. I am thinking we'd better get out of here while the getting is good. Then somebody else appears, then more villagers, this time unarmed; and one person has a rope. Soon there are about a dozen of us in all, trying to pull and push the truck up the incline for a hot, wet, sweaty, muddy hour.

We finally get the truck up to a reasonably secure resting spot. I assume we will now continue, but our driver, seemingly at his wit's end, turns the truck right around, and it slides immediately all the way back down to where we just came from, getting stuck again in the same place, over the stream. There are now about fifteen people and one rope, with which we all pull the truck up the muddy hill toward the direction from which we had originally come.

Once there, we smile politely, waving a fond farewell. We get in calmly, and the driver floors it, zooming the hell out of there, as fast as the wheels will whirl.

The whole thing—breakdown to fragile freedom—has taken almost two hours. My question is: What now?

Our driver says nothing as he takes us up another road, which ends near a channel in some tall mangroves. The tide is out, and under the trees we are looking at a lot of mud and a little bit of shallow water.

Vaughan asks the driver, "What's the plan?"

Driver smiles. "Plan," he says. He chuckles to himself. "Plan."

We sit in silence. A young girl in a blue sweatshirt with BROOKLYN written on it appears, followed by her little sister, who is wearing a pinkish, floral-print dress. Unlike me, they are scrubbed clean and spotless. They watch us with the large eyes of children, from what they seem to consider a safe distance.

There is an old wooden swing on the grass nearby. I get out to sit on it, and I make faces at the children. Vaughan soon follows. A man with his head wrapped in a turban and carrying—naturally—a rifle on his shoulder and cartridges on his waist walks up to the driver's window.

For the humor value, Pratt repeats something he said earlier. "Don't worry, no one gets shot accidentally here."

This time I won't get upset about it until somebody starts shooting. But this time, also, the driver is perfectly calm. We must be in a relatively safe part of the island. They confer. "O.K.," the driver says to us. "A boat will come here. We will wait."

And so we simply sit on the swing, working the caked mud off our shoes, our socks, our pants. Vaughan's face is streaked with mud, meaning mine must be too.

A mere hour and a half melts by, during which no one gets shot, threatened, kidnapped, intimidated, or even particularly frightened, before a very narrow outrigger canoe with a flop-flop engine arrives. We take our packs and step through the mud out to where there is enough water to float the canoe. Muddy water pours off our pants as we climb in, and we sit in the puddle because there are no seats—not that I was expecting seats.

My nerves are returning to normal; I am again feeling more like a visiting scientist than a terrified, would-be hostage. A strongly running incoming tide is flooding the mangrove forest as our boatman takes us through labyrinthine channels among the biggest mangroves I have ever seen. Thousands of fruit bats hang like eggplants in the exposed branches of the tallest mangroves. Among the most productive seafood nurseries in the world, mangroves shelter and feed trillions of juvenile fishes and a large array of other wildlife, and this forest growing out of the saltwater is just gorgeous.

In a few minutes, though, we come to some areas where the mangroves have been cut down and cleared over several acres. By way of explanation our boatman says, "Shreemp." Shrimp ponds are being dug here, not to feed locals but for export to rich countries. The ponds destroy the mangrove nursery areas whose fish feed the villagers. It seems a shame to see them going in here, liquidating the intertidal forest. Here I go again: The very moment I can stop worrying about imminent danger to my life, I resume worrying about conservation of nature and about social injustice.

Only about a fourth to a tenth of the Philippine's original mangrove forests remain, depending on which of several estimates is correct. Mangroves have been gouged for aquaculture ponds, cut for wood, and cleared for housing, and not just here in the Philippines. About half of the world's original mangrove forests are gone. In Indonesia, only 20 percent of the original mangrove forests remain, and the government has described the country's coral reefs and mangrove forests as being in critical condition, needing immediate rehabilitation; in 1995 the minister of the environment called on local people to begin planting mangrove trees and restoring the natural coral habitats.

We emerge from the overarching mangroves into a wide bay of islands under a light sky with high clouds. Behind us, behind the mangroves, Jolo Island rises into green hills of broken forest. Before us, palm-fringed dollops of sand and some large, flat islands line the horizon. Here and there, thatch-roofed bamboo houses stand on stilts in the open water. People live here in the bay itself, and we are motoring through a "village" of about two dozen such homes right now. A few families are standing outside their doorways, smiling and waving at us. Nearby, over an area of perhaps ten acres, the netlike contraptions from which these people make their living, growing seaweed, hang in the water from buoys at the surface. People in canoes are tending and harvesting the crop.

Vaughan explains that seaweed exports are worth hundreds of millions of dollars in the Philippines. He says this district is reputed to be among the best in the world for the quality of its seaweed, which is used in agar-based products ranging from cosmetics to ice cream. The stuff these people are growing finds its way into markets all around the globe, and into our households and foods.

Up ahead is the Cyanide Reform Program's mobile headquarters—a big, old, yellow wooden boat of about sixty feet, a floating dinosaur. Short rope ladders are lowered for us as we come alongside. Quite a few people line the rail, looking down at us. I am handing up my gear when I see that Perfecto is already aboard. He asks, "What happened to *you* guys?"

"Stuck in mud," I say.

The boat's bare, planked deck, aft of the pilothouse, is shaded by a wooden roof. The big diesel is sunken into a large, encaged cutout in the deck in sort of an exposed "engine room." The boat is a confusion of gear, permeated with the smell of diesel oil: diving masks, weight belts, plastic buckets, knives, snorkels, foam boxes, cardboard boxes, assorted clothing, an air compressor, kerosene lanterns, chairs, coiled breathing hoses, cots, a fire ax, rifles, cartridge belts (there is enough ammunition in view to fight a prolonged engagement with a medium-sized country—such as the Philippines), and about a million other things blocked from view by the dozen and a half or so people milling about. The people themselves include local divers, trainers with the Ecology Foundation, bodyguards, a captain, a mechanic, and a cook. Most are men, but one of the Ecology Foundation people and the cook are women.

The perspiring cook, shy and smiling, is stoking coals smoldering on the rear deck in a pit made from the bottom third of a fifty-five-gallon oil drum. She is a flat-nosed, red-skinned woman in a worn, loose, gray dress. Except for a few stray curls spilling onto her sweaty forehead, her thick black hair is pulled back tightly. She has been squatting at a small pile of fresh fish, preparing them for dinner. Her hands and bare feet are coated with slime, scales, gurry, and blood. She looks about thirty. Vaughan says she is probably seventeen or eighteen.

Perfecto is anxious to show us several fish caught today with nets for the aquarium trade. All of us think the nets have the potential to be these people's salvation. In one study, only about 30 percent of cyanided aquarium fish collected in the villages were still alive by the time they got to Manila, while the survival of net-caught fish was 95 to 98 percent. From 1960 to the late 1980s, the Philippines was the number-one supplier of decorative fishes in the world market. High mortality rates from exposure to cyanide, however, had given Philippine fish a bad name, allowing newcomers like Indonesia and Sri Lanka to corner a huge chunk of the market. In the early 1990s, the Philippine market share was in free fall, going from over $6 million dollars in 1990 to around $1 million in 1992.

I peer into the plastic buckets at a small variety of creatures bright with life: bumble bee–colored anemone fishes, lemon-yellow tangs, and highly valued clown triggerfish with their egg-yolk-colored "lipstick" and big white-polka-dots on black bellies. One fish in particular arrests my attention: a palm-sized fish upon whose indigo background is emblazoned a psychedelic thumbprint of alternating white and electric-blue asymmetrical, concentric rings—an astonishingly beautiful, almost impossible creature. Perfecto says with proud excitement, "This *imperator* is top of the line." It is the emperor angel in its juvenile colors, a fish commanding very high prices. There may be more of them left in Sulu than anywhere else.

As I am bowed over the bucket, transfixed by the emperor's Technicolor clothes, someone rests his fingers gently on my shoulder. "Our only problem is," a voice says, "we are racing against time." I turn and straighten up, looking into the beseeching face of a fuzzy-bearded man with a knit cap, pursed lips, thick glasses, and a slightly crossed eye. His name is Nazhar Muayudi. In an exceptionally soft voice he continues, "You have come to a place where we allow no one. We can control the area, but not the environment. We give an idea—the idea of how to care for the environment. I am a local people here. Most of us have not gone to school. Government programs seldom reach to an area like this. We are working seriously. We believe this program is very fruitful to elevate the livelihood of our people. Before, our people are engaged in cyanide fishing. But in the last few months, many people come and want to join us. Because they are already convinced cyanide is very destructive to the environment. They have already experienced how the fish die. And, of course, they have seen the corals die. We don't want to abandon the environment. All the people—not only our generation—will benefit."

I would not have thought the people in a place this remote could feel so affected. But I am seeing again that—as Johannes kept trying to emphasize, and as I saw in the Pacific Northwest—the key to survival is enlightened local control of natural resource use. And, again, this seems especially true when the market is distant and insensitive to the local depletions it can cause.

In most reef areas, though, the force of market demand reigns, unchecked by local control, and the social and economic effects are serious. Don McAllister calculated that 40 percent of the Philippines' fish yield was lost due to degraded habitat. This corresponds to depriving 3,000,000 Filipinos of seafood. It also corresponds to destroying 130,000 fishing jobs. If each fisher's employment helps support four other family members, then about 650,000 persons are *directly* affected by the loss of employment. Considering the commerce that might have flowed from those lost fish, it seems reasonable to estimate that loss of employment caused by fishery depletion affects more than 1,000,000 persons in the Philippines alone.

There was another estimate, too: that by the late 1980s Philippine fishermen's daily catches had dropped from fifteen or twenty kilos per day down to just to one to four kilos, a loss of between roughly 75 and 95 percent. More and more small-scale fishermen were catching only enough fish to feed their families and not enough to sell.

Fish is the most important food item in the Philippines after rice. Seafood contributes about half the animal protein consumed by Filipinos. It provides important vitamins and minerals to persons dependent on rice.

A former minister of social services and development wrote that 75 percent of Filipino children under four years of age suffer from malnutrition. Undernourished children do not reach their human potential and are more prone to physical and mental illnesses. Unemployed and improperly fed people are more prone to antisocial behavior. McAllister challenges us to consider the greater implications: How much of the Philippines' large and expensive standing army is required because of human misery and unrest stemming from environmental destruction? What is the cost of the burden unemployment and malnutrition places on health-care services and correctional institutions? As I've seen and heard today, none of these questions is unimportant, none of these issues exaggerated.

The big exposed diesel engine fires up with a tremendous clanking roar. Nazhar says, "Now we are going to the village on Dong-dong Island. You are very lucky. Few outsiders have seen how beautiful it is here. This is the last frontier in the Philippines."

Our yellow dinosaur chugs slowly along in calm water and humid air under a close, overcast sky. Islands and islets ring the horizon, and only a few far-flung huts and villages are visible in an immensity of water and a wide stretch of green coast. This indeed is very much the frontier, the outskirts, the edge, the end of the reach of settlement and development. Yet even here, the people say they are racing against time.

I am seated along the rail, watching the shoreline crawling slowly past. Nazhar pulls up a chair and sits in front of me, knee-to-knee, placing his hands lightly upon my shoulders and looking into my eyes. I feel uncomfortable. He continues softly, "We believe this is our treasure. Our products are ornamental fish, food fish, sea cucumbers, abalone, shells, sharks, sea horses, seaweed. Of all these products we are very much aware. We are looking for a livelihood so that we can eat. But we must not waste the coral. We must not waste the fish. Our religion teaches: You drink, you eat, but do *not* waste. This is the *most* fundamental commandment. Wasting is an evil. It is the product of the devil."

Talk of the devil usually presses buttons in me, but Nazhar's gentle voice is reassuring, like the calm, silver-gray sea sliding by. Nazhar points to one of the islands. "They used cyanide over there, but now we are working together. They are asking us to train them in catching with the nets. With our limited materials and abilities, we try our best to teach them, teaching my people the value of the environment. We have been inculcating the good and bad of catching fish and other marine products."

I often wonder whether my conservation values are a luxury affordable only to middle-class white westerners. But these people do not have the securities I have, or the options, nor are they being fed hysterical-sounding funding appeals by effete environmental groups. These are armed Muslims fighting for control of their own lives. In many ways, their interests are entirely different from mine, yet we have converged upon a similar assessment of the state of the reefs and the importance of the environment in securing human dignity and freedom. Interesting. So maybe conservation of nature is not just a Western, middle-class concept. Maybe it is a human need, a universal hunger.

Vaughan, still covered with mud and reminding me of how filthy we all have gotten today, is snoozing on a cot. How I envy him. Less than twenty-four hours ago I was in Hong Kong waiting for my canceled flight to be rescheduled. In the middle of the night I arrived in Manila with no sleep and got on another plane with Vaughan. Following today's events and last night's lack of sleep, I am being swept off my feet by a towering wave of exhaustion, a veritable tsunami of narcolepsy. Nazhar shows me to a bunk inside the wheelhouse, and I lay my wet, muddy, overfatigued body down alongside two loaded Browning automatic rifles. My head comes to rest beside a copy of the *Holy Quer-An.* I am not in Kansas anymore.

Some time later, Nazhar is tapping my toe. Fourteen hours after leaving Manila—two airplanes, a truck, and a boat ride later—we have arrived at Dong-dong.

I force myself up and wobble outside. We are approaching a dock swelling with onlookers: children, women, men. Ropes are thrown and we tie up. Voices mingle. The air carries a hint of smoke. The kids—mostly grimy—are in shorts and T-shirts. A few kids under ten wear only their birthday suits. One girl holds a stringer of fish called rainbow runners. The shoreline—white sand, backed by coconut palms—is crowded with bamboo-and-thatch houses on stilts, extending out over clear water. Many other houses sit back from the beach in the shade of the palms. The smiling people who have come to see us ashore include a scattering of copiously munitioned riflemen.

New-looking, brightly painted outrigger boats rest upon the beach. These, I am told, were supplied by the cyanide purveyors. I am made to understand that the villagers have recently run those people out of town—and kept the boats.

Vaughan, several of the Ecology Foundation people, several guards, and I dis-embark, followed off the dock by a small crowd of onlookers. The village, with a couple of thousand inhabitants, presents immediate contrasts: houses over water, and houses on dry land; young men carrying arms, others playing volleyball; smiles of welcome, and squints of distrust. A young woman pauses and looks at me sweetly; another, slender and shapely with a toddler on her hip, sweeps by, glaring a frightening and inexplicable look of wild defiance.

The talk is in murmurs—except for an occasional shout on the volleyball court—but there is plenty of activity. Many people are busy spreading seaweed out to dry, and bales of it are stacked alongside some of the houses. Chickens strut in perpetual motion across thoroughfares of well-worn sand. People in some of the shacks are selling snacks and refreshments.

Our entourage is led to one house and invited to sit on the porch. The most influential man in the village, a holy man, praying upon his beads, sits next to us. He says nothing at all.

A basket of cigarettes is offered. "No, thank you." Prawn crackers? "Yes, thank you very much."

Some women, many of them quite young, nurse babies on the steps of the huts. Vaughan remarks, "Jeez, every girl who's old enough is pregnant." From 1966 to 1986, while the productivity of the coral reefs dropped by at least one-third, the population of the Philippines almost doubled. Because of these two trends, the square kilometer of reef that helped support nine hundred persons in 1966 had to help support twenty-six hundred persons in 1986, almost three times as many. The country's population is expected to double again in the first third of the twenty-first century.

Perfecto says to me, "This is the typical community that we are trying to work with. Our task is really very challenging. Can you imagine, reaching out to these deprived communities? It drains our organization's resources. But this is where the challenge is—to enhance skills, to preserve corals."

A circle of kids, young men, and women has moved quite close, staring at us intently and inspecting us minutely. Many of these kids have never seen out-siders. Vaughan says the kids are already asking the adults, "Why are these peo-ple here?" "Just by our arrival," he says, "they are learning about the corals, the fishes, the cyanide." In most places, Vaughan says, villagers don't fish near the village anymore. "The areas have been too ruined. Those villages present too much of a logistical difficulty for us," he says. "Here, they still fish right near the village, so the entire spectrum of residents—elders, holy men, families, chil-dren—can be involved."

A couple of muscular young men bring a bunch of coconuts and set them down heavily, thudding the sand at their bare feet. Before Perfecto can say, "A welcoming drink," their machetes are whacking off the husks and opening the shell tops. Once we've received our coconuts, Perfecto smiles broadly, making a gesture of salute before we all take a deep sip. Vaughan says to me, loud enough for Perfecto to hear, "Without Pete to speak the local dialect and relate to the people, we wouldn't be able to work here."

A friendly man of about fifty sits down next to me as I am still sipping my coconut. He has an automatic rifle and a belt of cartridges. No big deal; no one gets shot by accident. Secondhand cigarette smoke seems to be a larger danger in this village.

Perfecto introduces us to this rifleman, explaining, "He is one of our local leaders. He is responsible for water and firewood." We smile and shake hands.

In the oncoming sunset, towering clouds are striking and piling up over the mountains in which the MNLF and the Abu Sayyaf rebels are hiding. The most heavily armed man I have ever seen, a cartridge belt loaded into an automatic rifle and another one hung around his neck, accompanies us out to the dock. Around the village, cooking smokes are now coming up through the thatched roofs, scenting the breeze as families prepare evening meals. Filipino pop music comes filtering faintly from a battery-powered tape player in one of the houses.

By sundown about twenty of us are back aboard the boat. I say "us," but I have no idea who most of these people are. There are only two cots—which the hardworking women commandeer without contest. Most of the men sleep side by side on large mats. Deliriously sleepy but not quite ready to lie among strange men piled like puppies, I put on my sweatshirt and rain gear, go up to the roof, lie on a towel, and shove a rolled-up T-shirt under my head. This expedition to Dong-dong, the grimy old wooden boat, the congressman's armies, cloud forests harboring revolutionaries and terrorists, the holy men, the disheveled thatch villages, chain-smoking men in fatigues dozing on mats surrounded by loaded rifles: It has seemed more an expedition into the heart of a world apart than an outing to—of all things—catch aquarium fish for living rooms in the United States. I would not have guessed that such seemingly frivolous hobbies could have at their origin such deadly serious business a world away. And so ends perhaps the longest—though for a while it seemed like it might become the shortest—and certainly the muddiest day of my life. I surrender my inert body to the dew drops.

First light: A slow-handed dawn brings the crowing of roosters and the Islamic call to the faithful. My hair and rain clothes are wet. I am chilly. But it takes the roaring sounds of the air compressors to bring me to full consciousness.

By the time I descend the ladder to the deck, we are already under way to the dive site. The engine-room mechanic, continually nursing the big diesel, controls the throttle based on signals from a makeshift bell that the captain rings by pulling a cord in the wheelhouse, making a clapper hit a suspended piece of pipe. The number of clangs directs the engine man to make the diesel run either faster or slower or slower still.

The air compressors are adding synergistically to the bone-vibrating noise of the engine. Scuba tanks are being carefully filled in a large plastic tub of cool water. These people have been trained well in scuba safety.

Perhaps a gun-safety course would be a good next project. The guards consistently walk with their guns horizontal, at every turn swiveling their line of fire through the midriffs of a dozen or more plain folk, including yours truly. Some like to keep a finger near the trigger; others like to rest the palm of a hand over the barrel. When a gun is placed at rest it is invariably horizontal. Men habitually lounge or doze with their own guns pointed into their brains, or at least their heads.

Some of the men are sorting dried, edible sea cucumbers. Our tireless young cook squats on deck, cleaning a dozen ballyhoo, her bare feet, as usual, covered with scales and slime and fish blood. Water for coffee is on the coals while a couple of fish bake alongside the kettle.

A few small flocks of sandpipers trickle by. I check their direction against the rising sun. North. Among the most migratory of animals, these frailties are headed from this tropic theater to face spring snowstorms on Siberia's tundra, where they will breed.

Grilled fish and rice is served, but only to us, the outsiders. The fact that I prefer the fried, vinegared cassava with sour green mangoes and raw ballyhoo brings giggles of approval and thumbs-up from the locals, particularly the cook. They explain that this is their everyday breakfast food, not meant for guests, and they are very pleased that I'm enjoying it. "This is our bagel," explains one of the more worldly men to a New Yorker he perhaps thinks is Jewish.

The suspended pipe-bell in the engine room clangs several times, and the mechanic idles the diesels down. We are off the tip of an island. Nazhar comes over, pats my shoulder very gently, and says softly, "Here the coral reef is quite very O.K., not yet touched by the diving. We are looking for the future of our people right here."

Four outrigger canoes and one large outrigger skiff that have run here with us from Dong-dong gather around our big yellow boat. The boat, by the way, is nameless, for lack of consensus. I have suggested the names *Philippine Queen, Big Yellow Taxi,* and *The Yellow Submachine (Gun).* Inexplicably, neither Pratt nor Perfecto have embraced any of my lyrical suggestions.

The current is running very hard. Vaughan and I will use scuba gear, while the fish catchers will be breathing off the "hookahs": long air hoses connected to the compressor pump on their outrigger skiff. Two netters and I will go down together, and Vaughan will accompany another pair. The fish catchers are wearing sweatsuits and homemade plywood fins.

We enter the water and descend thirty feet at a tide-swept angle to a sandy flat interspersed with coral heads. These isolated heads are better than a large reef for capturing fish with nets because the mesh can be strung around the individual corals.

Fair numbers of fish are present, but—as Bob Johannes and Larry Sharron had warned about the Philippines—everything is under six inches. The fish catchers, trailing the hookah hoses from their mouths and breathing off the streaming air bubbles being pumped to them from the drifting outrigger skiff above, look like weird, hooked fish.

Even on the bottom, we must work hard just to avoid being swept away. I reach for a rock to hold myself in place, incurring an immediate sting on the wrist from a small coral. I decide to seek shelter from the current behind the bigger coral heads. Each time I move to a new head, I am confronted by a moray about a yard long, staring at me from the lee of the shelter. Green eels predominate, but one is mottled yellow and black: a snowflake moray. They've got the place staked out.

The current is playing havoc with the net, and the divers abandon a couple of initial attempts at a set. This dive could have been better timed to coincide with slack water, but the trainees, all former cyaniders, show remarkable persistence in getting the net to work right. For me, just holding in the current is difficult. If I were doing this for a living, and I had once used cyanide, the difficulty would be vexing. Working the net looks virtually impossible. But working they are, and working hard. They are endeavoring under conditions that are exactly wrong for encouraging early successes. These young men are heroes, showing an understanding, forbearance, and commitment to the future that I have found rare anywhere in the world—for example, New England and the Pacific Northwest in my own country, where people often behave as though they have stopped thinking about tomorrow.

One trainee works for ten minutes to entrap a single emperor angelfish. He finally succeeds, carefully removing the struggling blue booty from the net and slipping it into his mesh-topped bucket. This little emperor is worth about $12 to him. Someone in the U.S. will pay about $150 to acquire it.

Next, the net goes around a coral head of large size and complex structure. Its shadowed interstices harbor a potentially lucrative array of fishes. You can see them by peeking into the holes. But the fish understand their security, and despite the divers' attempts at frightening them out, they will not break cover. The other divers join the attempt to drive the fish out and into the net. They won't budge. After some minutes the frustrated fishers give up and move on.

We drift in the current, into an area lacking corals and seeming devoid of fish. The bottom here is pocked and cratered. I look questioningly at Vaughan. He pantomimes an explanation, putting the knuckles of his fists together and then opening his palms and spreading his fingers while rotating his wrists outward. Explosion. Blast fishing. Much of the bottom is coral rubble, some of it still alive. But the structure, the coral community, is gone. I can see why many people have lost fingers, hands, and arms while they were doing this.

We find a standing coral head where the divers are lucky to get another emperor and one small sweetlips. The divers are very selective here, skipping numerous attractive fishes and shrimps and zeroing in on others. I wonder: Do they upset the ecology by removing these fish? A look around at the dynamite-blasted craters says to me, "Who cares if they do?" Compared to what has gone before, their determination with the nets is a vast improvement and a magnificent step forward to a simpler and better time.

One diver breaks a strap on his plywood fin and leaves for the surface. Another chases a beautiful yellow tang three times around a large coral head. The tang deftly avoids the net each time. The diver repositions the net and catches the fish, but it slips from his hand as he tries to put it in his zippered bucket, and it won't come out of cover again for anything.

He moves to a small, nondescript coral head that I would have swum right past. It turns out to be loaded: tiger-striped yellow pipefish, several kinds of shrimp, even a small grouper. While he is working, an anemonefish escapes from his bucket through an opening in the zipper. It is disoriented without its accustomed anemones; rather than darting away, it swims idly around us—*so* idly that I could catch it with my hand. The diver is so intent on catching rose-banded shrimps that he doesn't see the escaped fish hovering around him.

After sixty-six minutes underwater, we come to the surface. The take for the dive includes four emperor angels, several blue tangs, some domino damsels, anemonefishes, a bicolor angel, and three yellow tangs. This is the second net catch for these trainees. Experienced net catchers would get perhaps twice as many fish in a day (earning the equivalent of perhaps forty dollars each).

Ferdinand Cruz, International Marinelife Alliance's Cyanide Reform Program field director, has fought to get increased prices from Manila buyers for net-caught fish. Some have agreed. He says, "For blue tangs, fishermen used to get five pesos"—about twenty cents—"but now they get forty."

Vaughan says, "This way they obtain a comparably valued catch for fewer fish without cyanide, and what they like is that they can go back to the same coral head again and again, finding new fish there because the coral is alive and continues to draw and support them."

After a pause, Pratt continues, "The dealers who are making the big money selling these fish are doing none of the work. If people only knew what went into getting the fish they see and buy in aquarium shops."

Not least among the people who *are* doing the work, in my opinion, is Vaughan Pratt himself. While many people talk about sustainable development, Pratt and his coworkers have proven that retraining, detection, and enforcement can work. These efforts may yet succeed in transforming the Philippines from the tropics' worst case of coastal destruction to a model of rehabilitation, and the work here in Sulu is not an isolated example. Pratt once took Bob Johannes and me on an expedition to Canipo Island in the Calamianes group in northern Palawan.

One fisherman there told me the cyanide-detection lab is the best thing that has happened. It is "a great deterrent," he said, "because the jail terms are so serious." And what is a serious jail term? Several people had recently gotten eight-year sentences. First offense.

Canipo Island was the most pleasant remote village I've ever been in, with real energy instead of the sense of stagnation that characterizes many. About sixty brightly painted and properly registered boats lay ready for launching along the white beach. Another, bigger, one was under construction. About as many houses, some with electricity, stood under the coconut palms. The thoroughfares—even the pigpens—were clean, and the woven bamboo houses, some of the them two stories high, showed much individual expression in size, style, and shape (one was even hexagonal). A bamboo hut had been erected for showing movies. Local fauna included cats, chickens, puppies, ducks, and a swarm of plump children.

The villagers had formed a co-op called Kamil Amianan, which translates to Hook and Line. I asked one of the local leaders, a man named Caesar, for the secret to the village's vitality.

"Before, when they were blast fishing with explosives made from fertilizer, our people could hardly afford paddleboats," he said. "Now, with Hook and Line, and with the live-fish market, we can afford to send our children to school." With the area protected from cyanide, the catches have stabilized, and the take seems sustainable now for both fish and people. "That's why this place is special."

Johannes was deeply impressed, offering, "I'm so glad I came here. In most places there is so much cyanide and destruction associated with the live trade, but at least now I can say I've been to a place where the people are fishing responsibly, looking to the future, and prospering. This is the most encouraging thing I've seen in a long time."

Caesar replied. "We fought to make it this way."

We dined at the home of the fishing co-op's head. The house had a swept-sand floor and an indoor toilet, and the fishermen generously lavished a delicious (and valuable) meal of red grouper upon us and housed us overnight on the island. The bedroom I was given featured pictures of nine Catholic saints above the headboard (some of whom I had not spoken with in years), two rifles under the bed, and a wall calendar decorated with twelve young women in poses that made me miss home.

Downstairs, one man was not being received as well. He was the captain of a large, dilapidated old fishing boat that, along with its impoverished crew of over eighty boys and men, was being detained by deputies overnight for fishing illegally. The captain told me he had come all the way from Mindoro, 120 miles north, because cyanide and blasting had destroyed their fishing grounds there. He would be released in the morning after promising not to return, but his worries seemed far from over.

The makeshift bell in the engine compartment clangs a couple of times as our own captain signals to the motorman to throttle the diesel down as we approach

Dong-dong village. Again, about a hundred people gather on the dock to see the aquarium fishes we have captured today. One boatload of men, heavily armed, departs surreptitiously at our approach, but not surreptitiously enough that we don't notice them. It is the MNLF. They have been talking to Perfecto, who stayed onshore. They have heard we are here, and they want us to come to their village to train them to fish without cyanide.

On the dock, everyone is straining and jostling for a look into the buckets as the fish are sorted. The wildly improbable, gemlike colors and perpetual motion of the fresh-caught creatures captivate all, especially the children, putting them in a gleeful mood and giving them the giggles.

"This is environmental work at its best," Vaughan says. "It's really a social program."

The fish are transferred to perforated jars kept underneath the dock in the shade. A man points to one of the fish, saying to me proudly, "Thees ees thee clown treeggerfeesh." Happily, this catch is destined for the Ocean Park aquarium in Hong Kong, where these swimming jewels will continue to captivate people by the tens of thousands in the extraordinary new reef exhibit there (the largest in the world).

Pratt says, "The weakness for us is that the cyanide middlemen paid these catchers every day for the fish, and we can't do that yet."

Perfecto adds, "The issue here is survival, but the willingness for them to learn to fish clean is anchored on our ability to sustain a ready market for them. We need to set up co-ops and infrastructure from capture to market."

I ask Perfecto, who has been ashore all day, if he is coming back to *Big Yellow* with us. He seems to misunderstand the thrust of my question, and as several more heavily armed men board our boat, he says, "Yes, I am coming with you, but you did not have to worry, I had the Delta Force covering you all day."

We pull away from the dock and anchor a short distance from shore. New faces come and go continually in canoes. Onboard, amid the noise and smoke and smells of the deck, people are continually eating rice, cassava, fish—there is almost always something ready on the sooty fire. Our young cook works incessantly, with good humor and a quick-flash smile. She speaks no English, but after I try complimenting her cooking she makes a point of coming over to sit next to me in her rare moments off, gesturing requests for me to take more pictures of her with her boyfriend, who is part of the crew.

As the sun begins to settle, Nazhar himself settles next to me, saying softly, "You must come and visit us again in our beautiful place. Here, you have no worries. You are under our auspices, and no one will touch you. No one bad can get to you because you will always be under our protection."

Perfecto says to me, "The next time you visit, you must make more time to stay with us. I will show you more of our lovely corals. I will show you our wonderful mangroves. And—if you want—I will teach you how to shoot and disassemble an M16. It will be part of our cultural exchange." He chuckles.

By the time we finish eating and talking, this part of the world lies in darkness. I climb to the roof and look down into a galaxy of phosphorescence in the sea. In every heaven above float as many stars as seem possible to behold.

Three muffled shots report through the distant night. Someone paddling a canoe near the island is singing a strangely haunting melody in a voice full of beauty and all humanity, though the tongue to me is foreign. The song rolls across still waters and into the deep, blue-black universe beyond, a song from an ocean planet called Earth, a world of water, yet itself an island.

I spread my towel on the roof under the arching galaxy, lie down wearily in my clothes, and rest my eyes. I am thinking about irony, and hope, and the irony that hope is. The irony that ideals and hope can flourish at the tattered edges of human existence, the hope that if ideals can flourish here, they can melt civilization's jaded heart. Soon my thoughts begin to swim, and in a short while I am asleep.

Epilogue

It has been said—tongue in cheek—that animals were invented by water as a device for transporting itself from one place to another. That's an interesting perspective, especially considering that when animals left the seas in which life arose, they took saltwater with them, in their bodies—an internal environment crucial for cellular survival. We are, in a sense, soft vessels of seawater. Seventy percent of our bodies is water, the same percentage that covers Earth's surface. We are wrapped around an ocean within. You can test this simply enough: Taste your tears.

It was my first trip to Jamaica, and perhaps the only chance I'll ever have to see this lovely island. Yet Jamaica's coral reefs, where pioneering research on coral ecology was done in the 1950s, bear a reputation as the most unhappy reefs in the Caribbean: covered with algae (resulting from sewage and silt running off a populous island and from the algae-grazing urchins' mysterious collapse in the 1980s), bereft of large fish due to intensive trapping (someone remarked that the biggest fish left in Jamaica are wooden carvings in roadside stands), and, thus weakened, suffering further from batterings by a brutal procession of fierce hurricanes. With this in mind, being in Jamaica was a mixed blessing in the first place, but being there with some of the world's great marine experts, who had assembled to talk about global conservation issues, made it even more—let's just say "interesting."

On the first day, an impromptu snorkeling trip brought Dr. Les Kaufman of Boston University and Dr. Jane Lubchenco, president of the American Association for the Advancement of Science, to a typical Jamaican cove like the ones they had once known well when Kaufman was a student and Lubchenco a young instructor, about two decades ago.

Back in those days, the reefs were composed of branching corals reaching up toward the light: the wide-palmed elkhorn coral nearest the surface, the staghorn corals below them, the finger and fire and brain corals—all crowding and *building* the reef up and out as they competed for space. Jamaican reefs back then were almost entirely covered, festooned, and encrusted with living, growing coral (like the best reefs I had seen in Palau). Lubchenco described the sense of otherworldly, multi-sensory exhilaration she'd had back in the old days in Jamaica every time she dived: She shared her memories of being lost and dwarfed in the vertical coral columns, of the profusion of colorful fishes and other animals in and around the three-dimensional living structures, the water's bodily press and flow, the continuous crackle and popping of snapping shrimp and the scraping sounds of munching fish.

That was then. Now, as we surveyed the collapsed, weed-covered rubble pile the reef had become, Dr. Lubchenco, whose cool and considerable intellect had won her a Pew Scholars Award and MacArthur "genius" prize, fought back tears. The distinguished Dr. Kaufman, also possessed of an award-winning rational mind, was not even attempting to fight his own tears, and he grimly said it was like seeing a family member you know has died, but being unprepared for the first glimpse of her corpse. Lubchenco described the sight of the reef as "wrenching," but her expression bore more than that. It was a loss, she said, not just of the services the reef could provide for people—like food and shoreline protection against hurricanes—but of the opportunity for knowledge, and of a place that had inspired her. It was that lost source of inspiration that showed on her face.

And so the tears of scientists mixed with the water of the cove. The salt of the sea, which we all have carried in our bodies through long evolutionary history like our biological birth certificate, now returned to the place of its origin as though being laid to rest; the ocean inside humanity now mingled with the ocean outside in a display of sympathy and grief. Especially considering the weighty reputations of these scientists, it was a stunning, solemn moment.

Because I had not been there before, I did not have the same visceral reaction as they, but I hoped I would never feel quite so bad about the waters where I grew up as they were feeling here. And I thought back to seeing sharks at the surface of a slick summer sea, of fishing for bluefin tuna with my father and uncles and closest friends, when the world and I were younger. All these scenes were playing in my mind as I stood on that idyllic-looking Jamaican beach surrounded by jungle greenery, looking at the faces of those who once knew these reefs. I thought of the future and tried to divine the prognosis.

The next day was much better. We went scuba diving on a deeper reef, then snorkeling in another cove. Dr. Sylvia Earle, the great deep-sea explorer and passionate spokeswoman for marine protection, was with us this time, as was Florida Institute of Oceanography director Dr. John Ogden, who has helped achieve and defend a new management system for restoration of Florida Bay and the Keys, and Dr. Tom Goreau, whose father had done some of the first coral ecology research and whose grandfather had taken some of the first underwater photographs. I felt like an elementary school student among such formidable authorities. This time though, no tears for the reef. In this cove, for some reason, algae-grazing urchins were present in high densities. For some reason, here at least, they and the corals were trying to stage a comeback. And there were more fish than I had expected to see.

Dr. Kaufman surfaced, exclaiming, "This is fantastic. It's happening."

When his colleagues looked at him askance, reminding him that live corals covered only about 20 percent of the reef's surface and that the place had other problems and could hardly be termed recovering, Kaufman said, "Yes, but the two possible fates are duking it out, searching for which equilibrium the reef will go toward: further degradation or recovery."

And I thought: Doesn't that pretty much sum up the situation almost everywhere at this crossroads in history?

Which will it be, then: degradation or recovery, scarcity or plenty, compassion or greed, love or fear, ahead to better times or to worse? We will all, by our actions or inaction, help decide.

In the years since I began these travels in the early 1990s, the two possible fates for the world's oceans have, indeed, been duking it out, and the forces of good have landed a few solid punches.

Prompted by the combined voices of hundreds of conservation-minded people—ranging from members of small fishing-community associations to international environmental organizations—the United Nations enacted a worldwide ban on large-scale drift nets in the early 1990s. In 1995 the U.N. also agreed upon historic new standards for fishing on the high seas. Once this agreement enters into force (though only thirty ratifications are required and more than fifty countries intend to ratify it, the process takes several years), no area of the world's seas will be lawless any longer. The agreement includes a concept called the "precautionary principle," which says, in effect, that we must err on the side of caution— the first time a large-scale treaty has carried this concept. The United Nations also passed a fisheries Code of Conduct, setting out strongly worded guidelines.

In the United States, fisheries reform grew into a major conservation issue in the 1990s. Over 125 groups—from sportfishing clubs to scuba groups to conservation organizations to commercial fishing associations to scientific societies (perhaps the largest coalition ever assembled to work on an environmental issue in America)—united to overhaul the federal law governing fishing in the U.S., the Fisheries Conservation and Management Act. The law now requires fisheries managers to end overfishing for most species and requires rebuilding of depleted populations (bluefin tuna are one of the few exceptions, unfortunately). In New England, where devastating depletions caused such painful social disruption, strict new regulations have finally halted overfishing for most groundfishes, and some are showing increases for the first time in many years. Some sharks even got a break, with increasing attention at CITES meetings; halving of catch quotas off the U.S. East Coast; protection for great white, whale, and basking sharks in several countries; and scientists from around the world pooling their efforts to assemble a global action plan for shark conservation. The World Conservation Union in 1996 placed over a hundred species of marine fishes on its "Red List of Threatened Animals," a gesture that greatly raised the visibility of, and underscored the importance of, ocean depletions.

A few organizations decided to set an example by their own leadership. American long-line boats working off Alaska *asked* for regulations requiring that they use techniques to avoid catching albatrosses while deploying their gear (bird avoidance practices are now also required in the waters of Australia, New Zealand, and the Antarctic). And the largest buyer of seafood products in Europe, a corporate giant called Unilever, voluntarily lost millions of dollars by suspending their massive purchases of small fish; they decided that depleting the bottom rung of the marine food web was irresponsible and too risky to the future of their many seafood businesses. In Palau, Japan has offered to fund construction of a new Coral Reef Center, where the people of Palau and tourists from the world over would be able to learn about the many values of Palau's world-class coral treasures.

As if to cap a decade of real progress and to acknowledge how fundamentally the seas unify the world, the U.N. designated 1998 as the Year of the Oceans.

But for me personally, nothing speaks more eloquently about the possibilities for renewal than seeing the return of plentiful runs of striped bass coursing through my home waters, a spectacular success proving that tough management and respect for science really can turn depletion into abundance within a human lifetime.

Today many people are sensing that the seas need sympathy and that people who rely on the seas need action. In many ways the 1990s emerged as the decade when people finally began discovering the oceans. In 1995, *National Geographic*'s ten million subscribers worldwide read about the imperiled state of the world's seas. And as a fitting precursor to 1997's designation as International Year of the Reef, *Time* magazine's October 1996 international edition featured corals and fishes on its cover, as well as twelve pages of articles to go with the cover headline:

Global Agenda
TREASURES OF THE SEAS
We've plundered the oceans' gifts.
Can we now protect them?

Good question. A better one would be, "Will we choose to?" And perhaps we can help answer that by posing another question: "What if we don't?"

It has been said that the economy is a wholly owned subsidiary of the environment. Certainly, the salmon fishers in the Northwest and the women who live along Deer Creek know this—and *live* it. The reef fishers in Palau and Sulu and elsewhere are struggling to bring their life into line with this realization as they strive to protect and restore their corals, their economy, their sense of place, their future. When people speak of "saving the oceans," then, I offer this: We need the seas more than they need us.

But something else is needed in addition to a better understanding of services provided. People will seldom protect things having no perceived economic value, but as we have seen, people sometimes display an active unwillingness to protect even things *with* economic value. What values, then, *do* we really have? What values do we really need?

Today many typical people who do not particularly think of themselves as active conservationists or environmentalists apply the notion of "live and let live" to most species. Even if human use of species is deemed desirable, extermination is generally held unacceptable. Thus many people implicitly include non-human life in an unstated sense of extended community. They would not question a hawk's place in the sky, nor ask what good is a gazelle, nor wonder whether the world really needs wild orchids. Without stating it, they intuitively acknowledge other species' uncontested right to struggle for existence in life's harsh fabric. In so doing, they accept them into a family of the living.

Yet when told of the plight of, say, sharks, many of these same people still think it quite reasonable to inquire, "What good are they; why do we need them?"

In the 1940s, a forester named Aldo Leopold wrote of a "search for a durable scale of values." He called for extending our sense of community responsibilities beyond isolated humanity to encompass the whole living landscape, and he called this extension the "land ethic." Why? If for no other reason, to maintain a place for humanity. Such a notion was revolutionary at the time, but it has since become the core of conservation and environmental thought. Leopold loved to hunt and fish and use wood, but he sensed one inflection point: An action is right when it tends to preserve the integrity, stability, and beauty of a living community, and wrong when it tends to do otherwise. In other words, rightness lies in recognizing "enough," so that the future may be safeguarded.

What good, then, are sharks? Let's put all question of uses, products, and ecological significance aside for a moment. Perhaps we *most* need sharks—and seaweeds, starfishes, sea slugs, squid, salmon, swordfish, seabirds, and singing cetaceans—to test our ability to differentiate between right and wrong. If this answer seems silly, if refusing to answer the question of the value of sea creatures from an immediately utilitarian perspective—just one time—rings hollow, compare it to our unquestioning acceptance of the rightness of songbirds or elephants. The difference arises not because wet animals have lesser attributes than dry ones. Rather it is because we have yet to extend our sense of community below the high-tide line. Many still view the ocean as the blank space between continents. We need now a "sea ethic."

Some will dismiss talk of ethics as too emotional, too much a luxury in pragmatic times. I answer that cynicism, apathy, and greed are in fact undiluted and unquenched emotions, far less rational and thoughtful than ethics, and certainly less nourishing. They are counterproductive selfish indulgences we truly can no longer afford.

A teacher with fresh vision once offered me the thought that fishes help connect the world because the waters they swim in wash all shores. Such an expansive thought, helping as it does to gather the world together in our minds, does not require viewing the sea's inhabitants in unscientific terms. Recognizing our inter-relatedness does not imply notions of some unreal ocean utopia wherin all creatures swim at peace. No lions need lie down with lambs; mako sharks are welcome to attempt to bite swordfish in half, and swordfish may defend themselves violently. We can respect—we *need* finally to respect—the *reality* of the living oceans.

We can celebrate the seas' ability to bring humanity closer together because the oceans truly do so—in many ways that we have concretely seen. And it is a gentle and pleasant paradox that contemplating the connective, unifying power of the oceans can actually free our spirit. Simply by offering the sea's creatures membership in our own extended family of life we can broaden ourselves with-out simplifying or patronizing them. With such a mental gesture—merely a new *self*-concept—we may complete the approach to living on Earth that began with the land ethic. Just as the land ethic grew into the conservation and envi-ronmental consciousness of the late twentieth century, the sea ethic will logically expand our view of wildlife and its values throughout the oceans. We can then perhaps begin drawing around us a kind of conceptually reconstructed Eden in something like the original sense: humanity within the full complement of our natural endowment. We will find not least among our eroded endowment, and well worth regaining: our options.

So to embrace a sea ethic we need not idealize or distort the ocean's creatures. Indeed, up to now our view of the sea's living inhabitants can hardly have been more distorted. Instead, we have the opportunity to see them fully for the first time, as wild animals in their habitats, confronted with needs and dangers, equipped by evolution with the capacity and drive to manage and adapt and survive.

Such a perspective frees the mind and opens doors: to a lifetime of boundless inquiry, to a wealth of enriching insights and reflection, to the chance to be more fully human, to the possibility of making a meaningful contribution. The only prerequisites for taking this path are respectfulness and an extravagant desire for exploration—both impulses that build an elevated sense of vitality and purpose. The promise: that any honest inquiry into the reality of nature also yields insights about ourselves and the dramatic context of the human spirit.

For each of us, then, the challenge and opportunity is to cherish all life as the gift it is, envision it whole, seek to know it truly, and undertake—with our minds, hearts, and hands—to restore its abundance. It is said that where there's life there's hope, and so no place can inspire us with more hopefulness than the great, life-making sea—that singular, wondrous ocean covering the blue planet.

Selected Bibliography

BOOK ONE

Baker, C. S., and S. R. Palumbi. "Which Whales Are Hunted? A Molecular Genetic Approach to Monitoring Whaling." *Science* 265 (1994): 1538–39.

Bass, R. "The Heart of a Forest." *Audubon* (Jan.–Feb. 1996): 38ff.

Block, B. A. "Physiology and Ecology of Brain and Eye Heaters in Billfishes." In *Planning the Future of Billfishes, Part 2,* R. H. Stroud, ed. Savannah, Ga.: National Coalition for Marine Conservation, 1990.

Block, B. A., J. R. Finnerty, A. F. R. Stewart, and J. Kidd. "Evolution of Endothermy in Fish: Mapping Physiological Traits on a Molecular Phylogeny." *Science* 260 (1993): 210–14.

Brewster, W. "The Present Status of the Wild Pigeon (*Ectopistes migratorius*) as a Bird of the United States, with some notes on its habits." *Auk* 6 (1889): 285–91.

Carey, F. "Fishes with Warm Bodies." *Scientific American* (Feb. 1973): 36–44.

———. "Further Acoustic Telemetry Observations on Swordfish." In *Planning the Future of Billfishes, Part 2,* R. H. Stroud, ed. Savannah, Ga.: National Coalition for Marine Conservation, 1990.

Cousteau, Jacques. *The Silent World.* New York: Harper & Brothers, 1953.

Deriso, R. B., and W. H. Bayliff, eds. *World Meeting on Stock Assessment of Bluefin Tunas: Strengths and Weaknesses.* Inter-American Tropical Tuna Commission Special Report No. 7, 1991.

Evans, D. H., ed. *The Physiology of Fishes.* Boca Raton, Fla.: CRC Press, 1993.

Fordham, S. *New England Groundfish: From Glory to Grief—A Portrait of America's Most Devastated Fishery.* Washington, D.C.: Center for Marine Conservation, 1996.

Mowat, Farley. *Sea of Slaughter.* New York: Atlantic Monthly Press, 1984.

Partridge, B. L., J. Johansson, and J. Kalish. "The Structure of Schools of Giant Bluefin Tuna in Cape Cod Bay." *Environmental Biology of Fishes* 9 (1983): 253–62.

Russell, S. *Biological and Catch/Effort Data Collection from the Domestic Tuna Longline Fishery in the Northern Gulf of Mexico.* Baton Rouge, La.: Coastal Fisheries Institute, Louisiana State University, 1989.

Safina, C. "Bluefin Tuna in the West Atlantic: Negligent Management, and the Making of an Endangered Species." *Conservation Biology* 7 (1993): 229–34.

———. "Where Have All the Fishes Gone?" *Issues in Science and Technology* 3 (1994): 37–43.

———. "The World's Imperiled Fish." *Scientific American* 273 (1995): 46–53.

Tibbo, S. N., L. R. Day, and W. F. Doucet. *The Swordfish* (Xiphias gladius *L.*): *Its Life-History and Economic Importance in the Northwest Atlantic.* Ottawa: Fisheries Research Board of Canada, 1961.

Watson, Traci. "Why Some Fishes Are Hotheads." *Science* 260 (1993): 160–61.

BOOK TWO

Allendorf, F. W., and R. S. Waples. "Conservation and Genetics of Salmonid Fishes." In J. C. Avise and J. L. Hamrick, eds. *Conservation Genetics: Case Studies from Nature.* New York: Chapman and Hall, 1996.

Baker, T. T., A. C. Wertheimer, R. D. Burkett, R. Dunlap, D. M. Eggers, E. I. Fritts, A. J. Gharrett, R. A. Holmes, and R. L. Wilmot. "Status of Pacific Salmon and Steelhead Escapements in Southeastern Alaska." *Fisheries* 21 (1996): 6–19.

Bay-Hansen, C. D. *Fisheries of the Pacific Northwest Coast, Volume 1: Traditional Commercial Fisheries.* New York: Vantage Press, 1991.

Begley, S., et al. "Better Red Than Dead." *Newsweek,* 12 December 1994: 79–80.

Brown, L. R., P. B. Moyle, and R. M. Yoshiyama. "Historical Decline and Current Status of Coho Salmon in California." *North American Journal of Fisheries Management* 14 (1994): 237–61.

Caufield, Catherine. "The Ancient Forest." *The New Yorker,* 9 May 1990: 46.

Cone, Joe. *A Common Fate: Endangered Salmon and the People of the Pacific Northwest.* New York: Henry Holt, 1995.

Donaldson, I. J., and F. K. Cramer. *Fishwheels of the Columbia.* Portland, Ore.: Binfords and Mort, 1971.

Egan, Timothy. *The Good Rain.* New York: Vintage Books, 1990.

Emerson, Ralph Waldo. 1836. "Nature." In *The Portable Emerson,* ed. C. Bode. New York: Viking Penguin, 1946.

Ficken, Robert E. *The Forested Land: A History of Rain in Western Washington.* Seattle, Wash.: University of Washington Press, 1987.

Grier, N., E. Clough, and Anna Clewell. *Toxic Water: A Report on the Adverse Effects of Pesticides on Coho Salmon and the Prevalence of Pesticides in Coho Habitat.* Northwest Coalition for Alternatives to Pesticides, 1994.

Groot, C., and L. Margolis. *Pacific Salmon Life Histories.* Vancouver: University of British Columbia Press, 1991.

Groot, C., L. Margolis, and W. C. Clarke. *Physiological Ecology of Pacific Salmon.* Vancouver: University of British Columbia Press, 1995.

Harding, Walter. *The Days of Henry Thoreau.* Princeton: Princeton University Press, 1962.

Hunn, E. S. *Nch'i-Wána: "The Big River"—Mid-Columbia Indians and Their Land.* Seattle, Wash.: University of Washington Press, 1990.

Lynch, Eamon. "Logging Without Laws: A Timber-Happy Congress Suspends the Protection of Public Forests." *Audubon* (Jan.–Feb. 1996): 14–18.

Manning, Richard. *Last Stand: Logging, Journalism, and the Case for Humility.* Salt Lake City, Utah: Gibbs Smith / Peregrine Smith Books, 1991.

Maser, C., and J. R. Sedell. *From the Forest to the Sea: The Ecology of Wood in Streams, Rivers, Estuaries, and Oceans.* Delray Beach, Fla.: St. Lucie Press, 1994.

Mitchell, J. G. "Tree Sitters Protest as Old Redwoods Fall to Corporate Raider." *Audubon* (Sept. 1988): 78.

———. "War in the Woods: Swan Song." *Audubon* (Nov. 1989): 92.

———. "War in the Woods II: West Side Story." *Audubon* (Jan. 1990): 82.

Murphy, R. C. *Fish-shape Paumanok.* Great Falls, Va.: American Philosophical Society/Waterline Books, 1962.

National Research Council. *Understanding Marine Biodiversity.* Washington, D.C.: National Academy Press, 1995.

———. *Upstream: Salmon and Society in the Pacific Northwest.* Washington, D.C.: National Academy Press, 1996.

Nehlsen, W., J. E. Williams, and J. A. Lichatowich. "Pacific Salmon at the Crossroads: Stocks at Risk from California, Oregon, Idaho, and Washington." *Fisheries* 16 (1991): 4–21.

Norse, Elliott A. *Ancient Forests of the Pacific Northwest.* Washington, D.C.: Island Press, 1990.

Oregon and Washington Departments of Fish and Wildlife. Status Report. *Columbia River Fish Runs and Fisheries, 1938–1994.* Oregon Department of Fish and Wildlife and Washington Department of Fish and Wildlife, 1995.

Pearcy, W. G. *Ocean Ecology of North Pacific Salmonids.* Seattle, Wash.: University of Washington Press, 1992.

Reisner, Marc. *Cadillac Desert.* New York: Penguin, 1993.

Ryan, J. C. *State of the Northwest.* Seattle, Wash.: Northwest Environment Watch, 1994.

———. *Hazardous Handouts: Taxpayer Subsidies to Environmental Degradation.* Seattle, Wash.: Northwest Environment Watch, 1995.

Seideman, D. "Smoky the Spendthrift." *Audubon.* (May–June 1997): 20.

Shannon, L. V., R. J. M. Crawford, and D. C. Duffy. "Pelagic Fisheries and Warm Events: A Comparative Study." *South African Journal of Science* 80 (1984): 51–60.

Slaney, T. L., K. D. Hyatt, T. G. Northcote, and R. J. Fielden. "Status of Anadromous Salmon and Trout in British Columbia and Yukon." *Fisheries* 21 (1996): 20–35.

Stewart, Hilary. *Indian Fishing: Early Methods on the Northwest Coast.* Vancouver: Douglas and McIntyre, Ltd., 1982.

Thoreau, Henry David. 1849. "A Week on the Concord and Merrimac Rivers." In *The Portable Thoreau,* ed. C. Bode. New York: Viking Penguin, 1947.

Van Dyk, J. "Long Journey of the Pacific Salmon." *National Geographic* 178 (1990): 3–36.

Watts, Alan W. *Nature, Man and Woman.* New York: Pantheon, 1958.

White, R. J., J. R. Karr, and W. Nehlsen. "Better Roles for Fish Stocking in Aquatic Resource Management." *American Fisheries Society Symposium* 15 (1995): 527–47.

Wicker, T. "The Greening of the President, 1996." Unpublished article for *Audubon.*

Williams, Chuck. *Bridge of the Gods, Mountains of Fire.* San Francisco: Friends of the Earth, 1980.

Willson, M. F., and K. C. Halupka. "Anadromous Fish as Keystone Species in Vertebrate Communities." *Conservation Biology* 9 (1995): 489–97.

Book Three

Bonfil, R. *Overview of World Elasmobranch Fisheries*. FAO Fisheries Technical Paper 341. Rome: Food and Agriculture Organization of the United Nations, 1994.

Food and Agriculture Organization of the United Nations Fisheries Department. *The State of World Fisheries and Aquaculture*. Rome: Food and Agriculture Organization of the United Nations, 1995.

Hattori, S. "Preliminary Note on the Structure of the Kuroshio from the Biological Point of View, with Special Reference to Pelagic Fish Larvae." In *The Kuroshio: A Symposium on the Japan Current*, J. C. Marr, ed., Honolulu: East-West Center Press, 1970.

Johannes, R. E. "Reproductive Strategies of Coastal Marine Fishes in the Tropics." *Environmental Biology of Fishes* 3.1 (1978): 65–84.

———. "Traditional Marine Conservation Methods in Oceania and Their Demise." *Annual Review of Ecology and Systematics* 9 (1978): 349–64.

———. (Manuscript.) "The Science of Pacific Island Peoples and Marine Resource Management." Proceedings from the Conference on the Science of the Pacific Island Peoples, July 6, 1992, Suvu, Fiji.

Johannes, R. E., and M. Riepen. *Environmental, Economic, and Social Implications of the Live Reef Fish Trade in Asia and the Western Pacific*. The Nature Conservancy, 1995.

Leopold, Aldo. *A Sand County Almanac*. New York: Ballantine Books, 1949.

McAllister, D. E. "Environmental, Economic and Social Costs of Coral Reef Destruction in the Philippines." *Galaxea* 7 (1988): 161–78.

Myers, Robert F. *Micronesian Reef Fishes: A Practical Guide to the Identification of the Coral Reef Fishes of the Tropical Central and Western Pacific*. 2nd ed. Guam: Coral Graphics, 1991.

Nordhoff, C. "Notes on the Offshore Fishing of the Society Islands." *Journal of Polynesian Society* 39 (1933): 137–73 and 221–62.

Richards, Andrew. "Live Reef Fish Exports to Southeast Asia from the South Pacific." *SPC Fisheries Newsletter* 67 (1993): 34–36.

Roberts, Callum. "Effects of Fishing on the Ecosystem Structure of Coral Reefs." *Conservation Biology* 9 (1995): 988–95.

Rose, D. A. "An Overview of World Trade in Sharks and Other Cartilaginous Fishes." *TRAFFIC International*, 1996.

Rubec, P. J. "The Effects of Sodium Cyanide on Coral Reefs and Marine Fish in the Philippines." In *The First Asian Fisheries Forum*, J. L. MacLean, L. B. Dizon, and L. V. Hosillos, eds. Manila: Asian Fisheries Society, 1986.

———. "The Need for Conservation and Management of Philippine Coral Reefs." *Environmental Biology of Fishes* 23 (1988): 141–54.

Sadovy, Y. "The Case of the Disappearing Grouper: *Epinephelus striatus*, the Nassau Grouper, in the Caribbean and Western Atlantic." Gulf and Caribbean Fisheries Institute proceedings, vol. 45. Presented at the 45th annual meeting of the Gulf and Caribbean Fisheries Institute, Merida, Mexico, 1992.

———. "The Nassau Grouper, Endangered or Just Unlucky?" *Reef Encounter* 13 (1993): 10–12.

Smith, C. L. "A Spawning Aggregation of the Nassau Grouper, *Epinephelus striatus*." *Transactions of the American Fisheries Society* 2 (1972): 257–61.

Veitayaki, Joeli, Vina Ram-Bidesi, Elizabeth Matthews, Lionel Gibson, and Veikila Vuki. *Overview of Destructive Fishing Practices in the Pacific Islands Region*. Apia, Western Samoa: South Pacific Regional Environment Programme, 1995.

Index